REMNANTS

REMNANTS

EMBODIED ARCHIVES
OF THE ARMENIAN
GENOCIDE

ELYSE
SEMERDJIAN

STANFORD UNIVERSITY PRESS
Stanford, California

Stanford University Press
Stanford, California

©2023 by Elyse Semerdjian. All rights reserved.

No part of this book may be reproduced or transmitted in any form or by any means, electronic or mechanical, including photocopying and recording, or in any information storage or retrieval system, without the prior written permission of Stanford University Press.

Some material in this book has been adapted from the following articles and is used with permission:

Elyse Semerdjian, "Bone Memory: The Necrogeography of the Armenian Genocide in Dayr al-Zur, Syria," *Human Remains and Violence* vol. 4, no. 1, Spring 2018, 56–75. Copyright 2018, Manchester University Press. All rights reserved. Republished by permission of the publisher.

Elyse Semerdjian, "Phantom Limbs, Embodied Horror, and the Afterlives of the Armenian Genocide," in *Comparative Studies of South Asia, Africa, and the Middle East* vol. 42, no. 1, 182–195. Copyright 2022, Duke University Press. All rights reserved. Republished by permission of the publisher.

Printed in the United States of America on acid-free, archival-quality paper

Library of Congress Cataloging-in-Publication Data
Names: Semerdjian, Elyse, author.
Title: Remnants : embodied archives of the Armenian Genocide / Elyse Semerdjian.
Description: Stanford, California : Stanford University Press, 2023. | Includes bibliographical references and index.
Identifiers: LCCN 2022048339 (print) | LCCN 2022048340 (ebook) | ISBN 9781503630383 (cloth) | ISBN 9781503636125 (paperback) | ISBN 9781503636132 (ebook)
Subjects: LCSH: Armenian Genocide, 1915-1923—Psychological aspects. | Armenian Genocide survivors—History. | Women genocide survivors—History. | Human body—Symbolic aspects. | Collective memory—Armenia.
Classification: LCC DS195.5 .S459 2023 (print) | LCC DS195.5 (ebook) | DDC 956.6/20154—dc23/eng/20221028
LC record available at https://lccn.loc.gov/2022048339
LC ebook record available at https://lccn.loc.gov/2022048340

Cover design: Daniel Benneworth-Gray
Cover photograph: Loutfie Bilemdjian, a 17-year-old survivor from Aintab, was recorded as inmate 1010 at the League of Nations Rescue Home in Aleppo on May 17, 1926. Source: Registers of Inmates, the Armenian Orphanage in Aleppo, United Nations Archives at Geneva.
Typeset by Elliott Beard in Garamond Premier Pro 10.25/13.25.

Our bodies are the texts that carry the memories
and therefore rememory is no less than reincarnation.
—KATIE GENEVA CANNON[1]

CONTENTS

Note on Translation and Transliteration — ix

A Photograph as Prologue — 1

Introduction — 5

PART I *Bodies*

1 Zabel's Pen: Gender, Body Snatching, and the Armenian Genocide — 27

REMNANT 1: *"The Dance," Siamanto* — 45

2 Weaponizing Shame: Dis-memberment of the Armenian Collective Body — 47

REMNANT 2: *"Armenian Girls inside Arab Homes," Ruben Herian* — 60

3 Rescuing "Kittens" in the Desert: The Armenian Humanitarian Relief Effort — 62

REMNANT 3: *Letter from a Captured Armenian Woman, Keghanush Kuyumdjian* — 81

4 Recovering Survivors in Aleppo, Replanting Bodies in Syria's Armenian Colonies — 82

REMNANT 4: *"The Orphan Collection" (Vorpahavak), Armenian National Relief Organization in Constantinople* — 104

5 "Changelings" and "Halflings": Finding the Armenian Buried inside the Islamized Child — 105

REMNANT 5: *Aurora on Stage: Survival as Sideshow Act* — 124

| 6 | Aurora's Body, Humanitarianism, and the Pornography of Suffering | 126 |

PART II *Skin*

| 7 | What Lies beneath Grandma's Tattoos? Traumatic Memories of Inked Skin | 149 |

REMNANT 6: *Statement of Miss Eliza Shahinian* 163

| 8 | Wounded Whiteness: Branded Captives from the Old West to the Ottoman East | 165 |

REMNANT 7: *"The Removal of Tattoos and Carbonic Acid"* 183

| 9 | Removing the "Brand of Shame," Rehabilitating Armenian Skin | 184 |

REMNANT 8: *"Tattooed Like an Arab," Serpouhi Tavoukdjian* 199

| 10 | Counternarratives of Tribal Tattoos and Survivor Agency | 200 |

PART III *Bones*

REMNANT 9: *A Lamentation: "In the Deserts of Dayr al-Zur" (Der Zor çöllerinde)* 223

| 11 | If These Bones Could Speak: Early Armenian Pilgrimages to Dayr al-Zur | 225 |

| 12 | Feeling Their Way through the Desert: Affective Itineraries of "Non-Sites of Memory" | 240 |

| 13 | Bone Memory: Community, Ritual, and Memory Work in the Syrian Desert | 256 |

EPILOGUE
Bone on Bone 279

Acknowledgments 287
Notes 293
Bibliography 357
Index 371

NOTE ON TRANSLATION AND TRANSLITERATION

I have transliterated Western Armenian sources according to the Library of Congress system but without the diacritical marks. The subjects of this work spoke Western Armenian, an endangered dialect of Armenian and the Genocide's final victim. To honor this lost community and its dialect, I chose to retain Western Armenian pronunciation. For example, I refer to *Gochnag* instead of *Koch'nak*. In almost all cases I retained the *-ian* ending for Armenian surnames as opposed to the *-yan* frequently used in Eastern Armenian. Ottoman Turkish is rendered in the modern Turkish alphabet while Arabic transliteration conforms to that of the *International Journal of Middle East Studies*, but without diacritical marks.

REMNANTS

I

A PHOTOGRAPH AS PROLOGUE

FIGURE 1 *The Chekijian Family of Aintab. Source: Personal collection of author.*

This photograph was never meant to be a precious artifact. Simply mounted with glue on a piece of board and nailed to the wall of the Chekijian family home in the Armenian Quarter of Aintab, the nail holes on the upper-right and left-hand corners are scars of its earlier social life. A scratch down the face of my great-grandmother Vergine and a slash across the throat of the Chekijian daughter, Eliz, who didn't survive, foreshadow the frenzy of mass killing soon to be unleashed in the Ottoman Empire. I learned only later that both my aunt and I were named in memory of her.[1] Other scratches on the photograph trace decades of shuffling between homes across a newly created political border that would partition Turkey from Syria. Much like the community it represents, this photograph was not meant to survive a hundred years. Nor were the living bodies that sat for this studio portrait four years before the killing began.

Taken inside an Aintab photo studio around 1911, the photograph shows a little girl wearing a crisp white dress standing between her grandparents, seated in the front row and surrounded by their seven children. The child, my grandmother Hripsime, leans on her fez-wearing grandfather, who has a *kemer* wrapped around his waist, his money secured in the folds and held close to his slim frame. In contrast to the traditional Ottoman clothing of the family patriarch, the women wear black Victorian gowns, and their hair is coiffed in turn-of-the-century fashion. The brothers too are wearing Western-style suits: tradition and modernity are contained within a single frame.

The fez is out of place; it is Barthes's *punctum*.[2]

I am drawn to my own great-great-grandfather Hagop, seated at right in the front row. He and his brothers were tailors for the Ottoman military, and his fez, headgear instituted nearly a century earlier as a uniform for all citizens—Muslim, Christian, and Jew—stood in stark contrast to the clothing laws that had historically color-coded Ottoman communities by religion and social class. The unifying intent of the fez would be undermined by forces of nationalism, imperialism, and sectarianism that plagued the late days of empire.

My grandmother Hripsime was but seven years old when the Armenian Genocide began in 1915. As a young child who survived the genocide, she couldn't remember all that much. Maybe her lack of memory was a blessing, but for me, the historian of the family, it is an itch that I cannot scratch. The Ottoman military had relocated the four Chekijian brothers—tailors Hagop, Nazaret, Manuel, and Hovannes—from Kayseri to Aintab for the express purpose of making uniforms. The uniforms sewn by the hands of my great-great-grandfather and his brothers would be worn by the same men who would deport and kill Armenians throughout the empire. This memory collides into another of the Chekijian family being prepared for deportation. They were rounded up by Ottoman soldiers. Hagop came home to find his terrified family inside a horse-drawn cart about to be taken away. The soldiers, according to family legend, released the family when they recognized them as belonging to their very own tailor. Hagop's family was saved because of his complicated relationship (dare I say complicitous?) with the same military that slaughtered his countrymen.

Eventually, by means we do not know, little Hripsime and her mother, Vergine, the one whose face is scratched but defiant, found their way to Aleppo. My grandmother never shared the name of her missing father with my father. My cousin Berjouhi fills in the gap where my father's memory has been obliterated. She tells me that my great-grandfather's name was Nazareth Seykeljian and that he was "very clever" (*shad jarbig er*). A newlywed with two small children, he was forcefully drafted into the Ottoman military at the outset of the Great War and, like so many other Armenian men drafted into the labor battalions, never seen again.

A photograph is the only possession I have documenting my family on the eve of the *medz yeghern*, "the great crime" as the Armenian Genocide is often referred to in Armenian.[3] My own maternal family's complicity with the Ottoman military is a particularly shameful detail, but I reconcile that with my paternal grandfather, Youssef Semerdjian, who had fought with the Armenian Revolutionary Federation against Turkish forces in Aintab until he was forced to retreat to Aleppo in exile. Never knowing when the next war would start, he buried the rifle he used to defend his hometown within the family courtyard in Azizieh, Aleppo, waiting for the next opportunity to use it. When the French withdrew from Syria in 1946, my grandfather dug up the gun just in case another war broke out, but by then it had rusted and its wooden stock fell apart in his hands.

As I sift through archival records about the Armenian Genocide, they feel like the rotten debris from my grandfather's rifle; they barely resemble the vibrant, living community they represent. I have a sense that I may come across my grandmother's name in the records of "half-orphans," the children of widows collected in safe homes and orphanages in Syria. I feel butterflies every time I read the League of Nations intake records and orphan identity cards generated by European and American relief workers and come across a Semerdjian, a Chekijian, a Hripsime. An odd mix of dread and excitement overwhelms me when I consider the prospect of filling gaps to better understand how my own grandmother ended up in Aleppo—my own grandmother, a symbol, perhaps, for all the grandmothers lost and found. Grandmothers discovered after a century of hiding, those who whisper the truth about their pasts to their Muslim grandchildren in contemporary Turkey and Syria.

I have never found traces of my grandmother Hripsime in the archives; she exists only my family's memory archive. But the Chekijian family portrait has continued to inspire me with what it can and cannot tell me about my own family's history. I discovered the Chekijian family portrait in 2000 in an armoire belonging to my grandmother inside our family home in Aleppo. When my *tantig* ("little auntie") Eliz, the first of us to be named after a relative who had died in Dayr al-Zur, opened that armoire, it smelled like the Aleppo olive oil soaps she used to pack her clothes in to keep the moths away. I asked *tantig* to give me the original photograph. A stubborn woman, she hesitated but some how she handed it to me. Ravaged by a decade of war, I consider how this photograph—the only material family heirloom in my possession to survive the Armenian Genocide and the Syrian War—could have been lost forever in yet another war had my stern aunt, with whom I rarely won an argument, considered me a less convincing custodian.

In 2019, I met a branch of my family that had left Aleppo in 1946 for Armenia. While thumbing through photographs with my relatives in Yerevan on a hot, sticky afternoon, feeling drowsy after a heavy meal of *khashlama* and *kufta*, I discovered that my cousins have a pristine copy of the Aintab portrait. Life delivers surprises! Their portrait, without nicks or tears, looks as fresh as the day it was taken. Through their stories, my cousins Seta and Ani were able to fill in some gaps in my memory. But after catastrophe, some gaps can never be filled; heartache lingers.

The irony of having so little historical documentation of my own family's history is not lost on me—my profession is to reconstruct the history of everyday life and I have performed this act with the scant evidence left behind by marginalized women and non-Muslims in the Ottoman Empire. Analyzing this photograph with digital technology may reveal the dirt on the shoes of the family members, traces of the journey they took on an unpaved road to the photography studio in Aintab, but it cannot answer all the family mysteries that haunt me. There are not enough breadcrumbs to follow.[4]

My family, the Chekijians of Aintab, were tailors who sewed fabric together to make garments, including those worn by perpetrators who would murder their countrymen. I am a weaver of stories from the remnants they and others left behind. I follow in the footsteps of many other writers who have tried through fiction, art, music, and historical study to address the fragmentation of memory and traumatic silences of the past that Harry Harootunian has called "the unspoken as heritage."[5] Addressing this fracture requires radical acts of imagination because, for the survivor community, the violence of genocide is ongoing not only in the perpetrator's denial but in the unspoken. My own fragmentary memory of genocide inspires me to explore the stresses and limits of the historical archive that preserves some traces of the past while overlooking or actively effacing others. It is not easy to acknowledge the extent to which my own personal history has been erased by the atrocities described in these pages. We are still grappling with remnants a century later.

INTRODUCTION

FIGURE 2 *Seventeen-year-old Loutfie Bilemdjian of Aintab was abducted, bought, and sold to three different men before finally escaping to Karen Jeppe's Rescue Home in Aleppo. Source: "Registers of Inmates, the Armenian Orphanage in Aleppo" 1922–1930, inmate 1010, United Nations Archive at Geneva. Reprinted with permission.*

Name: Loutfie Bilemdjian **Father's Name:** Adour
Mother's Name: Mariam **Native Country:** Aintab
Age: 17 **Admission Date:** May 17, 1926

On the first outbreak of the deportation she was exiled with her parents and two brothers in the direction of Deir el-Zor. Traveling afoot [from Aintab], they reached Meskene. After a few days rest, the caravan started again for Deir el-Zor. On the road, the poor people were exposed to the attack by a band of plunderers, who, like a pack of wolves, descended upon them, robbed, and killed the people at their pleasure in the presence of the gendarmes, who, after the slaughter, shared their plundered booty. Loutfie's mother fell dead in the way of guarding her young ones. Her father and younger brother fell too. The older brother was lost and she herself came into the possession of a Tchechen, who sold her to a Kurd, the later passed her to a rich Turk named Mahmoud Pasha who sent her to his house in Veranshehir.[1] There she remained for 11 years till she got the opportunity to cross the border to Ras el-Ain from whereby our Hassitche [Hassaka] agent she was sent to us. Fortunately, on the day following her arrival, we gained information of her lost brother who had been at Marseille until a few months before. We shall take care of her until we succeed in locating her brother.

Left our care on May 19, 1926. Relatives, uncle in Aleppo[2]

Loutfie Bilemdjian's story was transcribed when she arrived at a Rescue Home ran by Danish humanitarian and League of Nations commissioner Karen Jeppe (1876–1935) in the spring of 1926. The entry provides a brief sketch of her ordeal as she was passed between men who bought and sold her near Dayr al-Zur, Syria. Loutfie was finally sold to a wealthy Turk in Viranşehir, a small town located between Urfa and Mardin in today's southeastern Turkey. Trafficked between a triangle of cities where the buying and selling of human cargo was heavy during the Armenian Genocide, Loutfie's image circulated along with those of other victims in European and American appeals for humanitarian aid funding. To audiences, her tattooed face spoke for itself as indelible proof of her enslavement and her experience as a "trafficked woman," in the human rights parlance of the period.

Loutfie's beauty is stunning. She surely attracted the eye of both slaver and humanitarian, but there is something particularly striking about the photograph taken in the studio adjacent to the Rescue Home office and later cropped and pasted to Loutfie's intake register. Many other women and children who appeared in that studio recoiled before the camera, its penetrating lens aimed at their battered faces and bodies to visually communicate the trauma described in the textual narrative. Loutfie, however, appears to sit comfortably before the photographer, meeting the camera's gaze. Other runaways wore tattered clothing—a tuft of fur for a shawl, rags for clothing. Loutfie, by contrast, is well-dressed, more proof that she was kept in an elite household. Perhaps she felt a tinge of shame about her tattoos, but instead of hiding her face, she pulled her embroidered cloak up over the back of her head for a degree of modesty before the camera.

For me, the intricate chicken belt buckle, perhaps carved from bone, stands out as a symbol of the care this young woman took in her appearance. Such care is affirmed again when I notice that the ∴ pattern tattooed on Loutfie's face is echoed in the dots and geometric designs on the dress she likely sewed herself. In the unusual case that another woman embroidered her garment, Loutfie still would have had some hand in the design work. The crow's-foot design that runs down her neck and chest is suggestive that the tattoo design may continue under her dress to possibly form the *hayat ağacı*, or "tree of life" motif.[3] Some versions of this motif encircle the breasts and extend all the way to the groin area and intend to offer its wearer blessings of a long, healthy life.[4]

Unmentioned in the entry are Loutfie's tattoos, which tell us aspects of her story that we might miss without closer observation. The dot on the tip of her nose and the .|. pattern on her chin indicate that she was captured somewhere between Ras al-'Ayn and Dayr al-Zur by the Wuld Ali, a tribe that constituted part of the 'Anaza confederation.[5] Transferred between three men—a Chechen, a Kurd, and a Turk—the details of her time among the 'Anaza is documented on the skin of her face rather than the written record. Observing these silences, I wonder, what other silences are there in the archive? What other ways might I view, read, and listen to archival documents for the minute traces of genocide experience?

In this book, I analyze the fragmentary evidence of Armenian survivors, paying special attention to the traces violence and memory have left upon the body of the archive and the actual bodies of Armenian victims and their descendants. The embodied trauma of victims of sexual abuse and forced marriage have been, at times, deemed too personal and too emotional to be worthy of historical study. Many stories have been held tightly as familial memories, while others have fallen into oblivion over time—this is most true for male victims of sexual abuse, whose stories have yet to be told. The story of sexual violence, while central to the objectives of genocide, are often relegated to a single-page mention within the existing historiography. But in the pages that follow I argue that thinking through and with the materiality of the body—as an archive of genocide experience that communicates emotional and affective knowledge discarded by the violence of traditional archives—can unlock traces of historical evidence that are worthy of study. By highlighting these ciphered bits of information, what I call *remnants*, I situate the material body of survivors as a repository of traumatic experience, bodies that also form sites of resistance where the memory of victims are preserved by their descendants.

Claudia Card has argued that genocide is an attack on "social vitality," the vibrancy and cohesiveness that "exists through relationships, contemporary and intergenerational, that create an identity and gives meaning to life."[6] Stamping out this vitality through cultural genocide and forced assimilation produces social death for the target group. In the case of Armenian women, they were most vulnerable to Islamization since Muslim patriarchal order and sexual regulations in Islamic law facilitated the assimilation of non-Muslim (*dhimmi*) women. For the Armenian diaspora, the tattoos that some women survivors bore have largely come to signify the shame of Islamization, mysterious visual artifacts from the largely successful attempt to eliminate the Ottoman Empire's Christian population from its eastern provinces.[7] Yet, the tribal tattoos themselves hold no religious meaning within Islam. The tattooed survivor is presented as a living (ethno)martyr within recent documentaries, while at other times a national stain, her tattoos a memory of the successful core genocide campaign to eradicate Armenian identity in historic Armenian homelands.[8] Occasionally, counternarratives disrupt our received wisdom by portraying the tattoos as badges of heroism and survival.

The women and children who survived the violent ethnic cleansing campaign are still referred to pejoratively in Turkey today as the "remnants of the sword" (*kılıç artığı*), those who were deported, raped, enslaved, and forcibly assimilated into Muslim households.[9] The sometimes incoherent fragmentary wreckage of what was once the Ottoman Armenian community is also referred to as "remnants" (Armenian: *khlyagner, pegor,* or *mnatsorats*) by Armenian contemporaries.[10] In the ruminations of Giorgio Agamben, remnants lie at the disjuncture between the drowned and the saved; they are the attempt to listen for the gaps in survivor testimony and reckon with the impossibility of witnessing for the true witness is already dead.[11] I seek to reclaim the concept of remnants as a tool of resistance against post-genocide aphasia and to locate the bodies of Armenian women and girls that have miraculously survived within a *mutilated historicity*.[12] Some texts are shared in their raw form between the chapters of this book as a means of drawing attention to both absences and traces that linger despite the state's attempts to erase them.

As I reflect on my family's trade as tailors, I am inspired by how the original terminology for text in Latin originates in the verb root *textere*, meaning "to weave"; the text itself is a series of threads that form a woven textile. Remnants are texts, but they are also bodies. Fragmented bodies, individual and communal, were disassembled in the process of genocide, a process I call *dis-memberment*. The bodies of victims were reassembled by humanitarians and nationalists after the war to recover remnants of the Armenian community. Visual, written, oral, and bodily texts of survival are fragmentary yet remain historically valuable for the information they contain. Rather than assigning these bits of fragmentary wreckage secondary status, I give them center stage to break open the archival record to offer an alternative reading of genocide experience.

Remnants are also immaterial traces of psychic intergenerational trauma as descendants grapple with fragmentary postmemory: secondary traumatic memories that are not rooted in personal experience but have instead been transmitted through image, narrative, and storytelling to form a range of communal memories. A fitting parallel is the transmission and remembrance of Holocaust postmemory, as Marianne Hirsch and Leo Spitzer explain of the Jewish survivor community:

These events were transmitted to them so deeply and affectively so as to seem to constitute memories in their own right. Postmemory's connection to the past is thus mediated not by recall but by imaginative investment, projection, and creation.[13]

The capacity for postmemory to form personal recollections helps us understand how it is that community members who did not directly experience genocidal trauma experience carry memories of dis-memberment, tattooed skin, and bones in the unmarked killing fields of the Syrian Desert. These memories are not shared for what they can offer empirically but instead for what reveal about the emotional weight of genocide that extends beyond the event itself—the genocidal erasure of Armenians from their ancestral homelands is ongoing.

Rather than use the term *postmemory*, I've chosen to use the term *prosthetic memory* to describe the intergenerational and mediated transference of shared memories and stories because the term captures how memory is an embodied practice.[14] Memory is stored within the body and genocide is remembered as body horror in which victims are forced to witness extreme violations of the body and desecration of the corpse. Furthermore, *prosthetic memory*[15] captures some the historic connection between memory and ritual in premodern human history, especially among Christian communities where the Eucharist, fasting, vespers, self-flagellation, and pilgrimage were embodied, temporally situated memories of Christ's suffering. Within ancient societies, human archives were people who were living, breathing repositories of memory, who embodied the religious and cultural texts they had memorized. Memory in our modern mediated culture works similarly, as historian of memory Alison Landsberg explains:

> Of course, this modern form of memory—prosthetic memory—shares certain characteristics with memory in earlier historical periods. With prosthetic memory, as with earlier forms of remembrance, people are invited to take on memories of a past through which they did not live. Some of the strategies and techniques for acquiring memories are similar, too. Memory remains a sensuous phenomenon experienced by the body, and it continues to derive much of its power through affect.[16]

Philosopher Maurice Halbwachs claimed memory is socially constituted to the extent that individuals draw upon the "group memory" transferred to them by others. While historically this transfer of memory occurred through storytelling, text, and church and state ritual, twentieth- and twenty-first-century media has greatly amplified and expanded group memory transmission.[17]

The age of mass media allowed for broad dissemination of printed and oral Armenian narratives of survival to the broader Armenian diaspora. The Armenian Genocide, like the Great War, occurred at the dawn of a new era of media-fueled prosthetic memory formation. That era continues today in the internet age, as stories of the genocide are broadcast with speed and breadth to audiences that extend beyond the Armenian community. Films, documentary journalism, and print and digital media—much of it authored by Armenians—continue to explore the legacy of the Armenian Genocide and make stories about it available to a wider audience. Over the last century, the memory of the Armenian Genocide has lived on, in part, through the transmission of memory through mass media, social media, and the internet, allowing it reach audiences beyond a single ethnic, racial, or religious grouping.

Prosthetic memory, as I see it, links past and present, and in the case of the Armenian Genocide, it opposes the uniformity of official memories shaped by the nation-state through violent erasure. Because the Ottoman Armenian community is now a diaspora dispersed across several nation-states (including Armenia), some memories lack official sites of memory and state monuments. These memories are what historian Mériam Belli has called "historical utterances," the messy, unofficial, and even at times unstable or inconsistent memories that lie outside official accounts.[18] Like phantom limbs of the amputee, prosthetic memories are still present and felt by subsequent generations by means of their engagement with the past through witnessing, storytelling, and memory work during pilgrimages to sites of mass atrocity. It is within this affective state that new knowledge is constituted. I honor these dissonant memories while also interrogating them for the stories they can tell us about embodiment and genocidal loss. Because the stories I share often fall outside the purview of state archives that have largely obliterated the voices of victims, it is important to share with the reader that I have a bone to pick with the archive.

THE STATE IN THE FIELD: A FEMINIST PROVOCATION

Rosie Bsheer has illuminated how the Saʻud dynasty shaped its state archives and "preservation" practices to consolidate its official version of state history. "Archive wars" violently erase evidence of and block access to an alternative past. She writes, "The archive question is also the state question. The state's material politics reveal how state power manifests, how the state itself is a sort of material practice, and how this materiality shapes and is shaped by the construction and destruction of history."[19]

The field of Armenian Genocide Studies has been held captive by the question of archives. Unlike Germany after the Holocaust, the perpetrator archive remained under the control of the state of Turkey. Historians are instructed to produce evidence while encircled by competing discourses of recognition and denial amid the ongoing attack on Armenian historical memory and the community's ancient cultural heritage by the perpetrator state. This ongoing violence certainly inflects the works we produce as a field. Most works examining this history have sought to use archival evidence to fortify positions of acceptance or denial of the Armenian Genocide. In these debates, non-Turkish archives have often been declared untrustworthy and eyewitness testimony more so. The official repository of Ottoman documents in the Prime Minister's Archives in Istanbul (Başbakanlık Osmanlı Arşivi) renders 1915 as the "Armenian problem" (*Ermeni meselesi*), an implicit denial that rejects the events as a question of state violence. The violent production of archive means that all scholars of this subject matter are, in the words of Heghnar Watenpaugh, working against "the relentless erasure of Armenian traces in Turkey, as place names and even Armenian inscriptions are obliterated from heritage sites and certainly informational placards affixed to objects created by Armenians."[20] The Prime Minister's Archives prominently displays its own self-published books on the subject, which include printed facsimiles, transliterations, and translations of documents that portray Armenians as rebellious traitors deserving of massacre during 1915 and mimic rhetorically the claims of the victim community in order to absolve the Ottoman Empire and its successor, Turkey, of guilt.[21] I mention these trends only to describe the ecology of Armenian Genocide scholarship as denialism and state policy overshadows scholarly production both inside and outside of Turkey.[22]

Regular controls are placed on the Ottoman archives by the Turkish government as each requested document is vetted, scanned, and monitored. Despite these controls, scholars have used Turkish state archives with the noble aim of proving methodically the intention and planning of the Ottoman state to deport and exterminate its Christian populations, beginning with the Greek Orthodox community and ending with the Armenians and Assyrians.[23] I am a beneficiary of studies of the Armenian Genocide that preceded this publication, but this book does not seek to prove that genocide happened. Instead, I seek at the outset to demonstrate how gender, patriarchy, and the body informed genocidal thinking. I seek to illuminate how abduction, conversion, and sexual enslavement, all practices rooted in older Ottoman practices, informed genocidal aggression against the individual and collective Armenian body. The body, and the skin, and the bones of Armenians bear witness to trauma as well as to the resilience of embodied memory. As such, although I engage some Turkish sources, I also refrain from overly fetishizing them, as I have in my own previous scholarship, in order to provide space for sources that amplify the voices of victims.[24] Critical studies of the archive continually point out its limits, but, as I see it, Armenian Studies has yet to absorb and engage these scholarly debates.[25] I suggest that we should approach the Turkish state archives not as a repository of Armenian Genocide knowledge but as a space of violent erasure and a subject in its own right.[26] The Ottoman archive is a sarcophagus full of "paper cadavers," for each document about an Armenian in the period under study is evidence of a crime, the imprint of a disappeared Armenian body violently removed from its indigenous land.[27]

This book interrogates the archive as an instrument of state building that effaces the social-psychic aspects of how Ottoman subjects experienced genocide, especially within a state that advocates denial as both foreign and domestic policy. While archives are certainly central to the work that historians do, they are not neutral in the face of power. They erase countermemories that threaten the state monopoly on historical narrative. What we end up with is a mutilated female subject, whose experience is obscured. In case it is not clear, my critique is issued as a feminist intervention against the disciplining effects of the state archive and a call to set new terms for how the Armenian Genocide should be debated. Our emphasis on bodies of evidence found in what is a national archive project has caused us to overlook perhaps the most obvious source for the history of genocide—the actual bodies of victims.

In this critical feminist rereading, I trace aspects of gender and embodiment in memoirs, letters, newspapers, biographies, oral histories, ethnography, photography, and film across a dozen archives in seven languages. This book blends disciplinary approaches to excavate the embodied experiences of genocide and memory or "what history meant in flesh and blood."[28] One could argue that Armenian history needs to be enfleshed by attending to the personal and individual stories of survival while also documenting the emptiness that remains, the shadows that represent hauntings as well as epistemological gaps that may never be filled. Yet, in addition to those sources, women's bodies themselves are treated as historical documents worthy of historical study through engagement with a number of interdisciplinary fields that I cannot claim to have covered comprehensively in this book. The reader may know these fields and the questions raised by them but due to lack of space and the desire for this book to be accessible to more audiences, I could not reference them all. I owe a great debt of gratitude to scholars in the field of Armenian Genocide Studies and Holocaust Studies who have laid the foundation for advancements in the field, including the developing subfield of Comparative Gender and Genocide Studies.[29] Through these readings of the body, I seek to contribute not only to Armenian Genocide Studies but to Middle East Studies, Gender Studies, the emerging field of Middle East Bodies Studies, and the field of Tattoo Studies, which remains a largely Eurocentric field.[30]

Though this work is a critique, I am not arguing to discard the archive completely. I am one of the archive's largest benefactors, having used over a dozen archives while researching this book alone while intentionally not privileging the perpetrator archive. Derrida called our archival obsession "archive fever," which he describes as "a compulsive, repetitive, and nostalgic desire for the archive" that should force us to interrogate our desires. Critically positioning ourselves before the violent production of the archive allows us to honor the living, breathing memories we continue to carry within our own bodies and minds.³¹ Remarkable is how a once vibrant Ottoman Armenian community has already been forgotten in the Turkish landscape as villages, place names, churches, and cemeteries have been obliterated.³² The work of activists to reactivate memory of lost communities can be found in an intervention by the Armenian leftist pro-democracy organization Nor Zartonk ("New Awakening"). The group erected a display of cardboard headstones to remind protesters that the site of the Gezi Park protest in 2013 was once the Surp Hagop Armenian cemetery before it was expropriated by the state after the Armenian Genocide.³³

We historians are trained to use what Hayden White has called "the middle voice," a form of narration that Holocaust scholar Dominick LaCapra has argued obscures the power relations between perpetrator and victim. LaCapra notes the implications of this position is morally unacceptable especially in cases in which the traumatized and their allies engage in forms of remembrance, mourning, and critical practice that he calls *"working through* trauma."³⁴ Bearing this in mind, I borrow from history's sister discipline of anthropology with the aim of writing better Armenian Genocide history and to disclose that writing this project was, for me, one of working through trauma. Afterall, the frequently used term *trauma* hails from the original Greek term for "wound." And the wounds for the Armenian survivor community have not yet healed, but my hope is that this book can move us in the direction of recovery.

In order to humanize the survivor community and make the storytelling more personal, I frequently refer to my interlocutors and many survivors by their first names. Using the first names of survivors and their descendants echoes the names of survivors, many of whom had lost all memory of their surnames, their lineages severed. In this historical narrative, I blend traditional archival sources and oral interviews with my own autoethnographic voice, the latter a disciplinary heresy for some historians. By periodically including my own autoethnographic entries, I remind the reader that I too have a subjectivity that inflects the collective memoir I narrate. The story of these displaced Armenians is also my story as I write from a position of exile. Acknowledging my positionality reminds the reader that historians shape the stories they tell and how the sources we use are mediated.

Primary sources or remnants are interlaced periodically to offer unfiltered spaces to draw the reader's attention to methodology and elevate trace voices they may have never heard before, among them a letter from an Armenian woman captive in Raqqa written to her father. Remnants are a reminder of the personal stories that have been lost in the politicized history of the Armenian Genocide. A feminist rereading of the Armenian Genocide demands radical acts of reparation because women have sometimes received only a single sentence or at most a single page of mention in histories of the Genocide. Yet women constituted half of all the victims and the primary victims in the death marches in the deserts of Syria where

Armenians, until the recent Syrian War, interacted with their human remains in acts of remembrance.[35]

I contend that we must center gender because mentioning it without studying it ignores how gender, sexuality, and patriarchy were central to the genocidal logic of the perpetrator.[36] For that reason, this work seeks to situate gender—read as not only the study of women but the relations between men, women, children, and by extension, community—front and center in order to examine more closely the way that the Ottoman state sought to dismantle Armenian vitality beginning with the family, and by extension, the historic indigenous Armenian community documented as far back as Herodotus's fifth-century-BC travels in Asia Minor. The state executed crimes of striking similarity and consistency that targeted the smallest unit of Armenian society to raze an entire civilization.

Furthermore, Islamization as forced assimilation operated along lines of gender that must be analyzed. It intended, in theory, to erase the victim's former identity and replace it with the culturally dominant Muslim identity of the genocide perpetrator, a process eased by patriarchal family structure. For some genocide survivors, assuming a Muslim identity was temporary; they were eventually rescued and reincorporated into the Armenian community.[37] Some Armenians reverted back to Islam, unable to be reformed back into Armenians. For others, conversion was a permanent state of being, a century-long performance that only recently crypto-Armenians have begun to publicly disclose.

Over the last decades, public discourse on Armenian grandmothers in Turkey emerged as a first step toward Armenian Genocide recognition. Carel Bertram has noted that Serdar Can's *Nenemin Masalları* (Tales of my grandmother) was the first biography of an Islamized Armenian grandmother, published in 1991 while he served a prison sentence in Diyarbakir for Kurdish resistance activities. From there, feminist voices like those of Fethiye Çetin emerged with the publication of *Anneannem* (My grandmother) in 2004, that ushered forth broader public discourse on hidden Armenians whose stories lay in the shadows out of fear of repression.[38] Many Islamized Armenians have followed Çetin to share their stories in films and published works.

However accepted these stories are by Turkish activists and artists, we must be mindful of how the rhetoric of grandmothers has, in other instances, enabled denialism. Within indigenous studies, Eve Tuck and K. Wayne Yang have referred to the fetishization of the (often fictitious) Native American grandmother among white descendants of settler colonists as "the move to innocence." In its North American iteration, the grandmother is frequently imagined as an "Indian princess," forming what Vine Deloria Jr. has called "the Indian grandmother complex."[39] Indigenous studies scholars have noted how the Native American grandmother is a fig leaf that obscures responsibility for genocide and affirms the futurity of the settler. Nora Tataryan Aslan captured this paradox when she illuminated how the discourse on Armenian grandmothers by Turkish liberals may have enabled a new form of genocide denialism that places the burden on the victim rather than affirming the perpetrator's responsibility for recognition and repair.[40] As the Armenian population of Turkey continues to dwindle, the figure of the Armenian grandmother offers a potent act of conscience and a symbol of reconciliation and repair for activists. For others, she is a symbol of genocidal success. Among these fraught images of Islamized women, the tattooed survivor looms like an apparition over the descendants of survivors who continue to struggle with traumatic memories of genocide that dis-membered their loved ones, their families, and their community.

BIOPOLITICS AND THE MAKING OF THE ARMENIAN GENOCIDE

While the Hamidiye Massacres (1894–1896), which claimed an estimated three hundred thousand Armenian lives, may have set a course for a broader genocidal campaign against the Armenians, Ottoman liberals agitated for a different future at the turn of the century. The 1908 constitutional revolution, enthusiastically received by Arab and non-Muslim subjects, offered a brief glimpse of hope in the multiethnic empire. Bedross Der Matossian vividly describes how a few weeks after the Committee of Union and Progress (CUP) took power, a celebratory ecumenical mass with Armenians, Greeks, Muslims, and Jews was held in Constantinople at the Armenian Holy Trinity Church located in the Balık Pazarı. The pathway leading to the church was lined with flags, and during the mass, the highest Muslim authority listened as the Armenian patriarch gave a patriotic speech. The mass was followed by a procession to Taksim Garden, where thousands of CUP supporters gathered to celebrate their common "Turkish-Armenian brotherhood."[41] The euphoria, however, was short-lived. Counterrevolutionary forces seized control of the party in 1909 and offered a stinging rebuke to Armenian supporters in the form of a pogrom against the Armenian population of Adana resulting in over twenty-thousand deaths.[42]

The universalizing message of citizenship and equality of late Ottoman liberalism collapsed further into xenophobic Muslim nationalism and a campaign of mass extermination that would destroy the empire's ancient Christian Greek, Armenian, and Assyrian communities on the eve of World War I. The cataclysmic loss of the Balkans in 1912–1913, coupled with horrific atrocities committed against the Balkan Muslim population by Christians, resulted in mass migration of Muslim migrants (*muhacir*) to Anatolia. The traumatic stories of Muslims who survived the pogroms in the Balkans fueled extremist calls for revenge, setting the stage for a counterrevolutionary coup led by Enver, Talaat, and Cemal Pasha, who seized control of government in 1913. The triumvirate formed a single-party dictatorship, which promoted Muslim chauvinism, boycotts of Christian businesses to support a "Muslim economy," and eventually the expulsion of Christians to avenge Balkan atrocities and political losses, beginning with the ethnic cleansing of Anatolia's historic Greek population that had lived in Anatolia before the empire's founding. This era of state formation was characterized by consolidation of Turkish Muslim hegemony over what remained of the Ottoman Empire.[43]

Late Ottoman social scientists offered ideological support for socially engineering the reduced empire, theorizing which bodies belonged to the state and which did not. The bodies of new Muslim émigrés from the Balkans would replace the Christians expelled through extreme policies. The Kurdish population, in their view, was assimilable, having a common religious heritage with other Muslims—though history has proven this particular assumption to be wrong. Among these Young Turk theorists was Ziya Gökalp, himself a Diyarbekir-born Kurdish sociologist, who believed that the emerging modern state should engineer its population through careful pruning and growth, writing in a poem that "the people are a garden and we are gardeners. Trees are not rejuvenated by grafting only, first it is necessary to trim the tree."[44] Informed by nationalist chauvinism, the final years of the empire were characterized by violent homogenization, focusing on the southeastern provinces where minority Christian Armenians (and Assyrians, often mistaken for Armenians but also specifically targeted with genocidal violence) were most heavily concentrated.

By 1914, the Ottoman government marched belligerently into global war alongside its German ally. That first year, during a fateful battle with Russia on the eastern front, in which Armenian battalions in Tsarist Russia joined to assist victorious Russian forces, 78,000 of 90,000 Ottoman conscripts perished; most of them froze to death while on campaign in the height of winter.[45] The Ottoman loss at Sarıkamış in January 1915, after years of campaigning against internal party enemies, incited politicians and soldiers toward a policy of expulsion for Ottoman Armenians.[46] While Ottoman troops had already begun carrying out random attacks on the Armenian population in retaliation for the casualties in Russia, which they blamed on Ottoman Armenians, not seeing them as distinct from those on the Russian side, the government organized disparate CUP paramilitary units into a formal Special Organization (*Teşkilat-ı Mahsusa*) that, along with Kurdish and Chechen irregulars, would carry out mass atrocities.

Talaat Pasha reportedly said, "I hate all priests, rabbis, and hodjas," affirming how the core of Young Turk ideology was secular if not atheist. Yet the party drew upon common symbols of Muslim identity to unite a diverse set of allies during the war.[47] In 1914, the mass deportation of the Greek population began, under the claim that they were a fifth column aligned with enemies of the empire; it was followed by the order to deport Armenians in 1915. Assyrians fell victim to state policy, resulting in the erasure of these Ottoman Christian communities and the death of 250,000 Syriac-speaking Christians in addition to an estimated 600,000 to 1 million Armenian casualties.[48] After the loss of Sarıkamış, Armenians were, after decades of Russian political rhetoric and material support from across the border, viewed as an enemy within. Over the course of the Armenian Genocide, 90 percent of the empire's historic Armenian community would be systematically erased from Anatolia to birth in blood the modern state of Turkey. Ümit Uğur Üngör captured succinctly the logic behind this murderous campaign, "No matter how much difficulty the Young Turks had in defining what 'Turkishness' was, it took them only a few years to define what Turkishness was *not*."[49] While the Ottoman state targeted its Christian communities, often using Kurds as surrogates, the state as early as 1916 began perpetrating violence against its Kurdish population.[50]

In his epic tome on the Armenian Genocide, historian Raymond Kévorkian writes that the Armenian Genocide emerged in two major phases.[51] The first phase of the genocide was characterized by conscription of Armenian men into the military (as labor battalions rather than combatants) and the disarming of the general population. Drafted men were disappeared. The second phase of the genocide was ushered in by mass arrests of Armenian politicians and intelligentsia on April 24, 1915. The initial deportation order was instituted formally a month later as the Sevk ve İskân Kanunu (Relocation and Resettlement Law). Using the euphemism of *tehcir* (forced migration), the temporary law of May 27, 1915, provided a similar image of punitive exile found in an earlier system of population transfer. The temporary law never mentioned Armenians by name but used the synonyms of espionage and treason so that executors of the order could "feel or sense" (*hissetmek*) whether populations were guilty or innocent of treachery; this gave génocidaires sweeping authority over their victims.[52] Genocide apologists typically overlook the mass killing that accompanied removal of Armenians from their ancestral homelands, prompting historians to underscore that "deportation" was used as code for genocide.[53] *Tehcir* drew upon Ottoman muscle memory but also innovated on these practices with a more deadly twist in the service of the emergent biopolitical state.

During these deportations, provisions (including money and clothing) were stolen as unprotected caravans were looted by Muslim villagers, marauders, and contracted perpetrators. The long death marches passed through gathering points, including Aleppo, but were pushed in the direction of two major zones in the Syrian Desert: Ras al-'Ayn and Dayr al-Zur. It was in the desert in July 1916 that officials would undertake a mass-killing campaign that characterized phase two of the Armenian Genocide.

Talaat Pasha once remarked in a conversation with Henry Morgenthau as the American ambassador urged the Ottoman government to change course, "I have asked you to come here so as to let you know that our Armenian policy is absolutely fixed and that nothing can change it. We will not have the Armenians anywhere in Anatolia. They can live in the desert but nowhere else."⁵⁴ Nearly two million people were exiled to the desert because the Ottoman government believed that the desert was an uninhabitable wasteland.⁵⁵ While many Armenians were killed at the outset of the deportations, many others were able to survive the harshest environments due to their own ingenuity; Armenian grassroots rescue networks offered relief to victims but also received assistance from local Muslim peoples of the Jazira region.⁵⁶ Many Armenians did, however, succumb to the extreme depredations of the deportation and the aridity of the desert. American consul in Aleppo Jesse B. Jackson estimated that close to three hundred thousand Armenians were killed in the Syrian desert within Dayr al-Zur Province during the second phase of the Armenian Genocide in 1916.⁵⁷ Mass violence was inscribed onto the bodies of men, women, and children. Armenian bodies needed to assimilate as Muslim Turkish bodies, or their bodies would be completely excised from the emerging modern Turkish state.

To remember the great catastrophe that befell the Armenian community, Armenian diasporans all over the world march, hold vigils, and protest on the anniversary of the arrest of 250 Armenian intellectuals on April 24, 1915, and the subsequent killing of over a million Armenians between 1915 and 1923. Among the most striking acts of remembrance is the citywide commemoration in Yerevan that ends with a procession uphill to Tsitsernakaberd, the "swallow's fortress" Armenian Genocide Memorial that overlooks the city. This horrific crime continues to be officially denied by the Turkish government. These ceremonies center on naming the dead and engaging in rituals to remember absent bodies of Armenian martyrs who were denied a proper burial.

BODIES, SKIN, AND BONES: A BOOK IN THREE [BODY] PARTS

The thirteen chapters of *Remnants* are divided into three parts: "Bodies," "Skin," and "Bones." The growing academic literature on the subject of the body has yet to merge with Armenian Studies and has only recently become more visible in Middle East Studies.⁵⁸ Scholars have discussed bodies as formative sites of historical, political, and social ideologies as well as a surface upon which sexual and gender identities are inscribed and enacted. Historian Kathleen Canning argues that bodies have remained immaterial to many scholars, who fail to see them as material repositories of experiences, affect, and memories.⁵⁹ Bodies are made in revolutions and unmade in war; they are defined through ideologies of colonialism, medicine, sexology, and criminology; and they are culturally contingent markers of gender, race, religion, class, and community. *Remnants* taps this interdisciplinary field of study to focus on the state project of mass violence and the undoing of the body as well as its restoration through humanitarian national and reparative memory work produced through prosthetic memory.

The chapters are not meant to be in perfect symmetry nor intended to be tidy narratives that offer complete resolution. *Remnants* embraces the fragmentary embodied memories of survivors and their descendants. I periodically interlace the text with what I call "remnants," historical artifacts such as photographs, newspaper clippings, archival letters, narratives, song, and my own autoethnographic entries both within chapters and as distinct interruptions between chapters. These interludes intend to draw attention to the fragmentation and loss experienced by Armenians during the genocide as well as highlight the fragmentary nature of my evidence. This book is a dare. And in it, I suggest that the body is a text and that, in turn, a book may take the shape of a traumatized body.

In part I, "Bodies," I describe how genocide unraveled bodies at both the individual and communal level. It was not by mistake that the architect of the Armenian Genocide, Talaat Pasha, used a medical metaphor to describe his desire to excise the Armenian "tumor" from the Turkish body politic, pathologizing a perceived lack of loyalty to the regime.[60] This struggle over bodies and belongingness was the byproduct of nation-building, the foundations of which were established through biopolitical regimes of the late Ottoman Empire that fused the language and ideas of racial science with nationalism. Use of medical metaphors describing minorities as "foreign elements" (*ecnebi unsur*) or "germs" (*mikrop*) affirmed the boundaries of purity and contagion. Aslı Iğsiz argues that like the internationalists in the League of Nations, Turkish nationalists articulated the architecture for the new citizenry in religious, ethnic, and racial terms, discouraging the mixing of heterogenous populations while seeking to violently separate or unmix populations into discrete national units.[61]

The mass killing of Armenians quickly came into conflict with earlier Ottoman (and tribal) sensibilities that saw feminine bodies and arguably feminized not-yet-masculine bodies (e.g., prepubescent children) as nonthreatening to the patriarchal order. The event that sought to extinguish the Armenian presence in Ottoman Asia Minor began on a much smaller level, with the destruction of the patriarchal Armenian family. It is here that Raphael Lemkin's etymology of *genocide* as the Greek *genos* ("family, kin, tribe, race") and the Latin *cidium* ("killing") is crucial to understanding the relationship of the individual to the broader community.[62] Recent scholars of gender and genocide, however, have illustrated that the primary target of genocide is a community's reproductive capacity.[63]

The separation of men from women through conscription left women and children vulnerable to attack; leaders within communities were publicly mutilated; the beards of Armenian priests were cut and their bodies flayed, symbolically removing patriarchal protection over feminized members of the community. If bodies themselves were not cut, maimed, or killed to extinguish their regenerative potential, the psychological effects of watching loved ones being mutilated and killed on the vital threshold of the family home or in the arms of their mother were meant to make life unbearable and deal a death blow to the family unit. The burning of live bodies within structures that scaffolded the community—homes, barns, city squares, and churches—completely erased an ancient indigenous community from its land.

Once separated from the patriarchal household and Armenian communal body, feminized bodies could be shaped into Muslims (Turks, Arabs, Kurds) as a raw-material product of relations between men. Women were surplus labor within a political economy of raiding, forcible marriage, and abduction, and there was a sense of proprietorship over women's and children's bodies within the patriarchal Muslim household, a patrimony affirmed by Islamic and tribal law.[64] The historical record certainly contains cases of beneficent Muslims (Turks, Arabs, and Kurds) who rescued Armenian women and children out of a sincere desire to save them from imminent death along the deportation routes.[65] No two stories of survival are the same; sometimes within a single Armenian survivor's story are examples of debilitating cruelty coupled with outstanding acts of humanity.

The biopolitical logic that brought about the near extinction of Ottoman Armenians from their indigenous homeland emerged from the same intellectual genealogy as the League of Nations. Both genocide and state-building efforts viewed national status and survival as tethered to numerical metrics proving deservingness. As historian Lerna Ekmekçioğlu has shown, at war's end, Armenians were at a disadvantage, having just lost over a million bodies. By encouraging marriage, reproduction, and recuperating those hidden within Muslim homes, Armenians could raise the numbers of Armenians counted as part of the nation.[66] Biopolitics, as Aslı Iğsız reminds us, relies on the same logic of calculation of numbers and space as necropolitics.[67] Americanized, Europeanized subjects would serve to root latent imperialism in Middle East postwar reconstruction or within Armenian humanitarianism, the raw biological material needed to reconstitute and even build a case for nationhood. As the largest modern humanitarian disaster at the time, Armenians needed relief funds, which prompted relief workers to quickly learn how to harness gendered iconography in photography, film, and media to gain the world's attention.

If the body is a book that tells the story of traumatic experience, skin comprises its pages. Part II, "Skin," focuses on the epidermis to exhume stories that have been neglected or left in obscurity. Skin is threshold of the body, the contact zone between the self and the world. Contact with skin through touch or gaze provokes affects of affinity, shame, or disgust as our skins mix with other skins in the world. How did the tattooed skin of rescued Armenian women and girls communicate both belongingness and otherness within the communities that they came into contact with? How did marked skin produce feelings of abjection and shame for tattoo-bearing survivors? Skin can produce powerful affects as both a literal and figurative parchment, a primal writing surface upon which words and symbols are inscribed.

Tattoos, for many audiences, were legible symbols of past captivity and/or assimilation that re-traumatized survivors, threatening them once again with alienation from their community by continually identifying them as Muslim at a time they were struggling to reclaim their Armenian selves. Tattoos were understood to be slave or pimp brandings, "Turkish symbols" or "devilish signs," all of which left Armenian women tainted. Armenian tattoos were conversely referred to as "symbols of valor and honor" by other survivors, who interpreted them differently, and as protective totems by the indigenous groups of Mesopotamia. For an entire century, tattooed Armenian women have lived in the shadows, covering their tattoos with makeup or hiring surgeons to remove tattooed skin from their bodies in an attempt to hide the shame of a people destroyed in their own native lands in Anatolia. This hidden shame has made tattoos (and by extension the survivor's own body) an undertapped historical record of genocide experience and a stinging memory within the survivor community.

The most immediate frame of reference for considering genocide tattoos is the Holocaust. The Auschwitz tattoo was what survivor Primo Levi called "the demolition of a man"; it defaced distinct Jewish human identities with mechanical numbers denoting point of origin and place in line at the time of registration.[68] The Auschwitz tattoo discursively linked survival and annihilation. The numerical series linked life and death. Food was not distributed unless the number was promptly shown at meal time, yet the tattooed numbers were also used to identify the corpses of inmates at the time of death. Importantly, the tattoo was used only within the camp where mass industrial killing was the most intense—Auschwitz.[69]

Both Holocaust and Armenian Genocide–era tattoos have been met with conflicting emotions of horror and reverence as marks of survival and martyrdom. The affective terror of tattoos prompted one Armenian to absorb the prosthetic memory of the Holocaust, transposing it onto a family memory of the Armenian Genocide when she noted, "On the inside of my grandmother's forearms, they had six-digit numbers that identified them in the camps."[70] The tattoos of Islamized Armenian women were not numbers at all. Yet, they were often applied forcefully by communities that often actively participated in the genocide. Indigenous tattoos are an expression of a habitus: the embodiment of the particular social logics of the community to which the marks belonged.[71] The tattoo symbols lost that meaning and were assigned another when women's bodies were reunited with the Armenian community. Tattoos were understood to be savage markings, but alternatively, among tribal communities of Mesopotamia, they were believed to be powerful totems where, ironically, they were meant to ward off evil and protect the wearer from harm.

While some discourses will be familiar to the descendants of Armenian Genocide victims who hold onto this painful memory, other narratives, such as the way the tattoos were interpreted and framed by missionaries, relief workers, medical doctors, the media, and the tribal peoples of Mesopotamia, may be lesser known. I approach these tattoos with an openness to their unexplored context, but do not mistake my scholarly attempt to understand the original purpose of these tattoos among the tribal peoples of Mesopotamia as an apology for genocide. This warning is issued specifically to genocide denialists, who use every opportunity, even the incidental survival of Armenians marked for death, as an opportunity to deflect blame. To efface the traumatic experience of victims for political gain is to misread this book. What I seek to illuminate is how tattoos have been historically overdetermined and to explain what has not been explained thus far: why they were applied on Armenian women's bodies by the communities that absorbed them. In this exhumation of the tattooed skin of survivors, conflicting narratives will collide, taking the reader along with them on the journey.

I leave the reader with Part III, "Bones," which explores what is left behind when the body, ravaged by the forces of nature, putrefies and decomposes: the bones that remain become a powerful symbol of the finite nature of life and of our struggle as humans against forgetfulness. Bones move us emotionally and inspire fear, disgust, reverence, and devotion. When unhinged from each other, the 206 bones that constitute our individual bodies can become unidentifiable and unknowable. Gender, ethnicity, religion, and race of bones cannot be determined by the untrained eye. Fragmentation of the body prompts us to project the fleshiness that was once there with our prosthetic memory. Sometimes, when we look closely, we see our own reflection in the phosphorous patina of bones. Mass grave sites obscure individuality—class, racial, and gender distinctions—which inspire those who witness them to imagine that "each deceased person had joined a collective dead, their bones interlaced in this membership through death."[72] As bones comingle with the earth, human remains become inseparable from the very land, sand, and soil that forms the bedding of our nationalist imaginations.

Focusing on Armenian pilgrimages to the killing fields where mass graves of the dead lie unburied except with the sediment of time, I theorize the meaning that these visits and the embodied interactions that survivors and their descendants have with both the land and the bones within the necrogeography of the Syrian Desert. These individual interactions with bones are vernacular practices within the a largely unmarked, agentic space that coproduces what I call *bone memory* in those who have made pilgrimage there. It is there, in the sands of the desert, that the bones speak and articulate their history to the living. We can hear their stories if we listen carefully.

Human rights scholar Sévane Garibian notes that Armenians "confront the question of the place and role of human remains in the community of the living in the aftermath of extreme violence."⁷³ Human remains have continued to be at the center of Armenian memory practices, and it is here that this book completes its cycle by focusing on the prosthetic memories enacted by descendants of Armenian Genocide victims in the desert. What does it mean then that Armenian bodies lay uninterred across vast swaths of desert and in the caverns and riverbeds throughout their ancestral homelands? How do Armenians cope with the psychic pressure to mourn the dead who have no headstones? Using the earliest firsthand accounts of visitors to the desert, as well as those of more recent pilgrims to the unmarked landscape of Dayr al-Zur, I illuminate how visitors interacted with the affective necrogeography of the desert. The pilgrim itineraries of Armenians who visited the sites of the dead, spaces that are now inaccessible and largely erased due to war, are reconstructed. Just as saintly bones were often on the move, so too are the bones of Armenian martyrs taken by the pilgrims who visit them in the Syrian Desert.

The final installment of the book is about the possibilities of a human archive, where *knowing in the bones* offers an antidote to the problem of state archives and the oblivion created in the wake of mass violence.⁷⁴ It also considers the way that the landscape, the literal as well the figurative landscape, has been transformed—bone on bone—once again by the mass graves and destruction the self-proclaimed Islamic State has left behind.

I return to Loutfie, the survivor who opened this introduction. For those who applied them, her tattoos were symbols of beauty and belongingness and served as protective amulets. For others, they were physical marks of assimilation among the Turkish, Kurdish, and Arab populations who abducted, adopted, or enslaved women and children during the Armenian Genocide. Those who saw Loutfie's photograph may have expressed shock and horror at what they viewed as her horrific disfigurement with tribal tattoos. We do not know if there may have been a time during her reabsorption into the Armenian community when feelings of shame began to surface, but to regard her tattoos simply as marks of slavery overlooks how they also inscribe her personal story of resistance and survival.

Loutfie's photograph was taken at the moment she transformed from the concubine of a wealthy Turk back into an Armenian. She left the Rescue Home only two days after her arrival, when she found a surviving relative in Aleppo and others in Marseilles. I like to imagine her new life among the many Armenian Genocide survivors who would settle in Marseilles after surviving genocide. Did she wear the latest French fashions in the 1920s, replacing her traditional embroidered dress, rooster belt buckle, and head covering? How did people respond when her neck tattoo peeped out above her dress? Did, despite her proud look in the photograph, her tattoos later cause her shame and discomfort? Was she able to eventually see them as badges of courage and survival? Maybe she found a doctor willing to surgically remove her tattoos or, like so many other tattooed survivors, she used makeup to cover the traditional Bedouin tattoo between her eyes.

Roland Barthes wrote, "It's true that a photograph is a witness, but a witness to something that is no more." So young and full of life when the photograph was taken, the photo now operates as a memento mori—Loutfie is now deceased and her photograph serves as a reminder of not only her remarkable survival but our own mortality.[75] We may never know the truth about what became of her life, but her photograph represents simultaneously her near-social-death experience, her survival, and her ultimate death since she is no longer with us. Loutfie, a native of Aintab, stands in for the stories of my own family members that will never be known because they were never documented in a register. She stands in for the persons whose names were never recorded and those who were never able to escape their captivity to tell their stories. *Remnants* grapples with fragments, be it a photograph, a tattoo motif, or a fragment of bone, to recognize the traces Armenians left behind in a deluge of biblical proportions.

Our journey begins with bodies, individual and collective, that were once rooted in the Armenian homelands in the Ottoman Empire.

PART I
Bodies

CHAPTER ONE

ZABEL'S PEN

Gender, Body Snatching, and the Armenian Genocide

> I longed to see acts of heroism but these were rare occurrences and usually performed by women.
> —KEROP BEDOUKIAN, *The Urchin: An Armenian's Escape*

On the balmy night of April 24, 1915, during the mass arrest of hundreds of blacklisted Armenian intellectuals in Constantinople, only one woman was viewed to be so dangerous that she was targeted for arrest, deportation, and disappearance: Zabel Essayan (1878–1943).[1] The slow destruction of the Ottoman Armenian community, beginning with the Hamidiye massacres (1894–1896), then the Adana Massacres (1909), and ultimately the Armenian Genocide, formed the arc of her life.[2] Among her copious writings was a 1919 report for the Armenian National Delegation that focused on the plight of Armenian women and children during the genocide.[3] In the report, she narrated how genocidal violence was informed by gender, something scholars would later show was not incidental but rather by design. The gendered body—and the cultural and social symbolism it contains—forms the social fabric of a community knitted together with norms and customs and bordered by taboos that if violated would unravel the social order. Genocide perpetrators target the systems of gender and sexuality that underpin the target community to enact their goal: to extinguish the life and futurity of a people. When it eliminates the reproductive capacity of both family and community, Elisa von Joeden-Forgey argues genocide commits "life-force atrocity."[4] However, the attacks on Armenian bodies during the Armenian genocide, as detailed by Zabel, were also rooted in a centuries-old Ottoman sex/gender system characterized by abduction, conversion, and slavery.

ZABEL ESSAYAN: WITNESS TO GENOCIDE

Zabel's career as an essayist, novelist, and feminist activist began at the end of the nineteenth century; her first poem appeared in print in 1895, followed by her first novel in 1905. In 1909, she was appointed by the Patriarchate of Constantinople to travel with a delegation of Armenians to address the needs of fellow Armenians throughout the empire from Kars-Bazar, İncirlik, Sis, and Osmaniye to Dörtyol, in the aftermath of a new round of pogroms in Adana.[5] Zabel's observations and writings on the Adana massacre were collected and originally published in 1911 as *Averagnerun mech* and later translated into English in 2016 as *In the Ruins*. Marc Nichanian has described the text as a genre-defying illustration of the impossibility of truly witnessing unfathomable mass violence.[6] Zabel documented the experiences of the most vulnerable members of the Armenian community: traumatized women, some still trembling with fear while others were nearly catatonic. She witnessed undernourished orphans whose parents had been murdered before their eyes—one of them was found still alive clasped in his dead father's hands.[7] *In the Ruins* bears witness to the catastrophe (*aghed*) that had befallen the Ottoman Armenian community. The scenes she described while walking among the ashes of a once-vibrant community are, in hindsight, a clear bellwether for the larger catastrophe that would unfold just a few years later.

During the arrests on the evening of April 24, 1915, Zabel slipped through the fingers of Ottoman authorities. She fled first to Bulgaria and then, when Bulgaria entered the war on the side of the Ottomans, she spent some time in Soviet Armenia, where she documented the testimonies of survivors, assisted with and organized the care of refugees and orphans, and continued her own writing. Though she had visited Soviet Armenia, she did not emigrate until she was offered a teaching post in literature at Yerevan State University in 1933.[8] As an activist, educator, and writer, she defended Armenian artists and writers such as Aksel Bakunts and Yeghishe Charents, who were under threat from Soviet authorities. This placed her in Stalin's crosshairs in 1937, prompting her imprisonment and torture in Baku. A researcher shared that a transcript of Zabel's interrogation is tucked away in the bowels of the Armenian National Archives in Yerevan. Tales about her death included possible drowning, but officially, all we know is that she died in Siberian exile in 1943. Like so many revolutionary Armenians who emigrated to Soviet Armenia in hopes of reconstituting a version of Armenia lost in 1915, Zabel survived one lethal form of authoritarianism in the Ottoman Empire only to be destroyed by another.

But back in the spring of 1919, when the final outcome of the armistice was still uncertain, Zabel sat before a typewriter in Paris to type a report addressed to the Armenian National Delegation, for whom she was an appointed inspector. The organization had prepared to advance the cause of Armenian nationhood at war's end on behalf of the surviving remnants of the nation. Zabel had written a report like this a decade earlier, but this time, rather than typing her observations in her native Armenian language from her red-colored home on the Asian shore of Istanbul, she typed her thoughts in French from a position of exile. She focused on the experiences of women and children, as she had before, but described far more vividly the sexual atrocities women and girls had experienced at the hands of genocide perpetrators, building on thoughts she had delivered at the Sorbonne just two months earlier.[9] Submitted to the Armenian National Delegation chairman, Boghos Nubar Pasha, "La libération des femmes et enfants non-musulmans en Turquie" (The liberation of non-Muslim women and children in Turkey) is arguably the first feminist analysis of the Armenian Genocide.[10] Zabel's writing has the hallmarks of early-twentieth-century feminist writing that focuses not only on women's victimhood but also the central role women should play in assisting the genocide's female victims as a form of feminist political action. Other documents written by Armenian women in the years that followed would also testify to the atrocities, including sexual atrocities, committed during the genocide.[11]

The opening lines of Zabel's report call attention to the abduction, conversion, and enslavement of young non-Muslim women by Turks during the war:

> From the beginning of the war, the Turks successively persecuted the non-Muslim nations which were under their domination. They massacred in place, deported, [and] massacred [once] again on the road to exile and in stages. Young women, girls, and children of both sexes were forcibly abducted, taken away or distributed to the Muslim population. It would be impossible to say the exact number of these unfortunates, but we are led to believe that the figure must reach and probably exceeds two hundred thousand [people]. The great majority are composed of Armenians [and] a very large number of Greeks. There are also Syrian and Assyrian women and children (Nestorians).[12]

Focusing on the intersection of gender and mass extermination (genocide as a concept had yet to be invented), Zabel describes the unraveling of non-Muslim communities and the targeting of women and children for sexual violence, mass deportation, and forced assimilation. Along the deportation paths from Constantinople to Erzerum, from Konya to Van, and from Aleppo to Mosul, non-Muslim women and children from the Greek, Nestorian, and Armenian communities were dispersed into Muslim homes. Muslim neighbors also sometimes benevolently took in women and children whose deported family members would never see them again. But absorbing children assisted the state's policy of separation and assimilation; a policy that was also facilitated through Turkish state orphanages and the monetization of Turkish adoption of Armenian orphans.

In addition to detailing the effect of abduction and assimilation—and related conversion and Islamization—on the Armenian community, Zabel described the enslavement and sexual violence that women experienced at the hands of Turkish agents. These were attacks on both the bodies of individual women as well as the collective Armenian community. Witnesses testified that perpetrators committed "rape, pillage, and murder, turning into massacre," which led Ambassador Morgenthau to describe the frenzied nature of violence unleashed on Armenians as an "orgy."[13] Overnight, women went from innocent daughters and modest wives to being forced into prostitution in brothels or being private concubines for both Turkish and German soldiers.[14] They were forced to endure inconceivable levels of sexual violence, which in some cases left women near death, only to endure the abuse again the next day.[15] Many of these rapes took place in front of family members or in public spaces to publicly usurp women's bodies from the patriarchal family unit. An eyewitness account from an Ottoman officer forwarded to the British foreign office described with horror how in Trebizond and elsewhere "[c]ases of rape of women and girls publicly are very numerous. They were systematically murdered after the outrage."[16]

Women's bodies were, therefore, at the center of genocidal design; their sexuality, Zabel noted, was "a cheap commodity; women were put up for sale in public squares and bazaars." They were trapped in a web of sexual violence that assured either their survival or death.[17] A century ago, Zabel's pen documented what later scholars of gender and genocide would confirm: sexual atrocity converts women's bodies into a medium of communication between men. In genocide, "the tools of domination that impose social hierarchies are selected in part for their efficacy; if they did not work, or were not thought to work, they would not be used," as Catharine MacKinnon would write. In other words, sex is the chosen weapon because it can do work that could not be performed with other means.[18]

Zabel's eleven-page report listed the names of those victimized by methodical kidnapping and rape, including girls as young as ten to fifteen years old and elderly women. A German officer kidnapped Elle Kalfaian, whom Zabel calls "the most beautiful girl in Erzeroum," dragging her through the streets to his house "despite her cries and protests."[19] In Erzindjan, the precision targeting of girls from the richest Armenian households aimed to upend social reverence for and untouchability of such women. "In Trébizonde," Zabel related, "the civil and military officers assembled the young girls of the notables, the most gracious, the best educated, in a public house [a whorehouse] for the members of the Committee [for Union and Progress]."[20] Social order was unraveled and hierarchies overturned when the daughters of nobility were converted into whores to service the sexual desires of German and Turkish soldiers. The sounds of tears and lamentation, she wrote, "only served to increase the joy of the sinister criminals and their bestiality."[21] Women who resisted the gendarmes and irregular killing squads made up of released criminals suffered torture and death.[22]

Like the historical record more broadly, Zabel's report is silent on the subject of sexual violence against men, but there are traces of it in the account of Meriam, a survivor who described how at the outset of the deportations "her husband was ravished and killed."[23] I hear the whispers of male sexual-violence victims in the shallow voice of survivor Roupen Gavour, who was only eight years old when the deportations began. He found work in the stables of a Kurdish home in Kharpert (Harput). But early one day, while drawing water out of a well to place in troughs for the animals, he heard the barn door slam. Mehmet bey, a member of the household described as tall and always wearing "Turkish clothes," stood before him blocking his way. Roupen said during his testimony, "Even then, I knew [what would happen]." He told the man that he was working and asked him to open the barn door, once, twice, three times. Mehmet bey instead pulled the boy down from second floor of the barn. Speaking through sporadic, traumatic wailing cries, the elderly man recalled his violation, remembering how "he [Mehmet] was a sex maniac. . . . Actually, he would come out and have sex with a cow or an animal" in the stable from time to time.[24]

Perhaps Zabel's report, as well as Armenian Studies scholarship more broadly, is silent on the subject of male sexual violence in order to spare male survivors further emasculation. The report illustrates further how women were specifically targeted as "victims of [repeated] collective rape" until they were taken away by a Muslim to his household.[25] There were entire troops tasked with raping women, often in public, "in front of many spectators." Zabel describes how, like a military drill, an alarm was sounded to mark the beginning of the mass spectacle of collective rape. She comments, "We are led to think that the Turks had organized these collective rapes [more] to insult our nation than to appease their passions. It is in a regular and repeated way that these crimes were committed."[26] The pattern of mass rape Zabel describes affirms how rape, as a weapon of genocide, was instrumentalized to shatter a community. Such intimate forms of violence destroy communities because sex is a relational exchange that is central to communal identity formation. By subverting these relations, the targeted population in genocide (including men) is gradually feminized and emasculated through violence. For survivors, genocidal rape is so unbearable that it has been called "worse than death" by victims.[27]

While the acts of abduction, conversion, and slavery detailed by Zabel were essential tools of Turkish domination of non-Muslim peoples during the war, they were not genocidal by design. Rather, they had been encoded body practices within the Ottoman Empire since the fifteenth century, making abduction, conversion, and (sexual) slavery habitual, remembered, and embedded patriarchal practices that could be exploited during the state's wartime extermination campaign. The Ottoman sex/gender system permitted men to pluck women's bodies out of the familial and communal whole during plunder. Reaching into this fleshly version of

Ottoman history illuminates how non-Muslim women's bodies were intertwined within Islamic, imperial, and non-Muslim legal views of sexuality, abduction, slavery, and marriage. Despite changes over time, Turks exercised Ottoman muscle memory as both statecraft and a sociocultural practice that reduced women to raw human material and surplus labor that could be harvested for the (re)production of household and, by extension, of the empire.

THE OTTOMAN SEX/GENDER SYSTEM

As the nomadic origins of the empire gave way to sedentary state building, two systems of slavery tethered to abduction and conversion—one military and the other domestic—emerged to form the backbone of Ottoman statecraft. Within an imperial "child levy" system (*devşirme*), abducted and forcibly converted boys formed the sultan's elite janissary corps from the fifteenth to the seventeenth century or were counted among the empire's more astute bureaucrats.[28] The second system, concubinage, as opposed to dynastic marriages that characterized the early empire, emerged in the mid-fifteenth century. Both systems were intended to absorb and assimilate abductees, forming them into devoted servants of empire. In a recent work, Marc David Baer argues that the child levy, which "forcibly transfer[ed] children of the group to another group," where they were forcibly converted to Islam and assimilated as Muslim, would by itself fit the modern definition of genocide.[29]

In her groundbreaking study of the Ottoman harem, Leslie Peirce illuminates how the institution of concubinage preserved dynastic wealth and a "posture of superiority" that was diminished in cross-dynastic marriages.[30] For both systems, non-Muslim subjects of the empire were exempted from slavery as "protected" (*zimmi*), in theory, as were Muslims.[31] Snatching non-Muslim bodies as war booty was to take place in non-Muslim lands on the Ottoman borderlands or inside enemy territory. Initially, the empire sourced slaves from conquered peoples in the Balkans, Russia, and to a lesser extent Africa, but when the Balkans split from the empire in the nineteenth century, the traditional supply of male slaves began to falter. Female domestic and sexual labor, however, were deeply rooted within the Ottoman sex/gender system and continued through World War I.

Anthropologist Gayle Rubin defines sex/gender systems as "a set of arrangements by which the biological raw material of human sex and procreation is shaped by human, social intervention and satisfied in a conventional manner, no matter how bizarre some of the conventions may be."[32] Adopting Rubin's terminology frees the appropriation of bodies and transfer of biological reproductive power from any particular gender system so that we can examine the struggle over sexual proprietorship as a universal feature of patriarchy rather than one embedded singularly within Islamic patriarchy.

In the late Ottoman Empire, patriarchy continued to be a challenge to progress even during the reform era known as the Tanzimat (1839–1876), which failed to abolish female slavery. Modernizing, liberal thinkers were unwilling to abrogate the male "sexual entitlement" enshrined in Islamic law; therefore, the Ottoman legal system left family law under the jurisdiction of shari'a. For women, this meant that marriage and dowry were still tethered to notions of proprietorship and patrimony, whereas rape continued to be considered a violation of [a male proprietor's] property.[33] The Qur'an 4:24 was interpreted to provide men legal sexual access to unmarried female captives, described as "those (women) whom your right hand possesses" (*ila ma malakat aymanukum*), affirming the popular notion that women's bodies could be possessed through either marriage or enslavement; both forms of bodily possession could involve abduction.[34] Kecia Ali, in her study of early Islamic juridical debates about marriage, has argued that jurists

> showed no hesitation in making analogies between wives and slaves or between marriage and commercial transactions. In fact, their central notion about marriage was that the marriage contract granted a husband, in exchange for payment of dower, a form of authority or dominion (*milk*) over his wife's sexual (and usually reproductive) capacity.[35]

Subsequently, the term *milk* has been used to describe both male proprietorship over wives and over slaves. Ali argues this would have been considered a normative analogy within premodern societies where up to a quarter of the population was enslaved.

Abduction, an extension of pillaging and raiding cultures of the past, had a larger association within marriage ritual for both willing and unwilling brides.[36] In the sixteenth century, however, abduction, especially of Muslim bodies designated to be free, was targeted by Ottoman imperial law that imposed horrifying penalties for men who violated another man's proprietorship over free Muslim bodies, among them castration for male abductors of boys and girls. For abducted boys, their dishonor was attenuated if they could demonstrate if they were unwilling sexual participants, the truest victims of sexual violation. For free Muslim girls and women, however, the social costs of abduction and sexual violence remained high. Married women abducted and forced to have sex with their captors were divorced by their husbands, and in order to maintain privacy and familial honor, cases were often settled privately to avoid scandal.[37] An honorable settlement was to sometimes have the victim marry her rapist.

Previously tolerated within Ottoman systems of slavery and law, non-Muslim zimmi in the late nineteenth and early twentieth centuries faced a confluence of sectarian violence, forced conversion, and female abduction, slavery, and sexual violence. Within the Ottoman legal order, non-Muslim Jews and Christians were a protected class, governed as a tax farm, which permitted limited autonomy in communal matters (marriage, divorce, and religious ceremonies) in exchange for a poll tax (*cizye*).[38] For zimmi men, if they learned languages, they could adapt to patterns of trade that could afford them opportunities to amass wealth as middlemen, merchants, and translators. Men who secured foreign citizenship exempting them from Ottoman law could elevate themselves above secondary Ottoman status. By the eighteenth century, community members became more vigorous about protecting communal boundaries, intensifying the policing of those borders as the empire modernized.[39] Historically, upward mobility through the military and civilian bureaucracy was closed to zimmi men unless they converted to Islam.[40] This system broke down by the mid-nineteenth century, when the empire instituted reforms that granted non-Muslims equal citizenship with Muslims, setting off some of the first sectarian-fueled riots in Syria and Lebanon.[41]

On the eve of Sultan Abdul Hamid II's infamous reign (1876–1909), Ottoman slavery was abolished by the short-lived 1876 constitution, which extended Ottoman citizenship to all subjects.[42] Slavery would not be debated again until the 1908 revolution.[43] Abdul Hamid II immediately halted the reform era upon ascending to the throne, and instead of liberating bodies, the state came to capture subject bodies through dual policies of centralization and Islamic revivalism.[44] Ceyda Karamursel has documented the failure of liberals to suppress slavery in the nineteenth century, when international humanitarianism focused on African slavery, bifurcating it from female domestic slavery dominated by Muslim Circassian women, which remained largely intact.[45] Ottoman Parliament minutes show that in the years leading up to the genocide, Armenian politicians continued to protest the continued enslavement of Armenian peasants in the eastern provinces after slavery had been abolished.[46] Ottoman sovereignty had always been elusive outside the metropole, where tribal allegiances and practices mattered and where Muslim families were able to avail themselves of surplus female labor through other means, such as polygamy. But it was the unique mix of late Ottoman sectarianism and the political economy of sex and gender that set the terms upon which state violence would be executed against non-Muslims in the twentieth century.

ABDUCTION AND STATE VIOLENCE AT THE END OF EMPIRE

While liberal Ottoman subjects experienced Abdul Hamid's repressive grip in one way, Armenians experienced it differently. Challenges to Ottoman sovereignty whether in the form of emerging Armenian ethnonationalism or local resistance to oppression were expunged with state-organized violence. The central government moved forward with yet another debilitating tax for the Armenians, forcing them to winter Kurds on their own lands in closer proximity to their households in addition to regular taxation. However, if we look more closely at the historical record, we learn that this additional tax burden was only one aspect of the tensions between the communities. Ongoing sexual violence against Armenian women and girls was yet another form of usurpation alongside the random violence of plunder and murder.[47]

Armenians used available avenues for justice in their attempts to recover abducted women and girls. An example is a high-profile 1889 case involving the abduction and rape of fourteen-year-old Gülizar near Moush by Kurdish tribal chieftain Musa Bey, who was known for his exceptional cruelty. The charges against him included rape of a woman named Ano and the bribery, theft, and extortion of surrounding populations, including Muslims. In one instance, he ambushed and tortured an Armenian named Ohan, burning him alive—the charges listed more instances of this particular crime.[48] After murdering Gülizar's grandfather, he abducted the girl, sparking a local crisis that garnered both national and international attention.

After bringing Gülizar to his household, Musa Bey forced the girl to convert to Islam against her will and marry his brother.[49] During her captivity, Gülizar was able to secretly notify her family of her whereabouts while sustaining death threats from Musa Bey and his men, all of whom were emboldened by accruing privileges for Kurdish strongmen in the Hamidian empire. During her abduction, Gülizar was pressured to convert to Islam. She was able to cunningly convince her captors that she had sincerely converted—her consent required by shari'a—while secretly planning her escape. Years later, Gülizar remembered being pressured to renounce her identity, saying, "I cried constantly. I couldn't get used to the idea of denying my faith, of becoming Kurdish." She had resolved to let herself starve. After burying her food in a corner of the room for a few days, her secret was discovered and she was given a severe beating.[50]

As her community agitated for her release, the local government retaliated by imprisoning and murdering Armenians for nationalist activities, including performing "national songs."[51] Meanwhile, Armenians from the provinces organized a protest at Kumkapı in Constantinople, the seat of the Armenian patriarchate, to agitate for official action against Musa Bey. Approximately fifteen hundred Armenians invaded the holy compound, breaking windows and accusing the patriarch of neglecting the needs of the community as violence erupted and many participants were arrested. After petitioning the Armenian Patriarch Khoren Ashikian in a formal complaint, the community's highest-ranking leader delivered the petition to the sultan at Yıldız Palace enumerating Musa Bey's abuses.[52] The Kumkapı compound was placed under armed guard for the protection of the patriarch.

Gülizar did not wait for leaders in Constantinople to secure her release. Instead she escaped of her own accord and reported her ordeal to the Ottoman Porte in an attempt to bring Musa Bey to justice for his crimes.[53] Recent scholarship by Owen Robert Miller has shown how the local Armenian community turned to Ottoman justice, condemning the warlord's cruelty while also organizing armed

Armenian resistance (*feday'i*) groups in the region to rally for the girl's release.[54] The Ottoman authorities limited Gülizar's participation allowing her to submit testimony in Bitlis rather than Constantinople in an attempt to mute public outrage that had migrated to Europe and the United States. While testifying, the girl was pressured by the Kurdish chieftain to testify that she had converted of her own accord. The chief prosecutor accused the Armenians of Moush of submitting false testimony.[55] Gülizar bravely refused to cave in to the pressure, declaring defiantly at the tribunal, "I am Armenian and will die an Armenian."[56] In the aftermath of the trial, the Ottoman authorities responded by arresting Armenian resistance activists and disarming the population, which sent the region into a cycle of violence.

Musa Bey was convicted and exiled to Mecca but quickly returned to Moush with impunity while the trial was still underway.[57] The trial became an opportunity for Musa Bey to, in the words of historian Ayşenur Korkmaz, acquire "legitimacy and sponsorship from the state" in order to strengthen his position.[58] Owen Miller has interpreted Gülizar's abduction alongside the massacre of Armenians in Sasun that would occur a few years later as illustrative of how sexual violence imbricated broader forms of state violence.[59] Not surprisingly, Musa Bey would play a role in the murder of sixty thousand Armenians of Moush during the Armenian Genocide twenty-five years later.[60]

Archival records further corroborate that it was not unusual for complaints about abduction issued from the Armenian community to Ottoman authorities to result in accusations of false testimony or worse, to be construed as Christians attempting to make true Muslim women commit apostasy. British parliamentary papers noted that on August 6, 1895, six Armenian boys complained that an Armenian girl from their community had been abducted by a Kurd. While the children reported that they heard the girl speaking Armenian—a language they, as Armenian speakers, would have recognized—the authorities were dismissive and instead claimed that the girl was not an Armenian but a Kurd. The court proceeded to accuse the children of trying to Armenianize the girl.[61] While whose claim in this case was legitimate remains ambiguous, it confirms that Armenians had little recourse to retrieve abducted women and girls because once a non-Muslim woman converted to Islam, retrieving her old identity as a non-Muslim would make her guilty of a capital crime. Abductions of minority women, not to mention larger crimes of violence against women, including femicide, continue to reverberate in contemporary Turkey. A woman, "Silva," who was abducted in 2010 shared her story in depth with journalist Avedis Hadjian. Her fellow community members naturally compared her ordeal to that of Gülizar a century earlier, illustrating how the gender violence of the present can trigger communal memories of past abductions.[62]

Historical tensions between Kurds and Armenians, reflected in these episodes of abduction, were instrumentalized by the state when it chose to enlist Kurds to punish Armenians. Jean Franco has shown how in cases of genocide, Latin American states instrumentalized minority indigenous peoples to perform their "savagery" on other "savages" (i.e., other indigenous peoples who were enemies of the state).⁶³ By outsourcing mass violence to marginalized peoples, the Ottoman state was able to reinforce its own image of the Kurds as uncivilized. With the shift toward Muslim nationalism in the last decades of the empire, the Ottoman government sought to bring Kurds, who had their own history of unruliness and tenuous relations with the Porte, more firmly under their grip.⁶⁴ Kurds, in this sense, became subcontractors of the state during the Hamidiye Massacres and again in 1915, when Kurdish loyalty was ostensibly purchased with Armenian "bait." According to Selim Deringil, this allowed Sultan Abdul Hamid to "kill two birds with one stone," assuring that only Kurds loyal to him would rule over the region and collect spoils, while ridding the empire of its Armenian problem.⁶⁵ Armenian rebellion created a pretext for state repression, which the sultan accomplished by producing his own Kurdish irregular force (Hamidiye). By mobilizing minorities in the Hamidye to attack and kill anywhere between 40,000 and 300,000 Armenians between 1894 and 1896, atrocities could be blamed on Kurds rather than the centralized Ottoman government, though the Western press vilified the monarch as "the bloody sultan" anyway.⁶⁶

The international community was aware of the persecution of Armenian Christians with the Hamidiye Massacres; however, the atrocities were framed in civilizational terms by Western powers, tapping into centuries of rhetoric that depicted the events as a primordial struggle between Islam and Christianity. Stories of forcible conversion to Islam coupled with the abduction of Christian Armenian women echoed powerful Orientalist tropes of savage sexuality and barbarism in the East, centuries-old European fears of Muslim violence dating back to the Crusades. Yet, the historical record shows forced conversion in earlier periods of Ottoman history was rare.⁶⁷ Forced conversion also varied by region since it was far more prevalent in the Ottoman-controlled Balkans than in the Levant.⁶⁸ We have to reach deeper into Ottoman muscle memory to find forced conversion as a tool of persecution, the foremost example being that of Sabbatai Tsvi, the Messianic Jew who led a mass movement in the seventeenth century. Marc Baer's in-depth study has shown that as a political threat to the empire, Tsvi was forced to lead the public mass conversion of his followers.⁶⁹ The ritual conversion was a humiliating, public display of loyalty and allegiance to the empire comparable to the political "conversion" of Muslim rebel leaders who contested the state and its sovereignty and were forced to profess allegiance. We could, then, think about these moments as public, embodied displays of abidance to Ottoman sovereignty and punishment for sedition against the sovereign in order to understand the outrageous displays of body spectacle during the Armenian Genocide.⁷⁰

In premodern everyday practice, socioeconomic incentives to convert motivated those seeking advancement. Armenian women, along with other zimmi women, strategically converted to annul their marriages; men strategically converted in order to reap the social rewards that included, among other things, tax-exempt status for members of the Ottoman military. In the nineteenth century, Ayşenur Korkmaz has found that non-Muslim women were increasingly under pressure to convert to Islam within exogamous marriages in the nineteenth century, even though Islamic law gave women the right to retain their personal religious identity.[71] Abduction, slavery, and conversion produced the empire—a ruling class of Ottoman bureaucrats and a hereditary dynasty that ruled for seven centuries.

The strict criteria for conversion to Islam was at odds with forced conversion practices during periods of repression. According to Islamic law, conversion to Islam must be completely voluntary and unforced, which is supported by the Qur'anic verse 2:256: "There is no compulsion in religion" (la ikraha fi'l din). During the premodern period, shari'a courts had procedures for conversion, including the requirement of witnesses and formulaic rejections of one's previous religion. In the period of reform beginning in 1839, the Ottoman Empire enacted specific measures "according to established practice and regulations" to ensure that conversion was completely voluntary.[72] Selim Deringil has shown how within the new procedure, the members of the convert's family and community needed to be present as witnesses to the event, requiring a face-to-face rejection of one's previous community, a full embrace of social death. The recitation of the required formula for conversion (*shahada*) needed to take place before the highest-ranking jurist, who would summarily issue a certificate of conversion. However, Selim Deringil discovered that these detailed legal requirements were not carried out for late-nineteenth-century Armenian mass conversions. Under threat of imminent death, Armenians attempted to convert en masse to spare their lives, but the Ottoman administration was reluctant to accept these conversions as legitimate, rejecting applications from the terrorized Armenian population. This left the converso population in limbo as they had converted in name only but were left without proof in the form of official documentation from the authorities. Even as communities insisted that their conversions were not coerced, spies were sent to check that communities had not reneged on their conversion, because previously some Muslim converts from the Hamidiye period had reverted back to Christianity.[73] On the eve of the Armenian Genocide, the state was ambivalent about accepting Armenian conversions due to this previous pattern of recanting conversion once the wave of political repression subsided.

When the deportation order was issued in spring 1915, as during the Hamidiye Massacres, the CUP government vacillated between allowing and forbidding conversion to Islam for Armenians who sought to spare themselves and their families. By June 22, 1915, Talaat Pasha ordered that Armenian conversions be accepted under the condition that the population still be dispersed within Anatolia to facilitate assimilation. Fuat Dündar documented how the central government quickly reversed this order three weeks later. In telegrams, the central government expressed suspicions about Armenian conversions: "Never trust conversions that happen in this way"; such converts "would not refrain from issuing intrigues under the guise of Islam."[74] Though it is impossible to determine just how many Armenians were Islamized and absorbed into Muslim households, recent studies of Islamized Armenians living in contemporary Turkey have underscored the incalculable loss, as many Turks and Kurds grapple with the realization that they are the grandchildren of both perpetrator and victim.[75]

In contrast to female conversion, male converts' bodies were ceremonially marked by an irreversible excision that rendered the body itself a document of conversion.[76] During the Hamidiye Massacres of 1895, six hundred Armenian men were circumcised en masse in Harput during a mass conversion ceremony.[77] In 1915, out of complete desperation, some Armenian men circumcised themselves to claim Muslim identity. Traces of these episodes suggest that male genitalia may have been examined as evidence of belongingness or otherness. In his survivor testimony, Sarkis Saroyan recalled how when he was four years old, "a mullah came and he changed my name to Sefer." He continued, "I felt a terrible pain. They burnt that part of my body as if by fire, put that excised piece of flesh in the sun to dry and kept it as proof." The Muslim family that later adopted him kept the skin as proof of his conversion during the genocide lest there be inquiries.[78] The transformation of Sarkis's severed foreskin into a document of conversion urges us to consider how male bodies were irreversibly marked upon conversion. Armenian women's bodies were unmarked by conversion to Islam, except in cases where tribal tattoos were applied by specific Muslim groups that practiced the tradition. Tattoo symbols like circumcision indelibly marked bodies with symbols of belongingness.

For many, conversion did not exempt them from deportation or death. During the genocide, Kurdish and Arab tribesmen either formally or informally converted Armenian deportees, focusing on assimilable bodies of women and children, absorbing them into their households. There are few accounts of Armenians undergoing formal conversion before Muslim clerics; instead, accounts describe conversions under duress in defiance of both Ottoman and Islamic law.[79] With deportations of Armenians underway, the remaining Armenians who had received exemptions as Protestants or Catholics began submitting petitions of conversion with the encouragement of the local officials.[80] The conversion of women and children in particular was eased by the structure of the patriarchal family, and Turkish orphanages were designed to mold Armenian children into Turks. On March 8, 1916, conversion to Islam was extended to Armenian women who married Muslim men, a process through which Armenian identity would be extinguished through patrimony within the sex/gender system of the Muslim family.[81] Slavery and polygamy, in particular, would be synonymous in Armenian women's experience during the genocide, their surplus labor extracted from them when they became second, third, or fourth wives in polygamous marriages or were forced into the institution of concubinage.

As for the assimilation of children, historian Nazan Maksudyan has documented how the empire managed the lives of children, be they street dwellers or orphaned and destitute children who filled police ledgers during the World War I. The practice of recovering and nationalizing children and placing them in orphanages was framed as humanitarian rescue and part of a state-building project that "recycled" the biological material of children to forge them into Turkish-speaking Muslim national subjects.[82] Affirming central coordination, the government offered cash to Muslim families in rural areas willing to take Armenian children into their homes, and by June 1915, it directed that orphaned children in the provinces be transferred to the households of reputable male notables. The discovery of an undated journal belonging to Talaat Pasha included demographic data for Armenians in all major cities and within it a special ledger for Armenian children transferred to Muslim homes.[83]

Separating women and children from their Armenian patriarchal household and transferring them to Muslim patriarchal households instrumentalized "social death" for the purposes of genocide.[84] The patriarchal family and traffic in slaves further excised surplus bodies from their communities. One child named Khatchadour recalled that near the deportee gathering point in Ras al-'Ayn three hundred to four hundred children were "sold like sheep in the village." He was purchased for three *mejidiye* coins by a Kurd from Diyarbakir—he was not the only victim to remember his price.[85] Nonthreatening because they were not yet men, young boys were assimilable bodies converted into shepherds and servants often living outside the household in barns with the livestock; women, by contrast, became domestic servants and field hands living within the household. Girls who were sexually desirable or beautiful—beauty is often defined in survivor testimonies as fair skin and hair, exotic traits in the locale that carried the highest value in this slave trade—could be spared death by becoming a wife or a concubine.[86] Locating these abducted women in the historical record remains a methodological challenge, but the photographic negatives of these missing women and children are visible, even within the perpetrator archive.

ARCHIVAL TRACES OF ABDUCTED ARMENIAN WOMEN AND GIRLS

One would think that the violent production of the Ottoman archives in Istanbul, Turkey, would have obliterated all traces of these abducted Armenian women; however, as with other missing bodies, traces remain. Zavier Wingham and Bam Willoughby have recently probed the archive for traces of Arap Bacı, a female Black slave figure whose black body was deleted from Ottoman history writing that favors the predominately white domestic kul/concubine dynastic slavery. Their scholarship has modeled how the archive can be used to critically insert Arap Bacı, as well as other marginal bodies, back into the historical record.[87]

When confronting the erasure of Armenian women victims, whose voices are largely obliterated, we find that narratives of denial are also a form of tacit recognition. These traces evaded the censor's gaze because when they are read with post-genocide amnesia, they affirm a nationalist narrative that absorbed women were rescued rather than taken captive, made wives rather than slaves, and became willing converts to Islam.[88] Such residual archival evidence should be thought of as film negatives that reverse lightness into darkness, distorting the broader historical picture.

The view from the Ottoman archives (formally named the Prime Minister's Ottoman Archives or Başbakanlık Osmanlı Arşivleri) reveals that surviving Armenians did not passively accept the abduction of their women and girls; the fingerprints of the survivor community mark the manuscript pages. After the armistice period, Armenians sometimes entered the homes of Muslim men to recover women and girls by force. In Ismit, a man named Hacı Bekir filed a complaint after two men entered his home to remove an unnamed Armenian girl "who was involved in the deportation and relocation" (tehcir ve tenkilde zi-i medhal olan).[89] In the course of the recovery effort, the adoptive Muslim father was injured in several places on his body, and the two assailants were arrested. Elsewhere, in Kastamonu province, two Armenian men, Boghos and Garabed Efendi, described as "Armenian orphans," most likely due to their experience as survivors of genocide, invaded the home of Akgözoğlu Mehmet Ağa, accompanied by the British police and other Armenians. They seized a girl named Hacer, whom the patriarch of the household had adopted nine years earlier, claiming that she belonged to the Armenian community.[90] A woman who belonged to another household "harem" claimed that she could procure a birth certificate and other legal documents that could prove definitively that Hacer was Turkish, not Armenian.

Within the perpetrator archive, we also find a complaint from the Armenian patriarchate in Constantinople seeking the return of an Armenian girl from Bilecik, whom they claimed had been forcibly married to a Muslim man by his father. The spouse's family responded that the girl had converted to Islam and willingly married. They also declared that she was from Eastern Karahisar, not Bilecik, implying she was not the person the patriarchate pursued.[91] In Sivas province, Annik and Satenig Baghdjian left traces in the Ottoman archives as Armenian community organizations along with family members agitated in vain for their release from forced marriages with Muslim men.[92] In another instance, the Ministry of the Interior received a tip that Şarkışla captain and gendarme Niyazi Efendi "took an Armenian girl as a bride for himself by force during the relocation" (tehcir esnasında şehrikışla'da bir ermeni kızıyla cebren tezevvüc ettiği ve mezbürenin) and the girl, being discontented, "wishes to go to her mother's household despite not daring to do so" (validesinin nezdine gitmek arzusunda bulunyor ise de cesaret edemediği).⁹³ Despite the claims of the Armenian community to the contrary, Meryem Abdalian, the woman at the center of the dispute, declared before two Armenian witnesses that she would neither leave her husband nor her six-month-old infant, showing how release could be hindered when the victim herself refused to cooperate.⁹⁴

In another case from Sivas, the family members of Arusyak and Yeghsabet Zadikoğlu from Amasya complained in court that their daughters were being held against their will.⁹⁵ Arusyak was being held by a man named Hekimhanlı Garib Ağa, but Yeghsabet, held by Elmas Ağa, insisted that she had converted, was married to him, had a child by him, and therefore would not leave him (arinzi'nin de ihtida ve izdivaç ederek çocuğu da olduğunu iftirak etmeyeceğini). The Armenian patriarchate compiled detailed lists of missing Armenian women and children, including the addresses of the Muslim households where they were kept. The patriarchate submitted their complaints at war's end in an attempt to vacate conversions per the terms of postwar treaties, but their claims were dismissed by Ottoman authorities.⁹⁶ Families and communities who tried to retrieve their loved ones from Muslim households after the war left their fingerprints behind in the archives.

Thinking about these traces of gendered violence that remain in the archive invites a return to Zabel's 1919 report, which opened our discussion. With her pen, Zabel supplemented these stories of community resistance and recovery with stories of individual women's acts of resistance. Armenian women's resistance to the forced deportations complicated the image of passive victimhood circulated in the Western press and demonstrated how women placed their bodies in harm's way to protect themselves and their community. "These gendarmes had complete power over the deportees." Zabel documents how several women of Urfa poisoned themselves rather than fall into enemy hands.⁹⁷ Women flung their bodies and those of their daughters into the Euphrates River in acts of benevolent suicide, preferring to drown than be subjected to sexual violence. "It happened that young girls, desperate to find a means for suicide," writes Zabel, "tried to win their captors by giving up all their jewels so that they would consent to kill them with shots from a revolver" rather than subject them to the sexual atrocities other women experienced around them.⁹⁸ "Some managed to flee after being raped; several were killed during their escape. A few succeeded in killing their captors, and the number of those who defended themselves with weapons was considerable."⁹⁹ In the context of a necropolitical state exercising absolute sovereignty over the right to kill, self-annihilation was for some a last expression of agency.¹⁰⁰

Other women chose to sacrifice themselves by taking up arms alongside men in battle. In an account Zabel obtained from a Turkish officer, "after the capture of the city by the Turks, when the officers and the soldiers looked for corpses to strip, they saw with great astonishment that there were several corpses of women whose breasts were decorated not with jewels but with bandoliers [sashes full of bullets]."[101] Some of them, like eighteen-year-old Miss Chainian from the city of Sivas fought valiantly, raining down "10 bullets from her Mauser [infantry rifle], [before she] was struck down by a gunshot."[102] The women in towns like Chabin-Hissar urged their men to disobey the Ottoman deportation decrees that would dispatch them to certain death and instead pick up arms to resist. "They preferred to die in the sanctity of their own homes rather than to suffer all kinds of insults on the path to exile," reports Zabel.[103] Although these martyred women were not able to offer first-person testimony, Zabel archived their traces to complicate her narration of women's victimhood by giving them names and agency; they were heroines rather than anonymous, passive victims.

Zabel's report was not limited to documenting atrocities and acts of agency; she also portrayed genocide as a crime informed by patriarchy. She urged Armenian women in the diaspora from Paris to Cairo to Constantinople to organize to help other women through what she called "the International Commission of Women."[104] This organization, she hoped, would make the rehabilitation of women victims a pillar of national reconstruction, consistent with a larger pattern of Armenian feminist and community mobilization to rescue female victims of the atrocities. In this sense, Zabel's career as a humanitarian activist reflects the organic grassroots organizing that Ottoman Armenians had conducted in the wake of the Adana Massacres and later during the Armenian Genocide. Historian Khatchig Mouradian has documented how Ottoman Armenians provided "humanitarian resistance," life-saving resources and aid, to other Armenians during the extermination campaign during World War I.[105] Armenians did not die passively.

In Mesopotamia, though, as many other survivors have noted, "in general, the Arabo-Islamic people had acted humanely towards the Armenian deportees"; Zabel nonetheless demanded that they return the women and children to the Armenian community, since rescuing future mothers for a rebirthing of Armenia was the only way to suture the community back together again.[106] This mission to rescue Armenians who were at risk of disappearing through the genocidal process of assimilation would be called the *vorpahavak* in Armenian, an "orphan rescue" that included Armenian children and widows, many of whom were Muslim wives, absorbed into Muslim households.[107] Zabel called for the increase in league orphanages that could shelter and rehabilitate Armenian children "delivered from Turkish hands." She called for special shelters for women—with a specific service for pregnant Armenian women—rescued from Muslim homes until they could be rehabilitated and repatriated to their homelands. Armenian women who had already organized relief efforts in Constantinople, Smyrna, Egypt, Russian (later

Soviet) Armenia, and America could be mobilized to assist in the *vorpahavak*. "The liberation of non-Muslim women and children," Zabel concluded, "is a work of justice, humanity, and civilization."[108]

In the waning days of empire, older methods of Ottoman statecraft—abduction, conversion, and slavery—emerged during the ethnic cleansing of Armenians from Asia Minor. Unassimilable elements—the men who managed non-Muslim sex/gender systems—were excised with an understanding that remaining biological raw material could be absorbed within the Muslim patriarchal household. Remaining bodies were transported to lands understood as uninhabitable from the perspective of the state: the Syrian desert. The dispersal of Armenians from their ancestral homelands was not a single event. Armenians who were not massacred outright were gathered in depots before being deported again. During these dispersals, Armenian bodies were snatched, converted, enslaved, and deported in order to give birth to a desired homogenous Turkish body politic. An essential element in excising the unwanted was the use of symbolic violence and sexual atrocity after ritualistically stripping bodies bare to completely unravel Armenian social order.

In writing about the particularities of collective rape, brothels, and the open sale of women and children's bodies to Muslim families, Zabel's writing forms a précis for us to consider how gender is at the center of genocidal thinking to the extent that in 1998 international law would rule that rape is an act of genocide and that guilt can be assigned not only to those who commit the act but to those inciting it.[109] For génocidaires, individual bodies are a metonym for the collective communal body. Destroying the individual body with extreme forms of mutilation and desecration of the corpse is not incidental but part of genocide's body work. The violence that unfolded in 1915, however, was illustrative of a mix of old and new thinking about gender and the non-Muslim zimmi body.

REMNANT 1

"The Dance"

by Siamanto (Atom Yarjanian) (1909)[1]
Translated by Tamar M. Boyadjian

And with the tears in her blue eyes drowning,
On a cinder plain, where Armenian life was still dying,
Such reported an eyewitness to our horror, this German woman:

This untellable tale, that I render to you,
5   I, myself, with these, my merciless human eyes,
from my unassailable home, through the window facing hell,
gnashing my teeth and frightful in fury ...
with my eyes, mercilessly human, I saw.
Reduced to a heap of ashes, this was in the city of Bardez;
10 corpses stacked up to the top of trees,
and from the waters, fountains, brooks, roads
your blood's murmur, contumacious ...
still, speaks its revenge to my ear, as such ...

Oh, don't be frightened when I tell you my untellable tale ...
15 Let humanity understand the crime of human against human;
under a sun of two days, on the road to the cemetery,
the evil of humanity against humanity;
Let the hearts of all those in the world know ...
That deadly shadow of a morning was a Sunday;
20 Dawning on the pile of corpses, that first and idle Sunday,
when in my room, from evening until daybreak,
cowering over the agony of a stabbed girl
with my tears, I was soaking her death ...
Suddenly, from afar a black, bestial crowd
25 Twenty brides with them, whipping [the women] vehemently,
Singing licentious songs of drunken revelry, they paused in the
    middle of a vineyard.

I, leaving the half-dead girl on her mattress,
I, came closer to the veranda of my hell-facing window ...

In the vineyard, the black crowd became a forest.
30 A savage, to the brides.—"You must dance!" he fulminated,
"You must dance, when our drum echoes."

And they started to whip the death-longing Armenian women's
    bodies, scourging them with fury . . .
The twenty brides, hand in hand, started their dance in a
    circle . . .
35 From their eyes, their tears were flowing like wounds,
Ah, how jealous I was of my wounded neighbor;
And so I heard, with this still snoring, [her]
cursing the universe, that poor Armenian woman with the
    beautiful face,
her sea holly, lily of a heart took wing towards the stars . . .
40 In vain, I moved my fists towards the crowd.
"You must dance," yelled the barbarous to the tempestuous:
"Until your death, you must dance, you infidel beauties,
with your breasts open, you must dance—smiling at us and
    unabsolved . . .
Exhaustion is not for you, neither is shame;
you are slaves; you must dance; naked and uncovered;
until your death you must dance, lewd and lustful;
Our eyes are thirsty for your movements and your death . . ."

Twenty dazzling brides dwindled to the floor exhausted . . .
45 "Get on your feet," they thundered, moving their bare swords
    like snakes . . .
Then someone brought a pitcher of kerosene;
Oh humanly justice, let me spit at your forehead . . .
Twenty brides, quickly, they anointed with that fluid . . .

"You must dance!" he fulminated, "alas a scent for you, that not
    even Arabia has . . ."
50 Then, with a torch, they inflamed the naked silhouettes of the
    brides,
And the carbonized bodies of the dance tumbled to their
    death . . .

From my dread, I shut the shutters of my window like a storm;
Approaching my solitary corpse, I solicited:
How am I to dig out my eyes? how am I to dig? tell me . . .

CHAPTER TWO

WEAPONIZING SHAME

Dis-memberment of the Armenian Collective Body

> The body is nothing more than a question. Will you slice this breast? Will you take this hand? The body lies in wait, vulnerable, unrhetorical. Along the road to Ras ul-Ain, as we neared, we saw a pile of hands.
> —MICHELINE AHRONIAN MARCOM,
> *Three Apples Fell from Heaven*

Atrocity is a form of body spectacle. Armenian poet Siamanto captured this sentiment in his poem "The Dance," written after the 1909 pogroms in Adana, events that foreshadowed the spectacular scenes of violence in 1915. Told from the perspective of a German woman onlooker, the poem describes a scene in which twenty brides were stripped of their clothing and coerced by whip to dance hand in hand before husbands, fathers, and Turkish officers. Forcing the victims to enact the joyous ritual of dance converts the festive communal ritual of a wedding into a carnivalistic prelude to death. Falling to the ground exhausted, the women were doused with gasoline and ignited with a torch, and in the words of the poet, "the carbonized bodies of the dance tumbled to their death."[1]

Having viewed the violent spectacle from her window, the narrator closes her shutters and questions her complicity as a witness: "How am I to dig out my eyes?" Although the narrator wishes she could unsee what she just witnessed, I seek to draw your attention more deeply into the difficult details of sexual atrocity. In genocide, women's bodies are severed from their community either through immediate annihilation or socially when captured bodies are forced to assimilate and birth a new nation. The late Ottoman Empire secured biopolitical futures for Muslims while subjecting non-Muslims to necropolitical violence by denuding, dragging, mutilating, burning, and publicly displaying corpses, forms of body terror that Adrianna Cavarero has called "horrorism."[2] When examining more closely the intent behind discrete acts of violence on the body—rape, mutilation, and murder—one discovers how the extremity of certain acts focus on the reproductive capacity of the body. These acts of genocidal violence work to fulfill an aim—not only the elimination of life but the victim's will to live and, even more importantly, his or her desire to reproduce future generations after traumatic scarring of the human psyche. These acts sought to extinguish Armenian life force and any hope of futurity.[3] Such theft of the body includes severing it from individual will by imposing the right to name, to use, and to dispose of the body in any way the génocidaire desires.

Abduction, conversion, and (sexual) enslavement of women suggests that genocidal intent surpasses individual death to encompass the broader goal of psychological, cultural, social, and communal extermination. In order to accomplish this aim, génocidaires and torturers force their victims to transgress socially and culturally constituted taboos—around, for instance, bodily comportment, clothing, food, and hygiene—transgressions that psychologically sever individual victims from the communal body. Anthropologist Mary Douglas argued in *Purity and Danger* that communal identities cohere through ethical codes and taboos that define and police the boundaries between that which is clean and that which pollutes. Forbidden acts (consuming certain foods and drinks, and engaging in certain behaviors, and bodily displays) are mapped upon the body, flesh, fluids, and excrement and can release powerful emotional sentiments of either belonging or, alternatively, feelings of otherness.[4] When they compel their victims to self-violate, torturers produce feelings self-loathing and abjection that psychologically sever victims from their community. By defiling the body and denying burial rites for corpses, génocidaires weaponize ethical and moral norms as tools for necropower to unmake bodies and worlds.[5] During the Armenian Genocide, the weaponization of shame compelled men, women, and children to engage in cultural taboos that enabled survival while simultaneously collapsing the norms that defined Armenianness.

This preparatory groundwork for genocide cannot be understood without gender for, in the words of Jean Franco, "symbolic acts of violence combine the upmost cruelty with extreme misogyny."[6] In the case of the Armenian Genocide, historian Matthias Bjørnlund has thoroughly catalogued the systematic gender-selective mass killing, or gendercide, capturing the carnivalistic atmosphere of rape, murder, and mayhem that women and girls experienced during the deportations.[7] The details of these sexual atrocities are not an easy pill for a reader to swallow. I fully recognize that listing these tortures will unsettle anyone who reads them. I have used evidence strategically to support my argument that these horrific acts, as misogynistic as they were, were performed with an intimate understanding of how gender, patriarchy, and social taboo operated in Ottoman Armenian society precisely because they because they could be forged into efficient weapons of mass destruction.

DIS-MEMBERMENT AND SEXUAL ATROCITY: BODY HORROR AS GENOCIDAL PRAXIS

Freeing up women's bodies for dis-memberment—either through abduction or worse sexual atrocity—was achieved through a systematic attack on Armenian patriarchal order. Perpetrators targeted the normative structures of the Armenian family and society that were underpinned by cultural constructions of honor, sexuality, femininity, and masculinity. Communal patriarchal codes emphasized the purity of Armenian women and girls, including preservation of their status as virgins until marriage to secure Armenian futurity through endogamy within the Armenian community or sometimes across Christian communal lines. Patriarchal customs shifted between communities based on urban, rural, and class distinctions, an understudied topic deserving of in-depth study.

It may surprise some readers to know that some aspects of Armenian patriarchy overlapped with those of the surrounding Muslim community prompting criticism among Armenian intellectuals. In her study of Armenian marriage, Hasmik Khalapyan observed that Armenian feminists criticized aspects of the Armenian patriarchal family yet did not cross the line between "improvement for the sake of the nation" and "abandonment of Armenian traditional roles."[8] Within Armenian families, brides complained of mistreatment in marriages in instances where they were reduced to servitude or oppressed by their mother-in-law. Armenian wives were expected to be modest and obedient not only to their husbands but to their extended family of in-laws.[9] Marriage ties bound Armenian families to one another and formed the fabric of Armenian social life. This fabric could be unraveled when gender relations were fractured with sexual violence as they were during the Hamidiye Massacres and again during the Armenian Genocide, when late-Ottoman biopolitics legally demanded, for instance, that non-Muslim wives convert to the religion of their Muslim husbands.[10]

We get a glimpse into these debates about Armenian patriarchy and a view from the Ottoman provinces in a late-nineteenth-century commentary titled "Social Problems: Marital Abuse in Our Region" (Engerayin khantirner: amusnagan dzeghdzmunk i kavars). The writer, Shahen of Van, argued that Armenian girls living in the province were subjected to abusive marriage customs, especially child marriage, by fellow Armenians. For example, Armenian girls were often promised in marriage at the time of birth, usually before baptism. He observed, "It is not rare to find 7- or 8-year-old brides there [in the villages]." These early marriages were coupled with cases in which "the weak gender" (dagar serin), his term for females, is forced against her will to marry. An unwilling bride in Hadjin, he notes, was threatened by her father, who said, "You are my possession. If I want I can bring you to the public square and sell [you]." While the girl cried as a result of her father's threats, in the end, she obeyed him and married against her will.[11] But not all girls were obedient. He added, "A very curious sight is when tearful brides escape from their new husband's house to their family home" to flee these arranged marriages.[12]

Boys also suffered from the abuse of early marriage. They were forced to travel abroad to work to pay off their wedding debts (with added interest payments) after marriage. Added to the list of social ills were the "seductions" of city life these men faced while separated from their new child brides. There is, Shahen argued, "no need to condemn from our side once again the results of early marriage because it is already condemned by doctors and healthcare workers."[13] He urged the religious authorities to condemn early marriages, which continued to receive the blessings of the church. But in his list of complaints, Shahen also pointed to corrupt marriage practices among Armenians that were condemned by the church, such as "remarriage" (grgnamusnutiun), which was his term for polygamy among Armenians. "Some of the villagers bring excuses that their wives are infertile or insane or excuses like incurable diseases. For that reason, they brought a new woman to their house and succeeded through an unknown priest to be blessed with a second and illegal union."[14] Accordingly, the religious authority worked to separate these men from their second wives. Shahen's social commentary on marital abuse in the late nineteenth century offers a small glimpse into debates about Armenian patriarchal practices in the Ottoman provinces. It was precisely Armenian male control over women that would be targeted as hostilities grew between neighboring communities in the late Ottoman period.

A major challenge to Armenian patriarchy was the abduction of women and girls, which should be understood as an extension of other forms of plunder that historically intersected with gender in the Ottoman realm. As intercommunal relations deteriorated and Kurdish privileges were extended by the state at the end of the nineteenth century, abduction and other forms of sexual usurpation grew worse. Perhaps the most extreme variation of sexual pillaging was the practice of "the right of first night" (arachin kishervairavunk), or the practice of offering consummation of a bride to someone other than the bridegroom, a practice called jus primae noctis in Latin. An Armenian source claims that Kurdish chieftains were applying this custom in the eastern provinces: "In Kurdish tribal environs, the kidnapping of Armenian girls had become customary law [sovoroyht er]. In some places, Kurdish feudal lords [avadaderere sahmanel] claimed for themselves the right of the first night [arachin kishervairavunk]." Such predation of women and girls was coupled with the privilege of free food and shelter in Armenian households for Kurds and Muslim travelers.[15]

Beth Baron has noted in her study of Egyptian nationalism that notions of honor are a collective construction in national consciousness. Violations of a woman's honor, symbolic of the nation, threatened to impugn the reputation of the broader community. Sexual violence has been historically framed as "rape of the nation" especially when used as a weapon of war by national enemies.[16] Honor in the context of the eastern Mediterranean world was to be protected by male relatives—fathers, brothers, other male kin, and, by extension, male neighbors. In the late nineteenth century, with the emergence of biopolitical states, both individual and family honor came under state control.[17] In cases where honor could not be protected, national honor could devolve into the opposing symbol of national shame.

Bearing in mind this broader Armenian social context, dis-memberment, or the severing of individuals from the collective communal body, was both a physical and deeply psychological affair. Elisa von Joeden-Forgey has argued in her study of gender and genocide that the initial acts of "ritual cruelties" form the interim stage of genocide and work to communicate meaning and construct a social reality for the perpetrator while simultaneously unraveling social bonds.[18] These acts, often described as "hysteria," "orgies," or "ecstasy of transgression," are a dance of desire enacted as masochistic fantasies onto the target population. After the mass killings of Armenians, the Kurdish saying "No man can ever think of woman's body except as a matter of horror instead of attraction after Ras-ul-Ain" captures how the spectacle of sexual atrocity was central to the extermination of Armenians. Genocide's body work affords the génocidaire an opportunity to make the victim into a plaything, a toy within a wider context of a game that grooms the killer by psychologically distancing him from the dehumanized victim.[19]

Examples from localities throughout the Ottoman Empire illustrate how "life force atrocities" were committed with a deep understanding of gender and patriarchy. Castrating men, especially men charged with protecting the home or community, and impaling women through the vagina, mocking coitus, converted the initial life-giving sex act into an unfathomable act of violence. Pregnant women were disemboweled, killing both mother and the exposed fetus in the process. Survivors describe babies being ripped apart or thrown like balls against walls in an attempt to kill them in one fell swoop, as if soldiers scored points in a game by doing so. Reports of soldiers tossing babies onto bayonets further fashions a living, breathing being into a toy to be stabbed for sport.[20] Importantly, survivors describe how babies were sometimes killed in their mother's arms or while they were nursing. Such spectacular violence meant to shut off life-producing capacity (again) for those who experienced the unbearable death of children during moments of maternal intimacy.[21]

Male patriarchs—husbands and priests, patriarchs of household and community respectively—were disappeared, tortured, mutilated, killed, and displayed within their own homes or in public squares in various states of degradation. In instances in which men had not yet been severed from the community through conscription or immediate killing, they were separated from what was an increasingly feminized deportee caravan.[22] Male authority was upturned when génocidaires forced men to dance before their wives and enact various other emasculating performances. Moreover, emasculation included actual castration and, in some cases, severed genitalia was placed into the mouth of the male victim to further humiliate him and his spectators.[23] The public severing of men and especially elders from the collective was an attack on communal order. Priests had their beards plucked—a symbolic castration—and sometimes were publicly flayed and dismembered, which serves to remind us that the spectacle of body horror is always a deeply political act.

In premodern political tradition, the sovereign would draw and quarter his enemies for crimes of the worst severity—a direct metonym for the amputation limb by limb of the communal body.[24] During the 1915 deportations, an eyewitness saw the corpse of an executed priest displayed with his decapitated head placed between his legs on the banks of Sev Chour (Black Water) near Van.[25] Such postexecution displays recalled humiliating punishments meted out to non-Muslims in earlier periods of Ottoman history, among them the placing of an Armenian *sarraf*'s decapitated head onto his buttocks or, in another case, the public crucifixion of a Jewish customs chief above the door of the Aleppo customs office.[26] Such humiliating executions were reenacted during the 1915 deportations. In one instance, two naked old men were "laid in such a position as to expose their persons to passersby, and on the abdomen of each was cast a large stone. They had evidently been murdered there at the noon hour and then the brutal guards had stopped to leave behind them the signs not only of violence but mockery and insult."[27] Armenian community leaders and revolutionaries were publicly tortured and humiliated, pre- and post mortem, their corpses hung publicly with signs around their necks declaring them traitors against the state. Such public displays of corpses confirm how bodies formed texts that communicate the power of the sovereign to spectators.

Public displays of punishment were embedded in Ottoman muscle memory, commonly reserved for "enemies of the state." The history of these penal traditions in the empire allows us to consider how *necroviolence*—denying the right of funerals and mourning—is a form of state-structured violence that has a deeper history. In this sense, death is not the end but only the beginning of state terror exacted on the body.[28] Such desecration obliterates post-life identity, denying an afterlife to the corpse though denying grave markers and ritual mourning that would instill communal memory. In this broader context, the spectacular deaths deracinated both living and dead Armenians from the land, denying the individual corpse, and by extension the community, a future.

DEFILING THE BODY, OBSCURING HUMANITY

Eliciting communal and individual shame through acts of necroviolence did the work of further dehumanizing the Armenian population in preparation for extermination. Witnesses described how women's breasts were cut off and fed to dogs, symbolically destroying the site of the body that would sustain and nourish future offspring. A survivor recalled, "I saw the Turks killing Armenians with hatchets. Some of them were cut into pieces and the pieces were given to the dogs which ate them."[29] Reducing humans to kibble for animals further subverts social hierarchies between human, animal, and thing. Such sport meant to render the humanity of Armenians unrecognizable through ritual mutilation and defilement. Reducing Armenians to a state of animality was observed by sympathetic spectators like German medic and photographer Armin Wegner, who described "swarms of orphans" with outstretched hands at the Armenian refugee camp in Ras al-'Ayn:

> At the sides of the camp, a row of holes in the ground covered in rags, had been prepared for them. Girls and boys of all ages were sitting in these holes, heads together, abandoned and reduced to animals starved without bread and food, deprived of the most human aid, packed tightly against the other and trembling from the night cold, holding pieces of still smoldering wood to try and get warm.[30]

Registered in his description is both sympathy with the oppressed and a recognition of how genocide rendered humanity virtually unrecognizable. The degradation of humanity is conveyed vividly Grigoris Balakian's description of an encounter with a begging child in Dayr al-Zur, who "looked more like a monkey than a human being," or a "ghost" or a "moving shadow." He failed to recognize the child as human until he spoke.[31] American consul Leslie Davis, who simultaneously held sympathy and at times antipathy toward Armenians, observed how deportees "resembl[ed] animals far more than human beings."[32] If the aim of the génocidaire was to produce a herd of inhuman prey, impossible to recognize as human subjects, eyewitness accounts offer the impression that the desired effect was achieved.

For perpetrators, "ritual cruelties" that forced victims to violate moral and ethical norms dehumanized Armenians by coercing them into acts of communal and familial destruction. As social norms were upended, Armenians at times did inhuman things like euthanize their children by drowning them in a river or, as in a case of a mother in Moush, enlisting older children to help murder the smaller ones. A survivor recalled with horror how, while trapped inside a burning stable, his mother ordered him to lie on top of his brother, pinning him to the ground as he screamed and squirmed so that he could be more effectively smothered by his mother.[33] Revulsed by what he viewed as Armenian cowardice, Consul Davis reported in Harput that Armenian "mothers have given their daughters to the lowest and vilest Turks to save their own lives."[34] Forcing people by circumstance to break familial bonds and violate their duties as sustainers for children produced feelings of abjection within those who survived.

Forcing Armenians to defile themselves took several forms, from forcing them to violate norms and customs to compelling them to do ritually unclean things such as eat impure foods. Such violations further extinguished Armenian identity and their intelligibility as humans to witnesses.[35] While the massacres were underway, government officials said it was a campaign to cleanse (*paklamak*) the land—an effective terminology that affirmed, in the mind of the perpetrators, that indigenous Armenians and other Christian communities targeted by the violence polluted the land.[36] The perception that the victim group was unclean was validated through symbolic ritual defilement and extreme deprivation. Reduced to performing the unthinkable to survive, starving Armenians were left to nourish themselves on a dog carcass washed up on the shore of the Euphrates or a dead donkey.[37] Deportees in some cases willingly picked through animal feces for undigested food particles or were forced to consume animal or human feces prior to being murdered.[38] In doing so, they crossed a crucial threshold by ingesting unclean food in order to live. Environmental conditions coupled with the enforcement from gendarmes simulated the routine of torturers who polluted the food of prisoners, forcing them to ingest bugs, spittle, and other unclean elements to survive. Forcing humans into such states are not accidental but by design. These forms of torture intend to produce embodied abjection and self-loathing in those subjected to it.[39] In this case, the death marches during the Armenian Genocide were comparable to a mobile prison deploying similar techniques of discipline to create, at the end, a group of barely human survivors forced to transgress boundaries of purity that produced affects of disgust and revulsion even within themselves.

The state of bare life encouraged some to convert to Islam for food, connecting life sustenance to violation of sacred religious boundaries. One witness saw children convert to Islam because they were starving. The boys were circumcised and offered a circumcision feast (*sünnet*) where their hungry bellies were fed.[40] The Armenians who still had money to purchase food were forced to pay gendarmes high prices to drink water from streams, and they were shot if they tried to approach water sources without paying. Zabel Essayan explained how the genocide created a perverse sexual economy in which deportees were forced to violate communal bonds by handing over young virgin girls in exchange for the right to drink water, making them complicit in the abuse of the life and dignity of others for survival.[41]

Some who had no access to water sources learned from other deportees like Stepan Miskjian to drink their own urine in the Syrian Desert to survive the desert heat.[42] Perhaps the most extreme violation of societal taboos documented during the genocide is cannibalism, a topic that is both sensational but reflective of the extremity of life during deportation. World War I was rife with examples of writers who invoked cannibal motifs metaphorically to describe the famine that seized the empire during the war—the result of killing off or conscripting agriculturalists and of a plague of locusts that attacked crops on a biblical scale. Karnig Panian wrote of how starving children in a Turkish orphanage in 'Aintoura, Lebanon, were desperately underfed, to the extent that they exhumed bones and pounded them into a powder for consumption. "The most difficult part was finding the bones to crush. We had to go outside the perimeter of the orphanage and look for them under rocks. We often didn't know what kinds of bones we were taking back to the others, nor did we bother trying to figure it out. We had sunk *that* low."[43] Questioning the provenance of the bones was largely rhetorical since hundreds of orphans died there; the Armenian orphans were likely eating the remains of other children to survive.

Traces of cannibalistic practices can be found in various testimonials of survivors near Dayr al-Zur, where life and death hung by a thread. Eyewitnesses spoke of "making *ghavurma* out of the dead,"[44] describing evidence of cannibalism on the bodies of the dead or cannibalism causing death.[45] In his detailed diary, Miskjian recalled gossip circulating outside Dayr al-Zur about a mother cannibalizing her child. Eventually, he stumbled upon a woman and her daughters dividing onto dinner plates the flesh of an elderly woman who lay mutilated within their quarters in an encampment. He confronted them by asking, "Do you know what you are doing?" and was countered with the mother's response: "What can we do to not die of hunger? In the old days in our villages, when we saw a dead person we were scared, but today we are in this situation."[46]

In another instance, a sensational account of cannibalism involved a woman, Dar Apris, who survived Dayr al-Zur after a massacre of women that left her beneath several corpses. She reported that she ate the flesh and drank the blood of the corpses atop her in order to survive for twelve days while trapped beneath them. This lurid tale shared in a local American newspaper described both Armenians and local Arabs stealing Armenian children.[47] The report claimed the local Arabs would come to the Armenian camp in Dayr al-Zur with fresh cooked meat for sale the day following an abduction. The accusations that parents (and Arabs) consumed their children paralleled reports of parents selling their children for money in order to eat—both violated sacred familial and communal boundaries. These tales set some deportees outside bounds, further dehumanizing them among other Armenians, who expressed disgust at the desperate ways that people sought to survive but narrated the broader catastrophic breakdown of order.[48] Yet, the anthropophagy metaphor forms a deep through line within survivor narratives about the genocide, or perhaps symbolizes the consumption of children through abduction and absorption within Muslim households. This assortment of taboo acts assisted in the portrayal of the target population as nonhuman so that killers could perform their work more efficiently and without remorse. In order to fully dehumanize the other, all symbols of humanity and human order needed to be shed, including clothing.

NUDITY AND THE STRIPPING OF SOCIAL SKIN

"A remarkable thing about the bodies that we saw was that nearly all of them were naked," wrote Consul Davis in a 1916 report about a scene of mass atrocity he investigated near Lake Gölcük/Lake Hazar.[49] Nakedness was an effective weapon; it further obscured the humanity of Armenians. In the Ottoman Empire, clothing was no small matter. Clothing contained the power to identify gender and social class, and for most of Ottoman history, sumptuary laws codified the relationship between clothing, religion, and ethnicity. Much of the clothing Armenians had worn to this point was hand-tailored, sometimes embroidered in unique styles passed down through female family members, who were expected to have some mastery in needlework. The care that went into clothing connected people genealogically to their ancestors and regional patterning. Those virtual skins, clothing and undergarments, littered the countryside as evidence of the procedural forced stripping that was a prelude to killing.[50]

Armenians recounted how those who were massacred were first forced to strip in order that their clothing could be preserved as spoils of war, sparing the garments from the tears, blood spatter, and damage when axes and hatchets did their bloody work. Taking clothes from dead bodies may have been taboo among Muslims. But obtaining them assured that the looted clothing bundles could find their way to city markets to be sold for profit.[51] In "an absurd sight," Muslim villagers wore "overcoats, frocks, jackets—various men's and women's European garments of the finest materials," all evidence of looting Armenian deportees.[52] I previously noted how the European fashions and hairstyles worn by some of my own relatives in the Chekijian family portrait were a sartorial sign of the adoption of European culture and language through Protestant schooling and the circulation of European tastes and habits more broadly.[53] Given this significance, stripping the body bare unravels social order by forcing victims to shed an outer layer of virtual skin, further severing the individual body from symbols that linked a person to family, community, culture, and ultimately the land. Forcing deportees to violate the boundaries of modesty further dis-membered the Armenian community and foreshadowed how Jewish men, women, and children would later be forced to strip communally, symbolically shedding their individual and collective human identities, before being herded into Nazi gas chambers for extermination.

From a more symbolic standpoint, stripping social skin was the final undoing of social order and a prelude to murder that signaled the absolute precarity of the victim and confirmed the absolute power of the perpetrator for all, including the perpetrator. Survivor Eva Chulian remembered how at Dayr al-Zur, "they disrobed us totally and we stood completely naked as the day we were born."[54] Several eyewitnesses registered shock at seeing not only caravans of half-dead Armenians marching through the desert but at the naked state that they were in after being stripped bare by the accompanying Turkish gendarmes. Denuding Armenian deportees suited genocidal aims by reducing humans to a lower species such that, in the chilling words of Hannah Arendt, killing them was "as impersonal as the squashing of a gnat."[55] In other words, humanity was made superfluous with the rhetorical power of "body horror," easing the psychological burden on perpetrators.[56]

Denuding victims also deprived deportees of one of their only sources of income during journeys when most of their possessions had already been already stolen. Many accounts describe Armenians sewing money inside their clothing for safekeeping in preparation for the deportations.[57] Armenians hid money in their bodies (hair, mouth, and other orifices) as resources to assist survival during the forced marches. Stripping them of that cash needed for survival assured higher casualties. A survivor observed that after marching men outside the village to murder them, soldiers and villagers "carried prisoner's clothes [back] in their arms."[58] It was not only clothing that was looted but any type of protective gear, including bedding and mattresses, leaving deportees completely unsheltered in foreign environments. Not only were the clothes stolen from the backs of Armenians surplus capital for marauding looters, corpses also held value. A witness noted that looters would sometimes pay a fee to Turkish gendarmes for the right to loot the corpses of dead Armenians. Sometimes these corpses were burned to ash to ease the looting of gold coins that remained lodged in the entrails of Armenians who had swallowed them for safekeeping.[59]

Deported from Samsun to Aleppo, Pailadzu Captanian wrote what was perhaps the first memoir by a woman survivor when it was published in 1919. She described how women were stripped by the Kurdish guards and forced to walk for days in the sun with no protection in what she called a "column of the naked [colonne des nudités] [that] had been turned into a slave market."[60] Taking away the clothes of deportees importantly expedited death by exposing them to the elements: the cool nights that caused hypothermia and the scorching hot sun of the desert. Due to extreme exposure, their skin was sun burned and blistered—skin that was also wounded by the beatings they received from guards. Some eyewitness accounts observed that skin was burned until the point of appearing discolored and even inhumanly green in color due to extreme damage.[61] As they walked, they used one hand to protect their heads from the sun and the other to protect their modesty; in other cases the "unfortunate females, in order to cover their nudity, put layers of mud" on their bodies.[62]

Nakedness was meant to produce feelings of shame within those reduced to this state. However, Muslim witnesses also felt shame at seeing fellow Armenians in such a state of degradation. Ambassador Morgenthau observed, "When they passed an Arab village in their naked condition the Arabs pitied them and gave them old pieces of cloth to cover themselves with. Some who had money bought some clothes; but still some remained who traveled thus naked all the way to the city of Aleppo. The poor women could hardly walk for shame; they all walked bent double."[63] In contrast to Morgenthau, Captanian noted that the local Muslim population mocked the naked women as they passed through villages and the countryside. Deportees understood well how the natural environment along with extreme deprivation, including denuding, was a genocidal weapon. Captanian explains clearly the methodology: "The goal of our journey through Anatolia was Dayr al-Zur. The authorities led the deportees on the longest path so as to systematically whittle them down through fatigue, hunger, thirst, murder and systematic looting. . . . The few survivors who had enough strength and resistance to survive the hardships and had the opportunity to escape the dangers on the road were exterminated in Dayr al-Zur by the *yatagan* [sabre] of the Turk."[64]

Unique among these traumatic recollections of denuding is the memoir of Yervant Odian, who perhaps because he was both male and a humorist had the fortitude to poke fun at his own nakedness after his filthy, shredded clothing was stolen by an Arab thief in Dayr al-Zur. He wrote, "They also took my headdress and shoes and left me as naked as the day I was born. Then, in a mocking tone, they said, 'Maas salami' [Have a good journey] and turned back. In a state of Adam's nakedness, I sat for a while on the ground to think what I should do."[65] Soon after, Odian encountered an old shepherd, who gave him a coat, but he was robbed of his clothing yet again by an Arab who accused him of stealing the coat. Odian remarks that Arab women began to call out "Mejnoun, mejnoun" (He's mad, he's mad!), construing the oddity of his nakedness to be a sign of madness, which he notes is also regarded a mark of holiness in Islamic mysticism.[66] Odian's narration interjects some humor into the tragic and very lethal condition of being completely exposed to the desert sun, but the story also illuminates how, in this instance, his naked body was viewed as stripped of humanity because, in this case, in the eyes of villagers he was divinely touched.

Yet, we cannot discount how Odian's maleness altered his experience. Female nudity, by contrast, was an important prelude to sexual atrocity. Captanian referred to the procession of women as "'the column of the naked' that was transformed into a mobile slave market. Easily inspected women were sold there like cows, informally, person to person, while others were auctioned." Nudity made the threat and enactment of sexual atrocity more profound as it exposed what Giorgio Agamben has called "bare life" (zoē)—life stripped of meaning and fundamentally outside the political order; life reduced to absolute vulnerability to the will of the génocidaire and by extension, state sovereignty.[67] Consul Davis noted at a site of massacre he investigated near Harput that "nearly all the women lay flat on their backs and showed signs of barbarous mutilation by the bayonets of the gendarmes."[68] Other women used their bodies to resist by committing suicide rather than succumb to sexual violence. In another instance, a woman coached women to urinate at the point that a gendarme attempted to violate them; in other words, she urged them to use their own bodily functions to provoke disgust rather than desire in a potential rapist.[69]

Shame and nakedness served to weaken the general population as an act of symbolic murder. Georges Bataille explains, "The act of stripping naked, in civilizations where it has full significance, functions as a simulacrum of the act of killing, or at least as an equivalent shorn of gravity."[70] Thus nudity was not just symbolically important; it was a tool for ongoing necropolitical violence (denuding, dragging, dismemberment, and public display) against state enemies and their corpses.[71]

During the Armenian Genocide, individual bodies served as a metonym for the broader communal body. Defiling bodies through ritual cruelty and symbolic (often sexual) violence was intended to have a nullifying effect on collective identity. Denuding bodies and forcing victims to engage in taboo acts to survive served to dis-member individual victims from the communal whole symbolically in preparation for mass murder. Bodies were physically separated through the dismantling of families, males from females, and extreme acts of symbolic violence that unraveled the material body. As with torture, defilement furthered such atomization, to advance the project of mass violence by shutting down empathic responses by undoing the humanity in the victim. Even fellow Armenians who survived the ordeal were repulsed at the extreme transgressions of social taboos undertaken for survival. Such unraveling of humanity was counteracted with the retrieval and recuperation of barely living Armenian bodies in postwar humanitarian missions. The earliest efforts began not with foreign humanitarians but surprisingly with Armenians who rallied to save themselves from the brink of annihilation.

REMNANT 2

"Armenian Girls inside Arab Homes"[1]

Dayr al-Zur, May 6, 1919

Armenian National Community in America,

Fellow Compatriots,
I have come to Dayr al-Zur with the job of sending deportees from here. Most of the deportees found here have gone to Aleppo, Mosul, and other places. Still, there is difficult work [to be done] here. In the desert among the Arabs, Kurds, and Circassians (or Cherkes) are thousands of beautiful girls and orphans. The English imperial military has kind regards but its policy does not allow us to make efforts to take back the many thousands of Armenians by force. For this reason, it does not want to excite the passions again or establish new problems. I, personally, cannot blame them. In the dominating situation, we Armenians could also not move in any other way. What remains is for us to approach this indirectly, such as taking [back these girls] by pleasing Arabs; and if necessary, we can even pay 1-2-3 gold [coins] to buy them back. I am making all the necessary preparations to take with me 1–2 men to travel through all the deserts, visit the villages and tents, taking with me gifts and other things for their sheikhs, which I will voluntarily hand over them. I have a little money. But to accomplish this goal, at least $40,000–50,000 is necessary. Armenian-Americans are not greedy—always giving and again they will give. I assure you that if there is a call put out to the people with this purpose in mind, we can immediately make this money conspicuous, especially if we tell them that here, or in Mosul, among the Arabs are our most beautiful girls, generally from Sebastia, Kharpert, and Aintab. My being here has already had a great moral and benevolent influence on the Armenians and made a scary and shaky impression on the Arabs. Every day 3 to 4 [women] from the harems come saying that the men responsible for the Armenians are here, (an American) [i.e., Herian].[2]

Personally, believe me when I say that this plan is dangerous work, but the heartbreaking letters that come from the desert prompt me to take this dangerous step in my life to rescue them in some form. The issue is simply this—the English imperial military takes only those who fearlessly announce that they want to return to their relatives; however, those who do not want to go are left among the Arabs. There are a number of reasons for those who did not want to come: some of them, which are very few, have gotten used to the life of the harems and they want to stay there; others do not know that revolution and change has happened in the world; some have children and they don't want to part from them; some think there are no Armenians left in the world, and if they leave their Arab husbands—who at the least feed them dry bread [*chor hats*[3]]— they will once again become helpless, homeless, and die; [and] some suppose that their family members have all died, and if they leave, where will they stay? On top of all this, add the fear and lies invented by Arabs. For example, they say that the British will gather and take them to the sea and throw them in and kill them or give them to the Turks, etc. They scare them with lies such as these. Most importantly, they say that if Armenians had any ruler [*der*],[4] they would have sent people to find them.

The only way to counteract all this is money. Arabs excessively worship silver [coins]. Everything is possible with money: it is possible to bribe the *shaykhs* [sheiks] and retreat peacefully. Immediately send me money through Baghdad or Mosul. The money I currently have was given to me by Archbishop Mushegh [the Archbishop of Mosul]. It is a trivial amount against what is needed—only close to $5,000. However, with this, I will start my work immediately and I am confident this work will bring good results.

Because of the grace of the English imperial military, our starving people can be fed, the lives of our orphans cared for. It is up to us to do what we can in to free these wretched people. Of course we have to adapt our work to the *policy* of England. At least for now, there is no other way. If there is more delay, after all the deportees leave, we will have to consider them all as lost.

I studied all the details of the Armenian massacres that occurred in Dayr al-Zur and its surroundings but for now I don't see the need to write about it.

Again, I beg you, my dear Armenian compatriots to do your best in order to send money. My whereabouts will always be known by the English imperial military, so they will send me the sum of money [you send to me]. Only, move at American speed and send money very fast! I sent a letter also to the Egyptian National Union [Yekibtosi azkayin miyotyan]. I have no hope that they will help me because the Armenian community of Egypt, first, is very slow, and second, the spirit of Armenian-Americans is lacking in them.

With love, greetings, and respect.

Yours,

Ruben Herian

CHAPTER THREE

RESCUING "KITTENS" IN THE DESERT

The Armenian Humanitarian Relief Effort

> I have to say that the job is very difficult and life-threatening every second, but as trade is very profitable, [rescuing orphans] is profitable in the sense that if I lose my life, instead of one the nation will gain hundreds.
> —RUBEN HERIAN, letter from Adana, April 6, 1919[1]

While under attack, while their people were being uprooted and murdered, and while hundreds of thousands were made into refugees, the Armenian community mobilized. They dressed as Bedouin sneaking into the crowd of deportees and within makeshift refugee camps to provide food and relief to their countrymen along the deportation routes. Armenians from abroad sent money and lobbied politicians, and some men, like Ruben Herian, an Ottoman Armenian who had emigrated to the United States before the genocide, returned to their homeland to join the struggle to rescue the innocents, who Herian called "kittens" in his coded messages. As the war ended, Armenians continued their own efforts to retrieve the remnants of their nation in Constantinople, Aleppo, and Beirut. Centuries of existence in Ottoman lands had established Armenian institutions scattered throughout the empire's metropoles—Jerusalem, Aleppo, Baghdad, and Cairo—that would form command centers for a massive humanitarian relief effort in which the victim community rescued its own.[2]

The voices of captive women and children held in Muslim homes can be found within a small trove of documents collected largely by a one-man rescue operation who worked in coordination with regional prelacies to rescue thousands of women and children. Herian is one example among many Armenians who joined the mission to rescue lost souls in the desert. These stories complicate any easy narrative of

Armenian victimhood and instead urge us to probe more deeply to discover how Armenians miraculously survived.

THE RESCUE OF ORPHANS AND WIDOWS AND ARMENIAN RESISTANCE

The story of Armenian rescue networks is about not just a story about Armenian institutions and community leaders, but also about everyday Armenians who shared information about the whereabouts of missing loved ones. While relief workers and clergy located and cared for missing Armenians, children did their part by informing new arrivals in Aleppo's orphanages of the whereabouts of their family members. Rumors of surviving Armenian remnants spread deep into the desert. Armenians conveyed messages via letters and children who served as "human newspapers," with messages concealed by mud written on their bodies. They hid messages in their mouths or tied them to their private parts to facilitate communication between Armenians while also evading the authorities.[3] Less informal communication eased reunions as well. In Raqqa, a local Arab resident recalled how a particular style of family embroidery reunited two sisters who had separately continued to stitch a pattern learned from their mother.[4] Family members from as far away as America and Canada wrote letters directly to the Aleppo prelacy listing the names and ages of missing family members. These letters were sometimes accompanied by elaborate descriptions of their physical features and even photographs to ease identification.

The story of the vorpahavak, the "orphan rescue," that stretched from Constantinople, Aleppo, Damascus, Baghdad, and Jerusalem has been told by other historians, and these works have rightly shifted our attention away from a flattened representation of absolute Armenian victimhood and toward what Khatchig Mouradian has called "humanitarian resistance," the nonviolent and extralegal ways that Armenians resisted the necropower of the Ottoman state.[5] The network involved high-profile Armenian political and business leaders, church committees, doctors and nurses, and local Muslim and Christian populations that facilitated rescue efforts on the ground during the first phase of genocide, in the spring of 1915, saving the lives of thousands of Armenians.[6] Armenians were not passively waiting for help, but helping themselves both individually and collectively by piecing together work and employing strategies of survival in the towns they were deported to. Ottoman authorities began to complain that Armenians had quickly revived themselves in places like Raqqa and Dayr al-Zur by 1916, prompting the empire to close avenues of survival in what Raymond Kévorkian has coined "the second phase" of the Armenian Genocide, beginning October 1915 until December 1916.[7] The genocide's second phase was characterized by the closure of concentration camps along the Euphrates River. Those who were able to survive this human-induced disaster were deported to Dayr al-Zur, where the third phase of mass extermination ensued, "to finish what they had started by relentlessly tracking down the handful of individuals who had benefited from some sort of protection."⁸ Despite these efforts to liquidate deportees, a clandestine network of Armenian humanitarians, some of whom disguised themselves as vendors to enter the camp's porous borders, snuck inside the camp to offer food and medical assistance.⁹ The recovery effort was mutually supported with individual letters of those seeking missing relatives and periodic reports from rescuers on the ground who published the details of their operations in the Armenian press.¹⁰

The rescue and reclamation efforts sought to claim as many Armenian bodies as possible to reconstruct a decimated nation and bolster efforts of the Armenian National Delegation in its efforts to affirm Armenian statehood in the postwar period.¹¹ In accordance with the League of Nation's focus on demography, negotiations would be strengthened by demographic numbers. Armenians were placed at a demographic disadvantage because of the massive losses they had suffered during the war. Lerna Ekmekçioğlu has shown how such loss made demographic recovery and a pronatal viewpoint imperative during reconstruction.¹² The reclamation of women's and children's bodies was part of a movement referred to in Armenian as the vorpahavak, "the orphan collection," which also included the collection of widows.¹³ This movement viewed the body as a site of resistance, rescue, and rehabilitation, recognizing that the genocide had targeted Armenian vitality.

Importantly, Armenian operations sprang forth during the first wave of the Armenian Genocide. The reclaiming of bodies after the war was sustained by the same biopolitical logic of states—that political power, including the right to self-determination, resided in demographic numbers. Although national independence had not always been a goal, the devastation of genocide had made it a point of consensus. Recovering bodies, then, was a necessary existential and political goal.

Historian Anna Aleksanyan has shown how as early as November 30, 1918, Bishop Torkom Kushakian, a Cairo-based member of a special committee for orphan collection formed by multiple Armenian agencies, sent a special fifteen-point program guideline for relief operations for rescues in Syria.¹⁴ The letter instructed organizations to extract all the Armenians they could, without qualification. "All Armenians whose names were changed and who were forcefully converted to Islam must be liberated and sent back, and if they are abducted by Muslims, everything should be done to save them."¹⁵ Archived in Paris and Yerevan, Armenian correspondence illustrates the sophistication of Armenian organizing prior to the constitution of the League of Nations and the drafting of postwar treaties.¹⁶

At war's end, the Armenian National Delegation estimated that 150,000 women and children absorbed into Muslim homes between Cairo and Baghdad were in need of rescue. The US vice consul in Cairo estimated there were 80,000 Armenian refugees in Aleppo, 6,000 of whom were girls trapped in Muslim households.[17] Outside the city, an estimated 40,000 orphans and girls were absorbed into Muslim homes along a corridor stretching from Urfa to Birecik to Raqqa and Ras al-'Ayn in the east.[18] The rescue operation to reclaim demographic strength was large but so was the reach of Armenian institutions. Within the empire's major metropoles, robust Armenian church institutions—the Armenian patriarchate of Constantinople headed by Archbishop Zaven Der Yeghiayan, Archbishop Mushegh Seropian of Baghdad, and Archbishop Ardavadzt Surmeyan of Aleppo, Archbishop Bedros Sarajian of Damascus, and many Armenian Catholics and Protestants—maintained their own relief efforts while corresponding with global political leaders and rescue workers.

Out of desperation, many of the women who had left Muslim households had been working as prostitutes. Historian Vahé Tachjian argues that Armenians were of two minds about wayward women who had turned to prostitution to support themselves during the war. Armenian elites both encouraged Armenian women to marry and (re)produce the nation and also viewed these women negatively in their individual writings. Some focused their ire on women who turned to prostitution to survive after being shunned by the community or reduced to poverty.[19]

The prelacy in Baghdad, heavily engaged in its own relief efforts, left behind evidence as to how it navigated the subject of Armenian prostitutes. In 1919, Archbishop Mushegh wrote Boghos Nubar to insist that all Armenian women and children be liberated from Aleppo's harems, no matter what the circumstance. While not all Armenians may have shared his view, Archbishop Mushegh affirmed that Armenian women held in Muslim homes were deserving of rescue, a view he dictated to the Armenian leadership in Paris from his prelacy in Baghdad.[20] In Baghdad, a portion of local Armenian efforts were specifically focused on retrieving deportees who through circumstance were "pushed to immorality," which Archbishop Mushegh estimated to be a substantial 80 percent of the refugee population.[21] Relief workers focused on treating the "shameful diseases" (maladies honteuses) suffered by rescued women and girls, including syphilis, chancroid, and gonorrhea.[22] Some of the hospitalized victims, the archbishop noted, were girls as young as ten and eleven years old. Emphasizing the magnitude of the problem, the municipality of Baghdad prepared a list of 150 known prostitutes—100 of them were Armenian women.[23] While providing a detailed account of prostitution, the shepherd of Baghdad's Armenian community noted that several more women were kept in Muslim homes as servants, unable to complain about the possible sexual abuse they suffered in those households.[24] Much of his efforts were spent trying to convince the British authorities to allow the Armenian community to rescue these women. Fearful of disruptions with the local Muslim population, the British authorities withheld their support and made rescues nearly impossible by demanding that the relatives of captured women and girls, many of whom had been killed in the massacres, appear in person in Baghdad to claim them.

Another noteworthy humanitarian appeal came from Calcutta, India, where a group of Armenians had settled hundreds of years earlier. In a pivotal speech, the Armenian Relief Committee of Mesopotamia (ARCM) chairman Mardiros H. Kouyoumdjian argued before an audience of Armenian compatriots and friends of Armenians that prostitutes were deserving of rescue and reincorporation into the Armenian community: "For the sake of our national prestige, it was our sacred duty to take a little more care of these, in order to prevent them from continuing the shameful and degrading profession, which they were forced to practice on account of hunger, misery, and unimaginable depravations."[25] In order to recuperate these women, the ARCM, besides running the Baqubah refugee camp and a few buildings for rescued Armenians inside Baghdad, established separate spaces for different categories of victim inside Mosul. According to the report, these included an orphanage housing 327 orphans, an alms house for poor and elderly indigent refugees, special houses for poor Armenian women unable to care for themselves, and private houses for 802 Armenian women. The committee created a specific program to recover and to recuperate Armenian prostitutes and a shelter to separate them from the rest of the female population. Rescue efforts were intensified because ideologically humanitarian workers believed that time could diminish the memories of being Armenian for Islamized children.[26] Armenian, European, and American humanitarians shared common views that women living among Arab and Kurdish tribesmen and within Turkish harems, generally speaking, had been "degraded and demoralized in the unwholesome and poisonous atmosphere."[27]

While the heads of church formed a natural base for Armenian relief efforts, local efforts included Armenian doctors and relief agents who worked at times independently while at other times in coordination with the international effort. These efforts were often combined with those of emerging governments, such as that of King Faysal, who briefly ruled from Damascus. The memoir of Levon Yotnakhparian shows how in cooperation with Archbishop Bedros Sarajian of the Armenian archdiocese of Damascus, Armenians initiated their own orphan relief effort in conjunction with King Faysal's government, dispatching Yotnakhparian and three other Armenians to retrieve Armenians from homes in the southernmost regions of Syria, in Jabal al-Druze and Hawran.[28] Armenians received added support from the Druze community, who sheltered and defended Armenian refugees. Arab newspapers, including *al-'Asima*—a publication supportive of King Faysal's brief governance in Damascus—issued a call to its Syrian readership to deliver "Armenians back to their nation." Yet, there was some confusion about whether residents were supposed to report or, alternatively, hand over Armenians to the authorities.[29] A bird's-eye view of the postwar Middle East shows Armenians mobilizing in cooperation with allies to save, locate, and retrieve other Armenians from Constantinople in the north of the empire to Damascus in the south.

The rescue of trafficked women and children in Aleppo would occur at a time the city was teeming with 150,000 Armenian refugees crammed into private houses, churches, and makeshift shanties in refugee camps. The city where hundreds of thousands had been deported was now becoming a place of settlement but without the capacity or infrastructure to hold so many people. Other refugees began to drift into the city in the postwar period to find loved ones or lend a helping hand as news of relief operations circulated. The Aleppo prelacy was the place where local and diasporan Armenians could send letters in search of their loved ones.

Though local Armenians of the Levant had already begun their campaign to retrieve bodies snatched during the war, Armenian national recovery was eventually prioritized by international law. Article 142 of the Treaty of Sèvres (1920) voided forced conversions to Islam in order to "repair so far as possible the wrongs inflicted on individuals in the course of the massacres perpetrated in Turkey during the war."[30] This clause in particular gave humanitarians legal grounds to transgress norms of Muslim patrimony and the shari'a that held conversion to Islam as immutable.

In addition to Sèvres, Armenian rescue efforts were aided by the 1920 Covenant of the League of Nations, which enshrined its dedication to the supervision of agreements pertaining to the traffic in women and children in Article 23c.[31] At the 1919 Paris Peace Conference, the Commission on the Responsibility of the Authors of the War and on Enforcement of Penalties was formed to prosecute a list of thirty-two war crimes, among them two related to crimes against Armenians: rape and the "abduction of girls and women for the purpose of enforced prostitution." However, the list of war crimes neither named Turkey specifically as the perpetrator nor the specific Greek, Armenian, and Assyrian ethnicity of female victims.[32]

By 1919, the Armenian mission to retrieve missing orphans in Syria was strained by Muslim complaints that it violated the sanctimony of the Muslim patriarchal household. Recovering lost Armenians subverted Muslim supremacy by offering too much power to non-Muslims who were, at the time, not citizens but foreign refugees. Though there were moments of tension between Muslim and Armenian populations during the recovery, the vorpahavak took on a different character in the north of Syria until it was halted in 1930.[33] Regionally, the Armenian prelacies in Aleppo and Baghdad were well poised to coordinate humanitarian workers, schools, and orphanages in the two cities on opposite ends of the great swath of desert where many Armenians lay in hiding, not knowing whether their community had even survived the cataclysm.

After the armistice in 1918, the league joined local efforts to retrieve an estimated three thousand Armenian orphans from Turkish homes from among the estimated four thousand to five thousand children scattered throughout Constantinople. These efforts were briefly halted in order to include Turkish participation in the relief efforts, after which there was a dramatic decrease in rescues, with only seventy-five orphans in a three-month period. Humanitarians like Emma Cushman, an American nurse who worked with the American Board of Commissioners for Foreign Missions and later Near East Relief (NER), and Dr. William A. Kennedy, a physician who represented the Lord Mayor's Fund for Armenia, set out to rescue orphans in the imperial capitol.

In Constantinople, the allies established the Neutral House first under their control but later administrated by the American NER to receive the flow of orphans making their way to the city in the aftermath of the war.[34] Early rescue operations by the local Armenian community, according to Patriarch Zaven, had little to no impact on the countryside.[35] The patriarch recalled in his memoirs how haphazard relief was outside the city when an Armenian-American arrived in 1919 to rescue some orphans from Ankara and Kastamonu with the blessings of the patriarchate; years later, the patriarch could not even recall the man's name, perhaps because the mission had been so insignificant. Another volunteer named Dr. Emirze rescued some Armenians in Kurdish and Arab villages around Urfa until his work was halted by the nationalist resistance in 1919.[36]

What was missing in those early years after the war was an international plan to rescue Armenians left behind in the Syrian Desert, the final line of deportation. Much of that work in those early years (1918–1921) was carried out almost single-handedly by Ruben Herian, whose mission was supported by the Armenian General Benevolent Union (AGBU) in Cairo and facilitated by regional prelacies in Aleppo and Baghdad.[37] Despite his slapdash humanitarian methods, Herian left behind a cache of archival traces that offer a glimpse into the humanitarian efforts of everyday Armenians searching for the remnants of their nation.

RUBEN HERIAN: "THE YOUNG MAN WITH GREY HAIR"

Co-founder of the Armenian National Movement and president of the AGBU Boghos Nubar had coordinated Armenian recovery efforts from Paris. An Ottoman subject from Cairo's Armenian community, Nubar advocated for the United States and European nations to support Armenian statehood at the conclusion of the war. A compact with the French minister of foreign affairs Georges Picot and British diplomat Mark Sykes—the men whose agreement redesigned the post-Ottoman Middle East—at the French embassy in London in the fall of 1916 set the terms through which Armenians would fight for the French in Cilicia in return for postwar statehood. The Armenian Legion was to eventually constitute the core of a future Armenian national army in post-Ottoman Anatolia.[38] Per the agreement, Armenians would send five thousand men to fight against Ottoman troops in Cilicia, under the supervision of French officers. An Ottoman Armenian immigrant to the United States, Ruben Herian, was among the men who volunteered to serve.

Born in 1869, Herian graduated from Tokat Armenian National School in his home town before moving to Constantinople and later New York.[39] Though he had spent only a small part of his life in New York, he referred to himself as "the American" in his publications and appeals to the Armenian press to encourage Armenian-Americans to donate more to rescue and relief missions.[40] After learning news of the Armenian Genocide, he left a successful business and a new life he had established as an immigrant in America to join the Armenian Legion. Herian personally arranged the transportation of twelve hundred Armenian-American men to assist the French and British forces in Palestine at the Battle of Arara (1918), where they successfully defeated the joint Ottoman and German forces on the southern front. Within two years, France would appease the Turkish forces and withdraw its support for the treaties it had yet to ratify. The result was the dismantling of the Armenian Legion and abandonment of Armenian self-determination by 1920.[41]

Despite his efforts behind the scenes, when the Armenian Legion was sent to the front lines in Palestine in 1918, Herian, then fifty, was rejected for being too old—even though he was known for his youthful appearance and nicknamed "the young man with grey hair."[42] A comrade wrote about Herian's noble service when he was left behind guarding a pharmacy where soldiers were given treatment in Zeitun: "He insulted his white hair, which had prevented him from going to the fight against his nation's enemy."[43] In an undated letter to his relative and confidante in America, Mirak, Herian described his motivation to join the Armenian Legion and how his rejection had inspired him to continue his struggle to liberate Armenians:

> My dear Mirak, I still feel very young and the spirit of vengeance burns inside me. Repression and intransigence against my tribe by the barbarians and savage Turks doubles my strength and power. What is life without honor worth? A nation which cannot protect the honor of its tribe by its own power has no right to live as a nation. Before coming here, I thought that people like me have no place in the army, but I'm pretty sure that I and people like me have their places.[44]

After the armistice, he mobilized his energies to help the Armenian community in a different way: rescuing Armenians absorbed in Muslim homes, in accordance with international treaties signed at the war's conclusion that assured repatriation.

Herian linked with the Armenian Relief Committee of Mesopotamia (ARCM), headed by Archbishop Mushegh Seropian in Baghdad, who would dispatch him to Dayr al-Zur on rescue missions. Like other humanitarian workers discussed in subsequent chapters, he focused his efforts around Jazira, the Euphrates, and the Khabour River basin, the last lines of deportation. The work formed a web of relief organizations that spanned Armenian institutions—the Armenian National Union, the Armenian General Benevolent Union, the patriarch of Constantinople, and the prelacies in both Aleppo and Baghdad—alongside Western humanitarian organizations such as Near East Relief and the League of Nations. Herian maintained regular contact with English and French authorities in the regions and carefully balanced their interests with his to retrieve the scattered fragments of his nation. The ARCM called his efforts "the Mission of Salvation" or "the Liberation Mission," and the global Armenian press from Fresno, California, to Aleppo raised donations for what they called The Desert Orphans Fund.[45] Armenians sent private letters to Herian describing how they had been tracking his progress in the Armenian press, saying things like "We read about your works in the Azk [Nation] newspaper that you have liberated people from Dayr al-Zor."[46] A global Armenian readership, largely in diaspora, learned of his mission from the opinion pieces he periodically published between missions. People sent money along with lists of names, ages, identifying features, and photographs of missing family members directly to Herian through the Armenian prelacy in Aleppo.

Herian's method was practical and grounded in action rather than the stiff bureaucratese of Western humanitarianism. His haphazard record keeping sparked criticism from the British officials who controlled eastern Syrian and thought his methods questionable. His overarching imperative was volume—retrieving as many Armenian women and children as possible "from the wilderness," each life representing futurity for the Armenian people.[47] The genius of Herian's operation was that it mirrored in reverse the very system that had unraveled the Ottoman Armenian community deported to the desert, where they had often been bought and sold to tribal households. Herian bought women and children back at an exorbitant price from the Bedouin. For example, one woman victim recalled being bought for the sum of seven sheep during the genocide; by contrast, Herian was offering solid gold coins for the release of women and children during his mission.[48]

At times, he pretended to be an American seeking to reward the Bedouin for caring for Armenians, while at other times he posed as a courier delivering funds to Armenians from their relatives far away. Herian was able to lure Muslims with promises of wealth to release the Armenians kept in their households.[49] He outlined his humanitarian methodology in "Armenian Girls inside Muslim Homes" (Hay aghchigner arapneru dunerun mech), where he describes the necessity to pay gold to buy back Armenians in light of the impasse reached with the British authorities, who were reluctant to enforce Article 142 of the Treaty of Sèvres out of fear of stirring tensions with the Muslim populations they now administered. The British were content to leave Armenians in the homes of Muslims unless they showed willingness to leave of their own accord. Of course, household scenarios were far more complicated since many of the women and children who sought to leave were not permitted to do so and were often abused terribly when they tried. As a businessman, Herian sought to use the tradition of gifting among the Bedouin to essentially buy back women and children at a price too high to ignore. To do so, he needed funding, so his dispatches often requested money from the global Armenian community for the purpose of retrieving lost souls.

While the rescue efforts in Mesopotamia were portrayed as effective, we do not have a complete picture since Herian, a humanitarian on-the-go, did not keep records nor write formal reports. While conducting his missions, Herian met other rescuers affiliated with either Aleppo or Baghdad. He would hand off the orphans to another rescuer, who would deliver them so that he could immediately return to Dayr al-Zur to continue the extractions. In one letter, the Armenian leadership sent him a coded message that a shipment of human cargo he had handed off to a priest had been received in Aleppo: "The Armenian women, girls, and 'kittens' sent by you were all given to us safely."[50] With pride, Herian recounted in an ARCM publication the number of women and children he had rescued between Syria and Iraq:

> My movements in the desert. First, I went to Gezireh and rescued 9 orphans, and then I proceeded to Shamatyeh and Khereyta, with five carriages, and liberated 45 boys and girls, then I went to Terban and Hawija, with six carriages, and ransomed 42. The latter place is four days' journey from Der Zor. Afterwards, I continued my searches in Meyadine and Aboukemal and brought home 17 more. I also went on horseback to Shawee and never returned empty-handed.[51]

He finished his letter by saying, "Today, I am sending 25 orphans into Aleppo." At the height of his efforts (see figure 3), he had purchased seven carriages and hired two nurses and was accompanied by paid guards to offer extra security during his desert missions.

At the time of rescue, Herian provided immediate health care to recovered Armenians, since many of them were sick and debilitated from years of forced labor. He also provisioned women and children with medicine, blankets, clothing, and food rations in the form of dried cheese and fruit and bread. In June 1919, after escorting orphans to Baghdad, he planned on returning to Dayr al-Zur to complete his work, claiming that he had nearly cleared the entire city of the Armenians held in Muslim homes.[52] While he was likely exaggerating, the Armenian National Union (ANU) estimated that Herian during his three short years of work had transferred 2,000 Armenians from Baghdad, and another 320–400 Armenians had been transferred by him to Baquba by boat down the Tigris; this was in addition to the ad hoc rescues in and around Dayr al-Zur.[53] This would make Herian's personal retrieval of Armenians from 1919 to 1921 comparable to that of Karen Jeppe, who achieved similar numbers in her Rescue Home over a decade.

FIGURE 3   Ruben Herian in Arab dress in a portrait taken in the Derounian Brothers Photography Studio in Aleppo, Syria. He and other Armenians dressed in local attire to disguise themselves during the rescue of orphans and widows. His personal correspondence shows that his Arabic was broken at best, but his sartorial transformation as an Arab may have helped him pass as local. Source: Ruben Herian, 420.65.23, enclosure 1. Reproduced with permission of the Armenian National Archive (ANA), Yerevan.

Some children, after years of indoctrination and natural assimilation among the tribes, were reluctant to come with Herian. One survivor, Almas Boghosian, recalled how traumatizing it was for her to leave with "the Americans" who rescued her in Suwwar, just outside the city of Dayr al-Zur. She was very small at the time of the deportations—approximately seven years old—and had bonded with the Muslim household she lived in describing them as "a good family." "I was lucky I end up in that nice house. Most of them have awful place." But she added, "They were just like my own family."[54] She recalled two important details from her rescue that situates it at about 1919. She remembered an edict calling for the Arabs to release all Armenians being kept in their homes as well as being picked up in a horse-drawn wagon one day, a scene that fits the description of the kind of wagon Herian used to retrieve Armenians in the region. Almas recalled being shipped directly from Dayr al-Zur to the Aharonian orphanage in Aleppo. She would have been easy for Herian and his crew to retrieve since her adoptive father had been murdered during a business trip to Dayr al-Zur, leaving only her widowed adoptive mother and sister in the house. In such dire straits, the widow could have been desperate for the gold coins he offered her while also being unable to form any resistance against the man and his entourage on her own.

An often-overlooked aspect of these rescues is how even Armenian rescuers were sometimes met with fear and uncertainty rather than recognition by their traumatized compatriots. Almas is a prime example of a child who had in her own retelling began to love her adoptive family. She described the separation from her second family as terrifying and traumatic: "I cried just like when I lost my mother and father."[55] Almas, who was about eleven at the time of rescue, would have never left the home of her adoptive parents if she had been given the choice. Generally speaking, children were not viewed as being capable of such a choice; their Islamization conducted by force was officially annulled by international treaty, which was enforced when possible by humanitarians.

In light of the reluctance of some Armenian children to leave Muslim households, the ANU wrote this to Herian: "Hearing that many Armenian children and women, fearing that Armenians will be massacred, refuse to be separated from the Muslims that found them. Therefore, to persuade them and give them faith that there is no such thing, we send you some pictures, which will make it easy to persuade and liberate them."[56] Enclosed was a photograph of a young man named Bedros for Herian to use as proof when approaching children "so that they could feel comfortable and be sure the liberated were being taken care of" in Aleppo. Rescued orphans like Bedros also contributed to the cause by rescuing others. He was sent back to Dayr al-Zur from Aleppo in order to help Herian buy clothes for the new batch of children he had rescued.[57]

Photographs were also sent as proof of life by loved ones searching for friends and family to help Herian locate them (figure 4). In one case, a boy named Hovannes would not leave the Shammar tribe that had adopted him in Dayr al-Zur until he saw a photograph of his rescued sister, proving that she was still alive.[58] In a letter to the British governor of Dayr al-Zur, the Armenian National Union also enclosed a photograph of a boy and his sister who were reunited in Aleppo as proof of the good work Herian was doing. The letter, sent to the governor at Christmas in 1919, affirmed Herian's self-sacrifice "to secure the best and most children" on behalf of the community.[59]

FIGURE 4 *This photograph of the orphan Maritsa or Mariam from Kharpert was sent with a letter from her Boston-based Uncle Reverend Hagop Parichanian to Ruben Herian in Syria. In this rare case, the photograph of the missing girl was archived.* Source: Ruben Herian, 420.65.15, enclosure 11. Reproduced with permission of the Armenian National Archives, Yerevan.

Muslims' outcry over the violation that such rescues posed to the sanctity of their families and homes prompted King Faysal to eventually withdraw his support for the rescue efforts.⁶⁰ After assuming control of eastern Syria, the British would give ultimate authority to Muslim fathers to provide or deny consent for the release of Armenian children they had absorbed into their household. Only with a patriarch's consent could a child be reclaimed by the Armenian community.⁶¹ Some British officials questioned Herian's methodology while others praised him, saying Herian "fully recognized the rights and difficulties of government" and that he "has never taken action that might had [sic] trouble, without first consulting the authorities."⁶² A memo from the British Military Office in Dayr al-Zur to the assistant officer of Mayadin, a city not far from Dayr al-Zur, provided the following terms for Herian's mission:

1. He is to arrange for you to see all the Armenians in Mayadin. You will see them alone.
2. Any woman married to an Arab, who wishes to do so, shall be allowed to leave her husband and go with you. In the case of there being children by the marriage, they will remain with the father, unless the father voluntarily relinquished his right to them.
3. Any Armenian woman or man (who is old enough to decide for her or himself) who chooses to stay where they are—will be allowed to do so.
4. All Armenian children will be sent with you whether they wish to go or not.⁶³

Through these criteria, the British memo sought to balance the desires for reclamation against the authority of Muslim patriarchs over their offspring with Armenian mothers. A frustrated Herian captured the British position in one of his personal letters: "The Englishmen are totally against forcibly taking them, unless they come of their own free will."⁶⁴

The Armenians of Aleppo sent praise of Herian's rescue efforts to the British governor in Dayr al-Zur, noting his "courage" and "self-sacrifice" and saying "the original methods he has been using to secure the best and the most children are greatly admired."⁶⁵ Herian's personal letters confirm that he was strongly aligned with the Ramgavar Party to the extent he would sometimes curse as "useless Dashnags," his fellow Armenians from a rival nationalist party, for not helping more.⁶⁶ Herian's goal was to rescue all who were stranded in Dayr al-Zur and its environs, though the orphans and widows of his hometown Tokat always held a special place for him. His letters also mention that the Tokatsi community had been mobilizing efforts in Constantinople as well—he contributed funds to their efforts.⁶⁷ He wrote:

I would very much like for the gentlemen rising like these hens to come here and travel 130 degrees under the sun and gather some "little kittens" [orphans]; alas, we cannot be humans. Sometimes I wonder if I am stupid or that nation lovers [nationalists] are smart, but to my strong conviction I cannot but act. The orphans will form the nucleus of tomorrow of Armenia; one more is a gain; they are the particles of my heart.[68]

The imagery in Herian's letters demonstrates the great cost of these missions to his own body while undertaking what he described as superhuman feats of rescue. To achieve his aims, he was prepared for self-sacrifice like a soldier in battle. These efforts took a toll on him and other humanitarians working to restore and reconstruct the remnants of the Armenian community.

Yet, the British authorities continued to seek more documentation of the lists Herian was procuring from Armenians abroad and composing himself in personal letters. He assured the authorities that he was tracking information, but his personal archive contains a messy array of documents that he kept on the run, certainly not the standardized modern record-keeping that would impress a seasoned British bureaucrat. Haphazard scribblings on random pieces of hotel stationery, the backs of business cards, or envelopes were illegible to the newly established British authorities. His style would contrast sharply with the formal, immaculate humanitarian records of the League of Nations. Yet every scribble represents the imprint of an Armenian body rescued from oblivion, a reverse negative of the disappeared bodies one can find in the Ottoman state archives.

On August 28, 1919, in a letter to the Armenian Relief Committee in Aleppo, the British assistant political officer in Dayr al-Zur who had previously praised Herian raised alarm about the delivery of number of children who had been brought to the city from the Khabour region:

> I repeatedly asked him to let me have a list showing the names of these Armenians whom he had sent to Aleppo, in order that I might be able to inform anyone making inquiries for them. Mr. Herian promised several times that he would make these lists out, but finally he left suddenly. He has neither given me any lists of names nor has he left any record with the Armenian Committee here.[69]

Herian's haphazard lists failed to comply with the bureaucratic order of the British, yet there were detailed lists of missing Armenians in letters sent to him through the prelacies in Aleppo and Baghdad to Dayr al-Zur. What he lacked was a scribe to compile in a register all he had compiled on the back of business cards, correspondence, and hotel stationery. One letter refers to a priest in Aleppo notifying worried community members that "Mr. Herian is Herian. [He] will go back to those areas again, so list your own losses," encouraging Armenians to document the missing.⁷⁰ The letters were from sent by Armenians as close as Aleppo and as far away as New York and Boston, all of them inspired by the articles Herian had written or articles about him published in the global Armenian press.

The letters Herian left behind offer bare bone ethnographic sketches of missing relatives—name, surname, place of birth, and age. Other letters contain remarkable fragments of information, considering that missing women and children were living in the most remote places imaginable. Some relatives knew minute details about whom the women had married, their new Islamized names, and even their home addresses. On November 3, 1919, Lousia Kazanjian wrote from Aleppo that her daughter Anna was now called "Zayna" and held by a Muslim man named Kassar who was a subject of the tribal shaykh Mouslat Pasha.⁷¹ Another letter writer knew that a friend of the family was being held by Sheikh Ali Sultan in the village of Ashret, a few days travel from Dayr al-Zur near the Khabour River in the region of Shaddadi.⁷²

In yet another letter, Priest Sahag Shamlian of St. Garabed Church in Üsküdar, Constantinople, offered a detailed description of his missing children and enclosed multiple photographs—missing from the archive but delivered in the original letter—to aid Herian's identification:

> Satenig is pretty, medium height, medium build, with round and large Armenian eyes, round face, red and white cheeks. My Haygantukht is hardly less than a bit fat; barely a little dark, but with round black eyes with round face, and very handsome and modest like Satenig. Both will now be around 17–18 years old.⁷³

The letter transmitted surprising details about the girls' locations, including their new addresses and the names of the men who had abducted them. Satenig, her father reported, lived in Dayr al-Zur with Hussein Chavoush, while Haygantukht lived with a wealthy jeweler named Yassen al-Sayyed. The girls reportedly stayed inside the home a lot and were rarely seen in public; "they are afraid to be seen or run away with the Armenians." He concluded, "I am posting a photo (taken in early 1915) that is a group photo of our village's girls' school, featuring Satenig and Haygantukht, whom I have named. I also enclose a photo of my Ardavazt, hoping that this will be quite useful." He also included a photograph of himself as proof of life: "Satenig will definitely come to us. And if they see our photo, I hope they both come together soon." The final lines of the priest's letter indicated that had no knowledge of the location of his wife, Aghavni, and asked that Herian inquire about her in hopes she was still alive. That Shamlian's letter focused on the rescue of his daughters suggests he had resigned himself to the idea that his wife may not have survived the deportations.⁷⁴ A notation in pencil on the front page of the archived letter says that one of the missing daughters was located by her uncle and already delivered back to her father. In the margins of these letters were references to both formal and informal networks of Armenians that assisted relatives in finding their loved ones. Advertisements in Armenian newspapers and local informants such as an unnamed "tailor" in Dayr al-Zur, Krikor Haigian, and his wife Satenig assisted Armenians searching globally for traces of lost loved ones.[75]

One can only imagine what kind of letters the Haigians had in their possession in Dayr al-Zur, material that never made their way into an archive. Among Herian's preserved letters is the rare voice of a twenty-six-year-old captive woman named Keghanush Kuyumdjian, who wrote a short letter to her father to ask him to find a way to rescue her from the household where she was held with her nine-year-old son from her former Armenian husband (see Remnant 3). The letter mentions correspondence that she had received clandestinely from her father through the very networks I have described. We do not learn whether she was, in the end, rescued from her situation.[76]

Family members frequently offered Herian direct financial assistance to carry out the rescues. Sometimes they took matters into their own hands to rescue their loved ones from eastern Syria. Such travails are also documented piecemeal among Herian's papers as his advice was sought on these individual missions. "Nishan Garmirlian, a native of Kayseriya [Kayseri], travels from the village of Munjunsun to Der Zor at his own expense to take his daughter who is there. He made many sacrifices on his way out of Egypt for that purpose. Therefore, I beseech you to help him, and to make it easy for him to reach his goal. For this we express our gratitude."[77]

Although he received funding from both individuals and Armenian charities, Herian's private letters reveal he was often cash-strapped. In one letter, he lashes out at the Armenian-American community for not sending enough money to rescue all the Armenians stranded in the desert: "In this great desert affair, the nation abandoned me. I wrote everywhere for them to help me financially, but no one answered my letter. Only through the Chamber of Immigrants Committee, with the help of Bishop Mushegh [in Baghdad], I was able to free many by putting my life in danger."[78] He noted in personal correspondence with Mirak that he had received 7,000 rubles from the bishop, which translated into 350 gold coins.[79] In the same letter, Herian reveals in confidence that he had spent five months' earnings from his retirement on the rescue operations. "My heart aches when I think that I am financially depleted, physically too old and unable to reach my goal. Not only is there no money but no men; this is not the work of one or two people."[80] It could cost Herian 50–200 rupees or even 1,000 rupees converted into gold coins to rescue a single child. On one occasion, Herian had to pay 1,800 rupees—a sum that does not include transportation, medical, and other expenditures—to secure the release of twelve under-age Armenian girls held by an influential unnamed tribal chief.[81] Aleksanyan notes that Herian, chronically short of funds, needed 30,000 gold coins to rescue five hundred women and children at the rate he was paying.[82] Similarly, Herian estimated that he needed a total of US$40,000–$50,000 to buy back the Armenians. "Move at American speed and send money very fast!"[83] To publicly entreat Armenian-Americans, Herian resorted to appeals to both Armenian ethnocentrism and American exceptionalism, while privately he resented that the Armenian diaspora was not doing more.

While Armenian intelligentsia sometimes expressed concern about the Armenians who had spent time in Muslim households, or worse, brothels, Herian and Armenian leadership in Aleppo and Baghdad appeared willing to accept nearly all Armenians, even the wayward, back into the fold. Certainly, it was known that Dayr al-Zur had become a center for prostitution, mostly servicing German and Ottoman officers. In one letter, we learn the limits of his generosity when he condemns Armenian prostitutes who bore children with Arab "dogs." He complained of these "Armenian prostitutes who seem to have become sweet and do not want to be separated from them [Muslim men]; some of them have babies from them." Instead of using the word for "babies," he insults the offspring of Muslim men, calling them "dog's kid" (shan tsak). Yet, he reserved the most vitriol for Muslim men who abused vulnerable women.[84] While the rescuer was not one to sit and philosophize about who was worthy to be saved, this letter and the overall attitude of the ARCM appeared to be that such women, however dark their pasts, were victims worthy of saving.

Herian's brief mission in the desert in coordination with global Armenian relief efforts offers a reverse image of the body snatching that characterized the genocide. Bought cheap with a few *mejidiye* coins or a couple of sheep, Armenians were purchased back with gold coin converted from dollars donated by the Armenian diaspora. Herian's mission was cut short first by the violent upheaval of the local Muslim population that responded to the intrusions into their households by attacking Armenians in Aleppo in 1919. Many members of the mob lethally targeted children and relief workers at Armenian orphanages in the city. In December of the same year, Herian's home in Dayr al-Zur and the Armenian church were looted and destroyed by local Muslims outraged by the vorpahavak and seeking revenge against those involved.[85]

Herian sought revenge for the plundering of the Armenian nation by snatching back its greatest wealth, its woman and children. In 1920, the French would assume control over Syria, changing the political landscape once again. Herian included ethnocentric remarks in his letters that reveal the range of emotions that drove him to extremes to rescue more and more children. He sometimes calls this drive to recover the remaining living bodies of Armenians "revenge" (vrej), which was also the title of a play he wrote in a small notebook that is archived with his personal papers.[86] In one personal letter, he began in English, "I don't give a d——," and continued in Armenian:

> I will work until my heart dies. I find pleasure in dealing with these Arabic-speaking little ones. The poor innocent kids come crying out to me saying, "Efendi ana mush Ermen, Ana Muslim" [Sir, I'm not Armenian, I'm Muslim], they say that out of fear, but when I bring them in and stay in an orphanage for a few days, they say, "Ana Ermen, Ermen zein, Arab pis" [I'm Armenian; Armenians are good and Arabs are dirty].[87]

Writing in broken Arabic with Armenian characters, Herian's letter to a confidant portrays his efforts to transform Islamized Armenian children in stark ethnocentric terms. He describes how he was willing to sacrifice his own dying heart for the pleasure of rescuing children. Other letters reveal how much he enjoyed the great affection the children held for him as their personal savior: "Saying 'father, father,' they kiss my hands. They worship me and this is a great payment for me."[88]

It is haunting to read the words Herian wrote in a 1919 letter: "I will work until my heart dies."[89] He continued his fundraising efforts for orphan rescue and planned on marrying an Armenian orphan and settling down in America. However, Herian would die two years later of a heart attack, in Cairo. Herian and others mobilized before the creation of international bodies in the region, but his work rescuing "kittens" in the desert would be continued by the Armenians who survived and a new figure who arrived in Aleppo: League of Nations commissioner Karen Jeppe.

REMNANT 3

Letter from a Captured Armenian Woman, Keghanush Kuyumdjian[1]

My dear father,
I was very happy to receive your letter. Praise the Lord. Through his infinite favor He rescued us from our enemies. Father, when I was made aware that you were alive, I felt so happy, I wish I had the wings of a bird to fly and come to you.

Father, I have two children here. One is Nazareth and the other from the Arab. When I received your letter, I wanted to come to Aleppo, but my son's father is not here and I have no money, so I beg my father to free me from this Arab.

Go to the church and beg! Again and again, I beg you to free me from here.
Concluding my letter, I remain your beloved daughter,
Keghanush Kuyumdjian, Raqqa

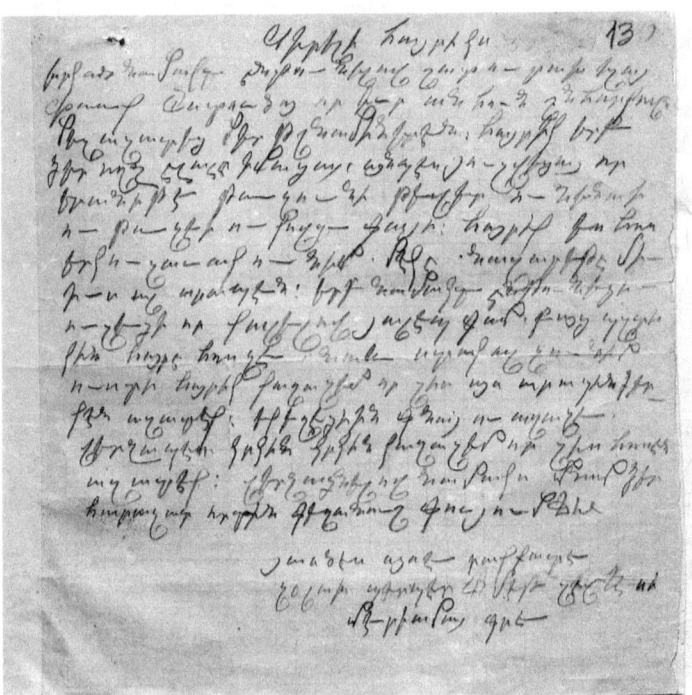

FIGURE 5 *A rare letter from a captive Armenian woman to her father appealing to him to rescue her. Source: Ruben Herian files 420.65.3, enclosure 13. Reproduced with permission of the Armenian National Archives, Yerevan.*

CHAPTER FOUR

RECOVERING SURVIVORS IN ALEPPO, REPLANTING BODIES IN SYRIA'S ARMENIAN COLONIES

As if heeding Zabel Essayan's call to establish an international relief effort to rescue the remnants of a scattered and displaced people, the League of Nations formed Neutral Houses or Rescue Homes in Constantinople, Adana, Aleppo, and Beirut for the recovery of Armenian women and children absorbed into Muslim households.[1] Reports of Islamized children were discussed and supported with five separate resolutions to advance a reclamation effort in coordination with the local Armenian patriarchate and other partners. The fourth and fifth League of Nations resolutions explicitly called for the establishment of "Neutral Houses" to temporarily house the rescued until they had the wherewithal to live independently.[2] Under these five resolutions, the British assumed control over the efforts, with the inter-Allied police enforcing extractions. Eventually, in collaboration with the Armenian Patriarchate of Constantinople, the British High Commission created the first Neutral House, in the Ottoman capitol symbolically on April 24, 1919.

For Syria in particular, the league continued what Herian and the Armenians had started: reclamation of women and children living among the Bedouin along deportation routes on the Euphrates and Khabur Rivers. Ultimately, the league would establish a Rescue House in Aleppo as a base of operations. For the Armenian community, a question loomed: to which nation would Islamized Armenian women birth children—the Arabs, Kurds, Turks, or Armenians? The identities of rescued children would be determined within the league's Rescue Homes by committee.[3]

Originally, Allied powers sought to exclude Armenian participation under the pretext of impartiality. However, after some lobbying by the patriarchate, the Neutral House came to be administered by American, Turkish, and Armenian representatives. Lerna Ekmekçioğlu has illuminated the urgency to reclaim women for the rebirthing of a new Armenian nation in the genocide's aftermath.[4] What ensued was a biopolitical tug-of-war between the emerging Turkish state and the Armenian community to claim reproductive bodies needed to birth the nation;

the struggle played out in league-run homes. In Constantinople, the Armenian community was represented by feminist writer and chairwoman of the Armenian Red Cross Zaruhi Bahri. After the Allied withdrawal, Bahri fled Constantinople with her family when Turkish authorities accused her of Armenianzing Turkish Muslim children at the Neutral House; she lived the rest of her life in Paris.[5]

The recovery efforts of the League of Nations were led by several exceptional women humanitarians who had worked most of their adult lives in the region. Two of these women were from Denmark—Maria Jacobsen, stationed in Jbail (Byblos), Lebanon; and Karen Jeppe, stationed in Aleppo, Syria. Both women would come to be called "mother" (*mayrig*) by the thousands of women and children they would rescue and raise in their homes, metaphorically reconstituting the dis-membered Armenian household as mothers to a dis-membered nation.[6] Jeppe described her work among Armenians as "mak[ing] them into human beings [again]," the restoration of humanity within the dehumanized humanitarian subject.[7] The Danish missionary's work supported the core relief networks established by unsung Armenian heroes who preceded her: teacher and humanitarian Berjouhi Bardizbanian in Istanbul, Dr. Khatchig Boghosian and nurse Almasd Santoorian in Aleppo, and humanitarian rescuer Ruben Herian in Mesopotamia.[8] A complex network of rescue stations and agents constituted a virtual Armenian underground railroad that reached deep into the Syrian Desert and would carry Armenian women and orphans to safety in the Aleppo Rescue Home. Local Arab and Armenian allies willing to work with Jeppe were crucial to recovery and to her eventual plans to establish rural Armenian settlements in Syria. The year Herian died, Karen Jeppe expanded and innovated vorpahavak efforts by employing Danish educational values to "restore" Armenianness, or at least a vision of what Armenianness should or could be in her view.

KAREN JEPPE: THE DANISH "MOTHER OF ARMENIANS"

A devout Lutheran Christian from Denmark, Jeppe spent most of her adult life, a total of thirty years, in the Middle East as an educator and relief worker among the Armenians.[9] Her thinking, Keith Watenpaugh has persuasively argued, moved beyond relief work and was at the forefront of modern humanitarian thinking that emerged during World War I.[10] A daughter of a school teacher in Gylling, Jutland, Jeppe too set out on a career in teaching, despite her father's desire for her to become a doctor. In 1903, inspired by a powerful sermon she had heard in Copenhagen by ethnographer and historian Aage Meyer Benedictsen (1866–1927) about the plight of the Ottoman Armenians during the Hamidiye Massacres (1894–1896), Jeppe traveled to the Anatolian city of Urfa (about 170 miles north of Aleppo). She assumed her first post as teacher there in an orphanage for a few hundred Armenians that German theologian Johannes Lepsius (1858–1926) had created in an old caravanserai at the German-Orient Mission.[11] The newly created Danish Friends of Armenians (Danske Armeniervenner) paid her fare to Turkey, and Jeppe took charge of ten boys sponsored by the organization, which wired 125 kroners each per year for their care.[12] In Urfa a decade before the genocide, Jeppe first experimented with a two-pronged education program: a modern curriculum combined with instruction in a skilled trade taught in surrounding workshops. This approach would remain her model for education and recuperation in the commune she would later create in Aleppo.

While in Urfa from 1903 to 1918, Jeppe immersed herself in the local culture, learning Turkish, Armenian, and Arabic. Fellow humanitarian Ingeborg Maria Sick described her colleague's symbiotic relationship with the local Armenian community:

> The members of this people she knew at once by intuition, understood them without explanation, because their mentality was akin to her own, understood both their good qualities—their aggressiveness and will to live, their unflinching faithfulness and patience—and also the faults they had of necessity developed under the terrors of the Turkish tyranny.[13]

Jeppe's connection with Armenians was so firm that she could cross boundaries that would been unacceptable for Armenian women. For example, when the deportations were initiated in Urfa in 1915, women and men took up arms against the Ottoman authorities to resist the onset of genocide in August. Many Armenians died during the Urfa resistance and Jeppe, an outsider and an unmarried woman, at one point took on the role of a priest by performing last rites for the fallen. Her position as outsider allowed her to transgress gender norms and boundaries, but the conditions of war necessitated Armenian women also transgress gender norms by carrying arms and fighting alongside men.[14]

During the siege at Urfa, Jeppe defied Ottoman orders by building an underground bunker to provide refuge for the Armenians hiding from the authorities. The fear of being discovered was daunting not only for Jeppe but for the twelve Armenians hidden under her floorboards. Armenian priest Der Karekin Voskerichian and his wife committed suicide by drinking poison while in hiding in her home in order to save Jeppe and others from the risks of concealing them.[15] Among those hidden under Jeppe's floor were a boy named Misak Melkonian and the Garabedian family who had adopted him. Jeppe would later adopt Misak as her own son, and he would work side by side with his adoptive mother to rescue, recuperate, and resettle dispersed Armenians in Aleppo.[16]

The violence Jeppe witnessed at Urfa, however, deeply affected her mental health and at times left her suicidal. Her mental health troubles, the result of witnessing the horrors of genocide, would continue to plague her throughout her life.[17] Devastated by what she had witnessed during the Armenian Genocide, Jeppe left the region in 1918 for three years to recover in Denmark.[18] When she returned, she came back energized to work with the League of Nations to recover dispersed Armenians in Mesopotamia.

JEPPE'S UNDERGROUND RAILROAD AND RESCUE HOME IN ALEPPO

Jeppe is perhaps best known for her appointment as commissioner for the League of Nation's Commission for the Protection of Women and Children in the Near East upon her return to the Near East in 1921. She feared joining the league because she was critical of the job it was doing, "dropping the work halfway, because they undertake no obligation to care for the liberated."[19] She claimed that she took on the position at the encouragement of the Danish Friends of Armenia, believing strongly that there was only a ten-year window for rescuing vulnerable Armenian girls and boys; after that, those children would be in their teens or early twenties, without marriage partners and families, and therefore still able to learn to reintegrate into the Armenian community.[20]

In early 1921, Jeppe quietly opened her reception home in Aleppo with the aim of creating "a camp," the term she used to describe the collective, but even with cash in hand, the "housing famine" the city was experiencing made it nearly impossible to find housing.[21] Jeppe's choice to concentrate her efforts in Aleppo was not accidental. The city was a transit center during the Armenian Genocide and afterward evolved into a center for reclamation efforts for several foreign governments and humanitarian agencies—the YWCA, Danish and German Orphanages, Near East Relief, and Jeppe's league and Danish Friends of the Armenians (De Danske Armeniervenner), alongside local Armenian institutions. Aleppo was a central gathering point for Armenians deported there during the first phase of the genocide and a site of humanitarian recovery in its wake. In spaces like Sabil Park and a site known locally as the "Hill of Bones" in Karlik, a cemetery that was once a military outpost, Armenians were held without shelter in makeshift camps where disease, slave auctioning, and sexual abuse were rampant.[22] Armenians who survived the ordeals of these gathering points were deported from Aleppo eastward, where they often disappeared in the towns of Meskene, Raqqa, and Dayr al-Zur.[23]

Conditions worsened in the refugee camps splayed throughout the city. Armenians were unemployed and starving in the ad hoc housing they had built from old gas tins and boards; the housing was "extremely unhealthy [and] lacking of every privacy, they were harmful morally just as well as physically."[24] The roads, which were unpaved desert paths more than anything else, were also a major hindrance due to their poor state. In the end, the reception home was built right next to Jeppe's personal home and next to the Baghdad railway tracks in a district that would later be known as Maydan. According to her report to the Danish Friends of the Armenians, the home was slated to open on September 1, 1922, and in the meantime, boys were encamped in tents in the gardens behind her home.

The loss of Cilicia—a region with a large Armenian population that the French had aimed to add to their mandate in Syria—to Turkish forces in 1920, the lack of French and English support for rescue operations in the region more broadly, and recent memory of a Muslim mob attack against Armenian refugees in Aleppo in 1919 meant that Karen Jeppe needed to employ subtle methods to extract Armenians who sought to flee Muslim households. Her letters and reports reveal that local Armenians and Arab allies offered crucial assistance in locating Armenians in various towns, villages, and Bedouin encampments in the Syrian Desert.

In early 1921 the Danish Friends of the Armenians dispatched Jeppe to found a shelter for Armenians in Aleppo, governed under the French mandate. A few months later, the League of Nations appointed her Commissioner for the Protection of Women and Girls in the Near East, a role that would open new possibilities for Armenian relief and developmental work. By 1922, Jeppe had built a complex network of stations along the Syrian-Turkish border, stretching eastward as far as Mardin, Hasakeh, and Dayr al-Zur to reach abused women and children in desolate areas. Jeppe's veritable underground railroad was a collaboration of several networks that ended at Baghdad railroad tracks in Aleppo, where her Rescue Home was built. The league offered meager funding, which she shared with other groups operating in the city. With less support from abroad, Jeppe wrote in 1922:

> It is slow work in this way especially as there are put obstacles to us from a party who ought to have supported us. I could obtain far better results in numbers if I rushed around in an automobile with soldiers and pulled out the Armenians from the houses, where I know they stay, but there is not the least doubt that my proceeding is far sounder.[25]

The clandestine network that spread the news of her operations attracted, in her opinion, "the most vigorous elements" who heard the call and came because "their own world has the strongest hold in them." In her assessment, two things motivated Armenians to leave: the will to free themselves from servitude and the will to rejoin and rebuild the Armenian community destroyed in genocide.[26]

The results of the network of rescue stations were profound. By 1924, over 600 Armenians were rescued, 187 in the first six months alone.[27] Her agents conducted these rescues in collaboration with Arab and Armenian men and women on horseback who scoured the countryside for survivors. Among the agents was Jeppe's adopted son Misak Melkonian and her assistant Leopold Gaszczyk, who toured the stations to oversee the networks of agents and informants.[28] Gaszczyk's Armenian wife, Horome, worked in the Rescue Home alongside Jeppe. Jenny Jensen, who observed desert operations with a tinge of romanticism, wrote that it was "a picturesque sight to see Misak standing there on the other [Euphrates] river bank with several of his Armenian men wearing the becoming Arab costumes."[29] Jeppe worked with clandestine agents, rarely named in her reports, including priests, a miller, Arab allies, and the Armenian community.[30]

The rescue stations Jeppe established ranged from official contacts—often listed without a name and simply as "my agent" to protect their identity in Jeppe's correspondence—to informal channels that spread by word of mouth. Among the unsung heroes who rescued Armenians in the desert were muleteers who recovered dispersed Armenians in remote parts of Syria and either led them to regional agents or personally transported them to Aleppo. Muleteers were crucial purveyors of information, collectors and deliverers of messages, including letters between Armenians held in Muslim homes and their family members in Aleppo or abroad.[31] Captive women could interact undetected with clandestine rescue agents and muleteers at public watering holes and in markets.

One agent, former merchant and Armenian Catholic priest Vasil Sabagh, who was typically careful to not incite the local population ran into trouble in 1925, while rescuing forty Armenian children. While rescuing the thirty-seventh child, a girl from Hassaka, local Arabs shot him down. Sabagh's death had a chilling effect on relief workers as a stark reminder of the risks involved as they transgressed Muslim households.[32]

Another violent encounter occurred when nineteen-year-old Dikranouhi, who had been trafficked by two different Arab men, fled to one of Jeppe's Armenian colonies in eastern Syria in June 1927. The scene intensified when "her possessor arrived with many armed men and claimed her, although in our territory she was safe." During the harrowing standoff, one of Jeppe's agents contacted Hadjim Pasha, since the man who possessed Dikranouhi was none other than her Muslim ally's son. Hadjim Pasha told the agent to "put her into a motor-car and send her to your rescue-home in Aleppo. The poor Armenians have suffered much from us. It is enough."[33] Upon arrival, Dikranouhi was able to locate her mother, who eventually joined her, but she also found her future husband, Benjamin, a fellow rescued orphan whom she married one year later.[34]

Later, Jeppe's team acquired an automobile to expedite their work thanks to a generous offer from an American benefactor named Miss Anna Gilpin.[35] Photographs of the Ford automobile and other sparkling specimens of modern technology used for speedy desert getaways signaled the sophistication of Jeppe's rescue operations to patrons abroad. She also included photographs of hardship when the car broke down, remarking, "The large number of 'dead' automobiles lying out there along the roads with broken axles, half burnt, or otherwise ruined does speak clearly about how easily it can go wrong."[36] The rescue station network that formed the backbone of Jeppe's underground railroad remained open until a plan to close them was announced in December 1927.[37]

From the time she began her work with the League of Nations, Jeppe conducted humanitarian work on a shoestring budget, prompting one to wonder how much more she could have done with generous support. In late 1922, Jeppe received the meager sum of £1,500 from the league, leaving her in need of raising £4,000 herself.[38] In 1923, the Near East Relief withdrew its resources from Syria, folding them into its Lebanon operation. By 1927, the league stopped providing financial support for her project, which meant shifting her work to that of a private charity and necessitating her appeals for donations from humanitarians abroad. The increased need for funding likely prompted Jeppe to reach out to less savory tabloid sources such as *The Slave Market News* in the UK to make the case that her work was still relevant and needed. She also offered newsletters and pamphlets photographs of the girls she rescued and helped produce a dramatic film representation of her rescue operations in 1926 to appeal to donors. These efforts to produce visual representations of her work meant to encourage support as well as remind people of the necessity of her mission at a time when the Armenian Genocide was fading from public memory. Meanwhile, displaced Armenians were still appearing on her doorstep as news of her work continued to circulate throughout northern Syria and southern Turkey. Jeppe received donations from Sweden, the UK Red Cross, and of course funding from those who read her reports in newspapers and pamphlets circulating in Denmark and England.[39] Her mission had to be both cheap and effective due to chronic underfunding, and her reliance on donations sometimes meant her dispatches to donors abroad had to be attention-grabbing.

RECOVERING ARMENIANS AND RESTORING HUMANS

In her first year of operation, April–August 1921, Jeppe reported to the League of Nations that she had rescued 100 girls and boys. Many of them were able to find relatives in Aleppo or even further away in France and America due to her efforts; the ones who found no surviving family members stayed with her at the Rescue Home until they were self-sufficient. By 1923, she was able to house 200 women and orphans, and the workforce of women in the sewing hall increased to 150 by mid-decade.[40] Four years into her operation, she had rescued a thousand Armenians. By 1926, Jeppe was caring for about 500 children and also providing aid to Armenian organizations inside Aleppo. In 1927, twelve years after the Armenian Genocide began, she rescued 325 children, her largest harvest of orphans in a single year.[41] Historian Edita Gzoyan has studied Jeppe's numbers closely, noting she and her network rescued more boys (591) than girls (463) over the age of fifteen. She explains that the gender disparity was due to the boys' location on the periphery of the Muslim households in which they worked as shepherds, often sleeping in barns with the animals rather than inside the home. Boys, in Gzoyan's assessment, suffered more abuse in these conditions. Physical and psychological distance had kept boys from bonding with Muslim families, whereas girls, living in closer proximity, were often absorbed into the family through marriage, which produced stronger attachments, making them less likely to flee.[42]

Another facet of Jeppe's recovery work in Aleppo that has been discussed by historians is her attitude towards Armenians and Muslims. In his study of Danish missionary work with rescued Armenian women and children, historian and biographer of Karen Jeppe Matthias Bjørnlund has argued that Danish missionaries and aid workers affirmed a typical belief of Western superiority toward both Armenians and Turks. However, critical views of Armenians were tempered by Jeppe's characterization of Armenians to the outside world as ideal subjects, or what Bjørnlund terms as being "(almost) like us," which emphasized the positive moral values of Armenians in her dispatches.[43] Jeppe's attitude toward Turks and Islam, however, was largely negative and likely shaped by what she witnessed and experienced first hand in Urfa during the Armenian Genocide. Recovering Armenians inside Syria was urgent because, as Jeppe explained, "It is in these districts that one must seek for the remainder of the women and children, who at the time were sold as cattle by the gendarmes to the residing Mahomedans or were robbed from the caravans or were saved from being slaughtered."[44] She added, "The Mahomedans had many reasons for seizing these women and children, ranging from pure human charity to the most savage lust."[45]

Jeppe's comments on the subject of religion, however, were often strategic and changed depending on audience. For instance, in her German-language report for Dr. Lepsius's Orient Mission in 1927, she emphasized the progress made toward the "spiritual education" of rescued children and the efforts to "weed out the bad seeds that have been sown," adapting the Parable of the Sower (Matthew 13:24–30) to the situation of Islamized Armenians.[46] Jeppe's Christian rhetoric should be viewed in light of how she reshaped fundraising appeals for different audiences due to chronic budget shortages. Further, as Keith Watenpaugh has noted, Jeppe's attitudes toward Muslims did change over time as her project in Aleppo evolved into one of cooperation with the Bedouin.[47] Jeppe rarely referred to religion in her papers, which is further evidenced by the absence of recorded baptisms registered at the Rescue Home. A small exception is the case of two children whose baptisms were recorded on the back of their intake registries without any additional commentary.[48]

But like many Europeans and Americans, Jeppe viewed Muslims through the lens of civilizational conflict, understanding the extreme violence she had witnessed as the product of religion more than an expression of emergent Turkish ethnonationalism. As a result, cultural and racial chauvinism inflects her views of Turks:

The standard of civilization of the Armenians at all, is on a higher level than that of those beings with whom the young people are forced to associate. Their race is far more developed, which will be most evident from the fact, that the Armenian nation never could sink to Islam but stuck to Christianity even subjected to the most incredible sufferings.[49]

Believing Islam to be diametrically opposed to Christianity, she argued in those early years in Aleppo that Armenians should not live under Muslim rule but instead, in the spirit of the League of Nations and the principles of self-determination espoused at the time, Armenians should have their own independent nation. Aslı Iğsiz has argued that the league's "historicist humanism" was embedded in a European intellectual tradition that conceived of human groupings in civilizational and racial hierarchies.[50] These human taxonomies inflected the league's postwar geopolitical redesign of the Middle East and supported the unmixing of bodies that had previously lived together into discrete national units. An independent nation would afford Armenians the space to recover that which was lost during the war and genocide. As the dream of self-determination faded, so did Jeppe's rigidity about Armenians living separately from Muslims.

As a result of the war, Armenians had been deprived of their homes, their folklore, and their artistic traditions. Jeppe notes how she found Armenians in a state of despair as their traditions fell into oblivion. For those who escaped, Jeppe recuperated them by returning to the system of education she had implemented in Urfa before the genocide: academic education coupled with vocational training. Her compound in Aleppo, therefore, contained institutions necessary to revitalize the community: a school, a hospital, a church, a kitchen, and several workshops and living areas for those who would take up residence. She believed that reviving the traditions would have the twofold effect of reviving important cultural crafts as well as generating income for widows and orphans.

The work of restoration began in the Rescue Home with Misak's "fatherly care," the counterpoint to the motherly care offered by Jeppe, both surrogates for missing parents.[51] Armenians would be, in her conception, integrated into the fabric of Syrian society by nurturing the whole person, which, according to the Grundtvig method of Danish education, considered the social, cultural, economic, linguistic, and religious aspects of personhood. In his close examination of Jeppe's informing ideology, Bjørnlund has argued that the "pragmatic nationalist essentialism" embedded in her project further secularized the Grundtvig philosophy and upheld "the nation or nation/state as destiny and as a human right."[52] Therefore, instead of making Danish values the center of education in the Rescue Home, the curriculum applied them conceptually while centering Armenian culture and heritage. Bjørnlund observed how Jeppe viewed her work in opposition to that of missionaries who sought to affirm Armenianness only to find inroads to Protestant conversion. Jeppe's was a nation-building project "to restore or strengthen group coherence by focusing on aid, education, industry, Armenian cultural heritage, and national restoration."[53]

Jeppe had a teaching staff of four Armenian women and one Armenian man along with an Armenian *mayrig*, or housemother. Armenian students (re-)learned Armenian grammar, natural history, geography, mathematics, and history.[54] The evenings were reserved for singing songs together, among them folk songs and perhaps hymns.[55] Jeppe's associate at the Rescue Home, Danish humanitarian Jenny Jensen, was far more vocal about the Christian teachings that formed part of the Armenian recovery effort. Jensen adopted the paternalistic tone of missionaries when she remarked, "They are all like little children in that respect, and they listen with interest to the Biblical stories. We would, by the way, be grateful for a series of large Biblical pictures to hang on the wall in the school room."[56]

A major aspect of learning to be Armenian again was linguistic conformity. While that might sound odd, we need to remember that Armenianness was never monolithic; Ottoman Armenians sometimes spoke Kurdish and Turkish as primary languages. During the Young Turk project to Turkify the population in the waning years of empire, ethno-religious privileges that had sustained a diversity of languages were eliminated in favor of Ottoman Turkish.[57] Many Ottoman Armenians used Armeno-Turkish—Turkish written with Armenian characters—in written texts. Ottoman Armenian identity was sustained in part through Armeno-Turkish bibles, recipes, lyrics, poems, novels, folk tales, histories, newspapers, and children's stories.[58] In this way, Jeppe's Armenian school claimed Western Armenian as the primary language for the creation of a modern Armenian national subjectivity, a homogeneity through which national belonging was being defined for many Ottoman subject peoples after the war. However, some Armenians would have been learning Armenian for the very first time in Aleppo.

Jeppe also created workshops for excess Armenian labor in the city, calling the work project "an entirely Danish venture," while reinforcing an essentialist notion of Armenian industry. "The Armenian is possessed of a wonderful gift to 'create bread from stones.' One family after another found a small corner where it might live and work which gave the food and even if much want still remained, the worst of it had been helped."[59] Jeppe originally received the idea for supporting Armenian handicrafts from fellow Danish humanitarian Ingeborg Maria Sick. At times, it seemed she considered them as a sign of Armenians' elevated civilizational and racial status: "The Armenians are a people artistically gifted, as witness their ancient beautiful books and writings with an abundance of drawings, their metal work and wood carvings, and not least the embroidery made by women since ancient times, to adorn their homes and their men, as well as their women."[60]

Armenian textiles were a lucrative trade item in many parts of the Ottoman Empire, an economy that was lost during the genocide.[61] Jeppe started a weaving factory that employed both men and women, but she closed it by the spring of 1921. Traditional Armenian embroidery embellished with gold silk threads was revived in the workshops and quickly sold out in fundraising bazaars in Denmark from the time Jeppe began selling them pre-war.[62] In addition to the bazaars in Copenhagen organized by the Danish Friends of the Armenians, the revived workshops in Aleppo supplied handicrafts to the Daells Varehus department store in Copenhagen, where they were sold to help finance Jeppe's efforts.

The revival of Armenian embroidery was not an easy project and served in many ways as a metaphor for Jeppe's broader recovery project to stitch a scattered and decimated community back together as nation. As she notes, patterns were easily found but dyers who remembered how to dye the threads in the old vibrant colors were scarce: "No woman had kept knowledge of the stitch."[63] However, after the loss of a million Armenians, few recalled how to prepare the materials for embroidery and weaving. After some trials, they found an Armenian dyer who could re-create the colors in such a way that they would not fade after washing. There was a "pleasure of working"; they worked not only for bread. Other Armenians joined in the communal effort of building the workshop and helping it thrive. In other words, the humanitarian viewed the project as not only restoring a national tradition but also as a form of work therapy for traumatized Armenian women living in the compound. Jeppe uses the metaphor of the phoenix to capture the spirit of Armenian revival: "If in reality it should regenerate as the new bird Phoenix from the ash of the old one, it must be imbibed by the Armenian genius."[64] In 1922, sixty women were employed in the workshop, and though they received wages for their labor, Jeppe admits it was not their sole source of income.

Teaching a craft (to women) and a trade (to men) not only promised revenue for self-sufficient households, humanitarian cost-savings, and work therapy but also addressed the underfunding that Jeppe often reframed as cost effectiveness by maximizing every dime she was given by donors. Armenians could be reformed on the cheap and their cultural wares sold in order to fund projects and move them toward self-sufficiency. To generate public support among Danish readers and drive fundraising, Jeppe often included specific profiles of children and details of their rehabilitation at the Rescue Home in her dispatches. The failure to provide this education and recuperation and thus the failure to fund projects like Jeppe's, readers were warned, could result in the possible return of women and children to Muslim homes.

Stitching the community back together was a monumental task. The genocide, in Jeppe's assessment, had reduced Armenians to slaves, and she compared them to Africans forced into chattel slavery in America noting they "have lived in slavery similar to that of the one in 'The Uncle Tom's Cabin' [sic]. They have been purchased and sold more than once, have drudged to obtain only unsufficient [sic] food and endured much ill treatment."[65] At the Rescue Home, "ill treatment" became a broad euphemism to describe the horrific abuses that damaged bodies. Humanitarian workers like Gaszczyk and Jensen used photography and intake files to document more fully the crimes Armenians had endured. Photographs of deformed and wounded children, women aged beyond their years due to harsh physical labor and all the psychological and physical effects of servitude are found in Jeppe's private collection of photographs now housed in archives in Denmark, Switzerland, and Armenia (figures 6, 7, and 8). Most of the photographs are unlabeled, making the context for the photographs elusive.

FIGURE 6 *A group of rescued young women whose names went unrecorded gather at Karen Jeppe's compound in Aleppo. Source: Karen Jeppe's private albums. Reprinted with permission of the Armenian Genocide Memorial Institute, Yerevan.*

FIGURE 7 Twenty-eight-year-old Zumroot Godjanian, originally from Urfa. During the genocide, she was forcibly married to an Arab, who sold her for the price of five sheep to another Arab with whom she lived for eight years. A Turkish carriage driver who claimed he was Armenian spotted her and said he would marry her if she fled with him. She arrived in Raqqa with her new husband but was informed by the local Armenian residents that the man who had rescued her was not Armenian at all but a Turk pretending to be one. Local Armenians helped her flee to Jeppe's Rescue Home in Aleppo ("Registers," inmate 345, admitted August 16, 1923, Archives of the League of Nations). A different portrait of Zumroot appeared on the cover of *Orient im Bild* on August 8, 1927. Source: Karen Jeppe's private albums, Armenian Genocide Memorial Institute, Yerevan, Armenia. Reprinted with permission.

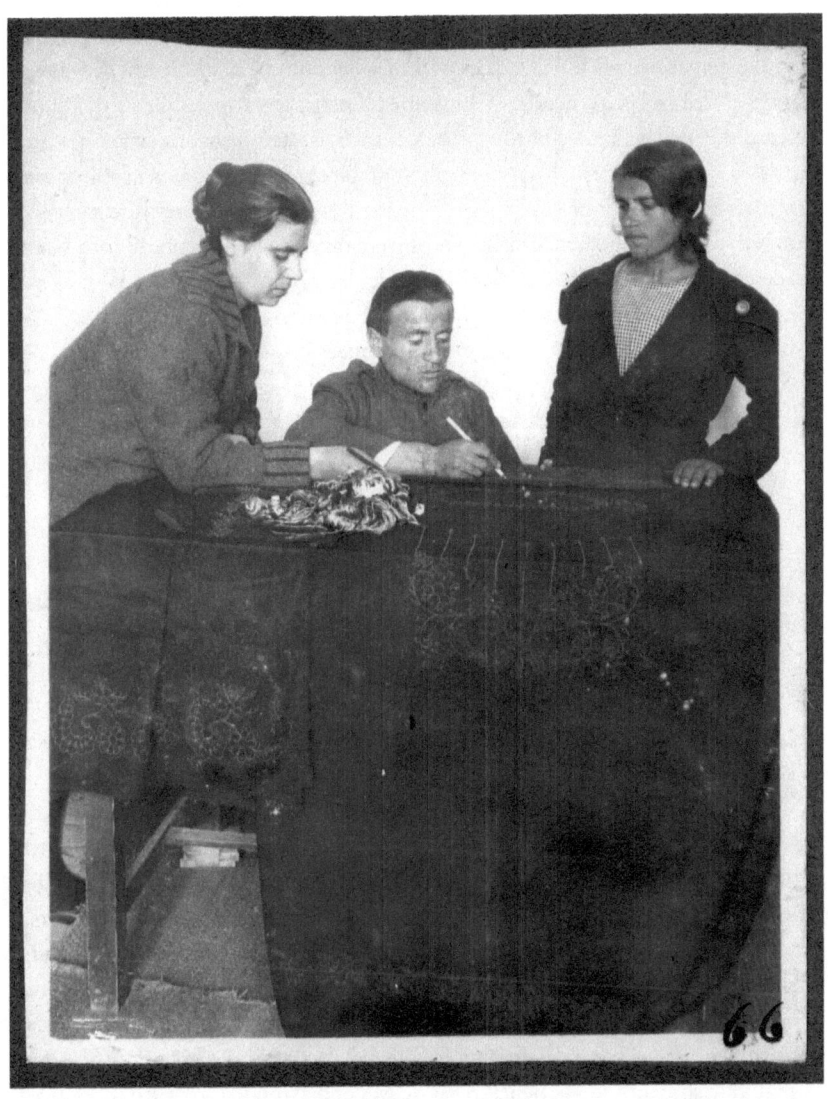

FIGURE 8 *Leopold Gaszczyk, assistant to Karen Jeppe, and his Armenian wife, Horome, teach textile techniques to an unnamed rescued girl bearing tribal tattoos on her face in the Rescue Home textile workshop. Source: Karen Jeppe's private albums, Armenian Genocide Memorial Institute, Yerevan, Armenia. Reprinted with permission.*

The five Jeppe photo albums housed in Yerevan are a vivid visual documentary of everyday relief work in Syria.[66] The photographs were most likely by Jeppe's Polish assistant Leopold Gaszczyk, who with his camera visually documented their humanitarian work in and around Aleppo. They include Jeppe's and Jensen's playful interactions with Arab allies within a Bedouin tent, where rescue workers enjoyed coffee and conversation.[67] But some photographs also detailed the wounds suffered during the course of the genocide, such as the image of a woman with a large scar on her left arm.[68] Another photograph shows the same scarred woman (arm covered) and her children united in the Rescue Home courtyard next to a stairwell, where many such family photos were taken. There are photos of a young girl receiving dental work; one photo in particular suggests she received some troubling news from the dentist.[69] The rescued Armenians suffered from a long list of illnesses, including gonorrhea, syphilis, tuberculosis, and trachoma, some of which are documented photographically.[70] Images of malnourished, underweight children provided visual evidence of the necessity of her work to feed and recuperate Armenian bodies and minds.

Many Armenians showed up at the home with impaired vision, mostly as a result of trachoma, and required eye surgery. One girl, Achkhen, was the offspring of her mother's forced marriage with a Kurd near Mardin. Jeppe wrote in broken English on the back of the six-year-old girl's intake record, "Achkhen very weak syphilis the eyes and ears are bad."[71] The collection includes images of blind children learning to read braille, Armenian children learning to read Armenian, and traumatized women and girls learning to sew and weave.[72] Jeppe's personal albums—an extension of her humanitarian record keeping—give us a glimpse into the scope of her work through the aperture of humanitarian photography.

But the most telling stories of abuse could be found within the short biographies she composed within each intake record, the only trace of what each individual woman and orphan endured. A memorable example of the kind of children Jeppe rescued was a shepherd boy named Elias. In his intake photograph, his cloak was open to show exposed ribs protruding under his nearly translucent skin and a festering wound on his abdomen. I thought Elias was under age ten but he was in fact a fourteen-year-old adolescent trapped in a smaller child's body due to malnourishment and disease. With bare feet and disheveled hair, his arms shortened by malnourishment hidden beneath his sleeves and extended outward in a Christ-like pose in the uncropped version of the photograph—this is how he appeared to humanitarian workers when the photograph (figure 9) was snapped within moments of arrival. His story was so powerful that it was shared with more detail in the *Armeniervennen* (Danish Friends of Armenians) newsletter. When Elias arrived on December 6, 1925, Jeppe wrote, "He had a wide, deep wound on his stomach. It was the effect of the medical treatment given by a Bedouin woman. She tries to cure his belly pains by putting burning rags on him."[73] Elias was suffering from dysentery, and the Bedouin woman seems to have used traditional folk medicine in an attempt to cure him. She perhaps inadvertently wounded him in the process, causing a secondary ailment for his body to fight alongside the dysentery.

After the photo session where the rescued were photographed in their original condition as a body of evidence, the boy was taken to the bath to be washed and dressed in fresh clothing. Elias exclaimed: "How wonderful! I have never been treated with such thorough care. One washes me, another pours water on me. No one has every treated me so kind."[74] But things grew worse for newly rescued Elias. Soon after his arrival, on advice from a doctor, Elias was hospitalized and died four days later. The story of the sick and emaciated shepherd boy powerfully illustrates that sometimes rescue was not enough because the body sometimes struggled to survive what it had just endured. In her 1927 annual report to the League of Nations, Jeppe offered a brief sketch of children who had arrived at the home only to

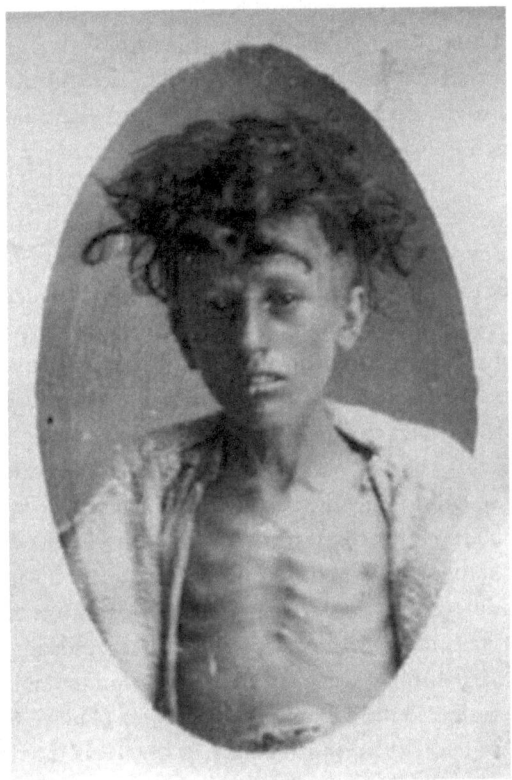

FIGURE 9 *Elias, a rescued shepherd boy originally from Urfa, suffered from a horrible stomach wound and dysentery. He died only four days after his arrival at the Rescue Home on December 10, 1925. Source: "Registers," inmate 887, United Nations Archive at Geneva.*

succumb to disease and exhaustion. Among them was a boy named Hovhannes, who after his rescue kept returning to the countryside to rescue more children. One day, he succumbed to a disease he had contracted during his rescue efforts, a small caravan of boys he had saved formed a procession to his tomb to honor him.[75]

THE ARMENIAN COLONIES IN SYRIA

When the League of Nations terminated financial support in 1927, Jeppe moved her work of restoring the Armenian community in Syria in a new direction. Jeppe mobilized her underground railroad as part of a sophisticated plan to move rescued Armenians out of Aleppo and implant them into the Syrian countryside to become self-sustaining farmers. Although Jeppe was an admirer of Zionist colonization taking root in British-controlled Palestine, Armenian settlements were not a statehood project, and they were sponsored neither by Armenians nor the League of Nations. Instead, international NGOs provided the cash to rent (rather than buy) lands for settlement from her long-time Arab ally and friend Hadjim Pasha.[76] Jeppe believed that rural settlement would isolate and protect Armenians from assimilation and the persistent work shortages in Syrian cities. During Mustafa Kemal's putsch to reclaim lands divvied up by Allied treaty, it was clear that the West had already turned its back on Armenian self-determination and an American mandate Armenia in Anatolia.[77] Armenians needed to carve a place for themselves inside Syria moving forward.

Jeppe's project to reconstitute the Armenian community included the restoration of both body and soul through the building of community settlements and the facilitation of marriages to plough-and-hoe-wielding Armenians in their new homeland. This work meant transitioning Armenians from refugees into citizens of Syria, a status they would eventually be granted in 1928 by the French, who had occupied Syria in 1920. French authorities had initially resisted Jeppe's colonization project and sought to slow the pace of Armenian settlement in the region, citing concerns about the associated cost and administrative duties.[78] But in actuality, the French harbored fears about Armenian settlement sowing unrest in the traditionally Muslim countryside, and Jeppe's approach sought to attend to that concern through cooperation with Arab partners. She first sought land near Alexandretta, where many historic Armenian villages were located and silk production and horticulture sustained them economically. This area known to Armenians as Musa Dagh is a region with great symbolic importance as the site of successful resistance to the deportations, which left parts of the region intact after the genocide.[79] At the time, it looked as though the mostly Arabic-speaking region of Alexandretta would remain under Syrian rule. It is fortunate that Jeppe did not opt for settlement there since a 1939 referendum resulted in the territory being ceded to Turkey with the blessing of the French.

Inspired in part by Zionist colonization efforts in Palestine and in part by necessity, Jeppe opted for establishing Armenian colonies in less settled regions of Syria with the consent and cooperation of Arab allies. The intention was to establish six agricultural cooperatives interlinked with the economic interests of surrounding Arabs rather than issuing any Armenian claims to self-governance. Armenians were settled in spaces like Tall Samn in 1924 and Tall Armen (Armenian Hill) nearby at Khirbat al-Riz and the Balikh River running north of Raqqa toward the Turkish border a year later.[80] In the first months of 1926, one hundred Armenian families were settled there and another hundred were preparing to join them. Another colony, called Sharb Bedros, was created on the Turkish border north of Tall Samn, and another in a place called Tineh.[81] Jeppe began exploring the region of Lattakia for yet another possible colony.[82]

Surrounding tribes, such as the 'Anaza, welcomed settlement in order to protect their lands from encroachment by both the French and tribal rivals.[83] Jeppe's main ally, Hadjim Pasha, would be crucial partner in these negotiations as he sought assistance in transforming the nomadic culture of the Bedouins into a more sedentary agrarian lifestyle with her assistance. "The Armenian colonization has to go hand in hand with the development of the Arab peasantry, and one must expect that the Bedouins will eventually be settled." She added in a report published in Denmark, "*Hadjim is building a house now*, that is a sign of the times."[84]

Jeppe considered the particular challenges of rehabilitating sexually traumatized Armenian women and girls who would be enlisted as wives to birth a new community in Syria. In a report to the League of Nations in 1927, Jeppe notes that 13 percent of the women rescued to that point were over eleven years old at the time of the genocide. "With very few exceptions, they were all violated as soon as they were captured, and in most cases, it was only the children who later tied them to their new homes."[85] Jeppe appears to have been successful at encouraging marriages between rescued Armenians for the purpose of sustaining the community. The Rescue Home register contains numerous entries of orphans who met and married each other in the home and refers to picture brides sought out by men abroad.

Meanwhile, in Aleppo, the Armenian community was facilitating similar matchmaking to reconstitute the community. Kerop Bedoukian described how his clever mother was able to convince an Armenian-American groom who came to Aleppo to find a wife to marry a woman who was once kept by a Muslim Turk. The former concubine had a one-year-old child from her former Muslim master but in the end the groom accepted her and the child.[86] The story reflects how even women who had been with Muslim men and bore them children were still marriageable to Armenian men. While some women found husbands abroad, many found their husbands locally or even within the walls of the Rescue Home. There are also references to endogamy among Islamized Armenians living within communities of Muslims; in one case, a mother married her Islamized son to an Islamized Armenian girl in the community prior to rescue.[87] Such marriages were to form the bedrock of the new settlements that Jeppe sought to establish throughout the countryside.

A group wedding in the Sharb Bedros settlement on November 25, 1928, allows us to witness how marriage and settlement worked in concert to implant Armenians in Syria. Behind the wedding party stood a series of conical-shaped beehive houses that were built by the grooms. Each home had three interconnected rooms: a lounge, a kitchen, and a small stable for the donkeys, sheep, goats, poultry, and pigeons they were rearing. The stables were built with the potential to expand as livestock increased. Generally speaking, after grooms built their homes, they would approach the Rescue Home in Aleppo to help them find a girl to marry. The brides would visit the village to meet the grooms ahead of time, but other than that meeting, they might not have seen their future husbands before the wedding ceremony.[88] It is important to underscore that these marriages were not love matches—Jeppe did not believe in romantic marriage. Marriage was completely utilitarian, and the household economy managed by a man and a woman was considered a building block for the reconstruction of the Armenian community in an artificial settlement. Despite her utilitarian view of marriage, Jeppe imagined these matchmaking events produced "excitement and joy" in both bride and groom.[89]

The mass wedding at Sharb Bedros served as a metonym for the reconstruction of the Armenian community and mirrored broader Armenian efforts to encourage marriage and reproduction after devastating loss. In the mass wedding photo (figure 10), Armenian Archbishop of Aleppo Ardavazdt Surmeyan is centered along with two other priests who had traveled nine hours from Aleppo to Sharb Bedros to conduct the ceremony. Jenny Jensen stood in as the Rescue Home representative alongside the archbishop's body guard to the left of the frame.

There is something striking about the photograph (figure 11) of a confident groom and his shy, uncomfortable bride who leans back slightly before the camera. Is she uncertain or performing the necessary modesty expected of new Armenian brides in the photo? Regardless, the shy bride will forever remain in obscurity as the caption "Babo and wife" obliterated her name from the historical record. Babo clutches his wife tightly with one arm, and the wedding photo of his brother in America symbolically brings his absent brother into his own wedding photo.[90] Though it is never explained in the accompanying text, one must wonder if the two brothers were the only survivors in their family and whether Babo's performance—that of a survivor committed to righting a wrong by marrying one of Jeppe's orphaned brides—symbolizes survival not only of his people but of his family lineage. He doubled the message of survival by displaying his brother's wedding photo within his own wedding photo.

Eight girls from the Aleppo Rescue Home were married in Sharb Bedros that

FIGURE 10 *A group wedding of Armenians in Sharb Bedros on November 25, 1928, was conducted by Archbishop Ardavazdt Surmeyan of Aleppo and two other priests. Danish relief worker Jenny Jensen, who reported on the event for the Friends of Armenia newsletter in Denmark, served as in loco parentis for the newlyweds. Source: The Karen Jeppe Archives, Gylling, Denmark.*

FIGURE 11 *Babo and his unnamed wife stand before their beehive-shaped stucco home in Sharb Bedros near Raqqa after their group wedding ceremony. His wife from Jeppe's Rescue Home looks shy next to Babo's firm stance before their new home, a structure he built with his own hands. Source: Reprinted with permission from the Armenian Genocide Museum Institute, Yerevan, Armenia.*

winter of 1928, and it was described as a joyous event by witness and surrogate mother to the brides Jenny Jensen.

> The wedding itself was very festive. It was a great honor for us to have none other than the bishop of Aleppo to perform the ceremonies. A big tent had been put up to host the act and later the dinner. At such an occasion both the French and Arab authorities are invited from Raqqa, and they usually show up each other and everyone. Life is not rich in events out there in the peasant country. To me, it was such a solemn ritual. I have been allowed to be a mom to these big children, and you friends back home understand that I stood there thanking God for letting me see those glowing faces.... Once more my thoughts wander to the day they arrived at the home, ragged, subjugated, lost—and now, what a difference! Young Christians, once more among their own people, knowing the road to salvation through Jesus Christ.[91]

The matchmaking events and group-marriage ceremonies were the cornerstone to rebuilding the nation. There is no reference to possible stigma for the brides, who very likely suffered terrible sexual and emotional abuse while in captivity. Babo and other men in the group photo still wear the traditional white *kufiya* of the Bedouin who had adopted them into their tribes before they were rehabilitated. The *kufiya* pricks at the viewer. It forces us to consider the limits of Jeppe's project of reforming Armenians forever marked by their new lives in Syria. The desert was to be greened with the implantation of young Armenians, the young trees they planted in front of the traditional beehive-shaped houses a metaphor for that promise. However, the "colonies" dissolved into the landscape within a generation—Jeppe's experiment failed.

It is here, in the space where Armenians were transplanted into Syrian soil that I bump into a prosthetic memory of my own transplanted grandfather, Youssef Semerdjian, an Aintab Armenian who spoke only Turkish and Kurdish when he arrived in Aleppo as a sixteen-year-old fleeing his town when the Armenian resistance, of which he was a participant, lost to Kemalist forces.[92] After he married my grandmother, Hripsime, another Aintabsti Armenian, in 1930, they had three children. When he constituted his new Armenian family in Aleppo, he worked hard to speak Western Armenian with his children. He regularly drew on his children's fluency in Armenian as he struggled to read the newspaper, pointing to words and asking them to tell him what the words meant. His name was Youssef as opposed to the ethnic Armenian version, Hosep, yet another sign that not all Armenian communities of Cilicia shared the same language and traditions.[93] So, Youssef learned to be Armenian, or a new version of being Armenian, in Aleppo alongside other Armenian refugees. His wife and children became his teachers.

While my grandfather struggled to learn Armenian in Aleppo, Karen Jeppe struggled to live with the toll her humanitarian work took on her body. Like Ruben

Herian, Jeppe's body eventually succumbed to the stresses she had placed on it. Danish colleague Maria Sick accompanied Jeppe to one of the rural Armenian settlements in 1935, where she developed symptoms of malaria and "her enfeebled body" was quickly overcome with a high fever that would not drop. From there, Jeppe was driven to a French hospital in Aleppo, where she died seven days later.[94]

Karen Jeppe's name has long been remembered by the Armenians of Aleppo. Kevork Garabedian, one of the twelve Armenians Jeppe sheltered under her floorboards in Urfa, wrote in letter that Jeppe wanted to be buried in Armenia, not Syria. "The Armenians must give her a resting place in the Armenian pantheon where their heroes abide in Erivan, as a token of their ever-lasting honour, she has so worthily deserved and their indebtedness so great to repay, so that future generations may come to know how a Danish Lady—an immortal heroine—has done for their forefathers in days of their distress out of the generosity of her heart and vicariously."[95] As she had performed the rites of priests in Urfa in 1915, she transgressed norms once again when she was buried in the Armenian Orthodox Cemetery in Shaykh Maqsud, Aleppo. Burial across communal lines is unheard of in a city that continues to bury each citizen according to their religious denomination to the extent that Orthodox Christians are buried separately from Catholics and Protestants. By being buried in the Armenian Orthodox cemetery, Danish Protestant Karen Jeppe was symbolically converted to Armenian Orthodoxy in death—she rests not far from my own grandparents' graves. The 10,000-square-meter lot in Maydan where Jeppe's operations took place was converted into the Karen Jeppe College, a high school that continues to serve generations of Armenians.[96]

The challenge of recovering Armenians required much more than recovering bodies, engaging in textile work, and establishing farming communities in Syria. Some of the rescued were barely able to survive their experience and, like the shepherd boy Elias, died within a few days or months of reaching sanctuary. After years of assimilation, the psychological effects made reentry into the Armenian community difficult, and some children fled Jeppe's home rather than refashion themselves back into Armenians. Even Jeppe expressed disappointment when children chose to return to the Muslim community when, in her words, "it seemed too difficult for them to adapt themselves to Armenian life, which means learning and thinking and in general a good deal of toil, as all civilized life does." With a tinge of civilizational rhetoric, the humanitarian noted though that those who had left to rejoin the Bedouin would sometimes return because the pull to rejoin the Armenian community was so powerful.[97] Those traces of children who ran away from the Rescue Home in Aleppo are a tacit recognition that recovering their original identity was a traumatic process as humanitarian workers probed deeply into the minds of children to recover their Armenian pasts.

REMNANT 4

"The Orphan Collection" (Vorpahavak)

by Armenian National Relief Organization in Constantinople (1919)[1]

And so—as you all know—Armenian orphans are not the only ones who have applied to be placed in orphanages. Thousands of villagers of both sexes who survived through a miracle—still remain with the executioners of their fathers and mothers. Forcibly converted to Islam, these children are worked like slaves, subjected to cruel treatment [*charachar*] and horrid threats [*ahargu sbarnalikneru*]. In fact, the aim of these barbarous measures is to prevent these children from returning back to their nation. These are children who—having the mass of their foreskin removed [through circumcision]—even during the war, were brought in groups to Bolis by powerful Turkish families, where they either were then crowded into orphanages or into harems. During the war, the [Ottoman] Turkish Empire brought these kids and mixed them in an orphanage or they were given the opportunity to be adopted into harems. From one day to another, a Krikor and a Sarkis became Ali or Mehmet, and a Hayganush and an Araxie became Aisha or Fatma. These are the children, who—even after one year of armistice, and despite all official and recurring announcements—are still waiting for their freedom. To Islamify these children forever—whether as a tradesperson, intellectual, official, mullah, or pasha—is indiscreetly the sacred mission of every Turk. The proof is in the following: each and every one of them, from differing social backgrounds, have made it through many kinds of difficulties—those deemed possible and impossible—in order to keep their prey [i.e., these orphaned children] captive in their hands. Armenian children were even uprooted from the homes of police officers.... We are not exaggerating if we say that it would not be uncommon to find, in every Turkish home in Bolis [Constantinople], from the most modest to the most wealthy, an Armenian orphan, especially an orphan girl, being kept there. The reason for this is twofold: the personal and the communal. The personal reason is that these orphans become free servants in these homes, who live off only the scraps left from their dinner table. The communal reason is that according to their beliefs, they believe they are saving their souls, while at the same time multiplying the number of Turkish people.

CHAPTER FIVE

"CHANGELINGS" AND "HALFLINGS"

Finding the Armenian Buried inside the Islamized Child

> So, the work goes on. Buried under the counterfeit consciousness of the changelings, bound there by monstrous nightmare terrors, are the memories of the tragedies which overtook their parents, their origin, even their names. Buried deepest of all is their religion, so that when at last brought to confess that he remembers his mother's grave and asked what kind of place it was, whether it had tall trees and pillar stones like the cypresses and stones of Turkish graveyards, [he] answered eagerly, "No, the graves were marked with 'guavour odounou' [the wood of the infidels]." Such is the name by which those stolen changelings know the cross.
> —ARAKEL TCHAKARIAN, "To the Rescue of Armenian Orphans," (1920)[1]

Among the challenges Herian, Jeppe, and other rescuers confronted when reuniting dispersed Armenian children with their families was that those who had been separated at a young age had little to no memory of their Armenian pasts. After years of indoctrination, transferred children held only faint memories of their parents, forgot their own identities, or worse, saw the Armenian people as mortal enemies. The children Arakel Tchakarian called "changelings" would not admit that they were Armenian, leaving relief workers to suss them out on their own.[2] A report of the League of Nations' Fifth Committee stated that "children torn from the Christian faith are often forced by ill treatment to disown even the little they remember of their past life." Jeppe observed that Armenian children were terrified to leave Muslim households because "their masters kept them from fleeing . . . by punishing them savagely, if they tried to escape." Due to this threat of violence, even after release from captivity, Armenians feared revealing their true identities.[3]

In Constantinople, Emma Cushman shared the challenges of rescuing these Armenian orphans, noting that while "decent self-respecting Turks" handed over the children to the relief workers, many others remained behind.⁴ Cushman wrote that affected children had been brainwashed in Turkish orphanages, where "they try to bring about not so much a change of name and locality but rather a complete change of mind in the child. These children for a period of time extending from one week to three months will deny strenuously that they are Christians."⁵

Children born to Armenian mothers and Muslim fathers posed another set of issues for rescue workers: they were attached to their Muslim households and sometimes rejected by the Armenian community or their own mothers. Islamic patrimonial law and family ties made identifying and extracting the children challenging and even dangerous. Jensen referred to these children as "halflings" (*halvt forvildede*), a term that also means half "savage" or "delinquent" in Danish, which implied that the children were "half-lost" in a moral sense. She may have felt this language was justified after hearing firsthand the horrific stories of rape, murder, slavery, and abuse experienced by rescued women and children.⁶ But the term captures the civilizational anxieties that children of mixed Muslim-Armenian parentage produced in the postwar era.

THE TRAUMA OF FORGETTING AND REMEMBERING

Rescuers faced several obstacles in identifying, recovering, and helping children with faint memories identify as Armenians again. The children were not passive in this process. One survivor, Almas Boghosian, recalled how when she arrived at the Ahronian Orphanage in Aleppo, older children knew her family and offered to write letters to her aunt in America on her behalf. Another child quickly identified her as hailing from Kharpert (Harput) because of the scar on her lower lip, a scar many people of the region bore that was created by a parasite carried by sandflies.⁷ While Almas's body served as a document in this case, in others proof of identity posed a formidable obstacle.

In postwar Constantinople, the Allied forces and the Armenian Patriarchate claimed that children were supplied with false paperwork and birth certificates by Turkish orphanages. Their names were stricken from seized orphanage registers and Muslim names superimposed to make it hard to track down their origins.⁸ An example of such a child is a ten-year-old girl, Melehat, who was rescued from the home of a Turkish police officer. She clearly remembered being Armenian. Among her memories were her father's profession, his imprisonment, going to church with her family, and deportation with her mother near Harput. However, Melehat's papers listed her parents as being Muslim.⁹

Orphanages housed Armenian Christians, non-Armenian Christians, and non-Turkish-Muslim Kurds because the state targeted all three populations for "internal colonialization," resettlement, and punitive deportation through the 1930s.[10] The aim, Keith Watenpaugh argues, was for children "to emerge as modern citizens whose Armenian and Kurdish identities were no longer an impediment to complete membership in the new national community."[11] Armenian authorities claimed that upwards of 50 percent of the children in Turkish orphanages were Armenian, totaling sixty thousand children. The rest of the missing children, estimated to be six thousand, were held in Turkish homes in Constantinople. Although Western humanitarians were suspicious of numbers provided by Armenians, they did note that a large portion of children in Turkish orphanages bore Kurdish names. Some of those children were likely Kurdish, but humanitarians claimed they were "Armenian hidden under a false name," described as either Turks or Kurds in Turkish orphanage registers.[12] Humanitarians also suspected that such children had been brought through Kurdish territory before arriving at the capital.[13] Document tampering made rescue work more difficult, prompting humanitarians to create a process for distinguishing Armenian children from Muslim children.

Armenian children were hidden not only behind names. Memories of being Armenian were buried deep in the psyche of traumatized Armenian children in the course of the genocide. Assimilation was a means of survival especially since many children were adopted by elite nationalist households in Constantinople.[14] One rescued eleven-year-old child named Sarkis in the Ottoman capital described how the Armenian was beaten out of him in the private home he had been taken to: "I forgot my language because whenever I spoke a word, they thrashed me hard enough to break my bones."[15] Similar abuse was common in state orphanages. Early telegrams from the Ottoman Ministry of Education in June 1915 articulated a plan to dispatch Armenian children less than ten years old to state-run orphanages for "training and education" (*talim ve terbiye*) weeks before the populations of Harput, Sivas, and Trabzon were deported.[16] On the southern front, the deportee population swelled, prompting Cemal Pasha, then governor of Syrian territory, to open orphanages. He explained his rationale in his memoir: "At that time, at the 'Aintoura monastery in Mount Lebanon, I was opening an orphanage that could take in a thousand Armenian children and I was also provisioning many Armenian orphans and widows in Damascus through the [Fourth] Army."[17] Cemal Pasha saw his efforts as humanitarian. Survivors, however, described their experience in Beirut as a form of brutal, and often lethal, assimilation comparable to the Indian boarding schools in North America.[18]

At 'Aintoura, Armenian identity was intentionally drowned through assimilation and systematic trauma, with methods that are best described as physically beating the Armenian out of the child. While Cemal Pasha had established another orphanage run by Armenians in Damascus, 'Aintoura engaged in a dual program of Islamization and Turkification of children who were, in the case of

Armenians, required to select a Muslim name upon entry, speak only Turkish, and proclaim the Muslim faith.[19] In this sense, 'Aintoura orphanage emerged as a laboratory of forced assimilation of non-Turkish children during the war. Similar to recent discoveries of Indian children's graves in the United States and Canada, the skeletons of more than three hundred children were discovered at the orphanage site in 2005. This horrific discovery forensically confirmed what American University of Beirut professor and interim director of 'Aintoura orphanage Stephen Trowbridge had documented after it was seized from Turkish authorities. Only 669 of the nearly 2,000 orphans admitted to 'Aintoura had survived the ordeal.[20] An Armenian cross gravestone (*khatchkar*) was installed in 2010 in memory of the child victims.

Starving children who sat in makeshift Armenian refugee camps in Syria were lured to 'Aintoura with the promise of food and shelter, provisions denied at the state level. Only children under twelve were selected since children beyond that age were considered adults. Younger children were also easier targets for the religious and cultural conversion that took place within the orphanage. A memoir by Karnig Panian illuminates the horrors of every day life at 'Aintoura, where rewards and punishments were meted out to mold Armenian and Kurdish orphans into Turks. The rewards included gifts of clothing and jewelry for girls, whereas boys were dealt blows and threatened with further physical violence until they accepted their new Muslim Turkish identity. If they failed to show signs of assimilation—speaking Turkish was a primary indicator—children were punished with food depravation and given beatings within an inch of death. The most brutal treatment was reserved for those who continued to use the Armenian language.[21]

Of course, such details of systematic child abuse are missing in the memoirs of Turkish nationalist feminist Halide Edib (1884–1964), written long after the armistice and establishment of the modern state of Turkey. She had first visited Lebanon in 1916 to inspect the state of Ottoman schools and orphanages at the invitation of Cemal Pasha. A skeptic at first, she was convinced that the orphanages worked as a "civilizing mission" for the empire's non-Turkish subjects after three visits to the 'Aintoura Orphanage in Lebanon in 1916, accepting the post of supervisor in January 1917.[22] Edib saw her work as that of a benevolent savior of destitute children who had "a look of depression and fragility about them all."[23] In her memoir, she recounts questioning Cemal Pasha about his Islamization policy: "You have been as good to Armenians as it is possible in these hard days. Why do you allow Armenian children to be called by Moslem names? It looks like turning Armenians into Moslems, and history someday will revenge it on the coming generation of Turks."[24] Cemal Pasha is portrayed as an ideal humanitarian when he reveals his motive for opening the orphanage: "I cannot bear to see them [Armenians] die in the streets."[25] Edib places the blame for instituting the orphanage onto the deceased Cemal Pasha while absolving herself of any complicity.

Though Edib's own view of her role at 'Aintoura has by and large been accepted, some scholars have disputed Edib's legacy to the degree that she has been the subject of heated debates in the field of Ottoman Studies over awards named after her and others complicit in the Armenian Genocide and the ongoing erasure of Armenians in Turkish nationalist historiography. While Elizabeth F. Thompson refers to her as Turkey's Joan of Arc, Keith Watenpaugh argues that her participation in forcible conversion, torture, and abuse at the 'Aintoura orphanage was engagement in acts of genocide—both scholarly points of view are a reflection of her dual legacy.[26] Edib and her champions often dismiss these accusations, yet 'Aintoura was not the only instance in which Edib was accused of the crime of forced assimilation of children. In 1920, the Armenian Patriarch of Constantinople, Zaven Der Yeghiayan, personally accused the feminist and her husband, Dr. Adnan Adıvar, of taking Armenian orphans into their home and forming them into Turkish Muslims.[27]

Having adopted a Turkish nationalist position after the war, Edib articulated what is now the nationalist script concerning orphaned children: Armenians were perpetrators of atrocities against Muslims, and the children were their direct victims.[28] It is possible that she also told these stories to Armenian orphans to further sever their identification with other Armenians. Indicative of this tendency to assign Armenians the role of perpetrator is the story Edib shared of a traumatized girl named Jale seeing Armenians massacring Muslims. She vividly recalled, for instance, the horror of seeing the neighborhood butcher's throat slit by an Armenian when her community was assaulted. Edib declares the girl was Kurdish, yet an international commission found this girl to be Armenian, not Kurdish as Edib claimed.[29]

Edib argued that at 'Aintoura children were transformed from a state of misery into bright, cheerful children, yet survivors Karnig Panian and Melkon Bedrossian described food depravation, beatings, forced performances of Turkishness, and sublimation of and punishment for performances of Armenianness at the orphanage—the body and cognition of children were violently inscribed by state power.[30] Body-centered performative violence is what Salwa Ismail has called "emplotted horror," violence that coerces compliance among witnesses by inducing affective fear, disgust, humiliation, and ultimately abjection.[31] Panian described this pedagogy of violence when he wrote about the public torture of orphans in the courtyard of the 'Aintoura orphanage before nearly two thousand child spectators.[32] Children like Panian were bastinadoed—the soles of their feet were beaten—sometimes a hundred or two hundred times to the point of passing out in the orphanage's courtyard and requiring admission to the orphanage infirmary.[33] The blows were delivered by the school director, who had been hired by Edib and had effectively converted the orphanage—a space associated with rescue and nurturing—into a torture chamber. Pedagogies of violence were inscribed not only onto bodies but into the space; an adjacent graveyard held the corpses of the children who had died as a result of beatings and denied sustenance reinforced the lessons at 'Aintoura. We will now move to the stories of children who survived forced assimilation and abuse in order to discover how humanitarians recovered the Armenian buried inside the Islamized child.

RECOVERING ISLAMIZED ARMENIANS FROM ALEPPO TO BAGHDAD

Humanitarians developed myriad ways to rescue the Armenian buried within the Islamized children they rescued. Some children had only vague memories of their parents and struggled to remember their own Armenian names. "We will call him Vartan because he does not remember anything from the time of his youth." Jeppe added poetically that, rescued from an Arab village, "the poor child has received more beating than eating."[34] But there were other Armenian children who seemed to easily remember their identity. For instance, Armen "never forgot he was an Armenian" and "spoke Armenian with his dear sheep when he was alone with them in the desert. In that way he did not forget his mother tongue."[35] Another boy, Puzant, who had lost his entire family and had been enslaved by an Arab, was found by one of Jeppe's agents near Dayr al-Zur. "It was wonderful to see Puzant's face when he the first evening heard the word hai = Armenian. His face was shining and he exclaimed 'Oh, how long a time has passed since I heard that word.' Before going to bed, the boys were saying their prayers and making the sign of the cross, and he said, 'Now I am at home again.'"[36] Puzant resettled in one of the Armenian colonies after his recuperation at the home.

The process of recovering Armenian identity was not without controversy, however, and on the ground, the "unmixing" of Armenian and Muslim populations was riddled with fear, trauma, and ethical dilemmas. While documentation and research were conducted for verification, some methods were far looser, inciting Muslim critics to accuse Armenians and Allies of forming Muslim children into Armenians. Importantly, teasing the Armenian out of the Muslim child produced the resentment of Turkish and Arab contemporaries. Because conversion within Islamic law is allowed in only one direction, toward Islam, reforming children back into Armenians, then, involved apostatizing through reconversion to Christianity. While reconversion was not something mentioned often by League of Nations commissioners, detailed descriptions of this process can be found in Armenian sources.

The religious aspect of recuperation is prominent in an Armenian essay by Sahag Mesrob titled "Their Name." The essay includes a photograph of the Islamized author as a young man wearing Bedouin clothing. Rather than speak of his own experience, he describes his humanitarian efforts to reclaim bodies and souls of children in an Armenian orphanage in Baghdad. The essay offers a glimpse into how Armenians were recuperated within the Armenian community:

> Everyday, barefooted boys with bare heads and girls who have Arab markings [tattoos] on their faces [ախտկիտուած են; lit. "they are dotted"] come to re-learn their lost language. They come together to be brothers in the same suffering and to eliminate the assimilation of years. Older children kept the pronunciation. They did not forget the cities and their names. They remembered their parents and criminal stories of their life. The younger children only speak Arabic. They forgot their parents and hardly remember their names. The youngest children forgot everything. Forgetfulness came to rest upon their powerful memories. A pity, they could never even remember their names. I put down the names of the ones who had names and arranged hundreds of them in one row for the first time. What can I do for the others? They don't remember even a word from their mother dialect but we can distinguish them with the seal/sign of the tribe [*tseghe*] which is different from Arab boys.[37]

For Mesrob, an important facet to becoming Armenian was to have an Armenian name. He was assigned the task of renaming the two hundred children he served in the orphanage:

> The first day was giving them names of Armenian heros [*feda'i*]: Nubars, Antraniks, Murads, Vahaks, Hrayrs, Vrouyrs, Jrayrs, Vahans, Vartans, more and more, but all these names were not enough. Day by day my unnamed boys increased. I was wondering how to make a method to find their names more easily (because they are many).... I was under pressure to find their names but not their birthplaces; the names of their mother and father and birthplace were lacking. What can I do to express the crime that they have passed through and what can I do to make this nation perpetuate? What could I do? Above all this, the cities and villages of the Armenians had their fragments in this wreck, but I do not know why I mostly put their birthplace as Zeitun and Shabin Karahisar.[38]

In the process of renaming orphans with Armenian names, Mesrob was able to convince a priest to conduct a new baptism for the children at the naming event. He requested that the baptism ceremony take place on Easter Sunday, with him standing as godfather for the entire group. In the course of the ceremony, the priest asked Mesrob, "What will be their names. Hurry please, say one right after the other." He replied "Vrej, Vrej, Vrej, father. All of them are Vrej. May they all be Vrej!" *Vrej* means "revenge" in Armenian. At the end of the ceremony, he wrote, everyone was in tears—the priest, the children, and the writer. "Suddenly, as the last godson was leaving the church, he shouted 'Vrej, father, Vrej (*Vrej hayrigs Vrej*),' accepting his new Armenian name."

Unlike Mesrob's religious reconversion of Armenian orphans, humanitarian accounts are far more secular, framing recuperation as a purely cultural and national project. Offering observations and details about the methods through which she and other relief workers determined Armenian heritage of Islamized children, Emma Cushman wrote:

> A case of this kind has come under my observation in the past few days. The child, a boy of twelve years, was placed for treatment in an international eye hospital, an American institution. He was sent in with other boys from the Turkish orphanage. He came with a Turkish name and a history of Turkish parentage. For two months he had been in this institution, had mixed with children of various nationalities and no one suspected that he was not a Turkish child. Suddenly, he began to sing Armenian hymns, and to speak in Armenian, not fluently of course, but a few words. When asked where he learned the hymns and also to speak Armenian, he said 'I spoke that language when I was little, then I sang these hymns.' He was asked what his name was at the time, and he readily gave an Armenian name.[39]

Through attentive observation, Cushman and other humanitarians worked to tease out the buried Armenian within Turkish children. The efforts to unmix Armenians from Muslim populations, however, were not without unsettling ambiguities.

One such ambiguity can be found in Kerime Serma, a sixteen-year-old living in the home of a Turkish military officer. Adopted as his daughter, Kerime was engaged to marry a Turkish man when she was brought against her will to the Neutral House. She sought to return to her Turkish father and fiancé—the report does not indicate if she was ever released to them. Another teenage girl when confronted with evidence that she was Armenian "confessed in tears that she was afraid to become Armenian again, because she had suffered much." She remembered she was the daughter of an Armenian lawyer named Sarkis Effendi Kendirian of Bitlis. She also recalled all the names of her seven siblings, one of whom was discovered at the Essayan Orphanage because they resembled each other so strongly. Sometimes, rescued children struggled to adapt and quickly ran away, such as Sarkis, a boy who "could not adapt himself to the life in the city and ran away from the Reception Home." In another instance, a boy named Ghazar, described as "a bad character" in Jeppe's registers, was returned to the Muslim community two weeks after rescue.[40]

There is no question that rescue was sometimes retraumatizing for orphans. Emma Cushman documented the recovery of "changelings," including their habit of emphatically professing the Muslim faith upon rescue. Among the children rescued in Constantinople was a girl named Virgin:

A 10- to 11-year-old. Brought from Eub Soultan, Dergahe Emuele [a neighborhood in Istanbul], Sinan Hodja Sheih Nourollah's house. A very beautiful and charming girl, they have kept her in "Muduriet" [police detention] three days in a subterranean den explaining to her that if she tells she is "Giavour" [Christian], the Armenians and the British will kill her. She kept silent under this terror for two days and confirmed that she knew nothing. By and by, her terror passed. She got used to us and began to relate that she was from Angora, her name Virgin, father's Vitchen [Vicken], mother's Foulik, sister's Josephine. During exile she has gone as far as Aleppo with her family; there they have separated her from them and brought [her] to Constantinople. She knows the Armenian letters, but cannot speak. She is a very sweet and affectionate girl. She is worth keeping in the Neutral House as a helper to the conductors. She shows an extraordinary pleasure for becoming Armenian again.[41]

The passage captures the terror children experienced during recovery efforts. It was only through a process of relationship building and trust that they would confess their true identities and experience the "pleasure for becoming Armenian again."

Armenian humanitarians engaged in the vorpahavak shared stories that illustrate the challenges of rescuing children who could not or would not remember their Armenian identity after a decade of assimilation and how their operations retraumatized those rescued children. After receiving the endorsement of Emir Faysal, the British High Command, and the Archbishop Bedros Sarajian of Damascus, Levon Yotnakhparian and three Armenian agents collected orphans in the area of the Hawran, Jabal Druze, and in private Muslim households in central Damascus.[42] Yotnakhparian told the story of an unnamed Armenian girl who lived with Dr. Lutfi, a Muslim doctor in Damascus. The harrowing account exemplifies how the recovery efforts of Armenian relief workers could be traumatizing for fully assimilated children.

When the Armenian rescue team with Yotnakhparian knocked on the door, the mother rejected their assertion that the girl was Armenian, saying "There is no Armenian girl here." But the Armenian rescue team had a witness—Bedross Karagouzian—the girl's neighbor from Urfa, who knew her family well. He was taken to her school and was ordered to pick her out of the class three times as a test to see if she was indeed the girl he remembered. He recognized her immediately, but they tested his memory further. "To test him a second time the 20 girls covered their heads and then opened their faces all at the same time. Again Mr. Bedross recognized the girl and pointed her out."[43] The third time the girls turned their backs and turned around at the same time, and he picked her out again. The girl was asked if she was Armenian; she insisted that she was not. Because she refused her identity, it posed a problem, and they were not able to extract her without a court battle.

Two days later, the court summoned the rescuers. The Lutfi family procured a midwife who claimed that she had birthed the girl to the Muslim mother. But the rescue team still insisted the girl was Armenian. The girl herself protested and cursed the Armenians who had come to take her away: "I am a Muslim girl and my father is Dr. Lutfi. I do not want to go with the gyavours [*sic*] [the infidels]."[44] The team of four along with her former neighbor testified that she was indeed Armenian. Yotnakhparian writes that he presented the final piece of evidence proving the girl was an Armenian orphan after he consulted health department records and found that Mrs. Lutfi bore a daughter eleven years earlier but the baby had died six months after birth. According to the records, Mrs. Lutfi never bore another child. This final piece of evidence proved the unnamed Armenian girl was indeed adopted, but the rescue operation was nonetheless traumatic for her. Yotnakhparian writes:

> She was consistently resisting. We picked her up and with the help of two soldiers, we put her in the carriage. We drove away. She was screaming, crying and constantly saying; 'Hey! Hey! Moslem brothers! The Armenians are taking your sister away. They are taking her so that she becomes a gyavour [infidel]. Save me! Save me!' She was shouting like that all the way. She also was trying to run away.[45]

When they reached the diocese of Archbishop Sarajian in Damascus, the unnamed girl saw his priestly robes and began screaming. At that point, Yotnakhparian writes that the archbishop slapped her face in an attempt to calm her down and then "we took her to our house. She tried to run away a few times, but we had locked the doors. By evening she started calming down a little."[46] While he felt that the forcible separation was necessary, he acknowledged the extraction retraumatized the girl. "We had to do what we did in order to bring back the lost Armenian orphans. There were thousands that we could not reach. They became Arabs and Moslems. This was a great loss for our nation, reduced in number after many massacres and tortures."[47]

The trauma of being re-identified as Armenian was exacerbated by fantasies and rumors that the children were being cannibalized. Edib and others used a potent dehumanizing anthropophagy motif to describe the reclamation efforts by which Turkified and Arabized Armenian children were converted back into Armenians. Efforts to tease out Armenianness from Islamized children generated fear among both Arab and Turkish intellectuals. From a Muslim perspective, the recovery effort committed the crime of inducing apostasy among vulnerable Muslim children. Orphanages largely controlled by Christian missionaries and relief organizations enforced the repatriation of Armenians demanded by the Allied-controlled League of Nations. Based on reports Edib had received from Turkish Red Crescent nurses, she feared that Muslim Turkish children, especially those who had no documentation, were being converted into Armenians, a forced conversion that mirrored the violent, forcible assimilation she herself had participated in at 'Aintoura. Mimicking the rhetoric of Armenian victims, Edib claimed the true parents of these orphaned children were Muslim Turks who had been murdered by Armenians:

> The children who were brought to the association were left in the care of the Armenian women, and these Armenian women, either by persuasion or threats or hypnotism, forced the Turkish children to learn by heart the name of an Armenian woman for their mother and the name of an Armenian man for their father.... When the children were brought in large numbers from the orphanages of Anatolia they were sent to the Armenian church in Koum Kapou [Kumkapı], a hot-pot which boiled the Turkish children and dished them out as Armenians. Some children tried to run away but were always brought back.[48]

Edib's cannibalism metaphor illustrates how orphanage and rescue homes figured within a biopolitical imaginary where raw human material could be dis-membered, snatched, rescued, restored, and reassembled into national subjects. In the process, Edib employed a classic xenophobic trope—the primal fear of being consumed by the savage other—a counter-image to missionary and humanitarian narratives that portrayed Christian women and children "consumed" through trafficking, enslavement, and murder.

These stories were not only believed by Turkish elites, but rumors of cannibalism also circulated among the children targeted for rescue. Children like Loutfie who was brought to the Neutral House in Constantinople had absorbed rumors of British and Armenians cannibalizing children.[49] Crying uncontrollably, the child shared her concerns in the following dialogue:

> The British officers gently asked her: "Why are you crying?"
> The child: "Why do you ask me why I am crying? I know as well as that the English and Armenians collect little children to eat them."
> The officers asked the child: "How do you know that?"
> The child: "Why, I have seen it with my own eyes."
> The officers: "How seen it with your own eyes? Tell us about it."
> The child: "Well, one day we went to visit a Turkish Lady who lived near us and every one of the persons in the house was in mourning and the Hanoum [lady] was crying bitterly. I asked her (as you have asked me) why she was crying and she answers: 'The little girl who was with us was stolen by the English and has been roasted and eaten. They say that the flesh of little children is very good to eat.'"[50]

For the two and a half months that followed, the girl continued to strenuously deny her Armenian identity. When asked who her parents were, she always gave the names of her Turkish family members. However, one day, a woman claiming to be her aunt arrived and the woman and child instantly recognized each other—her aunt called her by her Armenian name, Nevart. After that, when the little girl saw the man who had authored the article, she "hid her face in her hands in shame and ran away."[51]

Efforts to help children recover their Armenian identity were also hindered by the Turkish representative in the Neutral Homes, Nezihe Zeyneb Hanim, who once brought a Turkish woman to claim that an eight-year-old girl named Nadie belonged to her. When the woman and the girl did not recognize each other, Nezihe resigned in protest.[52] Emma Cushman explained within her small ethnographic entries that while children felt terrified at the prospect of revealing their Armenianness, they were more open after Nezihe's departure The resignation of the Turkish representative from the Neutral Home lifted a barrier to confessions by children like Hagop, who was taken from the home of a Turk named Tuhan Pasha in Nisantaşı, Constantinople: "Now that there was not any Turkish lady to terrify him, he was bold enough to confess his secret. The poor child has suffered beyond explanation and he is so frightened and has been so nervous that he speaks with difficulty and has a nervous movement of his eyes."[53] The child later admitted that when he had been held in a Turkish orphanage, the children were denied food and beaten for three days until they renounced their Armenian identity and became Turks. When he was absorbed in Tuhan Pasha's home, the lady of the house "used to beat him always," producing the terrified, pale, and "exceedingly thin body [that] tells us very plainly the sad story of the boy."

Armenian children of Muslim fathers must also have been affected by the prejudices of some rescue workers. One of Jeppe's associates in Aleppo, Jenny Jensen, described the awakening of Armenianness among the rescued children of mixed heritage in pejorative terms when she wrote: "The teacher tells about how wonderful it is to see how the dormant energy if awakened in the half-savage [Danish: *halvt forvildede*] children. The fatherly care and good nursing which Misak [Jeppe's adopted Armenian son] has given the children has awoken in them a feeling of gratitude and helped them forget the past terrible years."[54] Education, then, was conceived as having the power to overcome Turkish parentage of "halfling" children and reveal the Armenian hidden inside them, as in the case of one anonymous girl who was described by Jeppe in a letter: "D in the meantime is going to school with Armenian children, and truly becoming a real Armenian herself, in spite of her Turkish blood."[55]

SUBVERTING MUSLIM PATRIMONY

Stories of Armenianization scared not only Turkish elites and orphaned and adopted children but also Muslim families. And in this regard, Armenian children fathered by Muslims presented a particular challenge to rescue efforts. Some of the children placed in the Aleppo rescue home were clearly the offspring of Muslim fathers and Armenian mothers. Children sired by Muslim fathers loomed as a challenge to the Armenian patriarchal family. Many women recognized this challenge and simply abandoned their children when they escaped, knowing that it would invite trouble to escape with them. A full letter from Karen Jeppe reflects the policy that children fathered by Muslim men were not to be accepted without the permission of their fathers:

> I have received your letter about the woman Jeranig, but I profoundly suggest not to be able to touch the case, as it is entirely against my rule to receive Muslim children except in the case when the father gives them up on his own account. So far [at] the moment, I have to return them to you. If a statement can be made, that the father does not care for them, in a lawful form through the Turkish consulate, of course I will take charge of them. However, from a purely Armenian point of view, I do not approve of these half-cast children. They are no good anyhow. My advice is to send her back. Why should we trouble to educate these foreign children when we have so many Armenian children in need?[56]

Jeppe's refusal is framed in unusually harsh ethnocentric terms, calling the children of Armenian mothers and Muslim fathers "half-cast" and "no good," revealing her personal biases. In more general terms, relief workers feared that Muslim fathers might return at any point to retrieve their children, jeopardizing their operations. Yet Vahé Tachjian has argued that this view also existed among some Armenians, who viewed mixed offspring as unworthy of inclusion in the Armenian community. He writes that for some, "a Muslim who impregnated an Armenian woman represented, in the collective Armenian imagination, the Turkish executioner."[57]

However harsh, the dominant climate in the Rescue Home was one of acceptance. Sometimes the child's original Muslim name was recorded side by side with the Armenian name in the register. Intake records do not offer details about the separation of the mother from the Muslim father of the child. Images of childless women who fled after prolonged years of marriage suggests that they may have abandoned their children along with their husbands to return to their community. In other cases, there are traces of women who miscarried their children upon arrival, but the timing of these miscarriages hint that women may have induced their own abortions to avoid the stigma of bearing a half Muslim child at a time when they sought to reenter Armenian society. Furthermore, women could have also aborted to remove the burden of yet another mouth to feed when supporting themselves was uncertain.[58] Some editorials in Armenian newspapers encouraged women to abort the fetuses of Muslim fathers, while others encouraged the women to birth any offspring that might be claimed by the community to strengthen its numbers.[59] Other women chose to neglect the children they birthed rather than raise them as their own due to painful memories of conception through rape.[60] For example, a twenty-year-old woman named Beyzade from Harput was forcibly married to an Arab in Mardin. She bore the Arab three children and abandoned them all when a fellow Armenian helped her escape.[61] What is missing from the European humanitarian records are the profound anxieties heightened within Muslim communities when these children were taken.

Several of Edib's concerns have already been shared, but a secondhand anecdote recounted in her memoir captures outrage over the reclamation of absorbed children. Orphaned during the war, Kazim ended up in the American-run Near East Relief Center in Bebek, Constantinople, where "the Armenians got the benefit of the doubt."[62] Kazim remembered his Muslim father, but did he have an Armenian mother? We do not know, but the authorities proclaimed him Armenian despite his protestations. As if to add insult to injury, the boy was described as the son of a Turkish official in Adana—his Armenianization was an affront to Turkish supremacy enshrined within emerging ethnonationalism. He pleaded with a Turkish nurse to save him, but she could do nothing. Edib completes the story with nationalist flourish by including words that the child allegedly shared with the nurse: "Kazim is small, Kazim is weak, his fists cannot protect him, but the time will come when Kazim will be strong: then he will show the world that he is a Turk." Sentiments of cultural, religious, and national superiority were certainly inflamed by such a story that recounted the humiliation of Ottoman military defeat. Subverting Muslim patrimony paralleled the unraveling of the Armenian patriarchal household discussed in chapters 1 and 2. This violence, however, was conducted with Allied supervision and endorsed by international law.

In Aleppo, local Arabs were similarly outraged by the reclamation efforts taking place in the city in violation of Muslim patrimony and paternity. Such outrage resulted in xenophobic attacks against Armenians as the number of destitute refugees swelled in the city and was viewed as a threat to stability. Aleppo historian Kamil al-Ghazzi's scathing remarks against those who sought to extract Armenian women and children from Muslim homes in the city hinged on its violation of Islamic law: it subverted the sanctity of the household and Muslim marriage. The jurist recognized the primacy of Islamic law while ignoring completely the legal Armenian marriages the women were still committed to when their Armenian husbands remained alive. The author also made it no secret that he considered the wave of Armenian refugees to be a threat to the city, declaring Armenians "criminals" and "gangs." In his eyes, the theft of Armenian women and children from

Muslim homes was another manifestation of the disorder and violence Armenians brought to the city. The violent measures undertaken to retrieve Armenians from Muslim homes in the city inspired the most vitriol.[63]

In 1919, al-Ghazzi wrote, "The relatives of the children and women entered homes like a crime. They took the boy or girl by force or they used violence toward the caregiver or husband. They don't need to do that!"[64] While he did not blame Armenians for wanting the return of their children, he was outraged that home invasions were taking place with the assistance of the police. Furthermore, he saw this as an abuse of the generosity of Muslims who were willing to take Armenian women and girls as their wives. He offers a poignant anecdote about an unnamed Armenian woman peacefully living with her Muslim husband when her brother and Armenian husband arrived to reclaim her. Ignoring the violent separation from her first husband, al-Ghazzi focused on the violence the attempted retrieval incurred on the Muslim patriarchal household. The unnamed woman was taken to a church with a small window, where she was held in a small attic room and guarded by nuns—unusual because Armenians do not have nuns. The woman was urged to recant her marriage to the Muslim but held steadfast. The nuns "reminded her of her aversions [thakarata liha kul ma yujab nafratuha] so that she would not return to her Muslim husband. She did not pay any attention to their words."[65] Having given birth only a few days earlier, the separation of wife and child from the household was an attack on Muslim patrimony.

One night, the wife wrapped the baby tightly to her waist and leapt from the window to the ground below, injuring her ankle. At the same time, her husband, who had been imprisoned by the authorities at the time of her capture was released. She reunited with him at home, but was once again confronted by the police. This time the wife threatened, "If you try to return me, I will commit suicide." At those words, the police offered her another option: to sign a document promising that if the police were to come in the future and make demands, she would not resist. Al-Ghazzi concluded the story cheerfully, saying the Armenian wife remained with her husband and bore him several more children.[66]

These accounts provide evidence that extractions held the potential to inflame sectarian relations and incite hatred against Armenians. That extractions were traumatic for women and children as well as the Muslim families with whom they had bonded was not lost on humanitarians. Yotnakhparian noted empathically, after years of introspection,

> The people for whom we took away these orphan children had the right to resist. They saved the children from certain death, taking them in and looking after them like their own. They loved them and nourished them for four years. And here we come and pluck them away in one minute creating resentment and bad feelings.[67]

Whether due to "resentment" or "bad feelings," the stories shared by Edib and al-Ghazzi confirm growing Muslim hostility toward the Armenian-Allied reclamation project. Aleppo is a case in point. Over three hundred thousand non-Muslim (Armenian, Greek, and Assyrian) refugees that had descended on the city depleted precious resources and were straining the economy. On February 26, 1919, increased resentment against the Armenian refugees, including their collaboration with the French to form the Armenian Legion, resulted in attacks on Armenian shanties and orphanages.[68] The aggressive postwar dealings with the Allies, the partitioning of Syria from its economic hinterlands, the recruitment of minorities as colonial collaborators during and after the war, and the clerics and nobility who expressed the opinion that non-Muslims were transgressing Muslim order by behaving superior to Muslims resulted in communal violence against Armenian refugees, many of them orphans. On February 28, 1919, Sabun Khan Orphanage was overrun by a mob carrying long knives and guns and killing children, caretakers (*mayrigs*), and the director and teacher Garabed efendi.[69] Orphan Kerop Bedoukian was inside the orphanage at the time of the attack and describes the terror the orphaned children experienced when they were effectively orphaned again. Most striking in his account is his description of the mangled face of his "mother," an Armenian nurse who served the orphaned children.[70]

The death photo of the headmaster Garabed effendi's slain body splayed on a stretcher in the courtyard of Khan al-Saboun after the riot is yet another powerful visual reminder of boiling tensions between communities as the rescue effort triggered distrust and anxiety over postwar mixing and unmixing of bodies. While the dominant memory of many Armenians was the benevolent nature of Arabs who rescued Armenians, anti-Armenian propaganda in Arabic-language pamphlets created by the Ottoman authorities incited violence against generalized non-Muslim "infidels" in the name of protecting all Muslims during World War I.[71] Such propaganda was supplemented by juridical opinions (*fetva*) issued by clerics that declared Armenians traitors, condoning their murder and even promising entrance into heaven for doing so.[72] Certainly the influx of these ideas and the resentment of Muslim intelligentsia about recovery projects that placed non-Muslim Armenian and Allied desires above those of Muslims in Turkey and Syria fanned the flames of sectarian animosity. Muslims viewed their marriages to and adoptions of Armenian victims as beneficent acts and interpreted the postwar response of the Allied powers and Armenians as ungratefulness for the kind hospitality offered women and children in Muslim households. Specifically, Muslim husbands viewed their willingness to marry "dishonored" Armenian woman who would have, in their view, been cast off by the Armenian community as a further indication of their own beneficence.

The project to reverse years of assimilation was a primary objective of Armenian and Allied humanitarian relief workers. Identifying who was an Armenian after the war was slippery but part of the overall terrain of creating a distinction between those lost forever to assimilation and those who could be saved. Humanitarian rhetoric was influenced by the race-thinking of the time that supposed exposure to less civilized peoples was degenerative. Not all Armenians could be brought back from social death. While some had clear memories of being Armenian, others under the pressure of assimilation and domestic abuse, had psychically repressed any memory of being Armenian and feared the consequences of disclosing their true identity. Returning to the Armenian fold was traumatizing for children who had bonded with their Muslim families or, worse, had come to see Armenians as the enemy. Some children were rescued only to be lost again when they reverted back to being Muslims.

Amid the narratives of recovery and recuperation were photographs and experimental films that portrayed the harrowing experience of genocide victims and the recuperative power of humanitarianism.[73] The before-and-after photographs of rescued Armenians were the most powerful visual evidence. Images of rescued children draped in shabby, frayed tribal clothing were paired with shots of clean women and children sporting short-cropped hair and wearing European-style clothing, often white, symbolizing reform and redemption.[74] In this way, humanitarian photography fashioned recuperated Armenians as worthy humanitarian subjects rooted and thriving within their new living environments.

A potent example of this genre of humanitarian media is a black-and-white silent film commissioned by the League of Nations, which sought to promote efforts to terminate the trafficking of women and children.[75] Filmed in 1926, *A Rescue in the Desert* is a dramatic "reenactment" of the rescue of Astrig [Asdghig] and Lucia from the Bedouin desert community in which they lived and their recuperation in Jeppe's home in Aleppo.[76] After Lucia waves off a rescuer in a Ford automobile, an intertitle reads, "Nearby, in another tent, a girl Astrig [Asdghig] lives as a slave to the Bedouins since her childhood and is about to be sold to a harem" (figure 12). The reference to the harem, never mentioned in sixteen-year-old Asdghig's intake record at the home, was likely inserted to match her story to the league's mission to halt the traffic in women.

The reenactment achieved some realism by casting survivor Asdghig in her own role, rather than an actor. The film peddles her embodied experiences of captivity to generate moral outrage for the plight of Armenian women and financial support for the league's mission. In one scene, she is filmed with her back to the camera as she milks a goat in a basin, craning her neck to look at the camera. She rises and carries the basin to the other side of the tent, where Bedouin men are stereotypically lounging, swatting her occasionally with a stick as she works. After churning some milk in a goatskin bag, Asdghig brings a bowl from one side of the

FIGURE 12 *An uncanny moment when, with an uncomfortable giggle, Asdghig recognizes the Danish cameraman's filming of her reenactment in a Bedouin tent. She shyly wipes her tattooed face in embarrassment with her tattooed hand before continuing to churn milk in a traditional animal skin bladder, a task she likely performed when she lived among the Bedouin. While she works, the men sit drinking coffee and occasionally swat her with a cane. Source: Danish Film Institute.*

tent to the other, where the cameraman is located, and looks again straight into the camera, brushing her hand across her face in embarrassment. She is unsettled by being watched by the director's probing camera. In this dramatization, Asdghig, a girl who was rescued only a few months before by Jeppe's agents, steals the show with her continual glances at the camera (figure 13), recognizing the reenactment for what it is: both simulation and humanitarian spectacle.

After the rescue, Asdghig reappears as the epitome of a modern Armenian girl—clean, short-cropped hair, and wearing Western clothing—ready to be reunited with her Armenian family. During a powerful reenactment of a reunion between mother and daughter, Jenny Jensen and Lucia appear in the background wiping away tears. Is the reunion fictional or real? According to Asdghig's archived intake record, she was never reunited with her mother, and instead she left the home on August 8, 1926, when she got married and settled down in the rural town of Jarablous, perhaps as part of Jeppe's rural Armenian settlement project.

A Rescue in the Desert is one of many experiments with humanitarian film to reach donors abroad. To achieve this level of realism in this experimental documentary, no actors were used, and Jeppe appeared only in the first seconds of the

"Changelings" and "Halflings"

FIGURE 13 *While reenacting her arrival at the Rescue Home in Aleppo, Asdghig looks directly into the camera several times while Jenny Jensen and Leopold Gaszczyk compose the intake record preserved in the Rescue Home registry. A close-up of Asdghig's record with the affixed photograph finishes with a close-up of her actual register, which is now archived in the United Nations Archive at Geneva. Source: Danish Film Institute.*

reel. The victims simulating their rescue and recovery are centered yet their voices are heavily mediated by the Danish intertitles. Jeppe's photographs and *A Rescue in the Desert* were part of a genre of ethnographic visual culture that traded in images of individual Armenians who survived catastrophic loss and unimaginable tortures. But these were not the first moving pictures of their kind. Humanitarians had already experimented with documentary realism in *Auction of Souls*, starring real-life survivor Aurora Mardiganian, a film that continues to captivate our imaginations.

REMNANT 5

Aurora on Stage

Survival as Sideshow Act[1]

"There were seventeen girls and only sixteen crosses," narrated the dark-haired eighteen-year-old on stage. "There were seventeen of us girls tied naked across the backs of seventeen horses. The Kurd sheikh, Bekram Bey, drove us ahead of his band till we came to the ancient city of Diabekir [*sic*]. The gates of the city were closed and Bekram Bey did not want to bother with us anymore. Just outside the city walls there were sixteen great wooden crosses. There was one more girl than there were crosses. That is why I am here tonight—the other sixteen of us were crucified" (figure 14).[2]

Modestly dressed in a black jacket and a long skirt, with her hair pulled tightly back into a bun, Aurora's thin frame contrasted with the ornamented ceiling and pendulum-shaped chandelier of the opulent Loew's State Theater in Times Square. Her conservative dress stood in stark contrast to her matted black hair and nakedness that shocked us in the film immediately after her presentation. A row of naked girls were nailed to crosses. And while their hair was artificially lengthened to offer some modest covering of breasts, everyone still gasped. How the villainous Turks tortured those poor Christian girls!

When we walked into the theatre entrance, female ushers in Oriental dress greeted us in front of an ornamented Oriental façade erected for the opening event. My cousin said the opening in Minneapolis several months later was even more thrilling. Kurdish and Turkish raiders on horses had galloped through the streets, terrifying residents into buying tickets to see the film. The performance he saw featured live camels on stage, borrowed from the zoo! Can you imagine camels in Times Square? I am sure it was impossible to offer such a spectacular entry at the New York City premiere. The Minneapolis theater crew was even able to authentically re-create Aurora's experience, manufacturing a terrific sandstorm and a live slave auction! A menacing tribal sheikh purchased girls prior to Aurora's presentation, inciting the audience. My cousin says the auditorium was filled to the rafters and the audience was mesmerized by the story and the special effects that complemented the performance. Aurora was so overwhelmed at the Minnesota opening that she fainted on stage, leaving the audience in tears. There were reports that when she collapsed, the whole audience collectively gasped and a few members even screamed, fearing for her safety. Everyone realized that the girl was not only endangered on screen, but the poor urchin still suffers from her ordeal. Aurora said, "Until this very day, I get scared." She continues to move the desk in front of her hotel room door in case the Turks come after her again. When she lost consciousness while telling her story, it made front-page news in several newspapers the following morning.

Even though I had read about the plight of the poor Armenians over the last four years in the press and in my church newsletter, I was still shocked to see how the girls were stripped, tortured, and killed in ways unimaginable to us Christians in America. After seeing Aurora, "the sole survivor of half a million Armenian girls," on stage, "the Armenian Joan of Arc," I walked away more convinced that America must fight against the Turks. American Near East Relief must continue to support fellow Christians persecuted by Muslims! My church had a clothing drive, and I decided to volunteer to help clothe the starving, naked Armenians stranded in Syria. The film advertisement was right when it said, "See and hear this brave 18-year-old girl's story—it will make every woman's blood boil."

FIGURE 14   *An advertisement for* Auction of Souls *features an image of Aurora being crucified; she remarked in appearances and interviews that she was not crucified in real life. Source:* Moving Picture World, *May 31, 1919, 1296, 1297.*

CHAPTER SIX

AURORA'S BODY, HUMANITARIANISM, AND THE PORNOGRAPHY OF SUFFERING

At midnight on February 14, 1919, a few months after her debut, a girl who presented herself as Aurora Mardiganian appeared before a packed audience in a thousand-seat theater in Times Square. Prior to the screening of the eight-reel film *Auction of Souls*, an adaptation of her memoir *Ravished Armenia* published the previous year, Aurora, in the flesh, shared the story of her experience of the Armenian genocide and captivity among the Turks.[1] The first four reels of the film re-enacted Armenian life before the killings began. Other scenes featured half-nude women flogged and murdered on screen for refusing to convert to Islam and enslaved in Turkish harems.[2] Scenes typically censored were permitted for showings in the US because, it was argued, the sexual violence enacted on screen reflected the facts of Aurora's experience during the Armenian Genocide; though dramatized, the film was a documentary record of her testimony.

Still, ushers were required to bar anyone under twenty-one years old from seeing the film due to its explicit mix of sex and violence. The name of the film had to be altered from *Ravished Armenia* to *Auction of Souls* to placate moralists. Ironically, the sixteen-year-old survivor was, by theater standards, too young to view the violence she had reenacted in the film.[3] After Aurora survived the trafficking of women and children in Anatolia, *Auction of Souls* commodified her again, this time for consumption by American audiences. As if anticipating my argument, film advertisements informed audiences that Aurora's body itself was "a human document," forensic evidence of the crime of genocide that could be observed in a dual witnessing on film and stage.[4] Aurora's body was thus offered and read as evidence of a crime committed against the Armenian people, but its carnivalesque staging worked to satisfy audiences hungry for the realism of sideshows in the moving-picture age.

By the time *Auction of Souls* was released across the country, Aurora's mental health had declined and promoters had replaced the real Aurora onstage with seven Greek, Jewish, and even Turkish Aurora look-alikes, actresses who possessed her dark Middle Eastern features.[5] Was the girl onstage in Times Square, quoted as speaking perfect English by reporters in press accounts, Aurora or an Aurora look-alike? Aurora's participation in the film and tour, as well as the appearances of look-alikes, blurs the boundaries between simulation on screen and her real life. Mass media presented an outlet for witnessing the crime of genocide but posed other challenges for victims, who found themselves struggling to tell their story while being preyed upon by opportunistic humanitarians and Hollywood capitalists. The inaccessibility of her voice persisted even as her story was being performed by her embattled body and traumatized mind. The ongoing exploitation of Aurora's embodied trauma through mass media marketing and the urgency to witness human rights atrocities continue to generate ethical questions about humanitarianism and its representation of female victimhood to this day.

Aurora Mardiganian was an Armenian survivor who was crucified in celluloid for the noble purpose of raising over $117 million for Near East Relief to help her fellow Armenian Genocide survivors.[6] The exploitation of Aurora and her body has often been portrayed as living martyrdom evidenced in her symbolic crucifixion on screen. Her memoir alone sold 360,000 copies and was translated into several languages, and the *Auction of Souls* was shown throughout Europe, the US, and Latin America—reenacting her trauma in order to enrich the filmmakers and her sponsor Near East Relief at the cost of her own mental and physical health. Aurora's story can be told only because of the archival traces she has left behind, yet her story cannot fully be told due to the persistent mediation and fragmentation that left Aurora unable to narrate her own story.[7]

AURORA MARDIGANIAN: AN ARMENIAN BEAUTY SWEPT ASHORE

Before Arshalus Mardigian became American moving picture star Aurora Mardiganian (figure 15), she was an Armenian village girl in Tchemesh-Gedzak, about twenty miles north of Harput.[8] Some news reports claimed she hailed from a modest household, while others claimed her father was a silk and agricultural merchant.[9] Aurora's riches-to-rags story made her a real-life Armenian Cinderella, as the public reaction to her story confirms. She fell into the spotlight immediately upon arriving in the US, with June 1918 reports of a stunning Armenian beauty arriving ashore in search of her missing brother. Vahan Mardigian, her only surviving family member, had left for the US in 1905, before the Armenian Genocide.[10] Reports of the Armenian refugee Aurora amount to the first detailed biography published in American newspapers. The more salacious aspects of Aurora's story repackaged centuries-old Orientalist lore to readers eager to consume such spectacles, ushering in a two-year obsession with Aurora that quickly fizzled out.

Upon arrival in New York City on November 5, 1917, Aurora stayed with an Armenian tailor, Kevork Vardanian, and his family at 534 W. 178th Street in Wash-

FIGURE 15 *A portrait of Arshalus Mardigian turned Aurora Mardiganian, Hollywood star. Source: Armenian Genocide Memorial Institution, Yerevan, Armenia.*

ington Heights in Manhattan while she searched for her missing brother, who was never found.[11] The newspaper recounted some of Aurora's traumatic experiences in Turkey, interspersed with American nationalism as new immigrants served the reporter American ice cream and Armenian wine during the interview.[12] The young girl intended to work as a dressmaker in New York; however, fate had other plans for Aurora, as she quickly grabbed the attention of the press. Newspapers narrated her ordeal: "Everything seemed at peace when Turks descended like wolves on the fold. There was murder, rapine, arson."[13] The horrors of the Armenian Genocide were printed in newspaper ledes. Just as the Turks became wolves in the American press, Armenian women were described as prey "herded" by America's enemy, like "cattle" for slaughter (figure 16). Broadsheets featured lurid descriptions of soldiers disemboweling pregnant women, searching for hidden booty as the bodies of massacred deportees filled rivers.[14] The humanitarian urgency communicated through images of helpless Armenian women mobilized American support for the war effort and stimulated relief efforts already underway.

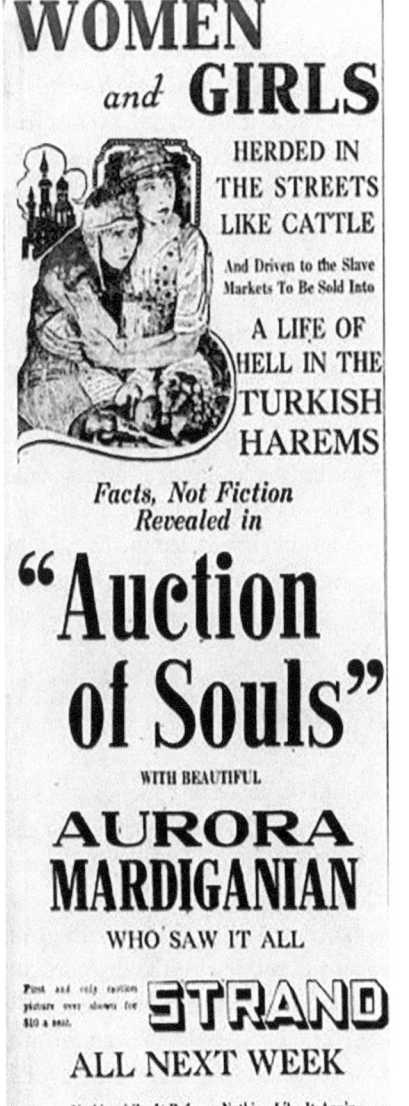

FIGURE 16 *An advertisement for* Auction of Souls *at the Strand Theater. Source:* News Scimitar, *July 8, 1919.*

Publication of Aurora's story in the *New York American* brought her to the attention of its editor, Henry L. Gates, who "was quick to recognize the commercial potential in Aurora Mardiganian" at a moment in which the war and Ottoman atrocities were of interest to the public.[15] Founded in 1915, New York–based Near East Relief (NER) served as an umbrella for various Christian missionaries and humanitarian societies working to ease the suffering of Armenian Genocide victims and spread American influence during the war.[16] The NER's fundraising drives were very successful, but Aurora's arrival in America presented a golden opportunity to raise millions for the relief effort.

Gates quickly organized a meeting between NER and Aurora. In a room in the Latham Hotel in late 1918, Aurora narrated her experience in Armenian, which was translated into English while Nora Waln and Henry L. Gates further "translated" the account into a story that would appeal to audiences. Nora Waln, publicity secretary for NER, gave the story shape as a memoir, which was later published with the organization's insignia imprinted on the cover page and a donation coupon printed on the final page of each copy. Though Waln did the work, Gates received credit as "interpreter" in the frontispiece of the original biography and was credited with authorship of the screenplay. Aurora's story underwent several mediations, unbeknownst to audiences. However, additional publications claimed that Aurora—who was given only a one-week crash course in English—was the author, as if she had the ability to tell her own story. Aurora's memoir was published in late 1918 as the war finished, and the film was made quickly thereafter, only pausing briefly when Aurora was quarantined with the Spanish flu.[17] The book and the immediate production of an accompanying film promised to spark interest in humanitarian relief and generate revenue long after the war's end.

AURORA'S BODY AND THE SPECTACLE OF *AUCTION OF SOULS*

Auction of Souls was finished in January 1919, and its debut in America was followed by distribution to audiences in Europe by the fall. Not only could an audience see her likeness on the screen, but Aurora's sexually abused pubescent body was displayed on stage for live audiences to observe both before and after the show. Her suffering in celluloid was to be experienced in a bizarre mash-up of nineteenth-century circus sideshows and modern film miracle. The discourse of Aurora's beauty individualized the broader story of thousands of women and girls abducted for the pleasures of the Turkish harem. In fact, advertisements informed spectators that Aurora had been sold for only 85 cents in a slave market in Bayezid to be delivered to the harem of Djevdet Bey.[18] Having endured sexual abuse and forced conversion to Islam, Aurora was trafficked again, this time by Hollywood to be consumed by American audiences hungry for stories of captivity, torture, and savage abuse in live performances.

Aurora's biographer Anthony Slide offers pointed criticism of the exploitation of Aurora when he writes, "She was to become the victim of another form of exploitation: capitalism and a society looking for a cause worthy of its white, Christian wrath."[19] Watching on screen and hearing Aurora's live testimony of captivity in a harem tapped into centuries of artistic and literary works about white, Christian women enslaved in Muslim harems, which had been amplified in the sexualized representations of war in Greece (1821–30), Bulgaria (1876), and the Macedonian insurrection (1902–3) leading up to the Armenian Genocide.[20] Stereotypical representations of women's bodies were continually appropriated as a metaphors for territorial boundaries to delineate self from other.

Many of the newspaper articles and advertisements promised audiences scenes from a real harem by recasting centuries-old images about the cruelty and despotism of the East. One attention-grabbing image, gleaned from the film, enacted a scene of sadistic fetish porn during the girl's conversion to Islam under the whip of a dark-skinned, muscular Muslim slave prepared to flog her while she prays behind an imam in a mosque, simulating conversion.[21] Within the same published excerpt from *Ravished Armenia* was a photograph of barefooted Aurora "weaving memories of her people into the beautiful laces that every Armenian girl delights to make." In this way, violent sadism was juxtaposed against domestic tranquility to transmit overlapping images of submissive femininity.

Brutal scenes of torture were consumed within the broader context of American war against the Germans and the Ottomans, a war the country had only entered the year before. Publishers were therefore eager to publish anti-Axis propaganda to rally the American public's support for a war that America had been late to enter. Nicoletta F. Gullace explains how the British had already developed relevant tropes in written and visual images of sexual violence during the 1914 occupation of Belgium, a year before the Armenian Genocide. Such images shaped British public opinion during World War I by harnessing the powerful familial and feminine images of "the rape of Belgium" to communicate obscure concepts of international law to English reading publics and to elicit both outrage and public support for the war effort.[22] Many of these tropes were adopted in America. Leshu Torchin writes that "in the Armenian case, the campaign was waged in a Christian register," reminding consumers of film and media reports that the victim population was not completely foreign but part of the same global "imagined" Christian community.[23] *Ravished Armenia* was able to harness images of sexual violence and religion to successfully rally mass support for humanitarian efforts in the Near East.

In her recorded testimonies later in life, Aurora conveyed in broken English, "I will not be Mohammed," emphasizing her resistance to conversion that underscored the religious aspect of the violence she experienced.[24] Media publics consumed horrors committed by the Turks as both anti-Axis propaganda and as salacious entertainment. In these representations of war, Armenian women, as well as Armenians in general, were feminized as prey, while the Turks and their Axis allies were predatory beasts. The connection between Aurora's personal story and geopolitics was underscored with a photograph of Talaat Pasha published in one of the graphics that accompanied the serialized version of her memoir; it visually connected the head of state and architect of the Armenian Genocide directly to her suffering.[25]

Although Aurora's abuse may have started with the Ottomans, it continued with her American handlers during the filming and promotion of *Auction of Souls*. In the first months after the film's opening, Aurora was still recovering from a broken ankle after falling twenty feet during a harem escape scene. Unable to walk, she had to be carried from scene to scene to complete the filming. Her custodian, New York journalist and screenwriter Mr. Henry L. Gates, the man who spearheaded the writing of her memoir and screenplay, recklessly encouraged Aurora to "step hard on her foot, claiming it would heal the break" while she continued to work on set.[26] In a filmed interview she gave later in life, Aurora showed printed photographic stills of her acting while part of her bandaged ankle was visible. Some news reports describe Aurora as being carried into the premiere of *Auction of Souls* on a chair due to her injury.[27] The physical injuries were compounded by the emotional stress she had already endured. She recounted how she would barricade her hotel room door during filming in California out of fear that the Turks would return to finish her off—a clear sign of post-traumatic stress that remained untreated by her employers.

A recent biography by Haik Demoyan and Lousine Abrahamyan further complicates her time as a ward of Mr. and Mrs. Gates. Aurora commented in an interview that while promoting the film, she was under extraordinary pressure to be a gracious and dutiful paragon of femininity at all times. In one instance, she was scolded by Gates's wife for not answering questions posed by curious Americans to "the Joan of Arc of Armenia" during a dinner party. Mrs. Gates scolded her, saying, "Young girls must always be gracious in the presence of their elders; in America, little girls were not allowed the privilege of 'moods' and moroseness in public." Aurora insisted that this was not a "mood" or "naughtiness," but only that she did not wish to speak with a mouth full of food. Ingeniously, she responded, "Each time I take a mouthful of food I like always a minute before I swallow it, and say in my mind a prayer to God that he will send another mouthful of food, just like mine, to my poor starving Armenia."[28] By deploying the rhetoric of the weak, Aurora framed her resistance to the pressure to perform into acts of piety and solidarity with still-suffering Armenians.

In the end, Aurora's attempts to resist her own exploitation were not enough. Due to her deteriorating mental health from the combined trauma of having survived a genocide only to relive it again for entertainment and humanitarian fundraising, her film tour was cut short in 1919 after a nervous breakdown. Accounts of her wounded ankle in the press are the only evidence that the *actual* Aurora Mardiganian appeared at any film openings. After she threatened suicide in the middle of promoting *Auction of Souls*, Mrs. Gates sent Aurora to a convent school. Suicidal, Aurora fled to New York City, where she contacted the philanthropist and NER chairwoman Mrs. Oliver Harriman, who had shown her some kindness in the past.[29]

Aurora's contract required live appearances for $15 per week to open *Auction of Souls* and lay bare her painful past—but she was never paid.[30] She commented years later, "I said I don't know what in that paper is. I said I don't understand my language much. I don't understand your English. And they said $15 was a lot of money. I was naïve. I didn't know nothing."[31] The actress-survivor's "moroseness" was cited as evidence against her when she sued the Gateses for breach of contract when she remained unpaid. Mrs. Gates's comments in the press included an admission that Aurora was traumatized: "The girl was suspicious of everything one did for her. Even when I was trying to help her, she thought I was going to do her some harm. I guess it was her experience in the war that has made her distrustful of everyone."[32] Cheerlessness made the girl useless for fundraising and film promotion efforts. The publicly suffering Aurora performed on film mirrored the quiet suffering she endured behind the scenes at the hands of her NER handlers, blurring the lines between the reality and performance of suffering. Then again, it simulated the absolute realism that the film sought to achieve from the outset. Aurora was to be a living artifact, a prop for NER's humanitarian effort, not a genocide survivor still suffering from trauma.

VIRTUAL REALITY: REENACTING THE ARMENIAN GENOCIDE ON THE BEACHES OF SANTA BARBARA

A beach in Santa Barbara was transformed into the set for *Auction of Souls*. The coastline had the look and feel of Western Armenia, which is still convincing a hundred years later. Mount Baldy stands in for Mount Ararat. Filming midwinter, Aurora recounted in her oral testimony how the girls were freezing upon the crosses placed on the beach; one actress was so sick that she drank whiskey to stay warm. Aurora claimed that during the simulated crucifixion, torture and terror became a reality with an alarming detail—the sick actress died from pneumonia during the filming of the iconic crucifixion scene.[33]

Another instance of simulation blurring the line between life and performance came when Aurora was paralyzed with fear by the sight of performers dressed as Turkish soldiers during a film shoot in Los Angeles. "The first time I came out of my dressing room, I thought they fooled me. I thought they were going to give me to these Turks to finish my life. So I cry bitterly. And Mrs. Gates say, 'Honey, they are not Turks. They are taking the part of those barbarics. They are Americans.' How will I know they are Americans? They talk English, their language. I have no Armenian around me, so I cry."[34] Hundreds of Armenians were cast as extras to enhance the authentic feel of the film along with impeccably made "Ottoman costumes." Yet, not all the outfits were convincing, and Aurora complained that the "gypsy clothes" she wore did not compare to the custom-made "long-sleeved and finely woven clothes" in Tchemesh-Gedzak.[35]

These moments of virtual reality on set remind us that dramatic silent films were a relatively new technology, having emerged in 1903, captivating audiences with their ability to convey real-life scenarios and action.[36] *Auction of Souls* producer William M. Selig was a filmmaking pioneer known for his use of natural backdrops, while director Oscar Apfel was known for his realistic portrayal of the horrors of World War I. By blending such achievements in realism, Slide observes, Apfel "created a film with such documentary-like feel that it was almost cinema verité," so real that film stills have found their way into lectures, onto websites, and into documentaries, where they are accidentally presented as documentary evidence rather than simulations because of their convincing documentary quality.[37]

The documentary quality of *Auction of Souls* was enhanced further by political endorsements and cameo appearances in the film. Known for his work compiling testimony of Ottoman war crimes with historian Arnold Toynbee in *Treatment of the Ottoman Armenians* (1916) (also known as "the Blue Book"), Viscount James Bryce endorsed the factuality of *Auction of Souls* in the *London Illustrated News*, writing, "All statements in the report were true, and if anything, fell short of the facts."[38] Former American ambassador Henry Morgenthau's cameo appearance featured a reenactment of a crucial conversation between himself and Talaat Pasha in which the premier of the Ottoman Empire revealed his plans to annihilate the Armenians, further simulated history.[39] The discursive linkages between the factual reports of the Armenian Genocide and the film blurred the lines between cinematic representation and history and give the film a documentary feel to this day.

While written and oral accounts of atrocities in the form of press accounts, pamphlets, government and humanitarian reporting, sermons, and lectures were normative modes of transmitting humanitarian knowledge in the US and Europe, *Auction of Souls*, Michelle Tusan argues, "pushed the boundaries of accepted narrative convention" with its graphic images of war atrocity.[40] Instead of a releasing the film immediately to the general public, there were private showings, including the League of Nations Union's twice daily viewings in London. The British government took issue with the film's realism; the Home Office investigated and Scotland Yard was asked to protect the public against indecency—namely, "exception taken to certain scenes dealing with women."[41] Concerns centered around objections raised by a Muslim religious leader, Mr. Amir Ali, who threatened to organize the Muslim community to boycott the film. The Foreign Office communicated in internal memoranda the concern that the film could inflame Muslim subjects in India and Egypt, producing an international crisis.[42] By the time British censors finished their work, all offensive references to religion had been deleted from the film, especially references to "Christians" on intertitles and the crucifixion scene that would sear the memories of so many viewers. *Variety* magazine assured audiences that "the management states not 50 feet of the actual story has been cut."[43] Scotland Yard promptly withdrew its objections to public showings after the modifications.

Film producers encountered censors early in the process, beginning with the British Board of Film Censors' rejection of the original title, which was also in the title of Aurora's memoir: *Ravished Armenia. Ravished*—a term synonymous with rape at the time—was not Aurora's naming but a choice by those who translated her experience.[44] The alternative title, *Auction of Souls*, was created to placate concerns of moralists. But the new title would have resonated with American audiences because of its similarity to *Traffic in Souls* (1913), a silent detective film about white European women forced in to prostitution in the US. Reinforcing its realism with the use of documentary newsreels of immigrants arriving at Ellis Island, *Traffic in Souls* shocked audiences with its representation of methods used to lure two newly arrived Swedish women into a life of prostitution.[45] For decades, activists had targeted global prostitution—referred to as "white slavery" and later "trafficking in women"—fearing that single white European women were being lured abroad for the purpose of sexual exploitation.[46] During the Great War, the established international discourse of "trafficking in women" was extended to the sexual enslavement of Armenian women in Turkey, which had the effect of rhetorically positioning Armenians as white, even if they were still racialized in other settings.

The marketing of *Auction of Souls* included a number of spectacular features that sought to authenticate Aurora's presence as "a human document" by tapping into older discourses of white slavery and Orientalism. Promoters erected extravagant façades emulating centuries-old Orientalist motifs on theater fronts. Photographs reveal what appears to be a wooden prop meant to look like Middle Eastern arcades, with artificial oil lanterns hanging from Oriental archways (figure 17). Film stills show Aurora and her co-star, fair-haired Swedish actress Anna Q. Nilsson, in the classic reclining pose of odalisques in the Romantic paintings of Delacroix, Gérôme, and Ingres. An *Auction of Souls* advertisement reproduced Gérôme's harem scene to visually link film to Orientalist paintings from a century earlier.

The image of languid women before Oriental façades lay in stark contrast to the behind-the-scenes truth of the traumatized teenager set to work herself to physical and emotional exhaustion upon arriving at Ellis Island. A stone-faced Aurora, flanked by two smiling women dressed in contrived Oriental costumes, stood in front of the backdrop, preparing to receive audiences coming into the theater. Aurora was not only in the feature, but she was *the* feature. From the right side of the photograph (figure 18), a man consumes the spectacle—two women in Oriental costume and one plainly dressed and demure Aurora in front the Oriental staging at the box office window in Milwaukee.

Advertisements posted on the façade inform audiences that Aurora would be present to speak to audiences about her firsthand experiences after showings. She was to be consumed by audiences, as the advertisement suggests "Aurora Mardiganian appears in person and on screen. The sole survivor of half a million Armenian girls. Fact not fiction."[47] But was the girl in the photograph Aurora at all? Or the mere specter of Aurora? An Aurora look-a-like?

FIGURE 17   *Display for* Auction of Souls *in front of the Princess Theater, Milwaukee.* Source: Motion Picture News, *July 19, 1919, 704, Archive.org.*

FIGURE 18   *Models wearing "traditional dress" flank a modestly dressed Aurora Mardiganian in front of the Orientalist* Auction of Souls *façade at the Princess Theater, Milwaukee. Many of these displays were embellished with marauding Kurds on horseback to excite audiences into attending.*
Source: Motion Picture News, *July 19, 1919, 704, Archive.org.*

By January 1920, advertisements for the film flooded the press as did coverage of Aurora's personal appearances in a rigorous promotion schedule that demanded three to four appearances per day.⁴⁸ Theaters offered a special "ladies only" matinee in which women were promised a more intimate, detailed discussion of sexual atrocities and bondage with Aurora after the film. The advertisement read:

> At the request of hundreds of ladies who have read little Aurora's story, "Ravished Armenia," this special matinee will be given in which Miss Mardiganian will describe fully and in detail her experiences while captive for two years in the slave markets and harems of the unspeakable Turk. She will speak intimately and confidentially as only one woman can speak to other women.⁴⁹

Aurora's rape was advertised specifically for female consumption, the target being maternalistic women humanitarians and consumers who craved more shock and outrage beyond the actual film. The creation of "the women's matinee" underscores a tacit understanding of the pornographic nature of Aurora's account, with explicit details about violence against women, including "impossible to forget" details of rape and grisly executions of women who refused to convert.⁵⁰

The sharing of intimate details on stage with women-only audiences, after so much excess reenacted within the film, exposes the need to continually entice potential audiences with new, increasingly graphic marketing strategies to increase ticket sales. The marketing strategies moved beyond charity to converge with capitalism and the emerging motion picture industry. The staging of Aurora followed the format of captivity narratives from women who lived among Indians in the American West, particularly the account of the tattooed American woman captives that featured prominently in freak shows, which will be discussed in chapter 8. Fitting a familiar pattern of testimonials from former captives held by savage others, Aurora was not just an actress but a survivor, a freak in a sideshow act throughout the staging and marketing of *Auction of Souls*.

Advertisements informed the public that "the heroine's part was played with amazing power and with a skill beyond the reach of art—it was not acted, it was lived."[51] The realness of Aurora's abused body was part of the marketing scheme. Some viewers were appalled by these acts and the final image: a row of crucified girls. Many reviewers commented that the girls featured in the film were chosen for their "comeliness" in order to entice male audiences to the theater. Sometimes the cinema verité quality of the film left viewers incredulous. An anonymous reviewer commented on the whiteness of the women actors, something that made the representation less believable: "to anyone who knows Armenia, these beautiful, white-skinned models were a 'scream,' for in Armenia such is not the breed." The reviewer described the film as "propaganda" not only for the war effort but for Christianity due to its religious overtones.[52]

Yet, the ability of humanitarian rhetoric to veer into "the pornography of pain" has a longer history in eighteenth- and nineteenth-century humanitarianism. Karen Halttunen has documented the emergence of a humanitarian concern for the pain of others in early-eighteenth-century Anglo-American rhetoric that emerged simultaneously with the production of erotica and humanitarian reform, both structured around cultural taboos.[53] In the case of Aurora, we can think about how objections to *Auction of Souls* may have been contesting not only the violent excesses she suffered on screen but also staged eroticized and embodied female suffering in particular.[54] The subjects of suffering were necessarily white, just as they were in romantic Orientalist paintings, making the objects of desire familiar but placed geographically elsewhere in this visual trafficking of bodies.[55] While in the nineteenth century, these white slaves were envisioned as white, European, female slaves of Greek or even Circassian origin, Lila Abu-Lughod has shown how this genre she calls "slave pornography" continues to be a multimillion-dollar industry to this day. Largely consumed by women living in Western countries, these narratives incite humanitarians to agitate for war—mobilized in the case of Afghanistan in 2001—in order to save the enslaved, burka-clad feminine other.[56]

Aurora's experience was represented by sadistic scenes of Turkish men flogging and raping helpless virgins, representations of a regressive male sexuality that served as a foil for enlightened, humane Euro-American masculinity.[57] Animalistic Oriental male sexuality persisted in the marketing of Aurora's story, including the simian-like Turk carrying Aurora that was used in a marketing poster for the *Ravished Armenia* memoir (figure 19). The image was inspired by a nineteenth-century sculpture of a gorilla carrying off a Stone Age woman, a representation of imagined Darwinian evolution that included interspecies sex, a metaphor for miscegenation that would later inspire World War I propaganda posters and later the blockbuster film *King Kong* (1933).[58] Similarly, the anti-German "Destroy this Mad Brute" (1917) poster featured a mustachioed, spiked-helmet-wearing gorilla carrying off a scantily clad blonde in its representation of sexual atrocity. The image crossed the Atlantic for use as a US Army recruitment poster in 1918.[59] In both instances, the victim is presented as light-skinned and scantily clad with fully exposed bare breasts, and as if that weren't enough to cudgel the viewer with a rape metaphor, the barbaric simian Hun bears a bloody phallus inscribed with the word *Kultur*. *Auction of Souls* posters followed these established tropes in their representation of raped liberty and inhuman brutality mixed with fears of miscegenation with atavistic Turks. The pornography of suffering fixed on such vivid literary and pictorial imagery to evoke "spectorial sympathy" yet, at times, overloaded the senses to the degree that consuming horrors was sometimes sexually arousing, revealing what Caroline Dean has called "the desire to be horrified."[60]

While some viewers consumed these images without question, critics like Sir Sidney Low penned scathing reviews of the film, denouncing it as pornographic war propaganda in its portrayal of "the wholescale violation of women, merciless floggings, shocking mutilations, every outrage that unchained lust and maddened cruelty could devise" and calling it a "a banquet of horrors."[61] Low described the crucifixion scene as the final course of the banquet: "girls... hanging naked from the crosses upon which they have been immolated." The critic's commentary illustrates how genocidal acts are themselves sensational because torture makes a spectacle of the victim's body that leave indelible visual reminders on the psyche and memory of witnesses. Such spectacles, real or simulated, affirm the power of the perpetrator. Genocidal acts are able to seize the attention of victims and spectators with sensational displays of violence in public space. Aurora's corrections later in life gesture to the ineffability of the violence she experienced and witnessed. Despite her best efforts to describe it, *Auction of Souls* still fell short of the terror she experienced in the face of Ottoman necropower.

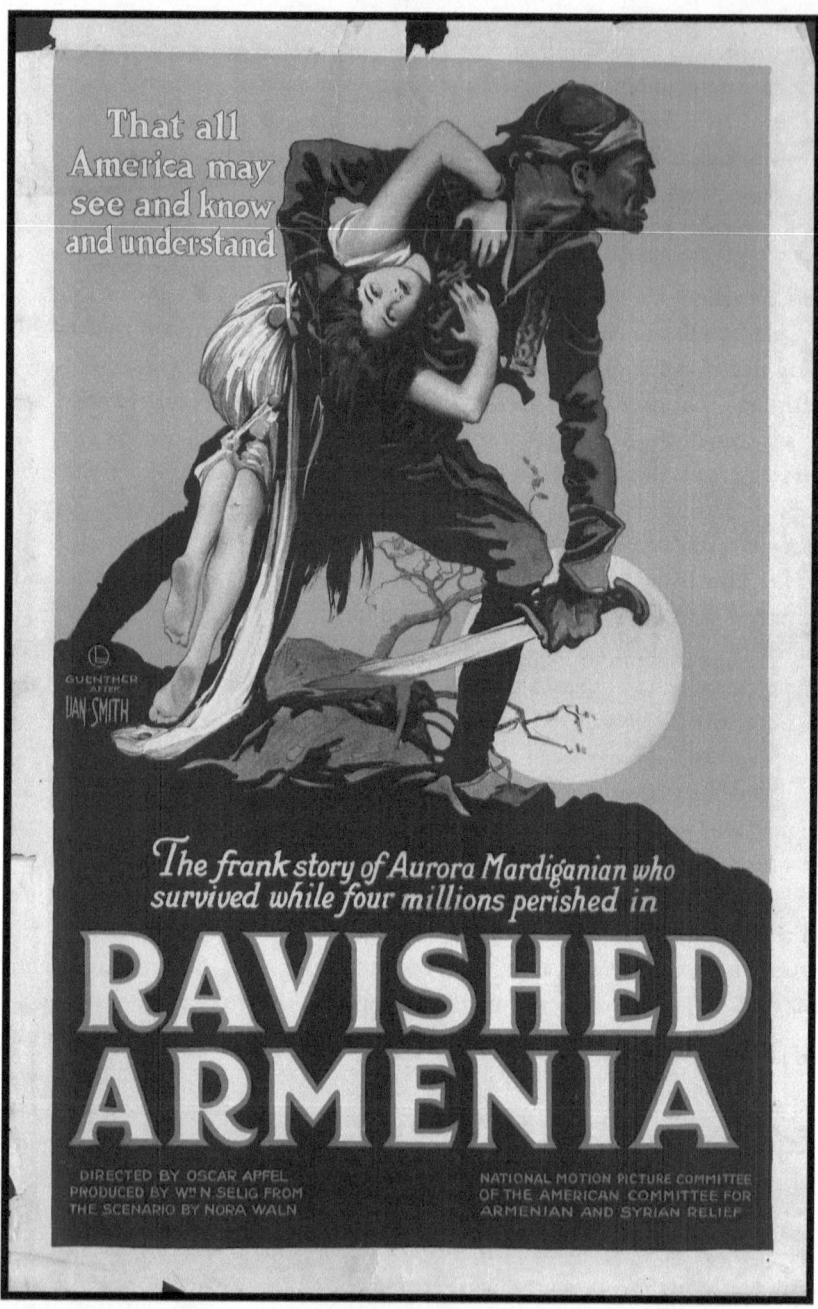

FIGURE 19 *A* Ravished Armenia *poster represents a simian-like Turk carrying off an Armenian woman, Aurora. The image is inspired by a sculpture by Emmanuel Fremiet (1824–1910)* Gorilla Carrying Off a Stone Age Woman *(1887) that reflected social Darwinist fears of racial miscegenation.* Source: Reprinted with permission from the National World War I Museum and Memorial, Kansas City, Missouri.

STRUGGLING TO NARRATE, STRUGGLING TO LISTEN

In two separate interviews, since spliced together into one at the Shoah Foundation Visual History Archive, Aurora offered a frenetic narration of her experience in broken English. As I listened, I struggled hard to piece together the story she was telling. I strained to hear her voice through the zig-zagging of narrative trauma. Even after studying her life, each statement seemed to be interrupted by another decontextualized fragment. Sometimes her narration was interrupted by the interviewers who cut her off by closing a clapboard in front of her face and yelling "Cut!"[62]

Noticeably, Aurora slips into Armenian when she discusses sexual violence. This is noteworthy because she is speaking clearly and fluently at that brief moment. Aurora narrates differently in Armenian than in English because even after decades of living in America, her English is nearly as broken as her narration. Interviews with Aurora in late life confirmed a mistranslation of her experience hinging on the translation for *impalement* from Armenian into English. She recounted, "The Turks didn't make their crosses like that. The Turks made little pointed crosses. They took the clothes off the girls. They made them bend down. And after raping them, they made them sit on the pointed wood, through the vagina."[63] Aurora was describing at that moment how sexual atrocity was performed after ritualized gang rape. In this instance, Turkish soldiers used their bayonets to form pikes upon which Armenian women were forced to impale themselves vaginally, mocking life-giving coitus, forcing them to participate in the theater of sexual atrocity. The virtual reality of the film crucifixion was less horrific than the fact of her experience yet still enough to produce the fury of censors.

Aurora's correction decades after filming illustrates the ineffability of pain. Elaine Scarry argues that the act of inflicting pain on others is an exercise in power that is simultaneously "language-destroying" and world-destroying as it renders the tortured unable to fully express what they have experienced. Even witnessing that pain "is the half-way point to the disintegration of language" and only serves to draw attention to the near absence of the victim as their agony "can only be dimly heard."[64] Peter Balakian has illuminated that this violation of both body and spirit, raping women to death with a sacred heritage object, the cross, was a means to kill a people. Everyday objects are "undone" through the process of using them in torture performances: a cross is no longer a cross once it is used for torture.[65] The use of the crosses in the film was also not incidental but underscored how Armenian Christianity was a central target of a genocide, which subsequently made it a rallying point for humanitarian cinema with the nailing of a silent pubescent girl to the cross as a surrogate Christ-like figure.

THE AFTERLIVES OF *AUCTION OF SOULS* IN ARMENIAN PROSTHETIC MEMORY

While Aurora's time in the spotlight was spectacularly bright, she quickly fell into oblivion, as did the film, which disappeared at some point in the late 1920s. Researchers scoured archives—including the Museum of Modern Art, where Aurora believed the film to be stored—looking for even a remnant of *Auction of Souls*. One forgotten reel had been discovered in the offices of a distributor in Paris. Mislabeled "Martyrdom of a People," the reel was difficult to identify since the viewer needed to know what they were seeing when they viewed the contents. Luckily, that viewer was an aspiring projectionist and survivor named Yervant Setian, who had viewed the film in Marseille in 1925.[66] The enclosure in the box contained erroneous supplementary notes attributing the enclosed story to a women named either Elisa Greyterian or Elsa Kederian.[67]

After his repatriation to Armenia in 1947, Setian deposited the film in the Armenian National Archives, where it remained in obscurity for nearly half a century.[68] It was there that a single twenty-minute reel was discovered in 1994 by Eduardo Kozanlian, an Armenian diasporan from Buenos Aires. After careful study of the excised bit of film, Slide and award-winning Armenian-Canadian filmmaker Atom Egoyan concluded that the segment of film found by Kozanlian is outtakes rather than the original film sequence. In 2009, Richard D. Kloian, the director of the Armenian Genocide Resource Center of Northern California, carefully edited and restored the video to the best of his ability. He inserted the intertitles using documents obtained from Slide, who approvingly remarked, "The result is a film that is dynamic, that lives, that holds the attention and engrosses the audience."[69] Yet, only a few of the intertitles on the surviving strip of film correspond to the original, perfectly preserved screenplay.

The restored film is, then, a reconstruction, a "re-membering" of the original skin of film. It is a simulation of a simulation that fittingly highlights how Aurora's experience has been continually mediated, her voice further obscured with each subsequent mediation. Like her experience, the remaining film fragments are decontextualized outtakes that are best understood as the material manifestation of the simulacra of Aurora, who no longer exists, in the sense that she was materially excised from the film even while living. No longer living, Aurora's story, it seems, is impossible to tell.[70] Shushan Avakyan captures this sentiment when she writes of Aurora: "She was actually to copy a copy of herself, giving birth to an extraordinary icon." Avakyan has persuasively argued that Aurora is far more elusive since the copy of her that survived was molded to suit an American and European audience primed by mass media culture to consume the spectacle of sexual atrocity.[71]

Much like a corpse recovered from a mass grave, *Auction of Souls*, a film that made millions of dollars, fell into oblivion only to resurface as a fragment in an archival exhumation. The only surviving fragment is believed to be director's cuts rather than the original film viewers would have viewed in theaters, an apt metaphor for the impossibility of witnessing. Some film fragments found their way into an Armenian language documentary in the 1950s that weaved *Auction of Souls* together with some war images from *All Quiet on the Western Front* (1930), making the remnant a historical puzzle that exemplifies the ethereal nature of memory, the slipperiness of simulation, and the vulnerability of the skin of celluloid to the ravages of time.[72] Aurora was all but forgotten, but both her memoir and the remnants of the film she starred in have inspired artists who have engaged the film, effectively reinserting it, after nearly a century hiatus, back into Armenian prosthetic memory.[73]

Aurora's resurgence in Armenian prosthetic memory and the affective power of her story come to the fore in a feminist reading of her life by Armenian-Canadian actress Arsinée Khanjian in *Auctions of Souls: Performing Memory* (2015).[74] Commissioned by the Maxim Gorki Theater in Berlin for the Armenian Genocide centennial, Khanjian wrote and directed a performance that reinterprets *Ravished Armenia* in order to ingeniously amplify Aurora's voice. The *Auction of Souls* film fragment, the text of *Ravished Armenia*, and a miraculously recovered video interview with Aurora in which she talks about her film and memoir are juxtaposed with carefully choreographed re-creations by two stage actors. The layering of text in this stunning example of performance art draws attention to the various mediations of Aurora's story in order to powerfully place the moments in which the genocide survivor critically inserts her voice in her native Armenian. This sets it apart from her meandering and interrupted English narratives that fail to offer the nuance and sophistication of her testimony in her native register.[75]

Importantly, Khanjian explained that she discovered a missing taped interview with Aurora from the 1980s, archived at the Zoryan Institute. After three and a half hours of questioning, the interviewer notified Aurora that the interview was over. Surprised, Aurora asked, "You're not going to ask me about my film?" The interviewer's crew had run out of film. And surprisingly, the crew had no sense of who Aurora was nor her exceptional experience as a survivor-activist who attempted to tell her story. As Khanjian pointedly notes, "The Armenian community somehow did not really listen to her," she suspects because "they didn't know who they were interviewing."[76] This prompted the actor to engage and resuscitate Aurora's life in a multimedia performance to create prosthetic memory so that she could be remembered.

Khanjian's feminist corrective offers a critical reading of Aurora's life story by drawing upon both her English language memoir and her Armenian testimony archived at the Zoryan Institute. The actor's detailed analysis of language, particularly how the original biography used euphemisms to describe scenes of violence, the ambivalence of which further obscured Aurora's experience. The haptics of touch—touch as intimacy, touch as harm—is explored throughout the performance with an examination of "kissing." Khanjian writes the word *kissing* on an overhead projector followed by a scene of a male actor reading a series of excerpts from Aurora's biography where the word *kissing* is used as a metaphor for sexual violence. This occurs while the male actor is suddenly assaulted by a female actress who forcibly kisses him, causing clear distress, inverting the masculine power in sexual atrocity. The forced kissing ends with the director walking to the overhead projector, an avant-garde analog technology. She writes on a tactile plastic film the definition of *touching*: "A touch or caress to signify attraction, reverence or sexual attraction."

It is here that Khanjian lucidly illustrates the ambivalences of touch and its affectivity as gateway to either eroticism or conversely pain or sexual violation. Through the performance, she underscores how touch can produce either sexual freedom or sexual oppression through the violent appropriation of women's bodies.[77] The performance continues to examine the ambivalences of language with the term *protecting* followed by *laughing*, the affects of laughing, smiling, hooting, joking, affects associated with joy reminiscent of Zabel's account that "the tears, the lamentations, the prayers," says an eyewitness, "only served to increase the joy of the sinister criminals and their bestiality."[78] The laughter of the male actor begins with a small giggle followed gradually with boisterous laughter that moves from joyous affect to a cackle and angered frenzy. This exploration of *laughter* chills the spectator to the bone as the actor convincingly conveys laughter's dual affects. Laughter is complicated within the broader context of killing, in which anger and delight comingle to produce the frenzied ecstasy of pure violence.

As spectators approached the Gorki Theatre to see Khanjian's performance in April 2015, they encountered a series of television screens installed by Khanjian's husband, filmmaker Atom Egoyan, featuring actresses reading sections of Aurora's memoir. Encircling spectators with Aurora's words to amplify the voice of the subaltern, multiple actresses read sections of the story, bit by bit, following one another, affirming that the story of a single girl echoed the experience of a nation. Egoyan astutely addressed this point when he said: "Aurora is a super-survivor. A survivor not only of the Armenian Genocide but also a survivor of the commercial exploitation of her story, and also to benefit from that sacrifice she made.... She is a sacred figure in our history."[79] And yet, Aurora was atypical as a "super-survivor" because the narrative was produced and circulated globally, yet the multiplicity of the actresses prompts questions about all the voices that were never heard but also whether Aurora's true voice was ever legible.

How then should we understand the power of Aurora's resurrection in Armenian communal memory after a prolonged absence? Film scholar Laura Marks has argued that "skin of film," is "a membrane that brings its audience in contact with the material forms of memory."[80] She calls this affective power *haptic visuality*, which invokes the sense of touch visually in the viewer and activates memory. The enactment of memory on film is always a multisensory, fragmentary, and disintegrated minefield or "bed of fossils."[81] Such images confront the viewer with that which cannot be represented, that ineffability of certain crimes in this instance, bringing it into dialogue with memory with evidentiary remains.[82] Both Khanjian and Egoyan address silences and traces left behind by Aurora and the struggle for her to be heard as subaltern. Even in its current fragmentary form, its haptic visuality continues to provoke strong emotional responses powerfully harnessed in *Auction of Souls: Performing Memory*.

A decade after *Auction of Souls* was released, Aurora married Martin Hoveian and gave birth to a son named Michael a few years later. After her husband's death, she continued to struggle with mental illness and suicidal ideation. Estranged from her son, she lived out her elderly years reclusively within Ararat Home, a retirement home in Los Angeles, and remained terrified that the Turks would return to murder her. Signs of mental deterioration can perhaps found in Aurora's late-life oral interviews in which she appears surrounded by mounds of storage boxes in her small apartment, sitting upon one of them while being interviewed.[83] Aurora died on February 6, 1994, but her once commodified body remained unclaimed for four years. Rather than receiving the burial of a Hollywood star, she was cremated and buried in a mass grave with 2,098 other unclaimed bodies by the municipality of Los Angeles. "The human document" that raised millions of dollars for humanitarian relief, in the end, was transformed into a discarded corpse buried in a pauper's grave marked only by the year of her death.

Diasporan Armenians have largely adopted the NER's version of Aurora's biography into their collective memory. Her story has even been enshrined in name through the Aurora Humanitarian Initiative, whose Aurora Prize for Awakening Humanity honors people dedicated to heroic acts of humanitarianism.[84] But such recognition was fleeting during her lifetime and, forgotten, she was not dignified with a respectable burial. Only the discovery of a fragment of film coaxed Aurora back into Armenian prosthetic memory. Cut, spliced, and vivisected, *Auction of Souls* was not preserved for posterity, and the lack of archival care suggests that her story was not even valuable to Armenians except incidentally and now only symbolically, rarely with any recognition of its tragic elements. What remains of *Auction of Souls* in communal memory, then, is but a chimera of the original woman.

How this sliver of film came into the hands of a diasporan Armenian in Argentina is itself an amazing story. In the last decades, Aurora's story has been told many times, often in celebratory ways. Khandjian's performance of Aurora's story drew upon her survivor testimony archived at the Zoryan Institute, giving it primacy over the actual film performance. After skillfully re-creating the survivor's story, Khandjian did the unthinkable. She brought a shredder on stage in order to destroy the veritable archive that she had carefully curated to inform her performance. Reinforcing this action, *Auction of Souls: Performing Memory* was not video recorded, which further amplified Khanjian's message about the power of memory in artistic practice and the ominous, obliterating power of forgetting.[85]

Visual representations of humanitarianism harnessed the rhetorical power of female bodies within a gendered grammar and iconography that came into fuller force through experimentation with new genres, photography, memoirs, and the moving picture. Humanitarian filmmaking emerged during World War I to summon and monetize moral outrage over the treatment of women in brutalized during the Armenian Genocide. Aurora's femininity and pubescence was not incidental to the staging of suffering but central to the decision of Hollywood traffickers to cast her. *Auction of Souls*, as an example of humanitarian filmmaking, reminds us that the images of sexual atrocities against Yazidi girls and women that we view privately today from our personal computers and smartphones are part of a larger history of representing female suffering.[86]

While women like Aurora left many traces of their stories behind, many women's stories have yet to be told. Like Aurora, they experienced embodied and psychic trauma during the genocide, but their experiences were imprinted as indelible tattoos that not only haunted them but continue to haunt the survivor community.

PART II
Skin

CHAPTER SEVEN

WHAT LIES BENEATH GRANDMA'S TATTOOS?

Traumatic Memories of Inked Skin

> For many years I had carefully cut out grandma from my world. I had meticulously wiped clean her tattooed hands.
> —SUZANNE KHARDALIAN, director,
> *Grandma's Tattoos* (2011)[1]

Hovering above the communal memory of genocide is the specter of the tattooed Islamized woman. Photographs of tattooed Armenian women survivors continue to wield a rhetorical power that I observed at a viewing of the documentary *Women of 1915* in New York City on February 23, 2017: the audience gave a collective gasp when images of seven tattooed women were collectively projected onto the screen.[2] Decontextualized, the tattoos did not need any explanation; their meaning was self-evident—the tattoos are overdetermined. Tattooed skin, like the petrified bones of our ancestors, is understood as evidence of a crime in the communal memory of Armenians. Yet, to this day we understand very little about why these symbols were engraved on the skin of women absorbed in Muslim households. The tattoo has come to represent both a literal and figurative wound that can never truly heal.

From humanitarian publications to photographic exhibitions, women and girls indelibly marked with tribal motifs on their faces, necks, chests, and hands produce an affective response among viewers. It is difficult to quantify how many rescued Armenians bore tribal tattoos[3]—a recent study speculates that more than 10 percent of those rescued may have carried the indelible marks on their faces and hands. In the years following their rescue, tattooed Armenian women attempted to make sense of their wounded skin marked with symbols belonging to a foreign culture. Some, such as filmmaker Suzanne Khardalian's grandmother Khanum, lived with their marks in seeming silence; others, such as Khanum's sister Lucia, rationalized their tattoos in one way or another; still others, such as Aghavni Kabakian, sought to have them removed surgically to wipe clean the traumatic tattooing that indelibly marked their skin and memory.

In more recent years, the next generation of Armenians have also attempted to make sense of the legacy of the tattooed women and their social death for their families and the Armenian people. Stories about Armenian women's tattoos press us to ask a deeper question: what role do tattoos play within the context of national shame felt by Armenians after the public torture of Armenian women and near annihilation of their community during World War I? Relief workers, missionaries, doctors, and survivors who adopted the view that the marks were shameful brands of slavery described these women as sex slaves or prostitutes. Some women internalized others' revulsion and sought to have their tattoos surgically removed in order to liberate their bodies by first liberating their skin.

AGHAVNI'S TATTOO

I was one of those little Armenian girls with rosy cheeks who had carved on her forehead the entire tragedy of her race.
—AGHAVNI KABAKIAN[4]

When the deportations began, six-year-old Aghavni Kabakian marched from the eastern Marmara town of Adapazarı.[5] Her younger sister Shakeh was with her, as was the little doll that she kept pressed to her chest during the entire march until it was pillaged by marauders. The girls were reunited by chance with their father in Eskişehir, but soon he and their grandmother perished from exhaustion and disease. Aghavni remembered the sound of her sister crying the entire 1,000-kilometer march south from the lush coast of their hometown to the dusty, tribal environs of al-Bab outside Aleppo.

The toddler Shakeh was abducted by *nawar* (Roma) soon after they arrived—a shock that sent Aghavni, "already an old woman of eight years," into despair. She lay on the ground in grief, waiting for death to relieve her of her suffering. "Wandering strippers of the dead" arrived to steal the rags she was wearing—her clothes had largely disintegrated. One of scavengers, a *nawari* man,[6] observed the amulet of Saint Gayane that had been sewn clandestinely into her garment by her grandmother in order to protect her from harm.[7] It was then that Aghavni opened her eyes. Believing that the girl had died and miraculously come back to life, the nawari man brought her to his tent to live with his family. During her time in his household, Aghavni was subjected to hard labor and physical abuse by other family members with such frequency that she took to hiding in the pasture with the cows to avoid being inside the home. But the family patriarch was different; he always took her side against those who tormented her under his roof.

One fateful day, Aghavni was tattooed like other nawar while the family patriarch was away. She recalled, "The neighboring Gypsy women tied my hands and feet and with large needles started to tattoo my face. I screamed from the pain and terror of the new experience while the children of the house beat my body with blows of sticks in order to silence me."[8] Why did the neighboring, as opposed to the adoptive, nawar have a sense of urgency to tattoo her? Did they seek to punish her as a foreigner or were her neighbors afraid that she would be identified during the many military sweeps in a region where many Armenian deportees were gathered? These questions remain unanswered not only for us but also for the narrator. Even if the motivations of the nawar had been uttered in her presence, Aghavni would not have understood what they were saying as a traumatized, non-Arabic speaking Armenian girl.

The tattooing event formed yet another rupture in her life, but also left her captor unsettled. For reasons unknown, the nawari patriarch "sold" Aghavni to a noble Arab named Hamid Bey in Aleppo the day after she had been tattooed. In this instance, being sold was more of a blessing than a curse, for in Hamid Bey's house, Aghavni was forbidden to do heavy work and treated like his very own daughter. Out of fear, she and two other Armenians who lived with him never set foot outside the home for three full years, believing all Armenians had perished off the face of the earth. In her fourth year as Hamid Bey's adoptive daughter, a priest and two representatives from Aleppo's Armenian prelacy arrived to take her away. King Faysal, who briefly governed Syria, had ordered that Armenians be rescued and reunited with their original community in compliance with an Allied treaty.[9] Hamid Bey had no choice but to acquiesce to the monarch's demands. Aghavni was overcome with tears as she held hands with her adoptive father, waiting to be delivered to the shelter for recovered Armenians.[10] Years later, whenever Aghavni visited Aleppo, she continued to be received warmly by her adoptive Muslim family as kin.[11]

In 1921, when she entered an American rescue home, Aghavni recalls: "I had almost forgotten my Armenian. I was speaking mixed Armenian and Arabic."[12] Although she was partially assimilated in body and spirit, she witnessed an unnatural scene of young girls holding the infants they had birthed in forced marriages and concubinage. She observed how many of these girls and women were tattooed just like her:

> This was the place where all the Armenian women and girls recovered from Kurdish and Arabic *ashirets* [tribes] in the vicinity of Aleppo were assembled. These included all sorts of hapless souls of all ages.... The faces of many of them were tattooed like mine. There seemed to be an air of indifference, a sort of fatalism on many of their faces.[13]

By reading "fatalism" on the faces of rescued women and girls, Aghavni suggests that tattoos are a window into the very soul of tattooed survivors. The women she saw were present before her but their interiors had been stripped, their souls had not survived the ordeal.

For Aghavni, then, her tattoos were a traumatic reminder of her near-social-death experience. "Stamped in my memory [is] a long list of sad images." For her, the tattoos were symbols of misery representing the entire experience of attempted annihilation. Her "stamped" memory mirrors the stamping of her skin that carved her tragic experience onto her forehead. "I was one of those little Armenian girls with rosy cheeks who had carved on her forehead the entire tragedy of her race."[14] Aghavni offers a verbatim reference to the Armenian term *jagadakir*, which means literally "written on the forehead," an Armenian compound noun that combines the noun for "brow" or "forehead" with the noun for "writing," which together mean "fate," "destiny," or even "doom." Feminist scholar of memory Hourig Attarian has argued that by inscribing the faces of Armenian women—often between the eyes upon the forehead—tribal tattoos territorialized the bodies of women while emblematically inscribing the terrible fate that had befallen the broader Armenian community.[15] Importantly, inscriptions on bodies connect to ways that punishment seizes the body, forming a virtual layer of imprisonment.[16]

These early impressions prompted the young survivor—like several other Armenian women survivors—to dedicate her entire life to poetically redeeming souls on the edge of annihilation as a nurse.[17] Aghavni and two others were selected to receive nursing scholarships for three years at a college in Constantinople. But before devoting her life to that service, she sought to redeem herself first by aggressively pursuing tattoo-removal surgery. "It was something I could not stand anymore. Look in the mirror."[18] Her motivations for tattoo removal began with a self-loathing that she describes eloquently in her memoir:

> As I grew older, however, a new type of suffering impinged itself on my consciousness. It was with a certain sense of dread that I approached my mirror each morning to fix my hair as I watched the blue marks of the tattoo which would mar the beauty of my face forever. Like indelible brands, each day and each moment, to the end of my life, they would remind me of the terrors of my exile days.[19]

Later, in an oral interview in 1986, Aghavni simplified the feelings she was having about her appearance: the tattoos had "given me a sense of depression." She felt stigmatized in nursing school—"they know I had no money and I had my face"—suggesting that her appearance was not only an emotional burden but an impediment to her studies.[20] The dream of tattoo removal became an "obsession" that led her to a life of studying medicine in hopes of one day finding a physician who could remove them so that she could be "cleansed of [her] spots." Removal would allow her to become "a respected woman" and fulfill a desire "to serve my unfortunate sisters."[21]

In Constantinople, Aghavni first approached an Armenian doctor about tattoo removal, but he quickly discouraged her from pursuing it further. She described the exchange:

> The very next day the Doctor sent for me and when I presented myself I was so excited I could not restrain my tears. A kind, patriotic man, he talked long to me, comforted me, and told me not to consider my marks as an insult, but, on the contrary, to regard them as the symbol of our people's martyrdom and he added, "there are thousands like you and they all are our worshipful sisters."[22]

The doctor's view contrasted with her own interpretation, a counternarrative of tattoo that argued tattoos were marks of survival and symbols of the national trauma she had survived. Despite the Armenian doctor's reframing, Aghavni stayed focused on her goal of facial tattoo removal.

Finally, in 1926, Aghavni met Near East Relief medical director Dr. Wilfred Post, a "famous surgeon" from the United States who had been visiting Constantinople, where she had attended nursing school at the Robert College.[23] "I at once called upon him and, with extraordinary boldness, begged him to operate on my face to eliminate the blue marks of the tattoo." Her appeals "impressed the great physician." Reluctant to perform the surgery during what was a short nonsurgical mission, Dr. Post was nevertheless sympathetic and persuaded by her genocide testimony. "I explained to him the atrocities which had been committed by the Turks and toward which the whole civilized world had practically maintained an indifferent stand."[24] He performed the surgery the very next day. Aghavni describes her transformation:

> A few days later when the last traces of the operation had healed, my acquaintances and friends viewed with wonder how the blue marks, like a miracle, had disappeared. For years I had been cut off from the social world, refusing to attend and to appear in public affairs lest I become the object of conspicuous notice because of my blue marks, but now I was just like everybody else, an accepted member of the social family, capable of looking people straight in the eye without being ashamed. I had the same impressions as one blind from his birth and he sees the wonders of nature for the first time.[25]

After the surgery, Aghavni was lifted from feeling "cut off from the social world." Her feelings of alienation were not just about being an outcast but a sincere perception that she was shunned by the Armenian community despite the Armenian doctor's attempt to reframe and accept her. American Red Cross and Near East Relief physician Dr. Mabel Elliot helped facilitate Aghavni's tattoo removal. Like other Americans and Europeans of her time, Dr. Elliot held strong opinions about the tribal tattoos applied to Armenian women, understanding them to be shameful marks of "those who had once been slaves to an Arab master," victims of sexual violence. As women who traversed the same circles in Constantinople, it is quite likely that exposure to Dr. Elliot and her views reinforced the stigma and self-negation Aghavni experienced after the war.[26]

Without explaining the specific tattoo removal procedure, Aghavni describes her post-surgery face as a rebirth through which she saw the world for the very first time. She never described what her tattoos looked like in her testimony, only their effect on her psyche. I searched in vain for a photograph of Aghavni in hopes of identifying her tattoos, but instead I found the reverse imprint that her tattoos had left on her US immigration record that references a distinguishing "scar on forehead & chin."[27] The profound shame she experienced when people looked her directly in the face, she argued, would disappear after tattoo removal. But did it? Was the surgery able to cleanse Aghavni of the stigma from which she so intensely suffered?

After losing thirty family members to genocide and finishing her schooling in Constantinople, Aghavni began a career as a school nurse in Damascus. It was there that a supernatural reunion would take place due to the persistence of a student named Layla. The girl had began asking questions about her nurse's personal life. Aghavni eventually relented and showed the girl a photograph of Shakeh, which she had framed in her office. Suddenly, both nurse and student began to suspect that they were related to one another. Layla called this premonition—a sense or perception that the two of them were related—"the voice of the blood."[28] The Armenian concept *ariune ge ganche* connotes that the blood of those linked by common familial or ethnic bonds can speak or call out to others. It suggests that Armenians can sense or detect the presence of other Armenians in close proximity and that such knowledge can be carried in the blood. The concept was such a revelation that Aghavni used it as the title of her memoir.[29] After seeing her own mother's portrait as a girl, Layla exclaimed: "What I want to tell you is, you are my aunt" (bidi illik inti khalti)!

To which Aghavni replied, "My sister is dead."

The girl returned, "My mother is Armenian."

Aghavni's head began to spin. She had lost every single family member during the deportations and had not held out hope that her baby sister, but a toddler when she last saw her, was still alive.[30]

In the month of Ramadan, Aghavni traveled to reunite with her sister Shakeh in Aleppo. The heart-wrenching reunion was short-lived and never repeated. Shakeh had married a Muslim Arab and "had seven children, one after another," Layla being the oldest. In her oral testimony, she noted that three more children were to follow. Mentioning the number of children Shakeh had birthed for her Muslim Arab husband emphasized her captured maternal labor within the patriarchal Muslim household. Islamized Armenian women's bodies were raw material for the propagation of Muslim children at a time when the Armenian population was marked for extermination and struggling to survive in the aftermath.

Aghavni recalled how, during the genocide, her sister was nearly tattooed by nawar: "To further disfigure her beauty, they prepared to tattoo her face." Unlike Aghavni, Shakeh escaped the needle. She was seized by the police before her beautiful face and European-like "golden hair" could be marred by her captors. From the police station, Shakeh took up residence in Aleppo, where she was married to a Muslim Arab. Despite the reunion, Aghavni never visited Shakeh again because their blood line was severed—they could never be sisters again.

> The joy of having found my sister is suddenly changed to sadness when I contemplate that she is forever lost to our family and our race. I even sin in thinking if it would not have been a thousand times better had all the Shakehs of our deportation shared the fate of those who perished in the desert of Der-ez-Zor and we had been spared the painful sight of their presence before our eyes.[31]

This difficult passage reflects her understanding that Shakeh, though alive, suffered an irreversible social death. Her "relationships, socially and intergenerational" were lost, completing the cycle of cultural genocide that had been set in motion in 1915.[32] For Aghavni, this was something far worse than dying as an Armenian martyr in the Syrian Desert. Perhaps Shakeh was a reminder of Aghavni's own near-social-death experience, reborn first with reabsorption into the Armenian community and later tattoo removal. When asked later in life why some women stayed in their new circumstances, Aghavni offered simply, "I don't know why" (chem keder).[33] It may have been too painful to contemplate how the conversion of Shakeh, the baby sister she had cared for like a mother as an eight-year-old during the deportation, had become a Muslim wife and mother who formed loving bonds that made leaving her Muslim family impossible. Shakeh as Muslim mother was forever dis-membered, severed from the family unit and the Armenian communal body.

Trauma and the destruction of family bonds clearly impacted Aghavni's adult life. She remarked, "I never wanted to get married.... It was psychological."[34] And yet, she did eventually marry an older man named Armen Khandigian at age 44 while living in Boston. He died a year after their marriage, after which she immediately applied for American citizenship. The timing suggests that Aghavni's marriage may have been one of convenience.[35] She married a second time eleven years later in Los Angeles. Her husband, Vahan Guleserian, was twenty-one years her senior. Marrying elderly men later in life not only allowed her to forgo reproduction but gave her a stronger position in the marriage as a younger wife to a frail man who may have relied on her nursing skills. Her caregiving role began on the deportation route and continued during her nursing career in Syria and America.

Aghavni's written and oral testimony is the most intact firsthand account of tattooing that I found in my research. And I found her in a footnote in Ryan Gingeras's *Sorrowful Shores: Violence, Ethnicity, and the End of Empire, 1912–1923* when he referenced the oral testimony Aghavni had given when she was in her seventies, her two interviews are archived at the Zoryan Institute in Toronto, Canada. While digging for more information about her, I found twelve pages of first-person written testimony she had published in 1961 in *The Armenian Review*, a Boston-based Armenian publication.[36] Gingeras's footnote described Aghavni's experience with "a local sheikh [who] bought, tattooed, and raped her."[37] After watching her videotaped testimony, I realized that the footnote characterized Aghavni's experience differently than her own oral and written accounts. She never described the nawar patriarch as abusive, and the Arab nobleman, Hamid Bey (the local sheikh?), is also described generously, as her adoptive father. Nowhere did she claim that either man had raped her.

I find this disjuncture productive. How did two researchers come up with very different understandings of Aghavni's experience? Afterall, Aghavni offered four full hours of oral testimony in Armenian interspersed with Arabic and English. I kept wondering whether the slippage between tattooing and rape was the result of the sheer violence of how she described being tattooed. Her tattooing account is so vivid that in the first draft of this book, I began describing the scene almost subconsciously as a "tattoo-rape." Her arms and feet bound, the tattoo needle serving as a phallus, all while neighbors beat her as she struggled mimics a scene of a gang rape. This was my own psychic leap as an author, and after review, I later deleted the term "tattoo-rape" from my reconstruction of her life. Even if Aghavni hadn't been raped, she certainly had been violated. And whatever forms her violation took, it left her averse to marriage, something she attested to in her own memoir. This imaginative leap is productive because these are not simple memory lapses on the part of researchers. The discursive links between tattoos, rape, and slavery are very real, common, and, importantly, deeply historical. Peeling back these layers to expose what lies under the epidermis reveals the deeper discursive and affective power tattoos continue to wield upon us. And a powerful example of the capacity of tattoos to move us emotionally is the documentary film *Grandma's Tattoos*.

WHAT LIES BENEATH GRANDMA'S TATTOOS?

Documentarian Suzanne Khardalian sparked a lively debate on the subject of embodiment and trauma when her documentary *Grandma's Tattoos* (2011) aired on al-Jazeera. The subject was the filmmaker's own grandmother, Khanum, a tattooed Armenian Genocide survivor who lived out her life in Lebanon after the war. Married with children and grandchildren, Khanum was emotionally distant and hardened as a result of her unspoken experiences. This left the traumatized survivor, in the eyes of her grandchild, not only mysterious but unlovable. "I never liked grandma. She never hugged me. Never kissed me. She never gave me a smile. And when she came down those twenty steps every morning, sat in a corner for long hours, we all felt ill from her suffocating presence."[38] Suzanne's haunted memory of her grandmother continued long after her grandmother's death, inspiring her to investigate her life and her "spooky tattoos."[39] The widely circulated documentary generated a robust discussion of tattoos in the Armenian community and beyond and has since inspired scholars to engage in more in-depth study of the tattoos that continue symbolize collective trauma for the survivor community.[40]

Suzanne is a prolific Armenian filmmaker who unflinchingly explores first-person testimonials of Armenian survivors. Among her thirty films, another, *I Hate Dogs—The Last Survivor* (2005), stands out as a terrifying story of a survivor haunted by his inability to bury his dead father, whose corpse he witnessed being consumed by wild dogs as he lay in hiding, during the mass killings in Dayr al-Zur. Living in Paris decades later, the survivor remains terrified of dogs, reliving his trauma every time he encounters one. Suzanne's work compels the viewer to witness the raw brutality of genocide and evokes a visceral response through the exploration of the corporeality of Armenian suffering. Whether someone is consumed as food by wild dogs or consumed sexually during the mass transfer of women, embodied trauma is centered in her productions.

Both films—*I Hate Dogs* and *Grandma's Tattoos*—are deeply affective and possess Marks's haptic visuality as they fuse together the experiences of embodiment, affect, and memory with the invocation of the senses (smell, taste, and touch).[41] Attentive to these sensory details in her filmmaking, Suzanne remarked in an interview with me, "Because I am very much interested in tactile pictures, the feeling, the touch, the smell—it is always in my mind when I make my films."[42] True to her interest, one of the first images we get of the filmmaker in *Grandma's Tattoos* is a close-up of her sifting through a pile of human bones with her hands at a mass grave site outside Dayr al-Zur.

By the time she began work on *Grandma's Tattoos*, Suzanne's grandmother had passed away. She therefore traveled to Hollywood to meet her great-aunt Lucia, who had been deported with her grandmother and abducted by the same man. The film's voice-over informs viewers that "she too has those spooky tattoos." Suzanne's grandmother and great-aunt had fled Adıyaman to the Euphrates River with their mother, where all three were abducted by the same Kurdish man, who aided their escape across the river in his boat. Suzanne's grandmother was given the Turkish name Khanum, while Lucia's was changed to Neseke. The filmmaker asks if Lucia remembers what her grandmother's real name had been, her Armenian name before the genocide, but her sister doesn't know. Like her ancestral homeland, Khanum's original name had been obliterated during the genocide. The two Islamized sisters lived for five years with their Kurdish abductor, whom

Lucia calls their "master," before being rescued. Exactly how they were rescued is not explained in the film.

When asked specifically about her tattoos (figure 20), Lucia brings her hands up near her face, noting, "Children used to have them done and we had them done too, my sister and I. It's a cross—I don't know."[43]

Suzanne asks, "What is written on your hands?" (inch krver e hos orinag).

Lucia, however, asserts, "It is a cross, Armenian [hos khatch e, haygagan]. This is a comb [sandr e]." Lucia emphasizes the Armenianness of her cross, placing *Armenian* at the end of the sentence as a punctuation mark. She interprets more of her tattoos, noting that "their flag" was tattooed on another finger (hos irentz troshagn e).

Suzanne follows up on Lucia's comment, asking whether it is "their flag," the star and sickle of the Ottoman flag, that is. Lucia concurs.

When Suzanne asks, "Who made the tattoos?" Lucia replies, "I don't really know. Children did them. Kids ten or eleven years old. It was we who chose to have them done."[44] Lucia does not appear to be ashamed of her hand tattoos. Her niece interjects when Lucia exercises her own interpretation of her tattoos, proclaiming that she chose to have them done as a child.[45] Suzanne remarks that Khanum, her grandmother, often wore gloves to conceal her tattoos, while Lucia does not.[46]

Lucia's explanation is dismissed by the filmmaker. Suzanne remarks in a voice-over, "I do not believe Lucia. What she is telling me doesn't make sense. An Ar-

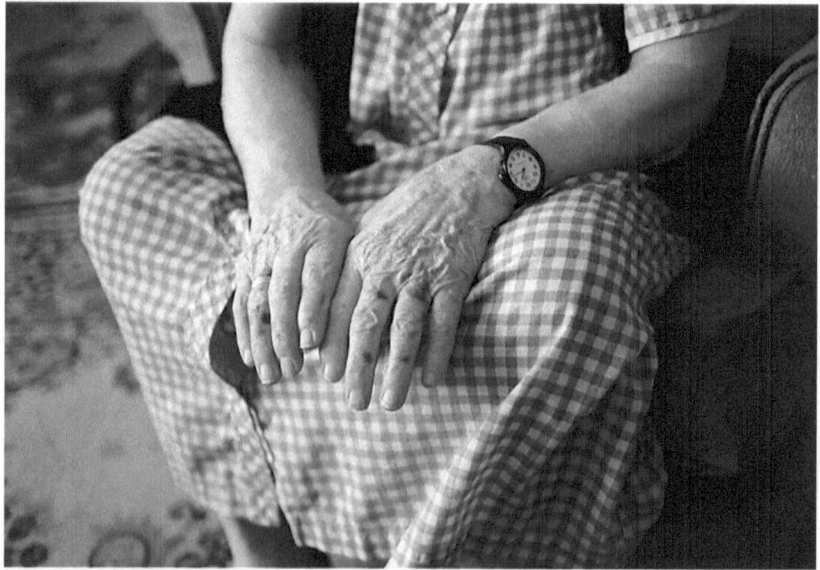

FIGURE 20   *Lucia's tattooed hands while she delivers her testimony. Source:* Grandma's Tattoos *(2011). Reproduced with permission of Suzanne Khardalian.*

menian girl would never willingly tattoo her hands and face with Turkish signs." Then, in a surprising turn, Suzanne offers her own interpretation of her aunt's hands, noting the presence of "a crescent moon" and "a Turkish flag," effacing national symbols that branded her great-aunt a Turk.

Lucia, however, says again that the tattoo on her hand is "an Armenian cross," effectively asserting her interpretation of the signs on her hands. The interview ends in frustration with Lucia saying, "It's enough to say the children did it. Let's leave it at that!" Suzanne understands this frustration to be her aunt hiding painful memories of abuse, but the scene is far more ambivalent.

When Suzanne returns the following day, Lucia is visibly angry and refuses to talk to her. We are left, much like the filmmaker, with more questions than answers about the tattoos and their purpose. The once talkative Aunt Lucia sits in silence. Is she traumatized by her tattoos and the memory of the Armenian Genocide, or is she angry for having her own explanation for her tattoos dismissed by the documentarian, a relative that she appears to barely know? Is Lucia's silence due to the recounting of the traumatic memory of her tattoos and abduction by her Kurdish "master"? We will never know. But the viewer is led to believe that Lucia is silent because the conversation may have revived her genocidal trauma. The viewer is led toward the conclusion the filmmaker had from the outset: the tattoos are shameful marks of sexual violence and slavery. As marks of Turkishness, the women who bear tattoos are the physical embodiment of forcible conversion to Islam.

The connection between tattoos and sexual violation is brought home in a scene when the filmmaker's mother transmits the prosthetic memory of the grandmother's sexual abuse to Suzanne. The culprit was the man who rescued Khanum's mother and children on the shore of the Euphrates. Lucia described the man as rescuing them "like in a dream," paddling them to safety on his boat; Khanum, however, had a very different memory. She was forced to sit on the man's lap during the journey across the river. She soon complained to her mother of feeling something hard beneath her: "The man is sticking something hard in my backside." Khanum, we learn, was molested during the river passage. Khanum's mother quickly took her daughter's hand to rescue her from molestation. At this point Suzanne has a revelation about the nature of her grandmother's trauma, concluding that her deep state of unhappiness was due to sexual abuse by her Kurdish (also referred to as Turkish) master. From there, the film concludes that her grandmother was raped, which leaves the filmmaker feeling "humiliated." This powerful turn in the documentary transfers a prosthetic memory, the humiliation of sexual assault, from the grandmother to a second-generation descendant.[47]

Specific memories of Khanum's sexual abuse quickly lead to speculation about a lifetime of sexual abuse and, shockingly, a previous life as a prostitute for which no support is provided in the film. Prostitution was certainly a reality for many women survivors who, in their desperation, turned to it to survive during and after the war. Khardalian's voice-over narrates, "The blue tattoos on her face and hands disgusted me. Devilish signs that came from a dark world. As a child I never dared to ask about her tattoos. Only now I realize what these strange marks meant. Only now do I know that they were the marks of violence and slavery."[48] For Suzanne, the tattoos are intimately linked with enslavement, producing a visceral affective response: disgust. The filmmaker is not alone; the triangulation of rape, humiliation, and prostitution in *Grandma's Tattoos* is dizzying yet illustrative of a long history of association of tattoos with crime and sexual deviancy, exposing why tattoos provoke, historically, such powerful emotions in us.

As a scholar, I find myself frustrated by the filmmaker's lack of engaged listening to her great-aunt's survivor account, yet to me there is no doubt that the filmmaker is clearly traumatized as she experiences the shameful prosthetic memory of her own grandmother's sexual assault.[49] Suzanne, like so many—and I include myself—is grappling with the fragments of the past and trying to make sense of them to achieve some understanding of what our grandmothers experienced. Yet, resolution is hard to achieve amid the fragmentary evidence that our grandmothers left behind. The scenes I have analyzed productively raise many questions for me about the power and spectrality of tattoos with the survivor community. The filmmaker is obsessed with the tattoos—as so many of us are. Even the Bedouin she meets along the Euphrates jokingly offered to give her a tattoo because she asked so many questions about them during a visit captured on screen. This brilliant moment of levity gestures back to the insatiable desire that tattoos can produce within us. It is our desire to know what they are communicating within the wreckage genocide has left behind.

The inked skin of Armenian women, however, is a complex, ambiguous, and even ambivalent site of individual, collective, and prosthetic memory of a genocide that used sexual violence as its primary weapon. With regard to the tattoos themselves, *Grandma's Tattoos* illustrates well how the symbols on inked skin are *empty signifiers* through which multiple discourses and contradictory interpretations are filtered. Devoid of an actual referent, tattooed symbols produce a variety of affective responses, moving between awe, pity, disgust, shame, tribal kinship, and desire.[50] They do so because, following Judith Butler's theorization of speech, the tattooed body communicates as speech and can communicate that which it does not intend. Butler explains, "The utterance performs meanings that are not precisely the ones that are stated or, indeed, capable of being stated at all."[51] In this sense, the communicative quality of tattoos is uncontrollable and delinked from their sovereign subject. I suggest that the loquaciousness of tattoos can help us understand how they can have a signification in one context that is very different from another. The repetition of speech can produce excessive resignification, the endless process of revision that can overdetermine meaning. This makes a return to the original context of Mesopotamian and Anatolian tribal tattoos all the more necessary. In the digital age tattoos are circulated more rapidly, which multiplies the targeted audience and amplifies dominant commonsense interpretations of tattoos that I seek to unsettle.

But there are reasons why tattoos captivate us beyond the slipperiness of their meaning. Recalling the original meaning of the word *trauma* in Greek, tattoos are actual wounds on the surface of the skin. In a traditional tribal tattoo application, a design is pricked with a needle then saturated with ink. Tattoos are, then, a representation of the physical and psychological wounds of our grandmothers. According to physician and trauma scholar Gabor Maté, trauma isn't only about an event. "Trauma is not what happens to you but what happens *inside you*."[52] That the tribal tattoos bore by Armenian women have come to symbolize this psychic trauma is not incidental. Our responses to them affirm how the concepts of trauma and wounding are inextricably linked to one another. When Suzanne explains her grandmother's sexual abuse to her sisters in an emotionally stirring scene, the tattoos are described as "a permanent reminder" of abuse. "It's like having an accident that scarred your face"—you will wake up to that reminder, that scar every day. The tattoos corrupted Khanum both physically and emotionally to the extent that her grandchildren confess that not only was she unloving but they too were unkind toward her. The tattoos and the underlying trauma they represented made her unlovable—an emotion Khanum likely felt as a trauma survivor. The tattoos and what they represent to the filmmaker, sexual abuse, made her feel "humiliated," a synonym for shame. The tribal tattoos that Armenian survivors bore have, therefore, come to represent collectivized national shame, a national wound.

For Armenians, the effects of social death and the affect of national shame are expressed by not only victims and their descendants but also those who observed their pain. A humanitarian pamphlet from 1926 asks readers: "What will her relations say when they see the photos of that poor tattooed woman, marked for life?"[53] The question suggests that witnesses play a role in creating the shame felt by women survivors and, by extension, the survivor community. Shame was frequently cited by women who, when reabsorbed into the Armenian community, felt stigmatized for their experience living among Muslims and bearing marks of assimilation on their skin. After the war, a humanitarian worker in Aleppo sensed that two tattooed women in Aleppo were experiencing shame in a rescue shelter. She wrote: "There was something about those two, as if they were ashamed. But how can it be any fault of their own to have been dragged from their loved ones and into the hands of violators. This injustice cries to heaven. God have mercy on those who are still prisoners of Islam."[54] One wonders if the humanitarian worker was sensing a "turning away" from her gaze.

Sara Ahmed has argued that public declarations of shame—in this case the national guilt expressed by Australian politicians for the destruction of aboriginal peoples and their cultures—can "bring 'the nation' into existence as a felt community."[55] Ahmed reminds us that the linguistic root of the word *shame* in the Indo-European tradition is "to turn away" from those who witness the shame. It is difficult for the person feeling shame to meet the eye of the witness because the affect of shame is not only turning away but makes the shamed "burn up with the negation that is self-perceived (self-negation)."[56] The affects of shame and social death, then, are ultimately the self-negation and abjection that so many forcibly assimilated Armenians, especially tattooed women, describe experiencing. For this reason, it is necessary to turn our attention to those Western observers who gazed upon tattooed Armenian women in order to better understand the ideological views of tattoos they brought with them to the war-torn Near East.

REMNANT 6

Statement of Miss Eliza Shahinian before the Committee on Immigration and Naturalization, House of Representatives, Washington, DC, in December 1922[1]

Miss Shahinian. "Do you promise you will be a Musulman?" I said: "Never mind. Since my parents have died upon the front of Christianity I am perfectly willing to die. But not to be a Mohamedan." And they said to each other, "Let us make picture on her face. Let her be no different. Everybody who sees her does not make a difference with our ladies." And I said: "No; let me die but not to do such things upon me." And they have beaten me awfully. So I was sick that time and they have done this to me that time I was unconscious.
Mr. Baker. That is, they put those marks on your face when you were unconscious?
Miss Shahinian. Yes.
Mr. Baker. Did they do it with the other young ladies the same?
Miss Shahinian. Yes; there were six more young ladies there and they have done worse to them than to me; those places on the face, on the lips, all black.
Mr. Vaile. Now, what is the purpose of putting those marks on these girls?
Miss Shahinian. So that there shall be no difference, Christian or Mohammedan. They do not know that I am a Christian or a Mohammedan because they are Mohammedan and they have the custom, their custom to do this upon the Mohammedan.
Mr. Vaile. All Mohammedan women wear the same marks?
Miss Shahinian. Yes.
Mr. Kalaidjian.[2] Each chief has his own mark put on his wives or concubines.
Mr. Vaile. That is what I was getting at. She has the brand of her particular chief?
Mr. Kalaidjian. Yes, that is it.
Mr. Baker. That will not come off, will it?
Miss Shahinian. I don't know if it will ever come off or not.
Mr. Kalaidjian. No; it is in the blood.
Mr. Vaile. Put in with a needle?
Mr. Kalaidjian. Yes.

Mr. Baker. How early do they commence to mark young ladies and Mohammedan girls?

Miss Shahinian. As soon as she is born, they may do that thing.

Mr. Baker. When she is a little baby?

Miss Shahinian. Yes.

CHAPTER EIGHT

WOUNDED WHITENESS
Branded Captives from the Old West to the Ottoman East

Tattooing—especially of female bodies—was understood as a counter-civilizational aberration that threatened the integrity and fidelity of the idealized white body in Western societies. *Tatau*, a word of Samoan origin, entered English vocabulary through colonial contact; the term captures the sounds of the tapping technique used with Polynesian tattoo instruments.[1] Though some Victorians took a liking to tattoos, dominant discourse affirmed that tattoos were synonymous with racial otherness and suggestive of miscegenation and acculturation.[2] The liminality presented by the tattoo, lodged both in and onto the skin as signs of potential transculturation, meant that tattooed subjects who sought reintegration needed narratives that stabilized their identity.[3] Racial ambiguities were resolved literally with stories of captivity and redemption or displayed with retouched photographs that would appeal to consumers of humanitarian mass media to resolve the racial dissonance that tattoos represented.

In her recent study of the League of Nations' anti-trafficking regime, Liat Kozma argues that mobilization to save white women from global prostitution was motivated by colonial fears of miscegenation between white women and native populations.[4] Lobbying efforts to stamp out "white slavery" centered on the perception that prostitution had been internationalized. League of Nations scholar Jeanne Morefield traces the relationship between the discourse of white slavery, "a misnomer that obscured the sexual abuse of women of colour," and "familial internationalism" in the emergence of a newly framed discussion of the "traffic in women in children" in 1921.[5] Transnational feminist activists in the 1920s sought to eliminate regulated prostitution by connecting it the issue to abolitionism and the exploitation of women globally.

Karen Jeppe's recovery work in Aleppo linked concerns about white slavery rooted in nineteenth-century fears of miscegenation to the experiences of tattooed Armenian women in the Ottoman Empire. Jeppe's testimony on the conditions of Armenian women in Muslim households was frequently transmitted to the league and incorporated into official reports and documents. Her dispatches and photographs of tattooed women were frequently summarized and reproduced—sometimes with touch-ups to emphasize and darken the tattoos—in popular humanitarian newsletters. These images linked the league's global mission to halt the enslavement, forced marriage, and sexual abuse to the ordeal of Armenian women and children. The racialization of tattoos in popular discourse fed assumptions that Armenian women were racially and morally tainted by their period of captivity with Muslim men. Some of the stories peddled in popular humanitarian leaflets and newsletters resembled captivity narratives of white women held captive by indigenous peoples of the American West. The sensationalism of the accounts sometimes pushed the rhetoric too far, and it came to a head in 1926 when two major figures in postwar Middle East, Karen Jeppe and Turkish feminist Halide Edib, debated the subject of tattooed Armenian women in the press.

ON CAPTIVITY NARRATIVES AND TATTOOED LADIES

A half century before the Armenian Genocide, tattooed American captive Olive Oatman set a precedent for how tattooed women's experiences would be shared as tales of colonial contact and captivity. In 1850, the Oatman family joined fellow Mormon settlers in a caravan of covered wagons headed from Illinois westward to the Colorado River in what is today California. On February 18, 1851, while struggling on treacherous terrain, other wagons turned away, but the Oatmans carried on only to be attacked by the Yavapai-Apache in what is present-day Arizona. The parents and four siblings were murdered. Thirteen-year-old Olive and her sister Mary Ann, age seven, were abducted and later traded to the Mohave, who gave the two girls distinctive geometric Mohave facial tattoos that later brought surviving Olive to fame as the first white woman tattooed by "savages."

The Oatman story was framed to meet societal expectations by Methodist cleric and ghostwriter Royal B. Stratton, who "constructed—indeed, created—their story" in a book titled *Captivity of the Oatman Girls* (1857).[6] The book, written as a first-person narrative in Olive's voice, described the scene of the girls' absorption into a Mohave community. Olive and Mary Ann, a sickly child who did not survive captivity, were given tattoos at a time they were plotting to escape. Though the girls assured the community that they had no intention to flee, the wife of the tribal chief summoned the girls outdoors, where tribal "physicians" applied "ugly marks" on their faces and arms.[7] Acknowledging a language barrier during her early days with the Mohave, Olive narrates through the biographer,

"They knew why we objected to it; that we expected to return to whites, and we would be ashamed of it then; but that it was their resolution we should never return, and that as we belonged to them we should wear their 'Ki-e-chook' [chin tattoo]."[8] The adoptive/abductor community explained that the purpose of marking the girls was so that other tribes would know to whom they belonged if they found themselves in foreign territory. Olive's ghostwritten biography claims that the tattoos were how the Mohave "marked all their own captives," implying that the tattoos had a relationship with slavery.[9] Despite Stratton's characterization, the tattooed girls did not hold slave status among the Mohave; instead, they were formally adopted into the family of the tribal chief and treated well, a correction that Olive made only after the publication of her memoir.

There was no space in the civilizational narrative and redemptive, biblical tone of the autobiography for Olive to be open about the complexity of her relationship with her adoptive Mohave family. The overt condemnation of Indians as "savages" and invocation of Christianity affirmed an eagerness to rejoin white society and to assuage fears of the transculturation present on her very skin. But Olive's life among the Mohave was complicated, evidenced by the warmness expressed toward the Mohave tribal chief Irataba, with whom she was reunited during a diplomatic mission in New York. At the reunion, Olive shook his left hand, an honorable greeting among the Mohave signifying the sacred oath of friendship, and spoke to him in his own native language.[10]

Outside the official published account, there were rumors that Olive was married to the chief's son and bore him two little boys who were abandoned upon her escape.[11] In these racially scandalous accounts, a close friend described Olive upon rescue as looking like a "frightened tattooed creature, who was more savage than civilized and who sought at every opportunity to flee back to her Indian husband and children."[12] Another account of her rescue describes signs of transculturation in Olive's struggle to speak English and in her woven bark skirt, the form of dress she and her sister wore with the chest exposed, according to custom.[13] But signs of acculturation were most evident on Olive's skin: "So completely was she disguised by long exposure to the sun, by paint, tattooing and costume that he could not believe she was a white woman. When he [rescuer Henry Grinnell] spoke to her, she made no answer, but cried and kept her face covered." In fact, Olive is described as covering her face, a gesture of shame in response to the fear, repulsion, and disgust expressed by her rescuers.[14]

Social stigma surrounding tattoos and time spent with racial others demanded that, in order to be accepted back into white society, Olive needed to present herself as unwavering in her loyalty to her white race and Christian faith. Within the broader context of nineteenth-century American settler colonialism, providential Protestantism and whiteness were intertwined pillars of American national identity—Olive did eventually leave Mormonism for mainstream Protestantism.[15]

Renarrativizing her experience was necessary because the popular stories about tattooed captives circulated in American freak shows suggested "that people of color could transform whites into people of color—ethnically and decoratively, as a means of exploitation and degradation."[16] After being ransomed and delivered back to white society, Olive signaled that despite her tattoos, she had not assimilated or "gone native."

Olive's tattoos set her apart from other formerly captive white women in the American West whose time among Indigenous peoples could not be observed easily upon their skin. Tattoos were not only marks of appropriation; they were understood to be visual evidence of the permeability of racial and civilizational boundaries, alluding to unthinkable transculturation between whites and non-whites.[17] Audiences could not only purchase Olive's memoir, republished in multiple editions, but they could witness the embodied evidence of captivity, the "indelible evidence of the scenes she has undergone," not only on her face but a tribal tattoo on her arm that was never photographed (figure 21). For seven years of performances after the publication of her memoir, for a fee, white audiences could see firsthand her tattooed skin.[18] Within the context of colonial spectacle and racial boundaries, such permeability between the races was often met with affective disgust. Affirming Mary Russo's argument that the grotesque body—in this case, the tattooed woman—presented an "open, protruding, irregular, secreting, multiple, and changing" boundary that upset the distinctions between male/female, human/animal, and, importantly, white/non-white. This is best illustrated by an unsettled spectator who described Olive as "an ambiguous being who is considered simultaneously and compulsively fascinating and repulsive, enticing and sickening."[19]

In her effort to decolonize the history of tribal tattoos, tattoo scholar and biographer Margot Mifflin compellingly challenges Olive's own characterization of her facial tattoo as a slave marking. In a careful study of Mohave tattoo aesthetics, Mifflin argues that the former captive's motif was the same one commonly worn by Mohave women: "The Mohaves did not tattoo their captives; they tattooed their own."[20] Like tribal tattooing in Mesopotamia, Mohave tattoos within their original context were blessings that served to protect and ensure passage to "the land of the dead" where the Mohave would commune with their ancestors, whereas to white settler colonists, a tattoo on a white woman "was every bit as damning, physically and culturally, as rape and miscegenation."[21]

Olive's story had several afterlives. The spectacular horror of tattooed white women was appropriated and exceeded by tattooed lady performers at various carnival and museum attractions in the United States and Europe. By the late nineteenth century, tattooed bodies were a common feature of sideshows but gained more mainstream notice at the 1901 World's Fair in Buffalo, where tattoos were presented as marks of atavism to viewing publics, ocular evidence of dominant

FIGURE 21 *Olive Oatman wearing a dress with tribal tattoos embroidered on her sleeves like the one on her arm. Her tattoo was available for private viewings at her public speaking engagements. Source: National Portrait Gallery, Smithsonian Institute.*

racial theories informed by social Darwinism.[22] Performances were accompanied by stories of the abduction, maiming, and rape of white Christian women by colonized peoples, affirming an understanding of tattoos as the forcible brand of the savage on pure, white bodies. Performances by "former captives" were not restricted to women; in his popular sideshow act in the 1870s, Captain Costentenus, "the Greek Albanian," described a harrowing tale of being tied down and forcibly tattooed from head to toe allegedly on the orders of the King of Chinese Tartary.[23] The scandalous spectacle of tattooed captives sold well at live shows, yet conformed with the cultural scripts of the late nineteenth century by framing tattoos, especially facial tattoos, as enacted against one's will—the only terms the public could accept. The monstrous, the beautiful, and their hybrid "monster beauty" were displayed before the public to evoke a range of emotions in the spectator—fear, adoration, and disgust. Freak shows also served a larger social purpose by producing disidentification with the freak performer and feelings of unity among spectators. Displays of extraordinary bodies surged at a time when colonial contact blurred racial and class boundaries between European colonizers and the peoples of the Global South.[24]

WHITE SKIN, INKED MASKS: RACE AND TATTOOED ARMENIAN WOMEN

Rebecca Jinks has argued that the general disposition of humanitarians toward tattoo-bearing Armenian women was one of disidentification.[25] Perhaps tattooed women and girls made some people recoil with affective disgust so much that they refrained from photographing them, as Jinks suggests, which may explain why photographs of tattooed women are largely absent from archives of major humanitarian and missionary workers. Yet, scholarship on sideshows and freakery disagree; some argue that the dominant societal impulse in both Europe and the United States was indeed to photograph, to stare at displayed freaks and extraordinary bodies. Kevin Rozario has shown that humanitarianism became a mass phenomenon only when donors marketed these images of humanitarian disaster as entertainment, fulfilling the desire to consume "delicious horrors."[26] As a result, turn-of-the-century humanitarians relied on accounts that would produce a conflicting set of emotions—compassion, sympathy, and revulsion and disgust—while carefully balancing accounts so as not to offer the "cheap thrills" found in pulp publications.[27] Arguably, these publications served as conveniently portable freak shows that could be consumed in the privacy of the home. Tattooed Armenian women and girls were consistently framed in these publications as recuperable humanitarian subjects so long as the scripts emphasized the tattoos as brands of slavery applied to unwilling white victims.

Taking cues from American captivity narratives, the English tabloid *The Slave Market News* shared the stories of captive Armenian women from 1924 to 1936. In 1926, the newsletter claimed that thirty thousand Armenian women were being "kept back by the Turk to satisfy his lust. These girls are practically Christian slaves," auctioned off in on auction blocks "like so many head of cattle to be taken away to the Harems of their corrupt purchasers."[28] *The Slave Market News* blended these stories with actual reports and images of Armenian victims that visually illustrate ongoing anxieties about white slavery and fears of transculturation among its readers using the same tropes as its American Christian counterparts.

Though the tone of *The Slave Market News* was outrageous, the periodical was able to convince many readers of its claims by citing reputable authorities in the form of politicians and humanitarian workers.[29] In Aleppo, Karen Jeppe and her associates sent dispatches and letters to the newsletter in order to elicit donations to support her underfunded mission. Large fundraising initiatives, such as the London-based Lord Mayor's Fund for Armenia, resulted in an outpouring of reader responses directly to Jeppe in Aleppo, thereby enhancing everyday engagement of the public as armchair humanitarians. Publishing the stories of individual victims persuaded readers to donate to fundraising campaigns or, as in one case, sell their jewelry to help liberate Armenians suffering in bondage.[30]

One story, under the headline "Slave Branding in the Twentieth Century," included photographs of two tattooed Armenian girls from Jeppe's collection, discursively linking tattooing to white slavery. The writer explained that the "poor faces" of the girls were "scarred for life." One abducted girl was held in a Muslim home along the Euphrates River, while another was passed between men and ended up in a "bad house in Baghdad," a euphemism for a brothel. Both girls ended up in the care of Jeppe, but the reader was left with a hard-hitting final message emphasizing the unnatural inversion of civilizational order: "If an Englishman dares to brand a dog like this the S.P.C.A. would probably prosecute him."[31]

The Slave Market News was not alone in linking tattoos to branding and slavery. Church newsletters in the United States published similar accounts, interpreting tribal tattoos as a variant of cattle branding or slave branding. One Baptist activist explained, "Many of those rescued had been branded with hideous tattoo marks indicating Moslem ownership, much the same as American ranchmen brand their cattle."[32] *The Slave Market News* used similarly incendiary rhetoric in 1924 when it claimed that "white children are bought and sold at 1 pound each," tapping into racial outrage among European audiences as they imagined white bodies exchanged like livestock.

> Large numbers of these Christian slaves have been found branded by tattoo marks.... It is foul inhumanity to enslave the helpless but it is the torture of hell to brand with tattoo marks the fair and innocent faces of white girls with their Moslem owner's mark. Cattle are branded in England lest they should stray and escape but in Asia Minor they brand white flesh and blood for the same reason.... WE CONSIDER THE FACT THAT WHITE WOMEN AND CHILDREN ARE BRANDED, TORTURED, OUTRAGED, ENSLAVED, BOUGHT AND SOLD IN THE LANDS WHERE CHRISTIANITY FIRST TOOK ROOT TO BE THE SCANDAL OF THE CENTURY AND A CRIME AGAINST THE CIVILISATION OF THE AGE.[33]

Atavistic marks branded white Christian bodies and inverted the perceived natural order among races, threatening the hierarchical order upon which Western civilization stood.

The Slave Market News's most powerful storytelling tool was Jeppe's photographs that invited audiences to fill in the gaps with their imaginations. Letters from readers asked that they publish more photographs. One contributor noted how, to their shock and horror, "Large numbers [of Armenian women] have been found branded by indelible tattoo marks, their fair white faces disfigured for life."[34] Accounts emphasized the dejection of survivors as their experience left them indifferent about life. "They have forgotten how to eat; when one offers them bread they throw it aside with indifference," having lost the will to live. "Dying anyhow" from broken hearts and illness, their owners permitted the slaves to "come home," affirming that tattooed women and girls were corrupted, discarded flesh.[35] Heartbreaking stories produced the desired affective response in the general secretary of the Friends of Armenia, who remarked that reading about the suffering these women endured "makes my flesh creep."[36]

The Slave Market News portrayed the recovery of Armenian women and girls in racial terms in order to amplify the larger message that rehabilitation could be effective in restoring racial boundaries unsettled during captivity. One exemplary story, "Rescued from Slavery," a story harvested from a Jeppe dispatch, told the story a twenty-two-year-old, identified only the initials D. S. to protect her privacy. Deported into the desert and suffering from starvation and thirst, the girl threw herself into water, in an attempt to end her life. She was discovered by an Arab girl who rescued her, but after staying with the poor family for a year or two, she was sold for twenty pounds to a "rich Sheik," who kept her in his household for thirteen years. Significantly, the narrative describes the rescued woman as being short and lighter-skinned than other Armenians, a detail that would surely enhance the reader's outrage. During her absorption into an Arab Muslim home, "she was tattooed, not only on her forehead, nose and chin, but the branding was put on the whole of her arms and hands, so marring every bit of good looks which she might possess."[37] When arrangements were made for her to marry, she ran away with the help of a fellow Armenian, eventually finding her way to Jeppe's Rescue Home. The account shifts to speculate on the woman's fate had she had stayed with the shaykh: "She would have been taken to a house where she would have been condemned to a worse slavery than before." By the end of the essay, D. S. is physically and emotionally transformed at Jeppe's Rescue Home in Aleppo. "Her mind has been awakened since she arrived in the Hostel, and from a sad down-trodden poor-looking Bedouin girl, she has developed into a bright cheerful-looking Armenian girl, responsive to kindness and eager for any little notice."[38] This vivid description of recuperation, even within a newsletter of dubious credibility, demonstrates how tattooed Armenian women were hardly "racial and cultural pariahs" in the eyes of relief workers but viewed as deserving, recuperable subjects of humanitarianism.[39]

"Slavery of White Children in the Near East" by A. Lancaster Smith illustrates well how *The Slave Market News* invoked Armenian whiteness at a time when Armenians were perceived as racially ambiguous or sometimes Asiatic in the West. This worked to affirm their deservingness as humanitarian subjects by eliciting strong empathic responses in its readership.[40] A provocative image of a young tattooed girl was captioned: "These two rescued white children are representative of thousands at present enslaved—the boy is not 'branded'—but the girl's face is tattooed with the Moslem owner's mark."[41] Already tattooed at the young age of ten years old, Mariam arrived at Jeppe's Aleppo Rescue Home in 1924. Orphaned before the genocide, Mariam was cared by her elderly grandmother in Kilis, but during the deportations, her grandmother gave her to a group of nawar encamped in Aleppo to save her life.

> Mariam was living for seven years with the Gypsy [nawar] wife under a tent. However, it happened that the Gypsies camped in Aleppo. An Armenian girl saw her on the fountain carrying water for sale. She recognized her as an Armenian girl, took a carriage and brought her right away to our Rescue Home. We also found out that she is Armenian so we admitted her to our Neutral House. As far as we know, she has no relatives.[42]

Mariam's chin tattoo is barely visible the photograph pasted to her intake record and her tattoos remain unmentioned in the accompanying biographical sketch. Yet the photograph in *The Slave Market News* emphasized this feature by darkening her tattoos using a retouching technique. The image was featured on a postcard and included in a supplement (figure 22) to encourage consumers of humanitarianism to increase circulation of the image. However, the retouching of Mariam's facial tattoos was so extreme that it left some people incredulous that her tattoos were real at all.

Responding to an inquiry about "alleged branding" of Armenian women and children by Turks published in *The Slave Market News,* British diplomat George William Rendel dismissed the allegation in a memorandum on March 10, 1925, concluding "the pamphlet was obviously of no importance and its evidence of no value."[43] However, the diplomat conceded that the allegations could also not be entirely denied. Within archived letters of correspondence were inquiries from humanitarians, the bishop of London, and British statesmen, who having read the pamphlet, expressed concern for the continued captivity of tattooed Armenian women and children.[44] The photograph in question appears to have been that of Mariam since the memo claimed the tattoos "appeared to have been drawn in on the negatives."[45] By highlighting the tattoos with retouching, Mariam's photograph had the unintended effect of attracting criticism, yet its emphasis on whiteness further activated a process that Keith Watenpaugh has called "unstrangering." For humanitarians, he argues, it was "less about assisting those who are strange and different, and more about helping those found to be knowable, similar, and deserving" in order to produce sentiments of solidarity.[46] The case of Mariam's

FIGURE 22 *This retouched photograph of Mariam, whose "face is tattooed with the Moslem owner's mark," standing beside another child, was first published in* The Slave Market News *in December 1924 and later as a printed postcard included in a 1926 supplement. Source: 12/43565/4631, United Nations Archives at Geneva.*

retouched tattoos, however, illustrates how rhetorical excess could sometimes fail to produce desired empathy.

By contrast, an image of a rescued Armenian girl was retouched in yet another way to erase indelible tattoo markings from her face. The unnamed girl who appeared on the cover of *The Aftermath* (1919), a YMCA booklet, allegedly bore scabbed patches that were the result of freshly made tribal tattoos upon arrival in Aleppo. "The girl escaped the life of the harem by masquerading as a boy—fighting as a soldier and working as a boy-servant."[47] Another image of the girl, this time wearing a pristine white dress, could be found inside the booklet. The photographs were reproduced in 1920 in *The Blue Triangle News* side by side as before-and-after portraits that proved the effectiveness of relief work detailed in the booklet. Immediately observable is the photographer's choice to resolve the issue of her tattoos, a suggestion of miscegenation, by removing them through the power of retouching (figure 23). This produced the desired catharsis among donors. The before-and-after images stood by themselves, decontextualized. The magic of makeup and photo retouching transformed the rescued girl, though upon closer examination, the photograph, now archived at Getty Images, shows there was likely permanent damage to her skin.[48]

The visual evidence of humanitarian photography is found not only in the reparation of the girl's skin with photographic retouching but in a spectacular

FIGURE 23 *A "before" image of this rescued tattooed Armenian girl in Aleppo was published on the front cover of* The Aftermath *(1919), a YWCA booklet. Her face was covered with dark, scabbed lesions from recent tattooing, and she wore male clothing and headress. The "after" portrait represents a transformed girl in a pristine white dress, and her tattoos have been removed by retouching the photograph. Source: Reproduced with permission of Getty Images.*

sartorial transformation. In the before photograph, the girl appeared very much like a boy with her male tribal dress, which was possibly staged. We learn that she had been working as a boy during her escape. This gender inversion may have been necessary for survival during her rescue due to the strict social regulations on women's movement. Men dressed as women and women as men to escape harrowing scenarios of mass violence—but her gender-bending dress may not have needed explaining to humanitarian audiences, who may have expected the blurring of societal norms after observing the outright civilizational transgression of a facial tattoo.[49] But the facial tattoo stands in stark contrast to the clothing she wears—her feminine tattoos would have certainly blown her masculine disguise. The former captive is transformed by a feminine white dress she dons in the after photo. The dress was certainly a luxury item in an environment where clothing was in short supply. It was likely borrowed since an archived group photograph of ten rescued girls who stayed with her at the YWCA shows the rescued girls wearing simple dresses, and some were not even wearing shoes.[50] The girl's humanitarian makeover is so transformative that I cannot identify her within the larger group photograph of tattooed rescued girls (figure 24), which is part of the same series of archived photographs taken in the YWCA shelter in 1919. The sensational visual and textual representations of recovered Armenian women and girls published in humanitarian newsletters and the press did not go unnoticed by Turks.

FIGURE 24   *Tattooed rescued girls at the YWCA in 1919. Two of these girls were singled out for individual portraits (see figures 23 and 31). Source: Reproduced with permission of Getty Images.*

DEBATING TATTOOS: KAREN JEPPE'S AND HALIDE EDIB'S DEBATE OF 1926

"It seems incredible that such things should have happened to white flesh and blood." opined a story about rescued women and girls titled "Branding by Tattooing" published in *The Slave Market News* pamphlet. Though her dispatches often contained more context and nuance, Jeppe confirmed the writer's view that tattoos were marks of imprisonment and slavery: "It is a perfect torture, inflicted with bundles of needles and a sort of fluidum that enters the blood, and for that reason is almost impossible to efface."[51] When asked if the tattoo marks could be removed, Jeppe responded that it was a painful and cost-prohibitive procedure for the poorer classes. For that reason, underprivileged girls would always have to bear tattoos and, she claimed, tattoo-bearing girls "will always be in danger of being recaptured" by Muslims. Jeppe offered a powerful comparison to her English readers: "The marking was mainly done to make running away more difficult, as the girl would be easily recognized as if she were a convict in prison clothes, walking down the streets of an English town."[52]

Jeppe's comparison of tattoos to prison uniforms—and her warning that tattoos subjected rescued women to the threat of recapture—starkly contrasts with her reports that the tribal tattoos Armenian women bore were declarations of membership to Kurdish and Arab communities.[53] The racialization effect of tattoos on Armenians as well as the implicit discourse of white slavery in Jeppe's remarks published in *The Slave Market News* tended to flatten the racial, ethnic, and national distinctions that Jeppe certainly understood as a person who had lived half her life in the region. The rhetorical excess of Jeppe and her associates in Europe provided fodder for critics, among them Turkish nationalist and feminist Halide Edib, who struck back in the press.

In a letter to *The Manchester Guardian* on January 13, 1926, Edib forcefully defended Turks against charges launched by a reader named "Churchman," a supporter of Jeppe who attacked Edib in the press after he learned that the Turkish intellectual had publicly denied reports that Armenian women were still held captive in Muslim homes.[54] In his letter, Churchman appealed to readers to donate to Jeppe's recovery efforts, noting that an £8 contribution was all it took to save an Armenian girl.

Living in forced exile after Mustafa Kemal began repressing his political opponents, including fellow revolutionaries, Edib was exposed to the stories and images that continued to circulate in Britain. A staunch nationalist, in her lectures she took the position that there was "no truth at all" in the claims of Armenians and the league that 30,000 Armenian women and girls remained in Muslim homes against their will. In her rebuttal, Edib first challenged the notion that recovered children at Jeppe's home in Aleppo had come from Turkish orphanages, arguing that Armenians had already been recovered during the armistice and the orphanages closed. Edib mocked his appeal for funding suggesting that Jeppe was trafficking in Armenians, buying Armenian slaves for her shelter: "Does that mean that Aleppo and the surrounding country, which has been under French control for six years, has a slave market, and that the French authorities allow the Moslem population to sell them to the Commissioner of the League [Jeppe] or the British missionaries?"[55]

The exiled feminist nationalist deployed the techniques of denialism when she claimed that Turks had been "exterminated and treated worse than wild beasts" by Armenians during the war, mirroring the charges of Armenians, the Allied Powers, and the League of Nations against the Ottoman government. This was a stark departure from Edib's earlier revolutionary writings, which had displayed sympathy toward the suffering Armenians in the aftermath of the 1909 Adana Massacres. In "Ölenlere öldürenler" (Those who died and those who killed), she expressed her deep feelings of shame as a member of the perpetrator group and her empathy for Armenians who had been reduced to "thousands of extinguished bloodlines" and "piles of bones."[56] This profound expression of collective grief stands in stark contrast with her later writings, which portrayed Turks as victims of Armenian violence. Historian Hazal Halavut has understood this shift in light of the elusive possibility of witnessing in Republican Turkey, especially as it was no longer possible to distance the Young Turks from the actual act of killings as Edib had been able to do earlier in Adana in 1909. Halavut captures the reasoning well when she writes of Edib, "Even in the few instances where she acknowledges the annihilation of Armenians, she seemed more concerned with how that made Turks appear to be a cruel people in the eyes of the Western World."[57] In later years, the feminist recanted her "motherly grief" over Adana, repressing any memory of solidarity for the Armenian people and for Armenian feminists expressed in earlier years.[58] In the immediate aftermath of the war, a now deeply nationalist Edib placed the blame for trafficking in women and children squarely on the shoulders of Arabs.[59] In her letter to *The Manchester Guardian*, Edib did not ignore the issue of tribal tattoos; instead, she asked of all English travelers to Turkey: "Have they met one single Turk tattooed or any Turk who knows the art of tattoo?"[60]

Edib specifically attacked "white slavery" rhetoric when she countered that Armenian women in Muslim harems were not slaves at all but were simply the wives of Turks. Jeppe eventually penned a response systematically disagreeing with Edib's characterization. "Until the Turkish-Kurdish war broke out last spring I still received girls from these harems," Jeppe wrote.[61] In this instance, the humanitarian underscored that Armenian women were still fleeing Turkey to find shelter with her in Syria, which contradicts the claim that repatriation was completed after the war. Jeppe argued that the girls she received were slaves, not wives because they were unmarried and forced to work without pay. Furthermore, she explained that nearly all of them suffered from sexual bondage: "Except for one, [the women and girls] had all been raped by the master of the harem. It is quite impossible to deny these facts."⁶²

Jeppe's response focused on the nature of her recovery of women. Recovered women were not purchased from Arab Bedouin but instead delivered through "a friendly solution" carefully negotiated so as to not disrupt relationships with the local community. She observed that although slavery was illegal in French mandate Syria, the territory in question was not fully governed by the state. At the end of her letter, Jeppe addressed the question of tribal tattoos:

> Then comes the question of the tattoo. I mentioned that the girls were often tattooed by the Mohammedans. When I discovered that the word "Mohammedans" was substituted with the word "Turks" in a certain kind of propaganda, I hastened to highlight that this was a misunderstanding. In reality the tattoos are, as far as I know, particularly done by Kurdish and Arab tribes.⁶³

Jeppe's final remarks are an admission to what she called a "certain kind of propaganda" that had lumped all Muslims together under the label "Turks" rather than distinguishing tattoos as a Kurdish and Arab tradition. This conflation was due to the ongoing use of *Turk* by Western observers to describe all Muslim populations, yet ethnic Turkish nationalism had already distinguished ethnic Turks from Kurds and Arabs. Jeppe's intervention at this moment stood in stark contrast to the sensationalist and largely decontextualized representation of tattoos that she had helped project to the world in *The Slave Market News*.

Jeppe submitted an annual report the same month as Edib's original letter in *The Manchester Guardian*. Though she may not have had the chance to have read Edib's letter yet, the report corrected at length some of the propaganda about tribal tattoos circulating within humanitarian and political circles. Her correction of various misconceptions is worth quoting at length:

> I want to mention the tattooing which has attracted much attention at home. The moral effects of this proceeding are sometimes very distressing, because the poor girls have a feeling of carrying a stigma for life on their faces, and in fact it often prevents them from coming home; they simply dare not expose themselves to the eyes of their compatriots. Physically it is a painful procedure when it is executed, but if no poison happened to enter the blood together with the fluid, it is harmless afterwards. Only in one case the hands of a woman have been so covered with tattooing that this may have been the cause of their being paralyzed. Whenever I have reported anything relating to this fact, I have written that the women were tattooed by the Moslems. As however it has come to my knowledge that in several articles in the press this word has been substituted by the Turks. I want to inform all my friends, that to my knowledge

the Turks are not tattooing the women; it is a custom belonging largely to the Kourdish [*sic*] and Arab tribes.⁶⁴

Though she offered a thorough correction of many misconceptions in her report, it did nothing to change the popular attitudes about tattoos perpetuated in the Western press and tabloid newsletters. *The Slave Market News* continued to publish photographs from her private photography collection, now archived with her private papers in Geneva, often without additional context or an accompanying article, through the 1930s.⁶⁵

Amid the polarized debate between two powerful women and their allies was a forceful response to Edib from Churchman, which captured a key aspect of the tattoos that had gotten lost in the war of words:

> With regard to the branding by tattoo marks, Mme. Halide Edib Hanoum can appeal to all the English travellers she likes: but the fact remains that numbers of women and girls have been rescued who have those horrible marks on their foreheads, chins, necks, and other parts of the body. If the Turks do not know "the art of tattooing" they know the art of deporting helpless women and children into the hands of those who do—a fact which is testified by rescue workers of unimpeachable authority.⁶⁶

Churchman's response to Edib affirmed that the true rhetorical power of tribal tattoos on Armenian bodies was not their ability to convey *who* tattooed the women but their capacity to bear witness to *what* had transpired: the forcible transfer of women and children as a strategy of cultural genocide.

Textual and visual humanitarian archives are largely untapped in terms of what they can teach us about gender, embodiment, and the Armenian Genocide. From these archives, we can learn how Western humanitarians viewed tattoos as both material and metaphorical inscriptions of slavery and sexual abuse. Decontextualized photographs of tattooed Armenian women who survived unthinkable crimes continued—and still continue—to circulate as portraits of prostitutes, though prostitution was never mentioned in the original archived image. Their easy dislocation from their original context recalls how photographs can become complicit in voyeurism rather than produce meaningful moral engagement with victims of war.⁶⁷ One of the most bizarre uses of Jeppe's personal photographs appeared in a 1931 edition of *Police Magazine* in Paris (figure 25). "Women's Hell: Not in Buenos Aires but in Asia Minor" (L'enfer de femmes: N'est pas à Buenos Ayres mais en Asie Mineure). The publication used the photographs to frame a larger cautionary tale about global prostitution, quoting extensively from an article published in *The Slave Market News*.⁶⁸ By then, the story of trafficked Armenian women and girls had likely receded into the background, giving the photographs new afterlives as generalized evidence of global prostitution. Armenian Genocide survivors were transformed into Argentinian prostitutes. As open or empty signifiers, tattoos had the capacity to enfold anxieties and fears and to reflect them back to a multitude of audiences.

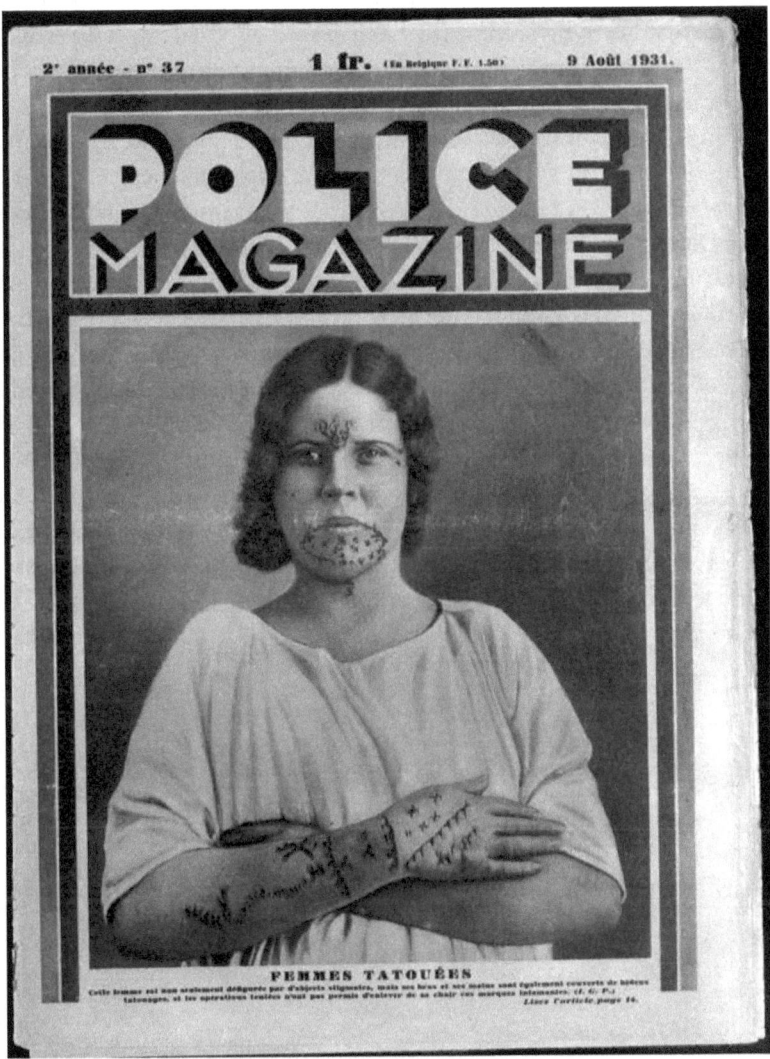

FIGURE 25 In 1931 Police Magazine *(Paris)* reprinted images of tattooed Armenian women on its cover to illustrate an accompanying article about the horrors of global prostitution. The images were from Karen Jeppe's private photographs (now archived as 12/43565/1463, at the Archives of the League of Nations, Geneva). Source: Reproduced with permission of Ville de Paris/Bibliothèque des Littératures Policières.

The heated debate between Jeppe and Edib over who was to blame for tattooed Armenian survivors illuminates how tattoos figured within the global humanitarian campaign against the traffic in women. Despite the subaltern dissonances in these images, rhetorically, these photographs, just like *Auction of Souls*, were intended to shock viewers affectively so that they would morally and financially support the mission to rescue trafficked women and girls. Among the anxieties projected were colonial fears of tattoos as atavistic marks suggestive of miscegenation or racial degeneration contracted, like a disease, by contact with the "savage" other. At a time in which Western societies sought to fix identity boundaries, tattoos shocked audiences with the threat of racial permeability.

But not all could be resolved. Whether "going native" in the West or "turning Turk" in the Ottoman East, tattooed bodies were displayed in text and image as objects of curiosity, the only cultural scripts available in American and European society. Despite the acclaim and popularity of these tales, its worth knowing that Olive Oatman spent most of her public life wearing a veil to cover her Mohave face tattoos—tattoo removal was not an option for her.[69] There was even a rumor that Oatman was institutionalized in an insane asylum, which in the Victorian context offered the stigmatizing sting of mental degeneration, perhaps viewed as further evidence of her time among atavistic others. The figure of Olive Oatman can help us understand how tattoo discourses constituted through nineteenth-century colonialism and race thinking would affect Armenian women decades later. Haunted by their very own skin, Armenian women sought modern medical solutions to permanently erase the ambiguity that rested on surface of their skin. Medical science was ready to help.

REMNANT 7

"The Removal of Tattoos and Carbonic Acid"

Hay pujak (Istanbul, 1922)[1]

There was once a blissful and a happy time, when only the blue marks of pilgrim tattoos (*hajji*) shone on shoulders and breasts,[2] which were the symbol of mortality, the proof of a pilgrimage to a holy place and a sign of zeal and devotion. But the hellish plans of warfare and the resulting awful exile caused the foreheads, lips, and cheeks of thousands of our young virgins to be brutally stamped under unknown tents in the depths of the deserts. The removal of these tattoos is now relevant, because there are many among us who carry these marks.

For some skin diseases, the healing properties of carbon dioxide ice, having been experimented with for the removal of tattoos, have had successful results and can be definitely accepted and applied as the ultimate form and remedy. In order to obtain carbon dioxide ice, you need to have a nickel-coated cylindrical, porous copper tool, on the inner side of which there is asbestos and a sheath.

As we pass the liquid carbon dioxide through the tool, some of the liquid—in its gassy state—leaks out through the holes, and what is left, freezes over the asbestos sheath. This chunk of ice can be easily cut off from the asbestos. This carbonic acid cylinder is made of a thick crystal and should be contained in a syringe from the bottom side. Crystal is a bad transmitter and there is no danger that the doctor's fingers would freeze. The area—where the ice is applied—reaches 80 degrees. The skin becomes white, and in a matter of one or two minutes, it becomes as stiff as glass and when removed, bleeding occurs locally within two to three minutes, some redness is noticed, blisters appear and as a result of the freezing, one could then see the degeneration [of the tattooed skin].

The depth of tissue degeneration is proportional to the duration of the application of the ice. In order to avoid degenerating deep into the tissue, one must wait two to three minutes after 20–25 seconds of ice application. After bleeding is detected, the procedure should be repeated at a temperature varying between -80 and +38 degrees, and thus, tattoos could be treated. At the end of the treatment, a fine white and an almost imperceptible scar will be seen instead of the [tattoo] mark, which will not look any different from the surrounding skin.

CHAPTER NINE

REMOVING THE "BRAND OF SHAME," REHABILITATING ARMENIAN SKIN

> Every time I hugged and cuddled her, I deliberately touched that mysterious part of her flesh. Her arm seemed to be split in two at that spot, as if the scar held some secret abyss under it.
> —HOURIG ATTARIAN[1]

Azniv was shunned by Armenians after the war. The indelible blue mark nested between her eyes was visual evidence of her life among the Bedouin who had rescued her from beneath a pile of corpses when she was about ten years old. During a massacre that took place outside Aleppo, Azniv received her first scar: the slash of a scimitar on her arm. "Next moment she was on the ground. She felt heavy. She felt crushed. She felt numb. She died. She couldn't move even if she wanted to. There was this terrible mass weighing down on her. It was a body, bodies, of persons who were talking, looking, breathing, hoping, dreaming only a moment ago."[2] It was there, hovering between life and death, that the Bedouin found her, the sole survivor in a heap of corpses. They gave her water to restore her back to life and said, "Do not be afraid my child, you are safe now." They, her rescuers, gave her a second scar: her forehead tattoo.

Upon reuniting with Armenian survivors in Aleppo in her early twenties, Azniv's cousin Zora rushed her off to the public bathhouse to wash off "all that dirt," to cleanse "the concentrated stench of camel urine embedded in her pores." People still complained about her smell, gossiping that she may not have bathed for the entire fifteen years that she lived among the Bedouin. Azniv was "a small, lively, delicate woman as gentle as her name bears witness," but she was deemed unmarriageable by the community despite having a great sense of humor, though there is a rumor that she may have later married for immigration purposes. Even as the stigma of that tattoo—signifying her time among the Bedouin—never washed off, she was still grateful to have been rescued, for the second time, and returned to the Armenian community. Decades later, she wrote a letter to her cousin in which she thanked her for rescuing her: "I will never forget what you have done for me.... If it were not for you, I would have rotted in that desert a long time ago."[3] Azniv never wore makeup to cover her tattoos, but she did eventually opt to willfully receive a third scar: a Jerusalem pilgrimage tattoo on her right arm. Perhaps that tattoo, in her view, could somehow efface the others with an affirmation of her true Armenian Christian identity.[4]

Azniv's story illustrates the psychological and social challenges that tattoos continued to pose for Armenian women even after rescue and reabsorption within the Armenian community. It is impossible to quantify the number of Armenian women who may have wished to have their tattoos surgically removed but lacked access or means. Those who did seek such treatment, however, have left behind traces in archival and media sources. Much like humanitarian filmmaking highlighting the plight of Armenian women during the genocide, as well as photography focused on Armenian women's tattoos, spectacular postwar accounts of Armenian women's tattoo removal were animated by the implication of tattooed Armenian women's bodily corruption. Recuperation as wives and mothers within the Armenian community, essential for the future, would be made possible through science's rehabilitation of the skin. Medical journals and the popular press published stories by and about doctors, many of them medical missionaries in the Near East, who were experimenting with techniques to remove the stain of captivity from the skin of Armenian women. And some of the world's most prestigious dermatologists, drawing on innovations in surgical skin care for those "disfigured" by war,[5] debated which surgical methods should be used to rescue these women from feeling imprisoned in their own skin.

STIGMA AND THE RECLAMATION OF TATTOOED ARMENIAN WOMEN

The urgency of Western scientific intervention for tattooed Armenian women was fueled by a popular perception that tattoos were veritable texts of Armenian women's sexual ordeal.[6] Media reports claimed that Armenian women had been tattooed by "Turk husbands," signaling the enemy's patriarchal hold over them either literally, if they had chosen to remain with or been forcibly returned to their presumptive captors, or psychologically, if they could not overcome the stigma of their tattoos. In either case, the tattoos were viewed as a hindrance to Armenian national development because it could, in some instances, threaten the marriageability of those who bore them. Tattoo removal, therefore, was viewed as rescuing not only individual women's bodies but the communal body of a decimated nation.[7]

Armenia's countrymen were praised for accepting these women back into the community as ethnomartyrs and mothers who would rebirth the nation. One anonymous report perceptively argued that while tattooed faces were considered beautiful among the Kurds and Arabs, "Armenians consider it a sign of disgrace."[8]

> The Armenians thus disfigured are returned to their homes with the story of slavery written plainly upon their faces, which they could not even hide with veils, as the Armenians do not follow the Moslem custom of veiling their faces. Sensitive to this public disclosure of their shame, many of these Armenian girls and women so branded have resorted to obliterate the tattoo, at the cost of permanent unsightly scars. Many others, unable to face the ordeal of returning, have preferred to remain in the Moslem households where they have been enslaved.[9]

Tattooed faces were viewed as a hindrance to Armenian national recovery because, on the one hand, as marks of punishment, they caused some women to stay imprisoned within Muslim homes while, on the other, they threatened to undermine tattooed women's recuperation as wives and mothers. The author concluded by affirming the urgency of tattoo removal in Armenian recovery efforts.

We have little information about how everyday Armenians felt about formerly captive women bearing tribal tattoos. One of the few scholars to address this historical lacunae is Lerna Ekmekçioğlu, who argues that as shameful as marked skin may have been for some, "the tattoos that many of the rescued bore on their faces and hands (an Arab and Kurdish tradition) did not necessarily leave them unmarriageable."[10] In her reading of the International Red Cross archives, Armenian memoirs, and diaries, Ekmekçioğlu has found that at an institutional level, Armenian relief organizations did not view the tattoos as stigmatizing and warranting exclusion from the reconstituted postwar Armenian community. The League of Nation's Rescue Home in Aleppo regularly documented the marriage of rescued tattooed Armenian women to Armenian men who were also rescued residents in the home. Oftentimes, the grooms had also been assimilated within Muslim homes. These marriages, inscribed on the back of the home intake records, are rarely consulted but seem to support Ekmekçioğlu's argument that marriageability may not have been an issue. Vahé Tachjian has shown how Armenian elites encouraged formerly captive Armenian women to marry and (re)produce the nation, while also viewing these women negatively.[11] Tachjian's finding suggests that rescued Armenian women did face some degree of prejudice, though Armenians who opposed reintegration may have been outnumbered by those who were accepting of these women for the cause of national recovery.

We know that tattooed Armenian women sometimes lived with profound feelings of abjection even after reabsorption into the community and (re)marriage to Armenians. One case of an unnamed twenty-year-old Armenian woman reveals how the psychological impact of tattoos kept women from continuing their lives. In 1921, a tattooed survivor, described as possessing rare beauty was brought to the University of Michigan hospital in Ann Arbor. Tribal tattoos adorned each corner of her mouth, the sides of her nose, her forehead, and under her bottom lip. She informed reporters that not only Americans but "fellow Armenians averted their gaze because they knew [what her tattoos meant], and she was always in tears because of it." An Armenian man proposed to her but she refused because "she bore the mark of a slave." When the unnamed survivor and her suitor learned of a skin grafting technique at University of Michigan hospital, he brought her to Ann Arbor. She promised to marry him after her tattoos were removed. After the successful surgery, in which "there was no hint of the ugly brand of the Turk," the young couple got married in Detroit.[12]

While tattoo removal may have facilitated one woman's marriage, it was a hindrance to another woman, who vividly recalled, "During my youth, a very polite Armenian youth met me. He admired my looks and knowledge of languages, but he said that without the blue tattoos on my pretty face, we might have gotten married. So, what the Arabs did with my face was the reason for me to remain all alone in my old age."[13] Other testimony, as well as records from the Rescue Home in Aleppo, suggests that many women with tattoos remarried, indicating that not all prospective grooms held the same opinion of tattooed brides.[14]

The story of a tattooed survivor, Nouritza, who was forcibly married to a Muslim man who deeply adored her, illustrates well how Armenian society in postwar Syria stigmatized rescued tattooed Armenian women while simultaneously accepting them back into the community. During her office visit for an eye ailment in Aleppo, Armenian ophthalmologist Samuel Meguerditchian serendipitously identified Nouritza as his own niece. He promptly arranged for her to visit him again so that he could sneak her back to their hometown of Kassab. Upon arrival, her relatives knew that the best way to help her settle into a new life was to marry her off to an Armenian, but no one would take her with "the dotted shadings, god forgive, on her hands, face, and lip" (al-daqdaqat al-tazlilat istaghfirulah 'ala idayuha wa wajihuha wa shafahuha).[15] The community arranged for Nouritza to marry a deaf man, another stigmatized member of the community. This suggests that the community believed that only a disabled Armenian man would take a woman whose past marred her face, as if it too were a disability. The Syrian-Armenian ethnographer, Kevork Apelian, added that Nouritza's new husband was so deaf that he regularly disturbed the neighbors with the loud sounds he made during sex. Was this disclosure meant to make a mockery of Nouritza and her disabled husband (in a society that heavily stigmatizes disability)? Still, the tattooed bride left behind a smitten Muslim husband, who searched high and low in hopes of her return. In a scene fit for a Hollywood film, her ex-husband found her in the streets in Kassab by repeatedly calling out her Islamized name, "Nur! Nur!

Nur!"[16] After a brief meeting with her former Muslim husband, Nouritza chose, despite her status in Kassab, to stay with her new Armenian husband. Like they did to Azniv, Armenians continued to stigmatize her, frequently referring to her as "the Bedouin," but she endured their ridicule because, in the end, she sought to live her life, however complicated, among fellow Armenians.[17]

Considering these examples of profound social stigma, many survivors took matters into their own hands to rid themselves of stigmatizing tattoo marks after reabsorption into the community. Historian Vahram Shemmassian has illuminated, "The tattoos imprinted on females according to Bedouin tradition could not be eradicated with any corrosives, thereby symbolizing the permanence of the deep emotional and psychological scars left behind by the genocide."[18] Considering their psychological weight, Shemmassian has found that many women sought to immediately remove stigmatizing marks from their bodies upon rescue and reabsorption into the Armenian community.

A magazine reported, "Many [women] have not waited to find a hospital but have scarred their faces beyond the power of medical skill to repair, trying with acids to burn out the marks."[19] Upon rescue, some tattooed women and girls used their fingernails to remove the marks with deep scratches.[20] Rescued among the Bedouin in Dayr al-Zur, a girl named Lucine in the Beirut-based, Danish-administered Bird's Nest Orphanage removed her chin tattoo by scraping it out with her fingernails, then scouring it with ash and lemon juice.[21] Another eyewitness saw girls in a Rescue Home in Adana using lemon juice to remove the "badges of slavery, of which they [were] very much ashamed."[22] Newspapers informed readers that "Armenian women have sought in various ways to remove the tattoo and in many cases have produced serious disfigurement" while trying to rid themselves of the marks on their own.[23] One survivor described how after she was ridiculed upon reentry into the Armenian community, her mother used nitric acid to try to remove her tattoos, which left her face scarred for the rest of her life.[24] Complete tattoo removal was impossible without invasive and painful treatments, prompting some to seek professional assistance.

There is early evidence that doctors in Marsovan (Merzifon), Aleppo, and Constantinople responded to women's pleas for tattoo removal by performing surgery on location. In 1920, the superintendent of the Near East Relief Hospital, Dr. J. K. Marden, successfully removed tattoos in Marsovan, though his surgical technique was not reported.[25] As she stands at a threshold, a woman from Karen Jeppe's private albums provides fragmentary documentary evidence of the cutting procedure used by many doctors in the Near East to rid Armenian Genocide victims of their tattoos (figure 26). Strategically placed scabs cover the areas of her face where here tribal tattoos had once been. Like so many photographs in Jeppe's collection, the photograph of one of the region's first tattoo removal surgeries provides no details such as the woman's name, the name of the surgeon, or a date.[26] Jeppe's resident physician Vahran Katchperouni listed tattoos among the many ailments rescued women were treated for (next to contagious diseases, trachoma, venereal diseases, and fistulas) in the Rescue Home. He did not, however, mention tattoo removal surgery though he hinted at the demand for it when he wrote: "Indeed they are all tattooed to their great despair and they desire to make these traces disappear at any cost as soon as they arrive because the tattoo not only disfigures them; it is the ineffaceable sign of their stay with the Turks."[27]

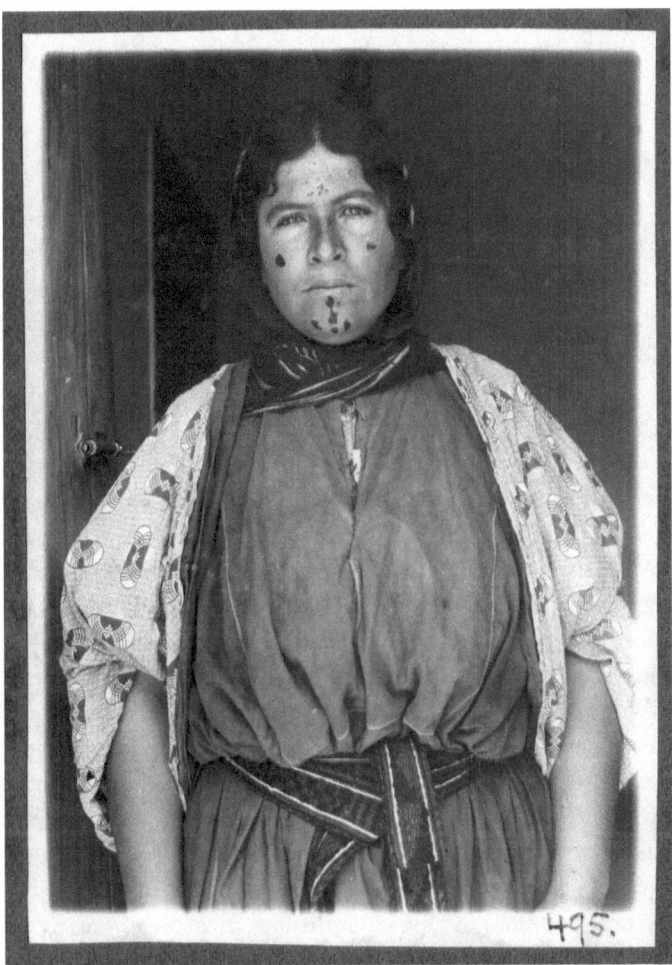

FIGURE 26 *An unnamed Armenian woman after tattoo removal surgery in Aleppo by an unknown doctor. The wounds suggest that the surgical technique was cutting the tattoos out of the skin with a scalpel. Jeppe kept this photo in her personal collection. Source: Album 60, photograph 495, Karen Jeppe Private Album. Reprinted with permission of the Armenian Genocide Memorial Institute, Yerevan, Armenia.*

In a 1930 report, Jeppe confirmed that tattoo removal surgeries were indeed taking place in Aleppo, but the high cost of the procedure made it accessible only to upper-class Armenian girls at the Rescue Home.[28] In addition, cosmetic surgeries were not foremost in the minds of medical humanitarians, who were treating victims for a slew of harmful diseases plaguing Armenians such as gonorrhea, syphilis, dysentery, scabies, trachoma, intestinal worms, and malnutrition.[29] While feeding and clothing the victims was a priority for humanitarians, for some women, removing the shameful yet indelible mark, the memory of forcible assimilation, was foremost on their minds.

SAVING FACE: EARLY INNOVATIONS IN TATTOO REMOVAL SURGERY

The doctor who surgically removed the tattoo of Aghavni Kabakian in Constantinople in 1926, Dr. Wilfred Post, was an early innovator in tattoo removals for rescued Armenian women. Post was a graduate of Princeton University Medical School in 1897 and the son of a medical missionary working at the American University of Beirut in Lebanon, where he had been born.[30] At war's end, the surgeon held the position of NER medical director and in this role led an inquiry on behalf of the organization to find a medically "safe and scientific way of removing tattoo marks without leaving a disfiguring scar."[31]

It is quite possible that before meeting Dr. Post, Aghavni Kabakian (chapter 7) had already read or heard about Post's successes in the field of tattoo removal in the United States. In 1920, the American press mentioned that both he and another prominent American dermatologist, Dr. George Washburn of Harvard University, were performing the tattoo removal surgery, likely by skillfully cutting away tattooed skin with a scalpel.[32] Washburn, a renowned former army surgeon, had built his reputation by restoring the disfigured faces of maimed soldiers during the Great War; he now turned his attention to Armenian war victims. In addition to reports on surgeons, American journals of dermatology contain traces of Armenian women's self-advocacy for tattoo removal. Their appeals stirred medical debates over which tattoo removal procedures—excising by scalpel, burning with acid, or plucking out by needle—had the most efficacy.[33]

The urgency of removing Armenian women's tattoos pushed still highly experimental tattoo removal techniques to the fore, garnering the attention of the nation's top dermatologists. In 1920, the *Archives of Dermatology and Syphilology* published a pre-surgical debate about which technique should be used to remove the tattoos of a twenty-four-year-old Armenian woman listed only as C. N., "who had been taken captive by the Turks and tattooed."[34] The proceedings report that her tattoos had been on her face for at least six years. Her husband explained, "She especially desired to get rid of them because, whenever she met any Turks on the street, they laughed at her."³⁵ But the woman cited the ridicule and shame she confronted on the street as her primary motivation for surgery. C. N.'s husband had been treating her at home, using citric acid with limited success. Dr. Fred Wise and Dr. John D. Fordyce presented her request to have the tattoo marks removed on her forehead, upper lip, and chin prior to surgery to a board of certified surgeons. Doctors were debating whether the scarring left behind by "needling" and electrolysis would be worth it for victims and whether the prospects of success were even worthwhile for surgeons; one doctor states that the "treatment of tattoo marks was thankless work, and they had best be let alone." Another physician advised that "scarring would be preferable to the condition now shown."³⁶

While some surgeons recommended incisions, others recommended non-scarring procedures that might leave little to no trace of the tattoo. A physician named Dr. Pels recommended desiccation—to extract all the moisture from the tattooed skin targeted for removal. In his approach, a fine needle was inserted into the skin while the patient was anesthetized, and with a small curette, the physician would scrape off and remove the now dead epidermis. The skin would later heal under aseptic conditions to avoid infection. Dr. Kingsbury recommended using carbon dioxide snow to treat the unnamed Armenian woman's face, the same procedure prescribed by Armenian doctors a few years later in Constantinople. In "The Removal of Tattoos and Carbonic Acid" (Vedkeru chinchuime yev penadzkhayin tutiun) published in the Armenian medical journal *Hay pujak* in 1922, the editors explained the benefits of carbon dioxide snow in removing tribal tattoos from the faces of Armenian women.³⁷ The urgency of removal was revealed in the opening lines: "The resulting awful exile caused the foreheads, lips, and cheeks of thousands of our young virgins to be brutally stamped under unknown tents in the depths of the deserts. The removal of these tattoos is now relevant, because there are many among us who carry these marks."³⁸ American reports, of course, made no reference to the indigenous doctors, who were tracking these surgical procedures, removing tattoos from the bodies of women survivors, and writing about their efficacy in their native languages.

Surgical innovations were covered in the American press with such sensational headlines as "Girl Disfigured by the Turks Reaches the U.S."; "How Science Cleansed Her of the Cruel Turk's Brand of Shame"; "Wants Method to Un-Tattoo the Armenians"; and "2 Girls Have Slave Tattoo Brand Removed."³⁹ Within these accounts were the words of actual surgeons, foremost among them Dr. Post, who affirmed the commonsense reasoning of the American public: tattooing was the byproduct of sexual enslavement and a barrier to full rehabilitation for Armenian victims. "The wearing of this brand, which shows that the woman has been an intimate of the harem, seriously interferes with the work of reconstruction and rehabilitation among such persons."⁴⁰ The tattoo narratives of American doctors, then, were framed by the broader mission to rescue the Armenian people and, by extension, their skin from captivity. No story captured the mission to recover Armenian skin better than that of Nargis Avakian.

RECOVERING NARGIS AVAKIAN'S FACE THROUGH MEDICAL WONDER

Nargis Avakian's tattooed face briefly captivated American audiences and forms the ideal case study of how tattooing and the recovery of indelibly marked skin were framed as medical, humanitarian, and media spectacles (figure 27). Nargis was described in the press as a fair Armenian girl "with a wealth of golden hair," reminiscent of youthful Aurora but with one major difference: tribal tattoos covered her face, hands, neck, and chest. She was "timid," "bashful," and hid her face in her hands during the interview. Nargis offered very few details of her life as a concubine; even her brother Nishan told the media that he tried to forget that he had rescued his sister from a harem and sought to avoid talking about the details.[41]

Nargis's ordeal intensified after the death of her parents, when she was bought and sold twice before being sold a third time in a slave market that had emerged in Urfa. Her third master, Abou Seraidz, "compelled her to submit to concubinage" and "gave orders that she be tattooed with the distinguishing marks of his tribe."[42] The newspaper described the markings as appearing "much the same as horses on the western plain are branded with the marks of the ranch to which they belong."[43] Christian women trapped in Muslim harems, it claimed, had been tattooed "from time immemorial."[44] The pastiche of images and details included an outlandish narrative of ritual tattooing at the rise of dawn, the ritual time when slave tattoos were applied according to "Arabian custom." This ritual timing at dawn also correlated with the opening daily prayer in Islam affirming the notion that the marks were those of Islamization. The tattoo was needled into her skin "with secret inks made from Oriental herbs." The eerie, cultic quality of the account was not enough to satisfy the appetite for "delicious horrors," so the account also included several provocative images.[45]

An illustration of Nargis's face pointed toward the rising sun and a series of random indelible marks were applied between her eyes, on her chin, and around her mouth. Meant to represent the girl's testimony, the image featured three turbaned and fez-wearing men holding down an abstractly cartooned Nargis depicted as nude from the waist up, a nod to classicism. The cartoon image served as a pretext to sexualize the tattooing event, peddling the pornography of pain of yet another pubescent Armenian survivor. The full-page spread included a reproduction of a painting by Jean-Leon Gérôme, *The Slave Market* (1871). Although many of the French artist's paintings were set in North Africa, the newspaper appropriated the image, implying that it represented the well-documented slave market in Urfa where Nargis had been bought and sold.[46] Through a combination of stories

Removing the "Brand of Shame," Rehabilitating Armenian Skin 193

FIGURE 27 *An in-depth story about Nargis Avakian's ordeal and tattoo removal surgery in America. Source: "How Science Cleansed Her of the Cruel Turk's Brand of Shame,"*Washington Times, *September 5, 1920.*

and images, journalists blended old and new forms of spectacle: the mystique of Orientalism alongside the wonder of medical innovation.

According to the report, Nargis's face was marked with a red-hot needle, emphasizing the sheer cruelty of her tattoos as torture scars. "Ordinary tattooing could be erased, but not this brand of the Arabs." The brand was so stigmatizing, the author remarks, that Nargis was "ashamed to meet her Christian kinfolk in the street."[47] The reader is informed that due to the indelible tattoos, she, like the American captive Olive Oatman, would be forced, due to social stigma, to wear a veil as Muslim women do to cover her face in public. Overlooking the previous surgeries that had taken place in the Near East, the report claimed, "What the scientists believed would save these Christian girls from the scars of their unavoidable shame, eventually was discovered, not in her native land, but in New York City."[48] Nargis's body, then could be redeemed through science within a specific narrative of American medical exceptionalism.

There is some evidence that this may not have been Nargis's first attempt at tattoo-removal surgery. Another American surgeon, Dr. Howard Fox, had at some unspecified date tried to remove the tattoos of a fourteen-year-old Armenian girl with the initials N. A. (whom I suspect was Nargis) using caustics, but it was unsuccessful.[49] Professor Edith Hansen of the Royal Copenhagen University, who would lead the surgical team that eventually performed Nargis's operation at the New York Institute, offered extended comments about the tattoo removal procedure to the press, noting that after surgery, "Nargis will be as beautiful as ever—more beautiful perhaps for the little lines and wrinkles that gathered also as the natural marks of her sufferings will have disappeared and the fresh bloom of youth will have been restored."[50] The restoration of Nargis's body, therefore, was not only about ridding her of facial tattoos, but about rehabilitating the entirety of her skin.

The premature corruption of a beautiful teenager bearing tattoos and wrinkles after contact with uncivilized others exposed how tattoo discourses were embedded within scientific racism in the previous century. Dermatological studies of tattoo removal mention earlier nineteenth-century debates in an attempt to contextualize Armenian women's tattooing as pathological.[51] The merging of disciplinary knowledge about physical degeneracy, deviancy, and "reading" the body for criminality (viewed as a disease located within the body), were commonplace in nineteenth-century scientific writings. A prominent scholar from the Italian school, Cesare Lombroso, suggested there was a relationship between criminal behavior and tattoos worn by criminals and prostitutes. The science of eugenics and phrenology emphasized that the entirety of the body (and that which is inscribed upon it) could be approached as a text whose signs could to be read and importantly indexed with photography and empirical study. Such data harvested from tattooed bodies could be harnessed by criminologists and eugenicists to halt the contagious spread of criminal tendencies, though they disagreed as to whether the source of such behavior was biological or sociological in nature.[52] In this context, tattoos were hieroglyphs saturated with meaning, which if decoded could assist the criminologist in not only understanding the criminal mind but aid in the identification of criminal disposition. The notion that tattoos could be read and deciphered also had its roots in arguments in early criminology that tattoos were a savage form of writing.[53]

"Reading" these tattoo specimens, alongside the cranium, physiognomy, and other "body signs," allowed scientists to demarcate the criminal body from that of the upstanding citizen; however, tattoo removal paradoxically blurred the boundary between these categories, troubling the discerning gaze of eugenicists and criminologists. Scientists experimented with silver nitrate, silver salt, and other methods as early as the late nineteenth century, and these experiments became more urgent in the treatment of disfigured soldiers during World War I in cases where gunpowder and carbon were lodged in the skin of combatants in ways that not only scarred but blackened the skin.[54] As for the Great War's other "disfigured" victims, Armenian women, "science set about its demonstration that the branded girl captives of the Turks and Arabs may eventually be restored to their unblemished beauty."[55]

Professor Hansen believed that the intention of the Arabs who enslaved Nargis was to inflict as much pain as possible on the girl's young, beautiful face. This, for her, was evident in the extensive damage done to the skin and cartilage:

> The Arabs had used a hand needle, which was very thick, and which was not even sharp. Evidently, they were too cruel to even sharpen their needle or use a thin one. The penetration was uneven. In many spots it went through into the inner flesh. In branding the girl's nose, they jabbed clear through the two skins into the cartilage. The places chosen for marking were the tender parts of the face—the temples, the nose, the brow, the region of under the lip.[56]

Driving a thick, unsharpened needle (perhaps a tool intended for textile work)—as opposed to the very thin needle used by tattoo practitioners—deep into Nargis's nose damaged the cartilage.[57] It is clear from the description of the needle (mentioned earlier as heated at the time of tattooing, which is atypical of traditional tattooing) and Nargis's damaged nose cartilage that her tattoo was not the work of an artisan tattooist. Instead it was violently and hastily applied by her captors to facilitate their work in human trafficking.

The tattoos around Nargis's chin were a common circle or dot pattern found on women in the Urfa region. The report notes that there are five dots representing the five daily prayers required in Islam. Along the chin is a complex * o * o * "star and five" (*najma wa khamsa*) pattern, which is also known as the "star and moon" (*najma wa qamar*) pattern in regional tribal tattoo practices.[58] While the motifs, with their open signification, can represent the five prayers in Islam, they can also represent the stars, moon, or be merely a decorative choice by the tattooist. The interpretation of the dots as representing Islamic prayers is challenged by the fact that there are more than five on her face. Furthermore, Nargis's forehead tattoo is described as looking like "a garden rake without the handle," the tattoo marks appearing "raked" into her skin. Other images show that the forehead tattoo did not form a complete line as it should have but instead was dotted because the tattoo ink was applied too deeply into the skin's layers during the violent tattooing event.[59] Although one account of Nargis's forcible tattooing claims, "Some artist of the slave owner's household gouged the flesh as a carver would dried wood," the dermatological evidence shows that her tattoo, from the standpoint of tattoo aesthetics, lacks artistry and precision. Perhaps the most bizarre aspect of her story was that men applied the tattoos. This detail flags Nargis's facial tattoos as extraordinary since tattooing was and continues to be women's work.⁶⁰

Ironically, the drawing of Nargis's tattoo removal (figure 28) actually preserved her tattoo motifs far better than the newsprint photograph. While the tattoo between her eyes faintly resembles an upward pointing arrow, a trident, it could possibly be an attempt to create what is known as either the "hen's feet" or "grouse's feet" (*rijil al-qatai*) motif found among Arab tribes of eastern Syria. This symbol, in Nargis's case, is not centered between her eyes, botching the symmetrical outward communication that a traditional forehead tattoo should have.⁶¹ Is this decentering of the tattoo the result of Nargis shaking her head while being tattooed, resisting the needle? Can we read the decentered motif as a sign of her resistance? We know that Armenian girls sometimes did refuse or resist, as in the case of a girl who tried to protect herself from the tattoo needle by" throwing herself in a shallow well"; she was eventually caught and tattooed under duress.⁶² While impossible to verify, the asymmetry and depth of Nargis's tattoo confirms my contention that the tattoo is not professionally executed. I suspect, therefore, that the male slavers who tattooed her were attempting to emulate the astronomical signs typically worn between the eyes of women in order to conceal her Armenian identity as they bought and sold her at an Urfa slave market. Arguably, Nargis wears in the most literal sense a mark of slavery—that is, her tattoo is a slaver tattoo. The intention behind her tattoo sits in opposition to traditional tattoos that were applied with the aim of absorbing Armenians into a tribal community.⁶³

FIGURE 28 *A diagram of Nargis's tattoo removal procedure illustrates the surgical technique as well as the shapes of her tattoos. Source: "How Science Cleansed Her of the Cruel Turk's Brand of Shame,"Washington Times, September 5, 1920.*

Described as a mysterious poison lodged under Nargis's flesh, the tattoo ink was to be extracted through a suppuration process, the skin carefully kneaded in order to separate the skin from the muscle beneath it. Then, compresses soaked in an unnamed medicated solution—likely tannic acid and silver nitrate, which in combination formed silver tannate within her skin—were applied to the face for a period of weeks. The compresses caused the top layer of skin to dissolve, allowing the tattoo ink to rise to the surface.[64] The doctor restored the "corrupted flesh" through this method of extraction, which produced pink skin resembling a sunburn. The restoration of whiteness, beauty, and Armenianness was achieved through modern science, "leaving Nargis as comely as ever," though it was certain to have left some scarring—a detail omitted from the report. Surgical restoration provided women survivors more confidence to be in public without meeting the perplexed gazes of bystanders. Importantly, such sensational stories affirmed how liberating enslaved, tattooed flesh was embedded within the larger medical mission to save captive Armenian women.

The editors of one local newspaper chose to place an advertisement for Poslam ointment—used to treat such skin ailments as eczema, scars, and acne—directly below their reprinted edition of Nargis's story. The advertisement proclaimed "Skin Treated with Poslam Quickly Heals."[65] The placement of the advertisement near a story about tattoo removal reminds us that tattoos were understood by doctors and the general public to be scars or wounds in need of medical intervention. One nineteenth-century physician described his procedure for scraping and needling tattooed tissue from the body as the excision of an infection or cancer, tattoos being yet another form of disease.[66] This was especially true as "the filthy habit" was linked to contagious diseases like cutaneous tuberculosis and syphilis. Press and medical discussions of tattoo removal affirmed the urgency of excising "marks of shame" to aid Armenian women's reabsorption into civilized society. The experience of shame and dejection was profound for stigmatized women not only in America but also those reabsorbed into Armenian communities, where the semiotics of tattoos communicated civilizational otherness.

Scientists and physicians used the metaphor of wiping skin clean—the restoration of beauty, moral decency, and whiteness—to describe the effects of tattoo removal, as in Nargis's case. These were the same metaphors used by Victorian scientists like Alphonse Bertillon, who wrote, "Before attempting to purify the criminal soul, ... we must first try to purify their bodies to get rid of the obscene, seditious tattoos they wear."[67] Late Victorian eugenicists and criminologists believed that bodies could be transformed into readable texts—which also meant, by extension, they could be reformed into tabula rasa or reinscribed as civilized with medical intervention. The face and head, long the subject of fascination for physiognomic science, "bore the outward signs of inner character," making them urgent body parts for redemption.[68] While tattooed bodies were sensationalized in the age of mass media, the historical record also contains traces of those who resisted the dominant or commonsense view of tribal tattoos. In these counternarratives, the tattoos that Armenian survivors bore are understood to be marks of heroism, survival, and resistance.

REMNANT 8

"Tattooed Like an Arab"

by Serpouhi Tavoukjian (1933)[1]

For some time there had been talk about having my face tattooed. As I have said, every Arab woman has tattooing, and this is thought to add much to her beauty. I did not wish to be tattooed, and still I did. I was afraid the Turks would get me again, and knew that if I were so marked, they would think I was an Arab and not an Armenian, and would never touch me. My [adoptive] father was anxious to have this done.

One morning, the artist they had arranged to tattoo me arrived. I did not object when she made ready to begin. This work is done by four fine needles tightly tied together. They are stuck deep into the true skin, but so rapidly that you can hardly see them move. The fluid used is not ink, but a blue dye made from the gall bladder of goats and sheep. These are dried and then ground into powder and mixed with water. When she was ready, the artist asked me to lie down on a rug spread in the courtyard. I did. I did not know that the tattooing would hurt. But when she began to prick my face and blood ran down, I kicked and screamed that I did not want to be tattooed, and begged her to let me go. However, the wives were there to help her, and one held my hands while the other sat on my feet. My protests were in vain. I must be made beautiful. I rose from the floor an Arab to all appearances.

When my [adoptive] father came home that evening, he was very much pleased with the improvement in my looks. He smiled and patted my shoulder and said, "My dear Helema, my little Arab girl."

CHAPTER TEN

COUNTERNARRATIVES OF TRIBAL TATTOOS AND SURVIVOR AGENCY

> An Arab took me to his home and told me, "My daughter, I know you do not have the same custom, but let me tattoo your face with blue ink so that they will not take you for an Armenian."
>
> —BAROUHI SILIAN[1]

Reading evidence against the grain, mining it for counternarratives can illuminate how survivors and perhaps how the tattoos themselves articulate lesser known aspects of the collective story of Armenian Genocide experience. Excavating what tribal tattoos communicate within their historical and cultural context engages in what anthropologist James Peacock has called "soft focus," a concept in photography in which the focal subject's image is softened so that it melts into the background making the context equally visible. In this case, such methodological openness and holistic breadth can offer unexpected insights as to the purpose tattoos served within their original context in Anatolia and Mesopotamia.[2]

There is a critical distinction to be made between those who willingly opted to be tattooed and those who were tattooed by force. There were women who, by circumstance, opted to be tattooed in order to conceal their identity because they were conspicuously untattooed while living among tattooed peoples. For the tribal communities that bore them, tattoos had the power to protect wearers from both metaphysical danger (from evil spirits) and corporeal genocidal violence (from Turkish soldiers and irregular killing units). While some tattooed Armenians were ostracized upon reentry into Armenian society, some sought to ease the burden of tattooed survivors by renarrativizing the tattoos as beautiful symbols of bravery. That the tribal tattoos of Armenian boys and men are largely unknown is illustrative of how tattoos have been ahistorically feminized and overdetermined as marks of sexual violence in Armenian postmemory.

Counternarratives of Tribal Tattoos and Survivor Agency 201

A warning to genocide denialists: examining these narratives is not an apology for their use as an instrument in cultural genocide and their power to deface Armenian identity. I do not seek to legitimize the tattoos but only to uplift an area of knowledge that could assist us in understanding more fully why the tattoos were applied to Islamized Armenians. I offer this intervention in order to avoid the pitfalls of the approximate or partial truths that circulate in the absence of context. The dominant framing of tattoos as shameful marks of sexual enslavement in visual and textual rhetoric has been already established in my own analysis in preceding chapters, but it still falls short of explaining the purpose the tattoos served within their tribal context. Scholars have yet to explain, for example, why the motifs that Armenian women and men survivors bore on their skin are identical to those of tattooed Arab, Kurdish, and Roma women—a fact that, by itself, suggests we need to probe deeper.

Viewing humanitarian photographs with what photography historian Gabrielle Moser calls a *disobedient gaze* can unsettle the tropes of difference that informed their production. Approaching these images disobediently allows us to not only view them as a distillation of the past; it can hint at potential viewing futures especially since photographs of tattooed Armenian women continue to circulate stirring painful memories within the survivor community.[3] We can listen for not only the missing context but locate dissonant traces of women subjects as survivors within images collected for a very different purpose at the time they were taken.

Our discussion thus far has adopted the view that tribal tattoos were traumatizing scars for Armenian Genocide victims; yet counternarratives embedded within survivor narratives portray tattoos as marks of survival and, within their tribal context, marks of beautification, protective totems, and tribal medicine. Can reading archival photographs and testimony disobediently allow us to arrive at new insights about the purpose and function the tattoos played in Armenian survival? Can our refusal to comply with the disciplining effect of camera and discourse allow us to view these images as trace genocide testimony on the bodies of women and men captured within the frame? What follows is a series of experimental readings of biographies and images of tattooed survivors that aims to locate their stories and, importantly, their agency as survivors by bringing "soft focus" to the tattoo inscriptions they bore.

SERPOUHI: TRIBAL TATTOOS AS LIFE-SAVING CAMOUFLAGE

The frontispiece of Serpouhi Tavoukdjian's memoir *Exiled* (1933), marketed as a teenage adventure tale, depicts her wearing traditional garments and head covering, simulating her four years among the Bedouin (figure 29). While the frontispiece borrowed from the Orientalist iconography of odalisques in Western art, it missed a crucial detail: Serpouhi never lived in a harem. She is sitting on the floor with her hand gripping a jug as if she were preparing to bring water from a village well, and the caption reads, "In Arab dress, and with tattoo marks on my face, I looked like this."[4] Despite the Orientalist marketing ploy, the text of Serpouhi's biography departs significantly from dominant descriptions of tattoos, making it worthy of deeper analysis.

Years earlier, along the Orontes River in northern Syria, a starving six-year-old Serpouhi begged, "O mother, please sell me. . . . Then we can eat again."[5] She remembered her mother selling her for about five American dollars at a slave market. Since her mother did not negotiate her own sale along with Serpouhi, mother and daughter would never see each other again. We learn, however, that the slave market sale was complicated because she was not purchased to become a slave but to become the daughter of a childless Arab nobleman.

On her way to meet her new father, Serpouhi was brutally attacked by Turkish soldiers. The local Bedouin accompanying her could not stand up to the Ottoman army and were unable to protect her. She escaped and miraculously found her adoptive father, Allel Moose ('Ali al-Musa), while wandering the desert. "When I came and stood breathless and bleeding before him, he greeted me like a father. His

FIGURE 29   *Serpouhi Tavoukdjian poses in Arab dress for the frontispiece of her memoir* Exiled *(1933). The caption reads: "The Author: In Arab dress, and with the tattoo marks on my face, I looked like this." Source: Serpouhi Tavoudjian,* Exiled: Story of an Armenian Girl. *Reproduced with permission of Review and Herald Publishing Association.*

eyes filled with tears, and he took his own white handkerchief and washed away the blood from my poor bruised face and tenderly dressed the cuts and bruises on my lacerated body."[6] The next day, Allel Moose dressed her as an Arab boy, draping his own sheepskin coat over her shoulders and placing a turban on her head to disguise her. Dressing as a boy was a safer way to travel in an environment where the bodies of Armenian girls and women were highly surveilled—this was the first of two moments in which her adoptive father camouflaged her for her own protection. At Abu Galgal—a small settlement of two hundred houses about twenty kilometers southeast of Minbaj—Serpouhi would become Allel Moose's daughter and, in her own words, he "proved to be indeed a real father to me."[7]

Upon her arrival, Serpouhi's adoptive family scrubbed her dirtied "black skin [that] peeled off like a shell under the strenuous scrubbing" to reveal new "clean" skin, her "Arab skin." The women also shaved all her curly, lice-infected hair to grow "Arab hair."[8] Along with these rituals of acclamation were tattoos that marked her full absorption into the community, described more fully in Remnant 8.[9] But the tattooing occurred after a crucial turn in her story. Serpouhi had more encounters with Turkish soldiers who were making periodic sweeps through the area in search of Armenians. Her fears turned out to be well-founded when she encountered a Turkish soldier who gave her a discerning glance. Terrified by being barely able to pass as Arab, Serpouhi willingly agreed to have the tribal tattoos worn by the women in her new community.[10] However, during the tattooing, she resisted the tattooist's hand, and similar to other women's experience, the women of Allel Moose's household pinned her down, holding her still while she was indelibly marked as belonging to their community. Her tattoo was both a violation and, with "soft focus," a tool of survival in an environment where soldiers were continually looking for Armenians hidden among the Bedouin.

VERGEEN'S "SYMBOLS OF VALOR AND HONOR"

Vergeen Meghrouni's survivor testimony was published posthumously due to the intimate details of abuse, rape, and the brutal murder of her mother by the Arab tribe that absorbed her near Ras al-'Ayn, Syria. During her captivity, Vergeen and another abducted Armenian girl waited for the arrival of an "artist" to tattoo them. We learn that the girls were given a choice as to whether they would accept the tattoos. While her fellow abductee flatly objected to the tattooing on the grounds that "when we are free, people will know we were with the Arabs and shun us,"[11] hopelessness drove Vergeen to go forward with the tattooing, or at least not to resist it. She was given a *disini*, a common sun-shaped motif, in the middle of her forehead and a dot motif on the middle of her lower lip. Like Serpouhi, Vergeen was transformed from an Armenian into a Bedouin by her tattoo. "Now, I was marked as one of them, a tattooed Bedouin," she remarked.[12]

Vergeen's tattoos do not appear to be a source of shame at this point in the story. The brutal rape she endured at the hands of her male captor, described with unflinching detail, is, however, clearly internalized as shame. In a vivid exchange, she reports telling her abductor when he forced himself on her: "I can't do what you want. My mother taught me that only my husband can touch me." She remembered how he laughed mockingly, telling her that since she was a Christian, he would never marry her but instead would make her his concubine. She refers to the sexual assault as "an indelible stain" that ruined her both physically and spiritually. "Here I was, not yet fully blossomed into womanhood; yet, I was tarnished for life."[13] Her Armenian companion assured her that when she returned to the Armenian community she would not be shunned but accepted because what happened was not in her fault. Vergeen fell into depression and had thoughts of suicide, an emotion she also had to sublimate in order to survive because she believed she would be killed by her captor if she were perceived to be mentally unstable.[14]

Shame enters Vergeen's story again when she considers her facial tattoos during her reunion with her fiancé Armen—the man to whom she was betrothed at a very young age before the deportations—in America. Armen fails to recognize her at first due to how much she has grown. Her shame is quickly countered by Armen's loving acceptance of her tattoos when he compliments her appearance. Vergeen demurs: "Unconsciously, I covered my tattooed chin: and Armen gently pushed my hand away from my face," saying "You don't have to hide those marks from me. . . . Please Vergeen, remember this: I will always regard those marks as symbols of your valor and honor."[15] She recalls, "I smiled in profound gratitude and buried my face inside my coat collar to conceal my happy tears from onlookers at the [train] station. My fears of rejection melted in that moment." Vergeen's personal shame is met with unconditional acceptance by her future husband. Despite Armen's reassurance, however, Vergeen had the tattoos surgically removed and typically wore makeup to cover remaining tattoo marks in photos for the rest of her life.

By reading survivor narratives more closely, we can discover how male loved ones intervened to reframe the tattoos in more positive terms as marks of beauty and courage. Armen, in this sense, was not unusual in his attempt to comfort a tattooed survivor. One man reframed his niece's tattoos to a prospective groom in Adana: "You should marry my niece. Isn't she pretty with those tattoos on her face that accentuate her blue eyes?"[16] While the uncle may not have been able to break the cycle of shame with his words, the prospective groom married his niece within the year, indicating his efforts were not in vain. The groom was one of many Armenian men who actively sought out Armenian brides, regardless of their status, after the war.[17] Renarrativizing tattoos should be viewed as acts of resistance and loving gestures of acceptance by Armenian men who sought to comfort traumatized women and girls.

I am not arguing that these moments in which counternarratives appear were enough to overcome women's personal trauma and profound sense of shame. But we lose sight of how Armenian men sought to alleviate the stigma women were experiencing when we ignore these narratives. Male compassion is a consistent theme that runs through many accounts of reunion and post-trauma rehabilitation. Less known is that some men and boys were also tattooed during their time among tribal communities.

TATTOOED MEN AND BOYS

Perhaps the most overlooked or unknown counternarrative is the tribal tattoos of recovered Armenian boys, which bear the same motifs as those that adorn the face, hands, and chests of women and girls. Though men's tattoos are well documented in existing Turkish ethnographies on traditional tattoos, I was able to find only two documented cases of tattooed Armenian male survivors in the course of my research.[18] Based on these limited examples, men's narratives about tattoos are not stigmatized, nor are they interlaced with the horrific tales of sexual violence that are typical of women's narratives.

Though no photographs of the tattoos exist, one survivor was given a series of tattoos on his right arm, which he claimed represented a long "Arab knife" or dagger (Arabic: *khanjar*; Turkish: *hançer*)," a crescent moon, and a "badly drawn" spider. The survivor, Hagop Arsenian, understood the crescent moon and star on his right arm to be Islamic symbols, though within the broader universe of Mesopotamian tattoos, the cosmological symbols had a deeper history. The spider was one of the many desert insects inscribed as protective totems within tribal tattooing of the region. He confirmed that he believed "these tattoos were [made] to disguise Armenians as Muslims and were done by local Muslims (mainly Arabs) to assist [save] them."[19] As in the counternarratives of women, the male survivor understood the tattoos as serving to camouflage his identity when his life was endangered.

Another male survivor, Edward Racoubian (b. 1906), was adopted at age eight by an Arab family near Ras al-'Ayn, when his ailing mother could no longer walk during the deportation. In his remarkable testimony, he recalls that his mother stayed a day with him to make him a new shirt and spoke in Turkish to an interpreter, who translated her final words to his Arab adoptive father. Soon after she was found drowned in the river—Edward eerily suggests in his testimony that she may have been murdered by the Arabs.[20] While in his adoptive father's home, he received "tattoos on my hands and body. They branded me as their own."[21] I wonder whether the survivor, now deceased, meant that he belonged *to* them or did he belong *with* them after being tattooed?

Edward's tattoos are prominently displayed in the photograph but not commented upon in the six-page unpublished testimony he left behind. Years after his liberation from the oppressive household, he returned to visit his adoptive Arab father, who begged "Abdalla" to forgive him for the severe beatings he had given the boy, mostly along his spine, which caused him back pain for the rest of his life.[22] Edward told his abuser that he had indeed already forgiven him and instructed the Arab to beg forgiveness from God instead. From his death bed, the Bedouin Arab confessed that he had built a mosque to atone for his sins against the Armenian boy he had both rescued and abused. Despite this, Edward did not discursively connect his experience of abuse to his tribal hand tattoos, as was frequently the case with women survivors.

We are left with a reminder of the tattooed survivor in two portraits by Levon Parian and Ara Oshagan (figure 30). The portrait of Edward's tattooed hands prominently displays the wheat (*buğday*) or ear-of-grain (*başak*) motifs that trail along their sides. With these tattoos, the tribal artist was perhaps giving the wearer the blessings of fertility and abundance. Importantly, these are the same tattoo motifs frequently worn by the Arabs who rescued him in Ras al-'Ayn, as well as several female survivors.[23] I can see the triangulated three-dot ∴ sequences on his fingers and a frequently used motif among the Bedouin Arabs that represents the crescent moon (*hilal*). Edward bears a *tarak* symbol along right wrist, which was also worn by women, blessing his hands for the production of fine workmanship. Yet, what is certain is that his hand tattoos do not elicit the sense of outrage that even a single x-shaped tattoo on a woman survivor's hand received in the American press a century ago.[24] Certainly, the absence of facial tattoos in these cases made the tattoos less stigmatizing and objectionable as a form of defacement for men. The facial tattoos of Arab and Kurdish men are documented in existing tattoo anthropology, but they are less extensive than the tribal tattooing typically applied to women.

Examining tattoo motifs more closely can illuminate the unspoken context to lives and experiences of Armenian women and girls who were tattooed with more frequency. I will now offer a series of experimental readings of five biographies and images in order to excavate stories from the embodied archives these survivors left behind.

THE GIRL WITHOUT A NAME

The girl without a name is seated center frame. I know it is her because her dress is striped exactly as it is in her individual portrait, yet she looks extraordinarily small sitting on a stool in this group photograph (figure 24). Both photographs, the individual portrait and the group portrait of tattooed Armenian girls, are archived at Getty Images, part of a collection of three images taken by the same unnamed photographer who encountered the girls in August 1919.[25] In the group

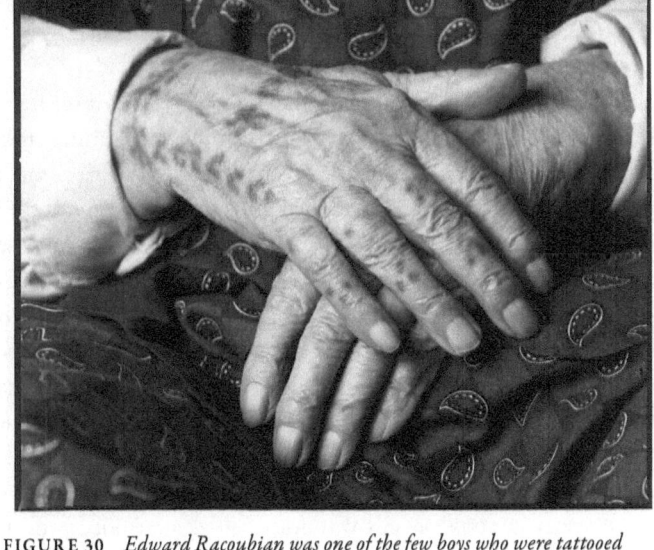

FIGURE 30 *Edward Racoubian was one of the few boys who were tattooed upon absorption into an Arab Muslim family home. His tattooed hands offer a glimpse into the counternarratives of tattoo often missed by commentators. Source: Photograph courtesy of Levon Parian and Ara Oshagan.*

photograph, teenage Armenian girls gather in the courtyard house that served as the YWCA shelter in Aleppo. Though all the girls are tattooed, only a few of the inked motifs are visible. The girls give the camera a stern glance, as if they were coached to look angry in an image destined for donors abroad. The clothing they wear ranges from tattered smocks to hand-me-down, high-necked Victorian and broad-collared dresses. One girl wears no shoes.

In the caption to her individual portrait (figure 31), the girl without a name was described as "hideously tattooed . . . to aid identification if she escaped from the horrible treatment." The caption embellished the violence already inscribed on the girl's tattooed body by adding another detail: she was expecting a child. Her folded hands accentuate her pregnant belly.

Beyond documenting her "hideous" tattoos, the photographer took some license with the girl's body, interpolating her through the humanitarian gaze. Her opened blouse bares not only her tattoos but her breasts in a "double exposure" that would have been as shocking as the tattoos to any viewer at the time. Under the pretext of documenting abuse, the photographer was either consciously or unconsciously emulating representations of bare-breasted North African natives that had been published in *National Geographic* a few years earlier, many of which had been staged to the extent that the hand of a man pulling back a blouse was inadvertently captured on camera.[26] We can see upon closer examination that safety pins are intentionally holding the girl's blouse open. Who put them there? The documentary nature of humanitarian photography created what Malek Alloula calls "the ethnographic alibi," a pretext to offer a little extra stimulus to a viewer already experiencing affective excess from the tattoos and the details in the photograph's caption.[27]

Reading the photograph with a "disobedient gaze," I can now see how the rescued girl's sorrowful expression may have just been the disciplining effect of the photographic process. It was easier to capture faces that were serious and unmoving. From a new perspective, the girl looks defiant as she looks down at the cameraman crouched before her. This pose also makes her look older and more seductive than she appears in the group portrait of young girls. In that group photograph of ten rescued, tattooed girls, her diminutive girlish frame, covered neckline, and stern gaze is devoid of any eroticism. In her individual portrait, her head is slightly tilted back, in a gesture emphasizing confidence but also suggesting sexual accessibility. It may have been this detail that prompted future audiences to assume the girl was a prostitute.

Recently, when this photograph was exhibited at the Museum of Natural History in Los Angeles in 2017, the girl was described as a tattooed prostitute in a caption that read: "Thousands of Armenian women were held as slaves and forced into prostitution. Their captors had the women tattooed on the arms and faces to identify them. This young woman escaped from a Turkish brothel with the help

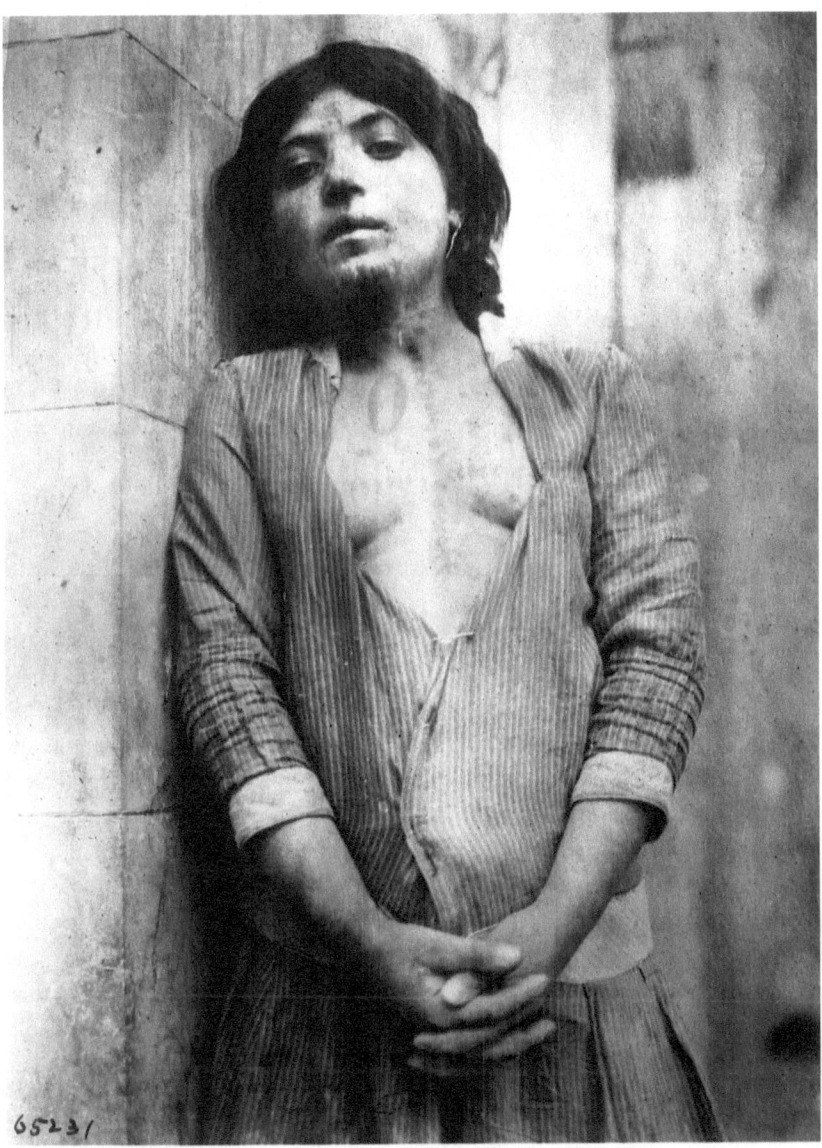

FIGURE 31 *In 1919, this photograph of a tattooed Armenian survivor in Aleppo was taken by an unnamed photographer. The original caption read: "An Armenian girl, recently rescued from a Turkish house and being cared for by the Y.W.C.A. workers at Aleppo, was hideously tattooed on the face and breast by her Turkish owner to aid identification if she escaped from the horrible treatment. She is about to become a mother—but she is only one of hundreds of such cases." Source: Reproduced with permission from the George Rinhart, Underwood & Underwood Collection, Getty Images.*

of the YMCA (Young Women's Christian Association) in Aleppo, Syria. But her fate remained forever etched on her face." The caption and its suggestion that the girl was a prostitute was reiterated in the *New York Times* coverage of the exhibit though she was never described as one in the original caption.[28]

That backward tilt of the head may have signaled sexual accessibility, but it also gave the photographer's seeking camera a better view of her tattoos, allowing them to speak to me a century later. The tattoos were applied professionally, and the tattooist's craftsmanship—professional tattooists in this tradition were always female—made the tattoo motifs largely legible within the frame. In other words, the blurring we see appears to be the poor quality of the image rather than the tattooist's skilled hand. From the standpoint of tattoo aesthetic, the ink traces the erotic zones of her body, a design that was not only considered beautifying but one that would elicit desire. Focusing on this context illustrates how the original intent of the motif stands in stark contrast to the unnamed humanitarian photographer's caption describing her as "hideously tattooed." Women who still bear tribal tattoos today note that their husbands are sexually aroused by the tattoos and the parts of the body they accentuate and beautify.[29] This suggests that both the placement of the tattoos and the opening of the blouse have one and the same function: the production of desire.

The girl's open blouse allows the tattoos to fill in some missing context erased in the archival process. I see the ^^^ and xxx shapes that crisscross her chest in a pattern called "the tree of life" (*hayat ağacı*) in traditional tribal tattooing of Anatolia. The motif forms the overall shape of a cross upon the girl's entire torso and though it stops above her belly button, it typically extends to the groin, connecting several erotic zones on the body. Some versions of this motif encircle and enhance the breasts. The cross shape is itself a powerful totem found on Muslim populations in Anatolia and Mesopotamia, but in this form, the tattoo blesses the wearer with a long, healthy life. The tree of life not only has protective powers when placed upon bodies; it appears in architectural features in both religious and secular spaces, as well as tombs, to bless the dead with an afterlife.[30] There is a faint suggestion that some of the x shapes that cover her chest may be star shaped-patterns * that double as life-affirming flower and fruit motifs, symbolizing the fertility of the woman bearing the tattoo. There is a mysterious outline of a stick body just above her navel at the end of the series of motifs.

Amid the tattoos covering her torso is a circular scar on her chest that resembles a brand. Was this mark the product of torture during or after the genocide? Was it made by one of the men who trafficked her or the household where she ended up? The horrifying scar speaks to what remains unspoken in the caption.

The communicative power of the girl without a name's "speaking scars," tattoo and brand, provide context where the caption did not. Tattoo motifs are never static, nor are they meant to be. Within the tribal universe to which they belong, tattoos were always context dependent, variable in interpretation, and their afterlives multiplied through the reproduction of her tattooed body in museums and online exhibitions. Which of its several meanings was the tattooist considering when she drew the tree of life upon the girl's chest? Was it a blessing? If so, how do tattoos and their affects make it possible for a blessing to be interpreted as a curse by a foreign photographer? Based on existing ethnography of tattoos in the region, it is very likely that the tattoo was applied at puberty, before the girl without a name was exchanged between men and transformed from a child into someone's concubine, wife, or even a prostitute.[31] Although the archived photograph is missing its context, "soft focus" allows for some new details to emerge that can further our understanding of not only the staging of the humanitarian photograph but clues to what the unnamed girl survived.

AGHAVNI: "THE LITTLE BRIDE"

"We call her 'The Little Bride,'" a humanitarian noted in the Aleppo Rescue Home intake record in 1925.[32] The rare inclusion of a nickname humanizes the fifteen-year-old runaway bride Aghavni Nersessian, who would have been about the same age as the unnamed girl in the Getty Images photograph.[33] By including her nickname and traces of her story, she is no longer just an object collected within the generic forms of the League of Nations Rescue Home, but a whole person whose harrowing story emotionally moved the humanitarian workers surrounding her. Aghavni does not recoil from the camera (figure 32). Her fierce gaze unflinchingly meets the camera, which makes her personality speak through the image. This gives us a good sense of why she made an impression on the foreign humanitarian worker who gathered fragments of her story:

> She had been forced to marry an old Arab, yet 8 days after the marriage she succeeded in fleeing to our house. A beautiful girl is she, but tattooed in an awful way. She remembers that she was deported with her parents. One day the caravan reached a valley near Rakka. The Arabs came over them. Aghavni's father was killed, she does not know anything about her mother. An Arab dragged her away and brought her to his tent. She remained there [for] 10 years and was then sold to another Arab with whom she was married.[34]

Aghavni's experience of being "sold" to an "old Arab" emphasized the cruelty and perversion at the heart of forcible transfers of young girls that continued well after the war. The girl had fled her situation one week after marriage, when sexual abuse certainly began or at least intensified, which gives us a glimpse into the extreme abuse endured by the Armenians left behind.

The humanitarian's description—"a beautiful girl is she, but tattooed in an awful way"—suggests that she was disfigured by her tattoo, despite the confidence

FIGURE 32 *Aghavni, inmate number 837, was nicknamed "The Little Bride" by the Rescue Home because she had fled from the old Arab man she had been forcibly married to a week earlier. Source: Reproduced with permission of the United Nations Archives at Geneva.*

conveyed in her pose. The tattoos themselves trouble the humanitarian gaze, forcing one worldview, that of the European humanitarian, to collide with that of the Arab tribe that had tattooed Aghavni. Aghavni's traditional *buğday çuvalı* (sack of wheat) motif resembles a series of three chevrons on her forehead between her eyes. The symbol is repeated in several images of tattooed women and a popular tattoo pattern in the region, frequently found on the throat and chest. The V-shaped pattern emulates not only a life-giving sack of wheat but is the shape of a womb, making the motif a blessing of fertility. The position of the tattoo between the eyes, in what is called a crown (*taç*) position, announces to anyone who encounters the young woman that she has been blessed.[35] Her chin is tattoo-free; the absence gives her forehead tattoo the communicative lead.

Aghavni has other tattoos, but they are not visible in the cropped portrait in the intake register; instead they can be found in a published version of her story retold to a broader Danish audience in the *Armeniervennen* newsletter.[36] The uncropped photograph communicated the story of trafficked women and children during the Armenian Genocide to its readership, members of the Danish Friends of Armenians. The full-body photograph features Aghavni in a floor-length dress, the exact clothing she wore when she escaped. She created some modest head covering by pulling her cloak up over the back part of her head. While at first the girl may appear to be wearing a traditional Muslim hijab, the staged photograph evokes classical paintings of the Virgin Mary, whose flowing headscarf draped to the ground. Aghavni's feet are not visible under the billowing fabric, giving her the appearance of a dove fleeing captivity, thus capturing the true meaning of her Armenian name.[37] As I consider Aghavni's absent feet, I also consider the powerful occasions in which tattooed Armenian hands were included in humanitarian portraiture in a way that gave them the power to witness.

VARTANOUSH'S AND JEGHSA'S HANDS THAT WITNESS

While it was rare to see hands in the photographs taken at the Aleppo Rescue Home, an image of thirty-five-year-old Vartanoush Kherbetjian gives hands the power to witness in humanitarian photographs. In her portrait, Vartanoush's tattooed face is paired with the intentional placement of her hands crossed on her chest (figure 33). Though it is difficult to know whether she or the photographer chose to position her hands this way, the gesture is that of a supplicant preparing to take communion. What stories are Vartanoush's weathered, tattooed hands telling us about her experience of genocide? As it turns out, Vartanoush's hands are testimony to one of the most remarkable stories of survival and resistance recorded at the Rescue Home.[38]

Before the war, Vartanoush was married to an Armenian named Sarkis Kherbetjian, who was drafted into the Ottoman military along with others. Miraculously, after three years of service, he returned home. Unfortunately, the deportation of fighting-aged men was underway as was the intentional feminization of the population. Fearing for his life, Vartanoush dressed Sarkis as a woman to conceal his identity. She was able to conceal his male identity for six months until he was deported from Geghi, north of Bingöl, along with his wife and son. His identity as a man was discovered during deportation by Ottoman gendarmes; they immediately killed him. The record, no longer mentioning her son, notes that during deportation, Vartanoush was abducted by an Arab who took her to his tent, using her as a servant for two years. She was then sold to another Arab, whom she served for four years until he was killed by a Kurd and she was sold off, yet again, to another Arab in Raqqa. The Arab in Raqqa had a wife and three daugh-

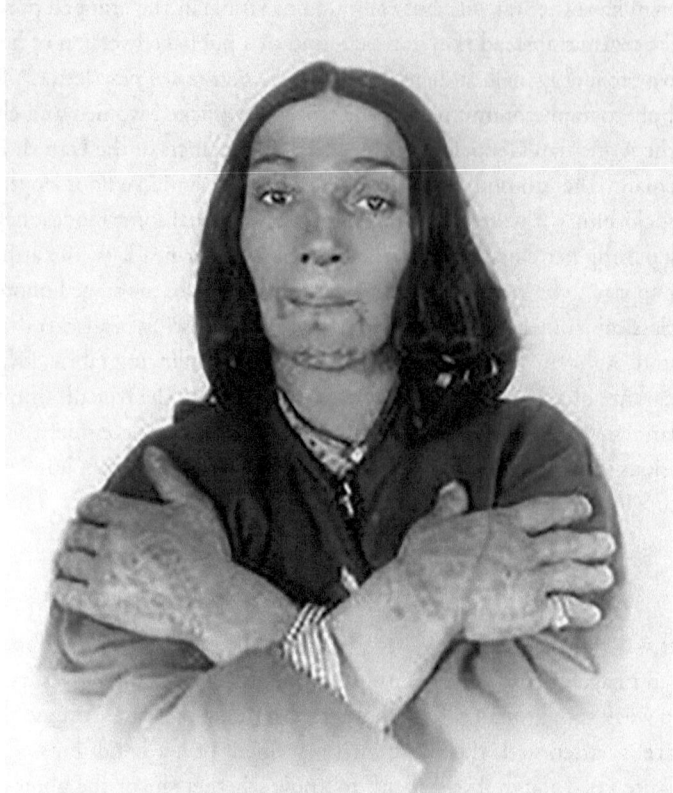

FIGURE 33 *Vartanoush Kherbetjian, age thirty-five. Vartanoush's intake photograph did not include her hands and her tattoos were barely visible. Jeppe kept the portrait of Vartanoush showing her hands in her private albums. Vartanoush was able to find her son and reach safety in the Rescue Home but died six months after arrival, her body unable to withstand what it had endured. Source: Reproduced with permission of Armenian Genocide Memorial Institute, Yerevan, Armenia.*

ters who were "very jealous" of Vartanoush and conspired to kill her. The women waited until the family patriarch was away on business to attack Vartanoush, beating her unconscious. Mistaking her for dead, they buried her alive. To her horror, Vartanoush awoke inside the grave. She was able to dig her way out of the grave with those overworked, tattooed hands and flee to Aleppo, arriving at the Rescue Home on April 16, 1925.

The very next entry in the Rescue Home register belongs to an Islamized Armenian boy named Aghabey, Vartanoush's now fourteen-year-old son birthed from her murdered husband Sarkis.[39] We do not learn how mother and son found each other, but like so many dispersed Armenians, the Rescue Home was where the remnants of the dis-membered Armenian community miraculously reunited.

Both mother and son arrived at the home on the same day, somehow finding each other upon Vartanoush's miraculous escape.

Returning to the photograph, Vartanoush's tattooed hands are testimony of her double survival, having survived the deportation and genocide and having defied death by crawling out of her own grave after being buried alive. In this sense, Vartanoush's hands are the Armenian equivalent of Whipped Peter's scarred back that formed photographic testimony of the horrors of American slavery. The wear on her hands tells yet another story, since, tragically, Vartanoush did not survive long after she arrived in Aleppo. She died six months later. Sobering evidence that survival was sometimes tragically short due to the extraordinary stress that genocide and enslavement placed on the bodies of victims.[40]

Another powerful example of hands that testify to the Armenian Genocide are those in the portraits of twenty-three-year-old tattooed survivor from Adıyaman Jeghsa Hairobediun [Yeghsa Hairabedian] (figures 34 and 35). Her portraits appeared not only in the Rescue Home registers but in Karen Jeppe's personal photographs scattered across archives in Gylling, Geneva, and Yerevan. The Danish humanitarian clearly had great fondness for Jeghsa, and the photographs may have been used in her fundraising lectures.[41] The story of Jeghsa's deportation, capture, servitude, and supernatural reunion with her mother was preserved in the Danish *Armeniervennen* newsletter:

> She was 8 then. Her father and an older brother were killed before her eyes. Her mother was torn away by a Kurd, and she suffered the same fate. She toiled from morning to night, still the cry sounded inside of her: "Let me find my mom!" Finally, her prayers were heard. She had to gather thistles and other brushwood from afar. One day, when she had walked far away, she met her mother, who was also gathering brushwood, and [Jeghsa] learned that she lived in a nearby village. How happy they were, a ray of sun had entered their existence. They met in secret, and after 15 years of suffering, they managed to escape and reach our home [in Aleppo].[42]

Two of the three surviving photographs of Jeghsa feature her tattooed right hand positioned mid-frame. Although her hand looks less weathered than Vartanoush's, each woman's mouth is downturned, their eyes gazing directly at the camera as if inviting the viewer to witness their testimony. Although the women have a decade between them in age, relief workers were quick to note that many women looked much older than their actual age to the extent that *The Slave Market News* printed an image of Jeghsa with the header "prematurely aged."[43] The accompanying article expressed surprise that Jeghsa was only twenty-three years old since she resembled, to the undisclosed author of the article, an elderly woman. Each year in captivity, we are told, ages an Armenian body by ten years. Another article described Jeghsa and other Armenian victims as having their fate inscribed

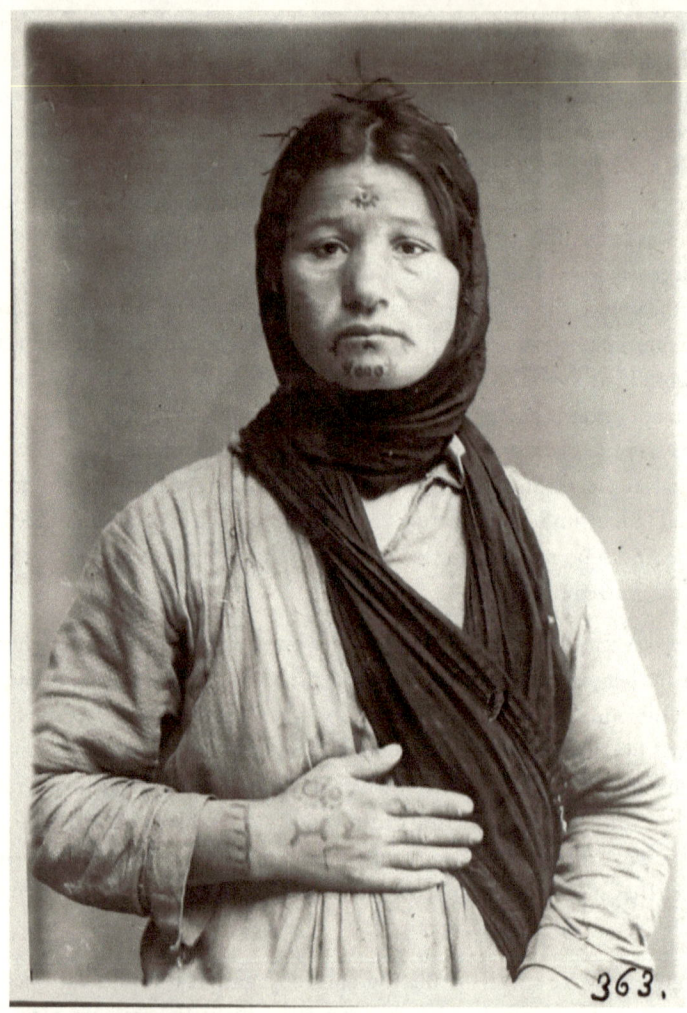

FIGURE 34 *Jeghsa Hairobediun [Yeghsa Hairabedian], a twenty-three-year-old survivor, appears to have held a special place in Karen Jeppe's work because she was photographed more than other rescued women and children. Two photographs in Jeppe's collection feature Jeghsa's tattooed face and hands such that the details of the tattoos are clearly visible. Source: Karen Jeppe's personal albums, photograph 363. Reproduced with permission of the Armenian Genocide Memorial Institute, Yerevan.*

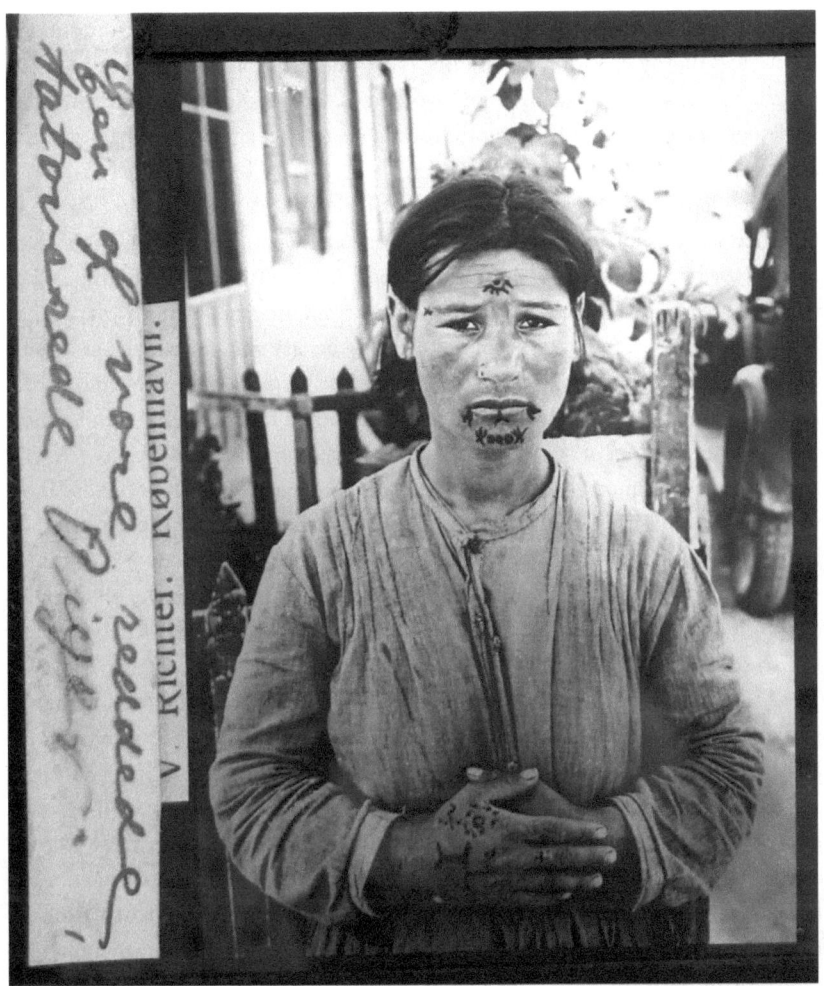

FIGURE 35 *A retouched photograph of Jeghsa highlights and accentuates her tattoos. The retouching, ironically, has preserved the motifs making them more legible. Jeppe often shared these photographs with humanitarian publications in Europe. Source: Reproduced with permission of the Karen Jeppe Archives, Gylling, Denmark.*

on their bodies. Jeppe wrote: "To see these young Christian women arrive, tattooed, abused. Torment was written on their faces that were aged before time."⁴⁴ References bodily corruption were not just a statement about the conditions in which captive women had lived and worked as servants for over a decade. They were suggesting that bodily corruption could result after a prolonged period living among uncivilized populations.

Karen Jeppe kept several photographs of Jeghsa in her private collection, none of which are captioned. Jeghsa's tattoos may have been retouched in the case of figure 35, which allows for the motifs to come into soft focus and communicate some context where none was provided. The *ceylan*, or gazelle, motif that Jeghsa bears between her eyes is a symbol representing beauty and grace. She has a mark on her right temple and a dot on the right side of her nose meant to emulate the nose ring commonly worn by Kurds of eastern Turkey. Jeghsa wears a comb (*tarak*) motif on her right wrist, a motif that Vartanoush wears on her right hand. Variations of the comb motif blessed any work the women did with their hands. Their weathered hands attest that they worked hard in those homes, possibly as weavers since a comb is used to consolidate rows of stitches on a loom. Yet, the sun-weathered brown patches of skin on their faces that are visible in the photograph are proof of a life of unimaginable toil. And their hands bear witness to both their unimaginable trials and their miraculous survival.

One hundred years later, the portraits and stories of tattooed faces and hands still elicit affective responses from viewers. These stories and images are rare, especially outside of the photographs in Jeppe's collections. Rebecca Jinks has speculated that photographers avoided taking photos of tattooed Armenian women because their tattoos made them uncomfortable.⁴⁵ But the stories these women and their tattoos have to tell are far more varied than the humanitarian and medical literature allows for—they demand we engage them disobediently to mine them for missing context with an eye toward decolonizing humanitarian photography for the purpose of writing a more inclusive history. The tattoos continue to hold currency for European and American humanitarians far more than they ever mattered to the local Armenian relief organizations assisting these rescues on the ground. If they had mattered, we would have more documents and records on the subject in Western Armenian.⁴⁶

It is significant, though, that Jeppe's mission focused on rescuing women from among Arab Bedouin and Kurdish populations along the Turkish-Syrian border, where higher concentrations of women practiced tribal tattooing. By examining images and stories of rescued tattooed Armenian women more closely, we can locate ciphered traces of the subaltern, plumbing these sources for unrecorded details missing from the written record. Reading images through this critical frame can grant the tattooed bodies captured in humanitarian photographs the power to witness and perhaps document hidden context and counternarratives. Among the untold stories of tribal tattoos is the universe within which inked skin was aesthetically pleasing and bore protective amulets and blessings for the wearer. In this reading, fertility motifs and the tree-of-life tattoo were meant to bless the wearer with a long life and rewards in the afterlife. Yet, for the bearers, these blessings were more often than not curses, painful memories of captivity engraved on their skin.

We must remember that the tattoo is, first and foremost, a wound.

I only began to understand the affective power of tattoos and the counternarratives they can reveal when I met the tattooed daughter of an Islamized Armenian woman along the Khabur River near Dayr al-Zur—a woman who was a living, breathing human archive.

I met Zahaya on my third trip to Dayr al-Zur, in 2008, when her son Sa'ad—an Islamized Armenian and a devout Muslim Arab of the Jabbour tribe—introduced me to her (figure 36). He had carefully collected memories of his grandmother, an Armenian girl who had been rescued by his grandfather, the district chief (*mudir al-nahiya*), on Tall Shaddadi in the spring of 1916. His grandmother was gathered with other girls the night before they would be marched to their deaths at the now infamous caves. The district chief was charged with guarding them over night, but instead he hid some of the girls in the village below. The story was harrowing as Sa'ad transmitted these prosthetic memories to me atop the hill that overlooked the village of Shaddadi next to the dry river bed that is now the Khabour River. The story was followed by a walk downhill to his mother's house to meet her.

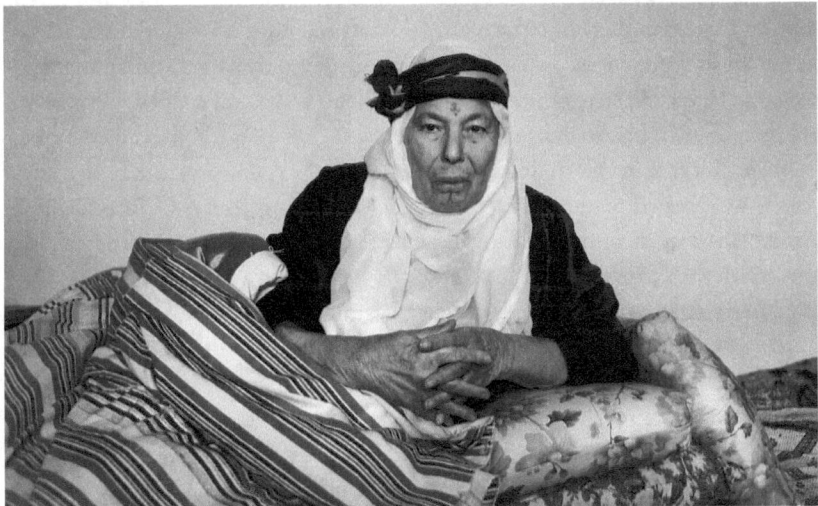

FIGURE 36   *Zahaya from Shaddadi, Syria, in 2008. She bears crosses on each of her thighs and a cryptic cross-shaped tattoo on her chin. Both were tattooed by her own Islamized Armenian mother. Source: Reproduced with permission of Kathryn Cook.*

Zahaya was a striking woman with light blue-grey eyes. She looked regal as she sat on a small couch with a blanket covering her lap. Unfortunately, she was crippled and could not stand without help. She shared what bits she remembered of her mother, Khanameh, the rescued Armenian girl from Aintab, who became the fourth wife of the district chief when she entered puberty. Her memory seemed weaker than her son's, or was it because we were strangers meeting for the first time? After traveling the deportation route from Aleppo to Dayr al-Zur to follow the path of my Armenian ancestors with traveling companion Kathryn Cook, my encounter with Zahaya was the apex of an intensely emotional journey—I started crying after weeks of playing the role of Armenian stoic during our trip along the deportation routes. This was surely weird for Zahaya. I tried to explain the history, where she was situated within it, and why I was emotional, but she didn't seem to register it. I heard one of the children of other wives in the polygamous household say dismissively in Arabic behind me, "Why are they here? Why does this matter to them?" I realized that Zahaya might be asking herself the same questions even though her son clearly knew why we were there. I realized mother and son didn't share the same interest in the past. Some people find it easier to move forward rather than look back.

It was Kathryn who asked Zahaya about the facial tattoo that lined her chin. The tattoo was an indigo cross, which complimented her blue-grey eyes. Zahaya told us that her mother had tattooed her herself. Kathryn asked if she had more tattoos on her body. It was then that Zahaya lifted the blanket from her lap and pulled up her dress to show us two large, darkly inked, cross-shaped tattoos, one on each thigh.[47] Seeing her tattoos was revelational. The cross motif is important both in Christian pilgrim tattoos and in Arab and Kurdish regional tattoo patterns. It can represent a cosmic star symbol or, alternatively, a talisman that protects the bearer. The cross motif is also believed to ward off sorrow.[48] But in the context of an Islamized Armenian mother, these symbols felt like an encrypted message. Survivors who could not express their Christian identities buried their secrets inside their bodies under their epidermal layer for survival. Was Zahaya's Armenian mother communicating her resistance to assimilation to us beyond the grave with these cross tattoos?

Zahaya's mother, known only by her Islamized name Khanameh—may not have left a single written record behind or a full account of her testimony. We don't even know her original Armenian name. But the woman who survived at Tall Shaddadi stamped her daughter with crosses as if to mark her as belonging to a Christian community that she would never know—marking her body like an enfleshed *khatchkar*, a cross-shaped memorial and tombstone, that represented the deaths of hundreds of thousands in the desert and the memory of all that was lost.

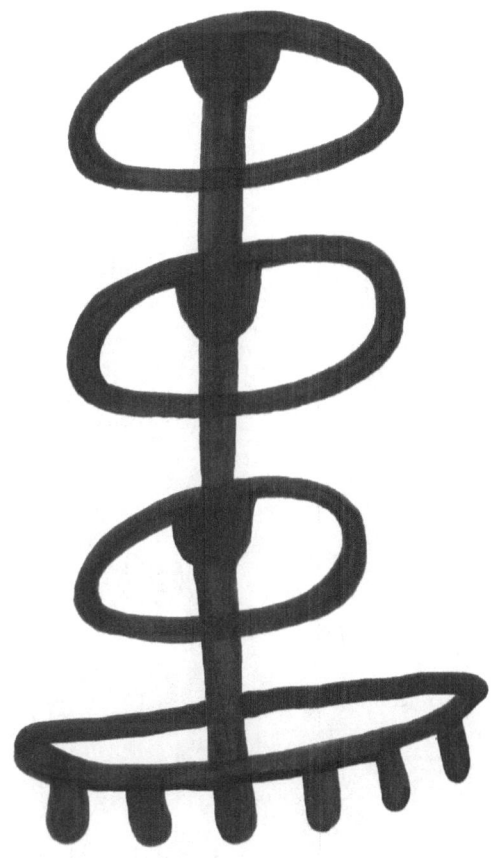

PART III
Bones

REMNANT 9

A Lamentation:
"In the Deserts of Dayr al-Zur" (Der Zor çöllerinde)[1]

Der Zor çöllerinde yaralı çoktur.	In the deserts of Dayr al-Zur, there are many wounded.
Gelme doktor gelme, çarası yoktur.	Don't come doctor, don't come, there is no remedy.
Bir allah'tan gayrı, hiç kimsem yoktur.	Other than God, I have no one.
Dininin uğruna giden ermeni.	Armenian who suffers for the sake of his religion.
Der Zor çöllerinde bayıldım kaldım.	In the deserts of Dayr al-Zur, I fainted, I swooned.
Harçlığım tükendi, evladım sattım.	I have no pocket money left, I sold my child.
Ana ben bu candan bıktım usandım.	Mother, I am worn down and fed up with my life.
Milleti uğruna giden ermeni.	Armenian who suffers for the sake of his nation.
Goyver ana goyver, gedelim çöle.	Let go, mother, let go, let us go to the desert.
Olalım çırçıplak arap'a köle.	Let us be a naked slave to an Arab.
Söylensin destanım, dillerden dile.	May they tell our story from one tongue to another.
Evladı uğruna giden ermeni.	Armenian who suffers for the sake of his child.

One verse of the lamentation was remembered differently by Yeghissabet Kalashian, a survivor from Musa Dagh:

> The deserts of Der-Zor are stony, impassable.
> The waters of the *get* [river] Euphrates are bitter and not potable.
> Water mixed with the blood of Armenians is undrinkable,
> Armenians dying for the sake of faith.[2]

FIGURE 37 *Vahan Papazian (1876–1973), known by the pseudonym "Goms," looks upon bones protruding from the soil in a during his pilgrimage to Dayr al-Zur in 1930. Born in Tabriz to a family originally from Van, the physician and revolutionary visited the region as a member of the Dashnag Party's central committee in order to support the Kurdish resistance movement against the Turkish government. Taken by Norwegian missionary Katharine Bodil Biørn, the photograph is among the earliest photographic evidence of both Armenian pilgrimage practices to Dayr al-Zur and the transformation of its landscape by genocide. Source: National Archive of Norway, Oslo.*

CHAPTER ELEVEN

IF THESE BONES COULD SPEAK
Early Armenian Pilgrimages to Dayr al-Zur

> If these stones, fields, and desert sands could
> speak, what stories would they tell?
> —GRIGORIS BALAKIAN[1]
>
> If only I knew the name of that skull.
> —HAMASDEGH[2]

"I wanted to bond with our people's grief, to make it part of my body and consciousness.... I wanted to go from Lebanon to Dayr al-Zur—that immense graveyard of our martyrs." Armenian essayist Hampartzoum Gelenian (1895–1966), known by his pen name Hamasdegh, scribed these words after his own pilgrimage in the Syrian Desert. First published in 1929, the essay "With a Skull" recounts Hamasdegh's encounter with "ribs ripped apart from spinal columns, knee caps and skulls," scattered fragments of bone comingling with and protruding from the soil. Hamasdegh described how in the gold-hued desert that comprised the killing fields, Armenian bodies "melded with the sands," an affective necrogeography, a landscape where land formations, human remains, and natural forces of erosion had congealed.[3] Moved by the scene, the essayist excavated the remains of a countryman from the desert floor: "It was from one of these sandy crevices that I removed, with both hands, a heavy, sand-filled skull, with awe and reverence, as a celebrant priest would raise the chalice with both hands during Mass" (figure 38). Invoking the moment in the divine liturgy when the holy wine is transformed into Christ's blood, Hamasdegh affirms the sacredness of Armenian bones to a sacrificed nation; his journey to the desert was an act of pilgrimage.

The sacred skull that Hamasdegh ruminates upon is no mere inanimate object; it communicates, signifies, and provokes the writer. "The shiny pallor of the skull

FIGURE 38 *Illustration that accompanied Hamasdegh's "With a Skull" (kangi me hed), in* Hamasdegh, *ed. Minas Minassian (Boston: Hamasdegh Jubilee Committee, 1969), 97. Source: Reproduced with permission of the estate of Minas Minasian.*

had almost acquired the color of ivory in the dry sand. Its sturdy array of teeth was powerful and expressive as a curse." For him, the skull was a speaking, living confidant during his journey. "We became travel companions the skull and I. Intimate friends sharing stories of green fields and desert days, me and the skull." The skull is rumored to have sat upon his desk while he composed the essay. Animated by the writer's pen, the skull pondered, the skull lived, the skull breathed, and the skull spoke wisdom to the author.

In the second part of the essay, Hamasdegh repeats, "If only I knew the name of that skull," as he imagines whom the skull may have belonged to among the caravans of Armenian deportees whose voices the author can hear in his head—yet I cannot help but notice how he imagines men of the cloth, pious men whose bones emerge from the earth as sacred relics. He asks, Did the skull belong to merchant and deacon of the church Mahdesi Arutin? Markar *vardapet*, a celibate priest and teacher? Or possibly Der Taghig, a priest conducting Mass as the massacres began? He imagines the priest supervising a dove-like children's choir dressed in white and singing in angelic voices as armed Turks and Kurds organized on the edge of town: "The church was now empty just like that skull, while the priest continued his celebration of Mass... and I heard the skull's incantations of the Holy Mass."[4]

In the final paragraph, Hamasdegh sacralizes the bones of Armenian martyrs, who Christlike, will be resurrected not by the Christian God but by the pre-Christian figure Haik, the mythical founder of the Armenian nation, whose trumpet will call the bones to form ranks of soldiers to reclaim their ancestral homeland. With an invocation of the ancient pre-Christian Armenian god of the harvest Navasard, Hamasdegh imagines green fields and a celebration of late summer bounty with a feast of lamb and produce harvested from the land. It is in those final lines that the scattered bones of Hamasdegh's (and my, for this is also my personal story of pilgrimage and bone memory) ancestors rise to act both as witness to genocide and historical agents in the making of a future Armenia within the affective necrogeography of Dayr al-Zur.

Hamasdegh's essay is illustrative of two main themes that emerge within pilgrimage narratives about the killing fields. The first is that, even for secular thinkers, bones—and human remains more generally—are sacred, consistent with religious conceptions of the sacred human body.[5] Second, and just as important, is the way that bones emotionally move pilgrims, some of whom became writers and creators of pilgrimage narratives, to remember their murdered countrymen. These memory works instruct how bone patina can project prosthetic memories to the survivor community, yet the mediated nature of these accounts can also impact those outside the Armenian community. Considering the affective power of bones instigates a shift in perspective from [live] human to [dead] bone agency prompts us to consider not only what we do with bones but what bones do to us.[6]

Human remains move us to tears and make us feel things that we would not feel without contact with them. While reluctant to go so far as to see bones as historical and political agents of resistance, Achille Mbembe notes that lifeless bodies quickly reduced to petrified bone have a "stubborn will to mean, to signify something."[7] Materialist scholars have urged us to contest the clear boundary between agent and object, arguing that the body should not be viewed as a perfectly contained vessel but instead as a leaky container that fails to hold its contents. Scholars have asked us to consider the complex exchanges between bodies, objects, and environment. The material turn encourages us to read sources differently and to think about how living bodies, environments, and bone remains interact with one another in ways that incite feelings, emotions, and embodied acts of remembrance.

Eyewitness accounts describe how Armenian bodies violently inscribed by Ottoman state sovereignty were transformed into human debris, strewn in the Syrian Desert. Bodies transformed into bone assumed a deferred agentic quality as both movers of contagion and inspiration within the ceremonies of survivors. The affective quality of bones has been observed by Armenian Genocide survivors and their descendants who have traveled to engage, excavate, and sometimes collect bones of victims within the necrogeography of Dayr al-Zur. Armenians make meaning with bones in the Syrian Desert, transforming them from discarded refuse into sacred objects of reverence. Some of the earliest visitors to these sites of mass atrocity, like Hamasdegh, were themselves genocide survivors who collected human remains to offer care denied their countrymen when they perished. Within this affective necrogeography, dis-memberment is re-membered through memory practices and ritual that give the dead the power to witness through the living bodies of pilgrims. As bones are reanimated in Armenian memory work and narratives about Dayr al-Zur, they form a potent antidote to the paradox of Auschwitz, as described by Agamben, that rendered victims incapable of witnessing.[8]

"Part III: Bones" engages in an interdisciplinary reading of memoirs, journals, poems, photo essays, and oral interviews,[9] in order to rehabilitate Armenian communal memory of Dayr al-Zur. Reconstructing the meaning of Dayr al-Zur to Armenians was made more urgent when a formal memory marker, the Armenian Genocide Memorial Museum and the Holy Martyrs Church at the center of the pilgrimage, was destroyed by an explosion attributed to ISIS in 2014. While the church is currently being reconstructed, recent events have underscored the precariousness not only of the memorial but of a region whose land and inhabitants have been ravaged by war over the last decade. The multiple layers of bone and trauma contained within the Syrian Desert pose a challenge to this reconstruction but also offer an opportunity to consider the shared trauma belonging to both Armenians and local Dayri Arabs over the last hundred years in this troubled border zone.

DAYR AL-ZUR: THE ORIGINS OF A DEATHSCAPE

Straddling the border of northeastern Syria and southern Turkey, the Euphrates and Khabur River basins have witnessed a century of violence. At the time of the genocide, northeast Syria comprised a segment of the Arabic-speaking boundaries of the Ottoman Empire. Many are familiar with the arbitrary boundaries of the modern Middle East designed by the Sykes-Picot Agreement (1916). Lesser known perhaps is that the Treaty of Sèvres (1920), negotiated between the Allies and the Ottoman Empire, recognized the formation of an Armenia, ambiguous as to whether it would be a mandate or independent entity, within parts of eastern Anatolia.[10] However, the armistice terms were rewritten as Turkish forces mobilized by Mustafa Kemal, the founder of the Turkish republic in 1923, advanced into Allied occupied regions, establishing the political boundaries that we recognize today. Yet, both states—Turkey and Syria—have unfaithful borders that threaten to betray states as the diverse groups that live there hold mixed allegiances. Arabs, Turks, Armenians, and Kurds have transnational affinities—hinting at the limits of the modern state's capacity to contain porous identities that flow across artificially created geopolitical lines.[11]

Near that fraught Turkish-Syrian border is Dayr al-Zur. Peter Balakian captures how even the name produces a powerful affect in the person who utters it. It "sticks with you, or sticks on you, like a burr or thorn: 'r' 'z' 'or'—hard, sawing, knifelike."[12] The cliffs along the Euphrates and Khabur basins formed deportation routes during the genocide as the landscape itself was weaponized. Dayr al-Zur is a place, but it is much more. It is a *deathscape*, a term that captures its significance as an assemblage of memory, emotion, ritual, and material bone where living, moving descendants re-member dis-memberment.[13] The symbolism of Dayr al-Zur as a deathscape was formed through prosthetic memory—that is, accounts that were transmitted in oral and written testimony, much of it published in the Armenian press in real time by deportees who witnessed it. In 1919, Yervant Odian recalled that upon learning of his destination during deportation, he knew "we were going to the one place whose name, for the last two years, every Armenian said with horror."[14] Grigoris Balakian, Peter's great-granduncle, described Dayr al-Zur as "the largest cemetery of the exiled Armenians" in his two-volume 1922 memoir titled *Armenian Golgotha* (Hay koghkotan).[15] Grigoris *vardapet* vividly describes the desert as a liminal zone dominated by the inversion of norms, where human ethics no longer applied. Armenian deportees were raided, abducted, enslaved, tortured, and dismembered by a combination of tribal groups, gendarmes, and Ottoman irregular forces.

> We saw caravans of women, completely naked because the Yeneze bandits who greeted the caravans had taken even their undergarments. We came across corpses as naked as the day they were born and with eyes gouged out; all their limbs had been cut off for sport and their bodies were swollen; their entrails were spilled out; during the daytime, the vultures would descend on these corpses and feast, while it was the wild animals' turn at night.[16]

Genocide performed its ultimate task in the Syrian Desert by making Armenians unrecognizable as humans even to fellow deportees as they were effectively prepared as animals prepared for slaughter.

Over time, the landscape became an unnatural environment manufactured by mass killing, a necrogeography, as witnesses encountered bodies and body parts in various states of decomposition. In 1921, Karen Jeppe noted, "Along the Eufrat [Euphrates] are still to be seen their discovered bones spread over the road, in like manner around the stations of the Baghdad Railway. In the deserts of Der Ser [*sic*] and Ras-el-Ajn [*sic*] they were slain in the thousands."[17] Survivor Kerop Bedoukian offers a powerful description of how mass killing formed the desert into a necrogeography in his memoir of survival as a child deportee. Rivers and brooks full of contaminated bodies in various states of decay under the hot sun altered the topography.¹⁸ In an unnervingly dispassionate account, he describes how, as a child, he became adept at judging how old corpses were based on the level of decomposition and oil patterns visible in the desert sands:

> The body oils on the sand were spread in a six-foot circle around each cadaver and each body seemed to be completely naked. . . . I forced myself to examine the stinking bodies to guess the time of their deaths. There was a time when the body melted completely into the sand under the hot desert sun—I thought this condition was reached in about six days. When I saw a baby still clinging to her dead mother's breast, I knew this death was quite recent.¹⁹

Such macabre observations allow us to reconstruct how the landscape became agentic, overflowing with corpses and contagion, due to the sheer volume of killing.

In 1916, a year after the initial killings of Armenian deportees, there were reports of typhus epidemics within the eastern provinces of the Ottoman Empire, and a gruesome paradox ensued. Armenian bodies that had been stuffed into village wells and flung from bridges and cliffs into ravines, valleys, and rivers, where they decomposed, invited disease back into the communities that had murdered them. Recall how Talaat Pasha had initially described Armenians as a contagion, a tumor on the empire; now, waterways choked with decomposing corpses left the water contaminated and undrinkable. With the outbreak of disease, the landscape itself had become a vector for disease that threatened non-targeted populations, including the Ottoman military passing though the same landscape. On some days seventy-five or eighty soldiers were dying from typhus.²⁰ Historian Raymond Kévorkian has shown that the cycle of contagion prompted a shift in Ottoman policy in an attempt to contain it.²¹ The land was to be cleared of all remnants of Armenians and future killing was to take place outside major towns to preserve the health of Muslims who were now threatened with disease.

The authorities began to devise new methods of disposal—mass burial and burning—to protect the Muslim population from the hygienic threat. Armenian deportees noticed how the ground was still moving as half dead Armenians buried in shallow graves struggled beneath the thin layer of earth: "Some of them were still alive, since the earth over them was moving."²² Grigoris *vardapet* laments that the burials he witnessed were not ritualistic but instead performed haphazardly by Muslim laborers who were brought in to cleanse the land of Armenian bodies. The priest's memoirs describe multiple pits, trenches, and natural caves that were used to dispose of bodies and control contagion. Scars on the Ottoman landscape were observable at sites where mass burials had been conducted months before:

> The land stretching before us from Islahiye seemed like a battlefield for the plain was covered with innumerable large and small mounds of earth. These were the graves of Armenians who had been buried fifty or a hundred at a time,

and though winter had passed, the mounds of earth had kept their convex shape—and alas, some were veritable hills.... When we were seized with the thought that these were human hills, filled with Armenians, ... our despair and demoralization reached such a level that we contemplated suicide.[23]

The "human hills" created by concentrated mass killing transformed the landscape of the Syrian Desert into an affective necrogeography. The observations of the mass scale of killings by Armenian deportees allow us to imagine that every hill and valley in the Syrian Desert contains the remnants of Armenians murdered there. Embedded in the necrogeography of the Syrian Desert are bones, fossilized memories brought to life by the living Armenians who engage in creative rituals of mourning and remembrance.

PROSTHETIC MEMORIES OF DAYR AL-ZUR: THE GENESIS OF PILGRIMAGE

In the years after the Armenian Genocide, Armenian pilgrims have narrated and imagined the remains of their ancestors and even themselves reflected in the sands of the Syrian desert.[24] Many Armenians who visited these sites to grieve over the Armenian bones in the desert never documented their visits. I discovered a passing reference to bone collecting in Dayr al-Zur in a letter Ruben Herian wrote to his relative Mirak, dated April 15, 1919. "Yesterday, I arrived here to visit the graveyard of 200,000 Armenians." While immersed in the work of collecting live bodies of women and children during the vorpahavak, Herian collected "fragments" (*pegorner*) of Armenians, a reference to bones, that he sent to "Cilicia," shorthand for the catholicos of Sis in Cilicia.[25] The rescuer added, "I am sending you a sample [*nmush*] inside this letter that shows the Turkish monsters' crimes, a real picture of the poor exiles wandering the deserts." Herian included short biographies of three women that he imagined the bones belonged to, stories he likely gleaned among the victims whose stories he had heard during rescue operations: "Aghavni, her shoes all wrapped in rags, her feet swollen, bloody, and full of wounds, refusing to walk. Ovsanna has interred her child who has died of hunger into the ground and is crying and praying. Azniv who is covered with torn clothes complaining with a desperate look to this civilized world."[26] The biographies enfleshed the bones he sent in the envelope forming them back into living subjects. Feminizing the bones in short biographical sketches was a tacit recognition of the feminized deportee caravans in Dayr al-Zur. Like Hamasdegh, Herian animated the bones narratively until they formed a picture of three individual women whose experiences should be remembered and mourned.

Writers left behind robust texts of their journeys, but some historical traces exist only in the memories of survivors. In 1928, a group of Armenians who had survived the genocide and continued to live in Dayr al-Zur traveled northward ten kilometers outside the city to a mass grave site located on the west side of the Euphrates River. They brought a crew of workers and large trucks to dig a large hole, eight to ten meters wide and three meters deep, and spent a week excavating the bones they found. Even little Janig Yeranossian, who was about ten years old at the time, helped to collect the thousands of bones. He recalled, "You could see all the white bones, skulls, lying on the ground." He claimed that somewhere back in Syria there is a photograph of him holding two bones in his little hands from the dig.

The local Armenians took the truckloads of bones and buried them near the large bridge in Dayr al-Zur on the Euphrates. The new grave was never marked and later was plowed and irrigated into pasture land by local Arab farmers. In the archived oral history, the interviewer asked Yeranossian whether he could go to Dayr al-Zur and still find the bones. He replied that there was no way that the bones could have remained intact that long: "Can bones remain for sixty years?"[27] Surely, he claimed, they had already dissolved into the soil. According to Yeranossian's memories, some of the bones from what may have been the first attempt at mass excavation were buried at a memorial in the original Surp Hripsimae Armenian Church in Dayr al-Zur, the church that predated the construction of the Holy Martyrs Church. He suspected that other bones collected during the community excavation were taken to Aleppo, Yerevan, Etchmiadzin, Beirut, and Damascus.[28]

Among the visits to Dayr al-Zur documented in the first decades after the genocide is an account by Armenian folklorist Tovmas Arapian. His journey in July 1935 was self-designed and conducted with a relative living in Raqqa who knew the region well. The group grew to four Armenian pilgrims, who rented a car to travel the length of the Euphrates from Meskene to Tel Abyad and Arab Pounar, working their way eastward toward "the slaughterhouse." Arapian described the experience of seeing past events in real time, illustrating how encounters with the necrogeography of the killing fields can trigger prosthetic memory. Arapian witnessed the ghosts of his own relatives upon seeing the scarred landscape full of holes and rocky spaces: "We were thinking that our martyred relatives were inside that place. Still, one after another, a human caravan was marching before our eyes. Hungry, thirsty, without sleep and tired, under the military's stick they were pushed to the slaughterhouse."[29]

While witnessing the past, the pilgrim simultaneously saw human remains in the lands he explored. "From Tel Abyad to Arab Pounar, the whole length, we saw many bones spread on the hills, in the caves, at the edge of the Euphrates." He saw the bones of his imagined kinsmen in the lush green fields and within the riverbed of the Euphrates. "With summer, the Euphrates's water was reduced so that we could see small hills in the river bed. We could also see our dear relatives there, fathers', mothers', brothers', and sisters' skulls and [other] bones."[30] The earth was

If These Bones Could Speak   233

transformed by the mass killing during and after the genocide as green pastures and rivers continued to bear the signs of what had transpired years before. Those on the journey collected bones to take with them, but Arapian did not explain the rationale for collecting human remains nor what was done with them afterward. For decades, Arab farmers churned up the bones of Armenians along the Euphrates while farming, spitting up the past with their plows.[31] But for others, excavating bones was more intentional: for the purpose of building a monument to remember the nameless victims in the desert.

MAKING A MONUMENT—THE EXCAVATION OF HARUTYUN HOVAKIMYAN, 1938

In 1938, three years after Arapian's self-designed journey, the first formal expedition to retrieve bones from Dayr al-Zur happened at the request of the Armenian catholicosate of Sis which by then had moved from its ancestral location in Cilicia to Antelias, Lebanon.[32] The Holy See chose Armenian Genocide survivor and orphan rescuer Harutyun Hovakimyan to lead the three-week expedition. His intimate knowledge of eastern Syria was obtained during his work recovering living bodies of Hadjin's orphans, whom he had collected and placed in rescue homes from 1927 to 1935.[33] In November 1938, he would set out on a different kind of rescue mission: the recovery of the remains of prominent Ottoman Armenian parliamentarians Krikor Zohrab and Vartkes Serengülian, who were reportedly nailed to the ground, tortured, beheaded, and dismembered near the Black Bridge [Karaköprü] outside Urfa.[34] Hovakimyan wrote of his mission in an unpublished memoir: "It is very dangerous but I had to do this because the archbishop gave me this mission to succeed by any means necessary, to not let these people who gave their hearts for the Armenian nation remain under the feet of the enemy."[35]

During his perilous journey, Hovakimyan traveled to the Jazira to cross the border into enemy territory. After meeting with Kurdish nobleman Ali Reza Bederkhan bey, he was smuggled into Turkey dressed as a Kurd. In his handwritten memoir, Hovakimyan pasted a photograph of himself in disguise bearing a French rifle given to him by the bey and riding a white donkey. He arrived near Urfa only to discover that Turkish guards were posted near the site where the Armenian politicians' remains were located, making it too dangerous to approach.[36] Unable to even approach the site of massacre, Hovakimyan returned to the Jazira region of Syria, the region of most intense mass killing, to locate and excavate bones of other important Armenians who perished in the desert.

The Armenian humanitarian interacted with local Kurdish chieftains and Arab elites whom he had previously worked with to rescue children in the region. He formed an alliance with the Kurdish 'Ali Reza Bederkhan and Syrian politician Hashim Atassi, the former governor (*qa'imaqam*) of Hovakimyan's hometown of

Hadjin. Atassi, described as "a personal friend" (*paregam*) who understood the "black fate" (*sev djagadakir*) of the Armenians. Atassi received him warmly in Homs, Syria, and helped secure permission from the Syrian authorities for Hovakimyan's mission to Dayr al-Zur.³⁷

Through his complex networks with regional Muslim leaders, the same networks Armenians had used to rescue live bodies were replicated during the recovery of human remains. The Syrian government in Damascus permitted Hovakimyan to exhume mass grave sites along the deportation route from Meskene, Raqqa, Ras al-'Ayn, Shaddadi, and Dayr al-Zur.³⁸ This time, Hovakimyan was instructed by the catholicos to look for the remains of a different martyr, Hovhannes Garanfilian *vardapet* of Zeitun, who had been arrested with twenty members of the Dashnag Party and exiled to Dayr al-Zur. Once again, Hovakimyan drew upon his contacts from the vorpahavak to locate the bones of the murdered celibate priest.

> In 1935, when I came to save the Hadjin orphans [during the vorpahavak], I met an Arabgirtzi named Krikor the tailor who was the *mukhtar* at the time of the genocide and had told me about the martyrdom of Zeitun's Archbishop Karanfilian *vardapet*. He is now deceased but his wife Satenig Haigian is there and can give me information about this *vardapet*'s corpse's [*adjoun*] location. I went to find Mrs. Satenig, a precious, honorable Armenian lady—deep inside her eyes are the suffering of her nation.³⁹

Digin Satenig Haigian (figure 39) did not write her own memoir, but she held in her memory the location of Hovhannes *vardapet*'s bones as well as the deceased priest's story.⁴⁰ She remembered the infamous governor of Dayr al-Zur Zeki bey, who was appointed in the summer of 1916 to expedite the extermination of Armenians. The governor tortured the priest to death in prison and, to cover up the event, registered his death as resulting from a typhus infection.⁴¹ Charged with washing of the priest's clothing, Satenig and her husband Krikor had held onto the priest's belongings only to have them confiscated by police after he was murdered. She told Hovakimyan, "Yes, I know in which hole the vardabed's bones are buried [alongside] well-known Toros Tchaghlassian of Kilis and also Director of the German Bank Sahakian Effendi of Aintab." She explained how her deceased husband Krikor wept when he took her to the site where the bodies were buried. Guiding the crew decades later, the widow retraced the footsteps of the twenty-minute walk outside to the bounds of Dayr al-Zur. "We walked with heads down" to the places her deceased husband had shown her, Hovakimyan asked himself, "Which one of these holes is the right one? Is it the place of the wind or the resting place of our sacrificed people's bones?"

At the site, there were both natural and manmade holes in the earth. They wasted no time and began digging. "With the bell ringer [of the St. Hripsimae Church in Dayr al-Zur], we started to work on the hole on the right side of the

FIGURE 39 *Digin Satenig Haigian, the survivor who guided Hovakimyan and his crew to the grave of celibate priest Hohannes Garanfilian vardapet of Zeitun at a mass grave site in Dayr al-Zur. Source: Harutyun Hovakimiyan, Hishadagaran, unpublished memoir, fond 450, list 2, no. 72, 172. Reproduced with permission of the Armenian National Archives, Yerevan.*

path. The bell ringer dug the hole in the sand and I shoveled it. After a while, we found ourselves in a frightening scene—while digging we found skulls without eyes, arm bones, and other things."[42] As the bones became visible during the dig, Lady Satenig, overcome with emotion, asked the crew to stop their work for the day. "'Let's go, Baron Harutyun. I cannot bear anymore!' the lady said crying, putting her hands on her face."

A handful of photos were taken during the expedition, but none are as powerful as the photograph of Hovakimyan and his crew snapped by an Armenian photographer bearing only the first name Onnig (figure 40). The only information accompanying the photograph says that it was taken at a site a twenty-minute walk outside the city where the desert begins to appear. Lady Satenig is conspicuously absent from the scene. The expedition leader holds a small skull missing its mandible. The smallness of the skull Hovakimyan cradles in his hand makes it appear like a reverse negative of the live children he saved during the vorpahavak. A second man gestures to the skull with his left hand while holding more bones, possibly a femur and hip joint, in his right.[43] The man crouched next to the hole is Baron Murat Keledjian, who owned an Armenian inn called Murat Hotel in Dayr al-Zur, and whom Hovakimyan described as "nation lover and full-blooded Armenian" (azkaser yev zdariun hay me). The man on the right of the pit is the bell ringer of St. Hripsimae Armenian Church in Dayr al-Zur. He is unnamed both in the archival photograph and in Hovakimyan's memoir, though he worked side by side with Hovakimyan to dig the pit while the others looked on. The man next to the bell ringer looks pensive, directly staring into the pile of bones with his head tilted downward in a way that completes a series of gestures affirming that the purpose of this photograph is to amplify a profound moment of witnessing.

Hovakimyan and the other men in the photo are dual witnesses. They witnessed the genocide firsthand as survivors but were also enlisted in gathering material proof of the trauma they and other Armenians experienced. The photo of Hovakimyan and his crew emphasizes the sheer volume of bones they discovered during their excavation, compelling the viewer to witness the war crime along with the crew. On the expedition, they gathered four boxes of bones from mass killing sites in Dayr al-Zur (including under the bridge), Margada, and Shaddadi and delivered them to the catholicosate in Lebanon.[44] It was there that a memorial chapel was constructed at the Holy See to hold the remains Hovakimyan had collected during his 250-kilometer expedition inside Syria. Fragments of skeletons and skulls were placed in a small chapel specifically designed as a memorial across from St. Gregory, the church of the Holy See of Sis; other bones may have remained in Dayr al-Zur. One document suggests that some of the bones Hovakimyan collected eventually made their way into the memorial at the Holy Martyrs Church a half century later.[45]

Moving forward to 1977, the local Armenian community in Dayr al-Zur consisted of only eighteen households. They prayed in the simple brick and adobe St. Hripsimae church built to service the community's remaining survivors and their descendants by the Aleppo prelate Ardavasdt Surmeyan in 1938–1939. The church also housed a memorial and bones excavated by locals. Archbishop Souren Kataroyan, prelate of Aleppo from 1977 to 2003, recalled just how "dilapidated and abandoned" the church had become over time. "When dignitaries from Armenia came to that abandoned church, as prelate I felt ashamed and it caused me

If These Bones Could Speak

FIGURE 40 *A 1938 expedition of Armenians led by Harutyun Hovakimyan, standing in an excavation near the Dayr al-Zur Bridge. Next to him is a local innkeeper, Murad Kelejian. In the background are the bell ringer of the St. Hripsime Church in Dayr al-Zur and an unknown worker who hides his face from the camera. In Hovakimyan's unpublished memoir, there is another photograph taken at the site in which the innkeeper Baron Murad stands in the pit. Additional photographs of this expedition are located in the Armenian Genocide Memorial Institute Archives, Yerevan, Armenia. Source: Reproduced with permission from the personal collection of Minas Minassian.*

to have one aim, and this aim was that the memorial for our martyrs should beautifully radiate within the heavens above Dayr al-Zur."[46]

Under Kataroyan's leadership and with the encouragement of Catholicos Karekin II in Antelias, he dedicated himself to constructing a proper memorial for those who perished in the killing fields. The work was facilitated by an anonymous benefactor who offered one kilo of gold to support the efforts, equivalent to a 30,000 Syrian lira down payment. Once the work was underway, the benefactor offered a second installment of gold valued at 800,000 Syrian lira to support construction. The catholicosate decided to host a competition for Armenian architects to design the church and memorial. The design contest was won by Lebanese-American architect Sarkis Bel Manoukian.[47]

The construction of the church and memorial was not without controversy. It relied on local Muslim laborers, who at one point while sculptors were creating the *khatchar* (traditional crosses that also served historically as gravestones), halted their work to ask a local Muslim cleric whether it was permitted for them as Muslims to create Christian crosses. Ultimately, the cleric they had consulted blessed their work, noting that creating crosses as paid work was not the same as worshipping them. While supervising the labor over a nine-month period, Archbishop Kataroyan traveled to Dayr al-Zur once every fifteen days, making the entire 335-kilometer round trip often in a single day. When the church and memorial were finally consecrated in 1990, Catholicos Karekin II visited the site from Lebanon and upon entry, the cleric fell to his knees, walking in supplication twenty-five meters inside the structure to fulfill a vow (*okhd*) he had made to see the project through to completion.[48]

Archbishop Kataroyan shared vivid memories of the day the Holy Martyr's Church opened. The first was a recollection about local Dayri Muslim women offering cool water from their doorsteps to the ten thousand Armenians who had descended on the town for the opening ceremony. Some of these Muslim participants shared with the pilgrims that they too were born of Armenian mothers. The second memory the archbishop recalled was even more profound. He remembered that among the visitors was a Muslim woman who entered the church courtyard and raised her sleeve to expose a tattoo on her arm. This tattoo was not a tribal tattoo like those of Islamized women in part 2, but was an Armenian tattoo that read Թագուհի (*taquhi*), a popular Armenian name that means "queen."[49] The woman explained, "My mother tattooed me here so that I would not forget my Armenian identity." By inscribing her true Armenian name onto her arm in indelible ink, her mother marked her as Armenian despite assimilation. The daughter of an Islamized Armenian survivor said before the prelate: "Let this be a penance for my sin that I took a foreign man as my husband. Despite this, I am still visiting the Armenian martyrs."

The bones Hovakimyan collected at Dayr al-Zur traveled to Antelias, Lebanon, the seat of the catholicosate, where they were placed in a courtyard memorial chapel. On December 17, 1938, on the occasion of the holiday of Christian martyr Surp Hagop (Saint James), ground was broken for a memorial in Antelias for "those who sacrificed their blood for our nation and our religion" only a few months after Hovakimyan had completed his journey.[50] The catholicosate said its intent at the time was to form "a place of pilgrimage which touches our hearts because thousands of Armenians will come to the memorial of the sacrificed generation to continue living as an Armenian and keep their Armenian nation going."[51] Archbishop Kataroyan also captured this sentiment in his recollections when he argued that the monument was created not only for the dead but for the nation that had miraculously resurrected itself from the ashes, a tribute not only to past but to future generations of Armenians. He believes that all Armenians carry with them an obligation to the past and the memorial is a reminder to those "reborn of a martyred nation."[52]

The religious significance of these memorials for the Armenian community was reinforced when the archbishop named a second chapel in the Syrian Desert at the mass grave site in Margada Surp Haroutiun, or "the holy resurrection."

The memorial chapel in Antelias would later house an altar on the eastward-facing wall; under it is an ossuary for the bones collected at Dayr al-Zur. Today, the ossuary remains in the chapel bracketed by two additional vertical glass ossuaries that climb toward the ceiling and displaying the bones under a dramatic soft yellow light reminiscent of Dayr al-Zur's desert sands. When I peered inside the ossuary for the first time in 2007, I saw myself in the reflection of the immaculately polished glass. It was so reflective that I saw myself among the anonymous bones: The bones and I were one. The bones and reflection seemed to transmit the prosthetic memory of the affective necrogeography of Dayr al-Zur to me at that moment.

I snapped my own souvenir photograph (figure 41).

Reflecting on the history and memory contained within the landscape of Dayr al-Zur only highlights how the bone remnants serve as mnemonic markers for pilgrims through which Armenians remember the past. In this sense, self and other and past and present are as blurred for the early pilgrims in the Syrian Desert as they were for me gazing into the glass ossuary at Antelias. The same blurry reflection that I witnessed on the glass pane also appeared to pilgrims whose itineraries and mourning rituals were enacted in the Syrian Desert in the late twentieth and early twenty-first centuries.

FIGURE 41 *The author looking at the bones that Hovakimyan collected in Dayr al-Zur in 1938, which are now in a glass ossuary at the Memorial Chapel at the Catholicosate of Sis in Antelias, Lebanon. Source: Photograph by author, 2007.*

CHAPTER TWELVE

FEELING THEIR WAY THROUGH THE DESERT

Affective Itineraries of "Non-Sites of Memory"

> **Every Armenian carries a map inside them.**
> —SUZANNE KHARDALIAN[1]
>
> **I have to go to the traces of Krikor Zohrab's remains (adjoun).**
> —A note penciled in the margin of
> Harutyun Hovakimyan's *Hishadagaran*

Two decades ago, I unwittingly followed the footsteps of other Armenians when I began searching for narratives to inform my own personal journey to the Syrian Desert. In an Armenian bookstore in Aleppo, I found a book by Aleppan-Armenian doctor Robert Jebejian, who along with photographer Hagop Krikorian, systematically reconstructed the Armenian deportation route from Aleppo to Dayr al-Zur and Ras al-'Ayn. The result of their research was the self-published *Routes and Centers of Annihilation of Armenian Deportees of 1915 within the Boundaries of Syria* (Aleppo, 1994). This volume served as a guide during my first trip to the desert in 2000. The now-out-of-print book was a crucial resource prior to the emergence of online, first-person pilgrimage testimonies, and even now it continues to have important documentary value since the region has become inaccessible and largely been destroyed in the recent fighting in Syria.

Jebejian and Krikorian documented sites of mass atrocity with text and images recalling the use of the camera in atrocity photographs of Armenian victims. Forbidden by Ottoman authorities, people like German humanitarian Armin Wegner smuggled his film of Armenian victims out of the region inside his belt.[2] The production and dissemination of images were primarily evidentiary, aimed at confirming the facts of genocide through the objective lens of the camera.[3] Decades later Jebejian and Krikorian created a monument in the form of a book for a place with few formal markers. Remarkably, Jebejian also made his home into a veritable monument, meticulously archiving thousands of Armenian newspapers, journals, photographs, and books in library named after his late wife, Violette—material that informed his reconstruction of the deportation pathways of 1915.

Pilgrimage itineraries to Dayr al-Zur are part the survivor community's broader search for and establishment of a monument to mourn the estimated half million Armenians who perished in the Syrian Desert. These abject, unmarked necrogeographies constitute what Roma Sendayka has called "non-sites of memory," which, in the context of her study of the Shoah, are defined as "abandoned, neglected locations, which nevertheless retain the right to commemoration, [and] generate a particular kind of affective aura that eventually becomes their trademark."[4] These spaces, she argues are haunted, producing strong somatic and affective responses in some visitors, but these hauntings can be neutralized through ritual and memorial. The Armenian Apostolic Church addressed the uneasiness of entering the haunted, unmarked space by erecting two formal memorials in 1990—one at Dayr al-Zur and the other at Margada. These were the first formal ritual spaces in the Syrian Desert. However, Armenians visited non-sites of memory, sites outside these official spaces, sometimes at times outside the prescribed ceremonial time of April 24. These journeys and rituals are of their own creation, making Armenian pilgrim itineraries unique acts of both official and unofficial vernacular memory work.

The designation of April 24 as ceremonial time began as the Great War came to an end; a committee of thirteen Armenian survivors in Constantinople organized a gathering of Armenians on April 24, 1919, in the centrally located Pera district, marking the first official commemoration for mourning and remembrance of the Armenian Genocide. They chose April 24 because on that day in 1915, nearly 250 Armenian intellectuals and politicians were arrested in an event known as Red Sunday (*garmir giragi*). The arrests and subsequent executions have since then been seared into communal memory.[5] During the 1919 commemoration, the Armenian procession moved through the city beginning at what was once the largest monumental structure in Beyoğlu—the Holy Trinity (Hagia Triada) Greek Orthodox Church directly positioned on what is today called Taksim Square.[6] The procession gathered at the Armenian Holy Trinity Church (Surp Yerortutiun), a stunning piece of Ottoman Armenian architecture designed by Garabed Balyan in 1838.[7] Common Armenian pilgrimage practices began with ceremonial processions of survivors retracing the steps of arrested Armenians throughout Istanbul on that fateful night on April 24, 1915. Unless cancelled by the authorities, as they were in 2022, genocide commemoration practices typically include visits to unmarked spaces such as the Haydarpasha train station, where politicians and intellectuals like Krikor Zohrab and Vartkes Serengülian were deported to the provinces and disappeared by Ottoman authorities.

It is unclear when April 24 became the ceremonial time to memorialize the Armenian Genocide for diasporan Armenians in the Levant. Armenians living in Syria and Lebanon, who lived near the killing fields of Dayr al-Zur, visited Dayr al-Zur either on their own or on organized outings with Armenian churches or clubs and associations in Syria and Lebanon and developed rituals of their own to respect their dead ancestors. As time progressed, diasporan Armenians maintained April 24 as a commemoration day throughout the world to protest the ongoing Turkish denial of the Armenian Genocide.[8] And in 1988, the newly independent Republic of Armenia set April 24 as a national day for Armenian Genocide remembrance, marking the first time any state had done so.[9]

Tsitsernakaberd—"the swallow's fortress" memorial and museum perched on a hill overlooking the city of Yerevan, Armenia—is the center of ritual activity on April 24, when "the entire country turns out for what is emotionally a funeral, a burial the victims never had."[10] The complex was created in 1967, much earlier than the church monuments in Syria. Tsitsernakaberd is a clearly marked, state-sanctioned site of official memory, representative of what Pierre Nora calls a "site of memory," a space where "memory crystallizes and secretes itself."[11] Within official state-sanctioned spaces, historical traces are selected and accrue symbolic power within material monuments. Official sites serve a functional use as a space where carefully curated memories are projected outward to the world. Tsitsernakaberd contains this official symbolic importance as the center of ritual conducted in commemorative time. As a national holiday in Armenia, April 24 includes the ritual of walking 3.5 kilometers to Tsitsernakaberd from the Yerevan city center—no small feat since the walk is uphill, which makes it a physically challenging, embodied act of remembrance.

By contrast, while conducting over a dozen oral interviews with visitors to the Syrian Desert, I learned that many traveled there outside of official commemorative time—that is, at times other than April 24. Some respondents from the diaspora informed me that they came to the desert whenever they had the opportunity to visit Syria.[12] The journey for many lasts from five to eight hours each way by bus or car from Aleppo and Damascus respectively. For someone coming from Beirut or Damascus, the journey entails an arduous sixteen hours of travel on a single day. Most of my interviewees went in groups that either they or the church had organized. These visits, which often last only a few hours, were organized in such a way that there was little time to explore Dayr al-Zur independently or to interact with local residents, indicating what I have come to interpret as evidence of visitors being unsettled by the traumatic associations they experience with the visit. Although these "non-sites of memory" in the Syrian Desert required long, difficult journeys, they, like graveyards, often leave visitors feeling unsettled or even ill. As haunted spaces, they were meant to be visited briefly and rarely entailed overnight stays.[13]

A recent report claimed that "Dayr al-Zur is to Armenians what Auschwitz is to the Jews. The most ghoulish thing about the place is that 95 years later the evidence of the massacres is everywhere."[14] Dayr al-Zur is also nothing like Auschwitz. There is a broader public memory of the Holocaust, and Auschwitz is a national museum, which has been maintained by the state of Poland since 1947. It is mostly Armenians and local Arabs who visit what are mostly unmarked sites left to the elements in decay. The precariousness of these sites has redoubled since a decade of civil war has erased the region's only historical markers. The only formal memorials in Dayr al-Zur—the Holy Martyrs Church and Armenian Genocide Memorial— and Margada—the St. Haroutioun Chapel and ossuary—were created by the Armenian Apostolic Church of Syria under the jurisdiction of the Armenian catholicosate in Antelias, Lebanon, not the government of Syria nor the government of Armenia. Because the markers pilgrims use to engage in formal mourning practices are relatively new (and so few), the empty, neglected necrogeography demands witnesses fill the space affectively with the prosthetic memories passed down by ancestors. Suzanne Khardalian captured this sentiment well when she remarked, "Every Armenian carries a map inside them";[15] this memory map, so to speak, is what guides their way in the desert. Pilgrims, with the assistance of local Arab and regional Armenian guides, *feel* their way in the desert, performing memory work and vernacular rituals within largely unmarked, abject spaces of atrocity. If we are to think of Dayr al-Zur as the largest cemetery of Armenian Genocide victims, how should we understand the relationship between the structure of the site and the past and present events that have shaped it? How have history and recent war in the region re/structured that geography and public memory of the space?

Armenian pilgrimage practices gained global attention with Pulitzer Prize– winning poet Peter Balakian's 2008 essay "Bones." His first-person account of his travels to Dayr al-Zur and Margada—an experience later expanded upon in the second edition of his memoir *Black Dog of Fate*—appeared in the high-profile *New York Times Magazine* and brought pilgrimage practices of Levantine Armenians in the Syrian Desert more fully into the consciousness of Armenian -Americans and English-speaking audiences more broadly.[16] Balakian has spent his career documenting the history of the Armenian Genocide, including the significance of Dayr al-Zur, in documentaries, news reports, nonfiction writing, academic articles, and poetry.[17] Just two years before the Syrian war began, Balakian visited all three pilgrimage sites in Dayr al-Zur, Margada, and Shaddadi to film a *60 Minutes* segment on the Armenian Genocide, which aired in 2010.[18] The significance of this story being told for the first time on a major media outlet gave the story vast dissemination forming a powerful prosthetic memory. In light of all that has happened in Syria over the last decade, Balakian's impressions are now more than nonfiction-essay writing; they are a veritable archive of Armenian pilgrimage rituals in eastern Syria that have been interrupted by the current war.[19]

Before the war, Armenian pilgrimages typically included visits to three memorial stations, only two of which—Dayr al-Zur and Margada—were formally marked with memorials in recent decades.[20] The trips would usually begin with the Holy Martyrs Church and the Armenian Genocide Memorial at Dayr al-Zur. Sometimes included in the Dayr al-Zur trip was the Busayra mass grave site. The second stop was typically Margada, where the St. Haroutioun Chapel is located.[21] These first two sites were destroyed during the Syrian War. The order of the stops follows the pathway of Armenian deportees who were forcibly marched on foot down the Euphrates River basin, gathered in Dayr al-Zur, and then marched along the Khabur River, while being murdered in stages along the way. The final site on the journey, the third station at Shaddadi, is one of the places where Armenian victims were gathered to be taken to caves in the desert and burned alive, though some survived to tell of what happened to them there.[22] I have used a combination of oral interviews, pilgrimage writings, and autoethnography to reconstruct these three stations of pilgrimage in and around Dayr al-Zur since trips have halted and may not start up again for some time.

STATION 1: DAYR AL-ZUR

As Levantine Armenians conducted annual visits to Dayr al-Zur in the decades after the genocide, the Armenian Apostolic Church made plans to construct a more formal complex containing a church, monument, and museum to replace the humble adobe St. Hripsimae Church used by the local Dayri Armenian community. After a design competition and a ground-breaking at the site in the mid-1980s, the memorial designed by a Lebanese-Armenian architect Sarkis Der Balmanoukian was completed in 1990.[23]

Upon completion, the Armenian Holy Martyrs Church (Surp Nahadagats), within which the Armenian Genocide Memorial and Museum is located, became the primary location, or first station, of Armenian pilgrimage to Dayr al-Zur. April 24 pilgrimages began at the church with a long requiem in the morning, followed by some patriotic songs and poems in the church courtyard. Within the walled complex, the Armenian Martyrs Church occupied the first floor of the church, where there are two Armenian crosses (*khatchkars*) and a small replica of the eternal flame at the Armenian state memorial in Tsitsernakaberd, Yerevan. Located on the bottom floor of the church was a memorial constructed from beautiful gold-toned marble that evokes the colors of Syria's desert (figure 42). At the center of the monument, a marble pillar lined with six gold-colored traditional *khatchars* reached up through the lower floor to the main floor of the building. At the foot of the pillar were the remains of Armenian Genocide victims, their bones carefully laid out in a circular glass ossuary—the closest thing to a proper burial the human remains have received over the last century. The memorial space is viv-

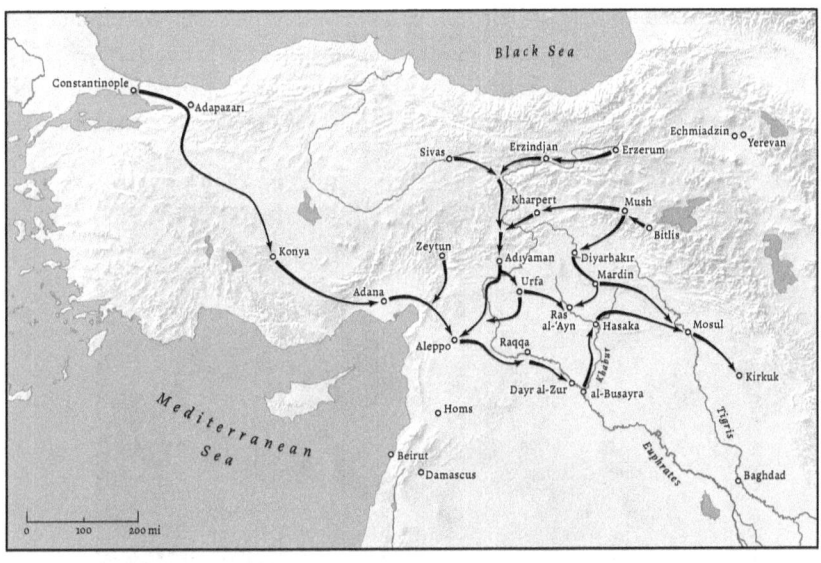

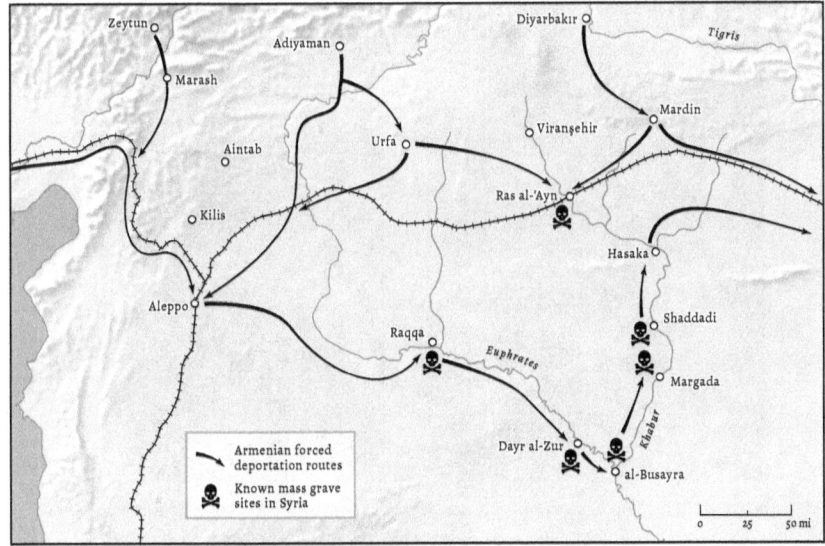

Armenian deportation routes and known mass grave sites in Eastern Syria.

idly described by Balakian: "Downstairs, under the sanctuary, there were archways and a giant marble pillar that rose up within a large opening in the ceiling. Circling the pillar were glass cases containing bones and soil. Hundreds of bones: partial skulls, femurs, tibias, clavicles, eye sockets, teeth. Case by case. Bones and more bones."[24] A local Armenian resident claimed that the bones that were later placed in the ossuary came from a grassroots excavation performed by Armenian community members in 1928, the only trace evidence of provenance that I was able to find in my research.[25]

FIGURE 42 *The Armenian Genocide Memorial inside the Armenian Martyr's Church in Dayr al-Zur prior to its destruction. The monument contained crosses (khatchars) that traditionally adorn Armenian gravestones, soil from the points of origin of Armenian deportees inside present-day Turkey, and bones encased in an ossuary around the base of the memorial. The structure was encircled by photographs of Armenian historic homelands affixed to the walls. Source: Photograph by author, 2007.*

The architecture of the monument combined with materiality of the warm golden marble and ossuary of the Armenian Genocide Memorial affected pilgrims who visited the site. One respondent eloquently described her reaction to the monument:

> I have extreme difficulty crying. My body tenses up and prohibits me from releasing tears. Something about the design of the church. There is a safety to the expression of sadness in that church. I felt that I could cry there. There was an intimacy to it. A warmth to it in the way the church was designed. It wasn't one of those old churches where you feel intimidated by the presence of a God. Rather, I felt embraced and humbled by the memory of what that church contains. You know how the architecture of the church can awake different emotions and can make you feel small or grand; it made me feel connected and it made me think about all that this land had been witnessing. If we want to be able to recognize the pain that we are going through today, people who live on this land, we have to remember the pain that the land withstood before.[26]

The ossuary contained earth and bone dislocated from their original contexts, which served as metonyms for the nation and the body. The viewer was immediately thrown into dual mourning when viewing both material objects—marble pillar and ossuary—within a single monument. The ossuary's carefully arranged pieces of bone, though fragmented, cohered into a whole to be mourned—the nation destroyed.[27] Small vials of soil encircled the pillar, each labeled with their point of origin—Ani, Aintab, Marash, Van—places from which Armenian victims were deported to meet their ultimate death in the desert. Both the earth and the human remains were hermetically sealed in glass and suggestive of ritual burial by sprinkling soil over the dead. Earth-filled jars were filled with soil taken from the homeland to which the exiled bones originally belonged, symbolically reuniting Armenian bodies with their homeland in final rest. In this sense, the memorial evoked religious and nationalist metonyms, simultaneously emphasizing the twin pillars of Armenian identity.

After their construction, the church and memorial complex in Dayr al-Zur were the center of pilgrimage activities by regional Armenians from Aleppo, Damascus, and Beirut. One pilgrim explained that the commemoration would start in the early morning of April 24, when a dozen buses would set out from Aleppo for a five-hour journey to Dayr al-Zur for mass and commemoration activities. Native Aleppan Harout Ekmanian remembered his annual visits with the Sahakian Elementary School and later in secondary school at the Karen Jeppe College. He recalled that on April 24 there was a caravan of cheap Abu Aziz buses with no air conditioning and plastic leather seats. "The rich kids had Walkmans. Some would sing Dashnag nationalist songs" on the way to Dayr al-Zur. The drivers were always Muslims for these annual trips, and "they would put *debka* music on to stay awake [while driving] and the Armenians would get upset." A joyful traditional dance music typically played at weddings and festivals, *debka* would have produced the opposite effect to the desired solemnness and Armenian patriotism desired on the trip. For Harout, it was an occasion to travel around the country, something that rarely happened for him as an Armenian, outside of the summer trip to Kassab that was common among Aleppo Armenians. As he remembered it, the trip had "no systematic representation of narrative explaining events." The presentation was "so general to the level you could ask a Bulgarian and they would know [more] about it." He recalled that there were no presentations on the Armenian resistance, the Battle of Sarıkamış, or even the regional impact of the genocide during the museum presentation. In Harout's memory, the trip, though collective, was completely unguided and did not include any instructional lectures or even a tour of the Armenian Genocide Museum. There was only a Mass and sermon by the archbishop or sometimes the catholicos.[28]

Another Armenian from Aleppo, Sosy Mishoyan-Dabbaghian, had a very different experience while traveling to Dayr al-Zur with a choir. She recalled how the time in the church was spent listening to a Mass delivered jointly by the Armenian archbishop of Aleppo and the catholicos of Sis, followed by lectures about the Armenian Genocide as hundreds of children sat on the floor around the ossuary and listened to the catholicos's call to remember, not to forget, and to demand engagement with "the Armenian cause" (*hay tad*).[29] In this sense, the Armenians on formal trips organized through the church received stronger nationalist messages, though those messages were delivered to Armenian citizens of Arab countries, urging them to resist the seduction of assimilation. In this way, the ceremonies conducted in and around the bones affirmed the boundaries between an "us"—Armenians bearing citizenship in Arab countries—and "them," the general population of Arabs, who are mostly Muslims. Sosy recalled, "We would surround the bones, sitting on the floor and listen to the one lecturing us.... When you see the bones, you feel you want revenge," but you also shed tears and have "feelings of sorrow for your ancestors."[30]

After the lectures, regional Armenians would hop back onto the bus for the five-hour journey home, which was followed by yet another Mass and commemoration at the Asdovadzadzin Church in Vilet, Aleppo, a church built by the catholicosate with donations from local Aintab Armenians in 1983. In those days, she recalled, the catholicos's voice would be blasted over speakers throughout the predominately Armenian neighborhood for the entire district to hear. But in 2012, when the uprising-turned-war intensified in Aleppo, Armenians quietly practiced a diminutive form of this ritual so as to not attract the attention of fighters in the area. As the war progressed, the trips to Dayr al-Zur completely halted.[31]

STATION 2: MARGADA

Located seventy kilometers north of Dayr al-Zur, Margada is a mass grave site where an estimated 80,000–100,000 souls perished on the road to Shaddadi.³² A vast swath of sparsely populated desert, one could probably pass Margada without even noticing it. There is little settlement there, which is typical of many mass grave sites in the desert.³³ It was deemed an uninhabitable space in the Ottoman imagination; the Turkish term *çöller* conveys the impression of a barren wasteland though it was never truly empty. Armenians were sent there under the guise of "resettlement" with the notion that Ottoman authorities viewed it as a space not fit for human life. Visible from the road is a large mound that upon closer examination is packed with innumerable human bones. The mass grave was unearthed in the early 1990s when the Syrian government was conducting oil exploration in the area.³⁴ Today, Margada is the only approximation of an excavation one will find in Syria, and its discovery, while completely accidental, gave momentum to the cause of creating a proper memorial to Armenian Genocide victims in the region. In 1999, the same decade as the Dayr al-Zur memorial complex and church was completed, St. Haroutioun ("Resurrection") Chapel was built by the Armenian Apostolic Church on the mass grave site to offer official recognition for those who perished.

Balakian eloquently archived the appearance of the chapel before it was destroyed in the war: "The floor was cool, and behind the altar was a wall of alabaster with a carved cross. With the evening sun pouring through a yellow glass window, the whole space was floating in saffron light."³⁵ The chapel was more of a memorial and ossuary than a church. The red-sandstone-walled structure contained a tiny one-chamber chapel that also served as a monument with a small triangular ossuary for the human bones that were displayed there (figure 43). The design of the chapel prompted visitors to remark that it was like a mausoleum, which, combined with its surrounding, induced emotional outpouring. The site is most memorable for millions of human bone fragments embedded in the hill surrounding the chapel. It was there, behind the Resurrection Chapel, where pilgrims would conduct excavations to collect bone fragments.

STATION 3: SHADDADI

Not far from Margada on the road to Hassaka is the third pilgrimage station, Shaddadi. As the hardline Ottoman governor Salih Zeki assumed control of Dayr al-Zur in the summer of 1916, he began carrying out orders of the central government to exterminate Armenian deportees outside the city following the new sanitary extermination protocol, according to historian Raymond Kévorkian.³⁶ Makeshift orphanages began deporting the ill-clothed, underfed, worm-infested

FIGURE 43 *The small ossuary at the St. Haroutioun Chapel at Margada, Syria. Source: Photograph by author, 2007.*

orphans.[37] During this second phase of the genocide, local Arabs were restricted from having more than one Armenian wife or servant in order to further prune an Armenian population that had miraculously survived. Governor Zeki bey's pogrom targeted the 18,000 Armenian women and children who had been detained for six months and were dying of hunger and disease in Dayr al-Zur. The authorities marched twenty-one convoys across the Zur Bridge in the direction of Shaddadi. The postwar indictment against the Young Turks estimated that 192,750 Armenians were exterminated by Governor Zeki in Dayr al-Zur from July to December 1916—among them 82,000 exterminated in the region of Marat, Margada, and Shaddadi.[38] At the time Armenians were forcibly marched along the Khabur River, the modern dusty town of Shaddadi did not exist. The town sprang up with the oil industry that developed decades later. Instead, a small village by the same name a few miles outside of the present-day town hugged the river's bend and was the scene of the march to the desert that ended at the caves.

I made my first trip to Shaddadi on April 24, 2000, right after the church ceremony in Dayr al-Zur. I headed out to the desert using Jebejian's book as a guide.[39] My journey was different than that of other pilgrims since it was of my own creation. I was accompanied by an American friend—a scholar of Arabic literature who also speaks Arabic as fluently as I do. My identity as diasporan Aleppan-Armenian created a different kind of experience with the local Arab population, many of whom have Bedouin heritage. Aboard a bus headed for Hasakeh, I started a conversation with a young Syrian man returning home from his military service. When I told him that I was looking for the caves, he told me that his hometown, Shaddadi, was my destination. There, he suggested I seek out a person he referred to as "the *shaykh*" on account of his being nobility within his tribe, not a clergyman. The shaykh knew a lot about Armenians.

As we approached the end of the long street that cuts through Shaddadi, a striking, blue-grey-eyed shaykh, whose name is Sa'ad Hammad al-As'ad, greeted me in front of his home on the edge of town. His first words to me were "Are you Aintabli?" I nearly fainted at the question because the man who identified me so quickly as an Armenian of Aintab origin was wearing a white headcover and a traditional white *jalabiya*, sartorial markers of Arabness rather than Armenian-ness. Was he Arab? I asked him how he knew I was Aintabli. He informed me that many of the Armenians who had come to see him over the years had hailed from Aintab because most of the people who passed by this town during the genocide had been deported from there. He pointed to the back of his house as if noting a pathway where deportees had passed three quarters of a century earlier. Then, he told me that his own grandmother was from Aintab and was deported, only to be rescued in Shaddadi.

Inside the cement house, Sa'ad sat in a living room ringed with elegant green cushions and arm rests as his young daughters quickly served us never-ending cups of tea. There he shared his story with me, which had been transmitted to him by his grandmother, an Armenian deportee from Aintab who had been named Khanameh by the Arabs who had absorbed her into their community. He did not know her family name but was told that her father was a *mukhtar* (neighborhood representative) in Aintab before the deportations. She and other small girls were brought by a gendarme to a small hill called Tall Shaddadi. The gendarmes ordered the chief of the district (*mudir al-nahiya*) to detain these girls until they came back for them. This chief was Sa'ad's great-uncle, Khatab 'Abdallah al-Fadhl, who hailed from a notable family of the Jabbour tribe. The Jabbour are vast; their members extend across the border into Iraq and northward into Turkey. According to his grandfather's account, preserved in Sa'ad's prosthetic memory, when the gendarme left, Khatab informed the surrounding residents and his family of the ominous future awaiting the girls. That evening the village quickly hid as many girls as they could among local families. Sa'ad's narration was one of rescue, a common feature of the narratives among the Bedouin, whereas women survivors and humanitarians would have likely referred to this event as trafficking in women and children, slavery, and even sexual abuse. This is where Sa'ad's prosthetic memory collides with others shared in earlier parts of this book.

Khanameh's Islamized grandson was waiting for someone to say thank you for saving her life. In fact, Sa'ad had the dream of visiting Armenia to be received as one of the many benevolent Arabs whose ancestors rescued Armenians in the desert. His dream was not only about prestige; he was in many ways proud of his memories of being the grandson of an Armenian as he communed with Armenian pilgrims. Twice when I visited him, he brought out a black business suitcase that served as a portable archive of the photos and documents containing information about his grandmother. In this way, I received Sa'ad's memories of the events at Tall Shaddadi as a context for what all sources agree came next. We traveled to the caves together that day so that I could learn about the events of Shaddadi through his blue-grey eyes (figure 44).

Survivor Dikran Berberian referred to this quiet place as the "abattoir of Shaddadi," where "girls less than ten years old [were] thrown into the Khabour [River]."[40] Sa'ad was similarly told that the little girls on Tall Shaddadi (figure 45), he emphasized, were too young for marriage and were destined for the caves in the desert. His grandfather confirmed this when he reported finding the dead bodies of little girls in a ditch nearby after the march from the Tall. His grandfather 'Ali took him into the desert, taught him the story and where the cave and its ditch were located, thereby preserving the family story for nearly a century for me to receive it during my visit in 2000 and again in 2007 and 2008. I began to think of Sa'ad, in this sense, as a human archive.

FIGURE 44 *Sa'ad Hammad al-As'ad leading the way to the caves of Shaddadi in 2007. Source: Reproduced with permission of Kathryn Cook.*

Feeling Their Way through the Desert

FIGURE 45   *Tall Shaddadi at sunset. According to Saʻad's grandmother, a survivor, Ottoman gendarmes gathered Armenian girls on the hill and placed local official Khatab ʻAbdallah al-Fadhl in charge of holding them overnight. He hid some of the girls within the homes of the village of Shaddadi. Those he was unable to save were marched out to the desert and killed at the nearby caves. Source: Photograph by author, 2008.*

Locals remark that they have been told by their elders that bodies washed out of the cave when it flooded after a large rainstorm.[41] Other accounts claim that Armenians were "put in natural cavities in the ground, sprinkled with kerosene, and burned alive" to carry out the sanitization project the Ottoman authorities instituted after the outbreak of contagious diseases from the mass killings. Two children who escaped the burning at the caves bore witness to the event upon returning to Dayr al-Zur—one died from traumatic shock brought on by the experience three or four months later.[42] A survivor of Shaddadi named Choushan reported that she was staying in a Turkish orphanage in Dayr al-Zur until one day the orphans were taken to a field and then thrown in a cave and doused with gasoline and burned. Choushan was eventually married to an Arab of the Jabbour tribe, the same tribe as Saʻad, who eventually let her leave willingly with the child she bore him to go to the Rescue Home in Aleppo. This small historical detail seems to confirm the benevolent version of events in Saʻad's narration.[43] Perhaps Choushan was one of those little girls huddled atop Tall Shaddadi.

Shaddadi has no formal marker. As a non-site of memory, the caves are marked by the memories of Armenians and Arabs who visit the site. Pilgrims must "feel" their way through while guided by local residents to the caves where the worst atrocities were enacted on innocents.⁴⁴ Descending into the caves is a feat of great difficulty since there are no stairs but only a pole for visitors to slide down to get inside the abyss. This journey is impossible for someone who suffers from old age or debility. Actress and storyteller Sona Tatoyan tempered the descent into the cave with some levity when she recalled visiting it with her aunt from Aleppo. "She literally had a blow out, and she wore nice clothes, high heels. It was like an absurdist comedy. I'm down in the cave, and she is up above with her makeup done [saying], 'Sona, *inch ganesgor?*'" (Sona, what are you doing?).⁴⁵

As my own arthritis due to old volleyball injuries set in, I was no longer able to climb down into the cave by my late thirties. On my first trip, when I could still descend, my travel companion was unnerved that we descended to such a place not knowing whether we would be abandoned there—we had met Saʿad hours earlier. I somehow instinctively trusted the man upon meeting him, but later understood how, in the company of the wrong person, throwing oneself down into a cave with strangers could be reckless. But memory-work in the Syrian Desert was not only an emotional or spiritual experience; it was also often physically gruelling, as pilgrims endured extreme heat and, in the case of the cave, required athleticism. My desire to descend was greater than any fear of strangers. Like other Armenian pilgrims, I had to witness what had happened deep inside the belly of the earth.

Pilgrims using the memory map they carry inside them "feel" their way into the desert. But without the memory map of my Arab guide, who later became my fellow Aintabli friend, Saʿad, I could not have found my way to the caves. The last time we traveled to the caves, in 2007, Saʿad had trouble finding his way. He was debilitated by diabetes, which was blinding him and damaging his extremities and nails. He refused to take insulin, thinking it was *haram*. A devout Muslim, he believed that the medicines he needed to survive contained pork. I frequently saw him in Damascus, where he received eye treatments. When I visited him at his daughter's home in Duwaylʿa outside the city walls, we continued our conversations and friendship. He and his wife both had diabetes and believed the disease came from the Armenian side of their families—I said nothing when they shared this assumption with me.

There was something dark and poetic about a nearly blind man walking through the desert in search for an unmarked cave that he had guided so many Armenian pilgrims to over the years. He has been the guide in this dark tourism for decades, to a historical site that is unprotected, unpreserved, unrecorded except in memory maps Armenians and their descendants carry inside them. I realized this might be one of our last trips to the site as his wife, Ghazalah, also the granddaughter of an Armenian survivor, was increasingly protective of his health—rightly so, as a scrape on his foot could take months to heal with his diabetes. GPS devices were forbidden in Syria, so on our last and final trip, I quickly scribbled out a map of our route in a notebook on my lap during the ride out to the cave. Worried about whether the knowledge of the cave's location would fade with Sa'ad's vision, I found myself attempting to archive his memory of the place. As we wandered back and forth across the desert, I feared that his knowledge of this tract of desert was lost, but suddenly a soldier stationed in a nearby post approached us and pointed us in the direction of the caves. He also informed us we were trespassing because the area was militarily sensitive, perhaps due to the oil excavation in the area. The episode revealed that the cave's location is common knowledge among locals. This reassured me that the prosthetic memories of this place will never be forgotten by the Arabs of the desert, who carry with them the memories of victim, rescuer, and perpetrator.

CHAPTER THIRTEEN

BONE MEMORY

*Community, Ritual, and Memory Work
in the Syrian Desert*

> To articulate the past historically does not mean to recognize it "the way it really was."... It means to seize hold of a memory as it flashes up at a moment of danger.
> —WALTER BENJAMIN, "Theses on the Philosophy of History" (1940)

> Are you bringing with you soil, or have you visited a farm/ranch, pasture outside the United States?" I put an X in the no column.
> —PETER BALAKIAN, "Bones" (2008)

In the summer of 2015, my family and I met up with a friend for lunch in Istanbul. Before we ordered our meal, she handed me a bag and asked me if I recognized it. THE MEMORIAL AT THE HOLY MARTYRS CHURCH, DAYR AL-ZUR, 1915 was written in blue capitalized Armenian script across a white plastic bag that I recognized from the Armenian Genocide Memorial gift shop. The town of Dayr al-Zur had been seized by ISIS the previous year, and the church complex that housed the memorial was intentionally bombed. My friend, a journalist, had spent significant time in Syria before and during the war, including a visit to the Syrian Desert with Armenian pilgrims. As she handed me the bag, my friend explained, almost apologetically, how she came to possess Armenian remains. I almost forgot to mention: she is Turkish.

Peering into the bag, I saw two human bone fragments that had been collected from al-Busayra, a town forty miles south of Dayr al-Zur along the banks of the Euphrates River. Like most mass grave sites in Syria and Turkey, al-Busayra has no marker. Instead, thousands of human bone fragments protrude from the earth's surface, as if the land itself is offering testimony, spitting up evidence from the earth for all to see. The two-story mound of dirt encasing human remains sits next to a schoolhouse; the schoolchildren serve as guides. During a visit to the site, a child pressed the bones into my friend's hand. Not knowing what to do with the remains she was given, she wrapped them in tissue and placed them in a tourist bag from the memorial for safekeeping. She kept the bones in her home for many years before sharing them with me. When considering how to respectfully relinquish the bones, she confessed that I immediately came to mind. I could not help but smile at the dark humor of the situation: two women exchanging human bones over a dish of kadınbudu köfte (lady's-thigh meatballs) on Istanbul's Asian shore with my five-year-old child running around the restaurant. The scene underscored our mutual obsession with the Armenian Genocide—a level of commitment that others would find grotesque.

At the time, I thought that she might have offered the bones to me because she knew that I too had visited the site and written about it in the Armenian press. Upon reflection, it now seems symbolic that it was that she, a Turkish citizen who offered me material evidence of a crime that her government refuses to recognize, this a few months after the Armenian Genocide centennial. She was offering me something from a place that I, an Armenian for whom this site held special symbolic value, could no longer visit due to war. The Syrian Desert has become over the last decade a place of danger yet again. The bones conjure all these sentiments for me at once. Yet, when I asked her more recently why she entrusted the bones to me, I received an unexpected answer. She explained that she chose me as custodian for the bones because I have a child to whom I can pass on the bones. With the bones comes the knowledge that is contained within them. For her, the bones represent Armenian history, the memory of a cataclysmic event that must be remembered and preserved for the next generation. These bones and the essential truth they contain were meant to be passed on.

When I became a custodian of bones in 2015, I had every intention of approaching the Armenian patriarchate in Istanbul to have them properly interred. It seemed to be the right thing to do. My friend was a Turk, a member of the perpetrator community. How would the patriarchate respond to her offer of Armenian remains collected from a mass grave? It would, however, be easy for me, as an Armenian, to hand them over. I imagined that the bones would be properly interred and consecrated, and the unfortunate woman whose body once carried these bones would be finally laid to rest. I imagined her to be a woman because most of the deportees during the Armenian Genocide were women and children. Could these remains belong to one of my own relatives who died in the deserts of Dayr al-Zur? Family members tell me that my namesake pictured in the Chekijian photograph may have died there (see figure 1). I will never know the identity of these bones. Hovann Simonian, one of the founders of the Armenian DNA project, told me that "the DNA of living people, whose hands manipulated the bones, is stronger than the original DNA." In other words, contact with the living can render DNA testing difficult or even impossible because the bones now carry my imprint transferred through touch.[1] These handled bones, then, will forever remain anonymous just like the unexcavated bones that lie scattered in the Syrian Desert. Anonymity, it seems, gives bones power within Armenian imaginaries.

I kept the tourist bag containing the bones in the foyer of my apartment in Istanbul that summer, contemplating the trip that I was going to make to Kumkapı, the neighborhood of Istanbul where the Armenian patriarchate is located. I thought about how I would explain how I came to possess them: in passive voice, not detailing the means by which I received them. At first, I was uncomfortable possessing the bones. I uttered prayers to the bones as I passed every time I entered and left the house. Yet, in the end, I could not let go of them. Somehow, I came to desire *my* bones. I have admitted this to no one till now, except to the friend who gave them to me. At the end of the summer, I rolled up the bag, placed it in a zip pouch inside my suitcase, and brought them home to America.

I confess, before I held the bones in my own hands, I had been critical of bone collecting, the practice through which Armenian pilgrims and local Arabs excavate human remains in the Syrian Desert. My primary objection to bone collecting was that this practice was destroying the empirical evidence that would one day provide scientific proof of genocide. However, the Syrian government permitted and then halted the only proper scientific excavation of the sites in the region just before the Syrian War. I used to be disgusted by the idea of touching, holding, and keeping bones. After that lunch meeting, however, my thoughts completely changed.[2]

I held the truth of 1915 in my hand.

Yet handling bones was the final exorcism of my own personal drive for the empirical truth about 1915. And while letting go of the drive to archivally and empirically prove the guilt of the Turkish government will be unsettling to historians as well as my fellow Armenians, it is not meant to dismiss essential truth of what happened in the Syrian Desert. Quite the opposite. Studying bones and memory practices only affirms that the truth surrounds us and lies within us. My intervention intends to serve as a final exorcism to break our archive fever.[3] I recognize the work of researchers who manage to empirically reconstruct events from ruination of war and atrocity, but I also recognize my own limits and the incomprehensibility of genocide amid the catastrophic debris it leaves behind that makes some forms of knowledge "beyond the threshold of detectability."[4] As I argued at the outset of this book, our impulse toward empiricism and genuflection before traditional archives in Armenian Genocide Studies inadvertently grants the perpetrator the power to set the terms of debate. This is a call to set our own terms as survivors, living historical remnants, and embodied archives of the Armenian Genocide.

We Armenians live with what Brian Massumi has called "the effect of the affects." The past continues to jolt bodies and minds like a lightning bolt, making the Armenians who still breathe "a medium of memory."[5] The stories I share contain a different kind of information that is just as important as archival knowledge. We could call it "knowing in the bones," a knowledge that is inscribed within the bodies of the living.[6] While some understand the bones in Dayr al-Zur as empirical evidence of a crime that took place there, respondents offered non-empirical, experiential, fragmentary, and affective accounts that are usually dismissed as too personal and emotional (dare I say "feminized"?) to have any historical value. These experiences are often excluded from formal archives and memorials as well as traditional histories due to their intangibility and lack of empiricism. These meaningful artifacts are almost always disregarded by Armenian Genocide denialists.

The bones of Armenian martyrs are enmeshed in memorial rituals and pilgrimages within the necrogeography of Dayr al-Zur, Syria. Armenians have developed formal and informal ceremonies and rituals with the bones of their martyred ancestors. Pilgrimages to these desert sites are a modern variant of historical pilgrimage practices, yet bones are more than relics. Bone rituals and displays are enacted in spaces of memory that lie outside official state memorials, making unmarked sites of atrocity more legible. These vernacular bone-memory rituals are of particular interest as we consider new archives and methods through which to study the Armenian Genocide.

Within the affective necrogeography of Dayr al-Zur, pilgrims perform both formal and informal immaterial micro-performances, or what Asef Bayat has called "quiet encroachments," a "politics of everyday life" enacted within strict authoritarian conditions.[7] Historically, Syrian Armenians were instrumentalized by the Hafez al-Asad regime to pressure Turkey during periods of escalated tensions in the late 1990s. At those times, the state allowed more aggressive Armenian Genocide commemoration activities, only to later suppress expression when relations between the nations warmed—a phenomenon that has garnered little to no scholarly attention. While Hafez al-Asad nearly went to war with Turkey over water shortages caused by the construction of dams, Bashar al-Asad's economic opening warmed relations with Turkish businesses, prompting suppression of Armenian Genocide discourse within Syria.[8] After 2004, new books about the Armenian Genocide were pulled from the shelves and memorial processions were ordered to be more muted; the martial drumming and chants that often characterized the commemorations stopped.[9] Armenian demands for recognition and justice were to be replaced with quiet, solemn expressions of grief, politely contained within church walls so as to not offend Syria's neighbor to the north during a period of improved diplomatic and economic relations.

Before the war, these "quiet encroachments" were certainly visible and policed by authorities. Armenian pilgrimages were nonthreatening; the state permitted visitors to continue these practices even as relations warmed between Syria and Turkey after 2004. Nor did pilgrimages stop after September 6, 2007, when Israel unexpectedly bombed a remote area of Dayr al-Zur province. All the respondents noted an increased presence of secret police (*mukhabarat*) after the Israeli bombing.[10]

I had experienced something similar when several secret police entered the home of my respondent Sa'ad in Shaddadi while I was interviewing him in 2008. I was repeatedly asked for my name and the name of my father. The follow-up question hinged on why my middle name was different from my father's first name, Nerses; the typical practice for both genders is to have the father's first name listed as a middle name on a Syrian identity card. During the second interview, likely with another police division since there are numerous branches, I was confronted with the exact same questions about my name. I lost my patience and said, "I am an Armenian from Aleppo. You know why I'm here, right?" The agent wearing the requisite black leather jacket said, "Of course I know why you are here. I'm from here. I know why Armenians come." Seeing the discomfort in Sa'ad's face, I knew my visits had now become a burden for him and his family, yet hearing the local Dayri *mukhabarat* acknowledge the truth of why I was there left me feeling very satisfied. Local *mukhabarat* also carry knowledge of the past with them, even when they are carrying out the task of intimidating Armenian pilgrims to satisfy Turkey's efforts to leave the past buried in the desert.

Dayr al-Zur is what Maurice Halbwachs would call a profane site, a space "inhabited by enemies of God." While many accursed spaces are avoided, others, for the sake of remembering the dead, are sacralized through ritual performances by pilgrim bodies atop the bodily remains of martyrs.[11] These micro-performances and interactions with the state matter even if they barely register as events in the historical record. Through the informal ritual displays and interactions of Armenians with bone, pilgrims co-produce communal memory within an abject, unmarked necrogeography. Like the liminal region within which they are situated, these Armenian memorial displays are vernacular encroachments that implant memory within a contested terrain that continues to be marked more by tribal bonds than state allegiance, which explains why secret police are sent to watch and monitor pilgrimage activities.[12] This borderland was elusive even before it was conquered by the Islamic State. Dayr al-Zur province's future is uncertain. Today, it is split between the regime in Damascus, on the one hand, and US-aligned Kurdish rule (called Rojava or the Autonomous Administration of North and East Syria), on the other.

By digging up bones with Armenian pilgrims, Arab residents perform what I term *empathic excavations*, which symbolically recognize the atrocities committed and simultaneously reinforce the collective memory of the history embedded in the very topology of the landscape. While the bone collectors are sometimes

Arabs, bone keepers are almost always Armenian. Scenes of Armenians collecting bones frequently appear in historical photographs and films about the sites, such that unearthing bones in and around Dayr al-Zur has been a consistent—one could even argue a clichéd—iconography of Armenian pilgrimage rituals for some time, most of it never preserved in writing and certainly not archived.

These memory rituals reflect what Walter Benjamin has described as an effort to "seize hold of a memory as it flashes up" by figuratively holding a memory in one's hand. Widely practiced by Armenians of the Levant, pilgrim bone keepers follow the footsteps of their ancestors and pilgrims before them in the Syrian Desert. Traces of these antecedent pilgrimages can be found in the letter Ruben Herian wrote in 1919 about his bone collecting practices and his decision to include human remains he had gathered in the envelope; in Hamasdegh's account of collecting the skull that he brought home with him from his dark pilgrimage to the desert; and in the writings of Tovmas Arapian when he recalled how during his travel to the killing fields in 1935, members of the pilgrim group began collecting bones instinctively along the way.

These prosthetic memories found in these early Armenian-language sources are echoed in Peter Balakian's documentation of bone collecting in a 2010 episode of *60 Minutes*, the voice-over noting ominously, "The most ghoulish thing about the place is that the evidence is everywhere." Peter's voice injected, "Look at this. We got kids who know this area picking up bones by the dozens."[13] The report expanded on Balakian's 2008 *New York Times Magazine* essay, "Bones": "I put my hand in the dirt, grazing the ground, and came up with hard white pieces." He continued, "'Our ancestors are here,' I muttered. Then I began, without thinking, picking up handfuls of dirt, sifting out the bones and stuffing them in my pockets. I felt the porous, chalky, dirt-saturated, hard, intangible stuff in my hands. A piece of hip socket, part of a skull. Nine decades later."[14] After filling his pockets with bones and dirt, Balakian describes placing them inside a ziplock bag and slipping them in his carry-on luggage to bring back home. The evidence is in the soil and in the memories of Armenian pilgrims and Dayri locals who carry the memories of their Armenian grandmothers (*hababas*) in their minds and in their very DNA as grandchildren of survivors.

Inspired by Balakian's essay, Armenian Genocide historian Khatchig Mouradian organized a group of four diverse intellectuals for a Dayr al-Zur trip in September 2009. The group made a one-day trip to the church and museum in Dayr al-Zur and the al-Busayra mass grave site. I interviewed Khatchig and several members of the group because of the unusual configuration of its members. Unlike others, this tour was not organized by the church or by specific members of the Armenian community. Instead, it was a group of Khatchig's own design: two Armenian and two non-Armenian witnesses—one Arab Lebanese-Syrian, the other Turkish. While there were opportunities to go to Dayr al-Zur on April 24 from

Lebanon, Khatchig noted, "I didn't just want to go there and weep and cry with other Armenians. I wanted to go with a Turk."[15] He invited a friend, journalist Amberin Zaman, to go, and when she accepted, he said, "I got my Turk!" indicating he sought to make the pilgrimage into a political act, one that would generate solidarity between Armenians and regional human rights activists. Amberin describes Khatchig's decision to take a Turk on his first visit to the site as "Khatchig's dream"; however, he frames it differently: "I always had an issue with getting large groups of people to go to a site in the absence of any larger broader acknowledgement. It's important to make it part of a broader experience and that is why David was there," referring to progressive Armenian activist and radio host David Barsamian. For Khatchig, going to Dayr al-Zur was a purely political act to the extent that he objects to referring to the trip as a pilgrimage.

In the course of the visit, a priest helped guide their tour and struck up a conversation in Turkish with Amberin. The fourth traveler in the group, Rania al-Masri, was shocked that the Armenian priest slipped into Turkish so easily. She asked him, "How could you speak Turkish here? You could speak Turkish anywhere. How can you speak it here?" Rania remembered, "He said, 'I speak Turkish to her because I speak her language so that she can really understand because people empathize when you speak to them in the mother tongue.' The strength of this man. I just wanted to kiss his hands. It still takes my breath away."[16] According to Amberin, she had asked the priest in Turkish, "Have any Turks ever come here before?" The priest had replied, "No, you are the first." This, for Amberin, was a profoundly disturbing realization. Others in the group observed she was visibly shaken by the possibility that no Turk had visited the site before her.

When they traveled to the mass grave at al-Busayra, Amberin recalled schoolchildren pressing bones into her hands, which is how she came to possess the bones that she later gave me in 2015. These empathic excavations are acts of profound witnessing performed in solidarity with pilgrims visiting the site. Yet Rania has a different memory of the same visit. She noticed the Muslim children who attend school on the site struggling to make sense of the bones, referring to them as "chicken bones." The kids imagined somehow that the mound of human bones that encircled their school were litter produced by massive meals of poultry. Rania, a professor and scholar of political ecology and the environment based in Beirut, recalled that the unearthed mass grave sites from the Lebanese Civil War are similarly understood as chicken bones by locals perhaps to psychologically distance themselves from the unsettling realization the remains they discovered are human.[17] Another possible and even grimmer explanation for this slippage between animal and human could be that the remains are too small to imagine being human at all—at the al-Busayra site, the victims were smaller-boned women and children.

Such psychological and emotional slippage affirms my argument that bones are not incidental objects of fascination. They produce strong emotional responses within us that can vacillate between disgust and reverence depending on context. Bones have evoked affects of transcendence dating back to the earliest collections of ancient relics within the Armenian community. The most treasured Armenian reliquary is St. Gregory the Illuminator's right hand, of which there are two. The right hand holds most benedictive power, in part explaining its value, as opposed to that of the left hand, as a relic. Not surprisingly, competing seats of Armenian Orthodoxy each hold right hand—one at the catholicosate of the Holy See of Sis in Antelias, Lebanon, and the other at Holy Etchmiadzin in Armenia.[18] The hand housed in Lebanon was encased in a gold reliquary embellished with realistic lines and wrinkles, created in 1927 by the Kalemkarian brothers, refugee craftsmen working in Aleppo. Possibly modeled after the arm of then sitting Catholicos Aram, the limb-shaped container was dressed in a partial red sleeve with gold embroidery, suggestive of a missing body. The saint's disembodied right hand has a straight, open palm. The object is held by the catholicos during ceremonies; it is kissed by believers; and it is placed on their heads to bless them as a reanimated saintly arm.[19] The Etchmiadzin version of St. Gregory's right hand has a very different reliquary encasement, created in 1657. Wearing a jeweled thumb ring and bracelets, this hand-shaped reliquary's fingers are in the sign of the cross, rather than a straight palm, ready to offer blessings when held by the catholicos in Armenia. Engraved in gold are scenes from the imprisonment and torture of the beloved saint and founder of the Armenian church at the hands of King Trdat. The right hands of St. Gregory bless with the power invested in relics but also remind us that the right hand was hacked from saintly bodies upon death. These elaborately designed and bejeweled golden cases elegantly conceal St. Gregory's post-mortem dismemberment, reframing it as wonder and mystery.

Karmen MacKendrick has shown how as objects invested with mnemonic powers, sanctified relics are "where memory is understood as the reproduction of a clear narrative line, as if the relics were illustrations in a history textbook."[20] The invocation of history at these sites through both formal and vernacular markers necessarily leads us to consider the communal memory embedded in the space as one where both identity and history is constituted. Rather than locate history as a temporally remote event, Jean-Luc Nancy considers it to be emotionally contained within the community and in a constant state of becoming:

> History—if we can remove this word from its metaphysical, and therefore historical, determination—does not belong primarily to time, nor to succession, nor to causality, but to community, or to a being-in-common. This is so because community itself is something historical. Which means that it is not substance, nor a subject; it is not a common being, which could be the goal or culmination of a progressive process. It is rather a being-in-common that only happens or that is happening, an event, more than a "being."[21]

Armenians convey this sentiment of "being-in common" to Armenians living and dead during their pilgrimages. The interaction of relics and memory invites us to consider the ways that fragments of bone symbolize our own inevitable fragmentation, a vivid foreshadowing of our own eventual decomposition.[22] Pilgrims who visit these material remnants of saints see themselves reflected, just as I saw my own reflection in the glass ossuary at the Armenian Genocide Memorial in Antelias, Lebanon. In Dayr al-Zur, bones together with the oral and written accounts project prosthetic memory to those who perform rituals in the killing fields.

AFFECTIVE NECROGEOGRAPHIES

When UK-based actress and writer Nouritza Matossian traveled to the region for a speaking engagement in 2001, a group of Damascene Armenians organized an impromptu trip to Dayr al-Zur. Nouritza recounted that as they approached Dayr al-Zur from Damascus, a five-hour ride, the passengers gradually grew quiet. When they stopped at a river to refresh themselves, she came to the realization that the same river had once been filled with Armenian bodies during the genocide. At St. Haroutioun Chapel in Margada, locals shared memories with Nouritza, narrating how the atrocity made an impact on the affective landscape within which they lived. A woman she met told her, "There is a plant—if you break the leaf, blood comes out." She noted that during the trip, she learned popular myths from the locals such as "local people never eat fish from this river"; collective memories of how the landscape looked during the genocide were transposed onto the present and into her consciousness.[23] Similarly, Peter Balakian captured how prosthetic memory imprints the memory of the survivor community when he wrote of his first glimpse of the Euphrates in Raqqa: "I was startled by how fresh and flowing and teal green the water was, not brown and sluggish as I had imagined it, and certainly not red with blood and clogged with corpses of thousands of Armenian bodies."[24]

These experiences occurred not only on the road to Dayr al-Zur and at the mass grave site in Margada but also at the Dayr al-Zur Suspension Bridge, a space that figures prominently in the imagination of Armenian pilgrims. The footbridge originally built in 1925 by a French architect was destroyed in 2013 during the Syrian War.[25] That bridge had been preceded by yet another, where on July 15, 1916, an estimated eighteen thousand Armenians perished as they were marched out of the city across the Euphrates. Though not the original bridge, the modern bridge alongside survivor narratives made legible an Armenian necrogeography visualized through prosthetic memory.[26] Adorned with festive lights, the suspension bridge was a major tourist attraction that converged with a promenade along the Euphrates, a space where locals and tourists would cool off in the evenings and enjoy food and drink. As a space of recreation, the bridge unsettled Armenian visitors who were there to mourn rather than recreate. Suzanne shared her experience on the bridge:

> I was imaging the women jumping in there, I was imagining you jump down and your head is crashed on those rocks. There were lots of young people because the university was just across—I don't know if you know about that. So young people were coming and going to their university. And hand in hand. And I said, "Oh my God!" This contrast of... do you know what has happened here? It is the same feeling that you go somewhere and you lie on the beach and there is this lake in Turkey which is exactly the same. You lie on the beach, you have your summer vacation, your children are running there, you have your cocktail or whatever, but do you know what you are lying on? And what is beneath you? And it's not very deep, only a few centimeters down.[27]

Such testimony reveals how the suspension bridge provoked not only memories of the genocide but of profound experiences of the uncanny, thus arousing, in the words of Sigmund Freud "dread and creeping horror." Uncanniness, the sensation of being unsettled (German: *Unheimlichkeit*), arises for some pilgrims to the extent that they feel physical sensations ranging from numbness to nausea and emotions that leave them feeling unwell.[28] Such unstructured, inexplicable, and ineffable experiences are beyond our capacity to explain and instead are experienced much like supernatural hauntings. For this reason, the suspension footbridge should be understood as an unmarked feature of the necrogeography of Dayr al-Zur.

Journalist Nora Perseghian, contributor and editor for the Armenian Revolutionary Federation newspaper *Aztag* in Beirut, Lebanon, went on an organized tour with an Armenian relief organization to Dayr al-Zur on March 24, 2010.[29] Nora's visit with a delegation of women coincided with the visit of Armenian president Serzh Sargsyan, who was joined by a representative of the Syrian government at the site, making the commemoration a larger political event. Her experience, documented in two Armenian-language essays, forms an illustrative counterweight to male writing that dominates the historical record. For that reason, I seek to elevate her experience as a woman pilgrim within Dayr al-Zur's necrogeography by engaging extensively with her writings.

In "Melodies from the Euphrates" (Ypradyan meghetiner), Nora recounts "feeling baptized again in the Euphrates River," a rich image of post-pilgrimage absolution at the site of mass trauma at the Dayr al-Zur Suspension Bridge. She condemns those living in the space today who unwittingly trample upon the dead, failing to understand the significance of the mass grave below the bridge. She recounts that during her visit, a Syrian soldier mocked Armenian pilgrims who came to Dayr al-Zur to photograph the Euphrates River, which for him was a trivial space. She told him, "They want to see the water and take photos." The soldier replied, "The water? They want to see the water? The water?" Nora writes, "They couldn't understand the value and meaning of that water for us"; they built restaurants where families were celebrating atop the unmarked site where Armenians had plunged to their death. The water is not only water; it was "a sea of blood ninety-five years ago."[30]

The normalcy at the site—including parties and celebration—forms the backdrop of a traumatic flash of prosthetic memory of women jumping off the bridge into the Euphrates to commit suicide. She accesses the memories of one survivor's testimony at the bridge: "Girls and women, three to four hundred in number, untied their belts, fastened themselves together and, one after the other, jumped into the Euphrates River, in order to not fall in the Turks' hands. The current of the river could not be seen then, the corpses had risen to the surface and were piled up one upon the other like a fortress."[31] Her memories recall those of survivors embedded in a lamentation: "Armenian girls going, going! One day death will come upon us, before becoming the enemy's wife. Let us find our death in the Euphrates."[32] The songs of other survivors, including a verse of "In the Deserts of Dayr al-Zur" (Der Zor çöllerinde; see Remnant 9), carry embedded memories: "The waters of the Euphrates River are bitter, you cannot drink a single cup! You can't drink water mixed with blood of Armenians."[33] These memories spoken and sung in survivor testimony informed Nora's memories atop the bridge.

Nora's account shifts to the second person, completing the projection, when she writes, "Finally, I saw you with my own eyes, not only on behalf of me, but also on behalf of those grandmothers and grandfathers who have told us about you, whose tears, if they had shed them in you, would have raised your river level remarkably."[34] Intimacy is expressed not to a person but to an agentic Euphrates that looks up toward her with pride and joy. The dead Armenian martyrs that lie on the river's bed rise with the river and with the women in her group, who have come from all over the world to remember the dead. Haptic memories emerge when her hands become wet with the tears of survivors as she recalls their testimonies; those same hands are wet with the river's water, a memory of touch. The river is transformed into a mix of blood and tears of Armenian Genocide victims, but the river is also personified as she imagines Armenian martyrs holding hands with the waves of the Euphrates to celebrate seeing their loved ones, their mothers and children. Land, memory, and Armenian history merge into one when she suggests that Dayr al-Zur is not a place but a text to be studied.[35]

Many pilgrims experience the convergence of themselves into the other, as their self-image blurs into the collective dead during episodes of mourning. Nora illustrates this when she writes, "Flowers are thrown in the river, into the graveyard of the Armenian martyrs, . . . where ninety-five years ago, instead of flowers, virgins threw themselves—noble and pure Armenian ladies, holy and dignified."[36] These metaphors took on new power when during her trip, flowers were tossed from the bridge into the Euphrates and the group of women pilgrims pledged to be "worthy of the young virgins who offered themselves ninety-five years ago to this very river." In the same ceremony, the women pledged to be loyal to their heritage and pass along the Armenian language to subsequent generations of Armenians. Though shocked by her experience on the bridge, Nora describes "feeling a bit more Armenian and a bit more determined to serve the nation and preserve its heritage" after her anointment at the river.[37] We will now move to a different set of unsettling experiences that shook some visitors to the bone.

UNSETTLING THE LIVING AND THE DEAD

> I am dreaming of bones. A bone boy came (uninvited) last night into my dreams. I made a picture of him while dreaming; he is an Arab boy and I cannot speak his language and he is holding his hands out to me, extended, as if an offering.
> —MICHELINE AHARONIAN MARCOM,
> *Draining the Sea* (2008)[38]

Prosthetic memory, alongside profound empathy for dead ancestors, blurs the lines between the living and the dead within Dayr al-Zur's landscape. Bone memory then is a re-membering of the broader community which is resurrected within Armenian mourning rituals. Through these rituals, pilgrims radically reimagine communal wholeness lost through the dis-memberment of mass violence. Such memories can produce both positive and negative affects within the bodies of visitors at the site. Some feel catharsis as their living bodies reunite with the dead, while others are unsettled to the extent they are physically unwell after visiting. These are not only resurgent memories but perhaps even manifestations of epigenetic trauma that has been carried within the bodies of survivors of catastrophic violence across generations. This "knowing in the bones" that genocide survivors have long spoken of is now supported by science.[39]

Around the time of Suzanne Khardalian's visit to Dayr al-Zur in 2011 to film *Grandma's Tattoos*, another mass grave of Armenian bones was discovered during routine construction by the Syrian military near the Margada site.[40] This prompted local guides to show her the discovery. Outside the chapel, Suzanne observed the Bedouin caretaker who had gone to extra lengths to make the space hospitable and less unsettling to pilgrims. She observed the plants that lined the pathway and was captivated by the ingenious way that plastic bottles filled with water were used to drip-farm the greenery to keep it alive in the arid desert. "I was more obsessed with that because... these little plants now they are sucking the nutrition that is in the soil, in that sand. Maybe this is reincarnation for some of them [Armenians] at least; all they need is water. It was so biological out there."

She contemplated how to navigate a space where earth and bodily remains were so tightly intermingled. This prompted Suzanne to think more deeply about the composition of the soil with each step: "I was worried about it all the time: am I going to step on someone's leg or someone's arm or someone's head? It was like I felt that I am in a trap, and coming to the church was somehow coming to a safe place."[41] An Arab boy dug up human remains behind the Margada chapel and offered them to Suzanne, who asked him, "What are you doing?" She then recalled, "This little boy is digging and finds a tooth and puts it in my hand, and I didn't know what to do. I remember the moment clearly. So, I closed my hand first. I said, 'God, I have a relative's tooth in my hand somehow. What do I do with it?' It was a very strange reaction I had. I dropped it back where it was. I know some people take things with them, but I couldn't do it. It was scary somehow to confront the remains of a person like that."[42]

"It was very moving—moving is not the right word; it was devastating." Novelist Micheline Aharonian Marcom described her pilgrimage to the Syrian Desert with actor, writer, and storyteller Sona Tatoyan—both are writers and creators engaged with the memory of the Armenian Genocide. Micheline and Sona found themselves unsettled, albeit in different ways, when they visited Margada in 2004. Sona had spent a significant amount of time in Aleppo but had never made the journey east. Micheline had read copious writings about the genocide while researching her novels and was moved to visit Dayr al-Zur after reading the late Robert Fisk's accounts of the killing fields in *The Independent*. "I read in an article by Robert Fisk that there were bones there and I wanted to go and see if it was true."[43] Micheline had corresponded with Fisk and ultimately became inspired to take the journey after Sona extended an invitation after reading Micheline's first novel, *Three Apples Fell from Heaven* (2004), the first of a trilogy that engages some of the remaining traces of Micheline's family biography within the broader story of the Armenian Genocide. Micheline considers the trilogy of novels she has penned to be a cenotaph, a memorial for the victims of the Armenian Genocide who were denied a proper burial.[44] She was working on the third novel in the series, *Draining the Sea* (2008), when she visited the Syrian Desert. Her travel companion, Sona, has similarly been engaged in creative memory work, including performances and writing a television series that engages Aleppan-Armenian characters who survived both the Armenian Genocide and the Syrian War.

Micheline would later interlace her memories of "the bone boy," a shoeless shepherd boy who appeared from the "moonscape" of the Syrian Desert, in *Draining the Sea*. Wearing an oversized white shirt, the boy approached the women and guided them to the bones behind the Margada chapel. "He is holding his right hand extended toward me and in a small and white brown pile in his hands, like a pyre, lie the bones of my ancestors—great-grandmother and young dead aunties, cousins—in this white and dusty and small collection that the boy has made on his way toward the schoolhouse, to class, he is running for he is tardy as usual." She continues, "He gently cradles their [ancestor's] old and eighty-three-year-old desert deserted bones, like a small palm offering, and he offers me my family's remains and runs from me then, into the desert."⁴⁵ Micheline recalled that during her visit to Margada, she dug her hands into the earth and excavated what both she and Sona remembered as an intact human arm. "I remember pulling out what was maybe part of an arm bone, and it came out intact. Then I just realized, sometimes you are in the desert and you realize you are in the sea. And I realized we were surrounded by these bones."⁴⁶

Sona remembered that Micheline had called her to come witness what she had unearthed:

> Micheline starts calling out my name, "Sona, Sona!" and she is by a mound and I go up. I had a still camera and a video camera around my neck. And in front of my eyes she pulls out a chunk of an arm. Literally. And as soon as it hit the air, it disintegrated in front of us. Like I said, I had two cameras around my neck but I was just having this experience I didn't take a photo or video of that.⁴⁷

The experience was profound as they watched the arm dissolve in their hands upon contact with the air. Sona reflected on the discovery of the arm, "realizing that is what happens to bones after ninety years of being left out in the sun and that we were walking all over them. That moment was extremely shocking because you realize that you are walking over the remnants of hundreds of thousands of dead bodies, decomposing."⁴⁸ Each pilgrim saved a few pieces from the arm as relics.

On their trip back to Aleppo, both women recalled how all four people in the car were silent in for a full hour—the haunting experience had captured their speech. They stopped at a hotel in the middle of nowhere that was used for local weddings. When they entered, they broke out into a fit of uncontrollable, disturbing laughter. Micheline recalled, "We needed [the staff] to find some wine. And Sona doesn't even drink. I was like 'God, we need to get drunk.'"⁴⁹ The desire to drink was an impulse to soothe the traumatic emotions bubbling to the surface as a result of an unsettling encounter with bones at the site.

Micheline noted that she and Sona processed the experience differently as writer and actor, each informed by their methodologies and experience. Micheline called her processing "compartmentalization," where the emotions were translated into an intellectual pursuit to reconstruct the history of the Armenians, which has been largely documentary since she explained that she had inherited only five sentences of knowledge from family members.⁵⁰ Such compartmentalization seems to correspond to Dominick LaCapra's notion of "working through" trauma—that is, critical practices through which people process trauma by documenting, remembering, and mourning traumatic loss. Although many of these concepts were applied to immediate victims of the Holocaust, they also extend to those who empathize with the trauma of ancestors subjected to mass violence.⁵¹

In contrast to Micheline, Sona experienced unmarked sites of mass atrocity both emotionally and corporeally, as a lightning jolt that resulted in illness during her subsequent trips to the region. On another trip, this time in Turkey, Sona lost sensation in her arm and grew nauseous after realizing, during a lunch break on the shores of Lake Gölcük (currently Lake Hazar), that she was once again treading on a site of mass murder. The lake was near her family's ancestral home of Harput. Sona narrated, "I got up and left in the middle of [lunch]... it was a visceral... my body was just.... It's not called Gölcük anymore. It took me a while to figure out [why] I was feeling so awful. 'Oh wait, is this *that* lake?'" It was *that* lake where many of the residents of her hometown of Harput had been murdered. Its shores accentuate the feeling of uncanniness now that the beach where nearly ten thousand residents lay dead is a tourist resort.[52] As a result of these jolts of memory, Sona was briefly hospitalized after her arm went completely numb twice in a single day. On her first hospitalization, her father, a physician, offered advice by phone to those tending to her, treating the inexplicable illness. Sona's experiences may correlate to LaCapra's notion of "acting out," or moments in which aspects of past trauma are reenacted or repeated, like flashbacks or even nightmares for victims and those who deeply empathize with their experiences as descendants who carry traumatic memories in their bones.[53] Or maybe they carry that memory in an arm.

Sona's loss of feeling in her arm raises productive questions about affect and trauma in haunted spaces of mass atrocity. What does it mean, then, that Sona lost her haptic capacity at one of these sites of atrocity? If we embrace the idea that the body can archive an absence, or a memory of dis-memberment, or what I call a phantom limb, a memory of haptic loss and the inability to touch and mourn a loved one, how can that memory come to be staged upon the body? While this essay cannot offer a scientific explanation for phantom limbs and embodied horrors experienced by some travelers to "non-sites of memory," it can still suggest that experiences of the uncanny and phantom limbs may register the attempt to grasp the inapprehensibility of unmarked spaces of mass violence.

It is the absence of care and ceremony that haunts these spaces.[54] I suggest that we consider the role of touch. Holding sand and touching the human bones that remain uninterred are deeply historical gestures. The haptics of pilgrimages to the sites, including both formal and informal exhumations, enact the role of tears and touch in mourning rituals that were denied the victims. It may indeed be the absence of ritual within these haunted spaces, the absence of markers memorializing the dead who lie beneath the feet of travelers, that prompts these experiences of the uncanny. It is this absence of ritual that has inspired pilgrims to create rituals of their own, embodied memory practices that include the collecting of bones belonging to martyred ancestors.

BONE COLLECTING AND RITUALS OF MOURNING

Margada was like walking through a graveyard without the gravestones. Not knowing how to interpret this necrotic terrain on which the dead are dispersed everywhere, visitors were unsettled with each step.[55] The unsettling mix of earth and bones at the site was also experienced by Sosy Mishoyan-Dabbaghian, who recalled that "when we went to Margada and touched the sand, you can feel the bones breaking in your hand."[56] At the site, "an Arab guard came to us and told us that here in every grain of sand you touch, you will find a piece of bone. And he told us about the cave [at Shaddadi] where the Turks collected Armenians and massacred them." It was there, at Margada, that Armenian pilgrims collected bones to take home with them. They referred to the human remains in Armenian as relics (*masunkner*) rather than bones, giving the memory work sacred nomenclature.

Sosy described how pilgrims wrapped the bones delicately in tissue at the site, though she herself took none. When I asked her why she took no bones, she replied, "I left it there in the place of eyewitness, and I wished them eternal peace and repeated quietly in my mind, 'Grandfather, there will come the time [for retribution] for sure, wait a bit longer.'" For Sosy, the site conjured the immediate memory of her grandfather, who had during his life narrated memories of how his father had been killed right in front of him in Harput. "[At Margada] I relived everything that my grandfather had told me with tear-filled eyes. He frequently would say 'Turkish dogs!' [shoon turk] every time he would recall what he had witnessed." Sosy's travels to Dayr al-Zur and Margada, then, served to reinforce prosthetic memories she had received from her grandfather. Not only was the pilgrimage thus connected with the site of massacre, but it served as a conduit for memories shared by surviving family members who were never deported to Dayr al-Zur but deeply connected to the process that produced it.[57]

Another pilgrim, Nouritza, admitted she had collected bones at Dayr al-Zur and taken them with her when she left.[58] When I asked her what she did with the bones and whether she kept them, she answered, "No, I buried the bones in Cyprus at the Armenian Church." She found it unethical to keep the bones as a souvenir of her pilgrimage. In her view, the bones needed to be laid to rest in sanctified soil: "They should be buried and treated with respect." This is where the photograph of her souvenir box purchased from the Dayr al-Zur Armenian Genocide Memorial gift shop enters the story (figure 46). The box contained several symbolic objects, all of them religious: a vial of soil to be scattered over the dead; two candles to be lit in prayer for the deceased; and a vial of incense to be burned at the "grave" site. The ceremonial box featured a wooden cross inscribed in Armenian with the words "Dayr al-Zur, April 24, 1915," which resembles a miniature grave marker for the pilgrim to either use on site or carry home as a souvenir. I asked her to interpret the symbolism of the two ears of wheat included among the items. She suggested that the wheat represented the bread typically received along with communion wine. While the bread represents the breaking of bread with Christ and his disciples at the Last Supper, it is also figuratively transformed into Christ's body during communion and consumed by parishioners. It seemed fitting that Nouritza recalled she had made another trip to Dayr al-Zur alone to spend more time there. During that trip she formed a prominent memory of making freshly baked bread with the local Armenians she had met.[59] The warm bread was broken and eaten with local residents, affirming the tie between bread, body, and community, the bread serving as metonym. Breaking bread with Dayri Armenians, as during the eucharist, invokes the memory of Christ's broken body on the cross and the breaking of Armenian bodies in the killing fields of Dayr al-Zur. As for the memorial box, Nouritza remarked that she used it in Cyprus to inter the bones in a space that she was familiar with, a space she thought of as safe: "I thought it was important to lay the bones to rest with that little box." It occurred to me only after interviewing her that Nouritza interred the bones on yet another difficult border, since Northern Cyprus was occupied by Turkey in 1974. The bones were taken from one contested conflict border and interred on another, following the movement of Nouritza's own exile.

There is something deeply unsettling about collecting human remains. The

FIGURE 46 *Souvenir box purchased at the Dayr al-Zur Armenian Genocide Memorial. Source: Reproduced with permission of Nouritza Matossian.*

practice awakens so many ethical questions within us. Understandably, some respondents grew uncomfortable when I asked them if they collected bones in Dayr al-Zur. Armenian respondents admitted to taking some bones, but often provided different reasons for taking them. A recurring sentiment was that the bones were proof of a crime, evidence that needed to be preserved. Micheline remarked, "I had this feeling that it should be reconsecrated but I didn't know how to do that. And it was also some kind of material evidence."[60] Whether for material evidence of a crime or a sacred act of memorialization, collecting bone evokes the ancient tradition of collecting fragments of dead saints, saints whose body fragments are displayed for a higher, more noble purpose. Some respondents created their own private ossuaries, mimicking the ossuaries for ancient saints. Sona Tatoyan placed the bones she had collected on a Buddhist prayer altar next to photographs of her deceased great-great-grandfather Abkar and her friend, the imprisoned Turkish philanthropist Osman Kavala, who was recently sentenced to life in prison in what Human Rights Watch described as "an outrageous miscarriage of justice." The bones are framed on Sona's mantle next to statues of Ganesh, "the remover of obstacles," and Guanyin, "the goddess of compassion."[61]

Nouritza sought to symbolically consecrate the bones in a space that was home to her; she did not feel it was ethical or moral to hold on to them. Suzanne found it unbearable to collect even the sand in the Syrian Desert because the sand itself contains decomposed remains of Armenian victims. Dayr al-Zur and its environs—earth, plants, water, and air—are saturated with the biological material of her ancestors to the degree she could not bear to take anything home with her. A local Dayri Armenian shared that it was considered taboo in his community to collect and keep bones. They were considered unclean objects, and interacting with them or even visiting a grave site demanded that one wash thoroughly upon entering the home.[62] Ambivalence lingers and some Armenians have shared their feelings of revulsion over bone collecting when I have presented my research publicly.

My own experience has moved from affective disgust toward veneration for the bones that sit on a bookshelf in a jewelry box that once belonged to an Ottoman Armenian. The box, gifted by the same person who entrusted the bones to me, is now housed in my bedroom. Veneration is an emotion that some of my respondents have echoed, whereas others felt it would desecrate or defile memory and even the sanctity of their home to keep the bones they collected.

THE WORK OF BONES

Armenian bone collecting rituals were captured in a 1936 photograph of Harutyun Hovakimyan in a bone pit in Dayr al-Zur. The bones from that excavation ended up in an ossuary in Antelias. Personal bone collecting conducted by Armenian pilgrims unconsciously replicates the original mission to collect and bless the remains of martyred ancestors. Displaying bones appears to be ethically permissible to the highest spiritual authorities if the body is testifying to something of great import—the memory of a miracle that is simultaneously the memory a great crime. "The bones of saints were often on the move," writes Thomas Laqueur; they were often held as souvenirs and powerful objects of reverence or, at other times, war trophies for perpetrators of mass violence. Armenians who grasp these bones seek to harness the history, power, and emotion that infuses their fragmented community members still embedded in the terrain.[63]

However, such open displays and keeping of bones are not universally adopted by Armenians. And sometimes art can communicate the ethical dilemma of bone collecting better than words. Photographer and journalist Diana Markosian cleverly addressed this ambivalence in a photograph published in *Smithsonian Magazine*.[64] In the course of her research, Diana found an Armenian man in New Hampshire who had been collecting Armenian bones in the Syrian Desert for some time and had gathered thirty bone fragments. The man shipped the bones to Diana for her to photograph for her article, but her artistic choice resisted the dominant mode of bone display. She chose to photograph the box unopened in her photo essay (figure 47). When I asked her about her choice to leave the bones unexposed in her photograph, she explained: "The box felt sacred to me. I didn't want to open it. I also didn't feel like I had the authority to open it—so I photographed it as an artifact rather than an object."[65] For Diana, the sacredness of the bones complicated her right to see them, much like the preparation of the Eucharist behind the curtain at the Orthodox altar and the Holy of Holies, where the sacred is placed out of view rather than seen by all. The sacred wine is covered by a veil that represents the separation between the worldly and the divine. In the photograph, the cardboard box serves as a veil for the sacred bones held within it. Diana's photograph of a cardboard box works as critical commentary on the display of Armenian bones found in historic essays, poems, and photographs. This reminder of the sacred power of bones seems to connect the totemic power of saintly relics past and present.

But this was not the only box of bones to be encountered during my research. During a visit to the Nubarian Library in 2019, I informed director Boris Adjemian that I was writing about Armenian bone collecting and Armenian pilgrimage practices in Dayr al-Zur. He smiled, saying he had something to show me, then led me into the guts of an archive originally curated by Aram Andonian while the genocide was underway. It was the stuff historians dream of, crossing the threshold of a private room where all the hermetically sealed books and documents are kept. On a shelf was a small brown cardboard box that resembled a rudimentary sarcophagus with a loose, roughly cut lid, perhaps whittled by a pocketknife. Inside the box (figure 48) was yet another box, a brand of tissues I recognized from my years in Syria. The tissues were not folded in a neat stack but instead were crumpled

FIGURE 47 *The cardboard box holding bone fragments that had been sent to Diana Markosian to photograph. The* Smithsonian Magazine *caption read: "Hundreds of thousands of Armenians were marched into the Syrian desert. Above, a box contains the bones of an Armenian who died there." Source: Reproduced with permission of Diana Markosian.*

FIGURE 48 *The makeshift sarcophagus that holds a Kleenex box filled with bones collected in Dayr al-Zur and archived in the Nubarian Library in Paris. Source: Photograph by author, 2019.*

to individually wrap about fifty small bones to protect them on their journey from Dayr al-Zur to the luxe district of Paris that they now call home.

The library staff was uneasy about the bones, creeped out by the prospect of touching them. They wanted the bones returned to their owner. When I asked who had donated them, I was told it was none other than French-Armenian photographer Antoine Agoudjian, a man who has spent the last thirty years of his life on a quest to document the memory of the Armenian Genocide. I blurted out, "I have to talk to this man!" At that moment, after researching the body, I descended upon Antoine's archived bones from Dayr al-Zur in one of the world's most important Armenian Genocide archives. I needed to know what he was thinking when he archived these human remains in a box of Kleenex, because inside my head, his archival practice had stirred bone memories.

The staff was uncomfortable with me talking about the bones tucked away in the library. I told them I would never speak of them without their permission. In fact, I was told they hoped the bones would be quietly removed by Antoine at some point because they were uncomfortable storing them. To this day, however, the bones are still stored at the library. I was finally given permission to discuss the bones for this book once they knew I was not interested in sensationalizing bone collecting but saw these practices as historically meaningful. The effort to archive bones is an extension of the work Armenians do with bones, whether collecting the bones of saints, keeping them in private ossuaries in their home, or handling them in the desert; they are all deeply historical gestures conducted within a climate of denial.

It is not easy to confront someone about the skeletons that he left in someone else's closet. In January 2020, I finally got up the nerve to contact Antoine. As with many research moments, our conversation was not what I expected. I learned that Antoine, inspired by the research of historian Raymond Kévorkian, the director of the Nubarian Library at the time, had been traveling to Dayr al-Zur since 1999. He has continued to visit the site during the Syrian War, making three visits in 2019 alone. Antoine was not traveling there for the explicit purpose of documenting the war, though he has published his photographs on the conditions in several European magazines. He went because of his "quest" to document the Armenian Genocide. During his trips, he documented not only the destruction of the Armenian Holy Martyrs Church but the city of Dayr al-Zur, which is now 90 percent rubble.

Antoine shared how he collected bones while in Dayr al-Zur and later donated them. When I asked where he had donated them, in order to test whether he was indeed the donor of the tiny cardboard sarcophagus at the Nubarian Library, he admitted that he had donated the bones to the archive and had kept no bones for himself. It was at that point that I confessed that I had seen the bones six months earlier. After a little chuckle, I asked why he donated the bones to an archive. Antoine described how he came to collect bones at the mass grave site at al-Busayra in 2001, the same mass grave site where the bones I was given had been excavated:

> Often the village of al-Busayra came up in the testimonials of survivors. I was thus on a quest, or if I may say an investigation into the traces of our memory. In this village located in eastern Syria, old people whom we had questioned about the traces of the Armenian genocide informed us of a piece of land where the Armenians were buried in 1915. We went there, dug and found, over several hundred meters, bones without graves. I collected some bones which I put in a box and then in the trunk of our vehicle. A few moments later, the police called us, arrested us and then interrogated us for several hours upon suspicion that we were looking for gold [i.e., possible heritage looting], then they released us. The next day, I mailed these bones to Raymond Kévorkian [then director of the Nubarian Library], thinking in my naïveté that it would be possible or conceivable to date them with carbon 14 or even determine the ethnic origin of these bones, thinking that they could constitute an irrefutable proof in the face of the Turkish state's denial. One must place this event in the rather peculiar time and context of my endeavor and especially the psychological state in which I found myself because I was the first one to have found this site loaded with memory.[66]

In an interview and subsequent correspondence, Antoine has referred to this drive to collect as "irrational," but if it is indeed irrational, I would argue it is because it is affective, based on a feeling or sentiment that comes from within, a drive that is at once psychic and embodied. Antoine captured this affectivity when he described the quest as a sensation, "a thirst" for the absolute truth of 1915. As part of Antoine's larger memory work in Dayr al-Zur, the bones were meant to be tested and archived as a preserved human document—a counterhistory to the violent erasures within the perpetrator archive.[67] His drive to archive and test the bones simulates the empirical methods Kévorkian himself attempted in Syria during an excavation that was halted by the authorities. It echoes the recovery of human remains in mass grave sites where DNA testing is possible with government cooperation—an option that is not available to the Armenian survivor community. In other words, the empirical drive reveals the desire for recognition, atonement, and repair that underlies our archive fever.

Whether stored in an archive or held in our hands, bones serve a mnemonic function for the Armenian survivor community. Holding bones is an attempt, in the words of Walter Benjamin, to "seize hold of a memory as it flashes up" by figuratively holding a tangible memory in one's hand. To grasp the bones of Armenians in the Syrian Desert is to attempt to tangibly apprehend lost bodies obliterated with genocidal violence and the archival truths denied or buried by the perpetrator state. We can consider the work bones do for those who *grasp*, a word that conjures both the physical act and intellectual apprehension, while also allowing history to be continually in motion as it flashes.[68] The act of grasping is, in other words, the work of memory.

Bone memory is a form of embodied memory work as pilgrims embark upon a grueling journey in which they walk, climb, and descend into pits. They excavate the dead with their bare hands and often keep the remnants as relics. The bones serve as a metonym for lost community members scattered in the Syrian Desert, a community reconstituted within the radical imaginary of pilgrims. Bones together with living pilgrims enact the memory of a community lost by merging the living with the dead. Karmen MacKendrick writes that "fragmentation evokes wholeness," because bones in fragments are able to, through their anonymity, conjure the collective memory of community.[69] In this way, relics should be understood as textbooks, which may explain the subconscious desire to archive them alongside works of history on the shelves of the Nubarian Library. Through bones, memory is both conjured and situated within a specific historical narrative. For pilgrims, community with the dead within the necrogeography of Dayr al-Zur has produced profound feelings of Armenianness, which raises an important question: now that access to the space, ritual, and memorial has been erased, how should Armenians be thinking about Dayr al-Zur in the future? The answer to that question did not lie in the deserts of Syria but in a small town in upstate New York.

EPILOGUE

BONE ON BONE

My interview with Peter Balakian happened on a drizzly spring day in upstate New York in 2017. The lush pastures full of beautifully spotted cows on the drive up struck me as an ironic setting for my journey to discuss the march our ancestors made to the parched landscape of the Syrian Desert. We had arranged, appropriately, to meet at a restaurant that served mezze, but to keep us out of the rain, my impeccable host offered me a mezze plate at his own dining room table. Peter's life has been dedicated to the traumatic post-memory of the Armenian Genocide. His creative nonfiction is now a historical archive of pilgrimage itineraries that have since stopped. As someone who, in the most literal sense, has grappled with bones, I had many questions for him.

Peter's *New York Times Magazine* essay "Bones" graphically recalled the moment he dug into the scorched earth of the desert to retrieve the relics with his own hands. While carrying the bones on his flight back to New York, he, like so many other Armenian travelers, saw the reflection of his countrymen representing more holistically a snapshot of all classes of Armenians who perished during the killings:

> I reached down into my briefcase and felt them through the plastic, glancing around to see if a flight attendant might be looking. What could I say? These are bones of my countrymen? I had visited a pasture of bones in the Syrian desert? This one might be from my grandmother's first husband, this one from a farmer from Sivas, this one a journalist from Aintab, this a mother from Adana. I put them back, down under my toiletry kit, and filled out my declaration card. "Are you bringing with you soil, or have you visited a farm/ranch, pasture outside the United States?" I put an X in the no column.[1]

Through these rituals and the imaginations of pilgrims, anonymized bones join the ranks of the collective dead, intertwined in collective membership. But the final sentence, referring to his puzzlement over where the human remains he collected fit within borders and customs regulations, cuts the reader to the bone.[2]

I had to ask Peter if he still had the bones he collected from Dayr al-Zur, and he responded matter-of-factly, "They are upstairs in my studio, in a glass container so I can see them. It's a bit the way they were displayed in the Dayr al-Zur church. They have spiritual meaning for me, and they connect me to the many members of my family who were killed in 1915."[3] From the second floor of his home, the bones he had collected in the desert hovered over us in his dining room.

Our conversation turned in a different direction when I asked him about the Syrian War and the destruction of the Holy Martyrs Church and Memorial at Dayr al-Zur, both issues weighed heavily on my mind. What happens when the bodies and bones of the dead continue to pile up? What happens when in Dayr al-Zur, Margada, and Shaddadi, spaces of ISIS occupation and mass killing over the last decade, fresh bones lie atop the older bones of a half million dead Armenians? What is the meaning of Dayr al-Zur in light of impending human extinction from global warming?

Such universal humanistic gestures are the bedrock of Peter's Pulitzer Prize–winning book of poems, *Ozone Journal*. The title poem is powerful in its non-linearity, which effectively emulates the jigsaw arrangement of genocide memory. Here the poet is a master weaver, stitching together what appears to be disparate fragments, memories, and experiences in order to offer a coherent story about human precarity in the face of global warming. The poem seizes upon Walter Benjamin's "flashes of memory," lightning flashes that interpolate the trials of Armenian survival, fatherhood, the AIDS epidemic, and global warming within its fifty-four stanzas. In *Ozone Journal*, holocaust is no longer for Armenians and Jews, but for every . . . living . . . thing. The prospect of genocide against a nation or ethnic group is transformed into the prospect of omnicide. Now all life is as precarious as a naked Armenian marching on the scorched earth of Dayr al-Zur.

As in life, memory is a series of seamless, timeless moments, and though the details of a memory are personal, their commonality underscores the precarity of individual and collective life. Peter recalls his cousin David, the moments of his life captured in the Xanax-induced memories of a brain ravaged by AIDS: "David was all memory as if a little Madeline were floating in tea."[4] Peter's daughter Ani also lives mostly as a memory flash, not present in the real time of the stanza. She lies at an arm's distance, a phone call away—a call she doesn't answer. His cousin David's body is ravaged by AIDS, and when his "body turned on itself," we are reminded of the environment of the desert that turned on Armenians who struggled to survive as their bodies betrayed them.[5] The Armenian condition is transformed into the universal human condition, and the prospect of genocide of a particular ethnic or racial group is effectively transformed into omnicide—that is, the death of all life on earth. When Peter writes, then, "All day I was digging Armenian bones out of the Syrian desert," experiencing the aftermath of genocide in Dayr al-Zur, he now sits on the precipice of another mass extinction.

The poet writes of "feeling the postmortem of the modern," the sense that death is not only in the past but also looming in all its spectrality over the present as a menacing hole in the ozone layer; an hour's exposure of plankton to the radiation coming through that hole would threaten the photosynthesis upon which all life hinges. "Ozone: major factor in making life on earth possible; O_3–allotropic, oxidizing, disinfectant, poisonous; pale blue gas, sharp, irritating—ignited by UV rays."[6] Peter meditates on a complex yet starkly simple equation: "No plankton, no world; who can take in the dread."

At one point in the poem, Peter crashes into a memory of the caves at Shaddadi: "At the caves, M. is obsessed with light flickering down—affect of the punctum." The reference to Barthes's punctum here stands in for something out of place, but it also calls to mind Barthes's description of the punctum as something that pricks, like "a wound."[7] Shaddadi is such a wound, a gaping hole in the ground, a natural formation but also something deeply unnatural and inexplicable. It is a void in which Armenian bodies were cast and burned alive, a prosthetic memory that overdetermines Peter's meditation on another hole, this one in the ozone layer, which threatens to incinerate all life on earth. The economized words of a poet best capture the experience of witnessing the caves of Shaddadi.

> M: Were thousands of Armenians stuffed in here?
> B: Fisk called them primitive gas chambers.

Here the poet recalls one of Robert Fisk's essays about Dayr al-Zur that describes how "the Ottomans engineered the first primitive gas chambers by driving thousands of Armenians into rock caves and asphyxiating them by lighting bonfires at the entrances."[8] The event was experienced by an Islamized survivor from Zeitun named Mubarak who escaped the inferno at Shaddadi. He narrated how after igniting the wood, Turkish soldiers blocked the entrance to keep Armenians from escaping. Armenians who survived further back from the opening moistened their mouths on the cavern walls for several days, and eventually, when the soldiers left, survivors used stones as stairs to crawl out of the cave. Mubarak recalls his mother being so overwhelmed by the experience that upon surviving, she abandoned him and his brother on their way to Iraq. Mubarak was forced to turn back to Shaddadi, where he was adopted by an Arab tribe.[9] The poet captures how to witness Shaddadi's caves is to experience somatically how the land and environment became a technology of death for deportees in the Khabour.

The poem, then, suggests that, like the dying Armenians on a death march in a parched desert, we all walk the precipice of mass extinction. Though we cannot hear the angel of death hailing us from the sounds of the "clunk clunk" or "drip

drip" of our air conditioners, the manmade chemical freon within them threatens the thin layer of invisible ozone upon which all life depends.[10] In this way, *Ozone Journal* humanistically takes the particulars of the Armenian condition and universalizes them as a meditation on the precarity of life amid the inevitable mass death of our entire species. Like Iraq War veteran Roy Scranton, who writes of the sense of doom beneath both a soldier's preparedness to die and his realization that inaction on climate change has already killed human civilization, Peter also asks, How does one live with this knowledge?[11] The genocide has imprinted the imminence of death on Peter as an Armenian with intergenerational trauma. We, the readers, are left uncertain not only about the future of Armenians but the future of humanity.

The necrogeography of Dayr al-Zur continues to absorb its dead. The Armenian Genocide Memorial in Dayr al-Zur was destroyed by an Islamic State bomb in September 2014 and much of the city lays in rubble after the US-led campaign against the caliphate, erasing not only monuments but spaces of life for everyday Dayris. These spaces are slowly being rebuilt, but they sit as precariously as the plankton in Peter's poem as a new round of war could render barely livable spaces unlivable. Reflecting on the mass killings memorialized by Armenian pilgrims can help us think about the layered history and ethical implications of the largely unmarked space where hundreds of thousands perished first during the Armenian Genocide and again in the Syrian War a century later.

Bone on bone, the stories of unknown victims and their remains are now stacked in the desert, part of a larger story we struggle to tell, for if so few remember the Armenians today, even fewer will remember Sunni Muslim victims in Dayr al-Zur—Arab tribesmen who resisted the repugnant black flag. Thinking about century-old Armenian bones in the desert should not detract from little-known reports of 202 mass graves where the Islamic State's approximately fourteen thousand victims were anonymously interred and forgotten.[12] These graves straddle the porous border of Syria and Iraq, a border symbolically destroyed by Islamic State, a border demolition broadcast to the world. The world watched in horror as Yazidi victims were trapped on Jabal Sinjar, starving and battling the forces that sought to annihilate them. Yazidi women were captured, enslaved, and raped, the violence reinscribed in the very lands where Armenian women and girls had been trafficked a century ago. However, Islamic State's other victims were Muslim and likely the descendants of Islamized Armenian Genocide victims absorbed into Muslim families. Mass graves once again dot the necrogeography of Dayr al-Zur and cities in eastern Syria, where Sunni tribesmen rebelled against Islamic State rule and an estimated seven hundred members of the Sh'aytat tribes, who absorbed many Armenians a century ago, were subjected to mass killings and even crucified publicly in Dayr al-Zur's city square.[13]

What should be remembered at Dayr al-Zur at war's end? How can Armenians work in solidarity with those who will, in the future, grieve with them for all that has been lost in the Syrian Desert? I posed this question to Peter, who replied:

> It would be important for the Armenian monuments to be remade. This is a historical ground with large ethical significance for the world—not just for Armenians. A small part of Dayr al-Zur could become a kind of Peace Park—if there were the right kind of leadership involved, and a place where human rights atrocities are reckoned with. Historical memory in public spheres matters to all nations, and as the largest graveyard of the Armenian Genocide, Dayr al-Zur is a tragic and morally important place and space.[14]

Within the intertwined histories embedded in the desert surface, Christian and Muslim remains are now comingled in a bone assemblage, prompting one to imagine Peter's shared memorial for the dead on the site at war's end. I vow to be there to build that memorial to our martyrs past and present alongside Dayri Arabs. I imagined doing this work with my interlocutor and friend Sa'ad al-As'ad, but I learned while completing this book that he did not survive the war. His town of Shaddadi was captured first by al-Qaeda's proxy, al-Nusra, in 2013 and later by the Islamic State, prompting him to leave for Turkey. According to his relatives, Sa'ad died in Ankara after a long battle with poor health. Ongoing clashes between US-aligned Kurdish battalions (called the Syrian Democratic Forces) and Islamic State sleepers combined with Turkish assaults on US-aligned Kurdish fighters that they have declared "terrorists" mean that the killing fields of the Syrian Desert are continually filled with new bones. Though we have unearthed the remnants of the past, it is now time to conclude our story, a story that has no ending.

Just as they provoked prosthetic memories in pilgrims who imagine their enfleshed countrymen and women in the desert, bones bring me back to the broader themes of this book, which include the fragmentary evidence, textual and embodied, that remain in the aftermath of genocide. Body parts have a long history of finding themselves in archives as spoils of colonialism, criminological empiricism, and scientific racism, but seldom do we consider the body as an archive of historical experience in its own right. Earlier parts of the book exposed where existing archives have left traces of lost bodies as "paper cadavers." Yet the fragmentary nature of this evidence exposes the violent erasure produced by genocide and state-induced amnesia. Ann Stoler has called this lapse of memory "colonial aphasia" in her critical study of colonial archives, a term that captures both an archival absence and a form of loss or dis-memberment that makes it difficult to generate a vocabulary through which to speak back at it.[15]

According to Derrida, the archive (*arkhē*) is produced through violent erasure that, in his assessment, is the sheltering of memory that simultaneously shelters itself from memory. From this perspective, the deluge of genocide that leaves behind only remnants, and of which only some were preserved, makes the process of recording memory all the more difficult. Archiving material bones in a private repository of genocidal evidence in Paris speaks back to this erasure by registering both absence and presence: bones without a body. The bones demand our attention because they are a reminder of both absent bodies and a community that was once whole. Being creeped out by bones is still an affective response to their presence, to the absent flesh and skin they conjure within us. I see this as a recognition of the profound power of bones over the living.

The final part of this book sought to produce its own veritable archive of memories and affect collected from those who traveled to the killing fields. Live bodies comingle with the dead to constitute a living/dead community of Armenians that enfolds past and present to the extent that, in oral interviews, pilgrims describe seeing the events that happened in the past before their own eyes within its affective necrogeography. This power of prosthetic memory compels the living to interact with the remnants of the dead, to enact Nancy's "community-in-being," a counterpoint to the genocidal violence that stripped bodies of clothing, dignity, and ultimately identities prior to killing.[16] Prosthetic memory and by extension material rituals that I call bone memory are an attempt to find a vocabulary for loss and a space for radical possibility within the conditions of genocidal erasure.

For women and children, the symbolic shedding of identity authorized their consumption as raw biological material for Muslim patriarchal families. The dismembering of bodies was largely symbolic, as was the nature of sexual atrocity that aimed to castrate men while impregnating the more malleable bodies of women with offspring in the forced birthing of modern Turkey within captive Armenian wombs. We cannot know how many Armenian grandmothers were appropriated for this purpose, but the Turkish discourse on grandmothers over the last two decades has done the feminist work of producing cognitive dissonance, pulling the memory of trafficked women who were coerced into birthing the Turkish republic into public memory. The feminist interventions of Turkish activist Fetihye Çetin, whose 2004 memoir *My Grandmother* (Anneannem) called attention to our lack of knowledge about the hundred thousand or more women who birthed the next generation of Turks, bravely coaxed those Armenian grandmothers out of the shadows and into the light of day.

Yet even such explicit feminist activism has been appropriated by and subsumed into a new rhetoric within what Talin Suciyan has called "post-genocidal habitus of denial" that absolves modern Turkey and its citizens of any responsibility for what happened while continuing to reproduce structures of inequality.[17] Armenian memories can be fodder for denialists who, like Halide Edib in 1926, would frame these women as merely the wives and mothers of Turks rather than women whose bodies were violently snatched and absorbed, through the mechanism of the Ottoman sex/gender system, as raw biological material for an emerging nation state. As Nora Tataryan Aslan suggests, accepting such responsibility would involve the demolition of the self, a sort of self-reflexivity that would call national myths, including the fetishization of Armenian grandmothers, into question.[18] In this way, Turkish liberal rhetoric about Armenian grandmothers mimics settler colonial narratives that fetishized the Indian grandmothers (always grandmothers, never grandfathers, for that would disrupt patrimony) that serve to deflect for white guilt and avoid meaningful reparation for the genocide of Indigenous Americans. The Armenian grandmother here has the power to absolve as she indigenizes the group selected for biopolitical life at the expense of dead husbands, fathers, and brothers.[19] Repair necessitates something more than symbolic inclusion; it demands standing in solidarity with the disappeared and disappearing minorities of the Middle East and unlearning the damaging, destructive, and exclusivist ethnonationalism that lies at the root of ongoing Turkish state violence not only against Armenians but against Kurds and Turks who dare to speak out.

And yet the surviving Islamized remnants of the sword were often feminine. The Armenian grandmother is a fact of this history. The abducted and absorbed bodies of women and children were viewed through a modern humanitarian optic during the orphan rescue (vorpahavak); however, the Armenian community valiantly rallied to rescue its own during the genocide and in its aftermath. Ruben Herian stands in for the many heroic men and women who risked their lives to retrieve Armenian women and children and bring them back to the community, only because his letters and even his random scribbles on the back of business cards were carefully archived.

Armenian women who turned to prostitution to survive, despite the social stigma, and Islamized Armenian children were recovered. They too were biopolitical material for the Armenian nation-building project during and after the war. Armenian views in this sense aligned with those of European and American humanitarians who sought to rescue as many bodies as possible. The occupying British and French authorities, along with Karen Jeppe, were careful to not take children born of Muslim fathers from their parents, though it is clear that some arrived in the Rescue Home, sparking the outrage of a Muslim mob that attacked an orphanage in Aleppo in 1919. Afterward, rescuing Armenians would have to be more clandestine along Jeppe's underground railroad, yet thousands of women and children who might have otherwise been rescued were left behind, dissolving into the majority Muslim population.

The optics through which humanitarians viewed the Armenian Genocide have been problematized by scholars who have examined the feminization of humanitarian appeals during World War I. This remains a feature of humanitarian appeals for support today, whose focus on the enslavement and mass rape of Yazidi women by Islamic State fighters is eerily similar to the Armenian women featured in humanitarian appeals a century ago. The media frenzy around Aurora Mardiganian is an early example of the exploitation of female suffering and the pornography of pain that inflect representations of humanitarian disaster. We are reminded that Aurora's body was abused by her captors and then again by Hollywood. Unclaimed, her body was cremated and discarded in a potter's grave upon her death in 1992. Aurora is a study in exploitation of the body through genocide, capitalism, and the struggle over memory since our memories of her were miraculously revived only a few decades ago. Through a critical rereading of Aurora's life, one can see how her body in pain prefigures motifs like *National Geographic*'s "Afghan girl" and the burka-clad woman suffering under the Taliban, both animating the cry for wartime humanitarian aid. The representation of the suffering feminine during World War I was amplified with the image of tribal tattoos that some rescued Armenian women wore on their faces, necks, chest, and hands.

I have argued that buried in the bodies, skin, and bones of Armenians is a history, a history that remains invisible because these tangible and intangible forms of knowledge are not always understood as evidence due to our archive fever. I have experimented with the idea that bodies are documents, an alternative archive that make it possible for us to imagine the possibilities of history writing liberated from our obsession with archives, especially those purged by states that deny the facts of history. This is not a call to place the archive into a shredder, as Arsinée Khanjian did so powerfully at the end her performance in *Auctions of Souls: Performing Memory*. It is a call to pay closer attention to the kind of erasures the privileged position of the archive produces and to think beyond them to tap into the living, breathing, human archive, a rich repository of memory and experience. It is a call for a kind of history informed by "knowing in the bones" that dabbles in disciplinary heresy, an infidelity born from the cumulative effects of mass violence. It is the call for a kind of history that allows us to attend to the silences within the archive and honor the living memory of the Armenian Genocide that lives within all who, like you, reader, sit with the subject long enough.

ACKNOWLEDGMENTS

I finished writing this book as a mix of fear, isolation, and denial set in during the COVID-19 pandemic. The analytical side of my brain could not help but reflect on the history of the immune system that forms the backdrop to the history I have written. After all, while Armenians endured the massacres, starvation, and death marches, they also suffered from debilitating diseases—cholera, typhus, and malaria—only to face down the Spanish flu at war's end. I came across a report that one of those survivors discussed in this book, Aurora Mardiganian, spent two weeks in quarantine in the Alexandria Hotel in Santa Barbara while filming *Auction of Souls*. Armenian survival was, therefore, complicated by the broader global struggle of humans against contagion. Armenian survival offers both lessons and warnings that should remind us of our vulnerability but also give us hope and strength for humanity's next confrontation, the standoff between humans and the warming planet we cohabit.

I would never have written this book without collaborative study with smart colleagues within the now defunct Global Studies Initiative Faculty Seminar at Whitman College. The program was the envy of other liberal arts colleges in the region and allowed professors like me to learn from others in a faculty seminar that invigorated my teaching and research in ways that I could have never anticipated. Through the seminar, I learned how to think beyond my discipline and push at the edges of history. This led me to engage in the disciplinary heresies evident in this book. A workshop called "Writing the Self," organized by my colleague Shampa Biswas, was another space where I first learned about autoethnography and began to integrate it into my writing practice. I thank Whitman, and especially my colleagues in the History Department, for continuing to support the advancement of my scholarship even when my primary site of research, Aleppo, Syria, was no longer accessible to me. I am especially grateful to my new intellectual home, Clark University, for selecting me as the next Robert Aram and Marianne Kaloosdian and Stephen and Marian Mugar Chair of Armenian Genocide Studies in the

Strassler Center for Holocaust and Genocide Studies. I look forward to writing this new chapter in my career.

An entire village was involved with the writing of this book. I am grateful for the support and stimulation I received from some amazing colleagues at the Society for the Humanities skin-themed fellowship at Cornell University 2016–2017. The feedback I received from other Society fellows at Cornell was pivotal to the development of these ideas. Thank you "Skin Sisters" Gemma Angel, Pamela Gilbert, Alicia Imperiale, Gloria Kim, Karmen MacKendrick, and Emily Rials, and a special thanks to the pink couch on the third floor of the A. D. White House, where many glasses of wine were poured. Part three of this book would not have been written without the encouragement of Gemma Angel, whose interdisciplinary genius continues to inspire. My gratitude to Timothy Murray for offering an amazing opportunity to learn from the intellects in our cohort. And for the record, we did want to have a live tattooing event at the final "Skin Practice" workshop in the spring of 2017, but inviting tattoo practitioners to simply speak about their trade proved less of a liability.

Among that Cornell cohort was Seçil Yılmaz, who helped in ways big and small as this project developed. It was Seçil's mother, Cemile Hanim, a Turkish woman, who, between dishes of *aşure,* helped me channel my tailor ancestors by teaching me to knit in Turkish ("*düz, arka, düz, arka*") on those blustery snow days in Upstate New York. This book comes from a place of healing that would not be possible without my relationships with Kurdish and Turkish allies who have expressed solidarity along the way. Foremost are my brave Kurdish and Turkish brothers and sisters who came together with Armenians to participate in the Armenian Genocide centennial events in Diyarbakir in 2015. The Armenian lyrics of the Onnik Dinkjian song we danced to that night on April 24 ring true: "The soul of Dikranagerd [Diyarbakir] is in all of our hearts."

I am especially thankful to Lerna Ekmekçioğlu and Melissa Bilal for their work on Fem-ARC, where I was able to present some of the contents of this book in an environment of respect and collaboration with Armenian feminist scholars. Lerna made many interventions, including recommendations for additional texts in Armenian so that I could archive as much as possible for future scholars to build on. Anthropologists Dawn Chatty and Alberto Savioli offered advice grounded in decades of fieldwork among the tribal peoples of eastern Syria—Savioli's dissertation on Syria's Bedouin in Italian is a crucial, one-of-a-kind source, especially since it may be another decade before researchers can safely return to the region.

The language of humanitarianism is a global one that demands fluency in many languages beyond my reach. I want to thank the American Research Institute in Turkey and Boğaziçi University, including the remarkable staff of instructors, for two summers of intensive modern Turkish. While I did translate many materials on my own, I benefitted from translation and translation checks from other scholars. My gratitude to Jana Byars, Matthias Bjornlund, Alptuğ Güney, Sosy Dabbaghian Mishoyan, Tamar Boyadjian, Bedross Der Matossian, and Rachel Goshgarian. I thank my fellow death studies traveler Mériam Belli, who has been a conceptual sounding board since our days at Georgetown; she along with my Whitman colleague Adeline Rother reviewed my French translations. This manuscript also benefitted from conversations with colleagues Aslı Zengin, Melanie Tanielian, Hülya Adak, and Erdağ Göknar for a blend of disciplinary heresy and much-appreciated solidarity during the COVID lockdown.

I am grateful to the generous researchers—Khatchig Mouradian, Vahé Tachjian, Stephan Astourian, and Vartan Matiossian—who shared sources and contacts, while archivist Mihran Minassian and documentarian Bared Maronian have given me access to photos and videos from their private collections. Khatchig Mouradian, Faedah Totah, Gemma Angel, and Marc David Baer read portions of the manuscript and offered crucial feedback. Thank you to my long-time friend Daniel Forbes, who read a chapter of the book and provided tattoo drawings that appear in the book design. Photojournalist Kathryn Cook encouraged me to write my own book on the Armenian Genocide during our travels on the genocide trail in Syria, Lebanon, and Turkey in 2007–2008 and in Diyarbakir in 2012, with our babies in tow. Gratitude goes to archivists Jacques Oberson at the League of Nations Library and Boris Adjemian at the Nubarian Library, who offered kindness and help from afar, connecting Geneva and Paris with the remote wilderness of eastern Washington. I am grateful to the Zoryan Institute and the Shoah Foundation for assisting me with access to oral testimonies of Armenian Genocide survivors during lockdown, and to Marc Mamigonian of the National Association for Armenian Studies and Research for sharing research materials. Jen Pope, Amy Blau, Chloe Daikh, and Lia Beatty offered critical research assistance. A special thanks to Jamie Warren who swept in with some editing and restructuring when I needed it most.

I thank my editor Kate Wahl for nurturing this project from inception to completion and for the astounding editorial skills of Barbara Armentrout. And I could not have written this book without my husband, Gibran Shamoun, and son Ibrahim, a.k.a "Abi," who always reminded me to take a break for *subhiyya*, whether I was ready for it or not. I am thankful to them and to my parents for their ongoing support for my scholarship, including my father who read the entire book and whose only comment was "It is too long."

Finally, it is important to name some of the impediments I have had to my research, including how the plague of war has shortened the lives of Armenians, Syrians, Assyrians, Kurds, and Turks. My now-deceased Aintabsti friend and interlocutor Saʿad Hammad al-Asʿad was among those who passed during the war. His only request was to go to Yerevan to tell his story and the story of his people, the Jabbour tribe. My hope is that I have documented his memories for others to hear now that he is gone. Many readers will know that my entire career was spent researching Syria, and the rest of my career just may be spent researching it from a position of exile. Losing a homeland once one hundred years ago and then losing one again has been devastating for many Syrian-Armenians. Figuring out how to express myself in light of the carnage in Syria has forced me to be more honest about the ties I share to the histories I write. Writing about this pain has been the largest challenge of my career. While the rest of the world has moved on, my hope is that the story of Armenian survival can offer inspiration to my fellow Syrian brothers and sisters who are still living precariously and to those living in exile. They have my solidarity, forever.

―――

This book is dedicated to my grandparents, Hripsimae Sekhildjian Semerdjian and Youssef Nerses Semerdjian (figure 49), originally of Aintab and later Aleppo. Each had their own individual story of survival during the Armenian Genocide. Their stories are largely left to oblivion because they never shared the details with their children. Some stories are too painful to pass on.

FIGURE 49 *Youssef Semerdjian and Hripsime Sekhildjian on their wedding day.*
Source: Author's personal collection.

NOTES

Epigraph
1. Katie Geneva Cannon, "Womanist Perspectival Discourse and Cannon Formation," *Journal of Feminist Studies in Religion* 9, no. 1-2 (Spring–Fall, 1993): 35. The Black feminist theologian is referring to rememory, a concept of reliving past trauma viscerally in the body introduced in Toni Morrison's novel *Beloved* (1987).

A Photograph as Prologue
1. On naming practices as "memory candles" see Carel Bertram, *A House in the Homeland: Armenian Pilgrimages to Places of Ancestral Memory* (Stanford, CA: Stanford University Press, 2022).
2. Barthes's much-studied notion of the punctum is described as a detail in a photograph that "pricks," "bruises," or "wounds," inciting the viewer to speak out the unspoken element in the photograph. See Roland Barthes, *Camera Lucida: Reflections on Photography* (New York: Hill and Wang, 1980, 2010), 27.
3. Vartan Matiossian, *The Politics of Naming the Armenian Genocide: Language, History and 'Medz Yeghern'* (London: I. B. Tauris, 2021).
4. Sato Moughalian mentions that a friend told her, "You know, you are one of the lucky ones. Your family left breadcrumbs behind." Mougahalian has meticulously reconstructed a biography of her grandfather, David Ohannessian, in *Feast of Ashes: The Life and Art of David Ohannessian* (Stanford, CA: Stanford University Press, 2019), 11.
5. Harry Harootunian, *The Unspoken as Heritage: The Armenian Genocide and Its Unaccounted Lives* (Durham, NC: Duke University Press, 2019), 7. Examples of writers and artists who have engaged fragmentary memories creatively in their works include novelists Nancy Kricorian, *Zabelle* (New York: Grove Press, 2009); and Micheline Ahronian Marcom, *Three Apples Fell from Heaven* (New York: Riverhead Books, 2004); and the art of Silvina Der-Meguerditchian, including her project *The Texture of Identity* (https://www.silvina-der-meguerditchian.de/works/the-texture-of-identity-ongoing/), which weaves family photographs into tapestries to symbolically reunite dispersed Armenians into a more coherent single textile.

Introduction
1. Viranşehir, as one survivor, Zabel, recalled, was where "they collected all the beautiful girls, and distributed them." "Registers of Inmates, the Armenian Orphanage in Aleppo,"

1922–1930 (hereafter "Registers"), inmate 961, March 25, 1926, United Nations Archives (UNA) at Geneva, Switzerland.

2. Loutfie Bilemdjian's story is shared in "Registers," inmate 1010, May 17, 1926, UNA. I have retained the original errors in English and spellings in Jeppe's own handwriting to retain the authenticity of the account. The account was composed in Jeppe's Reception Home in Aleppo, which was also referred to as Jeppe's Rescue Home. These records have been recently translated into Turkish in an important volume edited by Dicle Akar, Matthias Bjørnlund, and Taner Akçam, *Soykırımdan kurtulanlar: Halep kurtarma evi yetimleri* (İstanbul: Iletişim Yayınları, 2019).

3. In a fitting parallel with Loutfie's gown, tattooed former Indian captive Olive Oatman, whose story is shared in chapter 8, also wore a dress that suggested a hidden arm tattoo. Though the tattoo was never photographed, the arm embroidery on her gown hinted at the tattoo and likely emulated its design. See Margot Mifflin, *The Blue Tattoo: The Life of Olive Oatman* (Lincoln: University of Nebraska Press, 2009), 158.

4. Uysal Yenipınar and Mehmet Sait Tunç, *Güneydoğu anadolu geleneksel dövme sanatı beden yazıtları* (İzmir: Etki, 2013), 214–15.

5. Because there are few studies of tattoos within Syria, I drew on correspondence with a seasoned anthropologist of Syria, Dawn Chatty, who has worked among the tribes for over four decades. Through this correspondence she explained how a combination of tattoos represented specific tribal affiliation in Loutfie's case. Dawn Chatty, email correspondence, April 25, 2017.

6. Claudia Card, "Genocide and Social Death," *Hypatia* 18, no. 1 (Winter 2003): 63.

7. A recent book has argued that the Ottoman Empire orchestrated a genocide against all Ottoman Christians rather than Armenians specifically. See Benny Morris and Dror Ze'evi, *The Thirty-Year Genocide: Turkey's Destruction of Its Christian Minorities, 1894–1924* (Cambridge, MA: Harvard University Press, 2019).

8. Understudied, tribal tattoos have appeared in recent documentaries and exhibits, often accompanied with little context. See Bared Maronian, dir., *Women of 1915* (2016); and the Armenian Genocide Museum Institute's online exhibition *Becoming Someone Else ... Genocide and Kidnapped Women*. By contrast, Suzanne Khardalian's film *Grandma's Tattoos* (2011) provides more context to the tattoos through its ethnographic engagement with Syrian Bedouin.

9. Fethiye Çetin, *Anneannem* (Istanbul: Metis Yayınları, 2004) 81. Çetin's work was crucial to generating a discussion about Armenian grandmothers within Turkey. Subsequent to the publication of the memoir was the publication of a volume edited by Çetin and Ayşe Gül Altınay, *Torunlar* (Istanbul: Metis, 2009), later translated into English as *The Grandchildren: The Hidden Legacy of "Lost" Armenians in Turkey* (New Brunswick, NJ: Transaction Publishers, 2014). One contributor to the edited volume, filmmaker Berke Baş, released a documentary about her Armenian grandmother titled *Chanson de Nahide* (2009).

10. In Armenian, *khlyagner* (խլեակներ) can mean "wreckage," "fragments," or "remnants" of the uprooted and exiled Armenian nation. A word with similar meaning forms the title of an important novel by Hagop Oshagan, *Mnatsortats*, (Antelias, Lebanon: Dbaran giligioy gatoghigosutean, 1988). See Keith Watenpaugh on the term *khlyagner* in *Bread from Stones* (Berkeley: University of California Press, 2015), 14–15.

11. Giorgio Agamben, *Remnants of Auschwitz: The Witness and the Archive* (New York: Zone Books, 2000).

12. Marisa J. Fuentes, *Dispossessed Lives: Enslaved Women, Violence, and the Archive* (Philadelphia: University of Pennsylvania Press, 2016), 7.

13. Marianne Hirsch and Leo Spitzer, *School Photos in Liquid Time: Reframing Difference* (Seattle: University of Washington Press, 2020), 14; emphasis mine.

14. Carel Bertram calls these shared narratives "memory-stories" in her recent study titled *A House in the Homeland*, 7–8.

15. I have borrowed the term "prosthetic memory" from Pierre Nora's discussion of "prosthesis-memory" in "Between Memory and History: Les Lieux de Mémoire," *Representations* 26 (Spring 1989): 14; and Alison Landsberg, *Prosthetic Memory: The Transformation of American Remembrance in the Age of Mass Culture* (New York: Columbia University Press, 2004).

16. Landsberg, *Prosthetic Memory*, 8.

17. Maurice Halbwachs, *On Collective Memory*, ed. and trans. Lewis A. Coser (Chicago: University of Chicago Press, 1992), 38–40, 53.

18. Mériam Belli, *An Incurable Past: Nasser's Egypt Now and Then* (Gainesville: University Press of Florida, 2013), 3.

19. Rosie Bsheer, *Archive Wars: The Politics of History in Saudi Arabia* (Stanford, CA: Stanford University Press, 2020), 5–6, 28.

20. Heghnar Watenpaugh, *The Missing Pages: The Modern Life of a Medieval Manuscript from Genocide to Justice* (Stanford, CA: Stanford University Press, 2019) 18, 114.

21. Robert Melson coined this argument the "Provocation Thesis" in *Revolution and Genocide: On the Origins of the Armenian Genocide and the Holocaust* (Chicago: University of Chicago Press, 1992), 6.

22. Three noteworthy texts that explore the architecture of Armenian Genocide denial are Richard Hovanissian, *Remembrance and Denial: The Case of the Armenian Genocide* (Detroit: Wayne State University Press, 1999); Fatma Müge Göçek, *Denial of Violence: Ottoman Past, Turkish Present, and Collective Violence against the Armenians, 1789–2009* (Oxford: Oxford University Press, 2014); and Marc David Baer, *Sultanic Saviors and Tolerant Turks: Writing Ottoman Jewish History, Denying the Armenian Genocide* (Bloomington: Indiana University Press, 2020).

23. Though an incomplete list, genocide scholarship that draws heavily upon Ottoman Turkish sources includes Taner Akçam, *A Shameful Act: The Armenian Genocide and the Question of Turkish Responsibility* (London: Picador, 2007); Taner Akçam, *Killing Orders: Talaat Pasha's Telegrams and the Armenian Genocide* (London: Palgrave Macmillian, 2018); Hilmar Kaiser, *The Extermination of Armenians in the Diarbekir Region* (Istanbul: Bilgi University Press, 2014); Ryan Gingeras, *Sorrowful Shores: Violence, Ethnicity, and the End of the Ottoman Empire, 1912–1923* (New York: Oxford University Press, 2009); Göçek, *Denial of Violence*; Uğur Ümit Üngör, *The Making of Modern Turkey: Nation and State in Eastern Anatolia, 1913–1950* (Oxford: Oxford University Press, 2011); Hans-Lukas Kieser, *Talaat Pasha: Father of Modern Turkey, Architect of Genocide* (Princeton, NJ: Princeton University Press, 2018); and Ümit Kurt, *The Armenians of Aintab: The Economics of Genocide in an Ottoman Province* (Cambridge, MA: Harvard University Press, 2021).

24. On the subject of women, children, and Islamization, see Taner Akçam, *Ermenilerin zorla Müslümanlaştırılması* (Istanbul: Iletisim, 2014}; and Ibrahim Atnur, *Türkiye'de Ermeni kadınları ve çocukları meselesi, 1915–1923* (Ankara: Babil, 2005).

25. Rosie Bsheer offers an illuminating critique of the archive as a locus of state power in *Archive Wars*.

26. Ann Stoler, "Colonial Archives and the Arts of Governance," *Archival Science* 2, no. 1–2 (2002): 90.

27. "Paper cadavers" refers to a large archive 250,000 cards discovered in Guatemala that contain the only traces of the disappeared. Rather than study the cards as a repository of knowledge, Kirsten Weld studies the archival logics involved with their production as an archive. See Kirsten Weld, *Paper Cadavers: The Archives of Dictatorship in Guatemala* (Durham, NC: Duke University Press, 2014).

28. Rebecca West, *Black Lamb and Grey Falcon: A Journey through Yugoslavia* (New York: Penguin, 2007), 103.

29. Elisa von Joeden-Forgey, "The Devil in the Details: Life Force Atrocities and the Assault on the Family in Times of Conflict," *Genocide Studies and Prevention: An International Journal* 5, no. 1 (2010): 1–19; Amy Randall, ed., *Gender and Genocide in the Twentieth Century: A Comparative Study* (London: Bloomsbury, 2015); Mary Anne Warren, *Gendercide: The Implications of Sex Selection* (Totowa, NJ: Rowman & Allanheld, 1985); and Adam Jones, ed., *Gendercide and Genocide* (Nashville, TN: Vanderbilt University Press 2004).

30. For examples of Middle East body studies, see Murat C. Yıldız, "Strengthening Male Bodies and Building Robust Communities: Physical Culture in the Late Ottoman Empire" (Ph.D. diss., University of California, Los Angeles, 2015); Wilson Chacko Jacob, *Working Out Egypt: Effendi Masculinity and Colonial Modernity, 1870–1940* (Durham, NC: Duke University Press, 2011); Salih Can Açıksöz, *Sacrificial Limbs: Masculinity, Disability, and Political Violence in Turkey* (Berkeley: University of California Press, 2019). For tattoo studies, noteworthy examples are Nikki Sullivan, *Tattooed Bodies: Subjectivity, Textuality, Ethics, Pleasure* (Westport, CT: Praeger, 2001); Jane Caplan, ed., *Written on the Body: The Tattoo in European and American History* (Princeton, NJ: Princeton University Press, 2000). A noteworthy global example from this literature is Lars Krutak, *The Tattooing Art of Tribal Women* (London: Bennett & Bloom, 2007).

31. Good examples of critical discussions of the archive and the call from scholars for an ethnography of the archive are Jacques Derrida, *Archive Fever: A Freudian Impression* (Chicago: University of Chicago Press, 1998), 91; and Antoinette Burton, "Introduction: Archive Fever, Archive Stories," in *Archive Stories: Facts, Fictions, and the Writing of History*, ed. Antoinette Burton (Durham, NC: Duke University Press, 2005), 1–24.

32. Heghnar Watenpaugh has skillfully re-created the lost Ottoman Armenian worlds of Zeytun and Marash, two towns that were once home to large Armenian populations, in *The Missing Pages*.

33. Heghnar Watenpaugh, "Learning from Taksim Square: Architecture, State Power, and Public Space in Istanbul," *SAH Blog*, June 11, 2013.

34. Dominick LaCapra, *Writing History, Writing Trauma*, 2nd ed. (Baltimore, MD: Johns Hopkins University Press, 2014) 2–8, 22. Emphasis in original.

35. Armenian Genocide Studies has documented the experiences of Armenian women and specific atrocities committed against them. My argument is that genocide is gender history, and it is the optic through which genocide is best understood. See Eliz Sanasarian, "Gender Distinction in the Genocidal Process: A Preliminary Study of the Armenian Case," *Holocaust and Genocide Studies* 4, no. 4 (1989): 449–61; Donald Miller and Lorna Touryan Miller, "The Experience of Women and Children, " in *Survivors: An Oral History of the Armenian Genocide* (Berkeley: University of California Press, 1993); Ara Sarafian, "The Absorption of Armenian Women and Children into Muslim Households as

a Structural Component of the Armenian Genocide," in *In God's Name: Genocide and Religion in the Twentieth Century*, ed. Omer Bartov, with P. Mac (New York: Berghahn Books, 2001) 109–19; Matthias Bjørnlund, "'A Fate Worse Than Dying': Sexual Violence during the Armenian Genocide," in *Brutality and Desire: War and Sexuality in Europe's Twentieth Century*, ed. Dagmar Herzog (New York: Palgrave Macmillan, 2009), 16–42; Randall, ed., *Gender and Genocide in the Twentieth Century*; and Rubina Peroomian, "Women and the Armenian Genocide: The Victim, the Living Martyr," in *Plight and Fate of Women: During and Following Genocide*, vol. 7, ed. Samuel Totten (London: Routledge, 2009), 7–24. A series of articles and books have examined Islamization and the rescue of Armenian women and children from Muslim households; see Vahe Tachjian, "Mixed Marriage, Prostitution, Survival: Reintegrating Armenian Women into Post-Ottoman Cities," *Nations and Nationalism* 15, no. 1 (January 2009): 60–80; Vahe Tachjian, "Gender, Nationalism, Exclusion: The Reintegration Process of Female Survivors of the Armenian Genocide," *Nations and Nationalism* 15, no. 1 (2009): 60–80; Vahram Shemmassian, "The League of Nations and the Reclamation of Armenian Genocide Survivors," in *Confronting the Armenian Genocide*, ed. Richard Hovannisian (London: Routledge, 2003), 81–112; Lerna Ekmekçioğlu, *Recovering Armenia: The Limits of Belonging in Post-Genocide Turkey* (Stanford, CA: Stanford University Press, 2015); and Watenpaugh, *Bread from Stones*.

36. Catherine A. MacKinnon, "Genocide's Sexuality," *Nomos* 46 (2005): 313–56; and Katharine Derderian, "Common Fate, Different Experiences: Gender-Specific Aspects of the Armenian Genocide, 1915–1917," *Holocaust and Genocide Studies* 19, no. 1 (Spring 2005): 1–25,

37. Lerna Ekmekçioğlu's study *Recovering Armenia* has examined the specific burden rehabilitation efforts placed on women, who were urged to birth the Armenian nation during recovery. Another study similarly argued that motherhood is used to signify the uniqueness of Armenian women's national identity in Armenia: Sevan Beukian, "Motherhood as Armenianness: Expressions of Femininity in the Making of Armenian National Identity," *Studies in Ethnicity and Nationalism*, 14, no. 2 (2014): 247–69.

38. See Serdar Can, *Nenemin masalları* (Istanbul: Umut yayımcılık, 1991); and Fethiye Çetin, *Anneannem* (Istanbul: Metis yayınları, 2004).

39. Eve Tuck and K. Wayne Yang, "Decolonization Is Not a Metaphor," *Decolonization: Indigeneity, Education & Society* 1, no. 1 (2012): 3; and Vine Deloria, *Custer Died for Your Sins: An Indian Manifesto* (New York: Macmillan, 1969), 26.

40. Nora Tataryan Aslan, "Facing the Past: Aesthetic Possibility and the Image of 'Super-Survivor'" *Journal of Middle East Women's Studies* 7, no. 3 (November 2021): 348.

41. Bedross Der Matossian, *Shattered Dreams of Revolution: From Liberty to Violence in the Late Ottoman Empire* (Stanford, CA: Stanford University Press, 2014), 23–24.

42. Der Matossian has recently published a micro-history of the two waves of massacres against Armenians in 1909. See Bedross Der Matossian, *The Horrors at Adana: Revolution and Violence in the Early Twentieth Century* (Stanford, CA: Stanford University Press, 2022).

43. Erik-Jan Zürcher, "Young Turks, Ottoman Muslims, and Turkish Nationalists: Identity Politics, 1908–1938," in *Ottoman Past and Today's Turkey*, ed. Kemal Karpat (Leiden: Brill, 2000), 173.

44. Ziya Gölkalp shared this fantasy of cultural and linguistic homogeneity in his poem "Kızılelma (Red Apple)," cited in Üngör, *The Making of Modern Turkey*, 35.

45. Üngör, *The Making of Modern Turkey*, 59.

46. Marc David Baer, *The Ottomans: Khans, Caesars and Caliphs* (London: Basic Books, 2021), 429.

47. Henry Morgenthau, *Ambassador Morgenthau's Story* (Garden City, NJ: Doubleday, 1918), 20. Importantly, Jenny White has shown how Muslim identity continues to be centered in Turkish nationalism, blurring the lines between secularism and religion. See Jenny White, *Muslim Nationalism and the New Turks* (Princeton, NJ: Princeton University Press, 2012).

48. David Gaunt, Naures Atto, and Soner O. Barthoma, eds., *Let Them Not Return—Sayfo, The Genocide against the Assyrian, Syriac, and Chaldean Christians in the Ottoman Empire* (New York: Berghahn, 2017), 1; and Ronald Suny, *"They Can Live in the Desert but Nowhere Else": A History of the Armenian Genocide* (Princeton, NJ: Princeton University Press, 2015), xxi.

49. Üngör, *The Making of Modern Turkey*, 52; emphasis in the original.

50. Taner Akçam, "The Ottoman Documents and the Genocidal Policies of the Committee for Union and Progress [İttihat ve Terakki] toward the Armenians in 1915," *Genocide Studies and Prevention: An International Journal* 1, no. 2 (2006): 134. In *The Making of Modern Turkey*, Ümit Üngör has documented how the state began an internal colonization program that targeted Kurds by subjecting them to forcible assimilation while the Armenian Genocide was underway. The ongoing violence and forced displacement of Kurds continues to the present day; for examples of how political violence against Kurds is expressed within body discourses, see Açıksöz, *Sacrificial Limbs*.

51. Raymond Kévorkian, *The Armenian Genocide: A Complete History* (London: I. B. Tauris, 2011).

52. The discretion to deport at will meant that groups meant to be excluded, such as Islamized Armenians and Protestants, were sometimes subjected to deportation and violence. See Vahakn Dadrian, *The History of the Armenian Genocide: Ethnic Conflict from the Balkans to Anatolia to the Caucasus* (Berghahn Books, 2003), 221–22; and Yervant Odian, *Accursed Years: My Exile and Return from Der Zor, 1914–1919*, trans. Ara Stepan Melkonian (London: Gomidas Institute, 2009), 134.

53. Fatma Müge Göçek, "Turkish Historiography and The Unbearable Weight of 1915," in *Cultural and Ethical Legacies of the Armenian Genocide*, ed. Richard Hovanissian (New Brunswick, NJ: Transaction, 2007), 337–68.

54. American ambassador Henry Morgenthau comments on the prescreening of his telegrams, the contents of which were known to Talaat Pasha and conveyed to him during meetings. The memoir contains important information about personal contact between Morgenthau and CUP leadership. Henry Morgenthau, *Ambassador Morgenthau's Story*, 338; see 139, 393 for censorship.

55. Sam Dolbee has disputed the characterization of the Jazira region as desolate in "The Locust and the Starling: People, Insects, and Disease in the Late Ottoman Jazira and After, 1860–1940," (Ph.D. diss., New York University, 2018), 200.

56. Khatchig Mouradian, *The Resistance Network: The Armenian Genocide and Humanitarianism in Ottoman Syria, 1915–1918* (Lansing: Michigan State University Press, 2021).

57. Estimates are that a total of 600,000 to 1.5 million Armenians died during the Armenian Genocide. Göçek, *Denial of Violence*, 1; and Suny, *"They Can Live in the Desert But No Where Else,"* xxi, 326.

58. Examples of such studies include the classic Thomas Laqueur and Catherine Gal-

lagher, eds., *The Making of the Modern Body: Sexuality and Society in the Nineteenth Century* (Berkeley: University of California Press, 1987); Kathleen Canning, *Gender History in Practice: Historical Perspectives on Bodies, Class, and Citizenship* (Ithaca, NY: Cornell University Press, 2006); Joanna Bourke, *Dismembering the Male: Men's Bodies, Britain, and the Great War* (Chicago: University of Chicago Press, 1996). When bodies are explicit in scholarship in Ottoman Studies, scholars have largely focused on biopower—pronatal policies, demography, sexuality, disease, and medicine. Some examples include Alan Duben and Cem Behar, *Istanbul Households: Marriage, Family, and Fertility, 1880–1940* (Cambridge: Cambridge University Press, 1991); Gülhan Balsoy, *The Politics of Reproduction in Ottoman Society, 1838–1900* (London: Pickering & Chatto, 2013); Seçil Yılmaz, "Love in the Time of Syphilis: Medicine and Sex in the Ottoman Empire, 1860–1922" (Ph.D. diss., City University of New York, 2016); Emine O. Evered and Kyle T. Evered, "Sex and the Capital City: The Political Framing of Syphilis and Prostitution in Early Republican Ankara," *Journal of the History of Medicine and Allied Sciences* 68 (2013): 266–99.

59. Kathleen Canning, "The Body as Method? Reflections on the Place of the Body in Gender History," *Gender & History* 11, no. 3 (1999): 501.

60. Kuşçubaşı Eşref, an Ottoman special operations officer, described the directive to eliminate non-Turkish elements from the peninsula in Celal Bayar, *Ben de yazdım*, vol. 5 (Istanbul: Baha Matbaası, 1967), 1578, cited in Taner Akçam, "The Ottoman Documents and the Genocidal Policies of the Committee for Union and Progress," 133, 145; and Hülya Adak, "Identifying the 'Internal Tumors of World War I: Talaat Pasha'nın Hatıraları [Talaat Pasha's Memoirs], or the Travels of a Unionist Apologia into 'History,' " in *Räume des Selbst. Selbstzeugnisforschung transkulturell*, ed. Andreas Baehr, Peter Burschel, and Gabriele Jancke (Köln: Böhlau Verlag, 2007) 151–69.

61. Aslı Iğsız, *Humanism in Ruins: Entangled Legacies of the Greek-Turkish Population Exchange* (Stanford: Stanford University Press, 2018), 8.

62. Raphael Lemkin, *Totally Unofficial: The Autobiography of Raphael Lemkin*, ed. Donna-Lee Frieze (New Haven, CT: Yale University Press, 2013), 143–44.

63. von Joeden-Forgery, "The Devil in the Details"; MacKinnon, "Genocide's Sexuality"; and Adam Jones, "Gender and Genocide in Rwanda," in *Gendercide and Genocide*, ed. Adam Jones, 98–137.

64. Leslie Peirce, "Abduction with (Dis)honor: Sovereigns, Brigands, and Heroes in the Ottoman World," *Journal of Early Modern History* 15 (2011): 311–21.

65. Zabel Essayan is explicit in her analysis of the abductions of women and children that, generally speaking, Arabs did not share the same intent as Turks. "Within the Arab Mesopotamia, there are a great number of Armenian women and children. In general, the Muslim Arabs had acted humanely towards the Armenian deportees." Zabel Essayan, "La Libération des femmes et des enfants non-musulmans en Turquie," Armenian National Delegation 1–5, Correspondence for February and March, 1919, 1–11, Nubarian Library, Paris.

66. Lerna Ekmekçioğlu, "A Climate for Abduction, A Climate for Redemption: The Politics of Inclusion during and after the Armenian Genocide," *Comparative Studies of Society and History* 55, no. 3 (2013): 522–53.

67. Iğsız, *Humanism in Ruins*, 12.

68. Primo Levi, *Survival at Auschwitz: The Nazi Assault on Humanity*, trans. Stuart Woolf (New York: Simon & Schuster, 1993), 26–28.

69. An informative article titled "Tattoos and Numbers: The System of Identifying

Prisoners at Auschwitz" published by the Holocaust Museum Memorial describes how, during the tattooing process, the Nazis used a stamp full of interchangeable needles to outline the numbers on a prisoner's arm; after that step, the wound was rubbed with ink to form a tattoo. When the system was ineffective, the authorities returned to traditional tattooing with a needle. See https://encyclopedia.ushmm.org/content/en/article/tattoos-and-numbers-the-system-of-identifying-prisoners-at-auschwitz?series=18823.

70. Kate Murphy, "Ann Cavoukian," *New York Times*, Sunday Review, January 18, 2014.

71. Bourdieu defines *habitus* as "embodied history, internalized as second nature and so forgotten as history." Pierre Bourdieu, *The Logic of Practice*, trans. Robert Nice (Stanford, CA: Stanford University Press, 1980), 56.

72. Elizabeth Hallam, "Articulating Bones: An Epilogue," *Journal of Material Culture* 15, no. 4 (2010): 469–70.

73. Sévane Garibian, "Editorial," special issue: "Human Remains and Commemoration," *Human Remains and Violence* 1, no. 2 (2015): 4.

74. Yukiko Shigeto, "Smashing the Great Buddha, Crossing Lines: Tsushima Yūko's Nara Report," *Asia Pacific Journal* 16, no. 12 (June 15, 2018): 3, 10–11.

75. "If photography is to be discussed on a serious level," wrote Roland Barthes, "it must be described in relation to death." He draws the connection between photography and death induced by the death of his mother, and in another poignant example, he examines a photograph of a man waiting to be executed, alive yet soon to be dead. See Barthes, *Camera Lucida*, xi, 64–65, 94–95.

Chapter 1

1. Of those politicians, activists, lawyers, doctors, journalists, and artists arrested, 174 were executed by the Ottoman state. See the detailed account of Nesim Ovadya İzrail, *24 Nisan 1915 İstanbul, Çankırı, Ayaş, Ankara* (Istanbul: İletisim Yayıncılık, 2013).

2. In his skillful examination, Bedross Der Matossian has argued that the Adana Massacres should be understood in the greater context of ethno-religious violence originating in the nineteenth century, which includes the eruption of episodic violence in Ottoman Syria and the Balkans. See Der Matossian, *The Horrors of Adana*, 9–10.

3. Zabel Essayan, "La Libération des femmes et des enfants non-musulmans en Turquie," Armenian National Delegation Archives, 1–5, Correspondence for February and March, 1919, Nubarian Library (BNu), 1–11.

4. Genocide scholar Elisa von Joeden-Forgey describes the use of "wartime rape" as including "systematic mass rape," or what Zabel described in 1919 as "regular [repeated] collective raping of women," which includes forced maternity, forced prostitution, sexual mutilation, raping to death, sexual enslavement, forced marriage with génocidaires, and creation of public houses or rape camps to contain women for the purpose of sexual violence. See von Joeden-Forgey, "Gender and the Future of Genocide Studies and Prevention," *Genocide Studies and Prevention: An International Journal* 7, no. 1 (2012): 92; and von Joeden-Forgey, "The Devil in the Details."

5. Both Zabel and Arsaguhi Teotig are among the women whose writings have been translated by Melissa Bilal and Lerna Ekmekçioğlu in *Feminism in Armenian: An Interpretive Anthology* (forthcoming, Stanford University Press).

6. Zabel Essayan, *Averagnerun mech* (Istanbul: Aras, 2010, 2011); Zabel Essayan, *In the Ruins: The 1909 Massacres of Armenians in Adana, Turkey*, trans. G. M. Goshgarian,

ed. Judith Saryan, Danila Jebejian Terpanjian, and Joy Benjilian-Burgy (Boston: AIWA Press, 2016). It was translated into Turkish as *Yıkıntılar arasında*, trans. Kayuş Çalıkman Gavrilof, ed. Ardaşes Margosyan (Istanbul: Aras, 2014). Following Giorgio Agamben's analysis of the Shoah in *Remnants of Auschwitz*, Marc Nichanian has taken up the question of the impossibility of witnessing in *The Historiographic Perversion*, trans. Gil Anidjar (New York: Columbia University Press, 2009).

7. These accounts are narrated by Essayan in chapter 4, "The Orphans," *In the Ruins*, 21–55.

8. Hasmik Khalapyan, "Kendine ait bir feminizm: Zabel Yessayan'ın hayatı ve faaliyetleri," in *Bir adalet feradı: Osmanlı'dan Türkiye'ye beş Ermeni feminist yazar, 1862–1933*, ed. Lerna Ekmekçioğlu and Melissa Bilal (İstanbul: Aras Yayıncılık, 2006), 169–70.

9. Zabel's lecture at the Sorbonne, delivered in French, included slides of photographs taken by diplomats and journalists during the genocide. This speech was reproduced in Essayan (Yesayan), "Le rôle de la femme Arménienne pendant la guerre," *Revue des Études Arméniennes* 2 (1922): 121–38; it was recently translated by Mériam Belli as "Chronicle— The Role of the Armenian Woman during the War," *Journal of the Society for Armenian Studies* 28 (2022): 1–15, and cited in Lerna Ekmekçioğlu, "The Armenian National Delegation at the Paris Peace Conference and The Role of the Armenian Woman during the War," web project, "World War I in the Middle East" (NEH Summer Seminar 2012).

10. Essayan, "La Libération des femmes et des enfants non-musulmans en Turquie." For an English translation of the entire report, see Elyse Semerdjian, "Zabel Essayan, 'Liberation of Non-Muslim Women and Children,'" *Journal of the Society for Armenian Studies* 28 (2022): 1–14. The report has been consulted by a few historians. See Raymond Kévorkian, Levon Nordiguian, and Vahe Tachjian, *Les Arméniens: La quête d'un refuge, 1917–1939* (Presse de l'Université Saint-Joseph, 2006), 73; Lerna Ekmekçioğlu, "A Climate for Abduction, A Climate for Redemption," 522–53; Marc Nichanian, *Writers of Disaster: Armenian Literature in the Twentieth Century* (London: Taderon Press, 2002); Victoria Rowe, *A History of Armenian Women's Writing: 1880–1922* (London: Cambridge Scholars Press, 2003); Watenpaugh, *Bread from Stones*, 72–76; and Anna Aleksanyan, "Between Love, Pain, and Identity: Armenian Women after WWI," in *Women's Everyday Lives in War and Peace in the South Caucasus*, ed. Ulrike Ziemer (London: Palgrave Macmillan, 2019), 103–27.

11. Azkanver hayuhyats engerutiun, a woman's educational organization, was established by feminists in 1879. The organization published a book in 1920 documenting the atrocities via eyewitness accounts, titled *Témoignages inédits sur les atrocités turques commises en Arménie suivis d'un récit de l'épopée arménienne de Chabit-Karakissar* (Paris: Imprimerie Dubreuil, 1920); mentioned in Ekmekçioğlu, *Recovering Armenia*, 56n18.

12. All quotations directly from Zabel in this chapter are taken from my translation of Zabel's 1919 report. Semerdjian, "Zabel Essayan, 'Liberation of Non-Muslim Women and Children,'" 1.

13. Telegram from Henry Morgenthau to Secretary of State, July 10, 1915, National Archives, U.S. State Department Record Group 59, 867.4016/74; and Morgenthau, *Ambassador Morgenthau's Story*, 319.

14. Yervant Odian was recruited to help establish a brothel for Turkish and German soldiers in Dayr al-Zur after the outbreak of an unnamed venereal disease. To protect the soldiers, medically supervised and regulated prostitution was established. See Odian, *Accursed Years*, 196–98, 209–11.

15. Morgenthau, *Ambassador Morgenthau's Story*, 316.

16. Report by Lt. Sayied Ahmed Moukhtar Baas, in *British Parliamentary Proceedings*, ed. Ara Sarafian and Eric Avebury, 2003, Appendix III, 92.

17. Essayan, "La Libération des femmes et des enfants non-musulmans en Turquie," 2.

18. MacKinnon, "Genocide's Sexuality," 314, 328.

19. Essayan, "La Libération des femmes et des enfants non-musulmans en Turquie," 2.

20. Essayan, "La Libération des femmes et des enfants non-musulmans en Turquie," 2.

21. Essayan, "La Libération des femmes et des enfants non-musulmans en Turquie, 6.

22. Both the centrally organized Special Organization (*teşkilât-ı mahsusa*) and the affiliated killing squads known as *çete*, or "the butcher battalions" (*kasap taburu*), were known for their brutality against Armenian civilians. As Armenian arms were being confiscated by the authorities, the most criminal elements, primarily Circassians and Kurds, previously imprisoned for theft and murder were being armed and directed to assail Armenians. For more secondary discussion, see Kévorkian, *The Armenian Genocide*, 359, 409; and Akçam, *A Shameful Act*, 45–46.

23. *Ravished* has multiple meanings, but at the time, it was often a synonym for rape, leaving open the possibility that Meriam's husband may have been sexually assaulted prior to his murder. Meriam was rescued from her abusive Arab husband's home in Dayr al-Zur and brought to Aleppo. Tragically, she succumbed to tuberculosis soon after. Meriam, "Registers," inmate 923, January 13, 1926, UNA.

24. Interview with Roupen Gavour Gavourian (b. 1907), no date, no interviewer information, video in Armenian Genocide Oral History Collection, Zoryan Institute, Toronto. Roupen's story was originally shared with me by his descendants as a postmemory.

25. Zabel Essayan, "La Libération des femmes et des enfants non-musulmans en Turquie, 5. I have chosen to add the word *repeated* in brackets because what is being described here is continual and ongoing sexual abuse. Until the women and girls were either bought or abducted by another man who would then have private access to their bodies, any man or group of men could sexually abuse them at any time during deportation. From the accounts of women collected by humanitarian workers, the sexual abuse did not end after their transfer into Muslim homes; rather, it continued.

26. Essayan, "La Libération des femmes et des enfants non-musulmans en Turquie," 5.

27. Catherine MacKinnon uses this term to describe the case of Rwanda; "Genocide's Sexuality," 333. Similarly, Matthias Bjørnlund used the phrase "a fate worse than dying," uttered by a witness during the Armenian Genocide, as the title of his groundbreaking article that unflinchingly explores gender-based killing and sexual atrocity.

28. At the beginning of the eighteenth century, the Ottoman military was composed not only of slave soldiers but free-born Muslims, many of whom joined in order to avail themselves of its privileges and advantages, such as tax exemption. Ottoman historians have understood this shift as a marriage between economic and state interests at a time when the janissary system was aligned with the economic power of the guilds. The janissary title could be purchased for a price, offering an advantage to merchants who could profit more by avoiding taxes. Baki Tezcan, *The Second Ottoman Empire: Political and Social Transformation in the Early Modern World* (New York: Cambridge University Press, 2010), 210, 225.

29. Quoting from the U.N. Convention on the Prevention and Punishment for the Crime of Genocide, in Marc David Baer, *The Ottomans*, 47.

30. Leslie Peirce, *Imperial Harem: Women and Sovereignty in the Ottoman Empire* (New York: Oxford University Press, 1993) 29–31.

31. *Zimmi* is the Turkish term for Christians and Jews described in early Islamic writings as *ahl al-dhimma*, "the people of the covenant." Madeline Zilfi, *Women and Slavery in the Ottoman Empire* (Cambridge: Cambridge University Press, 2010), 98.

32. Gayle Rubin, "Traffic in Women: Notes on the "Political Economy" of Sex," in *Toward an Anthropology of Women*, ed. Rayna Reiter (New York: Monthly Review Press, 1975), 165.

33. Discussed in analyses of rape in Islamic law is that the proprietorship of men is embedded within the linguistic roots of terms connoting rape: in Arabic the modern term for rape is "usurpation" (*ightisab*), and it surfaces in Turkish as "to usurp" (*gaspetmek*). The most common modern Turkish term for rape is *tecavüz etmek*, which means "to rape, violate, shame or defile." See Elyse Semerdjian, *"Off the Straight Path": Illicit Sex, Law, and Community in Ottoman Aleppo* (Syracuse, NY: Syracuse University Press, 2008), 18–19; and Hina Azam, *Sexual Violation in Islamic Law: Substance, Evidence, and Procedure* (New York: Cambridge University Press, 2015), 106–8.

34. For descriptions of the restructuring of the Ottoman legal system in the age of reform, see "The Tanzimat," in *The Cambridge History of Turkey*, vol. 4 (New York: Cambridge University Press, 2006, 2008), 20; Boğaç A. Ergene, *Judicial Practice: Institutions and Agents in the Islamic World* (Leiden: Brill, 2009), 73–87; Selim Deringil, *Well-Protected Domains: Ideology and the Legitimization of Power in the Ottoman Empire 1876–1909* (London: Palgrave Macmillan, 1998), 45.

35. Kecia Ali, *Marriage and Slavery in Early Islam* (Cambridge, MA: Harvard University Press, 2010), 6–7.

36. Enactments of abduction are still part of some marriage ceremonies of some communities in the Middle East, evoking traditions in which the desire to marry was expressed by first kidnapping the bride. These traditions remain embedded in the Arabic term *zawaj al-khatifa* (marriage by kidnapping) used to describe elopement.

37. Peirce, "Abduction with (Dis)honor," 312, 316–17, 325.

38. The requirement to pay *cizye* was lifted in 1855. See Howard Eissenstat, "Modernization, Imperial Nationalism, and Ethnicization of Confessional Identity in the Late Ottoman Empire," in *Nationalizing Empires*, ed. Stefan Berger ad Alexei Miller (Budapest: Central European University Press, 2015), 442.

39. Elyse Semerdjian, "Naked Anxiety: Bathhouses, Nudity, and Muslim/Non-Muslim Relations in Eighteenth-Century Aleppo," *International Journal of Middle East Studies* 45, no. 4 (November 2013): 651–76.

40. Zilfi, *Women and Slavery in the Ottoman Empire*, 12–13.

41. Through two successive edicts—the Hatt-ı Şerif of Gülhane (1839) and the Hatt-ı Hümayün (1856)—the Ottoman government twice proclaimed that non-Muslim subjects were equal to Muslims. However, at the time of the first edict, Muslim resentment began to swell, and we can date the outbreak of modern sectarian violence in several parts of the empire to this time. Ussama Makdisi, *The Culture of Sectarianism: Community, History, and Violence in Nineteenth-Century Ottoman Lebanon* (Berkeley: University of California Press, 2000) 11, 63–66.

42. The 1876 Ottoman Constitution can be accessed at https://iow.eui.eu/wp-content/uploads/sites/18/2014/05/Brown-01-Ottoman-Constitution.pdf.

43. Ceyda Karamursel, "The Uncertainties of Freedom: The Second Constitutional Era and the End of Slavery in the Late Ottoman Empire," *Journal of Women's History* 28, no. 3 (2016): 141.

44. Heather Sharkey, *Muslims, Christians, and Jews in the Middle East* (New York: Cambridge University Press, 2017; Kemal Karpat, *The Politicization of Islam: Reconstructing Identity, State, Faith, and Community in the Late Ottoman State* (New York: Oxford University Press, 2001); and Hasan Kayalı, *Ottomanism, Arabism, and Islamism in the Ottoman Empire, 1908–1918* (Berkeley: University of California Press, 1997).

45. Karamursel, "The Uncertainties of Freedom," 140.

46. Abolition in the Ottoman Empire was an ongoing process. Even after pronouncements of abolition on paper and the halting of African slavery, the slavery of Circassians continued, based on claims grounded in shariʿa rulings affirming the practice. Abolition ended Circassian slavery in 1912, with a problematic law that slaves could purchase their freedom using bank loans from the Bank of Agriculture. Karamursel, "The Uncertainties of Freedom," 154.

47. In Islamic law, sexual violence was understood as a form of usurpation of another man's proprietorship over the sexuality of his wife in marriage. One Hanafi jurist argued, "The dowry [*mahr*] is an exchange for the vulva [*al-mahr ʿiwad ʿan al-budh*ʿ]." Such proprietorship is confirmed in some of the modern terminology for rape, such as either the Arabic *ightisab* or the Turkish *tecavüz*; both signify "usurpation." See Semerdjian, *Off the Straight Path*, 19.

48. Memorandum by Mr. Alvarez, Inclosure 12, and "List of Charges," Inclosure 13, in *Parliamentary Papers Turkey, 1890*, Correspondence Respecting the Conditions of the Population of Turkey and the Proceedings in the Case of Moussa Bey, no. 1 (1890–1891) (London: Harrison & Sons, 1891), 18–19; also cited in Owen Robert Miller, *Sasun 1894: Mountains, Missionaries and Massacres at the End of the Ottoman Empire* (Ph.D. diss., Columbia University, 2015), 91–92.

49. The story of Gülizar was written by her daughter Armenouhi Kévonian, *Les noces noires de Gulizar* (Paris: Parenthèses Editions, 1993); it was translated into Turkish as *Gülizar'ın Kara Düğünü* (Istanbul: Aras Yayıncılık, 2015).

50. Kévonian, *Les noces noires de Gulizar*, 41.

51. Consul Lloyd to Sir W. White, *Parliamentary Papers Turkey, 1890*, Inclosure no. 17, 21.

52. Memorandum by M. Marinitsch, *Parliamentary Papers Turkey, 1890*, Inclosure no. 80, 63–64. These events are summarized in Miller, *Sasun 1894*, 91–93.

53. Kévonian, *Les noces noires de Gulizar*, 137–139.

54. Owen Robert Miller, "Back to the Homeland" (Tebi Yergir): Or, How Peasants Became Revolutionaries in Muş," *Journal of the Ottoman and Turkish Studies Association* 4, no. 2 (November 2017): 287–308.

55. Stavridis to Djevdet Pasha, *Parliamentary Papers Turkey, 1890*, Inclosure 2, no. 6, 9.

56. Kévonian, *Les noces noires de Gulizar*, 87–88.

57. Kévonian, *Les noces noires de Gulizar*, 137, 149.

58. Ayşenur Korkmaz, "The Hamidian Massacres: Gendered Violence, Biopolitics and National Honour," *Collective and State Violence in Turkey: The Construction of a National Identity from Empire to Nation-State*, ed. Stephan Astourian and Raymond Kévorkian (New York: Berghahn, 2021), 110.

59. Miller, *Sasun 1894*, 85.

60. Owen Robert Miller, "Back to the Homeland" (Tebi Yergir): Or, How Peasants became Revolutionaries in Muş," *Journal of the Ottoman and Turkish Studies Association*, 4, no. 2 (November 2017): 300–301.

61. British Foreign Office, *Correspondence Relative to the Armenian Question: Reports from Her Majesty's Consular Officers in Asiatic Turkey* (Bitlis), Enclosure 2 in no. 3 (1896), 3–4.

62. Avedis Hadjian, *Secret Nation: The Hidden Armenians of Turkey* (London: I. B. Tauris, 2018), 83–84.

63. Jean Franco, *Cruel Modernity* (Durham, NC: Duke University Press, 2013), 52–53.

64. For the relationship between Kurds and the Ottoman Porte, see Janet Klein, *The Margins of Empire: Kurdish Militias in the Ottoman Tribal Zone* (Stanford, CA: Stanford University Press, 2011), 9–12.

65. Selim Deringil, "The Armenian Question Is Finally Closed," *Comparative Studies in Society and History* 51, no. 2 (April 2009): 349.

66. Estimates vary on how many Armenians died in the massacres. See Akçam, *A Shameful Act*, 42. French magazine covers represented Abdul Hamid with blood-soaked hands, sometimes with sword in hand. See Haik Demoyan, *Hayots tseghaspanutyan lusabanume hamashkharhayin mamuli aṛajin ejerin / Armenian Genocide: Front Page Coverage in the World Press* (Yerevan: AGMI, 2015).

67. These findings are specific for Aleppo and need to be tested for other parts of the empire. Elyse Semerdjian, "Armenian Women, Legal Bargaining, and Gendered Politics of Conversion in Seventeenth and Eighteenth Century Aleppo," *Journal of Middle Eastern Women's Studies* 12, no. 1 (March 2016): 2–30. Selim Deringil largely confirms my findings that conversion was rare before the mass conversions documented during periods of repression in the late nineteenth century and early twentieth century. Deringil, *Well-Protected Domains*.

68. Tijana Krstić, *Contested Conversions to Islam: Narratives of Religious Change in the Early Modern Ottoman Empire* (Stanford, CA: Stanford University Press, 2011), 6.

69. Marc David Baer, *Honored by the Glory of Islam: Conversion and Conquest in Ottoman Europe* (Oxford: Oxford University Press, 2008).

70. For the pedagogy of public punishment, see Michel Foucault, *Discipline and Punish: The Birth of the Prison*, trans. Alan Sheridan (New York: Vintage, 1995). Talal Asad cautioned against the Christian approach to conversion that emphasizes religious belief and faith over other considerations. See Talal Asad, "Comments on Conversion," in *Conversion to Modernities*, ed. Peter van der Veer (New York: Routledge, 1996), 263.

71. Korkmaz, "The Hamidian Massacres," 102.

72. Deringil, "The Armenian Question Is Finally Closed," 346.

73. Deringil, "The Armenian Question Is Finally Closed," 353.

74. Quoted in Fuat Dündar, *Crime of Numbers: The Role of Statistics in the Armenian Question (1878–1918)* (New Brunswick, NJ: Transaction, 2010), 108.

75. There is a growing body of scholarship on the subject of Islamized Armenians inside contemporary Turkey, including books published by the Hrant Dink Foundation. See *Sessizliğin Sesi: Diyarbakırlı Ermeniler Konuşuyor I –II*, ed. Ferda Balancar (Istanbul: Hrant Dink Vakfı, 2012 and 2014); *Müslümanlaş(tiril)miş Ermeniler: Konferans Tebliğleri Kasım 2013*, ed. Altuğ Yılmaz (Istanbul: Hrant Dink Vakfı Yayınları, 2015); Çetin, *Anneannem*; Altınay and Çetin, *The Grandchildren*; Laure Marchand and Guillaume Perrier, *La Turquie et le fantôme Arménien* (Paris: Actes Sud, 2013); and Hadjian, *Secret Nation*.

Testimony is offered in the documentary films *Chanson de Nahide* (dir. Berke Baş, 2009); *Bekleyiş* (The Waiting) (dir. Umut Bozyil, 2014); and *Vank'ın Çocukları: 1915 katliamında sağ kalan Dersimli Ermenilerin hikâyesi* (dir. Nezahat Gündoğan, 2016).

76. Derrida calls circumcision "a mark, a scar, a signature on the body." He also considers the ritual a public declaration of inclusion in the Jewish community bound by covenant with God. See Jacques Derrida, "Composing 'Circumfession,'" in *Augustine and Postmodernism: Confessions and Circumfession*, ed. J. D. Caputo and M. J. Scanlon (Bloomington: University of Indiana Press, 2005), 21.

77. Akçam, *Ermenilerin zorla Müsülmanlaştırılması*, 104.

78. Verjine Svazlian, *The Armenian Genocide and the People's Historical Memory* (Yerevan: Gitutiun, 2005), 67; and Bjørnlund, "A Fate Worse Than Dying," 37.

79. Such conversions of Armenians departed significantly from the conversion procedures registered at the shari'a courts in the early modern period. My own study of the shari'a courts of Aleppo shows that the few times Armenians did appear in court to convert, their conversion followed a formulaic recitation "honored in the Islamic faith" (*tusharrifu bi din al-Islam*). Converts were accompanied by two witnesses, and the entire event was registered in court before a judge. See Semerdjian, "Armenian Women, Legal Bargaining, and Gendered Politics of Conversion."

80. Report from Miss Alma Johanson from the German Mission in Moush dated November 18, 1915, submitted by Henry Morgenthau, National Archives and Records Administration (NARA) 59, 867.00/798, 9.

81. Dündar, *Crime of Numbers*, 109.

82. Nazan Maksudyan, "Agents or Pawns? Nationalism and Ottoman Children during the Great War," *Journal of the Ottoman and Turkish Studies Association* 3, no. 1 (May 2016): 139–50.

83. A coded telegram from the Ministry of Education was sent to ten provinces where coordinated attacks against the Armenian community were underway. It specifically directs that Armenian children be transferred to the households of elite notables living within those districts and villages. See DH.ŞFR 54/150, BOA June 26, 1915; the original Ottoman document is reproduced in Taner Akçam, *The Young Turks' Crime against Humanity* (Princeton, NJ: Princeton University Press, 2013), 318.

84. Orlando Patterson, *Slavery and Social Death: A Comparative Study* (Cambridge, MA: Harvard University Press, 1985).

85. Khatchadour Stepanian, "Registers," June 1, 1922, inmate 16, UNA.

86. The highest-value slaves in the Ottoman Empire were healthy, beautiful girls and childbearing women who were offered as tributes to the sultan. Muslim Circassian women continued to be enslaved because their aesthetic traits were desirable. See *The Concubine, the Princess, and the Teacher*, trans. and ed. Douglas Scott Brookes (Austin: University of Texas, 2008), 7.

87. Zavier Wingham, "Arap Bacı'nın Ara Muhaveresi: Under the Shadow of the Ottoman Empire and Its Study," *Yıllık: Annual of Istanbul Studies* 3 (2021), 177–83; and Bam Willoughby, "Opposing a Spectacle of Blackness: Arap Baci, Baci Kalfa, Dadi, and the Invention of African Presence in Turkey," *Lateral* 10, no. 1 (2021).

88. Some of the most damning evidence of the mass transfer of women and children has been documented by Turkish authors who frame these transfers as rescues deserving of praise. See Atnur, *Türkiye'de Ermeni kadınları ve çocukları meselesi*.

89. DH.KMS, 50/73–1, July 7, 1919, and DH.KMS, 50/73–2, July 7, 1919, BOA.

90. The document reports that the girl was released with the help of an Armenian auxiliary society (*ermeni muavenet-i seniyye cemiyeti*). See DH.İ.UM, 19/15-1, 34, 4, January 20, 1920, BOA.

91. DH-KMS, 50-2/41, 2 June 26, 1919, and DH-KMS, 50-2/41, 1 May 3, 1919, BOA.

92. DH-ŞFR, 98-140/1 February 12, 1920, BOA.

93. DH-ŞFR, 98-321/1, 1, April 27, 1919, BOA.

94. DH-KMS, 50-2/41, 5, August 24, 1919, BOA

95. The names of the girls are not transliterated consistently in the original document; I therefore approximated as best I could the original Armenian names. DH.KMS, 50/73-1, July 7, 1919, BOA.

96. DH-İUM, 19-7, 1-5, 11 April 6, 1919, BOA.

97. Essayan, "La Libération des femmes et des enfants non-musulmans en Turquie," 4, 6.

98. Essayan, "La Libération des femmes et des enfants non-musulmans en Turquie," 6.

99. Essayan, "La Libération des femmes et des enfants non-musulmans en Turquie," 6.

100. Banu Bargu, "Why Did Bouazizi Burn Himself?," *Constellations* 23, no. 1 (2016): 33.

101. Essayan, "La Libération des femmes et des enfants non-musulmans en Turquie," 7.

102. Essayan, "La Libération des femmes et des enfants non-musulmans en Turquie," 7.

103. Essayan, "La Libération des femmes et des enfants non-musulmans en Turquie," 7.

104. Essayan, "La Libération des femmes et des enfants non-musulmans en Turquie," 10.

105. Der Matossian, *The Horrors of Adana*, 18; and Mouradian, *The Resistance Network*.

106. Essayan, "La Libération des femmes et des enfants non-musulmans en Turquie," 8.

107. Lerna Ekmekçioğlu documents the debates within the Armenian community about the recovery of Armenian women during the vorpahavak and the need to recuperate women for the birthing of Armenians after the genocide. *Vorpahavak* means, in a literal translation, "orphan claim," but the rescue operation aimed from the outset to include widows, concubines, and other women being kept in Muslim homes. See Ekmekçioğlu, *Recovering Armenia*.

108. Essayan, "La Libération des femmes et des enfants non-musulmans en Turquie," 10.

109. Prosecutor v. Jean-Paul Akayesu, 1998. Discussed in Sherrie L. Russel-Brown, "Rape as an Act of Genocide," *Berkeley Journal of International Law* 21, no. 2, 350–73.

Remnant 1

1. Atom Yarjanian, pen name Siamanto, was born in Agn (current-day Kemaliye, formerly Eğin), off the shores of the Euphrates. He was arrested and massacred with other Armenian intellectuals on April 24, 1915. Siamanto composed this poem, among ten others, in 1909 after the Adana Massacres of the same year. This collection is titled *Garmir lurer paregames* (Bloody news from my friend) and was originally published in *Azadamard*, no. 8 (July 1, 1909): 1.

Chapter 2

1. Testimonies about Armenians being burned alive can be found in Amatuni Virabyan, ed. *Armenian Genocide by Ottoman Turkey: Testimony of Survivors* (Yerevan: Zangak, 2013), 64; Verjine Svazlian, *The Armenian Genocide: Testimonies of the Eyewitness Survivors* (Yerevan: Gitutiun, 2011), 181; Peter Balakian, *Burning the Tigris: The Armenian Genocide and America's Response* (New York: Harper Perennial, 2004) 274; and Bjørnlund, "'A Fate Worse Than Dying," 25. These atrocities mirrored accounts of atrocities against Bulgarian

Muslims that were circulated in Ottoman propaganda pamphlets and postcards. Stories of Muslim women stripped naked, forced to dance, and victimized by sexual atrocities were strikingly similar to those performed against Armenians a few years later. See Y. Doğan Çetinkaya, "'Revenge! Revenge! Revenge!' 'Awakening a Nation' Through Propaganda in the Ottoman Empire during the Balkan Wars (1912–1913)," in *World War I and the End of the Ottomans: From the Balkan Wars to the Armenian Genocide*, ed. Hans-Lukas Kieser, Kerem Öktem, and Maurus Reinkowski (London: Bloomsbury, 2015), 85.

2. Adrianna Cavarero, *Horrorism: Naming Contemporary Violence*, trans. William McCuaig (New York: Columbia University Press, 2011).

3. von Joeden-Forgey, "The Devil in the Details," 2.

4. Mary Douglas, *Purity and Danger: An Analysis of Concepts of Pollution and Taboo* (London: Routledge, 1966).

5. Elaine Scarry, *The Body in Pain: The Making and Unmaking of the World* (Oxford: Oxford University Press, 1987), 40–41.

6. Franco, *Cruel Modernity*, 79.

7. Bjørnlund, "A Fate Worse than Dying," 17.

8. Hasmik Khalapyan, "Marriage Law and Culture: Ottoman Armenians and Women's Efforts for Reform," *EVN Report*, July 19, 2019.

9. Henry F. B. Lynch, *Armenia: Travels and Studies*, vol. 2 (London: Longmans, Green, 1901), 220–21.

10. Korkmaz, "The Hamidian Massacres," 107.

11. Shahen, "Engerayin khantirner: amusnagan dzeghdzmunk i kavars," *Masis*, February 9, 1885, 671.

12. Shahen, "Engerayin khantirner," 674.

13. Shahen, "Engerayin khantirner," 674.

14. Shahen, "Engerayin khantirner," 674.

15. A controversy erupted when historian Taner Akçam mentioned "the right of first night" in the Turkish press, which resulted in a petition signed by 132 Kurdish scholars demanding an apology or, alternatively, evidence of the crime. Akçam responded by posting fifteen sources documenting the practice. See "Taner Akçam'dan 'ilk gece hakkı' ile ilgili eleştirilere yanıt," *Agos*, May 10, 2021. According to historian Stephan Astourian, who generously provided evidence of the practice to this author, bride abduction appears to be isolated in the regions of Moush and Sasun. Admittedly, more research is needed on this controversial subject. See M. S. Lazarev, *Kurdistan i kurdskaia problema (90-e gody XIX veka-1917)*, (Moscow: Nauka, 1964), 32–34; and Lynch, *Armenia: Travels and Studies*, vol. 2: *The Turkish Provinces*, reprint (Beirut: Khayats, 1965), 430–31, cited in Stepan Astourian, "Silence of the Land: Agrarian Relations, Ethnicity, and Power," *A Question of Genocide: Armenians and Turks at the End of the Ottoman Empire*, 60. Also see V. A. Bayburdyan who found a reference to the Kurdish "right of first night" and other privileges in archival manuscripts belonging to the catholicosate in the Matenadaran manuscripts library in Yerevan, Armenia, *Hay-krdakan haraberutyunnerě Osmanyan Kaysrutyunum XIX darum ev XX dari skzbin* (Yerevan: Hayastan, 1989) 53.

16. The specific example Beth Baron uses is of an attack on Egyptian village women by British forces in 1919. See Baron, *Egypt as a Woman: Gender, Nationalism, and Politics* (Berkeley: University of California Press, 2005), 41–50.

17. Baron, *Egypt as a Woman*, 42.

18. von Joeden-Forgey, "The Devil in the Details," 3.

19. Suny, *"They Can Live in the Desert but Nowhere Else,"* 314; and von Joeden-Forgey, "The Devil in the Details," 3–4.

20. Grigoris Balakian, *Armenian Golgotha*, trans. Peter Balakian with Aris Sevag (New York: Random House, 2009), 145. The original text was published as *Hay koghkotan: truakner hai mardirosakrutiunen: Berlinen tebi Zor, 1914–1920*, 2 vols. (Vienna: Mkhitarian daparan, 1922). Powerful testimony of destruction of fetuses can be found in *The Genocide in Me* (dir. Araz Artinian, 2006), https://youtu.be/xO8ogdmFmz4, 29:45–31:18.

21. A survivor recalled that a génocidaire uttered, "Gavurs [unbelievers] do not bear boys, see!" after cutting open a pregnant woman's belly to expose a female fetus. See Svazlian, *The Armenian Genocide and the People's Historical Memory*, 66; and Bjørnlund, "'A Fate Worse than Dying.'" 26.

22. Pailadzo Captanian noted that her husband and other men were gathered in a stable as her deportation caravan was forced to march on. Captanian, *Mémoires d'une déportée arménienne* (Paris: M. Flinikowski, 1919), 23.

23. Svazlian, *The Armenian Genocide: Testimonies*, 157.

24. Svazlian, *The Armenian Genocide: Testimonies*, 130, 109. It is worth recalling that not only priests but the famous Armenian members of parliament Krikor Zohrab and Vartkes Serengülian had their beards plucked prior to execution, a symbolic castration since the beard represented masculinity.

25. Svazlian, *The Armenian Genocide: Testimonies*, 122.

26. See Edhem Eldem on the execution of Yakub Houvanessian, a *sarraf*, or money changer, who died during torture but was beheaded post mortem and posed in a humiliating fashion. Eldem, "Istanbul from Imperial to Peripherialized Capital," in *The Ottoman City between East and West: Aleppo, Izmir, and Istanbul* (New York: Cambridge University Press, 1999), 173–74. For the execution of the Jewish customs chief (*emin al-gümrük*) in Aleppo, Musa w. Ishaq, who was accused of embezzlement and crucified (*salb*) over the threshold of the Khan al-Gumruk, see shari'a court record SMH (*sijillat al-mahakim haleb*) 25: 310:1212, Safar 5, 1059AH/February 18, 1649. The execution took place on February 13, 1649 (30 Muharram 1059 AH). A special thanks to Charles Wilkins, who shared his notes on this document, which is located in the archives of the Dar al-Watha'iq al-Tarikhiyya in Damascus, Syria.

27. Henry Riggs, *Days of Tragedy: Personal Experiences in Harpoot, 1915–1917* (London: Gomidas Institute, 1997), 57–58.

28. Aslı Zengin, "The Afterlife of Gender: Sovereignty, Intimacy, and Muslim Funerals of Transgender People in Turkey," *Cultural Anthropology* 34, no. 1 (2019): 83.

29. Hugh S. Miller "Salvaging the Womanhood of Armenia," *The American Woman* (April 1920), 17. Armenians were fed to dogs but also denied burials, a form of necroviolence that left their corpses to be consumed by hungry desert creatures. One survivor remarked "the dogs got enraged by eating human flesh." See Svazlian, *The Armenian Genocide and the People's Historical Memory*, 70. Hourig Attarian and Hermig Yogurtian documented the memory of a survivor, Pergrouhi, whose mother was consumed by dogs after a hasty burial "Survivor Stories, Surviving Narratives: Autobiography, Memory, and Trauma across Generations," in *Girlhood: Redefining the Limits*, ed. Y. Jiwani, C. Steenbergen, and C. Mitchell (Montreal: Black Rose Books, 2006, 16.

30. Armin Wegner, quoted in Peter Balakian, "Photography, Visual Culture, and the Armenian Genocide," in *Humanitarian Photography*, ed. Heide Fehrenbach and Davide Rodogno (New York: Cambridge University Press, 2015), 96.

31. Balakian, *Armenian Golgotha*, 248.

32. Report of Leslie Davis to Ambassador Henry Morgenthau, U.S. State Department Record Group 59,867.4016/392, reproduced in *United States Official Documents on the Armenian Genocide*, ed. Ara Sarafian, *The Central Lands*, vol. 3 (Watertown, MA: Armenian Review, 1995), 79.

33. Svazlian, *The Armenian Genocide: Testimonies*, 98.

34. Report of Leslie Davis, in Sarafian, *United States Official Documents on the Armenian Genocide*, 32.

35. Mary Douglas's classic study argues that community is constituted through laws that define what is pure and sacred versus what is not. See Douglas, *Purity in Danger: An Analysis of Concepts of Pollution and Taboo* (London: Routledge, 1966).

36. Balakian, *Armenian Golgotha*, 139.

37. Dawn Anahid MacKeen, *The Hundred-Year Walk: An Armenian Odyssey* (Boston: Mariner Books, 2016), 144; and Svazlian, *The Armenian Genocide: Testimonies*, 110.

38. Balakian, *Armenian Golgotha*, 337.

39. Salwa Ismail, *The Rule of Violence: Subjectivity, Memory, and Government in Syria* (New York: Cambridge University Press, 2018), 48–51.

40. Kerop Bedoukian, *The Urchin* (London: John Murray Publishers, 1978), 99.

41. Essayan, "La Libération des femmes et des enfants non-musulmans en Turquie," 3.

42. MacKeen, *The Hundred-Year Walk*, 145. MacKeen notes that urine is 95 percent water, which gives it life-supporting efficacy.

43. Karnig Panian, *Goodbye, Antoura: A Memoir of the Armenian Genocide* (Stanford, CA: Stanford University Press, 2015), 165; emphasis in original. Another survivor compared Armenians to "grazing animals" who ate ground-up bones to survive. Svazlian, *The Armenian Genocide: Testimonies*, 154–55.

44. Virabyan, *Armenian Genocide by Ottoman Turkey: Testimony of Survivors*, 137, 145. *Ghavurma* (Armenian) or *kavurma* (Turkish) is the name of a meat dish usually sautéed in butter or fat.

45. Peroomian, "Women and the Armenian Genocide," 12; and Richard Hovannisian, ed., *The Armenian Genocide in Perspective* (New Brunswick, NJ: Transaction Books, 1986), 178.

46. MacKeen, *The Hundred-Year Walk*, 195.

47. "Take Babies, Cook Flesh, and Sell It Back for Food," *Courier* (Buffalo), February 15, 1920. Nubarian Library.

48. It is not unusual for accounts of cannibalism to emerge during periods of deprivation, such as the locust famine during World War I. Najwa al-Qattan explores how hunger was articulated in "When Mothers Ate Their Children," *International Journal of Middle East Studies* 46, no. 4 (2014): 731.

49. Report of Leslie Davis, in Sarafian, *United States Official Documents on the Armenian Genocide*, 94.

50. Terence S. Turner, "The Social Skin," in *Not Work Alone: A Cross-cultural View of Activities Superfluous to Survival*, ed. Jeremy Cherfas and Roger Lewin (London: Temple Smith, 1980), 112–40; and Virabyan, *Armenian Genocide by Ottoman Turkey*, 103, 143.

51. Report of Leslie Davis, in Sarafian, *United States Official Documents on the Armenian Genocide*, 28.

52. Balakian, *Armenian Golgotha*, 101, 149.

53. Benjamin Braude, "International Competition and Domestic Cloth in the Otto-

man Empire, 1500–1650: A Study in Undevelopment," *Review: A Journal of the Ferdinand Braudel Center* 2, no. 3 (Winter, 1979): 437–51; Donald Quataert, *Ottoman Manufacturing in the Age of the Industrial Revolution* (New York: Cambridge, 1993); and Suraiya Faroqhi, "Declines and Revivals in Textile Production," in *The Cambridge History of Turkey*, 356–75.

54. Quoted in Svazlian, *The Armenian Genocide and the People's Historical Memory*, 51.

55. Hannah Arendt, *The Origins of Totalitarianism*, new ed. (New York: Harcourt Brace, 1958, 1973), 443, 457.

56. Cavarero, *Horrorism*, 9.

57. One Turkish captain confessed, "We found thousands of gold pieces sewn into the women's clothes." Balakian, *Armenian Golgotha*, 143. Authors have noted that rumors of Armenian gold linger in areas where Armenians used to live. Some residents believe it can curse them with bad luck. See Watenpaugh, *The Missing Pages*, 17.

58. Captanian, *Mémoires d'une déportée arménienne*, 31.

59. Sarafian, *United States Official Documents on the Armenian Genocide*, 84.

60. Captanian, *Mémoires d'une déportée arménienne*, 131.

61. Matthias Bjørnlund, "'A Fate Worse than Dying,'" 32.

62. Captanian, *Mémoires d'une déportée arménienne*, 99; and Essayan, "La Libération des femmes et des enfants non-musulmans en Turquie," 3. *Une fémelle*, a pejorative way of referring to female human beings, was used to emphasize the dehumanization of women in this process of stripping and torture. I would like to thank Adeline Rother for this insight.

63. Morgenthau, *Ambassador Morgenthau's Story*, 321. Morgenthau's testimony was also included verbatim in the "Blue Book," the first extensive documentation of survivor testimony compiled by Viscount Bryce with historian Arnold Toynbee, formally titled *The Treatment of the Armenians in the Ottoman Empire 1915–1916: Documents Presented to Viscount Bryce*, 2nd ed. (Beirut: G. Doniguian & Sons, 1979), 266. This book includes several references to Armenians being deported in a state of nakedness in the volume; see 20, 165, 262, 287, 289, 323, 416, 543, and 644 for more examples.

64. Captanian, *Mémoires d'une déportée arménienne*, 96.

65. Odian, *Accursed Years*, 163–64.

66. For an in-depth study of saintliness and madness, see Heghnar Zeitlian Watenpaugh, "Deviant Dervishes: Space, Gender, and the Construction of Antinomian Piety in Ottoman Aleppo," *International Journal of Middle East Studies* 37, no. 4 (November 2005), 535–65.

67. Captanian, *Mémoires d'une déportée arménienne*, 131; and Giorgio Agamben, *Homo Sacer: Sovereign Power and Bare Life*, trans. Daniel Heller-Roazen (Stanford, CA: Stanford University Press, 1998), 4–6.

68. Sarafian, *United States Official Documents on the Armenian Genocide*, 86.

69. Bedoukian, *The Urchin*, 34.

70. Georges Bataille, *Erotism: Death and Sensuality* (San Francisco: City Lights, 1986), 18.

71. Banu Bargu, "Another Necropolitics," in *Turkey's Necropolitical Laboratory: Democracy, Violence, and Resistance*, ed. Banu Bargu (Edinburgh: Edinburgh University Press, 2019), 213.

Remnant 2

1. For the original Armenian, see Ruben Herian, "Hay aghchigner arapneru dunerun mech," *Gochnag Hayastani*, 19, no. 35 (August 30, 1919): 1122–23.

2. Herian refers to himself in the third person as "an American" rescuer.

3. This term is idiomatic and refers to a deeply held notion in the region that bread is life-sustaining. Interpretively, it means their husbands feed them more generally.

4. *Ruler* (*der*) is used by Herian here to refer to a colonizing force that would look out for the Armenians' best interest.

Chapter 3

1. The phrase in brackets is illegible in Herian's original handwritten letter. I have offered an approximation based on context of the letter. Ruben Herian, 420.65.2, enclosure 25, April 6, 1919, Armenian National Archives (ANA), Yerevan, Armenia.

2. Earlier Armenian diasporas in the city of Aleppo are discussed in my chapter "Armenians in the Production of Urban Space in Early Modern Judayda, Aleppo," in *Requiem for Ottoman Aleppo/Alep à l'époque ottomane, un requiem*, ed. Stefan Winter (forthcoming). Also see Sebouh Aslanian, *From the Indian Ocean to the Mediterranean: The Global Trade Networks of Armenian Merchants from New Julfa* (Berkeley: University of California Press, 2014).

3. Mouradian, *The Resistance Network*, 98.

4. Syrian writer Ibrahim Khalil, inspired by these stories about Raqqa's Armenian community, included some of them in his short stories. Interview with Ibrahim Khalil, Raqqa, Syria, November 21, 2007.

5. For histories of the orphan rescue, see Nazan Maksudyan, "The Orphan Nation: Gendered Humanitarianism for Armenian Survivor Children in Istanbul, 1919–1922," in *Gendering Global Humanitarianism in the Twentieth Century: Practice, Politics and the Power of Representation,* ed. Esther Möller, Johannes Paulmann, and Katharina Stornig (New York: Springer International Publishing, 2020) 117–142; Boris Adjemian and Talin Suciyan, "Making Space and Community through Memory: Orphans and Armenian Jerusalem in the Nubar Library's Photographic Archive," *Études arméniennes contemporaines* 9 (2017): 75–113; Ekmekçioğlu, *Recovering Armenia*; and Watenpaugh, *Bread from Stones*. For broader histories of Armenian resistance during the genocide, see Kévorkian, *The Armenian Genocide*, 639–46; and Mouradian, *The Resistance Network*.

6. Mouradian, *The Resistance Network*, xx–xxvi.

7. Raymond Kévorkian's outline for the three phases of the Armenian Genocide continues to be the definitive breakdown of this evolution and unfolding of Young Turk genocide methodology; *The Armenian Genocide*, 662–64.

8. Kévorkian, *The Armenian Genocide*, 489.

9. Khatchig Mouradian, "Genocide and Humanitarian Resistance in Ottoman Syria, 1915–1916," *Études arméniennes contemporaines* 7 (2016): 87–103.

10. Western-language sources are used by far the most in studies of humanitarianism. This study has greatly benefitted from the accessibility of European and American archives. While there is an emerging scholarship that relies of Armenian language sources to discuss the vorpahavak, Armenian humanitarian documents have not formed a major focus of the broader scholarship. Some examples of scholars who have engaged Armenian humanitarian efforts during the genocide include Ekmekçioğlu, *Recovering Armenia*; Mouradian, *The Resistance Network*; Hagop Cholakian, *Karen Eppe* (Aleppo: Aravelk, 2001) 50–53; and Anna Aleksanyan, "Rescuing Armenian Women and Children after the Genocide: The Story of Ruben Heryan," *Armenian Weekly*, May 31, 2016.

11. Ekmekçioğlu, *Recovering Armenia*; and Watenpaugh, *Bread from Stones*. To see how

this movement of orphan relief compared with the one that emerged during the 1894–1896 Hamidiye Massacres dominated by missionaries and the American Board of Commissioners for Foreign Missions, see Nazan Maksudyan, *Orphans and Destitute Children in the Late Ottoman Empire* (Syracuse University Press, 2014), 116–23.

12. Ekmekçioğlu, *Recovering Armenia*, 33

13. The vorpahavak was described in detail by the Armenian National Relief Organization in Constantinople. See Azkayin khnamadarutiun *(*Armenian National Relief Organization of Constantinople), *Azkayin khnamadarutiun: enthanur deghegakir arachin vetsamsyah,* vol. 1, 1 May 1919–31 October 1919 (Constantinople: M. Hovagimian Publisher, 1920), 83–87.

14. Aleksanyan, "Rescuing Armenian Women and Children after the Genocide."

15. Aleksanyan, "Rescuing Armenian Women and Children after the Genocide," quoting from Ruben Herian, 420.65.5, 2, ANA.

16. Raymond Kévorkian and Vahé Tachjian, *The Armenian General Benevolent Union,* vol. 1 (Paris: Armenian General Benevolent Union), 62.

17. US State Department Record Group 59, 867.48/1261, Gottlieb to Secretary of State, May 22, 1919, NARA.

18. Vahram Shemmassian, "The Reclamation of Captive Armenian Genocide Survivors in Syria and Lebanon at the End of World War I," *Journal of the Society for Armenian Studies* 15 (2006): 114–15.

19. Tachjian, "Mixed Marriage, Prostitution, Survival," 88.

20. Letter from Archbishop Mushegh Seropian to Boghos Nubar dated March 20, 1919, Correspondence for February and March 1919, Nubarian Library.

21. French translation of an unaddressed letter apparently written by Archbishop Mushegh to Boghos Nubar Pasha, dated January 6, 1919, in box titled "Coupures angl. orphelins, femmes enlevies, etc.," Nubarian Library, Paris, 1–2. The letter has no addressee but on page two, Archbishop Mushegh addresses the intended recipient as "cher pacha," suggesting it was Boghos Nubar Pasha, the head of the AGBU. The letter was composed in French, like other reports of the time, for ready use in postwar deliberations in Paris. As with many of his other archived letters, Archbishop Mushegh offers a scathing criticism of British inaction in the face of exploitation of women in the city. In fact, another letter addressed to British authorities describes the British threatening the Armenian patriarch and the prelate with arrest for their attempts to rescue women and children. Letter from Archbishop Mushegh Seropian to Lieutenant Colonel Leachman, Political Officer, Mosul, Correspondance Arménie, January 3, 1919, Nubarian Library.

22. The author (or translator) of this document accidentally misspelled the term for gonorrhea. The often-used nineteenth-century term *blennorragie* was misspelled "bleu hagie." I would like to thank Mériam Belli for her help deciphering the misspelling in the original document.

23. French translation of a letter written by Archbishop Mushegh to Boghos Nubar Pasha(?), dated January 6, 1919. Letter from Archbishop Mushegh Seropian to Lieutenant Colonel Leachman, January 3, 1919.

24. I would imagine similar documents exist at the Armenian Prelacy in Aleppo; however, I have no access to such documents. They have not been openly made available to researchers.

25. Armenian Relief Committee of Mesopotamia, Speech Delivered by Mr. M. H. Kouyoumdjian at Galustan Park, Calcutta, February 13, 1920, Appealing for Funds in Aid

of the Armenian Refugee Orphans, published speech archived at Ruben Herian, 420.65.51, enclosure 5, ANA.

26. Telegram from Mark Sykes January 3, 1919, FO 371/3657/1749/F512, BNA.

27. This language is culled from documents found in the Aleppo Prelacy cited in Shemmassian, "The Reclamation of Captive Armenian Genocide Survivors," 114.

28. Yotnakhparian notes that while the effort was initiated by Archbishop Sarajian, Emir Faysal gave his full backing and provided the necessary paperwork to support the transfer. It is also worth mentioning that Faysal was continuing the work of his father, Sharif Hussein, who issued orders to care for Armenians and condemned the Armenian Genocide. See Levon Yotnakhparian, *Crows of the Desert: The Memoirs of Levon Yotnakhparian*, trans. Victoria Parian (Tujunga, CA: Parian Photographic Design, 2012). There is a documentary based on this memoir titled *Crows of the Desert: A Hero's Journey through the Armenian Genocide*, dir. Marta Houske, 2017.

29. *Al-'Asima*, May 19, 1919, reprinted in Nora Arissian, *Asda' al-abadat al-armaniyya fi al-sahafa al-suriyya (1930–1877)* (Beirut: Dar al-thakira, 2004), 112–13. King Faysal had two newspapers that served to deliver his message of "Syrianism" at a time when Syria as a state was being formed. These newspapers, *Halab* (Aleppo) and *'Asima* (Damascus), began publication in late 1918.

30. Article 142 in Treaty of Peace with Turkey, signed at Sèvres on August 10, 1920, Treaty Series no. 11, *British Parliamentary Papers* (London: H.M. Stationary Office, 1920) 33.

31. The Covenant of the League of Nations (1920), https://www.ungeneva.org/en/library-archives/league-of-nations/covenant#:~:text=The%20Treaty%20of%20Versailles%20was,a%20preamble%20and%2026%20articles.

32. See Articles 5 and 6 in Paris Peace Conference (1919–1920), Commission on the Responsibility of the Authors of the War and on Enforcement of Penalties, *Violation of the Laws and Customs of War* (London: Oxford University Press, 1919), 17.

33. This dating marks the last entry in the Rescue Home Registers kept by Karen Jeppe in Aleppo. The final registered child, Artin Deguiremenjian, inmate number 1880, was registered on October 9, 1930, UNA.

34. For more about the Rescue Home and Cushman and Kennedy, see Watenpaugh, *Bread from Stones*, 141–43.

35. Zaven Der Yeghiayan, *Armenian Patriarch of Constantinople (1913–1922): My Patriarchal Memoirs* (Monterey, CA: Mayreni Publishing, 2002), 185.

36. Both projects did not seem to have the impact of Herian and Jeppe's in Syria due to the mobilization of the Turkish army under Mustafa Kemal. Der Yeghiayan, *My Patriarchal Memoirs*, 186.

37. Der Yeghiayan, *My Patriarchal Memoirs*, 186.

38. Susan Pattie, *The Armenian Legionnaires: Sacrifice and Betrayal in World War I* (London: I. B. Tauris, 2018), 15–16, 24.

39. *Hérian*, (French) microfilm 13335, Nubarian Library, December 13, 1920, 1; and Arsaguhi Teotig, *Amenoun Daretsoutse, (1916–1920)* (Haleb: Kilikia Gratun Hratarakch'atun, 2009), 210.

40. For the original Armenian language editorial by Ruben Herian, see "Hay aghjikner arabneru dunerun mech," in *Gochnak Hayastani* 19, no. 35 (August 30, 1919), 1122–23.

41. The history of the Armenian Legion and the Battle of Arara was fully documented in Souren Bartevian, *Arara: Haygagan Lekiyone* (Izmir: Dabraqrutiun Keshishian, 1919); and Pattie, *The Armenian Legionnaires*.

42. Aleksanyan, "Rescuing Armenian Women and Children after the Genocide."
43. "Ruben Herian" *Joghovrty Tsayn*, July 14, 1921, no. 4135, 2.
44. Mirak (Մհրակ) is an unusual name, perhaps even a nickname for his relative and confidante. Ruben Herian letter to Mirak, 420.65.2 Enclosure 28, undated, ANA.
45. Aleksanyan, "Rescuing Armenian Women and Children after the Genocide," 2; and Shemassian, "The League of Nations and the Reclamation of Armenian Survivors," 120.
46. Letter to Ruben Herian from Garabed Baghdigian, 420.65.15, enclosure 8, February 14, 1920, ANA.
47. Letters written to Herian frequently refer to women and children being stranded "in the wilderness," which evokes a biblical image being lost, waiting to be redeemed. Examples can be found in Ruben Herian, 420.65.10, enclosure 1, April 26, 1919; 420.65.15, enclosure 10, April 13, 1920; and 420.65.9, enclosure 4, July 7, 1920, all archived at ANA.
48. See Khatoon, "Registers," inmate 1336, May 29, 1927, UNA.
49. Shemmassian, "The Reclamation of Captive Armenian Genocide Survivors,"127. Herian draws upon Orientalist stereotypes of the Arabs in his appeal to American Armenians, as well as essentialist ideas of American industriousness. See Herian, "Hay aghchikner arabneru dunerun mech," 1123.
50. Letter from the ANU in Aleppo to Ruben Herian in Dayr al-Zur, 420.65.8, enclosure 2, July 26, 1919, ANA.
51. Armenian Relief Committee of Mesopotamia, Speech Delivered by Mr. M. H. Kouyoumdjian at Galustan Park, Calcutta, Friday 13, 1920, 5–6.
52. Letter from Ruben Herian to Mirak, 420.65.2, enclosure 19, June 23, 1919, ANA.
53. "Hérian," Armenian Orphans, articles and biographical notes on Ruben Herian archived at Nubarian Library, 2. Herian lists the rescued orphans he took to Baghdad as 320 children in a letter to Mirak, 420.65.2, enclosure 19, June 23, 1919, ANA.
54. Interview with Almas Boghosian, 53473, March 12, 2011, Shoah Foundation Visual History Archive.
55. Interview with Almas Boghosian, March 12, 2011.
56. Letter from ANU Chairman and High Vartabed Zakarian to Rouben Herian, December 12, 1919, 420.65.8, enclosure 7, ANA.
57. Letter from ANU Chairman and High Vartabed Zakarian to Rouben Herian, December 12, 1919.
58. Hovhannes, "Registers," inmate 1062, July 14, 1926, UNA.
59. Letter from the ANU in Aleppo to the unnamed governor of Dayr al-Zur, 420.65.8, enclosure 8, December 12, 1919, ANA.
60. Kamal al-Ghazzi, *Nahr al-Dhahab fi Tarikh Halab*, 2nd ed. (Halab: Dar al-Qalam al-'Arabi, 1999), 3:556.
61. Memorandum from Political Officer of Mayadin to Ruben Herian, July 30, 1919, 420.65.42, 1, ANA.
62. Memorandum from Political Officer of Dayr al-Zur to Ruben Herian, August 28, 1919, 420.65.42, 3, ANA.
63. Memorandum from Political Officer in Mayadin to Ruben Herian, July 30, 1919.
64. Letter from Ruben Herian to Mirak, July 19, 1919, 420.65.2, enclosure 21, 1, ANA.
65. This letter from the Armenian Prelacy Archive is quoted in Shemmassian, "The League of Nations and the Reclamation of Armenian Genocide Survivors," 119.
66. Letter from Ruben Herian to Mirak, April 15,1919, 420.65.2, enclosure 18, ANA.

67. Herian notes in a letter that he formed a special association for Togatsti Armenians in order to raise funds for the relief effort. See April 6, 1919, 420.65.2, enclosure 24, ANA.

68. Letter from Ruben Herian to Mirak, July 19, 1919, 420.65.2, enclosure 22, ANA.

69. Memorandum from Political Officer of Dayr al-Zur to Ruben Herian, August 28, 1919, 420.65.42 enclosure 5, ANA.

70. Letter to Elder Priest Haroutiun Yessayan from Misak Sisserian January 5, 1920, 420.65.9, enclosure 3, ANA.

71. Letter from Lousia Kazanjian to Ruben Herian (addressed as "Honorable Sir"), November 3, 1919, 420.65.3, enclosure 9, ANA.

72. The village name is spelled Աշրէթ in Armenian. It is sometimes challenging to locate these places due to the Arabic written in the Armenian alphabet. Letter from Miss Yernige Toundjian to Ruben Herian, undated, 420.65.16, enclosure 5, ANA.

73. Letter from Priest Sahag Shamlian to Ruben Herian, October 7, 1919, 420.65.27, enclosure 2, 2 ANA.

74. Letter from Priest Sahag Shamlian to Ruben Herian, October 7,1919.

75. Some letters in the Herian archive refer to communication with "the tailor" and his wife in Dayr al-Zur. See letter to Elder Priest Haroutiun Yessayan from Misak Sisserian, January 5, 1920, 420.65.9 enclosure 3, 2, ANA.

76. Letter from Keghanush Kuyumdjian to her father, undated, 420.65.3, enclosure 13, ANA. The additional information about Keghanush's age and the age and status of her children was added in the margins of the letter by Herian.

77. Letter from the ANU in Aleppo to Ruben Herian in Dayr al-Zur, August 16, 1919, 420.65.12, enclosure 3, ANA.

78. Ruben Herian to Mirak, September 6, 1919, 420.65.2 enclosure 25, 2–3, ANA.

79. As the British system came to administer Iraq and eastern Syria, Herian would list donations in Indian rupees, Russian rubles, US dollars, British pounds, and Ottoman and gold coin. See letter from Ruben Herian to Mirak, July 19, 1919, 420.65.2 enclosure 22, 1–5, ANA.

80. Letter from Ruben Herian to Mirak, July 19, 1919, 420.65.2, enclosure 22, 5, ANA.

81. Armenian Relief Committee of Mesopotamia, Speech Delivered by Mr. M. H. Kouyoumdjian at Galustan Park, Calcutta, Friday 13, 1920, enclosure 6.

82. Aleksanyan, "Rescuing Armenian Women and Children after the Genocide."

83. Herian "Hay aghchikner arabneru dunerun mech," 1122. Herian refers to the Egyptian National Union in this passage, which is a union of the three Armenian political parties—Dashnag, Hunchag, and Herian's affiliate, the Ramgavar Party (Democratic Liberal Party of Armenia). See Mihran Damadian, *Im Husheres* (Beirut: Zartonk, 1985), 106.

84. Letter from Ruben Herian to Mirak, July 19, 1919, 420.65.2, enclosure 21, 1, ANA.

85. Aleksanyan, "Rescuing Armenian Women and Children after the Genocide."

86. The play is archived in the Ruben Herian collection; see *Vrej*, 420.65.1, ANA.

87. Letter from Ruben Herian to Mirak, July 19, 1919, enclosure 23.

88. Letter from Ruben Herian to Mirak, July 19, 1919, enclosure 24.

89. Letter from Ruben Herian to Mirak, July 19, 1919, enclosure 23.

Remnant 3

1. Letter from Keghanush Kuyumdjian to her father, undated, 420.65.3, enclosure 13, ANA.

Chapter 4

1. Shemmassian, "The League of Nations and the Reclamation of Armenian Genocide Survivors," 88.

2. Shemmassian, "The League of Nations and the Reclamation of Armenian Genocide Survivors," 88–89.

3. Edita Gzoyan, Regina Galustyan, and Shushan Khachatryan, "Reclaiming Children after the Genocide: Neutral House in Istanbul," *Holocaust and Genocide Studies* 33, no. 3 (Winter 2019): 399.

4. Ekmekçioğlu, *Recovering Armenia*.

5. Ekmekçioğlu, *Recovering Armenia*, 399–400; and Der Yeghiayan, *My Patriarchal Memoirs* (Monterey: Mayreni Publishing, 2002), 182. Zahrui Bahri shared the details of her experiences as the Armenian representative in the home in a series of three articles titled "Inch er chezok dune," *Aysor* (Paris), May 3–4, May 5, and May 6, 1953, Nubarian Library, and within her memoir *Giankis Vebe* (Beirut: n.p., 1995).

6. While the character of Jacobsen's Bird's Nest has changed over time, it continues to be an active sanctuary for orphaned and abandoned Armenian children and a boarding school for children whose parents can no longer support them. It is currently owned and operated by the catholicosate of Sis in Antelias, Lebanon.

7. Karen Jeppe, "Account of the Situation of the Armenians in Syria and of My Own Work amongst Them from the 1st of May til the 1st of September 1922," 15, 10158, De Danske Armenivenner 1919–1949, DNA.

8. The largely untapped writings of Armenian humanitarian Berjouhi Bardizbanian-Barseghyan were published in the Armenian newspaper *Hayrenik* and recently published as a memoir as *Khantsadz orer* (Beirut: Vahe Setian Publishing, 2016); for other unsung Armenian humanitarians, see Mouradian, *The Resistance Network*, 26–27.

9. There are several biographies and academic studies of Karen Jeppe's life from which I have gleaned information for this chapter. I am listing a few here in the order of publication: Ingeborg Maria Sick and Pauline Klaiber, *Karen Jeppe im Kampf um ein Volk in Not* (Stuttgart: Steinkopf, 1929); Hagop Cholakian, *Karen Eppe: Hai goghgotayin yev veratsnundin hed* (Aleppo: Arawelk, 2001); Jonas Kauffeldt, *Danes, Orientalism, and the Modern Middle East: Perspectives from the Nordic Periphery* (Ph.D. diss., Florida State University, 2006); Karen Jeppe, *Misak: An Armenian Life*, trans. and ed. Jonas Kauffeldt (London: Gomidas, 2015); Matthias Bjørnlund, "Karen Jeppe, Aage Meyer Bendictsen, and the Ottoman Armenians," *Haigazian Armenological Review* 28 (2008): 9–44; and Matthias Bjørnlund, *På herrens mark: Nødhjælp, mission og kvindekamp under det armenske folkedrab* (Copenhagen: Kristeligt Dagblads Forlag, 2015).

10. Watenpaugh, *Bread from Stones*.

11. Jeppe, *Misak*, xii.

12. See Ingeborg Maria Sick's obituary for Jeppe: "Karen Jeppe of Denmark and Armenia," *American-Scandinavian Review* 25 (1937): 19.

13. Sick, "Karen Jeppe of Denmark and Armenia," 19–20.

14. Two books in Armenian address the important subject of women *feda'yi*, a subject only sparsely mentioned in English publications. See Sona Zeitlian, *Hay gnoch tere hay heghapokhagan sharzhman mech* (Los Angeles: Hraztan Sarkis Zeitlian Publications, 1992); and Edig Minasyan, *Hay herosuhi ganayk* (Erevan: EBH hradaragchutiun, 2016).

15. Alternatively, Ingeborg Maria Sick writes that all twelve Armenians hidden in Jeppe's house survived, something contradicted by Armenian sources. Sick, "Karen Jeppe

of Denmark," 22. The suicides of Der Karekin Voskerichian and his unnamed wife are described in minute detail by Aram Sahakian, who claims to have been there when they took their lives. He writes the priest turned to him after drinking the poison to say, "My son, I believe you are going to live; live to relate to our compatriots how we met death. Tell them life and death as well should have a purpose. One day when you are free, relate to the world the heroic struggle and death of the people of Ourfa." Aram Sahakian, "The Twenty-Five Days of Ourfa," *Armenian Review* 26, no. 2 (1973): 44. There is evidence that Armenians were collecting poison when the deportation order was issued in places like Trabzon. See Letter from the Trebizond Consul Oscar S. Heizer to Ambassador Henry Morgenthau dated June 28, 1915, US State Department Record Group 59, 867.4016/85, 1, NARA.

16. Cholakian, *Karen Eppe*, 51–55. The relationship between Misak and the Garabedian family is described in an archived letter from Kevork Garabedian, "Miss Koren Yeppe: Mother," Baghdad, Iraq, n.d., DDA, box 10, folder A, DNA.

17. There is a pattern of humanitarian workers' mental health being damaged by what they witnessed. For example, Swiss teacher Beatrice Rohner suffered a similar mental breakdown from which it took years to recover. See Han-Lukas Kieser, *Nearest East: American Millennialism and the Mission to the Middle East* (Philadelphia: Temple University Press, 2010), 89.

18. The story of Jeppe's time in Urfa until her departure is told in chapter 7 of Bjørnlund, *På herrens mark*.

19. Karen Jeppe, "Account of the Situation of the Armenians in Syria," Baalbek, August 24, 1922, 9, DDA, box 10, folder A, DNA.

20. Jeppe, *Misak*, xxxv.

21. The housing shortage, as well as the use of tents for the encampment, is also addressed in "Frek Jeppe i Syrien," *Armeniervennen* 2, no. 11–12 (November–December 1922): 45. Jeppe, "Account of the Situation of the Armenians in Syria," 15, 17.

22. On Sabil and Karlik, see chapter 4 in Mouradian, *The Resistance Network*.

23. Robert Jebejian and photographer Hagop Krikorian documented these spaces inside the city of Aleppo in Jebejian, *Routes and Centers of Annihilation of Armenian Deportees in 1915 within the Boundaries of Syria* (Aleppo: Violette Jebejian Library, 1994), 24–26. See also Watenpaugh, *Bread from Stones*, 125.

24. Leopold Gaszczyk, untitled circular, Aleppo, February 1, 1946, DDA, cited in Jeppe, *Misak*, xl.

25. Jeppe, "Account of the Situation of the Armenians in Syria," 14.

26. Jeppe, "Account of the Situation of the Armenians in Syria," 14.

27. League of Nations, "Protection of Women and Children in the Near East," September 1, 1924, A.46.1924. IV. League of Nations Documents, 1919–1946, UNA.

28. Shemmassian, "The League of Nations and the Reclamation of Armenian Genocide Survivors," 101.

29. Jenny Jensen, "Fra Landsbyen'" *Armeniervennen* 6, no. 7–8 (July–August 1926): 24.

30. Cholakian, *Karen Eppe*, 72.

31. An example is a woman whose brother had sent her a letter and photo via muleteers who failed to deliver it. See "Registers," inmate 673, March 20, 1925, UNA. Others rescued by muleteers and brought to Jeppe's home include inmates 673, 788, 789, 794, 1051.

32. I was unable to determine what became of the thirty-seven rescued children or the circumstances surrounding the rescue. The story of Sabagh's murder is told in L. F. Gaszczyk, "Aleppo-Deir-ez-Zor und zurück," Aleppo, April 1946, DDA, 10158, DNA,

Notes to Chapter 4

5; letter from League of Nations Secretary General Eric Drummond to Rachel Chowdy, April 9, 1925, UNA 12/42731/4631; and Jeppe, *Misak*, xliii–xliv.

33. Dikranouhi, "Registers," inmate 1364, June 23, 1927, UNA.

34. Benjamin Sahagian, "Registers," inmate 1114, September 4, 1926, 2, UNA.

35. Karen Jeppe, "Fra Marken," *Armeniervennen* 4, no. 3–4 (March–April 1924): 11.

36. Jeppe, "Fra Marken," 11.

37. Karen Jeppe, *Report for the Commission for the Protection of Women and Children in the Near East*, Aleppo, July 1, 1926, to June 30, 1927, Publications of the League of Nations, Social IV.6, 1927, A27.1927.IV, 1, UNA.

38. Jeppe, *Misak*, xxxvi.

39. Jeppe, *Misak*, xxxiv.

40. Jeppe, *Misak*, xxxix, xlii.

41. Jeppe, *Report for the Commission for the Protection of Women and Children*, 1. On the numbers of women and children rescued, see Edita Gzoyan, "Rescued and Saved: Armenian Genocide Survivors at Aleppo Reception Home," *Armenian Weekly*, June 10, 2020.

42. Gzoyan, "Rescued and Saved."

43. Bjørnlund, "Karen Jeppe, Aage Meyer Benedictsen, and the Ottoman Armenians," 15–16

44. Jeppe, "Account of the Situation of the Armenians in Syria," 10.

45. Jeppe, "Account of the Situation of the Armenians in Syria," 10.

46. Karen Jeppe, "Karen Jeppes neuester Bericht," *Orient im Bild* 12 (1927): 64.

47. Watenpaugh, *Bread from Stones*, 139.

48. See the baptisms of Yeghsabeth, who is included on her mother Khatoon's intake record, "Registers," inmate 691, April 29, 1925; and also a baby with the Muslim name Zakia and the Armenian name Asaduhi, inmate 694, May 5, 1925, UNA.

49. Jeppe, "Account of the Situation of the Armenians in Syria," 14.

50. Aslı Iğsiz argues that historicist humanism, the approach through which human categories are understood in historical terms and peoples connected with their ancient histories, produced a racialized, segregated biopolitics in the postwar Ottoman Empire. See Iğsiz, *Humanism in Ruins*, 17–20.

51. Jensen, "Fra Landsbyen," 25–26

52. Bjørnlund, "Karen Jeppe, Aage Meyer Benedictson, and the Ottoman Armenians," 21.

53. Bjørnlund, "Karen Jeppe, Aage Meyer Benedictson, and the Ottoman Armenians," 9.

54. Karen Jeppe, "Das Gelübte," *Orient im Bild*, 5, 1929, 38; and Jensen, "Fra Landsbyen," 26.

55. Jeppe notes that Armenian folk songs in particular had a strong effect on Armenians during the process of rehabilitation. See Karen Jeppe, "Karen Jeppes Neuester Bericht," *Orient im Bild* 9 (1927): 64.

56. Jenny Jensen, "Brev fra Aleppo," *Armeniervennen* 5, no. 5–6 (May-June 1925): 17.

57. Der Matossian, *Shattered Dreams of Revolution*, 177.

58. Murat Cankara, "Armeno-Turkish Writing and the Question of Hybridity," in *An Armenian Mediterranean: Words and Worlds in Motion*, ed. Kathryn Babayan and Michael Pifer (New York: Palgrave, 2018), 175.

59. Jeppe, *Misak*, xxx; and Jeppe, "Account of the Situation of the Armenians in Syria," 13. Keith Watenpaugh used the expression "bread from stones," extracted from Jeppe's report, as the title of his book; see Watenpaugh, *Bread from Stones*.

60. Jeppe, "Account of the Situation of the Armenians in Syria," 6.

61. Although Armenians were present in several industries, Armenian production and trade in cotton and silk textiles throughout Eurasia had a long history. For example, Harput, a predominately Armenian city decimated during the genocide, had hosted Shaghalian, Hambartzoumian, Tevrizian, Enovchian, Tufenkdjian, Hindlian, Darakjian, and Demirdjian production facilities on the eve of war. See chapter 8 of Mesrob K. Krikorian, *Armenians in the Service of the Ottoman Empire, 1860–1908* (London: Routledge, 1977).

62. Sick, "Karen Jeppe of Denmark," 20–21.

63. Jeppe, "Account of the Situation of the Armenians in Syria," 6.

64. Jeppe, "Account of the Situation of the Armenians in Syria," 7–8.

65. Jeppe, Account of the Situation of the Armenians in Syria," 10; also cited in Watenpaugh, *Bread from Stones*, 136.

66. The albums are numbered 56–61 though the labels fell off two of them. Album 61 is an identical copy of album 56. I refer to Jeppe's photograph numbers in the following notes. See archive box Karen Jeppe Թպ-1, AGMI.

67. Karen Jeppe Թպ-1, photograph 69.

68. Karen Jeppe Թպ-1, photograph 295; and Dominika Maria Macios, "Leopold Gaszczyk—Unknown Photographer of Armenian Diaspora in Syria (1923–1947)," in *Art of the Armenia Diaspora*, ed. Waldemar Deluga, World Art Studies 20 (Warsaw: Polish Institute of World Art Studies, 2020), 99–101.

69. Karen Jeppe Թպ-1, photographs 497–498.

70. Karen Jeppe Թպ-1, photographs 1338, 1711.

71. I have adopted Jeppe's spelling for consistency. See intake records for Satenig Loosbaronian and Achken, "Registers," inmates 1337 and 1338, May 31, 1927, UNA.

72. Jeppe's personal albums are very different than the more Orientalist images taken by local Armenian photographer Vartan Derounian, which were compiled and published; they featured camels, barren countrysides, Armenian handiwork, ruins, mosques, suqs, and very little of Jeppe's humanitarian work in Aleppo. See *Karen Jeppes Arbajdsmark 44 Reproductioner Af Fotografier Fra Syrien Optaget af Den Armeniske*, Fotograf V. Derounian (København: Aleppo Udgivet af de Danske Armeniervenner, 1931), archived at AGMI.

73. Karen Jeppe, "Fra Optagelseshjemmet i Aleppo," *Armeniervennen* 6, no. 5–6 (May–June 1926): 21. Elias's intake record number is 887, dated December 6, 1925, in "Registers," UNA. The two renderings of this story by Jeppe and her staff frame the failed healing in civilizational terms implying inept care, lack of parenting, and inferior medical knowledge.

74. Elias, "Registers," inmate 887.

75. Karen Jeppe, *Annual Report of the League of Nations Commission for the Protection of Women and Children*, 1927, 12.63896.4631, 8, UNA.

76. Matthias Bjørnlund argues that Jeppe's approach to colonization was not imperial in nature. See Bjørnlund, "Karen Jeppe, Aage Meyer Bendictsen, and the Ottoman Armenians," 33.

77. This is the subject of Peter Balakian's *The Burning Tigris: The Armenian Genocide and America's Response* (New York: Harper Perennial, 2003).

78. She notes this in her September 5, 1925, report to the League of Nations titled *Report for the Commission for the Protection of Women and Children in the Near East*, lv.

79. Jeppe, "Account of the Situation of the Armenians in Syria," 17.

80. Shemmassian, "The League of Nations and the Reclamation of Armenian Genocide Survivors," 102.

81. Jeppe, *Misak*, lviii–lix; and Samuel Dolbee, "The Desert at the End of Empire: An Environmental History of the Armenian Genocide" *Past and Present* 247 (May 2020): 231.

82. Karen Jeppe, "Vore Aktiviteter i Syrien," *Armeniervennen* 6, no. 3–4 (March–April, 1926): 13–14.

83. Shemmassian, "The League of Nations," 101.

84. Jeppe, "Vore Aktiviteter i Syrien," 13–14. Italics in original.

85. Jeppe, *Report for the Commission for the Protection of Women and Children*, 3.

86. Bedoukian, *The Urchin*, 157.

87. Intermarriage among orphans can be found in sample records in "Registers," inmates 1164 and 1210, 1165 and 1405, 1179 and 1803, and 692 and 693, UNA.

88. Jeppe, "Karen Jeppes Neuester Bericht," 64.

89. Jeppe, "Karen Jeppes Neuester Bericht," 64.

90. Jenny Jensen, "Bryllup i Kolonierne," *Armeniervennen* 9, no. 1–2 (January-February 1929): 7.

91. Jensen, ""Bryllup i Kolonierne," 7.

92. Aintab Armenian Krikor Bogharian noted that Ottoman Turkish was taught as the mother tongue in primary school. See Vahé Tachjian, *Daily Life in the Abyss: Genocide Diaries, 1915–1918* (New York: Berghahn Books, 2017), 18.

93. Bedross Der Matossian has outlined the linguistic diversity of Armenians, including regional dialects, and the pervasive use of Armeno-Turkish even after the eighteenth-century Armenian Renaissance and standardization of Western Armenian in the nineteenth century. Importantly, Der Matossian concludes his article with a portrait of his Armeno-Turkish-speaking grandfather from Marash. See Der Matossian, "The Development of Armeno-Turkish (*Hayatar T'rk'erēn*) in the Nineteenth Century Ottoman Empire," *Intellectual History of the Islamicate World* 8, no. 10 (2019): 67–100.

94. Sick, "Karen Jeppe of Denmark," 25.

95. Garebedian, "Miss Koren Yeppe: Mother," 2.

96. Shemmassian, "The League of Nations and the Reclamation of Armenian Genocide Survivors," 95.

97. Jeppe, *Report for the Commission for the Protection of Women and Children*, 4.

Remnant 4

1. Azkayin khnamadarutiun (Armenian National Relief Organization of Constantinople), *Azkayin khnamadarutiun: enthanur deghegakir arachin vetsamsyah* volume 1, 1 May 1919–31 October 1919 (Constantinople: M. Hovagimian Publisher, 1920) 83–84.

Chapter 5

1. Arakel Tchakarian, "To the Rescue of Armenian Orphans," *Orient News*, part 1, 25, no. 2 (July 16, 1920): 4, editorial translated and archived at R638-12-4631-15100, UNA.

2. Yotnakhparian notes a case of this, which is discussed later in the chapter in the section "Recovering Islamized Armenians from Aleppo to Baghdad."

3. League of Nations, Fifth Committee, "Deportation of Women and Children in Turkey, Asia Minor, and the Neighboring Territories," Geneva, Switzerland, 1921–1922, 1 A.113.1921, UNA; and Karen Jeppe, "Interim Report from the Aleppo Section of the Commission of Inquiry," January 26, 1922, 2–3, 12.19111.1461, UNA.

4. League of Nations, Fifth Committee, "Deportation of Women and Children."

5. Emma Cushman shared these remarks in "Current Notes," *New Armenia* 13, no. 5

(September–October 1921): 77. Cushman's remarks are confirmed by Nazan Maksudyan's broader investigation of orphanages as a state tool for national indoctrination. See Maksudyan, "Agents or Pawns? Nationalism and Ottoman Children during the Great War."

6. I would like to thank Armenian Genocide scholar Matthias Bjørnlund for offering his translations and for his interpretation of the term *forvildede,* which could also mean "bewildered" or "confused." Jensen, "Fra Landsbyen," 24.

7. These details are mentioned in two interviews with Almas Boghosian: one from March 12, 2011, archived at Shoah Foundation Visual History Archive, and the other conducted with documentary filmmaker Bared Maronian on February 11, 2011.

8. False birth certificates in Turkish orphanages are documented by the deputy to the Armenian patriarch in Constantinople Arakel Tchakarian, "To the Rescue of Armenian Orphans," part 4, *Orient News,* August 8, 1920, 11, archived article, R638-12-4631-15100, UNA.

9. Melehat's parents were listed in her official papers as being named Fatima and Mehmet, yet her memory informed otherwise. See Emma Cushman, Index of Children Brought to the Neutral House, July 1920, 4, 12/15100/4631, UNA.

10. This campaign is the focus of Uğur Ümit Üngör's research that compellingly ties the Armenian Genocide to larger practices of ethnic homogenization of modern Turkey. See Üngör, *The Making of Modern Turkey,* especially chapter 3.

11. In this context, what was desired were citizens of a solely ethnic Turkish Muslim state since the empire had yet to collapse. See Watenpaugh, *Bread from Stones,* 144.

12. Little studied are the Kurdish children who were sent to Turkish orphanages during the war. Jeppe, "Account of the Situation of the Armenians in Syria," 9; and "Deportation des femmes et des enfants en Turquie, en Asie Mineure et dans les territoires avoisinants," Fifth Committee, Geneva, September 22, 1921, 1, 12/15/998/4631, UNA.

13. Shemmassian, "The League of Nations and the Reclamation of Armenian Genocide Survivors," 86; and Watenpaugh, *Bread from Stones,* 144.

14. Emma Cushman's report titled *Index of Children* offers evidence that many children rescued in Constantinople were rescued from the homes of Turkish elites.

15. Sarkis (Rafet), in Index of Children, 7.

16. DH. ŞFR 54/150, 13 Haziran 1331/ June 26, 1915, BOA.

17. Cemal Pasha, *Hatıralar* (Istanbul: İş Bankası, 2016), 340–41 The Ottoman Fourth Army was Cemal Pasha's division of the military stationed in both Lebanon and Syria. Historian Hilmar Kaiser has shown that it carried out the policy of forcible conversion rather than outright extermination policies of the central authorities in Constantinople. Khatchig Mouradian's reading of Armenian sources confirms that Cemal Pasha was assisting relief efforts in Aleppo, diverting grain to feed orphans, to balance his personal political interests in the region under his supervision. Mouradian concludes that is it possible to see Cemal Pasha as both a humanitarian and a perpetrator. See "The Ottoman Fourth Army's Orphanage Policy," in *Not All Quiet on the Ottoman Fronts: Neglected Perspectives on a Global War, 1914–1918,* ed. Mehmet Beşikçi, Selçuk Akşin Somel, and Alexandre Toumarkine, 79-80 (Istanbul: Oriental-Institut, 2020); and Mouradian, *The Resistance Network,* 49–51.

18. Keith Watenpaugh recently published a comparative study of the Pipestone Indian Training School in Minnesota and the 'Aintoura Orphanage; both are examples of "carceral humanitarianism," a lethal alternative for genocide against targeted indigenous groups. Watenpaugh is the first to suggest that the Indian boarding school model of

North America was directly absorbed by the Ottoman authorities through contact with American figures and institutions involved in Indian boarding schools. See Watenpaugh, "Kill the Armenian/Indian; Save the Man: Carceral Humanitarianism, the Transfer for Children and a Comparative History of Indigenous Genocide," *Journal for the Society of Armenian Studies* 29 (2022): 1–33.

19. Steven Trowbridge of the American Red Cross offered a report published as "How Turks Conduct an Orphanage: 'Aintoura: The Shelter of a Thousand Tragedies," *Missionary Review of the World* 42, no. 4 (April 1919): 287–88. In this report, he notes that less than half of the two thousand children brought to 'Aintoura survived the experience. Halide Edib has very different memories of 'Aintoura than the Armenian children who wrote about their experiences. Edib, *Memoirs of Halidé Edib* (London: John Murray, 1926), 417, 429.

20. Trowbridge, "How Turks Conduct an Orphanage," 287–88. In his memoirs, Cemal frames his work with Armenian widows and orphans as humanitarian assistance. See Cemal Pasha, *Hatıralar*, 340–41.

21. Panian, *Goodbye, Antoura*, 92–93.

22. Selim Deringil, "'Your Religion Is Worn and Outdated': Orphans, Orphanages and Halide Edib during the Armenian Genocide: The Case of Antoura," *Études arméniennes contemporaines* 12 (2019), 38.

23. Edib, *Memoirs*, 453.

24. Edib, *Memoirs*, 428–29.

25. Edib, *Memoirs*, 429. Hilmar Kaiser has recently written about how Cemal Pasha's policies toward Armenians defied CUP demands by permitting Armenians to continue to live in Syria and Lebanon, where central leadership sought to reduce the population through direct and indirect killing. He allowed Armenian children to live in orphanages established by his Fourth Army in defiance of orders, viewed by some scholars as a softer view than that of other contemporaries. See Hilmar Kaiser, "The Ottoman Fourth Army's Orphanage Policy, 1915–1918," *Not All Quiet on the Ottoman Fronts: Neglected Perspectives on a Global War, 1914–1918*, 73–101. Ümit Kurt challenges the view of Kaiser and others, showing that though Cemal Pasha's methods were different, his aim was consistent with CUP policy. See "A Rescuer, an Enigma and a Génocidaire: Cemal Pasha," *The End of the Ottomans: The Genocide of 1915 and the Politics of Turkish Nationalism*, ed. Hans-Lukas Kieser, Margaret Lavinia Anderson, Seyhan Bayraktar, and Thomas Schmutz (New York: I. B. Tauris, 2019), 221–45.

26. Elizabeth F. Thompson, *Justice Interrupted. The Struggle for Constitutional Government in the Middle East* (Cambridge, MA: Harvard University Press, 2013), 104; and Keith Watenpaugh, "Introduction," in Panian, *Goodbye, Antoura*, xiii; and Watenpaugh, "Kill the Armenian/Indian," 28–29. After leaving her position at the orphanage, Edib presented American University of Beirut president Howard Bliss with the 'Aintoura albums that included a series of photographs of cheerful, well-cared-for orphans. Antoura Orphanage Photograph Albums, 1915–1918, Ph:AO:1915–191, American University of Beirut Archives, Beirut, Lebanon.

27. Report from Armenian Patriarch Zaven of Constantinople, *La traité de blanche en Turquie*, November 1, 1920, 10 R638 12/9640/4631, UNA.

28. Hilmar Kaiser speaks directly about Edib's role as a "spin doctor" who explained Turkey to Europeans and Americans, some of whom defended her against the charge of forcible conversion practices under her watch. Kaiser, "The Ottoman Fourth Army's Orphanage Policy," 90.

29. Edib, *Memoirs*, 466–67.

30. Two memoirs offer detailed descriptions of children's experiences: Melkon Bedrossian's unpublished memoir examined by historian Selim Deringil is titled "Les mémoires de Melkon Bedrossian: Le récit mouvementé de notre déportation de notre village en Turquie 1905–1918," family archive of Jacques Bedrossian. The more accessible Karnig Panian memoir was recently translated into English and is titled *Goodbye, Antoura*.

31. Salwa Ismail, *The Rule of Violence*, 11.

32. Panian, *Goodbye, Antoura*, 93–94.

33. *Bastinado* is the Latin-derived term for the Ottoman punishment *falaka*. Because the hands and feet are sensitive areas of the body with more nerve endings, applying torture and beatings to those parts of the body is deemed most effective. At Aintoura, the children received fifty strokes for speaking Armenian. Panian, *Goodbye, Aintoura*, 92–93.

34. Vartan, "Registers," inmate 915, December 31, 1925, UNA.

35. Armen Kassabian, "Registers," inmate 1332, May 27, 1927, UNA.

36. *Hai (hay)* means "Armenian" in the Armenian language. Puzant Nizarian, "Registers," inmate 1270, March 19, 1927, DNA. I have included quotation marks around Puzant's words in order to delineate his direct speech. The original does not include those quotation marks.

37. Sahag Mesrob, "Yegherni hushartsan, anonts anune," *Aravodin darekirke* (Constantinople: Artsakank, 1921), 84. Sahag Mesrob's memoir, *Yegherni hushartsan* (Constantinople: Tpagr. M. Hovakimean, 1919), tells the story of his ordeal.

38. Mesrob, "Yegherni hushartsan, anonts anone," 84. Two places mentioned by the author—Zeitun and Shabin Karahisar—are known for the local resistance they organized during the initial phase of genocide in 1915. The Armenian national hero General Antranig was from Shabin Karahisar, making the place-names resonate with the notion of resistance within the Armenian psyche.

39. League of Nations, Fifth Committee, "Deportation of Women and Children in Turkey, Asia Minor, and the Neighboring Territories." UNA.

40. Sarkis, "Registers," inmate 47, no date, 2; and Vahan Avedissian, "Registers," inmate 159, November 28, 1922, 2, UNA.

41. Emma Cushman, Index of Children Brought to the Neutral House, July 1920, 12/15100/4631, 2, UNA.

42. The three Armenian agents were Yesayi Kereshekian [Krshkian], Garabed Kavafian, and Hovhannes Kavafian. Yotnakhparian, *Crows of the Desert*, 97.

43. Yotnakhparian, *Crows of the Desert*, 109–110.

44. Yotnakhparian, *Crows of the Desert*, 110.

45. Yotnakhparian, *Crows of the Desert*, 112.

46. Yotnakhparian, *Crows of the Desert*, 112.

47. Yotnakhparian, *Crows of the Desert*, 113.

48. Kumkapı is the location of the Armenian Patriarchate in Istanbul. Halidé Edib Adıvar, *The Turkish Ordeal: Being the Further Memoirs of Halidé Edib* (London: 1928), 17. This powerful passage from Edib's memoir was first analyzed in Keith Watenpaugh, "The League of Nations' Rescue of Armenian Genocide Survivors and the Making of Modern Humanitarianism, 1920–1927," *American Historical Review* 115, no. 5 (December 2010): 1332.

49. Tchakarian, "To the Rescue of Armenian Orphans," *Orient News*, part 1, 25, no. 2 (July 16, 1920): 3.

50. Tchakarian, "To the Rescue of Armenian Orphans," *Orient News*, part 7, 25, no. 5 (August 20, 1920):13–14.
51. Tchakarian, "To the Rescue of Armenian Orphans," part 7, 25, no. 5 (August 20, 1920): 13–14.
52. Emma Cushman, Index of Children, 10.
53. Emma Cushman, Index of Children, 16.
54. Jensen, "Fra Landsbyen," 24.
55. Jeppe is quoted in a letter to the editor by Laura Helen Sawbridge in *The Slave Market News*, July 1930, 2.
56. Cholakian, *Karen Eppe*, 80.
57. Tachjian, "Gender, Nationalism, Exclusion," 75.
58. Cases of miscarriages and stillbirths are mentioned in Feride, "Registers," inmate 1316, May 13, 1927, 2; Derouhi, inmate 1406, August 29, 1927, 2; and Vartanoush Der Avedissian, inmate 1792, November 14, 1928, 1, UNA.
59. Derorti, "Or Gertas Hay Gin," *Hay pujak* 3, no. 9 (July 1922): 150; and Dr. Yaghoubyan, "Hay Gnoch Aroghchabahagan Tere Hayasdani Mech III," *Hay Gin* 1, no. 19 (August 1, 1920). Both of these articles were originally quoted and analyzed in Ekmekçioğlu, *Recovering Armenia*, 545.
60. Donald E. Miller and Lorna Touryan Miller, *Survivors: An Oral History of the Armenian Genocide* (Berkeley: University of California Press, 1993), 101–2.
61. Beyzade, "Registers," inmate 920, January 12, 1926, UNA.
62. Adivar, *The Turkish Ordeal*, 18.
63. Al-Ghazzi, *Nahr al-Dhahab*, 3:556.
64. Al-Ghazzi, *Nahr al-Dhahab*, 3:556–57.
65. In the context of what was likely a forced marriage with a foreign Muslim, the text suggests that those interviewing the woman tried to induce her to feel "disgust" or "revulsion" or "antipathy" against her husband. Al-Ghazzi, *Nahr al-Dhahab*, 3:558. Neither the church nor the Christian district are named by al-Ghazzi.
66. Al-Ghazzi, *Nahr al-Dhahab*, 3:557. This story is also told in Keith Watenpaugh, *Being Modern in the Middle East: Revolution, Nationalism, Colonialism, and the Arab Middle Class* (Princeton, NJ: Princeton University Press, 2006), 205. Muslim backlash against the reclamation of children also took place in Istanbul. See Ekmekçioğlu, *Recovering Armenia*, 86.
67. Yotnakhparian, *Crows of the Desert*, 113.
68. Watenpaugh, *Being Modern in the Middle East*, 142n18.
69. Keith Watenpaugh situates this moment within the emerging Syrian nationalism of the period. He argues that Aleppo in particular had a mix of sentiments, including some who sought a position within the emerging Turkish state. Watenpaugh, *Being Modern in the Middle East*, 125, 153.
70. Kerop Bedoukian's eyewitness account is in *The Urchin*, 121, 140–46. One of the stories he shares is that of two boys who were lynched by the mob—ropes were tied around their necks and they were thrown in a well, but miraculously the boys regained consciousness and returned to the orphanage.
71. An example of a "seditious pamphlet" is one titled "To the People of Islam," which was sent by American consul Jackson to the US with a letter dated April 8, 1915, explaining that it had been circulated by Germans in Aleppo. See "Li jami'a ahl al-Islam," dated 1333 A.H./1915, 867.00/762, 353/Reel 6/ NARA.

72. Grigoris Balakian documented an interview with an Ottoman military captain named Shukri who said that the chief jurist of the Ottoman Empire had issued such a *fetva* calling for the annihilation of Armenians. See Balakian, *Armenian Golgotha*, 146.

73. Such visual rhetorical devices would also be used by other humanitarians to convey effectiveness, such as a publication by Armenian Relief Committee of Mesopotamia in Baghdad, which featured a before-and-after photograph of rescued Armenians. Speech Delivered by Mr. M. H. Kouyoumdjian at Galustan Park, Calcutta, Friday 13, 1920, 5, 2–6.

74. Ann McClintock has noted that white was a color frequently worn by women in Victorian Europe to invoke the "cult of domesticity"—that is, the properly defined woman's domestic sphere as "angel of the house." Ann McClintock, *Imperial Leather: Race, Gender, and Sexuality in the Colonial Contest* (London: Routledge, 1995), 160–62.

75. This description is derived from a 1926 dramatized 35-mm silent documentary with Danish intertitles detailing the rescue missions and work at the Rescue Home in Aleppo. The movie was commissioned by the League of Nations and filmed by an unknown director. Archived at the Danish Film Institute, the silent film represents a composite of rescue scenarios carried out by Jeppe's agents in her Ford automobile, and the Armenian escapees Asdghig and Lucia depicted in the movie are played by actual rescued Armenians. Several of Jeppe's employees are featured in the documentary, including Jenny Jensen and Leopold Gaszczyk, who sits at a desk and reenacts writing Lucia and Asdghig's intake records. Gasczyk's sister Johanna Paritzi and Jeppe's adopted son Misak Melkonian also appear in the film. Dir. unknown, *Karen Jeppe* (France: Pathé, 1926), Danish Film Institute.

76. Asdghig's intake record contains very little information because she remembered nothing about her past except her name and her birth place of Urfa. The intake record informs that she was rescued along with Lucia near Dayr al-Zur, where they lived in neighboring tents. Asdghig, "Registers," inmate 1046, July 7, 1926, UNA.

Remnant 5

1. This vignette assumes the voice of a woman spectator and is based on a number of reports woven together to give an impression of how *Auction of Souls* was staged and received throughout the country. Advertisements promised the film "will make every woman's blood boil," indicating that it was meant to produce a blend of morbid fascination and outrage through its pornography of suffering. See advertisement for Lyric Theater in Minneapolis, Minnesota, *Motion Picture News*, July 5, 1919, 318. A *New York Times* article lists the first New York showing as February 17, 1919. See "Show 'Ravished Armenia,'" *New York Times*, February 17, 1919, 11. The quotation from Aurora in the vignette describing the fear she lived with while filming and promoting the film is from her oral testimony archived at the Shoah Foundation Visual History Archive. The promotion of the film in Minneapolis was described as "striking advance advertising" in "Auction of Souls in Minneapolis, MN," *Motion Picture News*, July 5, 1919, 318.

2. "Thrilled Audience Cheers Aurora Mardiganian at First Showing of 'The Auction of Souls,'" *New York American*, May 11, 1919, L19.

Chapter 6

1. The advertisement in figure 14 lists the film as being seven reels. Film historian and Aurora biographer Anthony Slide has observed that the film was eight reels long, with each reel holding 10 minutes of film. See Anthony Slide, *Ravished Armenia: The Story of Aurora Mardiganian* (Jackson: University Press of Mississippi, 2014), 28, 259.

2. "Ravished Armenia in Film," *New York Times*, February 15, 1919,

3. Sévane Garibian, "Ravished Armenia (1919): Bearing Witness in the Age of Mechanical Reproduction: Some Thoughts on a Film-Ordeal," in *Mass Media and the Genocide of the Armenians: One Hundred Years of Uncertain Representation*, ed. Joceline Chebot, Richard Godin, Stefanie Kappler, and Sylvia Kasparian (New York: Palgrave McMillan, 2016), 37.

4. "What the Picture Is," advertisement by American Committee for Armenian and Syrian Relief (renamed American Near East Relief), reprinted in Anthony Slide, *Ravished Armenia*, 3.

5. References are taken from Slide, *Ravished Armenia*, 15, 25.

6. Slide, *Ravished Armenia*, 28.

7. Gayatri Spivak's pivotal essay concludes that the subaltern, in this case women, cannot speak nor represent themselves. Instead they are spoken for and represented by intellectual elites. See Spivak, "Can the Subaltern Speak?," in *Colonial Discourse and Post-Colonial Theory: A Reader*, ed. Patrick Williams and Laura Chrisman (New York: Columbia University Press, 1994), 66–111.

8. Haik Demoyan and Lousine Abrahamyan, *Aurora's Road: Odyssey of an Armenian Genocide Survivor* (Yerevan: AGMI, 2015), 9. Aurora's name was changed by her handlers.

9. The reference to Aurora coming from a "modest household" can be found in "Armenian Girl, 17, Tells of Massacres," *Sun*, June 25, 1918, 6. An account that gives her a more identifiably upper-class background as the daughter of a "prosperous merchant" is "The Most Pathetic Ambassadress in History," *News and Herald*, January 10, 1919. The latter version is confirmed in her biography by Demoyan and Abrahamyan, *Aurora's Road*, 12.

10. Archived interview, Aurora Mardiganian, AFF 137, Shoah Foundation Visual History Archive.

11. "Arrival of Armenian Girl Is Celebrated," *New York Tribune*, June 25, 1918; "Armenian Girl, 17, Tells of Massacre," *Sun*, June 25, 1918; Demoyan and Abrahamyan, *Aurora's Road*, 11. In a video interview, Aurora said she suspected that her brother might have moved to Canada in order to evade the draft during World War I. She noted that while touring with the film, she met a man who had met her brother with his wife and child in New York City. Despite her efforts to locate Vahan, the two were never reunited. Aurora Mardiganian, interview, AFF 53418, Shoah Foundation Visual History Archive, March 3, 1975.

12. "Arrival of Armenian Girl Is Celebrated."

13. "Armenian Girl, 17, Tells of Massacre," 6.

14. "Armenian Girl, 17, Tells of Massacre."

15. Slide, *Ravished Armenia*, 12.

16. Keith Watenpaugh argues that NER stood at the center of an emerging secular humanitarianism. Watenpaugh, *Bread from Stones*, 18.

17. Aurora Mardiganian, interview, March 29, 1984, AFF 53418, Shoah Foundation Visual History Archive.

18. Advertisement for an Aurora appearance at the Orpheus Theater in Duluth, *Duluth Herald*, October 22, 1919, 12. Aurora noted that the slave market was in Moush. Oral interview with Aurora Mardiganian, Shoah Foundation.

19. Slide, *Ravished Armenia*, 11.

20. Rana Kabbani has offered an extensive overview of misogynistic views towards women, including Christian women, from antiquity through the Ottoman period in *Eu-*

rope's *Myths of the Orient: Devise and Rule* (London: Macmillian, 1986); and Irvin Cemil Schick has examined gendered representations of war and atrocity from the nineteenth and early twentieth centuries in "Christian Maidens, Turkish Ravishers: The Sexualization of National Conflict in the Late Ottoman Period," in *Women in the Ottoman Balkans: Gender, Culture, and History*, ed. Amilia Buturović (London: I. B. Tauris, 2007), 273–305.

21. The graphic can be found in a serialized version of Aurora's memoir published as "My Two Years of Torture in Ravished, Martyred Armenia," *Washington Times*, October 6, 1918, 24–25.

22. Nicoletta F. Gullace, "Sexual Violence and Family Honor: British Propaganda and International Law during the First World War," *American Historical Review* 102, no. 3 (June 1997): 714–47.

23. Leshu Torchin, "*Ravished Armenia*: Visual Media, Humanitarian Advocacy, and the Formation of Witnessing Publics," *American Anthropologist* 108, no. 1 (March 2006): 215. Michelle Tusan argues that British humanitarian thinking was always rooted in Christian Protestantism rather than secularism. See Tusan, "'Crime against Humanity': Human Rights, the British Empire, and the Origins of the Response to the Armenian Genocide," *American Historical Review* 119, no. 1 (February, 2014): 50.

24. Aurora Mardiganian, interview, March 3, 1975, AFF 53418, Shoah Foundation Visual History Archive.

25. See Aurora's memoir in serial form as "My Two Years of Torture in Ravished, Martyred Armenia," *Washington Times*, October 6, 1918.

26. Slide, *Ravished Armenia,* 15. The photographs of Aurora's bandaged ankle are shown in the last moments of her videotaped interview, March 3, 1975 AFF 53418, Shoah Foundation Visual History Archive.

27. "Ravished Armenia in Film," *New York Times*, February 15, 1919

28. This version of events appears in Demoyan and Abrahamyan, *Aurora's Road*, 135–36.

29. Slide, *Ravished Armenia,*19, 25.

30. Slide, *Ravished Armenia,*12.

31. Slide, *Ravished Armenia,*13.

32. "Girl Ungrateful Says Former Ogden Woman," *Ogden Standard Examiner*, October 3, 1920, n.p.

33. Aurora mentions this troubling detail in her March 29, 1984, interview, AFF 53418, Shoah Foundation Visual Archive.

34. Anthony Slide has preserved Aurora's dialect in his transcriptions of interviews with her. I have chosen not to interrupt her natural speech. See Slide, *Ravished Armenia*, 15. Aurora frequently uses the term *barbarics* in her interviews to describe Muslim peoples.

35. Demoyan and Abrahamyan, *Aurora's Road*, 47.

36. The first silent film was *The Great Train Robbery*, dir. Edwin S. Porter (1903).

37. Balakian, "Photography, Visual Culture, and the Armenian Genocide," for the Armenian Genocide and Hamidiye Massacres in the larger context of atrocity photography that had emerged during the Crimean War in 1852.

38. "'Ravished Armenia' on the Films: 'Auction of Souls' an Indictment of Turkish Cruelty,'" *Illustrated London News*, November 8, 1919, 713.

39. This dialogue between Morgenthau and Talaat is reported in Morgenthau, *Ambassador Morgenthau's Story*, 335–39.

40. Tusan, "Crimes against Humanity," 69.

41. "Against 'Auction of Souls,'" *Variety*, January 20, 1920; Tusan, "Crimes against Humanity," 71–73.

42. Secretary of State's Inquiry regarding Mr. Amir Ali's Objections to Auction of Souls, January 24, 1920, HO 45/10955/312971/98.

43. Slide asserts that anti-Turkish references were of concern, but correspondence reveals many of the complaints were primarily from Indian Muslims. Slide, *Ravished Armenia*, 19.

44. The *Oxford English Dictionary* acknowledges that the term no longer has the resonance it once had; however, the "archaic" definition of *ravished* is "carried or dragged away by force; raped, violated; ravaged; (in early use) stolen, plundered." OED Online database.

45. "Traffic in Souls" is available in full on YouTube at https://www.youtube.com/watch?v=DDejjaFjhsg. See Bernard F. Dick, *City of Dreams: The Making and Remaking of Universal Studios* (Lexington: The University Press of Kentucky, 1997), 61.

46. Jeanne Morefield, "'Families of Mankind': British Liberty, League Internationalism, and the Traffic in Women and Children," *History of European Ideas*, 46 (2020): 6–7

47. "Milwaukee Manager Proves Hot Weather No Bar to Enterprise," *Motion Picture News*, July 19, 1919, 704.

48. Aurora Mardiganian, interview, March 3, 1975 AFF 53418, Shoah Foundation Visual Archive.

49. Advertisement for "Auction of Souls" in *The Daily Colonist*, January 20, 1920, 20.

50. These quotations are from Aurora's oral testimony where remaining fragments of her own narration are available. Aurora Mardiganian, interview, March, 3, 1975, AFF 53418, Shoah Foundation Visual Archive.

51. Advertisement, "This is Aurora Mardiganian," quoting Mrs. Oliver Harriman from an interview in *Harper's Bazaar*, in *Exhibitors Trade Review* 5, no. 23 (May 10, 1919): 1706.

52. "The Movies," *English Review*, May, 1920, 473.

53. Karen Halttunen, "Humanitarianism and the Pornography of Pain in Anglo-American Culture," *American Historical Review* 100, no. 2 (April 1995): 303–34.

54. "The pornography of sadism entered its heyday in the nineteenth century, when 'the English vice' became the central convention of English pornography." Halttunen, "Humanitarianism and the Pornography of Pain," 315.

55. Linda Nochlin, "The Imaginary Orient," in *The Politics of Vision: Essays on Nineteenth-Century Art and Society* (New York: Harper and Row, 1989), 33–59; Joan DelPlato, *Multiple Wives, Multiple Pleasures: Representing the Harem, 1800–1875* (Madison, NJ: Fairleigh Dickinson University Press, 2002); and Julia Kuehn, "Exotic Harem Paintings: Gender, Documentation, Imagination," *Frontiers* 32, no. 2 (2011): 31–63.

56. The slippage between sadomasochistic fantasy and Oriental sex prompted Annelies Moors to call it "hard-core Orientalism," in her review of Ayaan Hirsi Ali and Theo Van Gogh's film *Submission,* and Lila Abu-Lughod to call it "slave pornography." See Moors, "Submission," *ISIM Review* 15 (Spring 2005): 8–9; and Abu-Lughod, *Do Muslim Women Need Saving?* (Cambridge, MA: Harvard University Press, 2015), 96, 103.

57. Halttunen, "Humanitarianism and the Pornography of Pain," 318.

58. Emmanuel Fremiet's (1824–1910) sculpture *Gorilla Carrying Off a Stone Age Woman* (1887) features a nude white woman being carried off by a gorilla and followed on the heels of a less successful sculpture with a "negress" as subject in 1859. This connection between the marketing of *Ravished Armenia* book covers and this sculpture is docu-

mented in Demoyan and Abrahamyan, *Aurora's Road* and Eugene L. Taylor and Abraham D. Krikorian, "Notes and Queries Relevant to 'A Brief Assessment of the Ravished Armenia Marquee Poster' by Amber Karlins," *Journal of the Society for Armenian Studies*, 19(1) (2010) 137–145. For more on Fremiet see Marek Zgórniak, Marta Kapera and Mark Singer "Fremiet's Gorillas: Why Do They Carry off Women?" *Artibus et Historiae* 27: 54 (2006) 219–237.

59. The American version of the poster calling for enlistment in the US Army inscribed the land beneath the simian Hun's feet as America. Source: Hoover Institution Archives, Poster Collection, https://digitalcollections.hoover.org/objects/34265/destroy-this-mad-brute-enlist-us-army;jsessionid=E662C7348E134FB6B7B0DA27A29D416A.

60. Halttunen, "Humanitarianism and the Pornography of Pain," 318; and Carolyn J. Dean, "Empathy, Pornography, and Suffering," *Differences* 14, no. 1 (2003): 102.

61. Sir Sidney Low, "Propaganda Films and Mixed Morals on the Movies," *Fortnightly Review*, ed. W. L. Courtney, 107 (January 1920): 719.

62. These disturbing and insensitive interviewing techniques are captured in the oral interview archived at the Shoah Foundation, Visual History Archive.

63. Peter Balakian, "Raphael Lemkin, Cultural Destruction, and the Armenian Genocide," *Holocaust and Genocide Studies* 27, no. 1 (April 1, 2013): 70.

64. Scarry, *The Body in Pain*, 35–36.

65. While the cross was originally an instrument of death and torture for Christ, it later came to be a sacred object. Balakian, "Raphael Lemkin, Cultural Destruction, and the Armenian Genocide," 57–89.

66. *Auction of Souls* premiered at the Salle Gaveau Hall in Paris on December 11, 1919, almost a full year after the American premiere sponsored by the Ladies Armenian Society. Unlike its US and UK counterparts, the large Armenian diaspora in France played a role in its production, and the musical score was altered to include both European and Armenian works under the direction of Armenian composer Tigran Alexanyan and his orchestra at the hall. See Demoyan and Abrahamyan, *Aurora's Road*, 116.

67. Sévane Garibian has offered an extensive reconstruction of this chronology of events in "Ravished Armenia (1919)," 37.

68. Setian, like other Armenians in the diaspora, repatriated to the Soviet Republic of Armenia as part of a mass effort to urge Armenians to return to their historic homelands in the mid-1940s.

69. Slide, *Ravished Armenia*, 29. The fact that the remaining fifteen minutes of film contain this deleted scene seems to prove director Atom Egoyan's theory that the remaining footage is outtakes rather than the original reel shown in theaters, which means the contents of the final director's cut is even more unknowable.

70. Jean Baudrillard, *Simulations*, trans. Paul Foss, Paul Patton, and Philip Beitchman (Cambridge, MA: Semiotext(e), 1983), 11.

71. Shushan Avakyan, "Becoming Aurora: Translating the Story of Arshaluys Mardiganian," *Dissidences: Hispanic Journal of Theory and Criticism* 4, no. 8 (November 2012): n.p.

72. Slide, *Ravished Armenia*, 29.

73. What is unclear is when and how Aurora entered prosthetic memory inside Armenia. The newspapers collected by Aram Andonian in the Nubarian Library upon release of the film were almost exclusively from America.

74. Because the performance was unrecorded, I was dependent on interviews with Khanjian, including a video interview in which scenes of the performance were shared. See

Arsinée Khanjian, "Aurora: Performer of Memory," interview with Civiltas, October 12, 2016, https://youtu.be/FxRoiV763Hw.

75. In a recent interview, Khandjian observes how Aurora's testimony is "incredibly clear" in Armenian and disjointed in English. Also see Marie-Aude Baronian and Erica Biolchini, "Performance, Memory, and the Archive: A Conversation with Arsinée Khanjian," *Journal of the Society for Armenian Studies* 28 (2021): 183.

76. Baronian and Biolchini, "Performance, Memory, and the Archive," 183.

77. Hortense Spillers explores the ambiguity of touch in a brilliant lecture, "To the Bone: Some Speculations on the Problems of Touch," for the Gender and Sexuality Studies Program at Northwestern University, November 15, 2018, https://youtu.be/vM3EGoowAJk.

78. Essayan, "La Libération des femmes et des enfants non-musulmans en Turquie," 6.

79. Remarks by Atom Egoyan, "Ravished Armenia," St. Gregory the Illuminator Catholic Church in Toronto, Zoryan Institute, November 6, 2013.

80. Laura U. Marks, *The Skin of the Film: Intercultural Cinema, Embodiment, and the Senses* (Durham, NC: Duke University Press, 2000), 243.

81. Marks uses this example of disintegrated memories to understand the representation of memory in post-colonial and intercultural film. Some of these techniques include decontextualized images that fail to cohere around a single memory and the absence of sound or voice. See Marks, *The Skin of the Film*, 64.

82. Marks, *The Skin of the Film*, 51.

83. Aurora Mardiganian, interview, March, 3, 1975, AFF 53418, Shoah Foundation Visual Archive.

84. Nowhere in the description of the Aurora Humanitarian Initiative and the Aurora Prize is the namesake mentioned by name or described. See https://auroraprize.com/en/prize-about. Instead, one needs to click a link at the bottom of the page titled "Inspiration," https://auroraprize.com/en/prize-inspiration, and that page has a link ("Aurora Mardiganian") to a biography at https://auroraprize.com/en/aurora-mardiganian.

85. Baronian and Biolchini, "Performance, Memory, and the Archive," 16.

86. Nikki Marczak, "A Century Apart: The Genocidal Enslavement of Armenian and Yazidi Women," *A Gendered Lens for Genocide Prevention. Rethinking Political Violence*, ed. M. Connellan and C. Fröhlich (London: Palgrave Macmillan, 2018), 133–62.

Chapter 7

1. Suzanne Khardalian, dir., *Grandma's Tattoos* (Sweden: Deckert, 2011), https://deckert-distribution.com/film-catalogue/authors-documentaries/grandmas-tattoos/.

2. *Women of 1915*, dir., Bared Maronian, 2016, https://womenof1915.com/.

3. A very small portion of rescued Armenians actually bore tribal tattoos. During the course of her humanitarian work in Aleppo, Jeppe recorded every child and woman admitted in the Rescue Home, but only 1,664 entries survive. Although tattoos were a preoccupation of Western observers, they did not appear frequently in Jeppe's records. In the League of Nations Rescue Home Registers, some photographs clearly show women and girls with facial tattoos, while others are less visible. I was able to located twenty-two photographs of tattooed women and girls in the registers. Because these records have been digitized at the United Nations Archives in Geneva and are now publicly accessible, I am listing only the numbers of relevant intake records. See "Registers," 557, 597, 666, 686, 693, 749, 820, 832, 837, 897, 947, 950, 963, 986, 995, 1010, 1012, 1025, 1029, 1046, 1073, and 1099. I found textual references to tattoos in three of Jeppe's intake registers. Rebecca Jinks suggests that

more women may have been tattooed but the tattoos are not visible in photographs due to the development and emulsion techniques of the time. Her estimate of 10 percent is based on her identification of tattoos in 47 of 463 photographs of women and girls recovered by Jeppe in the surviving sixteen of nineteen registers archived in Geneva and Copenhagen. See Jinks, "Marks Hard to Erase: The Troubled Reclamation of 'Absorbed' Armenian Women, 1919–1927,"*American Historical Review* 123, no. 1 (February 2018): 100n44.

4. Aghavni Kabakian, "The Voice of the Blood," part 1, *Armenian Review* 14 (1961): 56.

5. Although Aghavni remembered her deportation as being in 1914, Ryan Gingeras has researched the survivors of Adapazarı and dates the deportations as beginning in July 1915. See Gingeras, *Sorrowful Shores: Violence, Ethnicity, and the End of Empire, 1912–1923*, 43.

6. There is a Roma or Dom (Arabic: *nawar*) community in Syria, many of whom live in and around Aleppo. Kabakian calls this group "Gypsy" in her memoir. The *nawar* community was also known in Syria for its tattooists, who serviced Bedouin communities, Alberto Savioli, "Le tribù beduine della Siria e l'arte del tatuaggio" (Ph.D. diss., Facoltà di Lettere e Filosofia, Università Degli Studi di Udine, 2003–2004), 105.

7. Kabakian, "The Voice of the Blood," part 1, 52–53.

8. Kabakian, "The Voice of the Blood," part 1, 53; recorded interview with Aghavni (Kabakian) Gulesserian, November 22, 1986, interview 2, archived at Zoryan Institute, Toronto.

9. Article 142, Treaty of Peace with Turkey.

10. Kabakian, "The Voice of the Blood," part 1, 55.

11. Recorded interview with Gulesserian, interview 2.

12. Recorded interview with Gulesserian, interview 2.

13. Kabakian, "The Voice of the Blood," part 1, 55.

14. Kabakian, "The Voice of the Blood" part 1, 56.

15. See Mesrob G. Kouyoumdjian, *A Comprehensive Dictionary, Armenian-English* (Cairo: Sahag Mesrob Press, 1950), 460. Hourig Attarian has analyzed the term *jagadakir* in her poignant analysis of her two great-aunts' forehead tattoos in "Narrating Women's Bodies: Storying Silences and Secrets in the Aftermath of Genocide," in *Gendered Wars, Gendered Memories: Feminist Conversations on War, Genocide and Political Violence*, ed. A. G. Altinay and A. Petö (London: Routledge, 2016), 257

16. Michel de Certeau, "Tools for Body Writing," *Intervention: Revolutionary Marxist Journal* 21–22 (1988): 7–11.

17. Recorded interview with Gulesserian, interview 2. Many Armenian women survivors worked in the nursing profession. Isabel Kaprielian-Churchill, *Sisters of Mercy and Survival: Armenian Nurses, 1900–1930* (Antelias: Armenian Catholicosate of Cilicia 2012).

18. Recorded interview with Gulesserian, interview 2.

19. Kabakian, "The Voice of the Blood," part 2, 65.

20. Recorded interview with Gulesserian, interview 2.

21. The second videotaped interview (Gulesserian, interview 2) at the Zoryan documents at length Aghavni's accomplished career as a surgical nurse, which included nursing Shukri Quwatli, the first president of independent Syria (1943–1949) while living in Damascus. She remarked, "I wanted to be a career woman, I wanted to travel the world."

22. Kabakian, "The Voice of the Blood," part 2, 66. Similar conversations in Constantinople occurred between elite Armenian women and doctors who attempted to dissuade Armenian women from aborting fetuses conceived when they were raped by Muslim men.

See Zaruhi Kalemkerian, "Badmutiun me Tornigis Hamar, Yerp vor Medznas," in *Giankis jampen* (Antelias: Dbaran Gatoghigosutian Giligio, 1952), 293–98.

23. Aghavni calls it "American University," her term for Robert College; the girls' campus is called the American College for Girls in Arnavutköy. Kabakian mentions disruptions with her studies around this time due to closures during the "Kemalist repressions." Kabakian, "The Voice of the Blood," part 2, 66–67. I discuss Dr. Post and innovation in tattoo removal methods in more detail in chapter 9.

24. Kabakian, "The Voice of the Blood," part 2, 67.

25. Kabakian, "The Voice of the Blood," part 2, 67.

26. Mabel Elliot, *Beginning Again in Ararat* (New York, Chicago Fleming H. Revell Company, 1924) 185, 244.

27. Aghavni Khandigian (nee Kabakian) Petition for Naturalization, U.S. District Court of Los Angeles, California, no. 215958, June 14, 1954.

28. Kabakian, "The Voice of the Blood," part 2, 70.

29. Sahag Mesrob uses this term frequently to describe the sensory experience of being around Armenians again after living among Muslim Arabs for several years. He writes "This is the voice of the nation's blood that calls and binds dispersed souls ..." (Յեղի՛ն արեան ձայնն է ասիկա, որ իրարու կը կանչէ, իրարու կը կապէ ցիրուցան հոգիները). See Mesrob, "Yegherni hushartsan, anonts anune," *Aravod-in Darekirke* (1921) 84.

30. Aghavni vacillates between English, Arabic, and Armenian in her oral interview. I included a few original responses as direct speech to highlight her voice. Recorded interview with Aghavni (Kabakian) Gulesserian; and Kabakian, "The Voice of the Blood," part 2, 69.

31. Kabakian, "The Voice in the Blood," part 2, 72

32. Card, "Genocide and Social Death," 63.

33. Recorded interview with Gulesserian, interview 2.

34. Recorded interview with Gulesserian, interview 2.

35. Aghavni's immigration record shows that Armen was eighteen years her senior when they married in 1953. Given her profession as a nurse, one might suspect that Armen was one of her patients and the marriage was in exchange for citizenship. Aghavni was a Lebanese national. See Aghavni Khandigian (nee Kabakian) Petition for Naturalization; and Marriage Record for Vahan Guleserian and Aghavni K Khandigian, California Marriage Index, 1960–1985, February 20, 1965, state file number 11189, 13, 569.

36. Kabakian, "The Voice of the Blood," parts 1 and 2. Her testimony was published in *The Armenian Review*, an important quarterly journal published by the Armenian diaspora community in Watertown, Massachusetts. It is one of many periodicals established within the Armenian diaspora in the wake of the genocide.

37. Gingeras mentions Aghavni's story in *Sorrowful Shores*, 201n53.

38. Khardalian, Suzanne dir., *Grandma's Tattoos*.

39. I have chosen to use first names for key figures and persons I have interviewed for this work in order to rhetorically personalize their stories. Suzanne Khardalian is one such case.

40. At present, *Grandma's Tattoos* is the most cited resource available to any researcher who seeks to explore the subject of tattooed Armenian women, and it certainly influenced my own decision to research the subject matter. Garibian, "Ravished Armenia," 36–50. A notable exception is the criticism of Lerna Ekmekçioğlu, who argued that *Grandma's Tattoos* is based on "ungrounded overgeneralizations." Ekmekçioğlu, "The Biopolitics of

'Rescue': Women and the Politics of Inclusion after the Armenian Genocide," in *Gender and Genocide in the Twentieth Century: A Comparative Perspective*, ed. Amy E. Randall (Bloomsbury, 2015), 236n69.

41. Marks, *The Skin of the Film*, 162.

42. Interview with Suzanne Khardalian, October 11, 2019. In this section of the interview, Khardalian made a profound connection between her past films on the Armenian Genocide and a new film she is making about the rape and enslavement of Yazidi women. She sees these events as interlinked in her forthcoming film "Inside her, Inside me: A Tale of Three Yazidi Girls."

43. I am offering some selected transliteration of the original Armenian dialogue that supports my argument about the textuality of tattoos. Khardalian invites her Aunt Lucia to "read" her tattoos. This scene emphasizes the legibility of tattoos that can be "written" (Armenian verb: *krel*) and thus read or interpreted by others. See Khardalian, *Grandma's Tattoos*.

44. Khardalian, *Grandma's Tattoos*.

45. Researcher Nazlı Hazar has noted in her ethnography of Yazidi women that children would sometimes tattoo each other out of boredom while shepherding. The children added that to them the symbols had absolutely no meaning. Hazar, "Silenced Memories: Yazidi Women in Turkey" (M.A. thesis, Sabancı University, 2020), 23.

46. This detail is mentioned in a synopsis for her next film, *Inside Her, Inside Me: A Tale of Three Yazidi Women*, on her academia.edu page, https://www.academia.edu/44962102/INSIDE_HER_INSIDE_ME_A_Tale_of_Three_Yazidi_Women.

47. The film jumps from the scene of Khanum sitting on the lap of a man during the voyage to the claim she was raped. It is unclear if there was more to the story that was not explained in the film due to editing.

48. Khardalian, *Grandma's Tattoos*.

49. Cathy Caruth, *Listening to Trauma: Conversations with Leaders in the Theory and Treatment of Catastrophic Experience* (Baltimore: John's Hopkins University Press, 2014).

50. In this sense, they are what Claude Lévi-Strauss calls "empty signifiers." See Claude Lévi-Strauss, *Introduction to Marcel Mauss* (London: Routledge, 1987), 63–64.

51. Judith Butler, *Excitable Speech: A Politics of the Performative* (New York: Routledge, 1997), 10, 15.

52. Gabor Maté, *The Myth of Normal: Trauma, Illness, and Healing in a Toxic Culture* (New York: Penguin, 2022), 20. Italics in the original.

53. "A Word Regarding Branding," *Slave Market News*, July 1926, 5.

54. The author was Jenny Jensen discussing two rescued Armenian women, Jeghsa Hairobediun [Yeghsa Hairabedian] and Maria Agha Sarkissian, in "Midt i Arbejdet," *Armeniervennen* no. 9–10 (September–October, 1930).

55. Sara Ahmed, *The Cultural Politics of Emotion* (Edinburgh: University of Edinburgh Press, 2014), 103.

56. Ahmed, *Cultural Politics of Emotion*, 103–4.

Remnant 6

1. Admission of Near East Refugees. Hearings Before the Committee on Immigration and Naturalization, House of Representatives, Sixty-Seventh Congress, Fourth Session on H.R. 13269, December 15–19, 1922, Serial 1-C (Washington DC: Government Printing Office, 1923), 109–12.

2. Reverend M. T. Kalaidjian, secretary for the Armenian Department of the YMCA in New York City, offered a statement and facilitated Eliza Shahinian's testimony at the hearing.

Chapter 8

1. Caplan, "Introduction," *Written on the Body*, xv.

2. Discourses of racial and social degeneration and tattoos are the subject of Gemma Angel, "Atavistic Marks and Risky Practices: The Tattoo in Medico-Legal Debates, 1850–1950," in *A Medical History of Skin: Scratching the Surface*, ed. Jonathan Reinarz and Kevin Siena (London: Pickering and Chatto, 2013), 165–80.

3. Jennifer Putzi, "Capturing Identity in Ink: The Captivities of Olive Oatman," *Western American Literature* 39, no. 2 (Summer 2004): 187–88.

4. While Liat Kozma carefully examines the emergence of the categories "white slavery" and "traffic in women," the latter replaced the former in the 1921 Convention for the Suppression of the Traffic in Women and Children, and she does not address its connection to the traffic in Armenian women during the genocide. Kozma, *Global Women, Colonial Ports: Prostitution in the Interwar Middle East* (New York: SUNY Press, 2017).

5. Morefield, "'Families of Mankind': British Liberty, League Internationalism, and the Traffic in Women and Children," 6–7.

6. Kathryn Zabelle Derounian-Stadola writes that "captivity narratives" became "the first American literary form dominated by women's experiences as captives, storytellers, writers, and readers." Derounian-Stadola, "Introduction," in *Indian Captivity Narratives*, ed. Kathryn Zabelle Derounian-Stadola (New York: Penguin, 1998), xi, 35. Pamela Gilbert explains how the genre was found in British literature and traveling shows in the nineteenth century. The narratives included stories of women who, due to circumstance, were pushed out of civilization and their bodies were inscribed by brutal savages (in either the American West or Pacific islands), which necessitated adopting rugged independence in order to survive, contravening strict Victorian norms. Pamela Gilbert, *Victorian Skin: Surface, Self, History* (Ithaca, NY: Cornell University Press, 2019), 333–34.

7. The arm tattoo was never photographed but it could, for a fee, be viewed during some of the live shows in which Oatman performed. Putzi, "Capturing Identity in Ink," 178.

8. Lorenzo D. Oatman and Olive A. Oatman, *Life among the Indians, or The Captivity of the Oatman Girls among the Apache and Mohave Indians* (San Francisco: Grabhorn Press, 1935), 133–34.

9. Oatman and Oatman, *Life among the Indians*, 134.

10. Upon the invitation of President Lincoln, Irataba visited the United States to negotiate the end of fighting between the Mohave and the US government. This included a personal visit, after which Irataba delivered the terms to the Mohave—they did not take the offer of peace seriously. If the story of Oatman's marriage to the son of the tribal chief was at all true, Irataba would have been her father-in-law. See Brian McGinty, *The Oatman Massacre: A Tale of Desert Captivity and Survival* (Norman: University of Oklahoma Press, 2014), 93, 176, 192.

11. While biographer Margot Mifflin has claimed this account was only a rumor, citing among other things Oatman's inability to have children when she was married to farmer John Brant Fairchild, another biographer, Jennifer Putzi, notes Susan Thompson Lewis Parrish, a close friend of the Oatman family, claimed Olive was married to a Mohave man, See Mifflin, *The Blue Tattoo*, 132; and Putzi, "Capturing Identity in Ink," 180.

12. Putzi, "Capturing Identity in Ink," 180.

13. A drawing of the Oatman girls wearing bark skirts can be found in the original publication of Royal B. Stratton's ghostwritten memoir of Lorenzo and Olive Oatman, *Being an Interesting Narrative of the Captivity of the Oatman Girls, among the Mohave and Apache Indians* (San Francisco: Whitton, Towne & Co.'s Excelsior Steam Power Presses, 1857), 160.

14. Testimony gleaned from Henry Grinnell, one of Oatman's rescuers, in "A Tour Through Arizona," *Harper's Monthly Magazine* 174, no. 29 (November 1864): 701.

15. Sarah Koenig, *Providence and the Invention of American History* (New Haven, CT: Yale University Press, 2021), 5.

16. Mifflin, *The Blue Tattoo*, 190.

17. Putzi, "Capturing Identity in Ink," 179.

18. Mifflin, *The Blue Tattoo*, 160, 164; and Putzi, "Capturing Identity in Ink," 178.

19. Mifflin, *The Blue Tattoo*, 165.

20. Mifflin, *The Blue Tattoo*, 167.

21. Mifflin, *The Blue Tattoo*, 47, 169.

22. Beverly Yuen Thompson, *Covered in Ink: Tattoos, Women, and the Politics of the Body* (New York: New York University Press, 2015), 24. Robert W. Rydell shows how World's Fairs sought to display the latest scientific thinking about bodies with didactic exhibits for popular consumption. See Rydell, *All the World's A Fair: Visions of Empire at the American International Expositions, 1875–1916* (Chicago: University of Chicago Press, 1985), 55–62.

23. A. H. Ohmann-Dumesnil, "The Successful Removal of Tattoo Marks and of Powder Stains," *St. Louis Medical and Surgical Journal* 78 (February 1900): 68.

24. Christine Braunberger examines tattooed women within the context of revolutionary aesthetics that questioned body norms in the nineteenth century in "Revolting Bodies: The Monster Beauty of Tattooed Women," *National Women's Studies Association Journal* 12, no. 2 (2000): 8–12. Of course, her story involved women who voluntarily tattooed themselves rather than captive women, but it exposes well the spectacle that involuntarily tattooed women would have been. Other studies have complicated the gaze of the spectator as it is met with that of the sideshow freak in a way that disturbs disindentification and instead reflects back to the spectator her own desires. Rachel Adams, *Sideshow U.S.A.: Freaks in the American Cultural Imagination* (Chicago: University of Chicago Press, 2001), 7–8.

25. Jinks, "Marks Hard to Erase," 97, 101.

26. Kevin Rozario, "'Delicious Horrors': Mass Culture, the Red Cross, and the Appeal of Modern American Humanitarianism," *American Quarterly* 55, no. 3 (September 2003): 419.

27. Rozario, "Delicious Horrors," 420, 436.

28. "The Unfinished Task," *Slave Market News*, July 1926, 3.

29. "Rescue of Armenian Women and Girls," *Supplement to the Slave Market News*, January 1926, archived with correspondence about the publication *Slave Market News* in FO 371/11545, E4504/663/44, BNA.

30. "A Message from the Bishop of London," *Slave Market News*, July 1926, 1. See also *Slave Market News*, July 1930, 2.

31. Emily J. Robinson, "Facts about Armenian Refugees and Slaves," *Slave Market News*, December 1924, 4.

32. W. Edward Raffety, "A Story to Awaken American Christians," *Missions: American Baptist International Magazine* 10 (1919): 819.

33. "The Brutal Mark of Slavery," *Slave Market News*, December 1924, 7. All-caps emphasis in the original text.

34. *Slave Market News*, January 1927, 5.

35. "The Unfinished Task" and "The Cry of 30,000 Women and Children," *Slave Market News*, July 1926, 3, 5, 8.

36. "The Cry of 30,000 Women and Children," 8.

37. "Rescued from Slavery," *Slave Market News*, July 1930, 1.

38. "Rescued from Slavery," 3.

39. Jinks, "Marks Hard to Erase," 94–95.

40. A. Lancaster Smith, "Slavery of White Children in the Near East," *Slave Market News*, July 1930, 7; and Janice Okoomian, "Becoming White: Contested History, Armenian American Women, and Racialized Bodies," *Multi-Ethnic Literature of the United States Journal* 27, no. 1, Contested Boundaries (Spring 2002): 213–37.

41. Most of the photographs published in *The Slave Market News* can be found within Karen Jeppe's private papers archived at the league of Nations archives within the United Nations Archives in Geneva, see an envelope with "The League of Nations" written upon it in R641 Société des Nations/League of Nations Archives, Section 12, Registry Files 1919–1927, Séries 38236–63896, dossier 12/43565/4631, UNA. Included among the photographs is the retouched image of Mariam printed in *Slave Market News*, December 1924, which was also made into a postcard for readers to circulate the image further.

42. Mariam, "Registers," inmate 557, June 18, 1924, UNA.

43. See *Slave Market News*, December 24, 1924. In response to repeated publication of accounts fueled by Jeppe's ongoing rescue efforts, George William Rendel underplayed the publication in a memo titled "Alleged Ill-Treatment of Armenian Women and Children in Turkey," March 10, 1925, FO 371/10864, E1490/228/44, 3, BNA.

44. See correspondence between the Bishop of London and British politician Austen Chamberlain in which copies of the pamphlet were shared. FO 371/11545, E4504/663/44, 251, BNA

45. Rendel memo, "Alleged Ill-Treatment of Armenian Women and Children in Turkey."

46. See Watenpaugh, *Bread from Stones*, 19.

47. *The Aftermath* (New York: YWCA, 1919), 11, in U.S.A. Records, box 337, folder 14, Sophia Smith Collection, Smith College.

48. The photograph now archived at Getty Images as "Former Turkish Slave Standing Against Wall" in the George Rinhart Collection appears in *The Aftermath*, 4. The image was reprinted with a different caption that did not retell her story but added that she was pregnant upon arrival, presumably from sexual abuse. See *Blue Triangle News* (New York: War Work Council, YWCA, January 6, 1920), 3. The original before photograph published in *The Blue Triangle News* was not found.

49. Some contemporaries of Olive Oatman also questioned her gender as they did other formerly captive women who spoke publicly. Oatman eventually stopped speaking publicly in 1870. Putzi, "Capturing Identity in Ink," 192.

50. "Girls after Being Rescued from Slavery," George Rinhart Collection, Getty Images.

51. Quoted in Lancaster Smith, "Branding by Tattooing," *Slave Market News* 1 no.25, (April 1930): 5.

52. Smith, "Branding by Tattooing," 5.

53. Karen Jeppe, "Annual Report of the League of Nations Commission for the Protection of Women and Children in the Near East," 1926, ALON 12/16489/4631, UNA.

54. Churchman was responding to the newspaper's summary of a lecture by Edib in which she denied Armenian women and girls remained forced to live in Muslim homes. He included references to League of Nations reports by Karen Jeppe as evidence to the contrary. See Churchman, "Armenian Women in Moslem Homes," *Manchester Guardian*, January 4, 1926; and Halide Edib's rebuttal in "Armenian Women in Moslem Homes," *Manchester Guardian*, January 13, 1926, 6.

55. Halide Edib, "Armenian Women in Moslem Homes," *Manchester Guardian*, January 12, 1926.

56. "Ölenlere öldürenler," *Tanin*, 254, May 18, 1909, 4, cited in Hazal Halavut, "Loss, Lament and Lost Witnessing: Halide Edib on 'Being a Member of the Party Who Killed' Armenians," *Journal of Ottoman and Turkish Studies Association* 8, no. 2 (2021): 313.

57. Halavut, "Loss, Lament and Lost Witnessing," 317.

58. Halavut, "Loss, Lament and Lost Witnessing," 316–17.

59. Selim Deringil examines the shift in Edib's rhetoric from defiant and revolutionary to nationalist in his article "Your Religion Is Worn and Outdated: Orphans, Orphanages and Halide Edib during the Armenian Genocide: The Case of Antoura," *Études arméniennes contemporaines*, 12 (2019): 33–65; and Lerna Ekmekçioğlu is preparing an article, "Use Consoling Words for Our Butchered Nation": Armenian Feminists' Post-Genocide Expectations from Their Turkish Counterparts," that closely examines the overtures Edib made to suffering Armenian sisters in the immediate aftermath of the war, demonstrating how her views of Armenians changed sharply in the mid-1920s.

60. Edib, "Armenian Women in Moslem Homes," 6.

61. Jeppe's rebuttal to Edib may have been published in English, but I was unable to locate the English version. The Danish version of Edib's letter to the *Manchester Guardian* and Jeppe's rebuttal were published in *Armeniervennen*, where the humanitarian acknowledges that propaganda was offering an inaccurate view of the tattoos. "En Diskusion: Karen Jeppes Svar," *Armeniervennen* 6, no. 78 (July–August 1926): 28–29.

62. "En Diskusion: Karen Jeppes Svar," 29.

63. "En Diskusion: Karen Jeppes Svar," 29.

64. Jeppe, "Annual Report," 1926, 4. Underlined emphasis in the original document.

65. Karen Jeppe's personal clippings from *The Slave Market News* can be located at 12.43565. 4361, UNA.

66. Letter from Churchman, *Manchester Guardian*, January 23, 1926.

67. The violence of photography as a moral problem is the premise of Susan Sontag, *On Photography* (New York: Farrar, Strauss, and Giroux, 1973), 10–11.

68. European publications sometimes printed photographs of tattooed Armenian women with little context, no context, or inaccurate context, suggesting that the nature of the photographs would be understood, known to readers on their own terms. See Chr. Winther, *Armenien og Karen Jeppe* (Copenhagen: Aug. Olsens, 1935); Henni Forchhammer, *Et Besøg hos Karen Jeppe* (Copenhagen: De Danske Armeniervenner, 1926); "L'enfer des femmes: N'est pas à Buenos Ayres main en Asie-Mineure," *Police Magazine* (Paris) 2, no. 37 (August 9, 1931): 14. The *Police Magazine* article drew heavily from the previously cited article by Smith, "Branding by Tattooing."

69. Olive Oatman's tattoos made an appearance in an AMC series *Hell on Wheels*, a

story about the building of the Transcontinental Railroad. I would argue that it was no accident that the tattooed character named Eva who bears Oatman's identical Mohave blue chin tattoos was depicted as a prostitute.

Remnant 7

1. Text translated from the Armenian: "Vedkeru chinchuim yev penadzkhayin tutiun," *Hay pujak* (Istanbul), 6 (1922): 84.

2. *Hajj* is the Arabic word for "pilgrimage," and *hajji* is the word for "pilgrim." The term is also used in Turkish and transmitted to Armenian. The author makes a reference to men having pilgrimage tattoos on shoulders and chests, though many pilgrims received far simpler inner-forearm cross tattoos.

Chapter 9

1. Hourig Attarian, "Lifelines: Matrilineal Narratives, Memory, and Identity" (Ph.D. diss., McGill University, 2009), 256.

2. Hourig Attarian has shared her powerful prosthetic memory of her paternal grandmother's cousin Azniv in her autoethnography "Lifelines," 255–56.

3. Attarian, "Narrating Women's Bodies," 258, 267.

4. Additional details about Azniv were shared with me by Hourig Attarian via email on August 13, 2021.

5. For a close study of the types of debilitating injuries Allied soldiers sustained during World War I, see Joanna Bourke, *Dismembering the Male: Men's Bodies, Britain, and the Great War* (Chicago: University of Chicago Press, 1996).

6. "Armenian Girls Branded," *Current History and Forum: A Monthly Magazine of the New York Times* 12, no. 1 (April 1920): 159.

7. Examples include "Armenian Girl, Tattooed by Turk 'Husband,' Arrives," *New York Tribune*, April 4, 1920, 2.

8. "Armenian Girls Branded,"159. This perceptive report names no author but relies on quotations from William T. Ellis, a Middle East correspondent with the *New York Herald*.

9. "Armenian Girls Branded,"159.

10. Lerna Ekmekçioğlu, "A Climate for Abduction, A Climate for Redemption," 54.

11. Tachjian, "Mixed Marriage, Prostitution, Survival," 91.

12. "Removes Brand of Slavery," *Arizona Republic*, October 27, 1921, 4.

13. Testimony of Sirena Aram Alajajaian in Svazlian, *The Armenian Genocide: Testimonies*, 412.

14. Testimony of Nouritsa Kyurkdjian in Svazlian, *The Armenian Genocide: Testimonies*, 412.

15. See the story titled, "Nouritza of the Tattooed Face," in Kevork Apelian, *Shahada mada al-hayat, min aram ila . . . aram/ Tsgyans nahadagutiun (aramen minchev. . . . aram)*, trans. Nora Arissian ('Anjar: Sava, 2006), 119–30. For a description of Nourtiza's tattoo design, see page 123.

16. Nouritza was called Nor in Armenian, which means "pomegranate," very similar to the name Nur, or "light," in Arabic. Nouritza had never formally divorced the previous husband in this tale; therefore, she was technically married to two men, as were many other Armenian women whose rescue was treated as a de facto marriage annulment by the community.

17. A photograph of Nouritza can be found in Apelian, *Shahada mada al-hayat*, 144, but her tattoos are not visible in the photo.

18. Shemmassian, "The League of Nations and the Reclamation of Armenian Genocide Survivors," 99.

19. "News and Notes of Missions," *Continent* 51 (January 18, 1920): 51.

20. Gottlieb to Secretary of State, May 22, 1919, Record Group 59, 867.48/1261, NARA.

21. Herant Katchadourian shares a memory of Lucine, his nanny, who was like a second mother to him. She never married or had children of her own but was instead completely devoted to him. See Katchadourian, *The Way It Turned Out* (Singapore: Pan Stanford, 2018).

22. Lemon juice and other home remedies used to fade the appearance of tattoos are listed in Fred Wise, "Tattoo Marks," *Archives of Dermatology and Syphilology* 2 (1920): 272–73; and James H. Tashjian, "American Military Mission to Armenia" part 6, *Armenian Review* 4, no. 3 (1951): 104.

23. "Armenian Girls Tattooed," *Denison Review* 54 (December 17, 1919).

24. Svazlian, *The Armenian Genocide and the People's Historical Memory*, 446.

25. "News Notes," *New Near East*, December 1920, 29. For Dr. Marden's tattoo removal in Marsovan, see "Collectors Levy Heavy Turk Taxes," *South Bend News-Times*, November 28, 1920, 3.

26. There are five albums belonging to Karen Jeppe at the Armenian Genocide Memorial Archive in Yerevan, Armenia. Many of the stickers that label the albums from 56–60 are now missing from the volumes. This photograph can be found in Karen Jeppe [թղ-1, album 60, photograph # 495. I would like to thank historian and archivist Gohar Khanumian at the AGMI for her insights on this photograph.

27. Vahran Katchperouni, "Rapport médical de la Maison de Réception de la ligue des nation á Alep, 1925–1926," 5, 12/49505/4631, UNA.

28. Smith "Branding by Tattooing," 6.

29. R. A. Lambert, "Aleppo," in *The Medical Work of the Near East Relief; A Review of Its Accomplishments in Asia Minor and the Caucasus during 1919–1920*, ed. George L. Richards, MD (New York: Near East Relief, 1923), 20.

30. After getting his medical degree at Princeton in 1897, Dr. Post returned to Turkey in 1904. Dr. Post had extensive experience as a medical advisor for the Near East Foundation during the war, and State Department records show that he served in a hospital in Konya and corresponded with the US government throughout the war. In 1917, he was named the director of two Red Cross hospitals in Constantinople. After serving as a medical advisor for NER in Egypt, Greece, and Turkey during World War I, he was named the organization's medical director (1918–1919) and spearheaded the battle against the typhus epidemic in Constantinople and relief after the Smyrna disaster of 1922. "Wilfred Post, 89, Surgeon and Medical Missionary," *Herald Tribune*, January 20, 1966; "Dr. Wilfred Post Surgeon on L.I., 89," *New York Times*, January 20, 1966; and "Class of '97,"*Alumni Weekly*, October 28, 1925, AC 104, Box 247, Seely G. Mudd Collection, Princeton University.

31. "News Items: Seek Doctors' Help in Removing Tattoo," *International Record of Medicine and General Practice Clinics* 110, no. 23 (December 6, 1919): 950.

32. Surgically removing tattoos with cutting continued to be advocated for among some surgeons. See Howard Fox, "Tattooing," *Archives of Dermatology and Syphilology* 2 (1920): 255.

33. Fox, "Tattooing," 255.

34. It is not stated which clinic was used for the procedure, but it could have been either the Vanderbilt Clinic, where Wise and Dr. John Fordyce often collaborated, or the College

of Physicians and Surgeons of Columbia University in New York, where Wise was the chief of clinic. See a biography of Wise in *Journal of Investigative Dermatology* 8, no. 6 (June 1947): 281–83.

35. Wise, "Tattoo Marks."

36. Wise, "Tattoo Marks," 272.

37. The only medical article in Armenian on the subject of tattoos and tattoo removal discovered in the course this research was "Vedkeru chinchuime yev penadzkhayin tutiun," *Hay pujak* (Istanbul) 6 (1922): 84. See Remnant 7. A survey of Armenian publications showed very little discussion of Armenian women's tattoos as compared with Western-language materials published by missionaries and humanitarians.

38. "Vedkeru chinchuime yev penadzkhayin tutiun," 84.

39. "'Girl Disfigured by the Turks Reaches the U.S.," *Citizen Times*, April 10, 1920; "Wants Method to Un-Tattoo the Armenians," *Star-Progress*, December 13, 1919; "How Science Cleansed her of the Cruel Turk's Brand of Shame," *Washington Times*, September 5, 1920; "2 Girls Have Slave Tattoo Brand Removed," *Detroit Free Press*, November 25, 1921.

40. "Wants Method to Un-Tattoo the Armenians."

41. "Girl Disfigured by the Turks Reaches the U.S.," *Citizen Times*, April 10, 1920; and "Armenian Girl, Tattooed by Turk 'Husband,' Arrives."

42. Unnamed in other accounts, it is unclear whether Abou Seraidz was an Arab or an ethnic Turk. Nargis is described as "the wife of a wealthy Turk" in "Armenian Girl, Tattooed by Turk 'Husband,' Arrives." It is unclear if this Turk is the same Turkish governor whose covetous eyes Nargis tried to avoid in another account.

43. "How Science Cleansed Her of the Cruel Turk's Brand of Shame."

44. There is no historical evidence whatsoever that concubines were tattooed in the Ottoman Empire.

45. Rozario, "Delicious Horrors," 422.

46. İrvin Cemal Schick shows how these war-time narratives have a long history. See Schick, "Christian Maidens, Turkish Ravishers," in *Women in the Ottoman Balkans*, 273–305.

47. "Girl Flees Turks' Torture," *New York Times*, May 6, 1920.

48. "How Science Cleansed Her of the Cruel Turk's Brand of Shame."

49. Howard Fox, "Tattooing," *Archives of Dermatology and Syphilology* 5 (1922): 255. Fox reported that the girl, "three years before, during the war, had been captured by the Turks and forced to become an inmate of the harem. As a brand of ownership, various bluish marks had been tattooed on her forehead, nose, temporal region and chin." If this is Nargis, Fox's article would indicate she attempted to have her tattoos removed once before.

50. See "How Science Cleansed Her of the Cruel Turk's Brand of Shame." Dr. Edgar T. Strickland from Sheffield University, England, was also visiting America at the time and had consulted other tattooed women described as "friends of the young victim."

51. A. H. Ohmann-Dumesnil, "Caroid in the Removal of Tattoo Marks," *St. Louis Medical and Surgical Journal*, February 1900, 177.

52. Cesare Lombroso viewed criminals as atavistic beings with primitive behaviors resembling inferior animals. Another criminologist argued another cause for criminality; Lacassagne maintained that "the social milieu [of the criminal] is the mother culture of criminality; the microbe is the criminal." See Alan Sekula, "The Body and the Archive," *October* 39 (Winter 1986): 26, 37.

53. Gemma Angel, "The Modified Body: The Nineteenth-Century Tattoo as Fugitive

Stigmata," *Victorian Review* 42, no. 1 (2016): 15. Some of these arguments are iterated in the studies of Kurdish and Turkish tribal tattoos. Such arguments, unfortunately, repeat the assertions of Victorian pseudoscience.

54. A 1889 medical journal reports that French dermatologist Dr. G. Variot had experimented successfully with tattoo removal methods involving silver nitrate, tannic acid, and a tattooing machine. This innovative method produced scabbing followed by new reddish-colored skin as it healed but no scarring like other procedures. This description is nearly identical to Nargis's procedure. See "A New Method of Removing Tattoo-Marks," *Journal of Cutaneous Diseases Including Syphilis*, 7 (New York: D. Appleton and Company, 1889), 108.

55. "How Science Cleansed Her of the Cruel Turk's Brand of Shame."

56. "How Science Cleansed Her of the Cruel Turk's Brand of Shame."

57. This is to acknowledge in some way the varied ways they were applied, but also to suggest a haphazard application more suggestive of symbolic Islamization than a tradition of tattoo that would be more finely applied by a professional tattooist.

58. Mümtaz Fırat, *Kaybolan izler*, 89; and Alberto Savioli, "Le tribù beduine della Siria e l'arte del tatuaggio" (Ph.D. diss., Facoltà di Lettere e Filosofia, Università Degli Studi di Udine, 2003–2004), 160.

59. "Armenian Girl, Tattooed by Turk 'Husband,' Arrives." The phenomenon by which tattoo lines appear to be dots is called "beading." Gemma Angel, "Recovering the Nineteenth-Century European Tattoo," in *Ancient Ink: The Archaeology of Tattooing*, ed. Lars Krutak and Aaron Deter-Wolf (Seattle: University of Washington Press, 2017), 110.

60. "Armenian Girl, Tattooed by Turk 'Husband,' Arrives." Krutak, *The Tattooing Art of Tribal Women*; Mümtaz Fırat, *Kaybolan izler: güneydoğuda geleneksel dövme ya da dek ve dak* (Istanbul: Yapı Kredi Yayınları, 2017); and Yenipınar and Tunç, *Güneydoğu anadolu geleneksel dövme sanatı beden yazıtları*. Serpouhi Tavoukdjian notes that the Arab family waited for the arrival of an artist to apply her tattoos, indicating the practitioner was not local but a professional who circulated through the communities periodically. Anthropologist Alberto Savoli has observed that in Turkey and Mesopotamia tattooists were women and that Roma (*nawari*) women were considered the most reputable. See Serpouhi Tavoukdjian, *Exiled: Story of an Armenian Girl* (Washington, DC: Review and Herald Publishing Association, 1933), 68–69; and Savioli, "Le tribù beduine della Siria e l'arte del tatuaggio," 106.

61. Savioli, "Le tribù beduine della Siria e l'arte del tatuaggio," 133, 138.

62. *The Aftermath*, 11.

63. Firat, *Kaybolan izler*, 152.

64. I would like to thank Gemma Angel for helping me determine which chemicals were used in this procedure—they were unnamed in the article. Experimentation with tannin and silver nitrate had been ongoing since Variot's discoveries in the nineteenth century.

65. "Would Remove Tattoos from Armenians Girls," *Star-Gazette*, December 12, 1919.

66. Ohmann-Dumesnil, "Caroid in the Removal of Tattoo Marks," 181.

67. Alphonse Bertillion, "Les Tatouages," 532–33, cited in Angel, "The Modified Body: The Nineteenth-Century Tattoo as Fugitive Stigmata," 18–19.

68. Sekula, "The Body and the Archive," 11.

Remnant 8

1. Excerpt from a chapter by the same title in Tavoukdjian, *Exiled: Story of an Armenian Girl*, 68–69.

Chapter 10

1. Barouhi Silian (b. 1900, Nicomedia), in Svazlian, *The Armenian Genocide: Testimonies*, 414.

2. James Peacock, *The Anthropological Lens: Harsh Light, Soft Focus*, 2nd ed. (Cambridge: Cambridge University Press, 2004), 145.

3. Gabrielle Moser, *Projecting Citizenship: Photography and Belonging in the British Empire* (University Park: Pennsylvania State University Press, 2019), 2–3.

4. Such stagings are frequently found in European art from the Romantic period and later appropriated by late Ottoman and even American photography studios. See Sarah Graham-Brown, *Images of Women: The Portrayal of Women in Photography of the Middle East, 1860–1950* (New York: Columbia University Press, 1988). Jug-bearing women are a common motif in turn-of-the-century Orientalist photography. The holding of earthenware is meant to evoke peasant labor and was appealing to even Ottoman bourgeoisie who sat for portraits. This staging aesthetic circulated even in humanitarian photographs; for her intake record, a survivor named Loucie posed barefoot and in Bedouin costume with a jug. Lucie Mardikian, "Registers" inmate 571, June 18, 1924, UNA.

5. Tavoukdjian, *Exiled*, 45.

6. Tavoukdjian, *Exiled*, 54.

7. Tavoukdjian, *Exiled*, 49. Abu Galgal (Abu Qilqil) is very close to Minbaj, a town many Armenian deportees passed on the deportation route toward Dayr al-Zur. This suggests that Serpouhi and her mother may have been at the Armenian refugee "camp" at nearby Meskene or in Minbaj where she was sold. Such encampments were not organized camps with walls but instead were a gathering of unsheltered Armenians surrounded by armed men. In other words, the boundaries of the enclosure were porous, allowing people to sneak in and out and easily traffic young girls and women. See Khatchig Mouradian, "Internment and Destruction: Concentration Camps during the Armenian Genocide, 1915–1916," in *Internment during the First World War: A Mass Global Phenomenon*, ed. Panikos Panayi, Stefan Manz, and Matthew Stibbe (London: Routledge Studies in First World War History, 2018), 145–61.

8. Lice-infected Serpouhi suffered from an illness that blackened her skin, and she fell into a fever. When her adoptive father was away, the wives of Allel Moose followed the protocol of many of the Bedouin and cruelly isolated Serpouhi from the tribe—an extreme quarantine in which the sick person is also denied life-giving sustenance and left to die. When he returned, he rescued her and brought her back to the community, where her hair was cut, her skin was scrubbed, and she recovered from the illness. Tavoukjian, *Exiled*, 64.

9. Tavoukdjian, *Exiled*, 64.

10. Tavoukdjian, *Exiled*, 68–69. Similarly, a respondent noted in an oral interview that the women in his family were tattooed in order to camouflage them more effectively from Turkish gendarmes. Sa'ad Hamad al-As'ad, Shaddadi, Syria, November 23, 2007.

11. Mae M. Derdarian, based on a memoir by Virginia Meghrouni, *Vergeen: A Survivor of the Armenian Genocide* (Los Angeles: Atmus Press Publications, 1997), 118–19.

12. Some of these tattoos are apparent in a photograph in Vergeen's memoir in her nurs-

ing uniform taken in a hospital. The tattoos are not apparent in other photographs due to her tattoo removal surgery and use of makeup to cover them.

13. Derdardian and Meghrouni, *Vergeen*, 107–9.

14. Derdarian and Meghrouni,, *Vergeen*, 107–8.

15. Derdarian and Meghrouni,, *Vergeen*, 249.

16. Robert Aram Kaloosdian, *Tadem: My Father's Village Extinguished during the 1915 Armenian Genocide* (Portsmouth, NH: Peter E. Randall Publisher, 2015), 255–56.

17. Isabel Kaprielian-Churchill has a remarkable study of postwar Armenian picture brides that reflects men's agency in accepting women survivors as wives. See Kaprielian-Churchill, "Armenian Refugee Women: The Picture Brides, 1920–1930," *Journal of American Ethnic History* 12, no. 3 (1993): 3–29.

18. Two examples of Turkish-language tattoo scholarship that feature numerous examples, including photographs, of tattooed men are Yenipınar and Tunç, *Güneydoğu anadolu geleneksel dövme sanatı beden yazıtları*; and Fırat, *Kaybolan izler*.

19. Racho Donef, "Interviews with Survivors of the Armenian Genocide," Armenian Genocide History, http://www.atour.com/history/AG/20030811a.html.

20. Edward Racoubian, "Testimony," unpublished manuscript, 3. I would like to thank Levon Parian for sharing this document with me.

21. Janet Kinosian, "Witness to Fire," *Los Angeles Times Magazine,* May 23, 1999.

22. Racoubian, "Testimony," 6.

23. The comb (*tarak*) has a range of possible motifs. Racoubian's wrist tattoo looks like a line with a series of hashes through it, sometimes chevrons, which is another variation on "the comb" motif. For the motifs found on Edward Racoubian's hands, see Fırat, *Kaybolan izler*, 111–12, and 118–19.

24. Here I refer to the story of Vardanousch Karagheusian, "Brand of Slavery Still on Her Hand, Armenian Girl Finds Asylum Here," *Eagle* (Brooklyn, NY), January 4, 1920.

25. All three photographs of tattooed rescued girls were taken in August 1919, likely by the same photographer. All three were part of the Underwood & Underwood Collection, which was later acquired by George Rinhart, one of the largest collectors of American photography. His collection is now held by Getty Images. For information on Rinhart and his collections, see Joan Bryant, *Black Subjects in Modern Media Photography: Works from the George R. Rinhart Collection* (Syracuse, NY: Syracuse University Art Galleries, 2020), 11.

26. Linda Steet, *Veils and Daggers: A Century of National Geographic's Representation of the Arab World* (Philadelphia: Temple University Press, 2000), 6–7. *National Geographic* published portraits of clothed and semi-nude North African women on the eve of Word War I. See "Here and There in North Africa," *National Geographic* 190, no. 4 (1914): 98–125. Many of the women of the Oulad Naïl tribe photographed in the series were dancers, perhaps even prostitutes paid to expose their bare breasts for the camera.

27. Malek Alloula, *The Colonial Harem,* trans. Myrna and Wlad Godzich, intro. Barbara Harlow (Minneapolis: University of Minnesota Press, 1986), 28.

28. The Musée du Quai Branly–Jacques Chirac featured the photograph in a traveling exhibition titled "Tattoos: An Exhibition" beginning in Paris in 2015. It arrived in Los Angeles in 2017. Elaine Sciolino, "Capturing the Spirit of the Tattoo," *New York Times,* May 6, 2014.

29. Coburn Dukeheart, "The Last Tattooed Women of Kobane," *National Geographic,* January 21, 2015, http://proof.nationalgeographic.com/2015/01/21/the-last-tattooed-women-of-kobane/. There may be a connection between increased religiosity and the dis-

appearance of tattooing among contemporary Muslim communities, although there are Muslims who argue that tattooing and Islam are compatible.

30. Yenipınar and Tunç, *Güneydoğu anadolu geleneksel dövme sanatı beden yazıtları*, 214–15.

31. The age of the unnamed girl in the Getty photograph is not documented. Since she is described as a "girl" by the photographer, I estimate that she must be fifteen years old or less. That would mean she was perhaps eleven at the time of the outset of the Armenian Genocide, placing her in the precarious position of being on the verge of puberty when the deportations unfolded.

32. Aghavni, "Registers," inmate 837, October, 8, 1925, UNA. Keith Watenpaugh refers to these rare inclusions of first-person commentary as "closeness" that "is itself a reminder of the reality of the level of cross-identification" that he documents among relief workers who saw their work as saving Christians in the Holy Land. See Watenpaugh, *Bread from Stones*, 39.

33. Our runaway bride shares the same first name as the tattooed nurse who opened part 2.

34. Aghavni, "Registers," inmate 837, October 8, 1925, UNA.

35. Sibel Abiç, *Dövme/Dek* (Mardin: T.C Mardin Valiliği, 2011), 32; and Yenipınar and Tunç, *Güneydoğu anadolu geleneksel dövme sanatı beden yazıtları*, 186.

36. Jenny Jensen featured both tattooed Aghavni and Nouritza in her article "Billeder fra Optagelseshjemmet," *Armeniervennen* no. 1–2 (January–February 1926): 5.

37. Jenny Jensen. See "Billeder fra Optagelseshjemmet," 4–5. In the Danish publication, Aghavni's name is misspelled "Arofni Nersissian." Aghavni appeared again in the booklet of photographs by feminist activist and educator Henni Forchhammer (1863–1955), who may have photographed her during her visit to Aleppo in 1926. See Forchhammer, *Et Besøg hos Karen Jeppe*, 9.

38. Vartanoush Kherbetjian, "Registers," inmate 686, April 16, 1925, UNA.

39. "Aghabey" is clearly his Islamized name. Though he had a memory of who he was and was reunited with his mother, his Armenian name is not listed. Rescue Home registers typically list the child's Armenian name while sometimes penciling the Islamized name next to it. Aghabey, "Registers," inmate 687, April 16, 1925.

40. There are several cases of rescued women, men, and children who died soon after rescue. See "Registers," Takvor [Takavor], inmate 587, July 11, 1924.; and Elias, inmate 887, December 6, 1925, UNA.

41. Jinks, "Marks Hard to Erase," 121.

42. Jensen, "Midt i Arbejdet," 36. I have retained some of the original misspelling of Jeghsa's name which is actually pronounced "Yeghsa" in Armenian for the sake of consistency. I was unable to locate her original intake record in Karen Jeppe's registers. Jeghsa's story was published by Rebecca Jinks, "Marks Hard to Erase," 119–23.

43. "Branding by Tattooing: Newly-Received Evidence," *Slave Market News* 1, no. 27 (October 1930): 1.

44. Jensen, "Midt i Arbejdet," 36.

45. Jinks, "Marks Hard to Erase," 101.

46. Amid the newspaper clippings compiled by Naim Andonian during and after World War I, I did not find articles and images of tattooed women from the Armenian press. See Coupures, angl. Orphelins, Femmes Enlevies (Cuttings, English. Orphans, Abducted Women), no accession number, Nubarian Library.

47. Although thousands of tattoos were snapped on this journey with photojournalist Kathryn Cook, I thought it would have been inappropriate to photograph Zahaya's bare thighs because the family is devoutly Muslim and it was our first and only meeting with her. See Kathryn Cook *Memory of Trees* (Heidelberg: Kehrer Verlag, 2014). Interview with Zahaya al-As'ad, Shaddadi Village, April 8, 2008.

48. Savioli, "Le tribù beduine della Siria e l'arte del tatuaggio," 124, 157.

Remnant 9

1. An Armenian folk song sung in Turkish by Armenian Genocide survivor Vartan Shapazian in 1939, archived in Library of Congress Archive of Folk Culture, https://www.loc.gov/item/2017701563/. Shapazian's version of the song has been transcribed and translated by the author.

2. Alternative variations of the song were documented in Svazlian, *The Armenian Genocide*, 568; and Yeghissabet Kalashian's is on 575. They are included here as a gesture toward the different memories held by survivors, including variations on song lyrics by Armenian deportees.

Chapter 11

1. Balakian, *Armenian Golgotha*, 250. I have included the missing question mark.

2. Hamasdegh, "Kangi me hed" (With a skull), in *Hamasdegh*, ed. Minas Minassian (Boston: Hamasdegh Jubilee Committee, 1969), 97–100. I have chosen to retain the original title "With a Skull" to emphasize the duality of Hamasdegh's real-life skull and the skull he imagines in the essay. The essay is translated beautifully into English by Tatul Sonentz in Hamasdegh, "Journey with a Skull," *Armenian Weekly Magazine*, May 11, 2010, https://armenianweekly.com/2010/05/11/hamasdegh-journey-with-a-skull/. I would like to thank Khatchig Mouradian for bringing this important essay to my attention.

3. M. J. Thornbush, "Introduction to the Special Issue on Necrogeography and Physical Geography," *Progress in Physical Geography* 4, no. 5 (2018): 541.

4. Hamasdegh, "Journey with a Skull."

5. Thomas W. Laqueur, *The Work of the Dead: A Cultural History of Moral Remains* (Princeton, NJ: Princeton University Press: 2015). Armenians' pilgrimages to sites where their ancestors were ethnically cleansed is the subject of Bertram, *A House in the Homeland: Armenian Pilgrimages to Places of Ancestral Memory*. Bertram has shared the personal stories of Armenian pilgrims who return to their homelands in Western Armenia/Anatolia. Her term *memory-stories* is comparable to *prosthetic memory*, a term I have adopted in this study due to its focus on narrative, media, and embodiment.

6. The touching and kissing of objects in sacred ritual by priests were not enjoyed by average people, but spectators were able to view and pray in proximity to the objects in ceremony. During the genocide, objects were stabbed and mutilated as were human targets. See Watenpaugh, *The Missing Pages*, 66, 103, 148.

7. Achille Mbembe, "Necropolitics," *Public Culture* 15, no. 1 (Winter 2003): 35.

8. Agamben, *Remnants of Auschwitz*, 164.

9. I have conducted a total of seventeen oral interviews with visitors to Dayr al-Zur. More information on these sources can be found in the Personal and Recorded Interviews in the bibliography.

10. Dawn Chatty, *Displacement and Dispossession in the Modern Middle East* (New York: Cambridge University Press, 2010), 161–63.

11. Dolbee, "The Desert at the End of Empire," 204.

12. Balakian, "Bones," *New York Times Magazine*, December 5, 2008.

13. The notion of -scapes through which to think of global assemblages was introduced by Arjun Appadurai, "Disjuncture and Difference in the Global Cultural Economy," *Public Culture* 2, no. 2 (Spring 1990): 1–11, 15–24; and the genealogy and meaning of the concept of "deathscape" can be found in Avril Maddrell and James D. Sidaway, eds., *Deathscapes: Spaces of Death, Dying, Mourning, and Remembrance* (London: Routledge, 2010), 4–5.

14. Odian, *Accursed Years*, 133.

15. Balakian, *Armenian Golgotha*, 241. The original text was published as *Hay koghkotan: truakner hay mardirosakrutiunen: Berlinen tebi Zor, 1914–1920*, 2 vols. (Vienna: Mkhitarian daparan,1922). I will refer to the author as Grigoris *vardapet* (celibate priest) to distinguish him from his great nephew, who shares the same patronym.

16. Balakian, *Armenian Golgotha*, 250.

17. Jeppe, "Account of the Situation of the Armenians in Syria," 9.

18. Bedoukian, *The Urchin*, 24.

19. Bedoukian, *The Urchin*, 32.

20. Report of Leslie Davis, in *United States Official Documents on the Armenian Genocide*, 50.

21. Raymond Kévorkian, "Earth, Fire, Water: or How to Make the Armenian Corpses Disappear, Destruction and Human Remains: Disposal Concealment and Mass Violence," in *Destruction and Human Remains: Disposal Concealment and Mass Violence*, ed. Elisabeth Anstett and Jean-Marc Dreyfus (Manchester: University of Manchester Press, 2012), 94–95; and Dolbee, "The Desert at the End of Empire," 212.

22. Testimony of Garnik Stephanian in Svazlian, *The Armenian Genocide and the People's Historical Memory*, 57.

23. Balakian, *Armenian Golgotha*, 242.

24. I recognize that *pilgrim* is a fraught term for it has a religious meaning as well as a settler-colonial usage. One respondent rejected my use of the term, but upon closer study, the rituals visitors perform are either religious or stand in for absent religious ceremonies for the dead. Because these visits are not a return to the Armenian ancestral homeland and they are brief in duration, they cannot be called "returns" either. For these reasons, I have adopted the term *pilgrimage* to describe them.

25. Ruben Herian, letter to Mirak, April 15, 1919, 420.65.2 enclosure 16, ANA.

26. Ruben Herian, letter to Mirak, April 15, 1919.

27. Janig Yeranossian's interview occurred in 1988, approximately sixty years after the genocide. Yeranossian, AFF 328, Visual History Archive, April 9, 1988, USC Shoah Foundation Archive

28. Janig Yeranossian also mentions a mass grave discovered by the French while digging a road eleven kilometers north of Dayr al-Zur on the road to Hassaka. While I was unable to locate a photograph of the old Surp Hripsimae church, one was shared in an interview with former Aleppo Archbishop Souren Kataroyan, "Տէր Զօրի Ս Նահատակաց մատուռը պետք է վերականգնի" (The Martyrs Church of Dayr al-Zur should be repaired), Horizon Weekly TV, July 12, 2021, https://www.youtube.com/watch?v=tg_H4G3Oews.

29. Tovmas G. Arapian, *Houshamadyan Siveregi* (Beirut: Sevan Press, 1971) 330.

30. Arapian, *Houshamadyan Siveregi*, 330.

31. Interview with Ibrahim Khalil, Raqqa, Syria, November 21, 2007.

32. After the Armenian Genocide, the catholicosate in the Ottoman city of Sis had its land expropriated by the Turkish government. The catholicosate relocated to Antelias, Lebanon, just north of Beirut, in 1930, where it remains to this day. Armenian Catholicos Aram I initiated a lawsuit at the European Court of Human Rights in 2016 to reclaim the confiscated church lands inside Turkey, but the claim was rejected by the court in 2017.

33. "Hishadagaran," *Hask* 1 (January 1939): 12.

34. Zohrab and Vartkes tried to intervene with the Young Turks but instead learned of their true aim to destroy the Armenian community. Both parliamentarians were encouraged to flee the country, but Zohrab courageously said, "To whom do you want me to abandon this people, without leadership or chief? I do not want to leave; it is my duty to remain on the front lines to the very last." On the evening of April 24, both Zohrab and Varkes were arrested. After detention in Galatasaray police station, the two men were transferred by boat to the train station at Haydarpasha station. They were deported to Aleppo and then Urfa, where they were to be transported to Diyarbakir for court-martial. Instead of being safely transferred, they, along with Armenian Archbishop Ardavazt of Urfa, were murdered by Çerkez Ahmed, who along with his Circassian *çetes* waited for them as they left Urfa on the road to Diyarbakir. Kévorkian, *The Armenian Genocide*, 533–34. Grigoris Balakian adds that along with other tortures, the men had their beards plucked out. Balakian, *Armenian Golgotha*, 105.

35. Harutyun Hovakimyan, *Hishadagaran*, unpublished memoir, fond 450, list 2, no. 72, 148, ANA. His name is spelled in archival accession records with a *-yan*, though Western Armenians typically used the *-ian* transliteration for -եան. Because orthography and translation are sensitive issues for speakers of Eastern and Western Armenian, I have chosen to retain this spelling for the sake of consistent transliteration for present and future scholars. I authenticated this accession number with the index and requested the memoir in July, 2019, but I was not given access to the memoir by the Armenian National Archives. It was through archivist Mihran Minassian—an employee of the Matenadaran and the Armenian National Archives in Yerevan and the only person who has access to the text—that I was given access to eight pages of the memoir, for which I am thankful.

36. Hovakimyan lists the names of the places he crossed from the Jazira into Turkey as Demkhiyya near Qamishli, Syria. Still as porous as it is, Kurdish clans and tribes are deeply connected to each other on each side of the border. Hovakimyan, *Hishadagaran*.

37. Hovakimyan, *Hishadagaran*, 148.

38. "Hishadagaran," *Hask* 1 (January 1939): 12.

39. Hovakimyan, *Hishadagaran*, 149; and Shemmassian, "The League of Nations and the Reclamation of Armenian Genocide Survivors," 100. The author also uses the Armenian term աճիւն (*adjioun*) to describe the "remains" of the victims he seeks to retrieve, not the word for "bones." *Adjioun* can also mean "ashes," among other things; see Kouyoumdjian, *A Comprehensive Dictionary, Armenian-English* (Cairo: Sahag Mesrob Press, 1950), 14. For more information on Archbishop Hovhannes Garanfilian *vardapet*, see Grigor Galustian, *Marash gam kermanig yev heros Zeytun* (New York: Hradarakutiun Marashi Hayrenagtsagan Miyotyan Getr, 1934), 172–74.

40. A woman named "the widow of Krikor Agha" is described in Karen Jeppe's papers as a rescuer who, as part of her network, opened her home to Armenian refugees in Dayr al-Zur. Jeppe, *Annual Report* (1926), 2. A letter from Jeppe confirming Satenig was an employee is reproduced in Levon Mesrob, ed., *1915: Aghed yev veradznunt* (Paris: Araks, 1952), 216.

41. When Dayr al-Zur governor Ali Suat bey was unwilling to implement orders against Armenians, he was replaced with a more obedient official, Zeki bey. Aram Andonian estimated that Zeki bey was personally responsible for the "cleansing" of 195,750 Armenians from Dayr al-Zur during the second phase of the genocide. Kévorkian, "Earth, Fire, Water; or How to Make Armenian Corpses Disappear," 105. See also Hilmar Kaiser, "Armenian Property, Ottoman Law, and Nationality Policies during the Armenian Genocide, 1915–1916," in *The First World War Remembered in the Countries of the Eastern Mediterranean*, ed. Olaf Fairshild, Manfred Kropp, and Stephanie Dähne (Beirut: Orient-Institut, 2006), 53.

42. Hovakimyan, *Hishadagaran*, 149.

43. Hovakimyan, *Hishadagaran*, 147.

44. "Hishadagaran," *Hask* 1 (January 1939): 12.

45. The claim that some of the bones were used for the Armenian Genocide Memorial in Dayr al-Zur was made in documentation at the AGMI in Yerevan that accompanied the photograph. I did not, however, find this claim elsewhere.

46. The complete story of the memorial was offered in an interview with Archbishop Kataroyan, "Տէր Զօրի Ս Նահատակաց մատուռը պէտք է վերականգնի."

47. Kataroyan, "Տէր Զօրի Ս Նահատակաց մատուռը պէտք է վերականգնի."

48. It is common among Eastern Christians to take a vow and make an offering upon its fulfillment. Karekin II's choice to walk on his knees is arguably the most humble offering a man in his position could make.

49. Taquhi was her given Armenian name. The archbishop did not mention her Islamized name in the interview.

50. Importantly, Saint James was beheaded in Jerusalem by King Herod Agrippa in 44 CE, executed alongside other disciples. St. James's head is a relic inside the twelfth-century Armenian Surp Hagop Church in the Armenian Quarter, the church of the Armenian Patriarchate of Jerusalem. The bones of his body allegedly made their way to Spain after his execution, where they too became relics.

51. The chapel was dedicated on April 24, 1938. The architect is listed as Vahram Altunian. The chapel was later renovated in 1993 by Dikran Kalustian. "Hishadagaran," *Hask* 1 (January 1939): 12.

52. Kataroyan, "Տէր Զօրի Ս Նահատակաց մատուռը պէտք է վերականգնի."

Chapter 12

1. Interview with Suzanne Khardalian.

2. Balakian, "Photography, Visual Culture, and the Armenian Genocide."

3. Wegner's photography is archived at United States Holocaust Memorial Museum. See Photographs of the Armenian Genocide from the Armin T. Wegner Collection, 56 photographs, accession no. 1987.88.1, RG-10.278. Noteworthy are Wegner's photographs of hundreds of Armenian deportees and murdered victims in Dayr al-Zur. Eyewitnesses and survivors commented on the importance of photography in providing objective, scientific evidence of the Armenian massacres. Anouche Kunth, "Traces, Bones, Desert: The Extermination of the Armenians through the Photographer's Eye," *Human Remains and Violence* 1, no. 2 (2015): 72–73.

4. For non-sites of memory, see Roma Sendyka's study of abject sites with no markers or recognition by the state. Sendyka, "Sites That Haunt: Affects and Non-sites of Memory," *East European Politics and Societies* 3, no. 4 (November 2016): 688.

5. Grigoris *vardapet* uses this term to mark April 24 in his own memoir, see *Armenian Golgotha*, 58.

6. The controversial reimagining of space at Taksim and the adjacent Gezi Park has been the subject of controversy since the 2013 Gezi Park protests. Taksim Square did not exist at the time of the 1919 procession. It was created by first destroying the old Ottoman barracks that existed there in 1940 to make room for Henri Prost's design for an open plaza similar to those in Europe. Gezi Park is expropriated Armenian land that was once the Surp Hagop Armenian Cemetery. In 2021, the Taksim Mosque was finally finished and now overshadows the Holy Trinity Church. For the historical controversies surrounding these spaces, see Heghnar Watenpaugh, "Learning from Taksim Square: Architecture, State Power, and Public Space in Istanbul," *Society of Architectural Historians*, June 11, 2013.

7. For details about the various locations where the ceremony took place on April 24, 1919, and Armenian women and feminist associations involved in the organizing, see Lerna Ekmekçioğlu, "Kalanlar: Savaş sonrasında ve tek parti döneminde İstanbul Ermeni Cemaati," in *1915: Siyaset, Tehcir, Soykırım*, ed. Fikret Adanır and Oktay Özel (Istanbul: Tarih vakfı yayınları, 2015), 543.

8. The first commemoration event was supposed to be held on April 11, 1919, but due to the illness of the Armenian Patriarch Zaven Der Yeghiayan, a ceremony was held on April 12–25 and the liturgy delivered by an archbishop at Saint Trinity Greek Orthodox Church at Taksim Square, Istanbul. On April 24, 1919, the Armenian patriarch delivered a liturgy that included prayers for martyred American missionaries. See "At the Origins of Commemoration: The 90th Anniversary Declaring April 24 as a Day of Mourning and Commemoration of the Armenian Genocide," Armenian Genocide Museum-Institute Foundation, http://www.genocide-museum.am/eng/31.03.2009.php.

9. The Armenian National Committee of America spent decades working on public recognition of the Armenian Genocide by a sitting US president. This acknowledgment was delivered by President Joe Biden on April 24, 2021.

10. The quotation is from "Turkey and Armenia's Battle over History," *60 Minutes*, February 26, 2010. When Kim and Khloe Kardashian visited the Tsitsernakaberd memorial on a trip to Yerevan in 2015—the Armenian Genocide centennial—it brought not only formal memory practices but the Armenian Genocide into awareness for a generation of Americans that were unfamiliar with it. See "Mother Armenia," *Keeping Up With the Kardashians*, season 10, episode 14, September 20, 2015.

11. Pierre Nora, "Between Memory and History," 7. Pierre Nora distinguishes history of what he calls "real memory." He describes a "site of memory" (*lieu de mémoire*) as a space "where memory crystallizes and secretes itself . . . a turning point where consciousness of a break with the past is bound up with the sense that memory has been torn—but torn in such a way as to pose the problem of the embodiment of memory in certain sites where a sense of historical continuity persists. There are *lieux de mémoire*, sites of memory, because there are no longer *milieux de mémoire*, real environments of memory." See also Nora, *Les lieux de memoire*, 3 vols. (Paris: Editions Gallimard, 1997).

12. Yael Zerubavel, *Recovered Roots: Collective Memory and the Making of Israeli National Tradition* (Chicago: University of Chicago Press, 1995), 7–8.

13. Roma Sendyka writes of "the aura of places that have been stripped of their "placeness" (a quality described in German by the term *Heimlich*)—of their potential habitability—and of their memory." See Sendyka, "Sites that Haunt," 688. Only one respondent I inter-

viewed, Nouritza Matossian, stayed overnight in Dayr al-Zur, and that was on her second trip to the region. Nouritza Matossian, interview, What's App, March 26, 2017.

14. "Turkey and Armenia's Battle over History," *60 Minutes*.

15. Interview with Suzanne Khardalian.

16. Balakian, "Bones." After Balakian's 2005 visit to Syria and another in 2009, he updated his memoir to include a chapter on Dayr al-Zur. See Balakian, *Black Dog of Fate: A Memoir* (New York: Basic Books, 1997, 2009). British journalist Robert Fisk also did much to publicize this space with American and European audiences, impacting public consciousness. See Robert Fisk, "The First Holocaust," in *The Great War for Civilization: The Conquest of the Middle East* (New York: Vintage, 2005), ch. 10.

17. Peter Balakian's writing on the Armenian Genocide is quite extensive and listed in the bibliography.

18. "Turkey and Armenia's Battle over History," *60 Minutes*.

19. See Balakian, "Bones"; Balakian, *Black Dog*, ch. 7, "Syria 2005"; Balakian, *Ozone Journal* (Chicago: University of Chicago Press, 2015).

20. A formal memorial was placed in Ras al-'Ayn by the Armenian Apostolic Church of Aleppo in 2008. The monument is a simple traditional white carved block with a cross (*khatchkar*), but I have not been able to personally verify whether it survived the destruction of the Syrian War.

21. Nicola Migliorino, *(Re)constructing Armenia in Lebanon and Syria: Ethno-Cultural Diversity in the Aftermath of a Refugee Crisis* (New York: Berghahn Books, 2008), 195.

22. Kévorkian, "Earth, Fire, Water; or How to Make Armenian Corpses Disappear," 89–117.

23. The Armenian National Institute has created a website catalogue of all Armenian Genocide memorials. "Der Zor, Syria, Armenian Genocide Monument and Memorial Complex," ANI, http://www.armenian-genocide.org/Memorial.110/current_category.72/memorials_detail.html.

24. Balakian, "Bones."

25. Former Dayr al-Zur resident Janig Yeranossian claims in his oral testimony that the bones within the now destroyed Armenian Genocide Memorial in Dayr al-Zur came from the 1928 excavation performed by local Armenians. See Janig Yeranossian, AFF 328, April 9, 1988, Shoah Foundation Visual History Archive.

26. Interview with Rania Masri, March 27, 2017. Although Masri traveled to Dayr al-Zur with Armenians, she is not Armenian, yet her eloquent description captures well the affective quality of the now-destroyed memorial.

27. Karmen Mackendrick, *Fragmentation and Memory: Meditations on Christian Doctrine* (New York: Fordham University Press, 2008), 123.

28. Interview with Harout Ekmanian, Skype, July 3, 2020.

29. *Hay tad* is the concept that Armenians should work toward justice for what happened to their people in 1915. This concept means different things to different people. For some, it is doing the political work of genocide recognition; for others, it is preserving their language, culture, history, which for many also includes marrying an Armenian and birthing the next generation.

30. This trip happened in 2000. Interview with Sosy Mishoyan-Dabbaghian, Skype, June 25, 2020.

31. Interview with Sosy Mishoyan-Dabbaghian.

32. See "Margadeh, Syria, Armenian Genocide Memorial at the Armenian Apostolic Church," ANI, http://www.armenian-genocide.org/Memorial.111/current_category.72/memorials_detail.html; and Kévorkian, "Earth, Fire, Water; or How to Make Armenian Corpses Disappear," 107.

33. Samuel Dolbee has examined closely the way that the Ottomans viewed the "desert province" (*çöl vilâyeti*). See Dolbee, "The Locust and the Starling," 9.

34. Balakian, "Bones."

35. Balakian, "Bones."

36. See Kévorkian, "Earth, Fire, Water; or How to Make Armenian Corpses Disappear," 105.

37. Kévorkian, *The Armenian Genocide*, 667.

38. Takvim-i Vakayi, no. 3540, May 5, 1919 cited in Raymond Kévorkian, "Earth, Fire, Water," 107.

39. I have previously published this account, created from my own ethnographic notes, in the Armenian press. See Elyse Semerdjian, "A Quiet Place along the Khabour: Rescue and Survival in 'the Abattoir of Shaddadeh,'" *Armenian Weekly Magazine*, May 28, 2010, https://armenianweekly.com/2010/05/28/a-quiet-place-along-the-khabour/

40. Dikran Berberian, "Le Massacre de Deir-Zor," in A. Andonian, *Matériaux pour l'histoire du genocide*, 12–15. The English is my translation, while the original French text is posted online: https://www.imprescriptible.fr/rhac/tome2/p2t51.

41. Interview with Sa'ad Hamad al-As'ad. Kévorkian offers a different version, which includes that some of the girls were killed on a mound, likely Tall Shaddadi. Kévorkian, *The Armenian Genocide*, 665.

42. Kévorkian, *The Armenian Genocide*, 667.

43. Choushan Melidonian, "Registers," inmate 1353, June 18, 1927, UNA.

44. Everyone I interviewed who traveled to Shaddadi relied on the memory of local residents to guide them to the unmarked caves.

45. Interview with Sona Tatoyan, Skype, September 21, 2020.

Chapter 13

1. Hovann Simonian, email communication, September 11, 2021. Simonian has been involved in the Armenian DNA project. See https://www.familytreedna.com/groups/armeniadnaproject/about/background.

2. With a team including a geneticist and a forensic anthropologist, Armenian Genocide scholar Raymond Kévorkian began an excavation of Ras al-'Ayn, another important mass killing site in Syria, before the war in 2009. After four days of field work, the excavation was suddenly halted by the Ministry of Land and Culture, though permission had been previously granted. The findings were never published due to a confidentiality agreement. Raymond Kévorkian, email communication, September 27, 2019.

3. Derrida, *Archive Fever*.

4. See Eyal Weizman, *Forensic Architecture: Violence at the Threshold of Detectability* (New York: Zone Books, 2017).

5. Roma Sendyka's reading of Massumi vis-à-vis "non-sites of memory" is incredibly useful. See Sendyka, "Sites that Haunt," 699–700.

6. I have borrowed the phrase "knowing in the bones" (*kimo ni meijite shiru*), which is attributed to Japanese critic Kobayashi Hideo. See Yukiko Shigeto, "Smashing the Great Buddha," 10–11.

7. Asef Bayat, *Life as Politics: How Ordinary People Change the Middle East* (Palo Alto: Stanford University Press, 2009), 51.

8. Fred Lawson, "The Beginning of a Beautiful Friendship: Syrian-Turkish Relations since 1998," in *Demystifying Syria*, Fred Lawson, ed. (London: Saqi Books, 2012), 111.

9. I am refraining from listing the titles of banned books in order to protect the authors. Mentioning this phenomenon and a banned book on a scholarly listserv a decade ago immediately caused the Syrian secret police to visit the home of the author. The change in character of the genocide commemoration activities is based on my personal participation on April 24 in 1999, 2000, 2001, and 2008.

10. Israel conducted a military operation called Outside the Box on September 6, 2007, which targeted an alleged nuclear reactor in the desert not far from Dayr al-Zur. Isabel Kershner, "Ending Secrecy, Israel Says It Bombed A Syrian Reactor in 2007," *New York Times*, March 21, 2018, https://www.nytimes.com/2018/03/21/world/middleeast/israel-syria-nuclear-reactor.html.

11. Maurice Halbwachs, *The Collective Memory*, trans. Francis J. Ditter and Vida Yazdi Ditter (New York: Harper Colophon Books, 1980), 139.

12. Many of the people I have interviewed have strong tribal affiliations with relatives spanning Syria, Iraq, and Turkey. Inside some homes, I have seen portraits of Saddam Hussein, long after his execution, indicating overlapping loyalties. The argument that the state has not been able to overcome these tribal affinities in eastern Syria has been expressed in Dawn Chatty, "The Bedouin in Contemporary Syria: The Persistence of Tribal Authority and Control," *Middle East Journal* 64, no. 1 (Winter 2010): 29–49.

13. "Turkey and Armenia's Battle over History."

14. Balakian, "Bones."

15. Interview with Khatchig Mouradian, Skype, March 24, 2017.

16. Interview with Rania Masri, March 27, 2017.

17. Interview with Rania Masri.

18. The two seats of Armenian Orthodox Christianity are the catholicos of Sis now seated in Antelias, Lebanon, and the Mother See at Etchmiadzin in Vagharshapat, Armenia.

19. Dickran Kouyumjian, "The Right Hand of St. Gregory and Other Armenian Arm Relics," in *Les Objets de la mémoire: Pour une approche comparatiste des reliques et de leur culte*, ed. Philippe Borgeaud and Youri Volokhine (Geneva: Peter Lang, 2005), 215–40. In addition to the Illuminator's hand, which confers authority upon each catholicos, Kouyumjian notes that he found about thirty different hand relics in the Armenian tradition.

20. MacKendrick, *Fragmentation and Memory*, 117.

21. Jean-Luc Nancy, *Birth to Presence* (Stanford, CA: Stanford University Press, 1993), 143, quoted in MacKendrick, *Fragmentation and Memory*, 119.

22. MacKendrick, *Fragmentation and Memory*, 123, 128.

23. Interview with Nouritza Matossian, March 26, 2017.

24. Peter Balakian, *Black Dog of Fate*, 335.

25. I was unable to determine whether the location of the current suspension bridge is the same as the bridge referred to in the memories of survivors. "*al-Jusr al-m'alaq fi dayr al-zur bina fransiyyun wa damra nizam al-asad*," Dayr al-Zur24, n.d., https://deirezzor24.net/.

26. Kévorkian claims that of the eighteen thousand, only one group survived the assault on the Zor Bridge on July 15, 1916. Kévorkian, *The Armenian Genocide*, 666.

27. Interview with Suzanne Khardalian.
28. See Sigmund Freud on *unheimlich* in "The Uncanny," trans. Alix Strachey, *Imago*, Bd. V. (1919), reprinted in *Sammlung*, Fünfte Folge, 1, http://web.mit.edu/allanmc/www/freud1.pdf, 1–2.
29. Nora Perseghian, "Ypradyan meghetiner," *Aztag*, April 24, 2010; and "Dzaghignere ichan hadz... Louysabasag anonts hishadagin," *Aztag*, October 7, 2010.
30. Perseghian "Ypradyan meghetiner."
31. Svazlian, *The Armenian Genocide and the People's Historical Memory*, 70.
32. In Turkish: "Giden, giden Ermeni kızlar! Bir gün ölüm bize düşer, düşmana avrat olmamaya, Yeprat'in icinde ölüm bulayım." Svazlian, *The Armenian Genocide and the People's Historical Memory*, 68.
33. In Turkish: "Yeprat getin suları acıdır, bir tas içilmez! Ermeni kanıyla su da içilmez." Svazlian, *The Armenian Genocide and the People's Historical Memory*, 70.
34. Perseghian, "Ypradyan meghetiner."
35. In her essay "Ypradyan meghetiner," Perseghian captures this notion when she writes: "Dayr al-Zur is not a desert, but rather the history of Armenians and the witness of the most horrible act of genocide against humanity."
36. Perseghian, "Dzaghignere ichan hadz."
37. Perseghian, "Dzaghignere ichan hadz."
38. Micheline Aharonian Marcom, *Draining the Sea* (New York: Riverhead Books, 2008), 58.
39. Many epigenetic studies have centered on the descendants of Holocaust survivors. Some of these scientific studies are synthesized in Resmaa Menakem's examination of trauma and racial violence, *My Grandmother's Hands: Racialized Trauma and the Pathway to Mending our Hearts and Bodies* (Las Vegas: Central Recovery Press, 2017).
40. Suzanne recalled that Syrian authorities may have been building a barracks when the bones were discovered during the groundbreaking. Interview with Suzanne Khardalian.
41. Interview with Suzanne Khardalian.
42. Interview with Suzanne Khardalian.
43. Interview with Micheline Aharonian Marcom.
44. Micheline Aharonian Marcom, *Three Apples Fell from Heaven*.
45. Micheline Aharonian Marcom, *Draining the Sea* (New York: Riverhead Books, 2008), 59.
46. Interview with Micheline Aharonian Marcom.
47. Interview with Sona Tatoyan.
48. Interview with Sona Tatoyan.
49. Interview with Sona Tatoyan.
50. Interview with Micheline Aharonian Marcom.
51. LaCapra, *Writing History, Writing Trauma*, 22.
52. I have written about this event and those experienced by others at Lake Gölcük. Semerdjian, "Phantom Limbs, Embodied Horror, and the Afterlives of the Armenian Genocide."
53. LaCapra, *Writing History, Writing Trauma*, 22.
54. I have written an essay about experiences of the uncanny and Sona's haptic loss; see Semerdjian, "Phantom Limbs, Embodied Horror, and the Afterlives of the Armenian Genocide."
55. The experiences of both Suzanne Khardalian and Sosy Mishoyan-Dabbaghian re-

flect well how non-sites of memory, where unmarked territory blends bones and land together as one, can produce hauntings similar to those studied in Poland by Sendyka, "Sites That Haunt," 694–97.

56. Interview with Sosy Mishoyan-Dabbaghian.

57. Sosy Mishoyan-Dabbaghian's grandparents visited Dayr al-Zur once when they took a diasporan Armenian there to witness the place, though they had not been personally deported there during the genocide. Interview with Sosy Mishoyan-Dabbaghian.

58. Interview with Nouritza Matossian.

59. Nouritza Matossian is an accomplished actress and author of *Black Angel: The Life of Arshile Gorky* (New York: Overlook Press, 2002).

60. Interview with Micheline Aharonian Marcom.

61. Interview with Sona Tatoyan; and "Turkey: Life Sentence for Human Rights Defender" Human Rights Watch, April 26, 2022, https://www.hrw.org/news/2022/04/26/turkey-life-sentence-rights-defender-osman-kavala.

62. Interview with Kevork Moutafian, July 13, 2020, Skype.

63. Thomas Laqueur, *The Work of the Dead*, 336.

64. Diana Markosian (photographs) and Jenna Krajeski (text). "One Photographer's Personal Endeavor to Track Down Survivors of the Armenian Genocide, 100 Years Later," *Smithsonian Magazine*, July 2015.

65. Diana Markosian, email communication April 9, 2017.

66. Email communication with Antoine Agoudjian, August 21, 2022.

67. Interview with Antoine Agoudjian, What's App, January 13, 2020.

68. David Eng and David Kazanjian, eds. *Loss: The Politics of Mourning* (Berkeley: University of California, 2002), 6.

69. MacKendrick, *Fragmentation and Memory*, 123, 128.

Epilogue

1. Balakian, "Bones."

2. Hallam, "Articulating Bones," 470.

3. Interview with Peter Balakian, May 26, 2017.

4. "The Proust effect" is referred to in the poem with the image of madeleine crumbs floating in lime blossom tea, which activates memory through scent and taste. Balakian, *Ozone Journal*, 40.

5. Roy Scranton, *Learning to Die in the Anthropocene: Reflections on the End of a Civilization* (San Francisco: City Lights, 2015)

6. Balakian, *Ozone Journal*, 38.

7. Roland Barthes uses the term "prick" frequently to describe details he analyzes. See Barthes, *Camera Lucida*, 116.

8. Robert Fisk, "The 1915 Armenian Genocide: Finding a Fit Testament to a Timeless Crime," *Independent*, April 6, 2014, https://www.independent.co.uk/news/world/europe/the-1915-armenian-genocide-finding-a-fit-testament-to-a-timeless-crime-9241154.html.

9. Seven-year-old survivor Mubarak was adopted by a woman in Shaddadi who kicked him out when she was no longer able to feed him during a famine. He was able to find another tribe to take him in and eventually spent the rest of his life with them. He could not recall his original Armenian name but remembered his survival at the cave vividly. Mubarak, interview AFF 349, Shoah Foundation Visual History Archive, June 1, 1988.

10. Balakian, *Ozone Journal*, 35.

11. Scranton, *Learning to Die*.

12. "ISIL's 'Legacy of Terror' in Iraq: UN Verifies over 200 Mass Graves," *UN News*, November 6, 2018. The Sh'aytat originally had an agreement with ISIS to not resist its rule, but that changed when the group abducted three Sh'aytat tribesmen. The tribe used social media to submit manifestos and a call to rise up against ISIS forces. As tribal leaders in the Dayr al-Zur region were forced into submission, ISIS made video recordings of tribal leaders swearing allegiance to the caliphate to circulate in an attempt to pacify the population. Karen Leigh, "As ISIS Advances in Eastern Syria, Local Tribes Stand in Its Way," *New Humanitarian*, August 1, 2014, https://deeply.thenewhumanitarian.org/syria/articles/2014/07/31/as-isis-advances-assessing-the-state-of-the-syrian-army.

13. For a bit of news coverage of the killing of seven hundred Sh'aytat tribesmen and more, see "Da'ash yu'adam arba'ah min 'ashirat al-sh'aytat al-suriyya," *al-Hayat*, October 27, 2014, http://www.alhayat.com/m/story/5312739; Paul Antonopoulos and Drew Cottle, "From the Arabian Peninsula to the Levant: Arab Tribes and the Syrian War," *Global Journal of Archaeology and Anthropology* July 5, no. 2 (July 2018), 1–5.

14. Interview with Peter Balakian.

15. Weld, *Paper Cadavers*, 2–3; and Ann Stoler, *Duress: Imperial Durabilities in Our Times* (Durham, NC: Duke University Press, 2016), 128.

16. "Being dead" is also a state of being.

17. Talin Suciyan, *The Armenians in Modern Turkey: Post-Genocide Politics and History* (London: I. B. Tauris, 2017), 22–25.

18. Nora Tataryan Aslan, "Facing the Past," 359–60.

19. Eve Tuck and K. Wayne Yang, "Decolonization Is Not a Metaphor," 10–11.

BIBLIOGRAPHY

Archives
Archives of the Rockefeller Foundation
  Archives of Near East Relief Foundation
Armenian Genocide Museum Institute (AGMI), Yerevan, Armenia
Armenian National Archives (ANA), Yerevan, Armenia
Başbakanlik Osmanli Arşivi (Prime Minister's Ottoman Archives) (BOA) Istanbul, Turkey
  Dâhiliye Nezâreti, Sifre Evrakı (DH.ŞFR)
  Dâhiliye Kalem-i Mahsus Müdüriyeti (DH.KMS)
  İdare-i Umumiye Evrakı (DH.İ.UM)
British National Archives (BNA), Kew, England
  British Foreign Office Records
  Home Office: Registered Papers
Burke Library, Columbia University, New York
  American Board of Commissioners for Foreign Missions Collection
Danish National Archives (Rigsarkivet) (DNA), Copenhagen, Denmark
  De Danske Armeniervenner (DDA)
Houghton Library, Harvard University, Cambridge, Mass.
  American Board of Commissioners for Foreign Missions Collection
Karen Jeppe Gylling Arkiv, Gylling Denmark
Matenadaran (Masrob Mashtots Institute for Ancient Manuscripts), Yerevan, Armenia
  Armenian Newspaper Collections
Mudd Library, Princeton University, Princeton, NJ
National Archives of Norway, Oslo, Norway
National Archives and Records Administration (NARA), College Park, Md. Foreign Affairs Records, Department of State
Nubarian Library (La Bibliothèque Nubarian) (BNu), Paris, France
  Correspondence for February and March 1919
  Coupures, angl. Orphelins, Femmes Enlevies
Rockefeller Archive Center, Sleepy Hollow, NY (RAC)
  Near East Relief Foundation Records
Royal Library Denmark (Det Kongelige Bibliotek), Copenhagen, Denmark
  Armeniervennen newsletter collection

Smith College Special Collections, Smith College
  Sophia Smith Collection
United Nations Archives (UNA), Geneva, Switzerland
  League of Nations Archives
  "Registers of Inmates, the Armenian Orphanage in Aleppo," 1922–1930, Records of the Nansen International Refugee Office, 1920-1947.
University of Southern California Shoah Foundation, Los Angeles, California
  Shoah Foundation Visual History Archive
Zoryan Institute, Toronto, Canada
  Armenian Genocide Oral History Collection

Human Archives
Personal Interviews
Antoine Agoudjian, What's App, January 13, 2020.
Micheline Aharonian Marcom, Zoom, June 22, 2022.
Sa'ad Hamad al-As'ad, Shaddadi, Syria, November 23, 2007.
Zahaya al-As'ad, Shaddadi village, Syria, April 8, 2008.
Peter Balakian, Hamilton, NY, May 26, 2017.
David Barsamian, Skype, April 4, 2019.
Harout Ekmanian, Skype, June 29, 2020.
Ibrahim Khalil, Raqqa, Syria, November 21, 2007.
Suzanne Khardalian, Skype, October 3, 2019.
Rania Masri, Skype, March 27, 2017.
Nouritza Matossian, What's App, March 26, 2017.
Sosy Mishoyan-Dabbaghian, Skype, June 25, 2020.
Khatchig Mouradian, Skype, March 23, 2017.
Kevork Moutafian, Skype, July 13, 2020.
Nora Parseghian, Skype, March 29, 2019.
Sona Tatoyan, Skype, September 21, 2020.
Amberin Zaman, Skype, March 21, 2017.

Recorded Interviews
Almas Boghosian (b. 1907), extended interview filmed by Bared Maronian, February 11, 2011, shared by Maronian and Armenoid Productions, Inc.
Almas Boghosian (b. 1907), March 12, 2011, Shoah Foundation Visual History Archive.
Roupen Gavour Gavourian (b. 1907), no date, no interviewer information, video, Armenian Genocide Oral History Collection, Zoryan Institute, Toronto, Canada.
Aghavni (Kabakian) Gulesserian, November 21, 1986, and November 22, 1986, Fresno, California, Armenian Genocide Oral History Collection, Zoryan Institute, Toronto, Canada.
Archbishop Souren Kataroyan, "Տէր Զօրի Ս Նահատակաց մատուռը պէտք է վերականգնի" (Der zori surp nahadagats madure bedk e veragankni), Horizon Weekly TV, July 12, 2021, https://www.youtube.com/watch?v=tg_H4G3Oews.
Aurora Mardiganian, March 3, 1975, in New York, and March 29, 1984, in Los Angeles, California, AFF 53418 , Shoah Foundation Visual History Archive.
Mubarak, June 1, 1988, AFF 349, Shoah Foundation Visual History Archive.
Janig Yeranossian, April 9, 1988, AFF 328, Shoah Foundation Visual History Archive.

Published Material
Primary Sources

Adıvar, Halidé Edib. *The Turkish Ordeal: Being the Further Memoirs of Halidé Edib*. London: Century, 1928.

Akar, Dicle, Matthias Bjørnlund, and Taner Akçam. *Soykırımdan kurtulanlar: Halep kurtarma Evi Yetimleri*. İstanbul: Iletişim Yayınları, 2019.

Apelian, Kevork. *Shahada mada al-hayat, min aram ila . . . aram/ Tsgyans nahadagutiun (aramen minchev. . . . aram)*.Translated by Nora Arissian. 'Anjar: Sava, 2006.

Arissian, Nora. *Asda' al-abadat al-armaniyya fi al-sahafa al-suriyya (1877–1930)*. Beirut: Dar al-thaikra, 2004.

Azkayin khnamadarutiun (Armenian National Relief Organization of Constantinople), *Azkayin khnamadarutiun: enthanur deghegakir arachin vetsamsyah*, vol. 1, 1 May 1919– 31, October 1919. Constantinople: M. Hovagimian, 1920.

Bahri, Zahrui. *Giankis Vebe*. Beirut: n.pub., 1995.

Balakian, Grigoris. *Armenian Golgotha*. Translated by Peter Balakian, with Aris Sevag. New York: Vintage, 2009. Original: *Hay koghkotan: truakner hay mardirosakrutiunen: Berlinen tebi Zor, 1914–1920*, 2 vols. Vienna: Mkhitarian daparan, 1922.

Balakian, Peter. *Black Dog of Fate: A Memoir*. New York: Basic Books, 1997, 2009.

———. "Bones." *New York Times Magazine*, December 5, 2008.

———. *The Burning Tigris: The Armenian Genocide and America's Response*. New York: Harper Perennial, 2003.

———. *Ozone Journal*. Chicago: University of Chicago Press, 2015.

Bedoukian, Kerop. *The Urchin: An Armenian's Escape*. London: John Murray Publishers, 1978.

Captanian, Pailadzo. *Mémoires d'une déportée arménienne*. Edited by M. Flinikowski. Paris, 1919.

Çetin, Fethiye. *Anneannem*. Istanbul: Metis Yayınları, 2004.

Dadrian, Vahram. *To the Desert: Pages from My Diary*. Edited by Ara Sarafian. Translated by Agop Hachikyan. London: Taderon Press, 2006.

Damadian, Mihran. *Im Husheres*. Beirut: Zartonk, 1985.

Demoyan, Haik. *Hayots tseghaspanutyan lusabanume hamashkharhayin mamuli arajin ejerin / Armenian Genocide: Front Page Coverage in the World Press*. Yerevan: AGMI, 2016.

Derdarian, Mae M., and Virginia Meghrouni. *Vergeen: A Survivor of the Armenian Genocide*. Los Angeles: Atmus Press Publications, 1997.

Der Yeghiayan, Zaven. *Armenian Patriarch of Constantinople 1913–1922: My Patriarchal Memoirs*. Translated by Ared Misirliyan. Monterey, CA: Mayreni Publishing, 2002.

Edib, Halide. *Memoirs of Halidé Edib*. London: John Murray, 1926.

Elliott, Mabel Evelyn. *Beginning Again at Ararat*. New York; Chicago: Fleming H. Revell Company, 1924.

Essayan, Zabel. "La Libération des femmes et des enfants non-musulmans en Turquie," Armenian National Delegation Archives, 1–5, Correspondence for February and March, 1919, 1–11.

Forchhammer, Henni. *Et Besøg hos Karen Jeppe: Skildring Fra Ed Resje Til Syrien Af Henni Forchhammer*. Copenhagen: De Danske Armeniervenner, 1926.

Ghazzi, Kamil al-. *Nahr al-dhahab fi tarikh halab* (History of Aleppo), 3 vols. Aleppo, 1922–1926.

Haygaz, Aram. *Bantog*. Beirut: Mshag, 1967.
Herian, Ruben. "Hay aghchikner arabneru dunerun mech." *Gochnak hayastani* 19, no. 35 (August 30, 1919): 1122–23.
Hovakimyan, Harutyun, *Hishadagaran*. Unpublished memoirs, fond 450, list 2, no. 72, ANA.
Jeppe, Karen. "Account of the Situation of the Armenians in Syria and of My Own Work amongst Them from the 1st of May til the 1st of September 1922," 15, 10158, De Danske Armenivenner 1919–1949, DNA.
———. *Misak: An Armenian Life*. Translated and edited by Jonas Kauffeldt. London: Gomidas, 2015.
Kabakian, Aghavni. "The Voice of the Blood." *Armenian Review* 14 (1961): part 1, 42–56, part 2, 65–72.
Kaloosdian, Robert Aram. *Tadem: My Father's Village Extinguished during the 1915 Armenian Genocide*. Portsmouth, NH: Peter E. Randall Publisher, 2015.
Kalemkerian, Zaruhi. "Badmutiun me tornigis hamar, yerp vor medznas." In *Giankis Jampen*. Antelias, Lebanon: Dbaran Gatoghigosutian Giligio, 1952.
Kerr, Stanley. *The Lions of Marash: Personal Experiences with American Near East Relief, 1919–1922*. Albany: SUNY Press, 1973.
Khardalian, Suzanne, dir. *Grandma's Tattoos*. Sweden: Deckert, 2011.
Kherdian, David. *The Road from Home: The Story of an Armenian Girl*. New York: Green Willow Books, 1979.
Kouyoumdjian, Mesrob G. *A Comprehensive Dictionary, Armenian-English*. Cairo: Sahag Mesrob Press, 1950.
Mardiganian, Aurora. *Ravished Armenia: The Story of Aurora Mardiganian*. New York: Kingfield Press, 1919.
Mesrob, Levon, ed. *1915: Aghed yev veradznunt*. Paris: Araks, 1952.
Mesrob, Sahag. "Yegherni hushartsan, anonts anune." *Aravod-in Darekirke*. Constantinople: Artsakank, 1921, 83–86.
Morgenthau, Henry. *Ambassador Morgenthau's Story*. New York: Doubleday, 1918.
Oatman, Lorenzo D., and Olive A. Oatman. *Life among the Indians, or The Captivity of the Oatman Girls among the Apache and Mohave Indians*. San Francisco: Grabhorn Press, 1935.
Odian, Yervant. *Accursed Years: My Exile and Return from Der Zor, 1914–1919*. Translated by Ara Stepan Melkonian. London: Gomidas Institute, 2009.
Panian, Karnig. *Goodbye, Antoura: A Memoir of the Armenian Genocide*. Stanford, CA: Stanford University Press, 2015.
Richards, George Lyman, ed. *The Medical Work of the Near East Relief; A Review of Its Accomplishments in Asia Minor and the Caucasus during 1919–1920*. New York: Near East Relief, 1923.
Riggs, Henry H. *Days of Tragedy in Armenia: Personal Experiences in Harpoot, 1915–1917*. London: Gomidas Institute, 1997.
Sahakian, Aram. "The Twenty-Five Days of Ourfa." *Armenian Review* 26, no. 2 (1973): 3–45.
Sarafian, Ara, ed. *United States Official Documents on the Armenian Genocide*. Vol. 3, *The Central Lands*. Watertown, MA: Armenian Review, 1995.
Svazlian, Verjine. *The Armenian Genocide and the People's Historical Memory*. Yerevan: Gitutiun, 2005.

———. *The Armenian Genocide: Testimonies of the Eyewitness Survivors.* Yerevan: Gitutiun, 2011.
Tavoukdjian, Serpouhi. *Exiled: Story of an Armenian Girl.* Washington, DC: Review and Herald Publishing Association, 1933.
Toynbee, Arnold. *The Treatment of the Armenians in the Ottoman Empire.* 2nd ed. Beirut: G. Doniguian & Sons, 1979.
Virabyan, Amatuni, ed. *Armenian Genocide by Ottoman Turkey: Testimony of Survivors.* Yerevan: Zangak, 2013.
Yotnakhparian, Levon. *Crows of the Desert: The Memoirs of Levon Yotnakhparian.* Translated by Victoria Parian. Tujunga, CA: Parian Photographic Design, 2012.

Secondary Sources
Abu-Lughod, Lila. *Do Muslim Women Need Saving?* Cambridge, MA: Harvard University Press, 2015.
Açıksöz, Salih Can. *Sacrificial Limbs: Masculinity, Disability, and Political Violence in Turkey.* Berkeley: University of California Press, 2019.
Adjemian, Boris, and Talin Suciyan. "Making Space and Community through Memory: Orphans and Armenian Jerusalem in the Nubar Library's Photographic Archive." *Études arméniennes contemporaines* 9 (2017): 75–113.
Agamben, Giorgio. *Homo Sacer: Sovereign Power and Bare Life.* Stanford, CA: Stanford University Press, 1998.
———. *Remnants of Auschwitz: The Witness and the Archive.* Translated by Daniel Heller-Roazen. New York: Zone Books, 2000.
Ahmed, Sara. *The Cultural Politics of Emotion.* Edinburgh: University of Edinburgh Press, 2014.
Akçam, Taner. *Ermenilerin zorla müslümanlaştırılması: Sessizlik, inkâr ve asimilasyon.* Istanbul: Iletisim, 2014.
———. *Killing Orders: Talaat Pasha's Telegrams and the Armenian Genocide.* London: Palgrave Macmillian, 2018.
———. *A Shameful Act: The Armenian Genocide and the Question of Turkish Responsibility.* Translated by Paul Bessemer. New York: Metropolitan Books, 2006.
———. *The Young Turks' Crime against Humanity: The Armenian Genocide and Ethnic Cleansing in the Ottoman Empire.* Princeton, NJ: Princeton University Press, 2013.
Aleksanyan, Anna. "Between Love, Pain, and Identity: Armenian Women after WWI." In *Women's Everyday Lives in War and Peace in the South Caucasus*, edited by Ulrike Ziemer, 103–27. London: Palgrave Macmillan, 2019.
———."Rescuing Armenian Women and Children after the Genocide: The Story of Ruben Heryan." *Armenian Weekly*, May 31, 2016.
Angel, Gemma. "Atavistic Marks and Risky Practices: The Tattoo in Medico-Legal Debates, 1850–1950." In *A Medical History of Skin: Scratching the Surface*, edited by Jonathan Reinarz and Kevin Siena, 165–80. London: Pickering and Chatto, 2013.
———. "The Modified Body: The Nineteenth-Century Tattoo as Fugitive Stigmata." *Victorian Review* 42, no. 1 (2016): 14–20.
Atnur, Ibrahim. *Türkiye'de ermeni kadınları ve çocukları meselesi, 1915–1923.* Ankara: Babil, 2005.
Attarian, Hourig. "Lifelines: Matrilineal Narratives, Memory, and Identity." Ph.D. dissertation, McGill University, 2009.

———. "Narrating Women's Bodies: Storying Silences and Secrets in the Aftermath of Genocide." In *Gendered Wars, Gendered Memories: Feminist Conversations on War, Genocide and Political Violence*, edited by Ayşe Gül Altinay and Andrea Pető, 257–68. London: Routledge, 2016.

Avakyan, Shushan. "Becoming Aurora: Translating the Story of Arshaluys Mardiganian." *Dissidences: Hispanic Journal of Theory and Criticism* 4, no. 8 (November 2012): article 13.

Baer, Marc David. *Honored by the Glory of Islam: Conversion and Conquest in Ottoman Europe*. Oxford: Oxford University Press, 2008.

———. *The Ottomans: Khans, Caesars, and Caliphs*. London: Basic Books, 2021.

———. *Sultanic Saviors and Tolerant Turks: Writing Ottoman Jewish History, Denying the Armenian Genocide*. Bloomington: Indiana University Press, 2020.

Balakian, Peter. *Burning the Tigris: The Armenian Genocide and America's Response*. New York: Harper Perennial, 2004.

———. *Ozone Journal*. Chicago: University of Chicago Press, 2015.

———. "Photography, Visual Culture, and the Armenian Genocide." In *Humanitarian Photography*, edited by Heide Fehrenbach and Davide Rodogno, 89–114. New York: Cambridge University Press, 2015.

———. "Raphael Lemkin, Cultural Destruction, and the Armenian Genocide." *Holocaust and Genocide Studies* 27, no. 1 (April 2013): 56–89.

Baronian, Marie-Aude and Erica Biolchini. "Performance, Memory, and the Archive: A Conversation with Arsinée Khanjian." *Journal of the Society for Armenian Studies* 28 (2021): 1–25.

Barthes, Roland. *Camera Lucida: Reflections on Photography*. New York: Hill & Wang, 1980.

Belli, Mériam. *An Incurable Past: Nasser's Egypt Then and Now*. Gainesville: University of Florida Press, 2013.

Bennet, Jane. *Vibrant Matter: A Political Ecology of Things*. Durham, NC: Duke University Press, 2010.

Bertram, Carel. *A House in the Homeland: Armenian Pilgrimages to Places of Ancestral Memory*. Stanford, CA: Stanford University Press, 2022.

Beukian, Sevan. "Motherhood as Armenianness: Expressions of Femininity in the Making of Armenian National Identity." *Studies in Ethnicity and Nationalism* 14, no. 2 (2014): 247–69.

Bjørnlund, Matthias. "A Fate Worse Than Dying: Sexual Violence during the Armenian Genocide." In *Brutality and Desire: War and Sexuality in Europe's Twentieth Century*, edited by Dagmar Herzog, 16–42. New York: Palgrave Macmillan, 2009.

———. "Karen Jeppe, Aage Meyer Bendictsen, and the Ottoman Armenians." *Haigazian Armenological Review* 28 (2008): 9–43.

———. *På herrens mark: Nødhjælp, mission og kvindekamp under det armenske folkedrab*. Copenhagen: Kristeligt Dagblads Forlag, 2015.

Bsheer, Rosie. *Archive Wars: The Politics of History in Saudi Arabia*. Stanford, CA: Stanford University Press, 2020.

Burton, Antoinette. "Introduction: Archive Fever, Archive Stories." In *Archive Stories: Facts, Fictions, and the Writing of History*, edited by Antoinette Burton, 1–24. Durham, NC: Duke University Press, 2005.

Butler, Judith. *Excitable Speech: A Politics of the Performative*. London: Routledge, 1997.

Cankara, Murat. "Armeno-Turkish Writing and the Question of Hybridity." In *An Armenian Mediterranean: Words and Worlds in Motion*, edited by Kathryn Babayan and Michael Pifer, 173–92. New York: Palgrave Macmillian, 2018.
Canning, Kathleen. "The Body as Method? Reflections on the Place of the Body in Gender History." *Gender & History* 11, no. 3 (November 1999): 499–513.
———. *Gender History in Practice: Historical Perspectives on Bodies, Class, and Citizenship.* Ithaca, NY: Cornell University Press, 2006.
Caplan, Jane, ed. *Written on the Body: The Tattoo in European and American History.* London: Reaktion Press, 2000.
Card, Claudia. "Genocide and Social Death." *Hypatia* 18, no. 1 (Winter 2003): 63–79.
Caruth, Cathy. *Listening to Trauma: Conversations with Leaders in the Theory and Treatment of Catastrophic Experience.* Baltimore: Johns Hopkins University Press, 2014.
Çetin, Fethiye, and Ayse Gul Altinay, eds. *The Grandchildren: The Hidden Legacy of "Lost" Armenians in Turkey.* New Brunswick, NJ: Transaction Publishers, 2014.
Cholakian, Hagop. *Karen Eppe.* Aleppo: Arevelk, 2001.
Dean, Carolyn J. "Empathy, Pornography, and Suffering." *Differences: A Journal of Feminist Cultural Studies* 14, no. 1 (Spring 2003): 87–124.
Demoyan, Haik, and Lousine Abrahamyan. *Aurora's Road: Odyssey of an Armenian Genocide Survivor.* Yerevan: AGMI, 2015.
Derderian, Katharine. "Common Fate, Different Experiences: Gender-Specific Aspects of the Armenian Genocide, 1915–1917." *Holocaust and Genocide Studies* 19, no. 1 (Spring 2005): 1–25.
Deringil, Selim. "'The Armenian Question Is Finally Closed': Mass Conversions of Armenians in Anatolia during the Hamidian Massacres of 1895–1897." *Comparative Studies in Society and History* 51, no. 2 (April 2009): 344–71.
———. *Well-Protected Domains: Ideology and the Legitimization of Power in the Ottoman Empire, 1876–1909.* London: Palgrave Macmillan, 1998.
Der Matossian, Bedross. *The Horrors of Adana: Revolution and Violence in the Early Twentieth Century.* Stanford, CA: Stanford University Press, 2022.
———. *Shattered Dreams of Revolution: From Liberty to Violence in the Late Ottoman Empire.* Stanford, CA: Stanford University Press, 2014.
Derounian, Vartan. *Karen Jeppes arbajdsmark 44 reproductioner af fotografier fra Syrien optaget af den armeniske.* Fotograf V. Derounian. Copenhagen: Aleppo Udgivet af de Danske Armeniervenner, 1931.
Derrida, Jacques. *Archive Fever: A Freudian Impression.* Chicago: University of Chicago Press, 1998.
———. "Composing 'Circumfession.'" In *Augustine and Postmodernism: Confessions and Circumfession*, edited by J. D. Caputo and M. J. Scanlon, 19–27. Bloomington: University of Indiana Press, 2005.
Deter-Wolf, Aaron, and Lars Krutak, eds. *Ancient Ink: The Archaeology of Tattooing.* Seattle: University of Washington Press, 2017.
Donef, Racho. "Interviews with Survivors of the Armenian Genocide." Armenian Genocide History, posted August 11, 2003. http://www.atour.com/history/AG/20030811a.html.
Douglas, Mary. *Purity in Danger: An Analysis of Concepts of Pollution and Taboo.* London: Routledge, 1966.
Dündar, Fuat. *Crime of Numbers: The Role of Statistics in the Armenian Question (1878–1918).* New Brunswick, NJ: Transaction, 2010.

Ekmekçioğlu, Lerna. "A Climate for Abduction, a Climate for Redemption: The Politics of Inclusion during and after the Armenian Genocide." *Comparative Studies in Society and History* 55, no. 3 (July 2013): 522–53.

———. *Recovering Armenia: The Limits of Belonging in Post-Genocide Turkey*. Stanford, CA: Stanford University Press, 2015.

Ekmekçioğlu, Lerna, and Melissa Bilal, eds. *Bir adalet feryadı. Osmanlı'dan Türkiye'ye beş Ermeni feminist yazar 1862–1933*. İstanbul: Aras, 2006.

Evered, Emine Ö., and Kyle T. Evered. "Sex and the Capital City: The Political Framing of Syphilis and Prostitution in Early Republican Ankara." *Journal of the History of Medicine and Allied Sciences* 68 (2013): 266–99.

Fırat, Mümtaz. *Kaybolan izler: Güneydoğuda geleneksel dövme ya da dek ve dak*. Istanbul: Yapı Kredi Yayınları, 2017.

Franco, Jean. *Cruel Modernity*. Durham, NC: Duke University Press, 2013.

Garibian, Sévane. "Editorial." Special issue, "Human Remains and Commemoration." *Human Remains and Violence* 1, no. 2 (2015): 2–4.

———. "Ravished Armenia (1919): Bearing Witness in the Age of Mechanical Reproduction: Some Thoughts on a Film Ordeal." In *Mass Media and the Genocide of the Armenians: One Hundred Years of Uncertain Representation*, edited by Jocelyn Chabor, Richard Godin, Stefanie Kappler, and Sylvia Kasparian, 36–50. New York: Palgrave Macmillian, 2016.

Gilbert, Pamela K. *Victorian Skin: Surface, Self, History*. Ithaca, NY: Cornell University Press, 2019.

Gingeras, Ryan. *Sorrowful Shores: Violence, Ethnicity, and the End of Empire, 1912–1923*. New York: Oxford University Press, 2009.

Göçek, Fatma Müge. *Denial of Violence: Ottoman Past, Turkish Present and Collective Violence against the Armenians, 1789–2009*. New York: Oxford University Press, 2014.

———. "Turkish Historiography and the Unbearable Weight of 1915." In *Cultural and Ethical Legacies of the Armenian Genocide*, edited by Richard Hovanissian, 337–68. New Brunswick, NJ: Transaction, 2007.

Grosz, Elizabeth. *Volatile Bodies: Towards a Corporeal Feminism*. Bloomington: Indiana University Press, 1994.

Guerzoni, Benedetta. "A Christian Harem: Ravished Armenia and the Representation of Armenian Women in the International Press." In *Mass Media and the Genocide of the Armenians: One Hundred Years of Uncertain Representations*, edited by Joceline Chabot, Richard Godin, Stefanie Kappler, and Sylvia Kasparian. New York: Palgrave Macmillian, 2016.

Gzoyan, Edita. "Rescued and Saved: Armenian Genocide Survivors at Aleppo Reception Home." *Armenian Weekly*, June 10, 2020. https://armenianweekly.com/2020/06/10/rescued-and-saved-armenian-genocide-survivors-at-aleppo-reception-home/.

Gzoyan, Edita, Regina Galustyan, and Shushan Khachatryan. "Reclaiming Children after the Genocide: Neutral House in Istanbul." *Holocaust and Genocide Studies* 33, no. 3 (Winter 2019): 395–405.

Halavut, Hazal. "Loss, Lament and Lost Witnessing: Halide Edib on 'Being a Memory of the Party Who Killed' Armenians." *Journal of Ottoman and Turkish Studies Association* 8, no. 2 (2021): 313–18.

Halttunen, Karen. "Humanitarianism and the Pornography of Pain in Anglo-American Culture." *American Historical Review* 100, no. 2 (April 1995): 303–34.

Harootunian, Harry. *The Unspoken as Heritage: The Armenian Genocide and Its Unaccounted Lives*. Durham, NC: Duke University Press, 2019.
Hirsch, Marianne. "Family Pictures: *Maus*, Mourning, and Postmemory." *Discourse* 15, no. 2 (Winter 1992–1993): 3–29.
Hovannisian, Richard, ed. *The Armenian Genocide in Perspective*. New Brunswick, NJ: Transaction Books, Rutgers University, 1986.
Iğsiz, Aslı. *Humanism in Ruins: Entangled Legacies of the Greek-Turkish Population Exchange*. Stanford, CA: Stanford University Press, 2018.
Jebejian, Robert, and Hagop Krikorian. *Routes and Centers of Annihilation of Armenian Deportees in 1915 within the Boundaries of Syria*. Aleppo: Violette Jebejian Library, 1994.
Jinks, Rebecca. "'Marks Hard to Erase': The Troubled Reclamation of 'Absorbed' Armenian Women, 1919–1927." *American Historical Review* 123, no. 1 (February 2018): 86–123.
Joeden-Forgey, Elisa von. "The Devil in the Details: 'Life Force Atrocities' and the Assault on the Family in Times of Conflict." *Genocide Studies and Prevention: An International Journal* 5, no. (2010): 1–19.
———. "Gender and the Future of Genocide Studies and Prevention." *Genocide Studies and Prevention: An International Journal* 7, no. 1 (2012): 89–107.
Jones, Adam, ed. *Gendercide and Genocide*. Nashville, TN: Vanderbilt University Press, 2004.
Kaiser, Hilmar. *The Extermination of Armenians in the Diarbekir Region*. Istanbul: Bilgi University Press, 2014.
Kaprielian-Churchill, Isabel. "Armenian Refugee Women: The Picture Brides, 1920–1930." *Journal of American Ethnic History* 12, no. 3 (1993): 3–29.
Karamursel, Ceyda. "The Uncertainties of Freedom: The Second Constitutional Era and the End of Slavery in the Late Ottoman Empire." *Journal of Women's History* 28, no. 3 (2016): 138–61.
Kauffeldt, Jonas. *Danes, Orientalism, and the Modern Middle East: Perspectives from the Nordic Periphery*. Ph.D. dissertation, Florida State University, 2006.
Kévorkian, Raymond. *The Armenian Genocide: A Complete History*. London: I. B. Tauris, 2011.
———. "Earth, Fire, Water: or How to Make the Armenian Corpses Disappear." In *Destruction and Human Remains: Disposal Concealment and Mass Violence*," edited by Elisabeth Anstett and Jean-Marc Dreyfus, 89–116. Manchester: University of Manchester Press, 2012.
Kévorkian, Raymond, Levon Nordiguian, and Vahé Tachjian. *Les Arméniens: La quête d'un refuge, 1917–1939*. Beirut: Presse de l'Université Saint-Joseph, 2007.
Kévorkian, Raymond, and Vahé Tachjian, eds. *The Armenian General Benevolent Union: A Hundred Years of History*, vol. 1. Paris: Armenian General Benevolent Union, 2006.
Kieser, Hans-Lukas. *Talaat Pasha: Father of Modern Turkey, Architect of Genocide*. Princeton, NJ: Princeton University Press, 2018.
Korkmaz, Ayşenur. "The Hamidian Massacres: Gendered Violence, Biopolitics and National Honour." In *Collective and State Violence in Turkey: The Construction of a National Identity from Empire to Nation-State*, edited by Stephan Astourian and Raymond Kévorkian (New York: Berghahn, 2021), 97–121.
Kozma, Liat. *Global Women, Colonial Ports: Prostitution in the Interwar Middle East*. Albany: SUNY Press, 2017.
Krikorian, Mesrob K. *Armenians in the Service of the Ottoman Empire, 1860–1908*. London: Routledge, 1977.

Krstić, Tijana. *Contested Conversions to Islam: Narratives of Religious Change in the Early Modern Ottoman Empire*. Stanford, CA: Stanford University Press, 2011.

Krutak, Lars. *The Tattooing Art of Tribal Women*. London: Bennett & Bloom, 2007.

Kurt, Ümit. *The Armenians of Aintab: The Economics of Genocide in an Ottoman Province*. Cambridge, MA: Harvard University Press, 2021.

LaCapra, Dominick. *Writing History, Writing Trauma*. Baltimore, MD: Johns Hopkins Press, 2014.

Landsberg, Alison. *Prosthetic Memory: The Transformation of American Remembrance in the Age of Mass Culture*. New York: Columbia University Press, 2004.

Laqueur, Thomas. *The Work of the Dead: A Cultural History of Mortal Remains*. Princeton, NJ: Princeton University Press, 2015.

Levi, Primo. *Survival in Auschwitz*. New York: Simon & Schuster, 1947.

MacKeen, Dawn Anahid. *The Hundred-Year Walk: An Armenian Odyssey*. Boston: Mariner Books, 2016.

MacKendrick, Karmen. *Fragmentation and Memory: Meditations on Christian Doctrine*. New York: Fordham University Press, 2008.

MacKinnon, Catherine A. "Genocide's Sexuality." *Nomos* 46 (2005): 313–56.

Maksudyan, Nazan. "Agents or Pawns? Nationalism and Ottoman Children during the Great War." *Journal of the Ottoman and Turkish Studies Association* 3, no. 1 (May 2016): 139–50.

———. "The Orphan Nation: Gendered Humanitarianism for Armenian Survivor Children in Istanbul, 1919–1922." In *Gendering Global Humanitarianism in the Twentieth Century: Practice, Politics and the Power of Representation*, edited by Esther Möller, Johannes Paulmann, and Katharina Stornig, 117–42. New York: Springer International Publishing, 2020.

———. *Orphans and Destitute Children in the Late Ottoman Empire*. Syracuse, NY: Syracuse University Press, 2014.

Marchand, Laure, and Guillaume Perrier. *La Turquie et le fantôme Arménien*. Paris: Actes Sud, 2013.

Marcom, Micheline Aharonian. *Three Apples Fell from Heaven*. New York: Riverhead Books, 2004.

Marks, Laura U. *The Skin of Films: Intercultural Cinema, Embodiment, and the Senses*. Durham, NC: Duke University Press, 2000.

Matiossian, Vartan. *The Politics of Naming the Armenian Genocide: Language, History and 'Medz Yeghern.'* London: I. B. Tauris, 2021.

Mbembe, Achille. "Necropolitics." *Public Culture* 15, no. 1 (Winter 2003): 11–40.

McGinty, Brian. *The Oatman Massacre: A Tale of Desert Captivity and Survival*. Norman: University of Oklahoma Press, 2014.

Mifflin, Margot. *The Blue Tattoo: The Life of Olive Oatman*. Lincoln: University of Nebraska Press, 2009.

Miller, Donald E., and Lorna Touryan Miller. *Survivors: An Oral History of the Armenian Genocide*. Berkeley: University of California Press, 1993.

Miller, Owen Robert. "Back to the Homeland" (Tebi Yergir): Or, How Peasants Became Revolutionaries in Muş." *Journal of the Ottoman and Turkish Studies Association* 4, no. 2 (November 2017): 287–308.

———. *Sasun 1894: Mountains, Missionaries, and Massacres at the End of the Ottoman Empire*. Ph.D. diss., Columbia University, 2015.

Morefield, Jeanne. "'Families of Mankind': British Liberty, League Internationalism, and the Traffic in Women and Children." *History of European Ideas* 46 (2020): 681–96.

Moughalian, Sato. *Feast of Ashes: The Life and Art of David Ohannessian*. Stanford, CA: Stanford University Press.

Mouradian, Khatchadour. "Genocide and Humanitarian Resistance in Ottoman Syria, 1915–1917." Ph.D. diss., Clark University, 2016.

———. "Internment and Destruction: Concentration Camps during the Armenian Genocide, 1915–1916." In *Internment during the First World War: A Mass Global Phenomenon*, edited by Panikos Panayi, Stefan Manz, and Matthew Stibbe, 145–61. London: Routledge Studies in First World War History, 2018.

———. *The Resistance Network: The Armenian Genocide and Humanitarianism in Ottoman Syria, 1915–1918*. Lansing: Michigan State University Press, 2020.

Nichanian, Marc. *Writers of Disaster: Armenian Literature in the Twentieth Century*. London: Taderon Press, 2002.

Nora, Pierre. "Between Memory and History: Les Lieux de Mémoire." *Representations* 26 (Spring 1989): 7–24.

Parla, Ayşe, and Ceren Özgül. "Property, Dispossession, and Citizenship in Turkey; or, the History of the Gezi Uprising Starts in the Surp Hagop Armenian Cemetery." *Public Culture* 28, no. 3 (September 2016): 617–53.

Patterson, Orlando. *Slavery and Social Death: A Comparative Study*. Cambridge, MA: Harvard University Press, 1985.

Pattie, Susan. *The Armenian Legionnaires: Sacrifice and Betrayal in World War I*. London: I. B. Tauris, 2018.

Peirce, Leslie. "Abduction with (Dis)honor: Sovereigns, Brigands, and Heroes in the Ottoman World." *Journal of Early Modern History* 15 (2011): 311–21.

Peroomian, Rubina. "Women and the Armenian Genocide: The Victim, the Living Martyr." In *Plight and Fate of Women: During and Following Genocide*, vol. 7, edited by Samuel Totten, 7–24. London: Routledge, 2009.

Putzi, Jennifer. "Capturing Identity in Ink: The Captivities of Olive Oatman." *Western American Literature* 39, no. 2 (Summer 2004): 177–99.

Qattan, Najwa al-. "When Mothers Ate Their Children: Wartime Memory and the Language of Food in Syria and Lebanon." *International Journal of Middle East Studies* 46, no. 4 (2014): 719–36.

Randall, Amy E., ed. *Gender and Genocide in the Twentieth Century: A Comparative Survey*. London; New York: Bloomsbury Academic, 2015.

Rubin, Gayle. "The Traffic in Women: Notes on the 'Political Economy' of Sex." In *Toward an Anthropology of Women*, edited by Rayna R. Reiter, 157–210. New York: Monthly Review Press, 1975.

Russell-Brown, Sherrie L. "Rape as an Act of Genocide." *Berkeley Journal of International Law* 21, no. 2 (2003): 350–74.

Sarafian, Ara. "The Absorption of Armenian Women and Children into Muslim Households as a Structural Component of the Armenian Genocide." In *In God's Name: Genocide and Religion in the Twentieth Century*, edited by Omer Bartov, with Phyllis Mac, 109–19. New York: Berghahn Books, 2001.

Savioli, Alberto. "Le tribù beduine della Siria e l'arte del tatuaggio." Ph.D. diss., Facoltà di Lettere e Filosofia, Università Degli Studi di Udine, 2003–2004.

Semerdjian, Elyse. "Armenian Women, Legal Bargaining, and Gendered Politics of Conversion in Seventeenth- and Eighteenth-Century Aleppo." *Journal of Middle Eastern Women's Studies* 12, no. 1 (March 2016): 2–30.

———. "Naked Anxiety: Bathhouses, Nudity, and Muslim/Non-Muslim Relations in Eighteenth-Century Aleppo." *International Journal of Middle East Studies* 45, no. 4 (November 2013): 651–76.

———. *"Off the Straight Path": Illicit Sex, Law, and Community in Ottoman Aleppo*. Syracuse, NY: Syracuse University Press, 2016.

———."Phantom Limbs, Embodied Horror, and the Afterlives of the Armenian Genocide." Special issue, "Death and Afterlives in the Middle East," edited by Aslı Zengin. *Comparative Studies of South Asia, Africa, and the Middle East* 42, no. 1 (2022): 182–95.

———. "Zabel Essayan, 'Liberation of Non-Muslim Women and Children.'" *Journal of the Society for Armenian Studies* 28 (2022): 1–14.

Sendyka, Roma. "Sites That Haunt: Affects and Non-Sites of Memory" *East European Politics and Societies* 30, no. 4 (November 2016): 687–702.

Shemmassian, Vahram. "The League of Nations and the Reclamation of Armenian Genocide Survivors." In *Looking Backward, Moving Forward: Confronting the Armenian Genocide*, edited by Richard Hovannisian, 81–112. London: Routledge, 2003.

———. "The Reclamation of Captive Armenian Genocide Survivors in Syria and Lebanon at the End of World War I." *Journal of the Society for Armenian Studies* 15 (2006): 113–40.

Sick, Ingeborg Maria. "Karen Jeppe of Denmark and Armenia." *American-Scandinavian Review* 25 (1937): 18–25.

Sick, Ingeborg Maria, and Pauline Klaiber. *Karen Jeppe im Kampf um ein Volk in Not*. Stuttgart: Steinkopf, 1929.

Sinclair, A. T. "Tattooing-Oriental and Gypsy." *American Anthropologist* 10, no. 3 (July–September 1908): 361–86.

Slide, Anthony, "Introduction." In *Ravished Armenia: The Story of Aurora Mardiganian*. Jackson: University Press of Mississippi, 2014.

Smeaton, Winifred. "Tattooing among the Arabs of Iraq." *American Anthropologist* 39 (1937): 53–61.

Steet, Linda. *Veils and Daggers: A Century of National Geographic's Representation of the Arab World*. Philadelphia: Temple University Press, 2000.

Suciyan, Talin. *The Armenians in Modern Turkey: Post-Genocide Politics and History*. London: I. B. Tauris, 2017.

Suny, Ronald. *"They Can Live in the Desert but Nowhere Else": A History of the Armenian Genocide*. Princeton, NJ: Princeton University Press, 2015.

Tachjian, Vahé. "Gender, Nationalism, Exclusion: The Reintegration Process of Female Survivors of the Armenian Genocide." *Nations and Nationalism* 15, no. 1 (January 2009): 60–80.

———. *La France en Cilicie et en Haute-Mésopotamie*. Paris: Éditions Karthala, 2004.

———. "Mixed Marriage, Prostitution, Survival: Reintegrating Armenian Women into Post-Ottoman Cities." In *Women and the City, Women in the City: A Gendered Perspective on Ottoman Urban History*, edited by Nazan Maksudyan, 86–106. Oxford: Berghahn Books, 2014.

Tashjian, James H. "American Military Mission to Armenia," part II. *Armenian Review* 4, no. 3 (1951): 92–106.

Tataryan Aslan, Nora. "Facing the Past: Aesthetic Possibility and the Image of 'Super-Survivor.'" *Journal of Middle East Women's Studies* 7, no. 3 (November 2021): 348–65.

Torchin, Leshu. "Ravished Armenia: Visual Media, Humanitarian Advocacy, and the Formation of Witnessing Publics." *American Anthropologist* 108, no. 1 (March 2006): 214–20.

Tuck, Eve, and K. Wayne Yang. "Decolonization Is Not a Metaphor." *Decolonization: Indigeneity, Education & Society* 1, no. 1 (2012).

Üngör, Uğur Ümit. *Confiscation and Destruction: The Young Turk Seizure of Armenian Property*. New York: Bloomsbury Academic, 2013.

——— . *The Making of Modern Turkey: Nation and State in Eastern Anatolia*. Oxford: Oxford University Press, 2011.

Watenpaugh, Heghnar Zeitlian. "Learning from Taksim Square: Architecture, State Power, and Public Space in Istanbul." Society of Architectural Historians, *SAH Blog*, June 11, 2013.

——— . *The Missing Pages: The Modern Life of a Medieval Manuscript, from Genocide to Justice*. Stanford, CA: Stanford University Press, 2019.

Watenpaugh, Keith. *Being Modern in the Middle East: Revolution, Nationalism, Colonialism, and the Arab Middle Class*. Princeton, NJ: Princeton University Press, 2006.

——— . *Bread from Stones: The Middle East and the Making of Modern Humanitarianism*. Berkeley: University of California Press, 2015.

——— . "Kill the Armenian/Indian; Save the Man: Carceral Humanitarianism, the Transfer for Children and a Comparative History of Indigenous Genocide." *Journal for the Society of Armenian Studies* 29 (2022): 1–33.

——— . "The League of Nations' Rescue of Armenian Genocide Survivors and the Making of Modern Humanitarianism, 1920–1927." *American Historical Reviews* 115, no. 5 (2010): 1315–39.

Warren, Mary Anne. *Gendercide: The Implications of Sex Selection* (Totowa, NJ: Rowman & Allanheld, 1985).

Yenipınar, Uysal, and Mehmet Sait Tunç. *Güneydoğu anadolu geleneksel dövme sanatı beden yazıtları*. İzmir: Etki Yayınları, 2013.

Yılmaz, Seçil. "Love in the Time of Syphilis: Medicine and Sex in the Ottoman Empire, 1860–1922." Ph.D. diss., City University of New York, 2016.

——— . "Threats to Public Order and Health: Mobile Men as Syphilis Vectors in Late Ottoman Medical Discourse and Practice." *Journal of Middle East Women's Studies* 13, no. 2 (2017): 222–43.

Zilfi, Madeline. *Women and Slavery in the Ottoman Empire: The Design of Difference*. Cambridge; New York: Cambridge University Press, 2010.

Zürcher, Erik-Jan. "Young Turks, Ottoman Muslims, and Turkish Nationalists: Identity Politics, 1908–1938." In *Ottoman Past and Today's Turkey*, edited by Kemal Karpat, 150–79. Leiden: Brill, 2000.

INDEX

Page numbers in italics refer to figures and Remnants.

abduction: archival traces of, 40–44; and captivity narratives, 166–67, 169, 171; and dis-memberment, 50, 55; Essayan on, 29–31, 299n65, 302n25; and genocide 11, 20, 23; of Khanum and Lucia, 157–58, 159; of Kherbetjian, 213; in late Ottoman period, 34–40; and marriage in the Middle East, 303n36; of Meghrouni, 203–4; and the Ottoman sex/gender system, 27, 31–34; of Shakeh, 150; and rescue efforts, 64, 67, 77. *See also* assimilation; captivity; dismemberment; sexual violence; slavery
Abdul Hamid II (Ottoman sultan), 34, 37, 305n66
abortion, 117–18, 332n22
Abu Galgal, 203, 343n7
Adana Massacres (1909), 15, 27, 28, 43, 47, 178, 300n2, 307n1 (Remnant 1)
Adjemian, Boris, 274
affect: and the body, 7, 18, 54, 284; and bones, 225–39, 259–78; and pilgrimages, 23, 240–55; and memory, 9, 10, 20–21; and tattoos, 149, 156, 160, 161–62, 170, 172, 182; and touch, 144–45, 157; and violence, 109. *See also* disgust; laughter; postmemory; prosthetic memory; shame; social death; trauma; uncanny
Aftermath, The, 174–76, 337n48. *See also* YWCA
Agoudjian, Antoine, 276–77

Ahmed, Çerkez, 348n34
Ahmed, Sara, 161–62
Ahronian Orphanage (Aleppo), 106
Aintab, 1–4, 102, 251
'Aintoura Orphanage (Lebanon): accusations of forced Armenianization at, 115; Cemal Pasha on, 107–10; conflicting reports about, 323n19; Edib's photos of, 323n26; starving orphans at, 55; Keith Watenpaugh on, 322n18; torture at, 324n33. *See also* orphanages
al-Busayra (Syria), 244, 256–57, 261, 262, 277
Aleppo: Ahronian Orphanage, 106; and Armenian rescue efforts, 65, 67, 75; girls at YWCA in, 206, 208, 210; Jeppe's rescue efforts in, 82–83, 85–103; Nersessian in Rescue Home in, 211; in *A Rescue in the Desert*, *123*, 326n75; and sectarianism, 118–19; and tattooing, 150–51, 161
Anneannem (My grandmother; Çetin), 14, 284, 294n9
Antelias (Lebanon), 238, 239. *See also* Catholicosate of Sis
Apelian, Kevork, 187
Apfel, Oscar, 134
April 24: arrests, 17, 18, 27, 28; as ceremonial time, 241–42; Neutral House founded on, 82; pilgrimages, 244, 247, 250–51, 261–62, 271

371

Arabs: "Armenian Girls inside Arab Homes," *60–61*; accused of cannibalism, 55; in captivity narratives, 172; commemoration and feelings about, 248; in "In the Deserts of Dayr al-Zur," *223*; and Hovakimyan, 233; and Jeppe, 86–87, 98–99; Kabakian's experience with, 150–51, 154; at Shaddaddi, 251–55; Shaddadi survivor adopted by, 281–83; and tattoos, 195, *199*, 200–220, 342n60; and white slavery, 178–80. *See also* Bedouin; Muslims

Arapian, Tovmas, 232–33, 261

Armenian Apostolic Church, 241, 243, 244, 249, 351n20

Armenian boys: and assimilation, 40, 108, 110–12; and dis-memberment, 54; and Herian's rescue efforts, 73–74; and Jeppe's rescue efforts, 88–89, 96–98, 103; lynching of, 325n70; and Muslim patrimony, 118; and sexual violence, 31; and tattoos, 200, 205–6. *See also* Armenian men; children; orphans

Armenian colonies, 98–102

Armenian Genocide Studies, 10–15

"Armenian Girls inside Arab Homes" (Herian), *60–61*, 70

Armenian General Benevolent Union (AGBU), 68, 70, 313n21. *See also* Nubar, Boghos

Armenian Genocide Memorial Complex (Dayr al-Zur): and bone memory, 256, 271–72, 325n25; construction of, 237–38, 243; destruction of, 228, 282; pilgrimages to: 244–48. *See also* Dayr al-Zur; pilgrimages

Armenian girls: and abduction, 34–36; in Arab homes, *60–61*; and the Armenian patriarchal family, 49–50; in *Auction of Souls*, *124–25*; captivity narratives and tattooed girls, 170–82; and dehumanization, 54; Essayan on, 29–30; and Herian's rescue efforts, 65–66, 70–71, 77; and Jeppe's rescue efforts, 88–89, 96; in prosthetic memories of Dayr al-Zur, 266; in Prime Minister's archive, 40–42; at Tall Shaddadi, 251–53; and tattoos of, 150–52, 158–59, *163–64*, *199*, 201–5, 206, 208–20. *See also* Armenian women; children; orphans

Armenian Golgotha (Grigoris Balakian), 229

Armenian Holy Trinity Church (Constantinople), 15, 241

Armenianization, 36, 117–21

Armenian Legion, 68–69, 120

Armenian men: and assimilation in Syria, 102; and conversion in the late Ottoman period, 38, 39; and dis-membering violence, 51–52; sexual violence against, 31, 302n23; and tattoos, 200, 205–6, *207*; women's tattoos and acceptance by, 204–5, 343n12. *See also* Armenian boys

Armenian National Archives (Yerevan), 28, 142, 348n35

Armenian National Committee of America, 350n9

Armenian National Delegation, 27, 28–29, 64

Armenian National Relief Organization, *104*

Armenian National Union, 70, 71, 73, 74

Armenian nation-building: and the Armenian Genocide Memorial Complex (Dayr al-Zur), 247–48; and Bilemdjian, 23–24; and biopolitics, 20; and Dayr al-Zur, 227, 238; and motherhood, 297n37; and *hai tad*, 351n29; and Herian's rescue efforts, 68, 75–76; and Jeppe's colonies in Syria, 98–102; and Jeppe's Rescue Home, 90–92; and Rescue Homes, 82–83. *See also* community; dis-memberment

Armenian patriarchate, 28, 41, 42, 65, 68, 82, 106, 257–58

Armenian Relief Committee of Mesopotamia (ARCM), 66, 69–70, 7, 326n73

Armenian Review, 156, 333n36

Armenian Studies, 11, 18, 31. *See also* Armenian Genocide Studies

Armenian women: and abduction, 34–36; archives and bodies of, 12; and Armenian Genocide histories, 13–15;

and assimilation, 7–8, 20; and *Auction of Souls*, 126, 130–39, 146; in *Auction of Souls* advertisements, 129, *140*; and captivity narratives, 165–82; and community regeneration, 307n107; and conversion, 37–38, 39–40; Essayan on, 27–32, 299n65, 302n25; and Herian's rescue efforts, 62, 64–67, 70–71, 77–80; in humanitarian photography, 120–23; and Jeppe's rescue efforts, 82–83, 85–89, 91–96, 99–103; and Muslim patrimony, 20, 117–19; in Prime Minister's archive, 40–42; in prosthetic memories of Dayr al-Zur, 231, 265, 266–67; resistance and agency of, 42–44; shame and dis-memberment through violence against, 47–59, 309n21, 311n62; and tattoo removal, 184–98; and tattoos, 20–22, 149–62, 200–205, 206, 208–220, 331n3. *See also* Armenian girls

Armeniervennen, 96, 213, 215, 338n61. *See also* Danish Friends of Armenia

Arsenian, Hagop, 205

Asad, Bashar al-, 259

Asad, Hafez al-, 259

As'ad, Sa'ad Hammad al-, 251–52, 254–55, 260, 283

As'ad, Zahaya al-, 219–20, 347n47

Asdghig (featured in *A Rescue in the Desert*), 121–23, 326nn75–76

Asdovadzadzin Church (Aleppo), 248

assimilation: at 'Aintoura Orphanage, 107–10; and conversion, 38–40; Essayan on, 29–30; genocide commemoration and resistance to, 248; and girls' reluctance to leave Muslim homes, 73, 89; Jeppe's colonies in Syria to prevent, 98; of Kurds, 297n50; and Oatman, 165, 167–68; re-Armenianization, 103, 110–21; and social death, 7–8, 14–15; and state violence, 37–40; as survival, 107; tattoos as symbols of, 21. *See also* conversion; Islamization

Assyrians, 11, 15, 16

Astourian, Stephan 308n15

Atassi, Hashim, 233–34

Attarian, Hourig, 152, 184

Auction of Souls, 123, *124–25*, 126–46, 326n1 (Remnant 5), 330n66, 330n69

Auctions of Souls (Khanjian), 143–45, 145–46, 286

Aurora Humanitarian Initiative, 145, 331n84. *See also* Mardiganian, Aurora

Aurora Prize for Awakening Humanity, 145, 331n84. *See also* Mardiganian, Aurora

Auschwitz, 21, 228, 243, 299–300n69. *See also* Holocaust

autoethnography, 13; and family history, 1–4, 102; and tattoos, 219–20; and pilgrimages, 239, 240, 250–55, 260; and bone collecting, 256–58, 274–76

Avakian, Nargis, 192–97, 341n42, 341n49, 342n54

Azkanver hayuhyats engerutiun (women's patriotic association), 301n11

Azniv (relative of Hourig Attarian), 184–85, 339n2 (chap. 9)

Bacı, Arap, 40–41

Baghdad, 64–66, 67, 71, 110–11

Bahri, Zaruhi, 83

Balakian, Grigoris, 53, 229, 230, 326n72, 348n34

Balakian, Peter: on the Armenian genocide and human civilization, 279–83; and bone collecting, 256, 261, 264; on Dayr al-Zur, 229, 246; on the Euphrates, 264; on Margada, 249; and pilgrimages, 243; rape with a cross, 141

Balkans, 15, 32, 37

Balmanoukian, Sarkis, 237, 244

Balyan, Garabed, 241

bastinado, 109, 324n33. *See also* violence

beards, 19, 52, 309n24, 348n34

beauty: and Armenian women's fates, 40, 46, 60, 293n1 (Introduction); of Bilemdjian, 6, 23; facial tattoos mar, 152, 155, 169–70, 186, 211–12; of facial tattoos, *199*, 200, 204, 210, 218; of Mardiganian, 127, 130, 138; and tattoo removal, 194, 195, 197

Bederkhan, Ali Reza, 233

Bedouin: Armenians disguised as, 62; Armenian women rescued from, 70–71, 103, 121, *122*; Armenian women saved by, 184, 251; Jeppe's cooperation with, 89, 99, 102, 179; medical treatment, 96–97; Mesrob in Bedouin clothing, 111; and tattooing, 160, 184, 188, 201–5, 206, *207*

Bedoukian, Kerop, 99, 120, 229–30, 325n70

Bedrossian, Melkon, 109

beheadings, 52, 233, 309n26, 349n50

Benedictsen, Aage Meyer, 83

Bilemdjian, Loutfie, 5–7, 23–24, 294nn2–3, 292n5

biopolitics, 15–18; and nation-building, 19–20, 64, 82–83, 115, 284–86, 319n50; and necropolitical violence, 47–59;

Bird's Nest Orphanage, 188, 317n6. *See also* orphanages

Blue Triangle News, The, 175, 337n48

Bodil Biørn, Katharine, *224*

Boghosian, Almas, 73, 106

bone collecting, 227–28, 231, 232, 233–38, 256–78, 279–80

bone memory, 22, 256–78, 284. *See also* prosthetic memory

"Bones" (Peter Balakian), 243, 256, 261, 279

branding, 171, 192, 210. *See also* violence; tattoos

Britain: and Armenian rescue efforts, 65–66, 68, 70, 75, 76, 313n21; *Auction of Souls* in, 134–35; and Rescue Homes, 82; press coverage of tattooed Armenian women in, 170–80

Bryce, James (viscount), 135

burials: at 'Aintoura Orphanage, 110; of Bones in Cyprus, 271; denied, 18, 48, 309n29; and the desert necrogeography, 228–38; of Jeppe, 103; Kherbetjian buried alive, 214; of Mardiganian, 145; *See also* bone memory; mass graves; ossuaries

Can, Serdar, 14

cannibalism, 54–55, 114–15, 310n48

Captanian, Pailadzo, 57, 58

captivity: *A Rescue in the Desert* depicts, 121–22; of Bilemdjian, 7; captivity narratives, 138, 165–82, 335n6; and denialism, 41; of Gülizar, 35; and Herian's rescue efforts, 70–80; and humanitarianism, 131, 137; and Jeppe's rescue network, 87; and the Ottoman sex/gender system, 33; of women and children, 42, 62, 102; and tattoos, 21, 151, 154–55, 185–86, 190, 192, 195, 200–219. *See also* abduction; concubinage; marriage; prostitution

Captivity of the Oatman Girls, 166–68

castration, 33, 51, 52, 284, 309n24. *See also* violence

Catholicasate of Sis, 233, 236–39, 243, 263, 348n32

Cemal Pasha, 15–16, 107, 108, 322n17, 323n20, 323n25

ceremonial time, 241–42

Çetin, Fethiye, 14, 284, 294n9

child levy system, 32. *See also* Ottoman sex/gender system

children, 285; and abduction, 33, 34–36; in Arab homes, *60–61*; and the Armenian patriarchal family, 49–50; in *Auction of Souls*, *124–25*; and bone collecting, 257, 262; bones of, 236, *237*; captivity narratives and tattooed girls, 170–82; and conversion, 39–40; and dehumanization, 53–55; Essayan on, 27–31, 43–44; and Herian's rescue efforts, 62–68, 70–71, 73–77, 79–80; Islamization of, *104*, 105–23, 323n25, 324n33; and Jeppe's rescue efforts, 83–84, 87, 88–89, 92–93, 96–98, 103; lynching of, 325n70; murdered, 51; and the Ottoman child levy system, 32; in Prime Minister's archive, 40–42; in prosthetic memories of Dayr al-Zur, 266; at Tall Shaddadi, 251–53; and tattoos, 20–22, 150–52, 158–59, 163–64, *199*, 200–206, 208–20, 334n45. *See also* Armenian boys; Armenian girls; orphans

Christianity: and Armenian identity, 110–16; and *Auction of Souls*, *124*, *125*,

130, 131, 135, 138, 141; and bones, 263, 271–73, 274; and captivity narratives, 167, 169, 170–71; and Dayr al-Zur as profane site, 260; and genocide commemoration, 242, 244–49, 350n8; and humanitarian photography, 213; and Jensen, 91; and Jeppe, 83–84, 89–90; and Orientalism, 37; and pilgrimages, 225–27, 233–38, 346n6, 347n24, 349n48; in Shahinian's testimony, *163*; and tattoo removal, 192, 193–94. *See also* Christians

Christians: and biopolitics, 15–18; and the Ottoman sex/gender system, 33–34; and prosthetic memory, 9; role in rescue efforts, 63; and tattoo motifs, 220; in Turkish orphanages, 105–6, 106–7. *See also* Christianity; zimmi

Circassians, 34, 304n46, 306n86

circumcision, 39, 54, *104*, 306n76

clothing: amulet sewn into, 150; and assimilation, 102; in *Auction of Souls*, 134; and the Chekijian family, 1–2, 4; and dis-memberment, 56–59; and gender, 326n74; Herian in Arab dress, *72*; Hovakimyan disguised as a Kurd, 233; and humanitarian photography, 6, 121, 201–3, 208, *211*, 213; and humanitarian films, 122; of Islamized Armenians, 110; money sewn into, 311n57; of Oatman, 167, 168, *169*

Commission for the Protection of Women and Children in the Near East (League of Nations), 85. *See also* Jeppe, Karen

Committee of Union and Progress (CUP), 15, 16, 38, 323n25

community: abduction and loss of, 40; assimilation and difficulty rejoining, 103; Bilemdjian's reabsorption into the Armenian community, 23–24; and bone collecting, 263–64, 278; and bones, 279, 283–84; conversion and rejection of, 38; dehumanization and destruction of, 53–56; gender and community resistance, 41–44; genocide and destruction of, 20, 27; and Jeppe rescue work, 90–92, 98–102; mothers' importance in rebuilding, 307n107; pilgrimages and the remaking of, 267–70; sexual violence's effect on, 30–31; shame and dis-memberment, 47–59; tattoos and social death, 149–62, 332n22; tattoo removal and belonging, 184–98; tattoos and shame, 203; and voice of the blood, 333n29. *See also* Armenian nation-building; dis-memberment; social death

concubinage, 23, 30, 32, 40, 151, 153, 211; and Avakian, 192; Meghrouni, 204. *See also* harems; prostitution; sexual violence; slavery; trafficking

Constantinople/Istanbul: 1889 protests in, 35–36; 1908 celebration of Turkish-Armenian brotherhood, 15; and author's story of bones, 256–58; genocide commemoration in, 241; Kabakian in, 152–54; mass arrests in 1915 in, 27; Neutral House in, 83, 115; rescue efforts in, 65, 68, 106–8, 112–13

conversion: and *Auction of Souls*, 126, 131, 132, 137; Essayan on, 29; forced, 35–36, 322n17; and genocide, 11, 14–15; and Islamic Law, 306n79; and the Ottoman sex/gender system, 27, 31–34, 44; Prime Minister's Archive and evidence of, 41–42; reconversion and Armenian identity, 111; Shahinian's testimony on, *163–64*; and starvation, 54; and state violence, 37–40; and tattoos, 159; Treaty of Sèvres voids, 67; in Turkish orphanages, 108, 323n28. *See also* assimilation; Islamization

crucifixion: in *Auction of Souls*, *124–25*, 127, 133, 135, 138, 139; and humiliation, 52; impalement mistaken for, 141; and memory of the cross, 330n65

Cushman, Emma, 68, 106, 112–13, 116

Damascus, 66–67, 107, 113–14, 154

"Dance, The" (Siamanto), *45–46*, 47

Danish Friends of Armenia (Danske Armeniervenner), 84, 85, 86, 96, 213. *See also Armeniervenner*; Jeppe, Karen

Dayr al-Zur: as affective necrogeography, 264–67; bombing of, 256; cannibalism at, 55; death march destination, 17; and the genocide's third phase, 64; Herian in, 70–80; and Khardalian, 157, 267–68; lamentation on, *223–24*; Matossian's trip to, 272–73; Mouradian's trip to, 261–62; nudity at, 57; in photographs, 349n3; pilgrimages to, 23, 224, 225–29, 231–39, 240–42, 242–48; as profane site, 260; Syrian War and the meaning of, 280, 282–83

Dayr al-Zur Suspension Bridge, 232, 236, *237*, 264–67, 353nn25–26

Davis, Leslie, 53, 53–54, 56, 58–59

deathscape, 228–31. *See also* necrogeography

decapitation, 52, 233, 309n26, 349n50

dehumanization: and the deathscape of Dayr al-Zur, 229; and dis-memberment, 51–52; and Jeppe's rescue work, 83, 88–98; and necroviolence, 53–56, 309n29, 310n43; and nudity, 56–59; of women, 311n62; of Turks in World War I–era media, 139, *140*, 329n58

denialism: and archives, 10–12, 13, 41; and Armenian grandmothers, 14–15; and bone collecting, 276, 277; and Edib, 109, 144–15, 177–79; 323n28; and feminism, 284; and genocide commemoration, 242; tattoo analysis not a basis for, 201

deportation: of Armenians, 17–18; of Bilemdjian, 5–6; of Chekijian family, 2; and conversion, 38–40; and the deathscape of Dayr al-Zur, 229; and dis-membering violence, 52; Essayan on, 29–32, 302n25; Jeppe during the deportation of Urfa, 84; of Kabakian, 150; Kherbetjian's experience of, 213; and nudity, 57–58; of orphans during second phase, 249–50; and pilgrimages, 244; routes, *245*; *Routes and Centers of Annihilation of Armenian Deportees of 1915 within the Boundaries of Syria*, 240–41; and tattooing, 180; women's resistance to, 42–44

dermatology, 185, 190, 192–97, 342n54

Der Yeghiayan, Zaven (Armenian patriarch of Constantinople), 65, 68, 109, 350n8

diaspora: and *Auction of Souls*, 330n66; author's experience as a member of the, 251–54; and genocide commemoration, 18, 242, 243; and Herian's rescue efforts, *60–61*, 70, 76–78, 78–79; Kabakian in, 155–56; periodicals in, 333n36; and prosthetic memory, 9–10; and prosthetic memory of Mardiganinan, 142–46; and rescue, 43; and tattoos, 7–8

disability, 187

disease, 65, 96–98, 189–90, 197, 230

disembowelment, 51, 129

disgust: and bones, 22, 262, 273; and forced marriage, 325n65; and taboo acts, 54–55, 59; and tattoos, 21, 160, 167–70; and violence, 109. *See also* affect

dis-memberment, 8–9, 14–15; and Edib's cannibalism metaphor, 115; and Jeppe's mission, 83; and pilgrimages, 228; prosthetic memory and re-membering, 267–70; and shame, 47–59; and tattooing, 149–62. *See also* Armenian nation-building; community; family; social death

disobedient gaze (Moser), 201, 208, 218

Draining the Sea (Marcom), 267, 268–69

Edib, Halide: and Armenian orphans, 108–110, 114–15, 118, 323n19, 323n26, 323n28; on Armenian women, 284; Jeppe's debate with, 166, 177–80, 182, 338n54, 338n59, 338n61; and nationalism, 338n59

Egoyan, Atom, 142, 144, 145, 330n69

Ekmanian, Harout, 247–48

Ekmekçioğlu, Lerna: on Armenian biopolitics, 20, 64, 82, 297n37, 307n107; on Edib, 338n59; on *Grandma's Tattoos*, 333n40; on tattoos, 186

Elliot, Mabel, 153–54

embroidery, 6–7, 56, 63, 91–92, 169, 263, 294n3

empiricism, 9, 258–59
epigenetics, 267, 354n39
Erzindjan, 30
Essayan, Zabel, 27–32, 42–44, 54, 144, 299n65, 300n4
euthanization, 53–54
excavations, 232, 233–38, 246, 249, 258, 351n25, 352n2; empathic excavations, 260–61
executions, 27, 52, 241, 300n1, 309n24, 309n26, 349n50
Exiled (Tavoukdjian), 201–2
exposure, 57, 58

family: destruction of Armenian patriarchal family, 19–20, 27, 40; and Herian's rescue efforts, 76–79; Muslim patrimony and the Armenian patriarchal family, 117–21; sexual violence and effect on, 30–31; shame and effect on, 47–59; tattoos and effect on, 154–55, 156–61; and the voice of the blood, 154, 333n29. *See also* community; dis-memberment
Faysal (king), 66, 75, 113, 151, 314nn28–29
femininity; and affect, 259; and Asdghig in *A Rescue in the Desert*, 122; and dis-memberment, 49–51; and tattoos, 152, 176, 165–82; *See also* gender; masculinity; motherhood; patriarchy
feminism: and the archive question in Armenian Genocide Studies, 10–15; and Armenian grandmothers, 284; and Edib's nationalism, 108–10, 177–78, 180; and Essayan, 28–32, 42–44; and Khanjian's *Auctions of Souls*, 143–45; and white slavery, 165–66
fertility, 206, 210, 212, 219
films: *A Rescue in the Desert*, 88, 121–23, 326n75; *Auction of Souls*, 124–25, 126–27, *129*, 130–39, 142–43, 145–46, 326n1 (Remnant 5); *Grandma's Tattoos*, 156–61. *See also* photographs; press
Fisk, Robert, 268, 281
Forchhammer, Henni, 345n37
France: *Auction of Souls* in, 142, 330n66; and Herian's rescue efforts, 68, 69, 70, 79; and Jeppe's colonies in Syria, 98; publication of photos of tattooed Armenian women in, 180–81
Freud, Sigmund, 265. *See also* uncanny, the

Gaszczyk, Leopold, 86, *95*, 96, *123*, 326n75
Gates, Henry L., 130, 132
Gates, Mrs. Henry L., 132, 133, 134
Gavour, Roupen, 31
Gelenian, Hampartzoum. *See* Hamasdegh
gender: and affect, 259; and the archives in Armenian Genocide Studies, 11–15; and the Armenian Genocide, 19–20; and Asdghig in *A Rescue in the Desert*, 122; and dis-memberment, 49–52; Essayan on, 27–31; and humanitarian exploitation, 131, 132–33, 135–39; and the Ottoman sex/gender system, 31–34; and representations of war, 327–28n20; and tattoos, 152, 176, 165–82, 200; and tattoo artists, 195–96, 210, 342n60. *See also* feminism; patriarchy
Ghazzi, Kamil al-, 118–19
Gingeras, Ryan, 156
Grandma's Tattoos (Khardalian), 149, 156–61, 333n40
grandmothers: al-As'ad grandmother, 219, 251, 252, *253*; author's grandmother, 1–4, 102, *291*; and biopolitics, 284–85; and bone collecting, 261, 266, 268; genocide recognition and Armenian, 14–15; and tattoos, 149–61
Greeks, 16
Gregory the Illuminator, Saint, 265, 353n19
Gölcük, Lake (Lake Hazar), 56, 270
Gorilla Carrying Off a Stone Age Woman (Fremiet), 139, *140*, 329n58

Hadjim Pasha, 87, 98, 99
Haigian, Digin Satenig, 78, 234–35, 348n40
Haigian, Krikor, 78, 234, 348n40
Hairobediun, Jeghsa, 215–19
hai tad, 248, 351n29
Hamasdegh, 225–27, 261
Hamidiye Massacres (1894–1896), 15, 27, 37, 39, 305n66

haptic visuality, 144–45, 157. *See also* touch
harems: and Armenian orphans, *104*; and *Auction of Souls*, 126, 130–31, 132; Avakian rescued from, 192, 341n44; and Herian's rescue efforts, *60–61*, 65, 66; and Orientalism, 135–36, 137; in *A Rescue in the Desert*, 121; and white slavery, 170, 174, 178–79. *See also* concubinage; prostitution; sexual violence; slavery; trafficking
Hay Pujak, *183*, 191
Hazar, Lake, 56, 270
Herian, Ruben, *60–61*62, 68–80, 231, 261, 315n49
Holocaust, 8–9, 21, 243, 300n69. *See also* Auschwitz
Holy Etchmiadzin (Vagharshapat, Armenia), 263, 353n18
Holy Martyrs Church (Dayr al-Zur): and bone memory, 256, 276, 325n25; construction of, 237–38, 243; destruction of, 228, 276, 280; pilgrimages to, 244–48. *See also* Armenian Genocide Memorial Complex; Dayr al-Zur
Holy Trinity Greek Orthodox Church, 241, 350n8
Hovakimyan, Harutyun, 233–36, *237*, 238, 239, 273, 248n35
humanitarian aid funding: and *Auction of Souls*, 127, 130, 133, 145; and Bilemdjian's image, 6; and films, 121–23; for Herian's rescue efforts, 70–71, 78–79; for Jeppe's rescue efforts, 88, 89, 92, 98, 215; and mass media, 171, 178, 182
humanitarianism: and 'Aintoura Orphanage, 322n18; and Armenian identity, 110–16; Armenian relief effort, 62–80; and Bilemdjian's photograph, 6; and biopolitics, 20; and Cemal Pasha, 107, 108, 322n17; and Jeppe's Rescue Home in Aleppo, 82–103; and League of Nations' "historicist humanism," 90, 319n50; and Mardiganian's exploitation, 126–46; and Muslim patrimony, 117–21; and the necrogeography of the desert, 284–86; and photography, 121, 326n73; sources and scholarship on,

312n10; and tattoos, 149, 161, 165–66, 170–76, 331n3, 337n48; and tattoo photos, 201, 205–220; and tattoo removal, 188–90. *See also* Herian, Ruben; Jeppe, Karen

I Hate Dogs (Khardalian), 157
impalement, 51, 141
"In the Deserts of Dayr al-Zur," 223–24, 266, 346n1
In the Ruins (Essayan), 28
Irutaba (Mohave chief), 167, 335n10
Islam: abduction and marriage, 35–40; and conversion in the early modern period, 306n79; and domestic slavery, 304n46; and orphan rescue, 106, 110–21; and the Ottoman sex/gender system, 33–34; and sexual violence, 303n33, 304n47; and tattoo motifs, 205–6, 210, 212, 218, 220, 344n29. *See also* Muslims
Islamic State (ISIS), 23, 228, 256, 282, 283, 285–86, 356n12
Islamization: of Armenian orphans, 73 *104*, 105–23; and Zahaya's al-As'ad, story, 219–20; and the child levy system, 32; endogamy among Islamized Armenians, 99–100; Herian's reaction to, 79, 80; and Kabakian, 150–51, 154–55; of Khanum and Lucia (*Grandma's Tattoos*), 157–59; and Kherbetjian's son, 214, 345n39; and state violence, 37–40; and survival, 54; and tattoos, 7–8, 14–15, 21, 149, *163–64*, 192; Treaty of Sèvres voids, 67. *See also* assimilation; conversion
Istanbul/Constantinople: 1889 protests in, 35–36; 1908 celebration of Turkish-Armenian brotherhood, 15; and author's story of bones, 256–58; genocide commemoration in, 241; Kabakian in, 152–54; mass arrests in 1915 in, 27; Neutral House in, 83, 115; rescue efforts in, 65, 68, 106–8, 112–13

Jabbour tribe, 219, 251, 289
Jackson, Jesse B., 18
Jacobsen, Maria, 83, 317n6. *See also* Bird's Nest Orphanage

James, Saint, 238, 349n50. *See also* Surp Hagop Armenian Cemetary
janissary system, 32, 302n28
Jebejian, Robert, 240–41, 250
Jensen, Jenny: in *A Rescue in the Desert*, 122, *123*, 326n75; Melkonian described by, 86–87; on orphans, 91, 106, 116; and Rescue Home photographs, 93, 96; and Rescue Home weddings, 100, *101*, 102
Jeppe, Karen, 83–103, 285; and *A Rescue in the Desert*, 121–23; on the desert deathscape, 229; Edibe's debate with, 177–80, 182; Herian compared to, 71; on Islamized children, 105, 110, 117; personal photo collection, 320n72; tattoos documented in photograph collection of, 188–90 *214*, 215–18; white slavery and Jeppe's rescue work, 166, 171–73, 180–81
Jewish people: Armenians compared to, 243; and Auschwitz tattoos, 21, 299–300n69; and Holocaust postmemory, 8–9; and Islamization in the seventeenth century, 37; and the Ottoman sex/gender system, 33–34; violence and humiliation of, 52, 56;

Kabakian, Aghavni, 150–56, 332n21, 333nn35–36
Karekin II (catholicos), 237, 238, 349n48
Kataroyan, Souren (archbishop), 236–37, 238
Kennedy, William A., 68
Khanjian, Arsinée, 143–45, 145–46, 286
Khanum (Khardalian's grandmother in *Grandma's Tattoos*), 149–50, 156–61, 334n47
Khardalian, Suzanne, 149–50, 156–61, 243, 265, 267–68, 273, 334n42
Kherbetjian, Vartanoush, 213–15, 218
Kozanlian, Eduardo, 142
Kushakian, Torkom (bishop), 64
Kurds: and Armenians in late Ottoman period, 34–36, 302n22; and biopolitics, 116, 298n50; Hovakimyan's relationships with, 233; and "right of first night," 50, 308n15; in Turkish orphanges, 106–7; and white slavery, 179–80; women stripped by Kurdish guards, 57
Kuyumdjian, Keghanush, 78, *81*

"La libération des femmes et enfants nonmusulmans en Turquie" (The liberation of non-Muslim women and children in Turkey; Essayan), 29–32, 42–44
language: and Armenian identity, 91, 102, 111, 112, 321n93; and Islamization, 107; and Kabakian's interview, 333n30; and Mardiganians's narration of sexual violence, 141
laughter, 144. *See also* affect
League of Nations: and Armenian rescue efforts, 67–68, 70; and demography, 64; historicist humanism, 90, 319n50; Jeppe's Rescue Home, 85–103; recordkeeping, 76; and Rescue Homes, 82–83; and *A Rescue in the Desert*, 121, 326n75; and white slavery, 165–66. *See also* humanitarianism; Jeppe, Karen; Rescue Homes
Lemkin, Raphael, 19
Lepsius, Johannes, 83–84, 89
Lombroso, Cesare, 194, 341n52
looting, 17, 56, 57, 58, 150

Manchester Guardian, The, 177–178, 178–79
Marcom, Micheline Aharonian, 47, 267, 268–69, 273
Marden, J. K., 188
Margada, 238, 243–44, 249, *250*; affective necrogeography of, 264–67; Marcom and Tatoyan at, 268–69; Matossian at, 271–72; Mishoyan-Dabbaghian at, 271
marriage: and abduction in the Middle East, 303n36; and the Armenian patriarchal family, 49–50; and assimilation, 89; and conversion, 37, 39–40; forced marriage, 20, 35–36, 41–42; and Islamic Law, 304n47; at Jeppe's Rescue Home and colonies, 99–102; of Kabakian, 155, 156, 333n35; and Muslim patrimony, 117–118, 119, 120; of Oatman, 167,

marriage (cont.)
335nn10–11; and the Ottoman sex/
gender system, 32–34; and rescue as
annulment, 339n16; and social death,
154–55; tattoos and marriageability,
184, 185–88, 204–5, 344n17
Mardiganian, Aurora, 123, *124–25*, 126–46,
286, 326n1 (Remnant 5), 327n11
Markosian, Diana, 274, *275*
masculinity, 31, 51–52, 309n24. *See also*
femininity; gender; patriarchy
mass graves, 22–23; at al-Busayra, 244,
256–57, 261–62, 277; at Dayr al-Zur,
224, 232–33, 347n28; at the Dayr al-Zur
Suspension Bridge, 264–67; in the
desert, 234–38, *245*; and ISIS, 282,
356n12; at Margada, 249, 267; *See also*
bone memory; burials; ossuaries
mass media. *See* films; photography; press
Matossian, Nouritza, 264, 271–72, 273,
350–51n13
Meghrouni, Vergeen, 203–5, 343n12
Meguerditchian, Samuel, 187
Melkonian, Misak, 84, 86–87, 90, 116,
326n75
"Melodies from the Euphrates" (Ypradyan
meghetiner; Perseghian), 265–66
Mesrob, Sahag, 110–11, 333n29
miscegenation, 139, 165–66. *See also* captivity; race; sexual violence
Mishoyan-Dabbaghian, Sosy, 248, 271,
355n57
Mohave, 166–67, 168, 335n10
Morgenthau, Henry, 17, 30, 58, 134, 298n54
motherhood: and Armenian nation-building, 43, 65, 99–100, 185, 186,
297n37, 307n107; and biopolitics, 19–
20; and dis-membering violence, 51–52,
53–54, 55, 309n21; Jeppe's humanitarian "mothering," 83, 90–91, 102; and
Muslim patrimony, 106, 117–21. *See also*
Armenian nation-building; community; grandmothers; reproduction
motifs (tattoos), 205–6, 207, 209, 210, 212,
218, 220, 344n23
Mouradian, Khatchig, 43, 63, 261–62,
322n17

Mubarak (rescued Armenian boy), 281,
355n9
Musa Bey, 35–36
Muslims: Armenians assisted by, 18, 20,
285; Armenians in the homes of, 31,
40–44; *60–61*, 62, 63–68, 69–80;
302n25, 306n83; reactions to *Auction of
Souls*, 135; and captivity narratives, 166,
172, 177–80; Essayan on, 299n65; and
the Holy Martyrs Church (Dayr al-
Zur), 237–38; and Islamization of Armenian orphans, 105, 106, 109; Jeppe's
attitude toward, 89–90; Jeppe's cooperation with, 98–99; Kabakian's experiences with, 150–51, 154–56; looting
by, 56; Mardiganian's description of,
134, 328n34; naked women mocked by,
58; and the Ottoman military, 302n28;
and the Ottoman sex/gender system,
33–34; and the patriarchal family, 284;
Muslim patrimony, 117–21; objections
to rescue efforts, 67, 75, 79, 87, 110–16;
and sectarian violence, 303n41; and
tattooing, 163–64, 187–88, 192, 205,
210, 344n29. *See also* Arabs; Bedouin;
Islam; Islamic State; Islamization
mutilation, 19–20, 44, 48, 59; and *Auction
of Souls*, 139; and dehumanization, 51–
52, 53, 55; and method, 8, 12
My Grandmother (Çetin), 284

names: and Armenian identity, 110–16,
238, 260; and author's family history, 1,
2, 3; girl without a name, 206, 208–11;
and Islamization, 64, 77, 105, 106–9,
157, 220, 251, 322nn8–9; and paper
cadavers, 296n27; and women's and
agency, 43
nawar (nawari), 150–51, 155, 156, 173, 332n6,
342n60
Near East Relief, 68, 70, 88, 327n16; and
Auction of Souls, *125*, 127, 130, 133,
145; and tattoo removal, 153, 188, 190,
340n30
necrogeography, 22–23, 225–39; and affect,
264–78, 284; and bone collecting, 259–
64; ISIS and the Syrian desert's, 282;

and non-sites of memory, 241, 243. *See also* deathscape
necropolitics, 20, 42; and necroviolence, 47–59, 309n24; 309n26, 309n29, 310n43. *See also* violence
Nenemin Masallari (Tales of my grandmother; Can), 14
Nersessian, Aghavni, 211–13, 345n37
Neutral Houses, 68, 82–83, 112–13, 115–16. *See also* Rescue Homes
non-sites of memory, 240–55, 270, 354–55n55
Nubar, Boghos, 65, 68, 313n21. *See also* Armenian General Benevolent Union
Nubarian Library (Paris), 274, *275*, 276–77
nudity, 52, 56–59, 311n62; and *Auction of Souls*, *124*, *125*, 139; in "The Dance," *46*; and the desert deathscape, 229, 230; and the humanitarian gaze, 208, *209*, 210, 344n26; in "In the Deserts of Dayr al-Zur," *223*

Oatman, Olive, 166–70, 182, 294n3, 335n11, 337n49; 338n69
Odian, Yervant, 58, 229, 301n14
omnicide, 280–81
Orientalism: and *Auction of Souls*, 124, 127, 131, 135–40, 329n56, 329n58; in Derounian's photos, 320n72; and forced conversion stories, 37; and Herian's stereotypes of Arabs, 315n49; in humanitarian photography, 201–2, 343n4; and tattoos, 192–93
orphanages: ARCM orphanage in Mosul, 66; Bird's Nest Orphanage, 188, 317n6; Essayaran calls for more League of Nations orphanages, 43; Edib on Turkish orphanges, 177–78; Islamization and Turkish orphanages, 29, 39–40, 106–10, 322n9, 322n18, 323n19, 323nn25–26, 324n33; Jeppe in orphanage in Urfa, 83–85; orphans killed at Shaddadi from Turkish orphanages, 249–50, 253; and Armenian identity, 110–16; sectarian violence at, 120, 285; starving orphans at 'Aintoura, 55. *See also* orphans; rescue; Rescue Homes; *vorpahavak*

orphans: in author's autoethnography, 3; Essayan on Adana Massacre orphans, 28; Bilemdjian, 5–7; and dehumanization, 53, 55; and Herian's rescue efforts, *60*, *61*, 62–68, 70–71, 73–77, 79–80; and Islamization, 39–40, *104*, 105–23, 306n83, 323n19, 323nn25–26, 324n33; in Jeppe's rescue efforts, 88–98; killed at Shaddadi, 249–50, 253; and Rescue Home marriages, 99–102; and *vorpahavak*, 43–44, 307n107. *See also* Armenian boys; Armenian girls; children; orphanages
ossuaries: Holy Martyrs Church in Dayr al-Zur, 244, 246–47, 248; Memorial Chapel in Antelias, 239, 264; private ossuaries, 273, 276, 280; Surp Haroutioun (Resurrection) Chapel in Margarda, 243, 249, *250*. *See also* bone memory; burials; mass graves
Ottoman Fourth Army, 107, 322n17, 323n25
Ottoman sex/gender system, 27, 31–34, 285
Ozone Journal (Peter Balakian), 280–82

Panian, Karnig, 55, 108, 109
Papazian, Vahan, *224*
patriarchy: Armenian patriarchal family, 19–20, 49–52; and genocide, 11, 14–15, 43; Muslim patriarchal family, 20, 154–55, 284; Muslim patrimony and the Armenian patriarchal family, 117–21; and the Ottoman sex/gender system, 31–34
patrimony, 20, 33, 39, 67, 106, 117–21. *See also* conversion; Islamization; marriage; patriarchy
Perseghian, Nora, 265–67
photography: and the author's family, 1–4; Barthes on, 300n75; Bilemdjian's story, 5–6, 23–24; Edib's photographs of 'Aintoura Orphanage, 323n26; genocide documented through, 240, 349n3; in Herian's rescue efforts, 73–74, 77; and humanitarianism, 121, 165–66, 170–76, 326n73, 337n48, 338n68; Jeppe's personal collection, 320n72;

photography (*cont.*)
in Jeppe's rescue efforts, 87, 93, 96–98; and Mesrob's "Their Name," 110; and Orientalism, 343n3; and Papazian's pilgrimage, *224*; Rinhart's collection, 344n25; and survivor counternarratives, 200, 201–2, 205–18; and tattoos, 149, 161, 180–82, 188–90, 331n3. *See also* films; press

pilgrimages, 22–23, 347n24; and Peter Balakian, 279–80; Bertram's work on, 346n5; and bone collecting, 256–78; to Dayr al-Zur, 225–39; and non-sites of memory, 240–55; Papazian's, *224*; and prosthetic memories, 10

Police Magazine, 180–81, 338n68

polygamy, 34, 39–40, 50, 220

Post, Wilfred, 153, 190, 191, 340n30

postmemory, 8–9, 200. *See also* prosthetic memory

press: and Herian's rescue efforts, 69, 70, 77; and Jeppe's rescue efforts, 88; and Aurora Mardiganian's story, 126–27, 128–33, 134, 137–39; on Muslim patrimony, 118; and prosthetic memory, 9–10, 243; and tattoos, 165–66, 170–82, 185, 188, 190–92, 192–97, 345n46

Prime Minister's Archives (Başbakanlık Osmanlı Arşivi; Istanbul), 11, 40–42

prosthetic memory, 9–10, 284; and *Auction of Souls*, 142–46, 330n73; of the author, 102; and Bertram's memory-stories, 346n5; and bone collecting, 256–78; and bones, 22–23, 225–39; in *Grandma's Tattoos*, 159–60; and non-sites of memory, 243, 251, 254–55; of Shaddadi in Balakian's poetry, 281–82; and tattoos, 21; and Zahaya al-Sa'ad's story, 219

prostitution, 30, 285, 300n4; and Armenian rescue efforts, 65–66, 67, 79; and *Auction of Souls*, 130; brothel for Turkish and German soldiers, 301n14; and Orientalism, 135–36; and images of tattooed girls, 208–10; tattoos equated with, 150, 159–60, 338–39n69; and white slavery, 165–66, 180–81. *See also* concubinage; harems; sexual violence; slavery; trafficking

race: and captivity narratives, 131; and Muslim patrimony, 117–21; and Orientalism, 135–39, *140*, 329n58; and Ottoman history, 40–41, 319n50; and science, 194, 197–98; and tattoos, 165–82; whiteness, 131, 135, 138, 165–82, 197. *See also* Orientalism

Racoubian, Edward, 205–6, *207*, 344n23

rape. *See* sexual violence

Ras al-'Ayn: Armenian children at, 40, 53, 205, 206; deportations to, 17; excavation of, 352n2; mass killing at, 229; memorial at, 351n20; and sexual violence, 51, 203

Ravished Armenia (Mardiganian), 126, 127, 130, 131–32, 139, *140*, 143. *See also* Mardiganian, Aurora

Red Sunday, 17, 18, 27, 28, 241. *See also* April 24

refugee camps, 53, 62, 66, 67, 85 343n7

relics, 226, 259, 263–64, 269, 271, 274, 278, 279; of Saint James, 349n50; hand relics in the Armenian tradition, 353n19. *See also* bone collecting; pilgrimages

"Removal of Tattoos and Carbonic Acid, The," *183*, 191

Rendel, George William, 173

reproduction: and Armenian nation-building, 43, 65, 82–83, 99–100; and biopolitics, 19–20, 27, 48; and dis-membering violence, 51–52, 309n21; and the Ottoman sex/gender system, 32–33. *See also* Armenian nation-building; community; motherhood

Republic of Armenia, 242

rescue, 41–44, 285; as annulment, 339n16; Armenian efforts, 62–80; and captivity narratives, 167, 172–77; of Islamized orphans, *104*, 105–6, 110–23; and Jeppe's Rescue Home, 82–83, 85–103; of Kabakian, 151; and *A Rescue in the Desert*, 326nn75–76; and Tall Shaddadi, 251–52; and tattoo removal, 184–

85, 186–90, 192–93. *See also* Rescue Homes; *vorpahavak*

Rescue Homes: and Armenian identity, 110–16; and Bilemdjian, 5–6; in captivity narratives, 172–73; and Jeppe's rescue efforts, 82–83, 85–103; and Kherbetjian, 213–15; marriages in, 186, 187; and Nersessian, 211–13; photos of tattoos in records of, 331n3; in *A Rescue in the Desert*, 123, 326n75; and tattoo removal in the records of, 188–90. *See also* League of Nations; Neutral Houses; rescue

Rescue in the Desert, A, 121–23, 326n75

"right of first night" (*arachin kishervairavunk*), 50, 308n15

Routes and Centers of Annihilation of Armenian Deportees of 1915 within the Boundaries of Syria (Jebejian and Krikorian), 240–41, 250

Sabagh, Vasil, 87
Sabun Khan Orphanage (Aleppo), 120
Sarajian, Bedros (archbishop), 65, 66–67, 113, 114
sectarianism, 33–34, 118–21, 303n41, 326n72. *See also* Turkish ethnonationalism
Selig, William M., 134
Semerdjian, Youssef, 3, 102, *291*
Serengülian, Vartkes, 233, 241, 309n24, 348n34
Seropian, Mushegh (archbishop), 65, 69, 313n21
Setian, Yervant, 142, 330n68
Sèvres, Treaty of, 67, 70, 228
sexual violence: and abduction, 34–40; and the archive, 7; against Armenian men, 302n23; Armenian orphans' experiences of, 106; in *Auction of Souls*, 126, 130, 137–39; in *Auction of Souls* advertisements, 129, *140*; in *Auctions of Souls*, 144; Balakian's interviews and the absence of, 156; and biopolitics, 284; and captivity narratives, 165–66, 168–70, 173; and dis-memberment, 50;

Essayan on, 27–32, 300n4, 302n25; feminist accounts of, 301n11; and genocide, 11; in "In the Deserts of Dayr al-Zur," 223; in Islamic law, 303n33, 304n47; and Mardiganians's use of Armenian, 141; Meghrouni's experience of, 203, 204; and Muslim patrimony, 118; Nersessian's experience of, 211; nudity as prelude to, 58; tattoos equated with, 150, 153–54, 159–60, 185, 191, 192–93; perpetrated by Turkish and German soldiers, 301n14; women's resistance to, 42–44. *See also* concubinage; prostitution; harems, slavery; trafficking

Shaddadi, 219, 244, 249–55, 260, 281, 283

shame: and Armenian communal dis-memberment, 47–59; Bilemdjian's potential shame, 6, 23; and captivity narratives, 167; and prostitution, 66; and tattoos, 7, 20–21, 149–62, 184–98, 204–5. *See also* affect; trauma; dis-membership

Shahen of Van, 49–50
Shahinian, Eliza, *163–64*
Shakeh (Aghavni Kabakian's sister), 150, 154–55
Shapazian, Vartan, 346n1 (Remnant 9)
Sharb Bedros, 99, 100–102
Siamanto (Atom Yarjanian), *45–46*, 47, 307n1 (Remnant 1)
Sick, Ingeborg Maria, 84, 91, 103, 317n15
60 Minutes, 243, 261
Slave Market News, The, 88, 170–73, *174*, 177–80, 215, 337n41
slavery: and abolition in Ottoman Empire, 304n46; and Armenian orphans, *104*, 110; Armenians compared to African Americans, 92, 215; and *Auction of Souls*, *124*, 126, 130–31; and beauty 306n86; Essayan on, 29–30, 31–32; in "In the Deserts of Dayr al-Zur," 223; nudity of women sold into, 57, 58; and the Ottoman military, 302n28; and the Ottoman sex/gender system, 27, 31–3; implied in *A Rescue in the Desert*, 121–22; and state violence, 39–40,

slavery (*cont.*)
  40–41, 44; tattoo removal liberation from, 186, 187, 188, 191, 192–93, 195, 196, 197; tattoos equated with, 21, 23, 150, 153, 159, 160; Tavoukdjian sold into, 201–2; white slavery and tattoos, 160, 165–82; white slavery and Orientalism, 135–37, 138–39, *140*; and Yazidi women, 282, 285, 334n42. *See also* concubinage; harems; prostitution; sexual violence; trafficking
Slide, Anthony, 131, 134, 142, 326n1 (chap. 6), 328n34, 329n43
social death, 7, 24, 38, 40, 121; and tattoos, 150, 152, 155, 161–62. *See also* affect; assimilation; conversion; community; dis-memberment; Islamization; shame
"Social Problems: Marital Abuse in Our Region" (Engerayin khantirner: amusnagan dzeghdzmunk i kavars; Shahen of Van), 49–50
suicide: and Grigoris Balakian's response to the deathscape of Dayr al-Zur, 231; Ghazzi's threat of, 119; Mardiganian's struggles with, 133, 145; Meghrouni's thoughts of, 204; and prosthetic memories of Dayr al-Zur, 266; as resistance, 42, 59; of Voskerichian, 84, 317n15
Surmeyan, Ardavazdt (archbishop), 65, 100, *101*, 236
Surp Hagop (Saint James), 238, 349n50
Surp Hagop Armenian Cemetery (Constantinople/Istanbul), 13, 350n6
Surp Haroutiun (Holy Resurrection) Chapel (Margada), 238, 243, 244, 249, *250*, 264
Surp Hripsmae Armenian Church (Dayur al-Zur), 232
Syria: Ahronian Orphanage (Aleppo), 106; Armenian rescue efforts in, 64, 65, 66–67; bone collecting, 256–78; Cemal Pasha's policies in, 323n25; deportations into, 13–14, 17; excavations halted in, 352n2; Herian's rescue efforts in, 69–80; Jeppe's rescue efforts in, 82–83, 85–103, 178–79; meaning making in the desert, 279–83; nawar in, 332n6; Nersessian in Rescue Home in Aleppo, 211; non-sites of memory in, 240–55; pilgrimages to, 225–39; in *A Rescue in the Desert*, *123*, 326n75; and tattooing, 150–51, 161, 203–20; tattoo removal in, 188–91

Syrian War, 243–44, 248, 256, 280, 282–83, 351n20

Talaat Pasha, 15, 16, 17–18, 19, 38, 40, 132, 134
Tall Shaddadi, 219, 220, 251–55
Taksim Garden, 15
Taksim Square, 241, 350n6
Tatoyan, Sona, 254, 268, 269–70, 273
"Tattooed Like an Arab" (Tavoukjian), *199*
tattoo motifs: 6–7, 195, 205–6, *207*, 210–11, 212, 218, 220, 344n23; tree of life (*hayat ağacı*), 7, 210, 219
tattoos, 20–22; and Arabs, *199*; and Armenian identity, 7–8, 15, 238; on Asdghig, *122*; on Bilemdjian, *5*, 6–7, 23–24; and captivity narratives, 335n6; and conversion, 39; and hajj, 339n2 (Remnant 7); and the Holocaust, 300n69; in Rescue Home records, 331n3; as text, 334n43; removal of, *183*, 184–98, 340n21, 340n32, 342n54; Shahinian's testimony on, *163–64*; and spectacle, 336n24; and survivor agency, 200–220; and trauma, 149–62; on Oatman, 294n3; and whiteness, 165–82; and Yazidi children, 334n45
Tavoukjian, Serpouhi, *199*, 201–3, 342n60, 343n8
tehcir (forced migration), 17, 41. *See also* deportations
textiles, 8, 91–92, *95*, 320n61
Thompson, Elizabeth F., 109
Three Apples Fell from Heaven (Marcom), 47, 268
touch, 20, 143–44, 144–45, 157, 258, 266, 270, 271. *See also* affect; bone memory; haptic visuality
Traffic in Souls, 135
trafficking: and *Auction of Souls*, 126; of Bilemdjian, 6, 7; Edib accuses Jeppe and Arabs of, 178; grandmothers discourse and public memory of, 284; humanitarian efforts to terminate, 121,

182, 213; humanitarian filmmaking as engaged in, 131, 133–39, 146; in refugee camps, 343n7; and rescue, 67, 87; and white slavery, 165, 335n4. *See also* concubinage; harems; prostitution; sexual violence; slavery

trauma: and Armenian identity recovery, 103, 110–16; and the body, 7, 11; and bones, 269–70; and death's immanence, 279–282; and epigenetics, 267, 354n9; of Gavour, 31; of Mardiganian, 127, 132–33, 136, 141, 146; and memory, 8–9; and nudity, 58; of orphans, 106–10; and photography, 6; of rescue, 73, 119–21; and the Syrian desert, 228, 236, 242, 253, 265–66; of tattooing and the comfort of Armenian men, 204–5; and tattoos, 21, 149–62; and work therapy, 92, 96; and writing, 13. *See also* affect

Trowbridge, Stephen, 108, 323n19

Tsitsernakaberd Armenian Genocide Memorial Complex ("the swallow's fortress"; Yerevan), 18, 242, 244, 350n10

Turkey: Armenian grandmother discourse in, 14; birthed by Armenian women, 284–86; birthed in blood, 17; expropriation of Church lands, 38n32; and genocide denial, 10–11; genocide survivors known as "remnants of the sword" in, 8; Syrian relations with, 259–60. *See also* Istanbul/Constantinople; Turkish ethnonationalism; Turks; Young Turks

Turkish ethnonationalism: and genocide, 15–18, 19; and Edib, 108–10, 177–79; and sectarianism, 118–21; and state violence, 34–40; *See also* sectarianism

Turks: and genocide commemoration, 259–60; US media depictions of, 128–29, 131–32, 138–39, *140*; as victims, 178; and white slavery, 178–80; as witnesses to genocide, 261–62. *See also* Turkey; Turkish ethnonationalism; Young Turks

uncanny, the, 265, 270. *See also* affect

United States: *Auction of Souls* reception in, *124–25*, 126, 130–33; *Auction of Souls* filmed in, 133–39; Balakian in, 154, 155–56; and captivity narratives, 166–70; genocide recognition in, 243, 350nn9–10; Mardiganian in, 127–30; tattoo removal in, 190–92, 192–97

violence: toward Armenian girls, 208, 210, 211, 214; toward Armenian orphans, *104*, 106–10, 323n19, 324n33, 325n70; in *Auction of Souls*, *124–25*, 126, 130, 137–39; in *Auction of Souls* advertisements, 129, *140*; in *Auctions of Souls*, 144; and biopolitics, 284–86; and Dayr al-Zur as deathscape, 228–32; Essayan on gender and, 27–32, 302n25; toward Garanfillian, 234; and genocide in *I Hate Dogs*, 157; Herian imagines, 231; in "In the Deserts of Dayr al-Zur," *223*; Jeppe on the effects of, 218; toward Jeppe's allies, 87; and Jeppe's mental health, 84–85; Kabakian's experience of, 150, 156; toward Kurds, 298n50; and Mardiganian's use of Armenian, 141; toward Meghrouni's mother, 203; against Muslim women in Ottoman propaganda, 307–308n1 (chap. 1); photographic evidence of, 240, 349n3; Racoubian's experience of, 205–6; in Rescue Home records, 93, 96–98; and sectarianism, 119–21, 303n41, 326n72; Shahinian's experience of, *163*; shame and dismemberment through, 47–59, 309n21, 311n62; and Special Organization, 302n22; and state archives, 11; and state violence, 34–40; and tattooing, *183*, 195; toward Zohrab and Serengülian, 233, 348n34. *See also* beheadings; branding; castration; sexual violence

vorpahavak (orphan rescue), 43–44, 62–80, 285, 307n107; and assistance locating remains, 233–34; and Jeppe's Rescue Home, 82–83, 85–103; and Armenian identity, *104*, 105–6, 110–23; sources and scholarship, 312n10. *See also* orphans; rescue

Voskerichian, Der Karekin, 84, 317–18n15

Waln, Nora, 130
Watenpaugh, Keith: on Edib, 109; on first-person commentary in Rescue Home records, 345n32; on Jeppe, 83, 89; on Syrian nationalism and the Turkish state, 325n69; on Turkish orphanages, 107, 322n18; on unstrangering, 173
Wegner, Armin, 53, 240, 349n3
whiteness, 131, 135, 138, 165–82, 197. *See also* race
"With a Skull" (Hamasdegh), 225–27, 346n2 (chap. 11)
Women of 1915 (Maronian), 149
workshops, 91–92, *95*
World's Fairs, 168–69, 336n22

Yazidi women, 146, 282, 285, 334n42, 334n45
Yerevan, 18, 242. *See also* Tsitsernakaberd Armenian Genocide Memorial Complex
Yotnakhparian, Levon, 66, 113–14, 119, 314n28
Young Turks, 15–18, 91, 178, 250, 348n34
YWCA, 174–76, 208–10

Zaman, Amberin, 256–57, 262
Zeki, Salih (bey), 234 249–50, 349n41
zimmis (non-Muslims), 7, 32, 33–34, 303n31. *See also* assimilation; Islamization; sectarianism
Zohrab, Krikor, 233, 240, 241, 309n24, 348n34
Zoryan Institute, 143, 156

The authorized representative in the EU for product safety and compliance is:
Mare Nostrum Group
B.V Doelen 72
4831 GR Breda
The Netherlands

www.ingramcontent.com/pod-product-compliance
Lightning Source LLC
Chambersburg PA
CBHW031750220426
43662CB00007B/350